NEW MEXICO'S MOSES

Querencias Series

MIGUEL A. GANDERT AND ENRIQUE R. LAMADRID, SERIES EDITORS

Querencia is a popular term in the Spanish-speaking world that is used to express a deeply rooted love of place and people. This series promotes a transnational, humanistic, and creative vision of the US-Mexico borderlands based on all aspects of expressive culture, both material and intangible.

Also available in the Querencias Series:

Nación Genízara: Ethnogenesis, Place, and Identity in New Mexico edited by
    Moises Gonzales and Enrique R. Lamadrid
Querencia: Reflections on the New Mexico Homeland edited by Levi Romero,
    Spencer R. Herrera, and Vanessa Fonseca-Chávez
El Camino Real de California: From Ancient Pathways to Modern Byways
    by Joseph P. Sánchez
Imagine a City That Remembers: The Albuquerque Rephotography Project by Anthony
    Anella and Mark C. Childs
The Latino Christ in Art, Literature, and Liberation Theology by Michael R. Candelaria
*Sisters in Blue / Hermanas de azul: Sor María de Ágreda Comes to New Mexico / Sor
    María de Ágreda viene a Nuevo México* by Enrique R. Lamadrid and Anna M.
    Nogar
Aztlán: Essays on the Chicano Homeland, Revised and Expanded Edition
    edited by Francisco A. Lomelí, Rudolfo Anaya, and Enrique R. Lamadrid
Río: A Photographic Journey down the Old Río Grande edited by Melissa Savage

For additional titles in the Querencias Series, please visit unmpress.com.

New Mexico's Moses

*Reies López Tijerina and the Religious Origins of
the Mexican American Civil Rights Movement*

RAMÓN A. GUTIÉRREZ

UNIVERSITY OF NEW MEXICO PRESS | ALBUQUERQUE

© 2022 by Ramón A. Gutiérrez
All rights reserved. Published 2022
Printed in the United States of America

First paperback printing 2023

ISBN 978-0-8263-6563-7 (paper)
ISBN 978-0-8263-6375-6 (cloth)
ISBN 978-0-8263-6376-3 (electronic)

Library of Congress Control Number: 2022933141

Founded in 1889, the University of New Mexico sits on the traditional homelands of the Pueblo of Sandia. The original peoples of New Mexico—Pueblo, Navajo, and Apache—since time immemorial have deep connections to the land and have made significant contributions to the broader community statewide. We honor the land itself and those who remain stewards of this land throughout the generations and also acknowledge our committed relationship to Indigenous peoples. We gratefully recognize our history.

Cover photograph by George Ballis
Designed by Felicia Cedillos
Composed in Adobe Caslon Pro 10.25/14.25

CONTENTS

Acknowledgments	vii
A Note on Ethnic and Racial Terminology	ix
Introduction	1
Chapter 1. The Social Origins of the Tijerina Clan	19
Chapter 2. The Origins of Pentecostalism	47
Chapter 3. Becoming an Evangelist	63
Chapter 4. Reies Tijerina's Ministry	75
Chapter 5. Of Revelation and Reies	97
Chapter 6. *Will He Find Any Faith on Earth . . . ?*	107
Chapter 7. The Valley of Peace	131
Chapter 8. Restoring New Mexico's Land Grants	149
Chapter 9. Of Prophets, Ancestors, and Tijerinas	191
Epilogue	223
Note on Translation	235
Appendix 1. *¿Hallará Fe en La Tierra . . . ?* / Will He Find Any Faith on Earth . . . ?	237
Notes	501
Bibliography	523
Index	533

ACKNOWLEDGMENTS

Many people and institutions were extremely helpful in making this book possible. First and foremost, I wish to thank the incredibly generous and knowledgeable staff at the University of New Mexico's Center for Southwest Research and Special Collections in Albuquerque. They acquired and processed the Reies López Tijerina Papers, which was the focus of my research over the course of almost ten years. Special thanks are due to Rose Díaz and Jacob Baca, who organized the papers and wrote the inventory for the collection, without which it would have been impossible to quickly find particular topics in this very large manuscript collection. Whenever I had esoteric questions about the provenance of a particular document, where I might exactly find this and that odd report or record, they both quickly offered their help in locating what I needed. The staff at the Center for Southwest Research were also very hospitable: Teresa Marquez, Tomas Jaehn, Christopher Geherin, and Samuel Sisneros.

During the 2011–2012 academic year, The Huntington Library and Botanical Gardens in San Marino, California, invited me to spend a year there as Los Angeles Times Distinguished Scholar. For this opportunity to work at one of America's premier research libraries, I thank Steven S. Koblik, the Huntington's previous director, as well as the past and present W. M. Keck Foundation Directors of Research Robert C. Ritchie and Steve Hindle.

Over the years of working on this book I had two incredible research assistants. Cecilia M. Rivas helped me translate Reies Tijerina's sermons from Spanish to English, while Freeman Faust and John Mitchell, then law students at the University of New Mexico, offered their expert reading and understanding the nuances of the criminal charges against Reies. Dale Sonnenberg shared his extensive video library of Reies Tijerina speeches and interviews. Enrique Lamadrid, Miguel Gandert, and Clark Whitehorn were all responsible for the acquisition of this book manuscript by the University of New Mexico Press, helping it along through the review process, and Sonia Dickey who managed its production.

Over the years several scholars have read draft chapters or the whole of this book and offered insightful comments and critiques, which have made the final book much better. Others shared their own essays and books on Reies Tijerina and offered to allow me to listen to the taped interviews they conducted with Reies, his wives, and his children over the many years. I thank them all in alphabetical order: Howard Brick, Dain Borges, Emma Borges, Rudy Busto, David Correia, Mario Joaquín Encinas, Neil Foley, David Gutiérrez, José Angel Gutiérrez, Gordon Mantler, Peter Nabokov, Lorena Oropeza, Sylvia Rodriguez, Phil Safir, Adam Saytanides, and Michael L. Trujillo.

A NOTE ON ETHNIC AND RACIAL TERMINOLOGY

Readers undoubtedly will find a number of ethnic, racial, and national identity terms herein that may not be entirely familiar. In Spanish the ethnic-national labels most frequently used are *mexicano* or the plural *mexicanos*, which simply mean Mexican. *Tejano* in Spanish is a person of Hispanic or Mexican ancestry residing in Texas under Spanish, Mexican, or American rule. The label *hispano* simply translates as Hispanic; it is a category most frequently used in New Mexico from the mid-nineteenth century to the present. The racial categories frequently used in colonial New Spain, then in independent Mexico were *español*, to identify a person of Spanish ancestry, *indio*, for an Indigenous person, and *mestizo* for individuals of mixed ancestry. Reies López Tijerina began using the racial category "Indo-Hispanos" around 1963 as a way of describing the racial and cultural mixing that had occurred in northern Mexico under Spanish, Mexican, and American rule, and to bring attention to the deep historical and cultural ties between indigenous nations and Hispanic settlers. Lexically, the term *Indo-Hispanos* originated in Central America in the 1950s, made its way to the Andean Republics, and appeared in the United States when Tijerina began using it.

In English the categories of identity used have slightly different meanings. "Ethnic Mexicans" is the broadest, indicating that such persons share a common identity as Mexicans regardless of their location or actual citizenship because of a shared language, culture, and history. Mexican Americans are persons who are legally American citizens. The same goes for Chicanas and Chicanos; they are American born and thus citizens but identify with their indigenous and European hybrid or mixed ancestry in oppositional ways.

Introduction

I have a dream.... It is a dream deeply rooted in the American dream. I have a dream that one day this nation will rise up and live out the true meaning of its creed. We hold these truths to be self-evident that all men are created equal.

—REV. MARTIN LUTHER KING JR.,
"I HAVE A DREAM" (AUGUST 28, 1963)

ON MAY 6, 1968, more than a month after the Rev. Martin Luther King Jr.'s April 4 assassination in Memphis, Tennessee, Reies López Tijerina traveled to Atlanta to pay his respects to Coretta Scott King, the slain leader's widow. Tijerina and King first met at Chicago's O'Hare Airport. King had just attended the National Conference for New Politics, held over the Labor Day weekend of 1967, and was leaving town. Tijerina was just arriving to attend the same conference. As a result of this brief interaction and knowing of each other's grassroots social justice movements, King invited Tijerina to lead an ethnic Mexican contingent from the American Southwest to the Poor People's March on Washington, planned for May 12, 1968.

En route to Washington for the march, Tijerina first stopped in Atlanta to offer his condolences to King's widow. When Coretta and Reies met, he told her about the *Alianza Federal de Mercedes* (Federal Alliance of Land Grant Heirs), an organization he was leading to gain justice for the poor mexicanos who had been robbed of their lands in the aftermath of the Mexican War. Like her husband who often preached of his dream of social justice and a republic free of racism with equality for all, Reies too had a dream. His dream was rooted in his religious commitments to personal salvation through social activism. He then proceeded to recount his dream to Coretta.

Late one April night in 1956, while evangelizing in Visalia, California, three angels descended from heaven on a cloud and landed next to Reies. "We came from afar for you and we will take you to an ancient kingdom," they explained. "There is no one else in the entire world who can do this work. . . . We have traversed the earth looking . . . [but] only [you] can do it." "What work?" he asked. "Secretary," they replied, which is how the terrestrial bird of prey that sits beside God's celestial throne is named. Instantly Reies was lifted onto the angels' cloud and began soaring through the heavens. They landed in a dark pine forest. "A horrible terror overtook me." He ran about nervously seeking an escape but encountered only a cemetery full of frozen horses. One of the horses, a white one, came to life and mounted on its back, Reies and the three angels took to flight anew. They eventually landed outside a walled kingdom, where thousands greeted Reies, cheering his arrival, hoisting him onto their shoulders, and entering the city's gates with enormous fanfare. In the distance Reies could see an old man, "the One," dressed in a flowing white robe, whom he presumed was God. Before long they were in conversation. God then held up a large silver key in one hand, and gesturing with the other, led Reies's eyes across the kingdom. "You will reign over all of this," God said, "and above you, only I." He gave Reies the key, asked him to sit on the celestial throne, and as he did, Reies was instantly back in Visalia. His body burning hot, Reies was sure he had experienced "a revelation" exactly as the one described in Revelation, the Bible's last book. Coretta Scott King listened attentively and politely thanked Reies when he was done.[1]

Reies Tijerina maintained that the work he undertook to peacefully recuperate the land, language, and culture of ethnic Mexicans in the American Southwest from 1946 until his death in 2015 originated in this dream. The desire to own land was what attracted many who first arrived in colonial America in peonage in the early 1600s. African Americans envisaged those "40 acres and a mule" promised after the Civil War, by which emancipated slaves hoped they would acquire property, establish their economic self-sufficiency, and finally build wealth to pass on. American pioneers too sought to materialize similar dreams of homesteads as independent property owners in the second half of the nineteenth century by migrating westward across the Mississippi.

Reies Tijerina was a man who remembered the major turning points in his life as catalyzed by dreams. There would be several other important ones with distinctive names. This one he called his "Visalia Dream," his "Super Dream." The Visalia dream stumped him for years, interrogating what this and that symbol could possibly mean, turning constantly to the Bible for potential interpretive clues, finding its meanings in the last book of the New Testament, Revelation. Trained as an Assemblies of God Pentecostal preacher, in 1956 he led a group of devotees into Arizona's desert, forming there a commune they called the Valley of Peace. They were sure that the Apocalypse was at hand, and they would be saved from its atomic destruction in the underground bomb shelters they constructed.

Reies's true and trusted Bible was the reference book he relied on to understand most of what transpired or he aspired to accomplish on earth. What was he to make of his angelic flight? Where was the ancient kingdom and the dark forest? Why had the frozen white horse come to life? Why had God granted him such immense authority? And the gifted key. What possibly could it mean? All these elements of the celestial kingdom appear in Revelation. Clearly the "supreme judge of justice" had authorized him as a modern-day Moses to lead the descendants of the ancient Kingdom of New Mexico to recuperate the lands stolen from them at the end of the Mexican War. The key he eventually interpreted as the Laws of the Indies, the Treaty of Guadalupe-Hidalgo, and the Constitutions of the United States and the State of New Mexico. The ancient kingdom was New Mexico, and the frozen horses were the *mercedes*, the colonial settlement land grants. Very few of the many women and men who joined the Alianza Federal de Mercedes Reies founded to recuperate the stolen land grants knew little of this prophetic vision that shaped the symbolic actions of the Alianza. Only the tightly knit circle of devotees who followed him to New Mexico after the implosion of the Valley of Peace commune were aware of its deep apocalyptic foundations. Had they known, most Alianza dues-paying members may have deemed it all rather bizarre.

Reies López Tijerina is not a name familiar to most Americans. If one were to ask a random group of people to name one or two of the major 1960s civil rights advocates seeking justice for America's racialized poor, most would instantly recall the Rev. Dr. Martin Luther King Jr. and perhaps, as a distant second, César Chávez. That King has a national holiday that marks his birth, and Chávez is similarly celebrated in California, certainly helps. In the American Southwest, where Reies López Tijerina forged much of his religious and political legacy, he is still much revered and now no longer so adamantly reviled. He died on January 19, 2015, which naturally dissipated much of the animus his fiercest critics once had. Time passed. So too have they.

For the *viejitos*, the old women and men who put their trust in Reies hoping he would recuperate their lands, he was the savior they had long awaited. For young Chicanas and Chicanos in the late 1960s he likewise was the embodiment of their emancipatory hopes and nationalist aspirations rooted in land. For these reasons, he is still vividly remembered in word and song, in history books and popular memory, and even in the legislative chambers of several Southwestern states. Reies Tijerina risked his life, repeatedly found himself and his family in harm's way while seeking social justice for America's racialized poor. His residences were fire-bombed five times. The cars in which he rode dodged bullets and attempts to ram his auto off roads. Several of his family members were sexually assaulted. The attackers wanted to humiliate Reies and show him how helpless he was at protecting his family and how his enemies remained a menacing threat throughout the second half of his life. He was surveilled by the Federal Bureau of Investigation for decades, and he was sentenced to state and federal prison terms largely because his prophetic sense of justice impelled him to uplift the ethnic Mexican population of the American Southwest. He attempted to revitalize their denigrated Spanish language, celebrating their maligned culture and reforming school curricula to stop depicting ethnic Mexicans as inferior, ignorant, and backward peasants with no real future in America.

To this day, many of those dispossessed of the original land grants Spain and Mexico bestowed upon them between the sixteenth and nineteen centuries to colonize New Spain's far north at their own expense, still gather to remember all they once had: their agricultural fields, livestock, timber, water, and enough food for every meal. They sing *corridos* (ballads) about Reies's advocacy on their behalf, recalling his courage, his stamina, his fearlessness before state power, and their faith that Reies and their divine maker in heaven would soon deliver them anew to their lands, freed of their suffering and oppression just as Moses led the Israelites out of Egypt. During Reies's life he failed to regain even a single acre of land for the members of the Alianza. By politicizing the history of property rights throughout the American Southwest, he helped cure the amnesia many had of how the United States waged war against Mexico from 1846 to 1848 and despoiled mexicanos of their lands. The Treaty of Guadalupe-Hidalgo ended the war on February 2, 1848. It promised those Mexicans who chose to remain in annexed territories that their lives, liberty, and property would be protected. They were not. Having slowly, but systematically, lost their land grants, by the 1960s ethnic Mexicans had been reduced to an impoverished racialized class deemed as wretchedly poor as Blacks in the American South. In 1966 then New Mexico governor David Cargo succinctly explained that a form of "economic Darwinism" dictated the politics of northern New Mexico. It was "the survival of the richest."[2] Those inequalities continue. In 2018 New Mexico had the third-lowest median household income in the country, followed only by Arkansas and Mississippi. In 2021, the First Nations of New Mexico had the highest mortality rates in the United States.

When Reies López Tijerina died on January 19, 2015, many obituaries marked his passing, describing in broad strokes his eighty-one years of life. He was described as a self-styled Moses, a fiery orator, a man who began his career as a Pentecostal evangelist staging revivals across the United States determined to lead mexicanos on both sides of the border from paths of damnation to eternal salvation. He waged a life-long messianic crusade to better the lives of the poor, constantly decrying the proliferation of nuclear weapons, warning that the world's end and Christ's millennial return were near. These accounts tell of Reies's radicalization, the long historical origins of land rights movement he led, his June 5, 1967, misnamed "armed raid" on the Tierra Amarilla Courthouse in northern New Mexico (it was a citizen's arrest), and his prison sentences. As he advanced in age and increasingly deemed himself an Old Testament prophet, even a messiah, he claimed he had been persecuted and figuratively crucified by the Jewish descendants of the House of Judah, just as they had marked for death a number of messiahs before and after they colluded with Pontius Pilate to condemn Jesus to his death on the cross. Reies claimed he was a direct lineal descendant of Abraham, Joseph, and Jesus, and as a modern-day Moses was still fighting to vanquish the "beast" (a reference to Rome's emperors and their colonial administrators as described in Revelation), to curb the blandishments of the wicked whore of Babylon (the fruits of Rome's colonial exploitation), promising to lead his followers to their stolen lands. Critics read many of these pronouncements, what detractors lampooned as the demented rants of a schizophrenic anti-Semite, which were right on target, but were much more complex in origin and exposition. He genealogically chronicled his ancestry, proved, at least to his own satisfaction, and possibly mine, that his Spanish ancestors were Jews who had been forced to convert to Catholicism in 1492. As *conversos*, these Sephardic Jews migrated to Spanish America to escape persecution.[3]

Historians of the Mexican American past in the Southwest have long honored Reies Tijerina as one of the paladins of the long Mexican American civil rights movement that quickened in the years following the Great Depression and gained political muscle when veterans of the Second World War returned home to unskilled, low-paying jobs, segregation, voter suppression, and white supremacy. José Angel Gutiérrez, one of the Chicano movement's important political leaders and founder of the Raza Unida Party in the 1960s, summed up Reies's accomplishments. "He did what Malcolm X and the Black Panthers only talked about. He waged war against the state of New Mexico and the United States government. Armed with the constitutional power of citizen's arrest, he set out after many high-profile individuals in state and federal positions, including the Chief Justice of the United States Supreme Court. He literally took possession and control of illegally occupied land in New Mexico."[4]

To celebrate such bravery before state power, historians routinely refer to Tijerina as one of the Four Horsemen of the Apocalypse. Galloping into battle by Reies's side were César Chávez unionizing farmworkers in California, José Angel Gutiérrez forging the Raza Unida Party in Texas, and Rodolfo "Corky" Gonzales in Colorado demanding economic opportunities for Chicanos/as through his Crusade for Justice. The apocalypse these scholars had in mind was not the religious one narrated by John of Patmos in Revelation, which inspired much of Reies Tijerina's life and language, but a secular one that was increasing uniting civic and political organizations in the 1960s into an oppositional movement seeking racial and economic justice for all, but particularly for Mexican Americans living and working in rural and urban places in the Southwest. They dreamed of creating a new America and the materialization of their American dreams, in which their citizenship would be recognized, their service to the republic as soldiers honored, with equal access to housing, employment, and educational opportunities as the GI Bill of Rights promised them, but which were never realized or reached down very far even though America was then putatively waging a war on poverty.[5]

Reies Tijerina entered the public sphere in 1946 as a twenty-year-old Pentecostal evangelist, trained and authorized by the Assemblies of God deep in the heart of Texas. He toiled tirelessly preaching the word of God, curing the sick, feeding the poor, demanding that sinners repent if they expected to enter the pearly gates of heaven as their bodies were lifted in rapture during the Apocalypse. But it was his frenetic energy, his fearlessness before state power, his electrifying oratory, and his full-throttled entry into American civil rights politics and attack on federal and state governments that ultimately gained Reies notoriety as one of the two most celebrated Mexican American political activists of the twentieth century. Determined to understand the structural origins of ethnic Mexican poverty, his unvarnished conclusion was that it was due to land loss. Decades after the Mexican War's military campaigns ended in 1848, a second, equally vicious struggle was waged against vanquished mexicanos to rob them of their property. This war was fought in the American Congress and courts, between lawyers and investors, between Anglo newcomers and Hispano old timers, and among vigilantes allied with various economic interests.

The Spanish Crown and Mexican Republic first awarded private and communal land grants (mercedes) to those willing to build buffer settlements in New Spain's far north. These colonization missions were self-funded but made particularly attractive because they came with titles of nobility, full municipal rights as *vecinos* (property-owning citizens), and the authority to use indigenous forced labor for their exploits. By the early seventeenth century, the silver mines of north central Mexico were producing half of the Spanish empire's wealth, coveted by its European colonial rivals England and France. The Kingdom of New Mexico had become a productive supply colony for these mines by the eighteenth century, temporarily thwarting European territorial ambitions and tempering the lethal raids of the nomadic and now mounted and armed Comanches and Apaches.

When the United States became the conquering sovereign over these former Spanish and Mexican terrains in 1848, ownership of the mercedes became entangled in sinister intrigues. There was massive fraud, the willful destruction of original settlement charters (*capitulaciones*) and deeds, collusion among American and Mexican politicians, between lawyers and elites, all intent on appropriating the land and its natural wealth in timber, minerals, game, and grazing terrain, masking their ownership, quickly flipping properties, and just as rapidly lining their pockets with ill-gotten gains. In 1901, the heirs of 301 New Mexican land grants stood before the United States Court of Private Land Claims demanding congressional validation of their mercedes, encompassing some thirty-three million acres. The Court certified only 87, totaling only three million acres. The remaining thirty million acres were mostly transferred into the public domain as property of the US government, subsequently managed by the US Forest Service, leasing these lands to large private and corporate interests, thus selling off these natural resources to which Hispanos no longer had access. This is how the contestation over the land grants began. Thus, thousands of mexicanos were transformed into landless peasants migrating from place to place as unskilled wageworkers, slowly descending into poverty and bare subsistence. During the Great Depression of the 1930s, many more lost their personal irrigated agricultural lots, their private garden plots, and even access to the communal lands that long had provided them with timber, water, and grazing grasses for their flocks. Many only realized what had legally occurred decades earlier when in the 1950s they were fenced out of their ancestral grounds. "*Cuando vino el alambre, vino el hambre,*" when the barbed wire arrived, so too did their hunger.[6]

Between 1901 and 1960 these increasingly landless peasants litigated, filed suit after suit, protested overtly by invading land, tearing down barbed wire fences, and torching farms and barns. When these tactics failed to get the government's attention, they simply ignored federal property boundaries, trespassed, refusing to purchase hunting, grazing, and fishing permits from the US Forest Service to use lands they once owned now in federal hands, defiantly hoping for arrest to force the government to prove ownership. They became constant irritants to the individuals and corporate bodies they deemed the desperados who had despoiled them of their mercedes. At every turn, from authorities high and low, they were told that they would never regain their lands. The old mercedes now legally belonged to others, and the full force of the law would be exercised by American courts and constabularies to assure that no one impinged on the sanctity of private property.[7] US Forest Ranger Phil Smith summarized the dominant Anglo narrative about this land loss when he said, "If these people [referring to hispanos] would let go of history a little they would get something done here. You cannot live in the past; you need to let go of the past to move forward. All people talk about is what they have lost; they cannot seem to get beyond this. It's sad. . . . It has become who they are."[8]

Contesting such imperialist fantasies that commanded forgetting among those vanquished and dispossessed by the Mexican War, Tijerina insisted on remembering. "If we recuperate the land, we will recuperate our culture. If we recuperate our culture, we can recuperate the family, and if we save the family, we will liberate ourselves from Anglo-Saxon domination."[9] To realize these goals Reies Tijerina and his first wife, María Escobar Chávez, began an organization based on the familiar and well-respected mutual aid society model. The Alianza Federal de Mercedes, headquartered in Albuquerque, was legally incorporated on February 2, 1963, the 115th anniversary of the signing of the Treaty of Guadalupe Hidalgo, which ended the Mexican War. The Alliance's goal was to forge these heirs into a larger political force, eventually perhaps into a political party, to recuperate their lands, challenging the shenanigans used to rob them. The petitions, the letters, the marches, the sit-ins, the fasts, and land invasions the Alianza staged pushed Reies Tijerina into America's political consciousness, onto civil rights activist maps of the United States, and into J. Edgar Hoover's FBI gaze as a dangerous rabble rouser who had to be silenced. Neutralized.

Discredited. Put away. Yes, even killed. All were tried and most succeeded, save for his assassination.

Hoover feared that Tijerina, like several Black Power leaders, might emerge as a messianic prophet and savior to Mexican Americans in the Southwest. Reies certainly had the training, the oratory, and ardent desire for that role, which he realized to some extent. That is perhaps why in 1969 the National Broadcasting Company (NBC) aired an hour-long exposé—*Reies Tijerina: The Most Hated Man in New Mexico*—meant to "educate" viewers across the country as to who this man, this closeted Communist, this rabid Castroite, this hypocritical pietistic Bible-thumping sexual psychopath really was.[10] That was the tone and tenor of those who were discrediting his cause.

This book delves into the social and cultural world into which Reies López Tijerina was born, his life and loves, and all the major religious and secular issues he devoted his manic energy to. A survey of the published books that focus on him are quite lopsided in scope and temporal sweep. They mainly address his land grant activism between 1963 and 1969, but some include a few years before and after. Of course, these works briefly and rapidly survey his social origin and religious ministry, then intensively delve on Tijerina's leadership of the Alianza, the organization's radicalization, and its rapid demise while Reies served time in a federal psychiatric prison ward, where he was diagnosed as suffering from schizophrenia, with an evident bipolar disorder from which he had probably suffered since he was a teenager. The issues Reies devoted the remainder of his forty-five years of life are rarely mentioned.

My goal here is to narrate Reies's religious formation and how it logically morphed into his political activism, which initially focused on land grants but soon expanded to multiracial coalitional politics among Native Americans, Mexican Americans, and African Americans. I do this by focusing the arc of history into which he was born, delving deeply into the first thirty-five years of his life, the period during which he was forged as an Assemblies of God evangelist, turning to his 1960s Alianza activism only briefly to sketch continuities, because the basics of this story are already well known. Then I turn to his life's story anew from his incarceration in 1969 and then to his release from federal prison to his death in 2015. The only sustained education Reies ever had, secular or religious, was a two-year course of study at the *Instituto Bíblico Latino Americano* (The Latin American Bible Institute; hereafter LABI) near San Antonio, Texas, which took him three years to complete because of suspensions. There he learned his Bible theology, how to prepare and deliver sermons, the importance of prophecy to Christians, and the absolute centrality the Book of Revelation held for Pentecostals. So spiritually armed, Reies entered a world in 1946 that he saw corrupted by sin, in desperate need of repentance. He preached this message tirelessly for twelve years, from 1946 to 1958, punctuated by Reies's Visalia Dream, his Grand Vision, when he and God, together imagined a salvific future, to which Reies committed the rest of his life. It was a life of preaching and politics, with the Bible and human law as his interpretive secular silver key.

The larger argument herein is that when Reies in 1958 moved full throttle into the political realm on behalf of the poor, joining the ranks of the many in the United States then actively seeking civil rights for racialized minorities, he never stopped being an evangelist. His Pentecostal formation was deeply engrained in his psyche, in his daily language, and at the very core of his moral and ethical temperament. He did not simply erase or forget all of this when he became active in social-movement politics seeking justice for those who had lost their lands in the last half of the nineteenth century, determined to eradicate the most egregious forms of racism and white supremacy, and to valorize the language and culture of mexicanos. In this book I have resisted separating his language and action into distinct, mutually exclusive religious and political realms, as some authors have done. Instead, I show the continuities and relationships between the two. Reies judged the secular exactly as he measured the religious. Both were one in his mind.

Elisions of Tijerina's rhetorical complexity by previous biographers requires that we read and listen to the totality of his words, both those uttered or penned in Spanish and English. Much of what Tijerina said was delivered to monolingual Spanish-speaking audiences or broadcast over Spanish-language radio. The Alianza's press releases and weekly updates "*Noticias de la Alianza Federal de Mercedes*," published in Albuquerque's *News Chieftain*, were in Spanish. English-speaking biographers either could not read these Spanish texts or simply ignored them. Take, for example, Reies Tijerina's massive autobiography, *Mi lucha por la tierra* (My Fight for the

Land), published in Mexico City in 1978. In this book he offers readers a synthesis of his life from 1956 to 1976, plotting a map of his trials and tribulations modeled on those Moses experienced leading the Israelites out of their Egyptian captivity. It is a long 575-page book, issued in an edition of 5,000 copies, which did not circulate much beyond Mexico. An abridged translation appeared only in 2000, edited by an old political ally and confidant, José Angel Gutiérrez, titled, *They Called Me "King Tiger": My Struggle for the Land and Our Rights*.[11] Reies Tijerina hated the José Angel translation, constantly denouncing him for having excised the religious language that was so central to his autobiography. Hoping to expose English monolinguals to Tijerina's Spanish-language texts, the appendix of this book reproduces the sermons Reies penned and preached between 1946 and 1955, published as ¿*Hallará Fe en la Tierra . . . ?* (Will He Find Any Faith on Earth . . . ?), followed by my English translation of these sermons.

Scholars have argued recently that Reies Tijerina's theories of imperialism and colonial oppression were forged by his observations and connections to Third World liberation movements, particularly those articulated by Cuban and Vietnamese national revolutionaries during the 1950s and 1960s. Tijerina's sermons from the 1940s show otherwise. While he was a student at the LABI, he studied the New Testament intensively, and his imagination was powerfully gripped by the ways John of Patmos, the presumptive author of the New Testament's Book of Revelation, described the Roman Empire's colonial exploitation of Judea's Jews, the murder of Jesus, the destruction of the Jewish temple in Jerusalem in 70 CE, and the persecution of Jesus's followers in Rome's Asia Minor colonies. This is how Reies first learned the meaning of imperialism, colonial exploitation, and state-motivated repression of conquered and defeated ethno-religious groups. He often referred to Rome's emperors and their local prefects as "the beast" and described the blandishments colonial exploitation offered Rome's citizens as the "debauchery of wicked whore of Babylon," with the goddess Roma as the emblem of idol worship.

In the 1960s Tijerina certainly knew of other contemporary nationalist, anticolonial struggles. His personal papers, housed at the University of New Mexico's Zimmerman Library, contain many newspapers from the 1960s and 1970s reporting on Puerto Rico's independence struggle, Palestinian demands for a homeland, Native American attempts to regain their ancestral lands, the progress of the war in Vietnam, and American attacks on the Cuban Revolution wrought by the economic blockade and Bay of Pigs failed coup.[12] On June 9, 1967, J. Edgar Hoover ordered FBI agents to raid Reies's living quarters, hoping to find evidence of his ties to Communist organizations. All they found was a copy of Ernesto "Che" Guevara's *Guerilla Warfare* (1961). But these anticolonial struggles were not what first and most fundamentally shaped his analysis of imperialism. Yes, many young women and men in the 1960s hailed Reies as northern New Mexico's "Che," or even as the Emiliano Zapata of the Southwest (a reference to Mexico Revolutionary peasant hero).[13] But in 1943, as a student at the LABI, Reies intensively studied why Jerusalem's Roman prefect, Pontius Pilate, crucified Jesus and later waged a war of extermination against Judea's Jews. Why did Rome's Emperor, Cesar Augustus, demand that his colonial subjects venerate him as a deity, commanding offerings to venerate the empire's goddess Roma?

Most of what is known about Reies Tijerina rests in studies focused on the creation and declension of the Alianza Federal de Mercedes between roughly 1963 and 1971, a period of eight years. His longer biography, the years before and after the land grant struggle, or from 1926 to 1958, and from 1969 to 2015, remain largely opaque. Roughly seventy years of Reies's life still remain unexplored or disconnected. Enter any library and search the subject catalog for Reies López Tijerina. What you will find is a group of books initially published in the late 1960s and early 1970s. These include: Michael Jenkinson, *Tijerina: Land Grant Conflict in New Mexico* (1968), Peter Nabokov, *Tijerina and the Courthouse Raid* (1969), Richard Gardner, *¡Grito!: Reies Tijerina and the New Mexico Land Grant War of 1967* (1970), and Patricia Bell Blawis, *Tijerina and the Land Grants: Mexican Americans in Struggle for Their Heritage* (1971). As the books' subtitles indicate, they were framed by the incendiary passions of the moment in which they were written and published, enmeshed as their titles imply in "conflict," "raid," "war," and "struggle." The United States was then waging a brutal imperial war in Vietnam, and in the minds of many, it was impossible not to compare the logic and tactics of the war there and the state repression being waged at home. Tijerina constantly and caustically protested the war in Vietnam and urged young Mexican American men to resist the draft and military service in this predatory imperialist war in which they had no stake. The battles young Mexican Americans were morally obliged to wage were here, at home, in the United States, to recuperate their lost land in the American Southwest, not across an ocean in Vietnam. "If we have to go to Vietnam and you have these lands rights (at home) which have been stolen from you by the federal government you might as well fight for them here," he argued.[14]

Between 1971 and 2005, little more was published on Tijerina. Then, in 1999, Reies donated his personal papers to the Zimmerman Library at the University of New Mexico, allowing researchers to judge for themselves all the good, the bad, and the ugly of his documented life to that point. The Reies Tijerina Papers were opened to the public without restrictions on June 5, 2005. Housed in the Library's Center for Southwest Research, the collection's scope is as comprehensive as any researcher can hope. More books followed that made use of his archive: Rudy V. Busto, *King Tiger: The Religious Vision of Reies López Tijerina* (2005), Jake Kosek, *Underhistories: The Political Life of Forests in Northern New Mexico* (2006), Gordon K. Mantler, *Power to the Poor: Black-Brown Coalition and the Fight for Economic Justice, 1960–1974* (2013), David Correia, *Properties of Violence: Land Grant Struggles in Northern New Mexico* (2013), Lorena Oropeza, *The King of Adobe: Reies López Tijerina, Lost Prophet of the Chicano Movement* (2019), and José Angel Gutiérrez, *Tracking King Tiger: Reies López Tijerina and the FBI* (2019). Except for Busto's book on Tijerina's religious ideology, and Mantler's study of Reies's role in the 1968 Poor People's March on Washington, DC, studies of the Alianza years dominate.

I first met Reies Tijerina as a boy at a gathering of the Alianza, which I attended with my mother around 1964. She was one of the many hispanas whose family lost their 1739 Tomé de Dominguez land grant and wanted to learn what Reies might do to gain its return. At that age Tijerina left little of an impression on me. I heard his name in our home now and then, but never in a sustained way. I eventually went off to graduate school in New York and Wisconsin and was not really following events back home in Albuquerque, except for news of the wretched effects the war in Vietnam was having on neighbors and friends. In 1978, as a history doctoral candidate, I returned to New Mexico to undertake dissertation research on the Spanish colonial Kingdom of New Mexico. From that point on, Reies and I intersected quite regularly. We first became friendly because we were often the only two readers using the microfilm editions of the Spanish, Mexican, and Territorial Archives of New Mexico housed at the State Records Center and Archives in Santa Fe. We were both studying social reproduction; he focused on land, I on marriage and family formation. When he could not decipher esoteric seventeenth- and eighteenth-century Spanish paleographic script, he would ask for my help. Our paths continued to cross at conferences and public events in the 1990s. My own interest on Reies's life and ministry was ignited by the ceremony the University of New Mexico's Zimmerman Library hosted when his papers were opened for public use on June 5, 2005. For a few days after, I poked around his massive archive. Call it fate, call it providence, call it my own long-held interest in the history of religion. One of the first items that grabbed my attention were forty-five sermons he had preached between 1946 and 1955.

Fascinated by them, I telephoned Reies who was then living in Uruapán, Michoacán, Mexico, asking permission to translate his sermons into English. That was the genesis of this book. He granted permission with condition. He wanted to see my translations as they progressed, threatening to terminate our verbal agreement if he disliked what he read. Agreed. Reies reminded me how other translators had sanitizing his textual corpus, excising or ignoring his religious thought. I assured him that it would be quite impossible for me to secularize his sermons. They were about God, sin, redemption, and the Apocalypse. On that score I was safe.

Reies liked my translation, quibbled about my punctuation, which I explained simply made for easier reading in English. Having learned how to read and write English and Spanish from the Bible, Reies mimicked its stylistically penchant for long run-on sentences connected by one semicolon after another. That was the extent of my grammatical emendations, adding only an occasional footnote to illuminate arcane biblical referents.

In the chapters that follow, let us turn first to Reies Tijerina's genealogy and ancestral history. In flights of fancy, he said many times that his ancient clansmen originated in the Holy Land, in Assyria, and from there migrated across North Africa and into the Iberian Peninsula, before embarking across the Atlantic to the Spanish Caribbean, to Mexico City, and from there to Texas. Here the origins of the mercedes, the land grants Spain and then Mexico awarded to those willing to colonize frontiers, are described and traced, how the Mexicans of Texas, known as *Tejanos*, lost their land and were transformed into migrant farm workers in the decades after the Texas Revolution and American annexation. All these transformations unfold through Reies's family history. In chapter 2 we turn to the origins of Pentecostalism and the Assemblies of God to fully understand the ideological origins of the Gospel message Reies eventually preached and the rituals necessary for the total embodiment of the apostolic faith. From here, what follows in chapter 3 is a foray to the Latin American Bible Institute, which the Assemblies of God established to train ethnic Mexicans who wanted to become evangelists. Reies Tijerina arrived there in September 1943, ready to develop a closer relationship with God and to learn how to spread his message. Once he learned how to read and interpret the Bible, how to write and deliver sermons, and how to stage Pentecostal revivals, he went off as an evangelist spreading the news of salvation. Chapter 4 describes Reies's life as a preacher and the nature of his revivals. In chapter 5 I offer an analysis of the Bible's last book, Revelation. This is the biblical text that describes Christian end-time, recounting in horrific detail how God will punish the world for its sinfulness, what will occur during the world's final days, when Jesus Christ returns to rule triumphantly for a thousand years. Without this focus on the political context in which Revelation was written by John of Patmos, the chapter that follows would be impossible to fully understand.

Chapter 6 offers an analysis of the sermons Reies preached, penned, and published in 1955 as a book titled *Will He Find Any Faith on Earth . . . ?* His answer to this question was no. In January 1956 Reies led a small group of his most devoted followers into the Arizona desert to start a religious commune he called the Valley of Peace where they went to await the Apocalypse. It did not arrive. Internal dissention did. Plagued by accusation of incest and adultery, Reies's desire to live polygamously as the ancient prophets had, led the Heralds of Peace to begin scattering. This was when Reies had his Super

Dream, and as a result of what that vision inspired, Reies renounced his life as a preacher for that of a social activist. All of this is described in chapter 7. In chapter 8, Reies Tijerina's arrival in New Mexico is narrated. He promised the old timers that he would recuperate their lost land grants, forming the Alianza Federal de Mercedes to gather the dispossessed and petition the government toward this end. Here I delve into the events that led to a seizure of federal lands, and what followed legally, politically, and socially. In chapter 9 we find Reies serving his federal prison sentence for the invasion of a part of the Kit Carson National Forest, his treatment for schizophrenia by prison psychiatrists, his release, and his reading of his FBI file in 1979. He had long been paranoid about his government surveillance. Here he read exactly what the government had done to silence him starting in 1963 and how he and his family suffered as a result. Around 1980 he became obsessed with his genealogy, again prompted by his FBI file, first tracing his clan's migration from Spain to Texas, then backward from Spain to Genesis to establish his messianic origins and to accuse the descendants of the Jewish House of Judah as those who had plotted to kill him. The chapter closes with the hardships his wives and children suffered from the moment he started his evangelistic ministry to his death.

CHAPTER I

The Social Origins of the Tijerina Clan

SEPTEMBER 21, 1926, WAS a punishing day for Herlinda López. Nine months pregnant, her belly protruded as she waddled through cotton fields near Falls City, Texas, dragging a bag with nearly a hundred pounds of pickings. Working under a blazing Texas sun, her throat parched and wanting for water, she stopped to brush aside the sweat on her brow and moved on. Quietly she prayed her day be done. Suddenly she bent over in pain from birthing contractions. She made her way back to the one-room house she occupied with her husband Antonio Tijerina. The hours passed. The tempo and intensity of her contractions quickened, and as they did, so too her shrieks and cries. A boy! They named him Reies, or King. He was born right there atop Herlinda's cotton-stuffed sack, which initially doubled as his crib, or so the legend goes. Herlinda returned to the cotton fields a few days later. She had no choice. The harvest was almost over and if she was to keep her family fed during the winter ahead, there were still many cotton bolls left to pluck.

Much later, during the 1960s, civil rights activists often compared Reies López Tijerina to his namesake, Dr. Martin Luther King Jr. Both were reverends. Both were Protestant ministers using biblical prophetic messages to advance the cause of racial justice in the United States. Tijerina resisted the analogy, tartly insisting that the "king" in his name was more accurately connected to the kings of Spain and to Jesus Christ, the King of Kings. As Reies explained it, the Tijerinas originated in Spain and migrated to the New World in the early sixteenth century. How they got from the Iberian

Peninsula to Texas, how their numbers grew and fared over the course of almost four centuries, and how this history profoundly shaped Reies Tijerina's world, memories, and political activism, is our focus here.

Between 711, when the Moors first invaded the Iberian Peninsula, and 1492 Iberia's Catholic monarchs waged a constant war to subordinate Islam and to reestablish Catholic control. The peninsula's two most powerful kingdoms—Aragón and Castilla—were made one through the marriage of King Ferdinand and Queen Isabella in 1469 and, by so doing, finally marshalled the forces to vanquish Islam, laying the foundation for the emergence of modern Spain. This 1492 victory was followed months later in October by Christopher Columbus's landing in the Americas, planting the seeds for what became a global empire, reaching all the way from Europe to the Philippines. Roman Catholicism became Spain's official state religion in 1492, ordering that Muslims and Jews convert or face expulsion. Under threats of death many fled, scattering across the Mediterranean. Those Jews who remained and converted, known as conversos, naturally were deemed suspect and flaccid in their imposed faith. When Cuba, Mexico, and Peru were finally under Spanish control by the 1530s, many conversos migrated to the Americas, hoping there to escape the anti-Semitism they faced in Spain.[1]

In the early 1980s, Reies Tijerina became obsessed over his genealogical origins for reasons that will unfold more fully later in this book. In short, it was to substantiate his belief that he was a messianic Jewish prophet of Old Testament lineage. He found a converso couple named Diego Texerina and María Hernández living in Porcuna, in Andalucía, who were originally natives of Tejerina in the Kingdom of León. Diego and María's son, also named Diego, ventured to the New World. Perhaps escaping persecution. Perhaps seeking adventure. We do not know. Embarking at the port of Cádiz on October 19, 1510, he was listed as passenger number 123 on a ship bound for Santo Domingo on the island of Hispaniola. Over time, Diego Texerina's descendants moved to Cuba, then to Mexico, helping to colonize Monterrey. There the genealogical trail disappears. A José Texerina emerged in historical records anew in 1748, when the viceroy of New Spain granted him license to establishment the town of Santiago de Valladares, in what is now the northern Mexican state of Coahuila. Such areas attracted conversos believing that in sparsely populated places they could prosper and might practice their natal faith clandestinely.²

During the seventeenth and eighteenth centuries, there were many Inquisitorial inquests launched against colonial settlers in Nuevo León and Nuevo México, targeting conversos accused of secretly practicing Judaism. Some were tortured and waterboarded until they confessed that they obeyed the "law of Moses." They were publicly garroted until they died, their bodies then burned at the stake. Historian Solange Alberro found that between 1571 and 1700, thirty-four to thirty-seven persons were consumed by such flames in New Spain. Not many, granted, but just enough to vividly emblazon such punishment in the imagination of conversos.³ Many of these investigations were trumped up, politically and economically motivated, and eventually dismissed. Nevertheless, accusations of crypto-Judaism were always enough to wreak havoc on one's life and livelihood. The behaviors these dockets described, which were guaranteed to provoke suspicion and land one before the Inquisition, were not attending Sunday Mass, changing bed linens on Friday, publicly cursing the name of God, saying that Mary, his mother was not a virgin, not obeying the clergy, lighting candles on Friday night, and so on. Some of these behaviors were indeed Jewish Sabbath ritual fragments. Often Spanish residents in the New World turned to the Inquisition to settle more mundane squabbles over local power and were only occasionally about deeply disguised Jewish identities.⁴

The charter of incorporation (*capitulación*) José Texerina obtained to establish a town in 1748 included for himself and those who accompanied him titles of nobility as *hidalgos*, enormous grants of land called mercedes, and the exploitation of indigenous tributary labor. The Tijerina males who descended from these colonists eventually moved north to what became Laredo, Texas, sometime in the late eighteenth- or early nineteenth century. Reies Tijerina vividly remembers that as a boy, Santiago Tijerina, his paternal grandfather, constantly told him stories about the land grant (merced) the king of Spain had given them.⁵

Genealogical records show that in the 1750s José Texerina (now spelled Tixerina) fathered a son also named José, who likewise begat a son, Javier, who in turn sired a son named Antonio. This Antonio's surname finally appeared in records as "Tijerina." He took a bride named María Antonia, who birthed their first son in 1832. They christened him Julian who was Reies Tijerina's paternal great-grandfather. He married Guadalupe Ortiz, who birthed three sons: Francisco, Fernando, and Santiago. Santiago Tijerina was Reies's paternal grandfather. He is remembered to have lived to the age of eighty-seven, was interred in Laredo, Texas, in 1947, and so probably was born in 1860.[6]

Family lore holds that the Tijerinas thrived in Laredo, where they were livestock ranchers. Living with kin and kith in extended webs of social relations, they enjoyed a modest but comfortable rural life. They did not live like the grandees of central Mexico, but they certainly relished the trappings of local nobility, the status of vecinos, as independent property-owning men with full civic rights, enjoying the service of servants, and pride in family name. God fearing and church going, most of them said that they believed in the one, true Christian God, and if as conversos they did not, they dared not whisper such things. In this unforgiving terrain that they worked so hard to tame, the Tijerina women and men became as tough as the scrub brush their cattle chewed on and as leathery as their hides. Their sense of superiority was rooted not only in their descent from Spanish conquerors but also their lordship over land and indigenous labor. What was more fantasy than fact, a delusion so common among settler classes in colonial situations, was the belief that their bloodlines were pure and superior to those of their *mestizo*, or racially mixed, neighbors. The sex ratio on New Spain's northern frontier had many more single Spanish men than marriageable Spanish women. Biological mixing occurred. Whether they knew it or not, or wanted to admit it or not, the area's nobility had more in common racially with the *indios* and mestizos they lived among and loved but whom they so demeaned as racially impure inferiors.

Mexico declared its independence from Spain in 1821 and soon thereafter opened its borders to immigrants, believing that "to govern is to populate." Streams of settlers, mainly from the American South, rushed into Texas, vowing to abide by Mexico's laws, promising conversion to Catholicism and mastering the Spanish tongue. In return they were given access to cheap land and the right to keep their black slaves. This last concession was revoked in 1829, Mexico hoping thus to stem their immigrant invasion. Mexican Texans, or Tejanos, were quickly outnumbered. As Anglo ascendancy in Texas increased in the 1830s, so too their desire for independence grew. In 1835 an alliance between Anglo and Mexican Texans declared themselves independent as the Republic of Texas. In the first forays to suppress the rebellion, Mexican troops scored bloody victories at the Alamo and Goliad. These defeats ignited Anglo rage, soon avenged, eventually routing Mexican forces from Texas in 1836.[7]

No sooner was their Republic birthed than calls for its annexation into the United States were realized in 1845. Feigning a boundary dispute with Mexico, the drums of war sounded in Texas in 1846, resounding all the way to the halls of Congress. War was declared against Mexico on May 10, 1846. President James Polk maintained that Mexico had "invaded our territory and shed American blood on American soil," which was simply not true.[8] Hostilities lasted from May 10, 1846, to February 2, 1848, when the Treaty of Guadalupe-Hidalgo ended the war.

The treaty vowed that the United States would protect the rights of Mexicans who chose to remain in conquered territory, granting them full citizenship as whites, and assuring that their liberties and properties would be respected as if they had been bequeathed to them by the United States itself.[9] Senator Alexander Stephens of Georgia ridiculed the objective of President Polk's war. What Polk desired was not a "peace with Mexico but a piece of Mexico."[10]

Even before the independence of Texas was won in 1836, Anglo settlers began venting their rage against Tejanos for no apparent reason other than that they were Mexicans, or so Tejanos claimed. Violence, intimidation, lynching, and the destruction of Mexican property became a blood sport overnight in hopes of getting ethnic Mexicans to abandon their lands. Martín de León, an aristocratic landholder in Victoria, was driven from his home and had all his livestock seized in the 1840s. Laredo's José María Martín complained in the 1850s that Anglos "began a movement to clean out the Mexicans. They would rant at public meetings and declare that this was an American country and the Mexicans ought to be run out."[11] Juan Seguín, San Antonio's mayor between 1840 and 1842, and a leading patriot during the independence revolt, experienced much the same. Seguín referred to the interlopers as "scum" who were even targeting Mexican elites "whose only crime was that they owned large tracts of land and desirable property."

Seguín openly defended his countrymen against racist and war-crazed Anglos. They were denying Tejanos their constitutional rights, Seguín complained, relishing a perverse satisfaction when they terrorized Mexicans and treated them "worse than brutes."[12] Seguín and his family fled to Mexico to escape the violence in 1842. Hundreds followed. Those who were able to sell their lands did so for a pittance, knowing that if they delayed, they would surely be killed and strung from posts. Reies Tijerina's paternal great-grandfather Julian, who had lived on his merced in Laredo for well over fifty years, died defending it from such an assault. The Tejano towns of Victoria, San Patricio, La Bahía, and Refugio were razed by Anglo vigilantes. Seething with resentment and vowing retribution, Tejanos took refuge in Mexico and retaliated as soon and as often as they could.[13]

The rhetoric of conquest Anglos vaunted was of their white supremacy, their God-given mastery to lord it over racially inferior descendants of Indians, that it was their Manifest Destiny. Levi Woodbury, who hailed originally from New Hampshire, described the battle raging in Texas as between "men of the true Saxon race" who previously had been "humiliated, and enslaved to Moors, Indians, and mongrels."[14] Tejanos theoretically enjoyed the full rights of American citizenship. De facto, as Senator John C. Calhoun argued in 1848, that privilege was reserved for "the Caucasian race—the free white race." It would be a "fatal error," he continued, to place "the colored race on an equality with the white."[15]

As the decades passed, Santiago Tijerina, Reies's grandfather, frequently gathered his kin to remind them of what Tejanos had experienced under Jim Crow, the nature of vigilante justice, and its enforcement by the *pinches rinches*, the cursed Texas Rangers. Santiago Tijerina died in 1947, but before he did, he often reminded his children and grandchildren exactly how he got the deep dark scar he had around his neck. "The Texas Rangers were killing all the heirs who had documents or proof that they were descendants of the land grants." One afternoon they arrived at his ranch, accusing him of stealing cattle. Without interrogation, without even a shred of proof, they strung him up from a tree, a noose around his neck. Had the local judge, who was a family friend, not arrived when he did, protesting that the Rangers had the wrong man, Santiago's body would have been left dangling from that tree. His scar had a history.[16]

As a young boy, Reies Tijerina paid little attention to his grandfather's stories, dismissing them as fanciful old man talk. Then one Saturday in 1949, while evangelizing in Victoria, Texas, Reies heard a similar story from an Anglo man from Cuero. He engaged Reies in conversation for more than four hours, explaining how Anglos had stolen Tejano lands. It would begin, the old man declared, by an Anglo pretending to be a Tejano's friend and offering to buy his land.

> At night the Anglo's gunslingers and rustlers would kill the workers of the *hacendado* and kill the cattle and terrorize the workers ... then the Anglo would come, talking casually ... he would offer him a gift, maybe a bottle of liquor ... he would have a dance ... the Anglo would ask him to dance with his own daughter. He would convince him that he was a real friend. At night the Anglo's men would murder, but he wouldn't kill the owner until he signed the paper ... finally he was persuaded by all this organized murder, so he signed the document and he was given the gold. So when he was leaving the ranch, the Anglo would say, "Pancho, what gate are you using? The east, the north, the south?" And he would tell him and in the brush the Anglo's gang would come and kill everybody and get the gold and put some Indian arrows into the bodies.[17]

The story rang true, exactly as his grandfather Santiago had recounted a decade earlier. Had Reies queried old timers about the veracity of such accounts, he would have understood how true they were. An elderly resident of San Benito, Texas, named Arturo, recounted how his ancestors lost their lands and the nobility the king of Spain had granted them. "They slowly killed us. They would shoot our animals and force us off the land." Then availing themselves of American law for similar ends, they would "fail to send us tax forms, so we never knew when to pay our taxes," Arturo continued. "Then one of them would claim default on the land, pay the taxes, and become owner of our land. Since they had the sheriff and the lawyers, and since our people didn't understand the language or their system, they stole the land under our house."[18]

Texas became a hotly contested battleground fought over by Anglos and Tejanos for control of the state's resources between 1850 and 1915. In 1859, what became known as the Cortina Wars, broke out in Brownsville, when Bob Shears, the city's marshal, badly beat a *ranchero* and his former servant for public intoxication. Juan Nepomuceno Cortina, one of the area's wealthiest Tejano landowners, came to their defense, shooting the marshal in the arm. Cortina was charged with attempted murder. He retaliated by holding Brownsville captive for six months. Calling his countrymen to arms November 23, 1859, Cortina described Texans as "flocks of vampires, in the guise of men . . . [who invaded the area] without any capital except the corrupt heart and the most perverse intentions." Writing to his fellow Tejanos Cortina noted, "Many of you have been robbed of your property, incarcerated, chased, murdered, and hunted like wild beasts, because your labor was fruitful, and because your industry excited the vile avarice which led them." Repelling several attempts by the Texas Rangers to quash Cortina's rebellion, a fragile "peace" was restored by federal troops in December 1859.[19]

Violence in El Paso, Ysleta, and San Elizario came next as the sites of the Salt War of 1877, provoked by the state's secret appropriation of the salt beds mexicanos had depended on for consumption and trade for more than a century. Texas awarded the beds to the Texas and Pacific Railroad, which in turn sold them to El Paso judge Charles Howard. When Howard demanded payment from the mexicanos mining salt that he claimed as his, they revolted, killing him and his assistants. It took federal troops to reestablish a fitful peace.[20]

This history of racial conflict, state repression, and the alienation of their mercedes led some Tejanos to demand succession through revolution. Hatched in San Diego, Texas, not far from Mexico's border, on February 20, 1915, their "Manifesto to the Oppressed Peoples of America" complained that they had been "robbed in a most perfidious manner by North American imperialism." The United States ignored the "daily lynchings of men . . . now dictates itself to the lynching of an entire people, an entire race, and entire continent . . . [this] hatred of races which closes the doors to schools, hotels, theatres and all public establishments to the Mexican, black and yellow, and divides the railroads and all public meeting places into areas where the savage 'white skins' meet and constitute a superior cast." Promising "equality and independence" for Mexicans, Blacks, Indians, and the Japanese, the "liberating army" intended to kill "every North American over sixteen years of age," sparing only women, children, and the elderly. The plot was foiled and the revolution's leaders executed, but the provocations that led to the plan were not forgotten.[21]

Between 1821 and 1930 the makeup of the population of Texas was remade in the 1830s, in the 1870s, and in the 1910s. Immigration rather than natural growth accounted for much of the change. Under Spanish rule in 1800 Tejas listed 7,000 settlers. As a result of the empresario settlement grants awarded to Anglo immigrants, by 1827 Tejas had grown to 18,000, with Anglos representing 67 percent of the total. On the eve of independence in 1836, Texas counted 39,000; Anglos numbered 30,000, or 77 percent. The first US Census in 1850 enumerated 154,000, with Anglos now forming 84 percent. Over the next fifty years, the population of Texas grew exponentially. By 1900, the state had 2,426,700 residents, with whites constituting 93 percent, and ethnic Mexicans only 7 percent, or 165,000. The impact of the Mexican Revolution on trans-border migration into Texas was evident by 1930. Between 1910 and 1930, the ethnic Mexican population grew from 226,466 to 683,681; Anglo whites now numbered 4,283,491, out of a total of 4,967,172, representing 86 percent of the total.[22] The turbulent origins of the 1910 Mexican Revolution, its violent population displacements northward, and its aftermath explains the demographic growth reported in 1930; peasants seeking to feed themselves and refugees in search of safety formed the majority of these migrants. The rest can be attributed to the rapid expansion of cotton farming and the development of sugar beet production, which were both labor intensive pursuits that could only profit if they had abundant, cheap, unskilled labor. The US Immigration Quota Acts of 1921 and 1924 severely restricted the entry of European and Asian laborers. Mexico provided the closest abundant supply.

This demographic growth was simultaneously accompanied by an occupational transformation. In 1850, 41 percent of the state's ethnic Mexican population were farmers, livestock raisers, sheepherders, herdsmen, and cowhands; in 1870, 22 percent were; and by 1900, they represented only 19 percent. Transport and trade in 1850 (i.e., cart men, teamsters, merchants, clerks) accounted for 23 percent of ethnic Mexican laborers, but only 7 percent by 1900. Mexican skilled laborers (i.e., carpenters, tailors, shoemakers, blacksmiths) were 35 percent of the total in 1850, but only 10 percent in 1900. The greatest occupational transformation was in "service" and "unspecialized labor." In 1850, 0.6 percent of Mexicans were service workers, rising to 16.7 percent in 1860, before dropping to 11 percent in 1900. "Unspecialized labor" likewise rose from 0.3 percent in 1850, to 55 percent in 1900. Aggregating "service" and "unspecialized labor," by 1900, 67 percent, or two out of every three Mexicans were employed as unskilled laborers, while in 1850 less than one out of every hundred had been. In 1850 Tejanos dominated transport. By 1860 they were displaced first by Anglo competitors and then by the railroad in the 1870s.[23]

From the 1870s to the 1890s, the vast grasslands of central Texas were enclosed where once cattle freely fattened before slaughter in St. Louis and Kansas City. Fenced land at first protected watering holes against overgrazing and cattle rustling. But the enclosure of large swaths of land laid the foundations for their transformation into cotton plantations. The construction of railroad networks throughout Texas accelerated the process. In 1860 cotton production amounted to 432,463 bales, 805,284 bales in 1880, and 2,971,757 bales in 1920, yielding one-third of all domestic cotton production in the country. By 1930 Texas tenant farms produced two-thirds of the crop.[24] As cotton became king in Texas, ranching and livestock production were displaced, absorbing much of its labor. During this changing use of cheap manual labor, ethnic Mexicans, blacks, and poor whites competed as sharecroppers and tenants, grubbing, tilling, tending, picking, and ginning cotton.

Texas cotton farmers favored ethnic Mexican workers over poor whites and blacks because, as was often crudely explained, Mexicans were short and built close to the earth. Nature itself predisposed them to planting and plucking. One grower reasoned in 1920 that the Mexican was "specifically fitted for the burdensome task of bending his back to pick the cotton and the burdensome task of grubbing the fields." Mexicans too were obedient. They endured harrowing labor conditions without complaint. Poor white workers rarely did. Whatever shelter Mexicans were given, as primitive and as uninhabitable as it might be, they made the best of what they were given without audible grumbles. Alone among their own, of course they wagged their tongues in Spanish saying exactly what they thought of their low wages, poor treatment, and the ghastly conditions in which they toiled.[25]

Between 1910 and 1930, half of all the ethnic Mexicans who sought work in Texas came as families; the rest were mainly single men, with far fewer women and children. Texas employers preferred families because they were much more stable, usually remaining in the United States when their work was done or returning as sojourners yearly. Since such families were only paid seasonally, from planting to harvest, when their work was done they were gone. And since most lacked the financial means to return to Mexico, they stayed put nearby. To survive they turned to kin, friends, churches, and welfare agencies, thus shifting the burden of support from their employers to the state and to local charities. African American agricultural workers who hailed from the American South demanded wages all year long as was custom on Southern plantations. This was why Mexican laborers were preferred, not because of their stature, not because of their humility. It was their low cost, pliability, managed stability, and the winter subsidies others paid to maximize grower profits.[26]

The World of Antonio Tijerina and Herlinda López

Antonio Tijerina and his wife Herlinda López, like the many other Tejanos who lost their ancestral lands between 1850 and 1900, were soon among those left destitute by the Wall Street stock market crash of 1929. The Great Depression intensified their plight, forcing them to migrate from field to field, sometimes as sharecroppers, other times as fieldhands, eking out a bare subsistence however they could. Like most old-stock Tejanos and recent Mexican immigrant arrivals, they often worked side by side from dawn to dusk, making just enough to survive, rarely enough to meet all their needs, always in debt, never accumulating enough to buy tools much less to purchase a plot or home. When conditions were good, when Antonio Tijerina was lucky enough to negotiate a share-cropping agreement with an Anglo farmer, he, his wife Herlinda, and their six children—Anselmo, Margarito, Ramón, María, Reies, and Josefina—took up residence at a particular ranch, planting, watering, weeding, and moving on when the harvest was done.

Cotton picking in Texas also was migratory family work timed by the plant's developmental cycle. The work was tedious and backbreaking. If other options existed, it was not work anyone willingly coveted. Experienced adult men could pick anywhere from seven hundred to a thousand pounds of cotton a day; their wives and children much less. The first time young Eddie Stimpson picked cotton near Plano in the 1930s, he gathered a three hundred-pound haul. "I had to crawl home.... I went to bed without eating and could not rest or even hardly move. The next morning I could not get up. For two days I had to stay in bed. My mother would rub me down, put hot pad and hot iron and bricks on me to draw the soreness out."[27] The work offered no shade, save for the hat on one's head, which tempered some of the sun's blaze where summer temperatures normally reached 105. It was desiccating work. The young withered and suffered heat strokes. The inexperienced crawled home aching from the monotonous routine. And everyone complained about the lack of clean drinking water, which was rationed and in short supply, and the lack of sanitary facilities.

Reies Tijerina was told that he went into these fields as an infant riding the tail of his mother's cotton-picking sack. By the time he was four years old, he too was picking cotton by his mother's side. By age eight he was pulling along his own hundred-pound sack.[28] Every hand was necessary to produce a family's daily bread. If they arrived early enough and stayed long enough at a particular farm, Antonio sometimes got permission to plant a garden next to their living quarters.[29]

Having enough food to feed the Tijerina family of eight was a constant challenge. Herlinda foraged edible herbs and plants to supplement their diet of corn, beans, chili, and potatoes. Meat was beyond their means. When they settled for a season, they sometimes raised chickens or a hog; something quite impossible when following crops from place to place. During the years of the Great Depression the search for food became particularly desperate. Antonio, Herlinda, and their older boys scavenged broadly, collecting whatever seemed to have some utility and sale value. Daily, Antonio would seek edibles in city dumps.[30] Herlinda fashioned "a bow out of an automobile spring and an arrow out of scrap metal" to hunt jackrabbits and was apparently also quite adept at catching snakes, which she sold for seventeen cents a pound.[31]

The Tijerina boys—Anselmo, Margarito, Ramón, and Reies—spent most of those days of the Great Depression helping to put food on the family's table. Reies recalled that early every morning, while it was still dark outside, one of his siblings would go to the homes where milk had been delivered and help the bottles walk away. Reies and Margarito became experts at hunting field rats. "We'd dig them out of their holes and eat them," explained Reies, "you know, they're good."[32] Barefoot and dirty the Tijerina brothers rummaged through trash for anything that might fetch a penny. They collected and sold old rags, iron scraps, worn rubber tires, and bottles. Their weekly hauls never amounted to much, but still, if they managed to earn five dollars, that was a lot. One day, as Reies tells it, he and his older brother Ramón sold their scraps. When Ramón got the cash, he went to the movies, spending most of it on himself. "That night my father waited with a big whip. Ramón got a big whipping that night. The whipping never left my mind."[33] Reies remembered with delight the day his orphan friend Raúl took him to an alley behind the homes of the rich. In the garbage cans "I found food, food, and more food, big pieces of fried chicken, roast beef, bread, pieces of fruit, cake, candy. My hungry days were over," or so Reies hoped. All that ended the night they were caught by the police.[34]

"All my friends were the same, and I was content," said Reies, satiating his hunger from trash cans. "I didn't know any better."[35] But for mexicanos who ate only if they scavenged, it was particularly humiliating. Even harder to endure, said Rosa Rosales, were the denigrating Anglo taunts and curses, their constant complaints and condescension, spoken always with an air of superiority even by poor whites. With considerable bitterness Rosa remembered how Anglos in West Texas treated her while picking cotton,

> I would hear people always talking about "*esos migrantes*" [those migrants]. "Look what they did," "Look how they left this place," "They're so dirty," "You can't leave anything out while they're round." . . . I had heard these remarks so often that I thought they were talking about gang members or people in trouble with the law. One day my husband was talking of some trouble, and I said, "Oh, it was probably *esos migrantes*." He looked at me and asked who I thought "those migrants" were . . . "*nosotros somos migrantes*" [we are migrants]. I felt so ashamed and dirty that I cried. I said, "You mean all those times people were talking about me and my family as if we were no good?"[36]

There were more than a few nights the Tijerina children went to bed hungry. Antonio and Herlinda often did not eat to make sure their children did. One such day occurred in 1930 while the family was picking and shelling pecans at John Mathas's Ranch near San Antonio. Reies remembered the day vividly; it was a story he repeated many times. Breakfast that day was a half-cup of a pecan bark tea and another half-cup for dinner. Undernourished, Reies fell into a deep, comalike sleep for more than twenty-four hours. Herlinda and Antonio took him for dead and summoned the local priest to help arrange his burial.[37] In the midst of considerable wailing Reies awakened.

> They were making the coffin and they were crying.... And I remember that I was cold when I got up ... my family got completely shocked. Shocked! And then, the next day, and throughout the years, my uncles used to talk about me. "There goes the dead boy," you know, "there goes the resurrected boy."[38]

In this dreamy state of consciousness, Reies remembered walking through lush verdant fields bursting with colorful spring flowers. Birds were flying about and chirping beautiful songs. It was a joyful place because Jesus Christ was by his side. They were walking together:

> I was feeling through his hand and my hand. He never talked. He didn't say nothing, I felt something through his hand, you know, I was sure as long as he had me by his hand ... I didn't have to worry for nothing.... And we were traveling in a little narrow road and I was pulling, with my other hand, I was pulling a little red wagon.[39]

Did Reies's comalike experience really happen? Was it a dream? Or was it the distorted morality tale about death and resurrection his mother told him? It is impossible to know. Whatever the story's origin, the memory remained indelibly marked in Reies's psyche, recalled as his "little death" and "stroll with Jesus Christ." As an adult he frequently repeated the story to signal to his congregation that since his early childhood he had had a very intimate relationship with Jesus Christ, and still walked with him hand in hand. Skeptics may justifiably wonder how a four-year-old boy could possibly remember such an early childhood dream. Simple. As Reies explained it, whenever he was startled, upset, or began to cry, his mother would take him in her arms, rock him gently, repeating the details of his dream. Quickly it calmed him.[40]

The gender division of labor in the Tijerina household took identical form in most ethnic Mexican homes. Antonio managed everything that faced the outside world; all that had to do with the fields, work contracts, delivering the family's labor, settling accounts, and dealing with outsiders. Sharecropping was risky business for mexicanos in Texas. Always at the mercy of powerful farmers, always disadvantaged before the law, all too often they failed to negotiate written contracts and, lacking mastery of the English language, they frequently did not understand exactly the terms of their verbal contracts. During the Depression, as cotton prices fell, its profitability depended on labor superexploitation. Some farmers even claimed that the best way to assure workers were obedient was to keep them at the brink of starvation. "The man working for food not only works regularly," boasted one farmer, "he works gladly; he takes orders cheerfully, is seldom sullen—all in all, he's the most satisfactory farm worker."[41]

On many farms, workers obtained their staples—beans, flour, salt, sugar, coffee, potatoes, corn—on credit at the owner's commissary. When the harvest ended and it was time to settle debts and collect their pay, ledgers routinely showed that wages equaled or failed to cover purchases, with no recourse.[42] Memories of dead Mexicans, lynched, their lifeless bodies hanging from trees, their heads impaled on posts, reminded them of what happened to "greasers" and "wetbacks" who dared protest, who had the temerity to talk back or even to grumble out loud. A young woman named María remembered what fate her uncle Eduardo suffered in Texas in the late 1920s. He had always done exactly as he was told by his employer.

> One day, his boss was angry about something and my uncle didn't exactly agree with him, so they exchanged words. At the end of the day, when the workers started for home, the boss told him to stay.... That night he didn't return home.... My cousin went to talk to his boss, but he said that Eduardo had left after redoing his job. Days passed.... they found my uncle in a nearby wooded area. His body was riddled with bullets and

covered with cactus. The older people took him to the river to clean him and pluck the thorns from his body.

Eduardo's burial had to wait until late that night because the family feared the blood sport of the Ku Klux Klan, which was a basic fact of life.[43]

Denying sharecroppers their wages and forcing them off the land just after harvest were common practice. Antonio Tijerina fell victim to both forms of fraud. It happened once. It happened twice. Reies claimed it happened seventeen times, though that seems hard to believe.[44] How gullible and powerless could Antonio have been? Perhaps this was a morality tale Reies wanted his audiences to hear, exaggeration or not. One day while Antonio was tending the crops, a group of unknown Anglo men arrived and "tried to hang my father—they had a rope around his neck because they wanted his crop."[45] On another occasion the landlord dispatched a knife-wielding thug to evict the Tijerinas from the farm they were tending. Antonio fought back. As he did, his attacker cut a deep gash across the hamstring of one of Antonio's legs. He survived. The injury left him partially crippled. On many days Herlinda "had to hoist him on her back and carry him to the fields in the morning and carry him back at night."[46]

The Depression year of 1931 was particularly dreadful for Antonio, Herlinda, and their children. They were sharecroppers on Albert Stevens's ranch just outside of Poth, Texas. For some reason Reies was frequently awakening from sleep at night, screaming, sobbing, and shaking uncontrollably. "This car would come driving toward our house by itself, without any driver. It would come closer and closer without a driver, and I would begin to tremble. I was afraid Stevens would think we had stolen it and would come and shoot one of us." This is why Reies said he cried. Herlinda would immediately comfort Reies, urging him to remember his "little death" and walk with Jesus, and soon he would fall asleep again.[47]

Reies was a few months shy of five but clearly sensed that Albert Stevens was a dangerous man. Everyone in the family was on edge whenever he came around. After the Tijerinas had spent an entire season planting wheat, barley, corn, cotton, and beans for him, he arrived with his two sons to settle accounts. At gun point Stevens demanded the Tijerinas leave. Antonio refused. He wanted his pay. Stevens's sons, both mounted on horseback, lassoed Antonio with a rope and dragged him off, leaving his entire body covered with rope burns and bloody, dirt-filled abrasions. In the days that followed, Antonio demanded justice from Poth's local judge. Antonio wanted his family's wages. "Tony," the judge replied, "Albert is an outlaw, no law can control that man. Don't make trouble, just take your chickens and hog and go, or you will lose them too."[48]

The Tijerinas left. They had no choice. Broken in spirit, Antonio humiliated before his children, Reies remembered that his father never recovered psychologically after this dastardly deed. He fell silent and hardly ever said a word, "only half a man, just walking around like meat with eyes, that's all."[49] In moments of anxiety Antonio would shake uncontrollably. "Once he began trembling he never stopped. . . . [He was] terrified all the time, too timid to even speak out. . . . When he talked to the ranchers he would forget the few words of English he had and would tremble and limp away." Reies vowed after witnessing all this that he would never allow anyone to treat him so.[50]

The Tijerinas moved. They went to the next town, to the next place, at a dizzying pace. The names of those towns, "Whiteface, Wilson, Levelland, Forestville, Poth, the names run like stripes through my mind," Reies recalled.[51] "We picked beans and melons. We picked cotton, 25 cents a hundred pounds, chopped cotton, 10 cents a row, topped turnips and hoed onions and cultivated broom corn and shelled pecans."[52] Living anywhere they could, in shacks, under bridges, many nights the sky was their roof. When the Tijerinas were sharecroppers, their lives had a certain autonomy, less surveillance, more protection, and some stability for the children. But when they had to hit the road, the work conditions of seasonal migrant were more brutal, more unpredictable, exposing them to many more dangers for uncertain pay.[53]

Mexicanos had to contend with exploitative employers, with the state-sponsored violence of the Texas Rangers, with vigilantes, and increasingly, with the terror white supremacist Ku Klux Klan members directed at them. On pay day mexicanos had to be particularly vigilant because "Klansmen . . . were trying to take that money."[54] Reies remembered some incredibly gruesome stories of robbery and murder, which only intensified the misery Mexicans suffered during the Depression. "I remember when we were working near Fredericksburg and had been paid for our work, my father and the other men would guard the road so that our money wouldn't be taken away from us. I remember the dark night and those model Ts going by on the road and the men whispering, 'the Klan.'"[55]

The tensions that sometimes pitted Mexican Americans against Mexican immigrants quickly evaporated whenever Klan killings and cross burnings occurred. "The Klan has made [us] . . . a solid group again," explained one mexicana in 1924. "We were drifting apart, away from the church, away from our old friends. But [Klan violence] has brought us all together again."[56] Fearing that mexicanos might face "greater bitterness and prejudice than they now suffer," a pair of Presbyterian church ministers urged their congregations to keep their "churches entirely clear from any connection with the Ku Klux Klan," lest they offend fellow Christians.[57]

Herlinda López's children remember her as the one who kept the family tightly knit through all the challenges they faced in the early 1930s. As the mistress of the household, she worked a double day, not only childbearing and childrearing, but cooking, cleaning, sewing, and washing clothes as well. Daily, she rose early to empty the chamber pots and to chop wood so that she could stoke the stove to cook breakfast. When the children were dressed and fed, to the fields they went. At night the routine in reverse was much the same. Herlinda returned to the stove, heating water to cook, to wash dishes, and to bathe. Clothes had to be mended and cotton flour sacks fashioned into shirts and dresses. In the one-room house in which they lived, all the evening's rituals occurred under the glow of a kerosene lamp. The family's meager possessions hung from nails on the walls: a calendar, pictures of loved ones, and images of Jesus, Mary, and the saints.[58]

Herlinda López and Antonio Tijerina were members of different churches. Herlinda had been baptized and raised a Catholic, but only attended services at Christmas and Easter and when baptisms, matrimonies, and burial rites occurred. Like many ethnic Mexicans in the first quarter of the twentieth century, she was deeply suspicious of the institutional Catholic Church, of its clergy, and of its cozy relations with the powerful. Yet Herlinda's belief in a merciful and almighty God was said to have been deep and firm. She "read the Bible a lot. . . . She prayed before meals and in the evening." Like so many other ethnic Mexican Catholics in the 1930s, her veneration of Christ, the Virgin Mary, and local saints was rooted in notions of reciprocity between humans and the divine anchored in the home. She would beg the intercession of those in heaven for favor on earth and in return she offered prayers, candles, and flowers, promising pilgrimages to shrines, praying novenas, and invoking the names of Jesus, his mother, and the saints in moments of duress. *Ay! Jesús mio! Ayudanos mi virgencita*, she was known to mumble. Oh! My Jesus! Help us my dearest virgin![59]

Antonio Tijerina was baptized a Catholic at birth. But as he grew older and wiser, he realized a basic fact about Anglo power in Texas or, for that matter, about white supremacy in the United States. In the localities where he had to find work, white Protestants controlled the economy. White Protestants controlled local politics. White Protestants controlled the law and constabulary. They "don't like Blacks and don't like Catholics." Antonio "became a Protestant out of fear," explained Reies, hoping he would suffer less abuse from his employers, face less harassment from the Texas Rangers, and perhaps find better paying steady work.[60]

Herlinda López died on April 21, 1931. Earlier that year, en route to Colman, Texas, to pick cotton, the Model T auto in which she was riding flipped into a ravine. She was tossed from the car and suffered massive chest injuries. At the San Antonio hospital where Dr. Robert B. Green patched her up, he discovered that she had a very advanced case of breast cancer. From that point on she never recuperated, hardly ever left her bed, rarely slept, and was always in agonizing pain because they did not have the money to buy her pain killers. Many nights when Reies could not sleep, he remembered his mother's agonizing moans and cries. She expired just moments after birthing her tenth child Cristóbal.[61]

Herlinda's reproductive history and death reflected wider trends in fecundity and mortality among ethnic Mexicans in Texas. In 1900 mexicanas between the ages of fourteen and forty-four, on the average, birthed four children. Infant mortality was high among them; only one out of every ten infants survived to the age of one. Out of every three infants Anglo women bore, two survived to that age.[62] By 1924 the life chances of ethnic Mexican infants had improved considerably, reports Elmer T. Clark of the Methodist Episcopal Church, South. "The Mexican baby has one-third the chance to live that is possessed by the average baby," by which he meant white baby.[63]

Herlinda López married Antonio Tijerina in 1919. In their twelve years together, she conceived and birthed ten children; seven survived to adulthood. When Antonio married Herlinda at age thirty-one, he had already been widowed twice by wives who died giving birth. Robert N. McLean and Charles A. Thomson, two Presbyterian ministers seeking converts in New Mexico and Colorado in 1924 concluded that "in large families, with more than five or six children, there is a high mortality rate; often more than half of the children have died. For instance, here is a family of thirteen children, of which eight have died; another of seven children, of which five have died. Here is another, however, of six, of which five are living."[64] A young Mexican immigrant confided in 1925 to another Presbyterian proselytizer, Mr. Vernon Monroe McCombs, that his wife had birthed three children in the first three years of marriage but died giving birth to the fourth. Living in poverty and without a support network in the United States, he plaintively turned to McCombs and asked: "Now what can I do?"[65]

Antonio Tijerina faced the same question in April 1931. He sought a foster family for his newly born son Cristóbal. Nasario Vásquez, Herlinda's brother raised him as his own. The Tijerinas completely lost track of him for twenty-seven years, reestablishing contact in 1961. This "adoption" was a source of considerable friction between Reies and his father, still festering in 1972. Writing his son Reies on March 2, Antonio angrily scolded him for the questions yet again asked in a recent letter. Antonio resented being pestered by Reies as to why he, Antonio, had put Cristóbal in someone else's care. "I am going to tell you the complete truth. I am tired of your many questions on this topic. Understand that she [your mother] told me to give this child to Nasario. Why did you have to tell him [who his parents were]? He is not your child." Antonio bristled over Reies's belated paternalism. It was none of his business. Reies felt otherwise and quickly offered his bother succor.[66]

With Herlinda's passing and without an infant in tow, the family joined the itinerant mass of agricultural laborers, migrating constantly from 1931 to 1936. Faced with much tighter labor markets and lower wages in Texas, in 1936 Antonio took his family to Michigan where he had heard that work could be found in the state's sugar beet fields. Antonio "was so tired of the hard work in Texas and his inability to save any money." To Michigan they went.[67]

Sugar beet production in the United States began in 1900. By 1920, ninety-eight factories produced more than a million tons of sugar. Three major regions of the country eventually dominated its production. In the West, California planted the most extensive acreage employing poor whites and ethnic Mexicans. In the mountain west, sugar beets were grown in Colorado, Utah, and Idaho, drawing its labor mainly from northern Mexico and New Mexico. And in the Midwest, the crop was planted extensively in Michigan, Ohio, and Wisconsin, where Mexicans and Tejanos provided the work.[68]

Early every spring, from 1936 to roughly 1945, the Tijerinas boarded one of the large trucks that routinely ferried mexicanos from Texas to Michigan.[69] Reies had vivid memories of these treks, packed together "with many other families on a great semy [sic] cattle trailor [sic]."[70] Trucks initially had no covering, exposing the migrants to the elements, relying on the cold wind to dry them after rain and to cool them during summer's heat. "We were packed like sardines . . . thirty adults and twelve children," recalled María López about the back of these trucks. "The journey was three days of pure hell because the drivers rarely stopped except for gas."[71] Eventually the trucks were covered with canvas tarps to offer some protection from the elements during long hauls. On older trucks lacking functional exhaust pipes the covering created carbon monoxide death traps, which took the lives of numerous children. "Even with all this they brand us lazy. Never mind that our desire to work might cost a family member," Juanita Valdez raged.[72]

The northward trek to Michigan passed through Oklahoma, Missouri, Illinois, and Indiana, places that greeted them with racist taunts whenever they stopped for food or gas. One elderly South Texas mexicano remembered wanting to purchase a meal in 1930. "We walked in, and they stared at us like freaks. The owner told me that one of us could place the order, but we'd have to wait for it out back because they didn't allow Mexicans in their restaurant." Though the owners of the restaurant "were White trash, somehow we weren't good enough to eat there."[73] At another stop Tejanos were similarly denied sit-down service but allowed to purchase takeout. They ordered eight cheeseburgers, paid, got their order, and left. Back on the road "we realized that each burger was just two buns with an onion slice in the middle."[74] At "one of these stops," María López "needed to get some hot water for my baby's formula." The "restaurant had a sign that read 'No Mexicans, No Negroes.' We wanted water, but we had to wait till an Anglo lady came and got it for us. She made us pay fifty cents for a ten-ounce bottle of hot water."[75] At the gas station where they had stopped, a Tejana recalled urgently needing the restroom. It was locked and displayed a No Mexicans Allowed sign. "I decided to stand up to the owner of the gas station so I asked him for the key. He was cold and mean and asked if I had read the sign. I said, 'Yes, but we're not Mexicans, we're Texans.'" He grudgingly gave her the key. Her revenge, she said, was dropping the key down the toilet and locking the door when she and her mother were done.[76]

From April to November the Tijerinas worked in Michigan, then returned to winter in San Antonio. Life in Michigan was bleak, often cold in comparison to temperatures in San Antonio, made all the more ghastly by their housing. In this there was equality among beet workers. They all lived in run-down shacks and abandoned railcars. "Usually we'd find broken windows, rat droppings all over the floor, and faraway rest rooms that were always plugged," recalled one family's matriarch.[77] Imelda said that her family's shack in Michigan was a battleground for "rats and roaches. At night you could see them commuting along the two-by-fours over our heads. At first we couldn't sleep, but soon exhaustion took its toll and we learned to ignore." Despite her ghastly quarters and low wages, Juanita Valdez never complained.[78] "Sure, you can complain," but experience taught her that the smallest protest provoked farmers to instantly fire them. They then "tell you to leave. Then you won't have a job, and he might just call other farmers and tell them you're a troublemaker." Without housing, without a job, Juanita said her family knew that if they were to survive, they had to endure their work conditions silently.[79]

Work in the beet fields, like cotton picking, was mostly done by families because they were deemed more stable and came with young hands that were ideal for several aspects of the work. Two steps of sugar beet production were mechanized. First, tractors prepared the soil for planting in early April, then liberally seeded to maximize plant germination. The next steps were done by hand. Adult workers "blocked" or removed all but the biggest plants, followed by children on their hands and knees thinning further. While the plants matured, workers watered and weeded. When company chemists determined that the beets had reached their maximal sugar content, usually in early October, a lifter would be drawn by horse through the fields, digging up the beets by their roots. The workers would then pluck and gather them into rows. Next "toppers," each carrying an eighteen-inch-long knife with a hook at its tip, would lift the beets with the hooked end, cut off the leaves, and hurl them into wagons. At the processing plants, torrents of hot water washed the beets delivering them to cutting knives and shredders, finally landing in boiling vats where they first yielded their sweetness as molasses before being swirled into white sugar, then packed and shipped.[80]

When their first harvest ended, Antonio Tijerina concluded that their work in Michigan was just as hard as cotton picking in Texas. It paid only a little more. As one beet worker explained, her family had traveled thousands of miles on the back of a truck, had daily performed back-breaking work, living in abysmal camps, and, at the end, we had "no money to show for it."[81]

The children of these agricultural migrants often complained both about the trek and the work. "I hated it," explained Monica, of her summers in Michigan's beet fields. "I knew I was going to spend the summer working long hours under the sun. Often I would ask, 'Why do we have to go? Why can't we stay?'" Her parents would give her a blank, silent stare. "I would get no answer."[82] What Monica hated most about leaving Texas every spring for Michigan and returning in early October, was that they departed before the school year ended and returned way after classes had started. She was always falling behind, slowing her advance to the next grade.

The minimal education the Tijerina children got during the 1930s was typical of what other migrant children experienced. "I only had about six months of school in all, because we were always on the move," Reies Tijerina lamented.[83] And besides, he did not like going to school because the other children laughed at him for arriving barefoot, in dirty, tattered clothes. To suffer less humiliation, he slowly gathered his pennies from selling paper, scrap metal, and rags until he had enough money for a pair of shoes. His father took him to town, bought an affordable pair, and returned to his neighborhood shouting: "*Mire! Mis sapatos!* [sic]" (Look! My shoes!) His shoes, Reies boasted, properly fit. Other mexicano children were not as lucky.[84] Recalling his childhood in south Texas during the 1940s, Hilario confessed that only two of the family's six children had ever set foot in a school. "My brother and I had to go to school barefooted and the children made fun of us." One day a traveling shoe salesman knocked at their door. His father decided to eliminate this excuse for not attending school. The man "had a very poor selection of shoes, so he sold us shoes two sizes too big. He said, that would make the shoes last a long time. My father liked that," recalled Hilario. "The first day we wore them, we had a hard time waddling the mile to school. The children, who always noticed everything, saw our big shoes and decided to call us 'ducks.'" Hilario and his brother felt so humiliated by the laughter that they never returned to school.[85]

The first record of Reies and his siblings attending school comes from Poth, Texas, in 1935. The experiences he, Anselmo, Margarito, Ramón, María, and Josefina had were not particularly pleasant and apparently ended after one week. None of the Tijerina children spoke English and when the teacher caught Reies's older brother Ramón speaking Spanish, she spanked him in front of the class. "Ramon left the school when the teacher was not looking. I looked out the window and there, about a quarter of a mile away was Ramón running home. We all left the school the next day. I did not learn one English word during that week." But even if the children had wanted to stay, they could not. Antonio had fallen way behind in paying rent and they were evicted the fall of 1935. With nowhere to go, they returned to San Antonio to live with Antonio Tijerina's sister Josefina.[86]

Back in San Antonio, Ramón, María, Reies, and Josefa attended the Buckner Fanning Christian School, where they were all put in the same class. As they still spoke no English, Mrs. Grace, their teacher, paid them little attention. While instructing the other students in reading "she would give us clay to play with," which she must have deemed pedagogically uplifting destined as they were to life as dirt farmers. The inattention apparently did not bother them, for what Reies remembered most was that "Mrs. Grace was an angel. She never bothered us." One day she even visited their house and gave their father "35 cents for family food." This schooling too did not last long. They had to move "from place to place until spring when the early field work started."[87]

In 1936 Reies and his sister Josefa attended a rural school near Edinburg, Texas, where their teacher, Mrs. Stanley, would pick them up and take them to school every day. With such an attentive teacher, a small class size, and two months of attendance, Reies finally felt that he was learning something and joyfully recalled those days. Thanking "the God of my mother," Reies proclaimed, "nothing stood in my way now, so I felt. . . . In two weeks they promoted me to the second grade. I was excited. I saw a new world before my eyes. My Spanish reading and writing was improving fast." Again, that progress stopped. The bitterness of Michigan's sugar beet fields beaconed again.[88]

Antonio Tijerina found himself ill and bed ridden in 1936. Reies's eldest brother, Anselmo, found work at a Works Progress Administration camp in New Mexico. Margarito, his sixteen-year-old brother, became the household head, making good on the sharecropping arrangement his father had contracted with a Mr. Joe that spring. Margarito plowed and planted more than two hundred acres of corn, beans, and wheat. Just before his crops were ready to harvest, Mr. Joe forced the Tijerinas out without pay. "Margarito was very upset." What could they do? What they did was to pick cotton near San Antonio, then Seguín, Corpus Christi, and finally in "the west part of the state, where the cotton grows late." Reies said that he took this all in stride, given that he had a sick father, was only eleven years old, and had no real power or status to change things.[89]

Reies and his siblings were back in San Antonio by the fall of 1938, intermittently attending the Frank Johnson School until 1940. As was common in Texas schools then, Reies's name was Anglicized on his official transcript as "Ray," listed as "white," fully vaccinated, without any apparent diseases. His father Antonio was listed as employed on a Works Progress Administration program, which was not true. Antonio was sick and Anselmo replaced him. In autumn 1938, at age twelve, Reies was still enrolled in the first grade, attending a total of ten days in a classroom with children who were six years old, half his age. Winter attendance in 1939 was much better; 40.5 days during January and February, or two full months. By March the family was on the move again. Reies's teachers—Mr. Shultz, Mr. Williams, Mr. McMurry—all gave him As for the classes he had attended. In 1939–1940, a Mr. Galbart registered 28 days of attendance in the second grade. By the winter of 1940, Reies was recorded in Mr. Yaeger's third grade class, but his report card showed no attendance. Reies recalled one rather blunt exchange with his teacher that year who was lecturing on how the United

States was "the land of the free and home of the brave." Reies raised his hand. "Why do you teach English only? Is there no room in the land of the free for my language and my culture?" He asked again, "if this country is called the land of the free and home of the brave, but who were the braver; the whites or the Indians?" The teacher bristled. Reies did not like the answer he got. He never asked another question, or so he claimed. This was the last extant record of Ray Tijerina attending elementary school.[90]

At fifteen years of age, Reies was quite out of place around his third-grade classmates at Johnson School, who were eight and nine years old. Whatever his discomfort, he dropped out mainly because his father needed him to work. It was time to migrate to Michigan's sugar beet fields. Though Reies's teacher begged Antonio to leave Reies behind because of "his bright mind," Antonio had to ignore the plea. In Michigan there was work and housing, something they did not have in Texas. They were back in Croswell, Michigan, for the third time by spring 1941.[91]

One afternoon that summer, while Reies and his sister Josefa were home alone, an itinerant Baptist preacher named Samuel Galindo knocked at their door, asking to speak to the family's head. The preacher was ministering to the mexicanos in the area. Antonio Tijerina was not home. Galindo began a conversation with Reies and Josefa, who became so rapt in what he had to say about the Bible that their two hours together rapidly flew by. When Galindo "saw that I was an enthusiast and that I liked listening to him," he gave Reies a Spanish-language copy of the Bible.[92] From that moment on, Reies claimed that his life was completely transformed. Though his Spanish-reading ability was rudimentary at best, he nevertheless "began to read the Bible from the first page of Jenisses [sic]." That night after his father and brothers returned from work exhausted, from his bed Antonio listened to Reies read the Bible. The readings continued nightly, with his siblings feigning interest only "when I came across an exciting episode."[93]

Reies was fully absorbed by the Bible. Not even an old bicycle a neighbor gave him competed for his interest. He was now spending whatever free time he had underlining biblical passages that "were most attractive to my soul." His brief public schooling had failed to inculcate American nationalism in the form of stories about the founding fathers and revolutionary heroes. He knew nothing about George Washington or Abraham Lincoln. Now, he was riveted by the bravery and wisdom of the prophets, by Abraham, David, Ishmael, and Moses. The Bible's constant use of the words "justice, mercy, truth, humility" moved him profoundly, deducing that God, the grand architect of the universe and the source of all life, most valued judgment and justice.[94] These two words were gradually etched in his mind and soon were bellowing forcefully and constantly from his mouth.

In the months that followed, both Reverend Galindo and a Methodist minister named Reverend Gold regularly visited the Tijerina home for Bible readings and prayer. In turn, the Tijerinas on Sundays traveled to Galindo's church in Deckerville, Michigan, and then to Gold's in Sandusky. "I began to talk to Protestants and especially to Baptists and Methodists there in Michigan, and that was when I began to decide on the religious life and made plans to go to Bible school."[95] Galindo persuaded Reies to become a Baptist. From that point on, Moses and the Old Testament's prophets became his idols. "I gathered up the strengths and liberties of justice out of the lives of those Biblical men of old."[96] His grandfather Santiago found Reies's conversion abhorrent and shunned him. "He wouldn't speak to me after that, he didn't speak to me for years." Finally, when Santiago Tijerina was on his deathbed in 1947, the two reconciled.[97]

Throughout 1942 Reies begged his father to send him to study "the ways of God and the *valientes* [the valiant ones] of Justice." Where exactly he should go to pursue these studies provoked considerable discussion. Quite by chance he learned from his sister María that the babysitter Reverend Samuel Galindo employed wanted to become a missionary and planned to enroll at the Assemblies of God Instituto Bíblico Latino Americano, then located in Saspamco, Texas, on San Antonio's outskirts. This is the reason Reies chose the school. Neither he nor his father had money for his matriculation and toiled that summer gathering it.

Reies spent the summer of 1943 in Michigan's sugar beet fields preparing himself to "become a champion of God's Justice and to speak and teach it to the people of this world." He prayed. He fasted. He read the Bible daily, meditating on its words and stories. He wanted to be spiritually ready for the rigorous religious training he expected at the Institute. He was. Reies believed that he was going to one of the "most holy of places" on earth, where heavenly angels were said to visit the students daily "like in ancient times."

By September 1943, Reies had the cash for a year's tuition and board.⁹⁸ Before he left, he took a more radical step. He abandoned the Baptist Church, receiving Holy Spirit baptism from Fred Gómez, his pastor and close friend in Saginaw.⁹⁹

At age seventeen Reies was largely a self-taught man. He had learned to read and write in Spanish from his older brother Anselmo with the Bible as his textbook.¹⁰⁰ Nurtured in hunger, hardened though poverty, forged under the heat of Jim Crow's racist sun, he was determined never to forget his Christian values.¹⁰¹ Reies was confident, frequently defiant. By then, too, he had developed an intense sense of justice and nerves of steel. "I remember fighting in the fields because the rancher didn't clean the fields good enough," complaining about work conditions when he was about fourteen or fifteen years old. "I felt driven by this inner force to defend my rights, to tell them they weren't paying us enough or doing right by us." Though Antonio would scold Reies for such behavior, cowering and visibly trembling when he witnessed such confrontations, Reies persisted. So cantankerous, so confrontational, so verbally dexterous was he becoming, that he quickly gained a local reputation as an *"abogado sin libros,"* a lawyer without books.¹⁰² That is why others constantly sought his aid, giving freely.

The life experiences of a poor Tejano sharecropper and itinerant farmworker living in a racist, segregated society instilled in Reies Tijerina the moral and ethical values that eventually anchored the rest of his life. In this chapter we explored the historical and socioeconomic world into which Reies Tijerina was born and matured as a young man. In the next we turn to the Apostolic Faith, to the religious revival that swept the United States at the beginning of the twentieth century. This spiritual awakening left many speaking in tongues and healed. Reies Tijerina was one of the many so profoundly transfixed by this "new" embodied experience of the Pentecost that he enrolled at the Assemblies of God Latin American Bible Institute in 1943. We focus first on the moment American Pentecostalism was born and rapidly flourished, before returning to Reies's enrollment in Bible school.

CHAPTER 2

The Origins of Pentecostalism

DECEMBER 31, 1900, WAS a moment of solemn expectation for many Christians. Christ had not returned to earth on December 31, 1899, on the eve of the new millennium, as many had hoped and prayed. Perhaps they had misinterpreted prophecy. Perhaps Christ was angry at the world. Since he had not yet arrived, was it possible that his second coming would occur instead at the end of 1900? No one knew. In the heartland of America, on the outskirts of Topeka, Kansas, a group of radical Christian evangelicals gathered, confident that their prayers would be answered on that New Year's Eve. That was when Christ would arrive anew on earth.

Charles Fox Parham, a Holiness minister who established Topeka's Bethel Bible School, gathered seventy-five of his students to bear witness to Christ that night. They believed they would witness the second Pentecost as described in Luke's Acts of the Apostles. Jesus's early followers were baptized anew with the Holy Spirit, signified by the tongues of fire that rested on their heads: "When Pentecost day came around, they had all met in one room, when suddenly they heard what sounded like a powerful wind from heaven, the noise of which filled the entire house in which they were sitting; and something appeared to them that seemed like tongues of fire; these separated and came to rest on the head of each of them. They were all filled with the Holy Spirit and began to speak foreign languages as the Spirit gave them the gift of speech" (Acts 2:1–4).

Those gathered in Topeka prayed that night. They sang songs of benediction to the lord, hoping he would hear their sweet hymns plaintively calling for him to return. On January 1, 1901, at about 7 p.m., Agnes Ozman asked Parham to lay his hand upon her so that she might be filled with the Holy Spirit. As he did, "I began to speak in tongues, glorifying God," Ozman testified. "I talked several languages. It was as though rivers of living water were proceeding from my innermost being." Parham was equally amazed. "I had scarcely repeated three dozen sentences when a glory fell upon her, a halo seemed to surround her head and face, and she began speaking in the Chinese language and was unable to speak English for three days."[1]

What happened in Topeka, Kansas, that first night of 1901 was the beginning of what would be called the Pentecostal movement. This moment of fully embodied religious enthusiasm still rages today as the most dynamic religious revival Christianity had witnessed since the days of St. Paul. Reies Tijerina was so taken by its egalitarian culture that he became one of its evangelists, staging revivals akin to those described below.

Charles Fox Parham was the person initially most responsible for the movement's start. Born in Muscatine, Iowa, in 1873, at the age of nine Parham believed he had been called to the ministry; at age thirteen he converted to Methodism; and by age nineteen he started preaching locally, without license, eschewing denominationalism, rejecting water baptism, and embracing sanctification, a belief that through the gift of grace one's entire body and soul were cleansed or made "holy," which is how the Holiness movement got its name. Parham identified with the Holiness movement until 1894. Believing that he had to preach "true" Bible Christianity, he did so, naming his devotions the Apostolic Faith. He took up itinerant preaching announcing Christ's millennial return, convinced that the Apostolic Faith could not be experienced in denominational churches, which he insisted were dead and dull. He called sinners to repent, promising to heal them through prayer. His ministry in those years consisted of five elements: "Salvation, Healing, Sanctification, the Second Coming of Christ, and the Baptism of the Holy Spirit," as Sarah, his wife explained.[2]

Parham eventually founded the Bethel Healing Home and Bible School to prepare missionaries to preach "this Gospel of the Kingdom . . . as a witness to all the world before the end of the age."[3] Students enrolled. What they shared was a belief in the Bible as literal truth and ultimate authority, a yearning for Christ's Second Coming, and a desire to experience the Holy Spirit in more profound ways, through spiritual healing and tongues speech, technically known as *glossolalia*.

Stories emanating from Topeka's Bethel Bible School rapidly began attracting women and men who yearned for a total religious embodiment of their faith. While many adepts, called *saints*, were lifted, rapt, and left agog, the curious soon disappeared, finding the rituals theatrical antics, derisively calling them "Holy Rollers." Parham closed the Bethel Bible School in 1901 and moved on, continually preaching the fundamentals of his Apostolic Faith in Iowa, Missouri, Oklahoma, and Texas. He settled in Houston for a time, where he met William J. Seymour, who ultimately catalyzed the Apostolic Faith into a much larger religious movement. Seymour was born on May 2, 1870, in Centerville, Louisiana. Eager to escape southern racism, this child of former African American slaves had drifted from place to place seeking Christ since 1895, briefly enrolling in Bible schools along the way. In 1905 he settled in Houston, met Parham, and quickly experienced his own Holy Spirit baptism and gift of tongues speech.

Seymour tried to enroll in Parham's Bible school to deepen his Apostolic Faith, but Texas law prohibited blacks and whites from being educated side by side, something Parham fully endorsed. He was a rabid segregationist and white supremacist, who thought it was sinful for blacks and whites to mix. At his services sanctuary seats were reserved for whites only. Blacks had to stand in the rear and were never allowed to approach the altar to receive Holy Spirit baptism simultaneously with whites during revivals.[4]

After much coaxing, Parham finally agreed to admit Seymour provided he sat in the school's hallway and listened to lessons through an open door. So began Seymour's formal education, relying on the Bible as his only textbook. Students read it, reflected on it, memorized it, and were constantly tasked to find the scriptural foundations for repentance, sanctification, healing, and the works of the Holy Spirit. The only book of the Bible that received special attention was Revelation because of its importance in describing what Parham believed was the approaching millennium of Christ's return.[5]

At the age of thirty-six in 1906, Seymour accepted an invitation to pastor a small African American Holiness Church in Los Angeles. Soon after he arrived on February 22, he ran afoul of his patrons, was locked out of the church, and took up residence with a young African American couple named Edward and Mattie Lee. By early March others were joining the three in their prayer circle. Edward Lee, a janitor at the Los Angeles First National Bank, always prayed during breaks. One day while praying, Lee was swept up into heaven by the apostles Peter and John. Together they "lifted their hands to heaven and they began to shake under the power of God and began to speak in ether tongues." Lee reported all this to Seymour's prayer circle. Convinced that Lee's vision required special action, they undertook a ten-day fast, meeting nightly to study Luke's Acts of the Apostles, which described the first Pentecost. By the third day of their vigil, Edward Lee was feeling quite ill. The group prayed over him and collectively concluded that the moment was ripe for his Holy Spirit baptism. Seymour and a fellow preacher laid their hands on him, prayed, and immediately he fell to the ground speaking in tongues.[6]

News of what happened at Lee's home "spread like fire," attracting many who genuinely sought salvation, reported Frank Bartleman, who participated in these events and became the movement's first chronicler.[7] All they needed now was a place to accommodate the burgeoning crowds seeking baptism. Seymour rented an old abandoned two-story church at 312 Azusa Street, opening the doors of his Azusa Street Mission on Easter Sunday, April 15, 1906.

"Weird Babel of Tongues; New Sect of Fanatics is Breaking Loose; Wild Scene Last Night on Azusa Street" is how the April 18 edition of the *Los Angeles Daily Times* reported what happened that Easter Sunday. "Colored people and a sprinkling of whites" were speaking in tongues, letting out "a gurgle of wordless prayers." The report continues:

> The bounds of reason are passed by these who are "filled with the spirit," whatever that may be "You-oo-oo-gou-loo-loo come under the bloo-oo-oo boo-loo" shouts, shouts of an old colored "mammy," in a frenzy of religious zeal. Swinging her arms wildly about her she continues with the strangest harangue ever uttered.... One of the wildest of the meetings was held last night, and the highest pitch of excitement reached by the gathering, which continued in "worship" until nearly midnight. The

old exhorter urged the "sisters" to let the "tongues come forth" and the women gave themselves over to a riot of religious fervor.[8]

Days later, on April 18, a major earthquake leveled San Francisco. Much of the city was destroyed by fire. Those gathered at the Azusa Street Mission immediately interpreted this as another sign of Christ's approaching millennial return. One "speaker had a vision in which he saw the people of Los Angeles flocking in a mighty stream to perdition. He prophesied awful destruction to this city unless its citizens are brought to a belief in the tenets of the new faith."[9]

Within a month, thousands were attending services at the Azusa Street Mission. Seymour preached a simple gospel message of repentance, restitution, sanctification, healing, Holy Spirit baptism, and Christ's approaching return, following exactly Parham's norms. In the first issue of *Apostolic Faith*,[10] a free four-page newspaper that began circulating broadly, Seymour explained that "Baptism with the holy ghost is a gift of power on the sanctified life; so when we get it we have the same evidence as the Disciples received on the Day of Pentecost, in speaking in new tongues."[11] The physical embodiment of Holy Spirit baptism, Seymour claimed, was tongues speech.

Those who attended revivals at the Azusa Street Mission testified that they were exuberant events. "Meetings begin about ten o'clock in the morning and can hardly stop before ten or twelve at night, and sometimes two or three in the morning, because so many are seeking, and some are slain under the power of God," reported *Apostolic Faith*.[12] "The place was never closed nor empty," attested Bartleman.[13] "Wave after wave of revival swept the people . . . crowds were weeping over sin one minute and praising God for pardon the next," recalled Methodist minister A. G. Garr. Men and women openly repented for their sins. There were shouts, fits of joy, and sweet songs that did not require musical accompaniment. "No one could understand this 'gift of song' but those who had it," continued Bartleman. "It was indeed a 'new song' in the Spirit. When I first heard it in the meeting a great hunger entered my soul to receive it. I felt it would exactly express my pent up feelings. I had not yet spoken in 'tongues.'"[14]

There was loud praying. There were bodies swaying. There was singing among those "carried into ecstasy of amens and hallelujahs. Emotion mounted higher and higher," said Garr.[15] Then there was testifying. "People told of those who were healed, of those who were relieved of the sting of poverty, of those who were filled with the Spirit of God." Some recounted their dreams and visions. Trances possessed some. Others fell to the ground as if listless. For what was transpiring, explains Bartleman, was that "God took strong men and women to pieces, and put them together again, for His glory. It was a tremendous overhauling process. Pride and self-assertion, self-importance and self-esteem, could not survive there. The religious ego preaches its own funeral sermon quickly."[16] As women and men were so transformed, they prayed for sinners. They prayed for the sickly and for the infirm. "The mission people never take medicine. They do not want it," reported *Apostolic Faith*. "They have taken Jesus as their healer, and He always heals."[17] On hearing the Gospel many testified that they had been healed of their physical and psychological pains.[18] Those who arrived using crutches, those dependent on prosthetics, left them behind as mementos of the healing that had occurred at 312 Azusa Street.

Florence Crawford arrived at the Azusa Street Mission in 1907, having gone through life seeking "something real." While dancing one night she heard a voice, "Daughter, give me thine heart." Three more times she heard the words before she understood that they were God's calls. Though she regularly prayed and fasted, she felt lost because her body and soul had not yet been sanctified. For years she traveled to places where the doctrine of sanctification was taught and practiced. She frequently attended prayer meetings and revivals, but nothing happened. "The hunger, the craving, the thirst that was in my heart, no human could know unless he had it," Crawford explained. God finally led her to the City of Angels, to 312 Azusa Street. Here, after a week's prayer, "fire fell and God sanctified me. The power of God went through me like thousands of needles." Three days later Florence was baptized with the Holy Spirit and received glossolalia's fire.

> A rushing mighty wind filled the room. This tongue that never spoke another word but English began to magnify and praise God in another language. I was speaking Chinese and it was the sweetest thing I ever heard in my life. The power of God shook my being, and rivers of joy and divine love flooded my soul. Oh, it was wonderful!

Florence Crawford had suffered three bouts of spinal meningitis as a girl, which had left her slightly blind and her body badly deformed. She walked only with the support of a metal prosthetic harness and could see only through thick glasses. In the days that followed her Holy Spirit baptism and tongues speech, the community again prayed over her. "God instantly healed me," she said, abandoning her harness and glasses. She never relied on them again.[19]

What was particularly unique about those who gathered at the Azusa Street Mission was that they were of every race and color, a multitude of nationalities, women and men, young and old, worshiping together in the African American section of town. "We were delivered right there from ecclesiastical hierarchism," affirms Frank Bartleman.[20] The services were egalitarian. "The people are all melted together . . . made one lump, one bread, all one body in Christ Jesus. There is no Jew or Gentile, bond or free, in the Azusa Mission," reported the December 1906 issue of *Apostolic Faith*.[21] At services people sat in a square facing each other, no one was elevated over others, with no one orchestrating what would happen there. "We did not even have a platform or pulpit in the beginning," continues Bartleman. "All were on a level. The ministers were servants, according to the true meaning of the word. We did not honor men for their advantage, in means or education, but rather for their God-given 'gifts.'"[22]

A. A. Boddy traveled from England to the Azusa Street mission in 1912. She too wanted spirit baptism. She returned to England where she became a Pentecostal leader. This what she witnessed in Los Angeles:

> It was something very extraordinary, that white pastors from the South were eagerly prepared to go to Los Angeles to the Negroes, to have fellowship with them and to receive through their prayers and intercessions the blessing of the Spirit. And it was still more wonderful that these white pastors went back to the South and reported to the members of their congregations that they had been together with Negroes, that they had prayed in one Spirit and received the same blessing as they.[23]

News of the Azusa Street Mission revivals disseminated rapidly by word of mouth, through letters, and around the world through an extensive network of Protestant missionary newspapers. Missionaries working in distant lands, who found it difficult to learn local languages, were naturally drawn to the idea that Holy Spirit baptism manifested itself as speaking in foreign tongues. Those who in turn had been baptized and spoke in tongues took this newly found ability as a supernatural sign that the Apocalypse was approaching and that they had to spread the gospel worldwide. *Apostolic Faith* made this connection explicit in its September 1906 issue:

> The gift of languages is given with the commission, "Go ye to all the world and preach the gospel to every creature." The lord has given language to the unlearned, Greek, Latin, Hebrew, French, German, Italian, Chinese, Japanese, Zulu and the languages of Africa, Hindu and Bengali and dialects of India, Chippewa and other languages of the Indians. Esquimaux, the deaf mute language and, in fact the Holy Ghost speaks all the languages of the world through His children.[24]

From that moment on Holy Spirit baptism was evident only through glossolalia, though by the 1940s it was uncoupled because too much of it seemed feigned. Reports from American missionaries around the world began affirming tongues speech as the supernatural sign of the approaching millennium and the urgency of the gospel's spread.[25]

As the embodied experience of the Pentecost at the Azusa Street Mission became known, it began to occur in many other places almost simultaneously; in Rochester and Nyack, New York; North Bergen, New Jersey; Akron and Cleveland, Ohio; Portland, Oregon; and Pittsburgh, Pennsylvania, and among the missionaries who formed the Christian and Missionary Alliance, then one of the largest Protestant organizations. "There is busting out in many centers a revival which is surely a visitation of God upon the earth and which may be the beginning of the final outpouring of the Holy Ghost which is to immediately precede the coming of the Lord," reported George N. Eldridge to those that had gathered for the Alliance's tenth annual convention in March 1907.[26]

The human diversity and egalitarianism that Pentecostal renewal had made possible in Jim Crow America frayed, almost as rapidly as it had been born. "All souls are equal in the eyes of God," congregants proclaimed, but increasingly tensions arose over authority and leadership that were rooted in race, gender, and class divides. Charles Fox Parham was responsible for the breach, making his way to Los Angeles in October 1906. "To my utter surprise and astonishment," he wrote, "I found conditions even worse than I had anticipated? [W]hite people [were] imitating . . . the crude negroisms of the Southland, and laying it on the Holy Ghost."[27] He rebuked the congregants for their "animalism" because they crowded the altar, "with Blacks and Whites milling around like hogs," a sight he claimed that would have brought "the devil a blush of shame. . . . [B]ig buck niggers" were laying their hands on whites. How could such things be done in the name of the Jesus Christ?[28] Parham tried but was unable to wrestle control of the mission from Seymour. He departed, vaunting the accomplishments of the Ku Klux Klan, particularly their "fine work in upholding the American way of life."[29] African American embodiments of the Holy Spirit, which awed some revival participants, frightened most whites. They fled and started their own segregated prayer circles.

White flight intensified in 1908, followed by the expulsion of "poor illiterate Mexicans," who had been brought to Azusa Street by Abundio and Rosa López. Why? We do not know. Frank Bartleman witnessed and reported on the 1909 event in his book, *How Pentecost Came to Los Angeles. How It Was in the Beginning* (1925). He is sparse and cryptic, writing only that he was shocked by this "murdering the Spirit of God."[30] Abundio and Rosa López were immigrants from Guadalajara, Mexico, who had migrated to Los Angeles to work building the Southern Pacific Railroad. Roughly two months after the Azusa Street Mission opened, they were baptized in the Spirit and spoke in tongues.[31] Expelled from the Azusa Street Mission, they responded by intensifying their evangelizing, preaching the word of God widely throughout the American Southwest and across the border in northern Mexico. Anywhere poor Mexican farmworkers toiled, Abundio and Rosa could be found, heralding the approaching fire of God. Calling sinners to repentance and redemption, such important fellow Pentecostal preachers like Luis López, Ramón Ocampo, and Francisco Llorente all traced their spirit baptisms to the Azusa Street Mission. Romana Carabajal de Valenzuela, one of the first Mexican women Pentecostal evangelists in California eventually founded La Asamblea Apostólica de la Fe en Cristo Jesús, which grew into many churches that extended far into central Mexico.[32]

Brothers Guadalupe and Vicente García arrived in California's Imperial Valley to pick cotton in the late 1920s. Epifano Cota, their labor contractor, was an Assemblies of God pastor. The brothers were soon reborn and in 1930 went south to evangelize in the Mexican state of Durango. Mexicanos deported during the Great Depression saw this as an opportunity to spread the faith among the displaced.[33] Francisco Olazábal, perhaps the most successful Pentecostal evangelist of his age, preached to hundreds of thousands. In 1916, Olazábal, like many of the thousands who came to the United States fleeing the Mexican Revolution's violence between 1910 and 1917, received his Holy Spirit baptism and then began staging enormous healing crusades throughout the American Southwest and Puerto Rico. His life was cut short by an automobile accident in 1937.[34]

As the Pentecostal movement grew, it constantly fractured along inherent fault lines. Eschewing emergent hierarchies and authoritarianism, Pentecostals often fought to restore what they called the ideals of the primitive church. They wanted to rescue Christianity from its sterility, returning to apostolic times when the charisma of Christ and his disciples was accessible to all. At the beginning of the twentieth century, their critique was that Protestant denominations had grown into large, hierarchical, and bureaucratic organizations, with rigid top-down distributions of power, authority, and resources and services that were cold, remote, and dull. Their clergy were mostly elite white men. They were highly educated, trained in seminaries and colleges, who preached esoteric sermons on theological points of little importance to the laity. In short, the living embodiment of Christ through one's entire body, mind, and soul had been stifled in Protestant churches, whose ministers were more interested in power and money than in the human condition and redemption.

In contrast, Christians who began explicitly calling themselves Pentecostals in the 1920s were largely self-educated, laboring people of color, with few resources. When they gathered, they did so mostly in their private homes without pomp or fanfare. The Bible was their only guide, and they sought no guidance from organized churches. They were firm in announcing Christ's millennial return, the need for personal sanctification, healing, Holy Spirit baptism, and tongues speech. They were living by Christ's ideals, or so they thought, just as they imagined Jesus's early followers had in apostolic times.

The critiques leveled against Protestant denominationalism in 1901 by adepts of the Apostolic Faith, constantly repeated themselves within the Pentecostal movement, provoking schisms, fracturing faith communities, prompting flights to create new home churches. Were they living as the apostles had in Jesus's time? Were they hewing closely to Christ's words? Were their lives sanctified? Were their assemblies growing too large, too wealthy, too worldly? Were their members succumbing to the vanities and comforts of capitalist society? These were the questions they constantly asked. These were the questions Reies Tijerina would later shrilly pose and answer. Ministers, referred to as "saints," and their congregants often answered these questions differently. Pentecostal community churches that had grown comfortable in their practices expelled dissidents, urging them to purse their purer apostolic faith somewhere else, further afield, in new communities of their own. As we will shortly see, this is what Assemblies of God pastors in Texas asked Reies Tijerina to do in 1950. They had soured of his reformist "new message" and "new" biblical interpretation. It was time for him to move on. He did, as do we, turning to the formation of the Assemblies of God, the Pentecostal denomination Reies first joined when he enrolled at the Latin American Bible Institute in September 1943.

The Origins of the Assemblies of God

The Assemblies of God, currently the largest Pentecostal denomination in the world, emerged out of the religious enthusiasm women and men first experienced in Topeka in 1901, initially denominated the Apostolic Faith. In the decades that followed a complex landscape of mostly household churches sprouted across the United States and around the globe, that had no formal institutional connections or formal management structure. Out of this fluidity, of sifting, of shifting, of searching, the Assemblies of God emerged and gradually took form. For the first thirteen years of their existence, congregations resisted governance or organization, fearing that the charismatic fire of the Pentecost would be extinguished through the development of bureaucracies and leadership hierarchies, which they constantly denounced as the evil that had infested older Protestant denominations and rendered them deadening.

The Assemblies of God intentionally eschewed the word "church" in their name, fearing what sociologist of religion Max Weber called the "routinization of charisma" would surely transform them into the same sort of churches against which they had rebelled with their loud, vibrant, tactile, and sensually embodied apostolic faith. Necessity forced their hand. The rapid growth of educational institutions, publishing houses, missions, missionaries, and a massive apostolate, by 1914 required management. The First General Council of the Assemblies of God was convened in 1914 in Hot Springs, Arkansas, to publicly incorporate, to brand and codify their Pentecostal theology and evangelization methodology, and to create organizational structure to oversee the vast array of activities and religious networks their movement had birthed.

At this 1914 Council meeting, the Assemblies of God divided the globe into distinct districts. A Latin American district was formed specifically to evangelize ethnic Mexicans on both sides of the US-Mexico border. Alice E. Luce and Henry A. Ball, two of their most dynamic missionaries, were chosen to lead the district. Luce began her missionary career in India and had just returned to the United States in 1914, when she was asked to refocus her energies on ethnic Mexicans. Ball, a convert from Methodism, had joined the Assemblies just a few years earlier and immediately began proselytizing among Mexican farmworkers in south Texas. He was widely respected for the enthusiastic revivals he organized and for the widespread dissemination of Assemblies of God news through *La Luz Apostólica* (The Apostolic Light), the Spanish-language newspaper he published.[35]

Luce's forte was pedagogy and mission formation. Ball was an organizer par excellence. Together they became a dynamic duo. Luce believed that for missions to succeed they had to be self-governing, self-supporting, and self-propagating, explicitly embracing Roland Allen's "three-self" rule outlined in his 1912 book, *Missionary Methods: St. Paul's or Ours?*[36] Each assembly had to be self-governed and economically independent, relying solely on itself and local resources for their growth and expansion or, conversely, for their abandonment. The missionary's task was to preach the gospel, to gather converts into an assembly, and once that was done, to move on to a new place, repeating the process again and again. Assemblies of God evangelists were imagined as itinerant preachers, continually cautioned not to think of themselves as permanent pastors. Pastors had to emerge organically from their converts, particularly from those most physically and psychically transformed by the word of God who would serve as living testaments of their embodied faith, their sanctification.[37]

Luce, who was then considered one of the most dynamic missionaries in India, quickly won enthusiastic praise for her energetic proselytizing among ethnic Mexicans. Assemblies of God publications constantly celebrated her successes, explaining in detail how she had rescued mexicanos from "degradation," from "sin," and from the "evils of the world." In the December 1930 issue of the *Latter Day Evangel* magazine, Luce asks readers: "Does it pay to make some sacrifice to give the Gospel to those strangers within our gates?" Yes! Absolutely, she replied, describing the great joys Mexicans experienced through conversion, noting that many of them had become so devout that they had received the gift of tongues. Sure, the work was slow. Sure, it was difficult. Indeed, it was costly. Often it was marked by insurmountable obstacles and backsliding. But if the Assemblies of God were to win the war they were militantly waging against sin and the Roman Catholic Church for the hearts and minds of Mexicans in the Latin American District, their financial support for this work of love and charity was absolutely crucial. Send cash. Here is sister Luce's address.[38]

By 1926 Alice Luce concluded that the evangelization of mexicanos would only advance significantly through the recruitment of ethnic Mexican ministers who understood the culture, who spoke Spanish fluently, and who knew the daily challenges of the unskilled itinerant laborers the Assemblies of God sought to convert on the cotton farms of Texas, the sugar beet fields of Michigan, the auto plants of Detroit, and the many other places they toiled. After sustained lobbying, the Assemblies of God granted Luce and Ball permission to establish two Latin American Bible Institutes in 1926. The *Instituto Bíblico Latino Americano*, the one Reies Tijerina and his first wife María Escobar attended, was located initially in Saspamco, Texas, near San Antonio, and relocated to Ysleta, Texas, just outside of El Paso, in 1945, where it remains. The second one, the Berean Bible Institute, was established in San Diego, California, and was moved in 1940 to its present location in La Puente, California, in greater Los Angeles.

Building two Bible institutes to serve the Latin American District was a daunting task. The start-up and operational costs were immense. The Council of the Assemblies of God offered Luce and Ball little financial support, insisting that they had to be independent and self-sustaining. For that to happen, tuition had to be charged. It was kept affordable, which meant that the instructors were almost all Anglo volunteers. Luce characterized the struggles she faced establishing these institutes as enormous but necessary. In the June 6, 1936, issue of the *Pentecostal Evangel* she reports that the LABI had graduated its first ten students. They immediately began ministering in rescue missions and prisons. Brimming with pride, she continues:

> The Latin American people make splendid Christians and their willingness to sacrifice personal interest and their devotion to the Lord is inspiring.... Graduates ... are making effective ministers of the Gospel not only in the U.S.A., among their own people, but also among the Spanish-speaking people in Mexico.[39]

H. Mary Kelty, one of the Institute's first teachers, was equally ebullient about these graduates: "Think of those precious lives snatched from the darkness of sin and Roman Catholicism."[40] Luce and Ball had reason to boast. The Latin American District of the Assemblies of God, created in 1914 with only seven ministers, six assemblies, and one hundred members, by 1940 counted 174 ministers, eighty assemblies, and more than five thousand saints, with many more camp followers on the cusp of conversion, and even more sitting on the fence.[41]

The LABI offered a two-year course of study, with instruction from September to May. This nine-month school year allowed students to return home for the summer to earn the second year's tuition. The first year's curriculum included courses on prophecy, Christian doctrine, preaching, and Bible study. Homiletics, divine healing, Holy Spirit baptism, and pastoral theology filled out the second. The books students were assigned were almost entirely authored by Alice Luce. She had supervised their translation into Spanish and into many other languages for use around the world. She penned tomes on Pentecostal theology, on homiletics, and edited a popular hymnal still used worldwide. Most of Luce's books are in print, deemed canonic, time-tested works that teach students the basics they need to succeed as Assemblies of God evangelists.[42]

From 1926 to 1942, the size of each entering class was small, enrolling between ten and twenty students yearly, never counting more than forty pupils in residence at any one time. Most of the students were women. Women were numerically dominant and prominent in the founding of the Assemblies of God, as evident in the first physical embodiments of Pentecost. The foreign missionary personnel were largely women. They staffed Assemblies of God schools, publications, and missions. All that changed after the start of World War II. Women were pushed into the background, into much more marginal and auxiliary roles in the governance of the Assemblies of God, with men increasingly becoming its leaders, evangelists, and pastors.

In the next chapter we turn to Reies Tijerina's arrival at the Latin American Bible Institute, the education he got there, and his evangelical career in the Assemblies of God.

CHAPTER 3

Becoming an Evangelist

AT THE AGE OF seventeen, Reies López Tijerina arrived at the Latin American Bible Institute in early September 1943, then located in Saspamco, Texas, nineteen miles southeast of San Antonio. LABI later moved to the outskirts of El Paso because Saspamco was very difficult for students to reach by bus or train. LABI sat on an active 165-acre working farm, with livestock, an orchard, and extensive fields of corn and hay. The site had a church, several faculty houses, an administration building with classrooms, offices, and food services on the ground floor, and a men's dormitory upstairs. A separate women's dorm with outdoor toilets for everyone's use was nearby. The two bath houses, like the administrative building, were too expensive to heat or cool, so only cold water ran through its veins.

Kenzy Savage was appointed LABI's superintendent on May 27, 1943, just months before Reies arrived, a post Savage held until 1947. He knew the Tijerinas because they were active members of San Antonio's Templo Cristiano, which Kenzy had previously led. His first goal at LABI was to stabilize its finances, immediately staging Pentecostal revivals across Texas to attract more tuition-paying students. He succeeded. By that September he had enrolled seventy-five students, twenty-five more than the previous year, graduating twenty-four in 1944 and twenty-seven in 1945. "GLORY! God's blessings are beyond measure!" he proclaimed when he reported his success.[1]

The institute's curriculum was designed to forge ethnic Mexican students who had no formal education and knew even less about the Bible but were eager to spread the word of God as Assemblies of God ministers. Classes were conducted entirely in Spanish to prepare them for evangelizing in foreign missions. Ministering to ethnic Mexicans, even among those citizens living in the United States, was considered a foreign field.[2]

Reies Tijerina rapidly chafed under the school's strict behavioral codes and orthodox curriculum. "For the first two months I kept quiet and to myself, but the deeper we went into the history of the church and the doctrine of the church and the religious ministry life style [sic], the more I felt that I was being geered [sic] in the wrong path." He found his classes too insular, too narrowly focused on the dogmas of the Assemblies of God.[3] When Reies, as a teenager, first accepted the Bible as his guide, "it seem [sic] so simple to find communication with God. So Easy. But now the more I went into the world of religion the harder it seem [sic] to get closer to God." He complained to his father Antonio about the "boring and anti-brotherhood education that I had found in the place." Reies expected a sanctuary of charity and love, with students who were honest and kind. Instead, his classmates were "stilling [sic] my belongings, cursing and swearing and fighting." He had few friends. And of the angelic visitations he arrived expecting, well, it "was not so."[4]

The instruction LABI offered its first-year students was as orthodox as Reies complained, cleaving closely to the Bible, relying almost exclusively on it to teach the precepts of faith. Students were expected to learn the Bible's lessons through rout memorization, instantaneously citing chapter and verse to anchor whatever moral a preacher wished to instill or to address whatever problem a community faced. They were taught to seek out, identify, and critique error, constantly interrogating textual and interpretive accuracy to avoid subtle infiltrations of heterodox ideas. This indeed was the sort of questioning that invariably nurtured doctrinal schisms in the Assemblies of God, animated by conflicting personal egos, deep resentments, and petty jealousies, but which were always disguised as truth-seeking, truth-telling, and divine intervention. As we will see shortly, later in 1950, this sort of doctrinal schism profoundly bedeviled Reies's ministry.

In her book *Probe the Spirits, to Assure They Are God's* (Probad los Espiritus, Si Son de Dios), Alice E. Luce urged her LABI students to be vigilant about exactly such things:

The prevalence of these false doctrines is due in foundation to devils as was prophesied in Revelation 16:13–14. "And I saw emerge from the mouth of the dragon, from the mouth of the beast, and from the mouth of a false prophet, three spirit worlds, like frogs, because they are prodigal demonic spirits, who appear to kings of all the inhabited earth, to gather together for the war of the great day of God almighty."[5]

What Anglo teachers at LABI feared, or at least what they said most frightened them, was that Mexicans might imbibe the devil's "error" and be led astray. Here was a variant of the "White man's burden," bringing salvation to benighted Mexicans while keeping students tightly under their teachers' heavy-handed disciplinary control, frequently with the paddle. Such close supervision continued even after graduation when newly trained ministers began preaching on their own, leading their own assemblies, but still very much "supervised" by their white elders.

Preaching was the fundamental skill every missionary had to master. The Institute devoted an enormous amount of energy and time to assure that its graduates mastered this skill. Luce's *The Messenger and His Message: A Handbook for Young Workers on the Preparation of Gospel Addresses* (1925) was the tome used for this task. The first half of the offered practical advice on how to research, prepare, and deliver a sermon; the second half contained a variety of themes, with corresponding biblical quotations so that neophytes could easily reference these pages when pressed for the inspiration that the Holy Spirit had not delivered as rapidly as needed.[6] God's message provided students with the perfect words with which to preach. The student's task was to deliver them so persuasively that they effectively entered "the hearts of the hearers."[7] Students were discouraged from delivering sermons on politics, social problems, current events, and scientific discoveries. A "true preacher is one who has a definite call and a definite message; in the words of Paul he is 'separated unto the Gospel of God.'" Faithfulness to God's word took precedence over all. Ask yourself: "HAVE I FAITHFULLY DELIVERED THE MESSAGE WHICH GOD WAS SENDING TO THOSE PEOPLE THROUGH ME?" This was the question every homiletics student had to ask and answer affirmatively.[8]

For the word of God to enter deeply into the minds and hearts of their auditors, Luce insisted that sermons had to consist of four parts: introduction, presentation, application, and culmination. The introduction gathered up and summarized collective experiences because "only that which touches them enters their hearts."[9] Sermons had to draw on scripture to convey God's own words. Biblical passages needed to be selected with several criteria in mind: clarity, pedagogy, and interpretive robustness. "The preaching that unveils JESUS to them as the all-sufficient Savior, Sanctifier, Healer, Teacher, Guide, Baptizer and Coming King is the kind of preaching that will feed their souls and produce definite results."[10] The culmination was "the final struggle which decides the conflict." That struggle was the resistance unbelievers displayed to content they had heard for the first time. For this very reason a sermon could not be "too long, labored or verbose."[11]

Personal reminiscences, distracting mannerisms, improper dress, and exaggerated diction were all verboten. Avoid a "shrill, piping, screechy voice." If the preacher's words were gently to enter the coarse, hardened, and resistant hearts of sinful auditors, they themselves had to be paragons of tenderness and love.[12] They had to lead lives of virtue, marked by utmost personal dignity and vigorous physical health. To be efficacious instruments of Christ's miraculous power, pastoral aspirants had "to drink in the Lord's life for daily health, that our bodies may be filled and energized moment by moment with the Spirit's power."[13]

Reies's first year at LABI ended in May 1944. He departed with considerable doubts, uncertain if he would return for the second term. He spent that summer working with his family near Sandusky, Michigan, earning his tuition and fees should he choose to return. Antonio Tijerina listened to his son's complaints patiently. "Lets [sic] Pray for them," he gently advised. They did daily and prayed too for the many suffering from the violence and destruction caused by World War II. Antonio's two eldest sons had been drafted into the military, Anselmo in 1941, Margarito in 1942. "The name Adolf Hitler was mentioned enough times to stay in my mind," Reies recalled. Whenever talk of the war against Germany and Japan dominated his auditory spaces, Reies panicked, froze up, and instantly broke into a cold sweat. Perhaps he reasonably expected that soon he too would be drafted. Talk of war so unnerved him that he took cover under a bed and refused to emerge for hours, until he had calmed himself.[14]

World War II was impossible to ignore. Anselmo and Margarito frequently wrote to their wives from the European front. When such letters arrived, the family would gather to hear them read aloud. They recounted horrible "sad stories."[15] Why the war then raging in Europe and Asia so rattled Reies can only be understood if one imagines him at the time as a God-fearing soul, seeking redistributive justice to improve the plight of the poor, abandoned, and those forgotten amid the destruction of a world war. He often described the training he received at LABI as preparing him to wage war against sin and Satan, ready as the biblical *Valientes*, or valiant ones, to serve as a fierce gladiator for the Lord. The word *valientes* in the Old and New Testaments was used to valorize those who were mighty and brave in their struggles against evil. He could not fathom a war of bullets and bombs aimed at innocents, which had as its only goal the advancement of the imperialist aims of the "beast." Perhaps this is why Reies froze. Perhaps he feared that the Selective Service Administration would draft him. Reies's understanding of sin was complex. It was physical, embodied, palpable, and, between 1942 and 1945, very visibly lethal and global, and later understood as genocidal when the extent of ethnic cleansing became known.

Whatever his gnawing reservations, in September 1944 Reies put them aside and returned to LABI, encouraged that his older brother Ramón and Ramón's recent bride, Ester Escobar, were matriculating in the Institute's first-year class. With his older brother nearby, Reies now felt less isolated, less vulnerable, less alone. When a romance developed with a pretty, young woman from Monte Vista, Colorado, named Vicky Rivera, who had enrolled in the entering class, things became all the more cheerful. Reies soon met his first love and gave what he said as his first romantic kiss to a woman. "I liked her very much," Reies reminisced. "We talked twice. I kissed her once, and that was the beginning of my first problem." This was how Reies narrated his love for Vicky in his 1978 autobiography. When I interviewed him three decades later, a very different story emerged, one not of innocent youthful romance but of sexual harassment. "I grabbed her and kissed her, and she reported it. She was doing very poorly in school. The superintendent said: either you or her will go. I was very macho and so I decided to leave."[16]

All the school's spaces and activities were strictly gender segregated and carefully chaperoned to prevent romantic attachments and premarital sex.

There were many more females than males at the school and teachers well understood what sexual rivalries and potential havoc such gender imbalances could provoke. Young male students were not allowed to mix with female students in public or private, nor were amorous relationships allowed. According to students then at the Institute, they claimed that they knew of no romantic relationships of any sort. Only when students started to arrive as married couples, as Ramón and Ester Tijerina did in 1944, were they accommodated with different housing arrangements.[17]

When LABI Superintendent Savage, learned of Vicky and Reies's budding romance, they were both suspended. "The young man [Reies Tijerina] was suspended from the school the Christmas vacation of 1944 for not complying with the rules stipulated by the school on friendship with female students." This is how his official institute transcript read.[18] Reies argued bitterly with Savage about the expulsion, accusing him of racism toward Mexicans. Reies had visited the racially segregated Assemblies of God Bible Institute for white students in Springfield, Missouri, and there he had seen that "boys and girls intermingled, held hands, and kissing each other, not only in private but in public." Savage was enforcing a different, stricter moral code on his ethnic Mexican students "that you and your Anglo people never observe."[19] Reies's observation about the racial segregation of Anglo and Mexican students rang true. All the students at LABI were ethnic Mexicans. All the teachers were Anglos. The lone exception was Miss Ester Basón, the piano and singing teacher, who was Mexican and a part-time volunteer.[20]

Despondent by this turn of events, Reies returned home to winter with his father, who's yearly migratory harvesting trek already had looped back to San Antonio. By now, too, all of Reies's brothers and sisters were married and no longer residing in their small and modest familial home. It fell to Reies to care for his father.[21] Reies passed the winter of 1944–1945 in San Antonio and in the spring once again migrated to Michigan. In early April 1945, he received his own draft notice and reported as instructed to a US. Army recruiting station. Reies did not relish the idea that he would be forced to cross the Atlantic Ocean to "kill people I had never met before." Germany's unconditional surrender to the Allied Powers on May 8, 1945, came just days before his physical exam. The doctors found a small cyst in Reies's throat, which much later grew larger and eventually cause him searing pain when he preached loudly and for long periods of time. Reies was found medically unfit for military service. By then, World War II was ramping down, decreasing the demand for new recruits.[22]

Antonio Tijerina fully understood his son's passionate desire to become a Pentecostal evangelist and pestered him to appeal his expulsion. Antonio argued that Reies's older brother Ramón and his wife Ester were at the school, and they too now needed Reies to help them brave the challenging curriculum and culture there. Reies appealed. He was allowed to return conditionally, provided that he end his relationship with Vicky Rivera. Agreed. Reies returned in September 1945. When the Institute got no appeal from Vicky Rivera, they concluded their disciplinary problem had been resolved.[23] Or so it seemed.

Unbeknown to anyone, Reies and Vicky had been writing to each other frequently since their expulsions. In July 1945, Reies traveled to Colorado to see her. Much to his dismay, Vicky was dating another man with whom in public she seemed quite in love, openly demonstrating a certain level of physical familiarity. Crushed, confused, but still quite utterly smitten, Reies admitted being now even more lovesick and uncertain about what he should do. He remained in Monte Vista for a month, found work, hoping that he and Vicky would ignite their love anew. His wooing failed. He began his journey back to Texas with a more level head, stopping to visit old friends in the mountain village of Tierra Amarilla, in northern New Mexico, during the first week of August 1945, just miles from Los Alamos, the birthplace of the atomic bomb.[24]

Apocalypse Now: August 6–9, 1945

Unbeknown to most Americans, during that first week of August 1945, B-29 bombers flew 1,400 missions over Japan. As antiaircraft sentinels detected American bombers approaching, sirens constantly shrieked. That week millions of fliers fell from the sky warning: "Evacuate or Die!"[25] Hiroshima's 300,000 residents had hardly begun to stir on August 6 when sirens cried out anew. Quietly, almost silently, the Enola Gay approached with the world's first atomic bomb, packing an explosive power equivalent to 20,000 tons of TNT, the biggest explosive force then known.²⁶ At 8:15 a.m. (Japanese time), the bomb was dropped, exploded, and unleashed a blinding light. Those who survived said that it was "not of this world, [but] the light of many suns in one. It was a sunrise such as the world had never seen, a great green super-sun . . . [of] dazzling luminosity." It seemed as if one were witnessing the very beginning of time, that moment when God said, "Let there be light."²⁷ The bomb's heat reached 5,400 degrees Fahrenheit, instantly vaporizing everything for miles. Where 70,000 men, women, and children stood at 8:15 a.m., by 8:16 only their ashen shadows remained. "My God, what have we done? My God, what have we done," wrote Robert Lewis, commander of the Enola Gay's crew in his logbook that day, as he saw "the entire city disappear."²⁸ Nagasaki met a similar fate on August 9, 1945.

Reies Tijerina, like 98 percent of the American public, rapidly learned of the bomb's destruction of Hiroshima. "DEADLIEST WEAPONS IN WORLD'S HISTORY MADE IN SANTA FE VICINITY" was the *Santa Fe New Mexican*'s headline on August 6.²⁹ For most war-weary Americans who wanted Japan punished, the narratives President Harry S. Truman and his advisors spun about the necessity of dropping the bomb sufficed. The United States had completely obliterated Japan's ability to wage war and, with the bomb, was sending a threatening missive to Germany and the Soviet Union.³⁰ Japan surrendered on August 14, 1945, ending the war. President Truman explained American actions thus: "The Japanese began the war from the air at Pearl Harbor. They have been repaid many fold." Dropping the bombs "was an awful responsibility which has come to us. We thank God that it has come to us instead of to our enemies; and we pray that He may guide us to use it in His way and for His purposes."³¹

The United States and its allies won World War II. This was a moment of great celebration, not of woeful lamentation. It was time to forget the past and to ponder atomic energy's radiant future. This was the dominant message the American government wanted its citizens to imbibe. Truman embargoed all photos and firsthand reports from Hiroshima and Nagasaki to shape American public opinion. It worked. Eighty percent of Americans thought the bombings justified in 1945.³²

Did the residents of Hiroshima and Nagasaki deserve such death and destruction? Reies Tijerina was one of the many devote Christians who loudly condemned the murder of more than 200,000 Japanese innocents. What was most disgusting, particularly to Reies, was that Christians were "thanking God for what the Atom Bomb had done to Japan. . . . I felt bad and sick to my stomach to see no one feeling pity for the Japanese people." Most Americans quickly shrugged off the nuclear holocaust, rapidly forgot the atrocities of World War II, reveling instead in the country's postwar prosperity and the fruits of its rapidly expanding global empire.[33]

Reies could not and insisted he would not forget. Tutored in the Bible's prophecies, his mind instantly raced to the Book of Revelation:

> The first angel sounded, and there followed hail and fire mingled with blood, and they were cast upon the earth: and the third part of trees was burnt up, and all green grass was burnt up. And the second angel sounded, and as it were a great mountain burning with fire was cast into the sea: and the third part of the sea became blood; And the third part of the creatures which were in the sea, and had life, died; and the third part of the ships were destroyed. And the third angel sounded, and there fell a great star from heaven, burning as it were a lamp, and it fell upon the third part of the rivers, and upon the fountains of waters; And the name of the star is called Wormwood: and the third part of the waters became wormwood; and many men died of the waters, because they were made bitter. And the fourth angel sounded, and the third part of the sun was smitten, and the third part of the moon, and the third part of the stars; so as the third part of them was darkened, and the day shone not for a third part of it, and the night likewise. And I beheld, and heard an angel flying through the midst of heaven, saying with a loud voice, Woe, woe, woe, to the inhabiters of the earth by reason of the other voices of the trumpet of the three angels, which are yet to sound! (Rev. 8:7–13)

In Revelation, Reies found all the signs of the Apocalypse, of Christ's rapidly approaching return to earth to rule triumphantly for a thousand years. In the sermons he subsequently preached, he urged repentance for "one could already see the light," the light of the Apocalypse, the light of Christ's return. Ironically, even President Truman saw it this way. For in the days following the "Trinity test" of July 16, 1945, which tested the atom bomb, Truman wrote in his diary that the bomb was "the most terrible thing ever discovered. ... It may be the fire destruction prophesied in the Euphrates Valley Era, after Noah and his fabulous Ark."[34]

By the beginning of September, Reies was back at LABI to finish year two of his program of studies. The school had been relocated to Ysleta, Texas, on the outskirts of El Paso. Reies was a little older, thought he was a lot wiser, and had become much more confident than when he arrived in 1943. He now engaged his teachers and classmates in heated debates, quarrelling about the content of the curriculum and about the approaching apocalypse. As Reies explained it, "Now I clearly saw the organized church as the greatest stumbling block between men and God."[35] The relationship the Assemblies of God had forged with the state was too close, too cozy, too accommodating to the sinister, worldly power of the "beast," which did not square with the teachings of Jesus Christ. The Assemblies of God were fixated on the accumulation of money, depriving the poor and those in need solely to undertake massive construction campaigns, building countless sumptuous churches and schools. Such activities were deadening the charisma the Holy Spirit had given Christians at the Pentecost, leading many ministers to forget Christ's command that they feed, cloak, and shelter the poor, orphans, and widows.

He leveled searing critiques about the institutional sexism and racism his teachers barely disguised. Though previously many women had held leadership roles in the Assemblies of God, by the mid-1940s Mexican female graduates were not allowed to preach on their own, to form or to lead congregations independently, though they had no reservation about admitting them into its Bible institutes and charging them tuition to prepare them for these roles. On rare occasions, single women were permitted to travel to remote corners of the world as missionaries, but only if the Assemblies of God deemed them particularly gifted, were fully informed of all the social and sexual risks such assignments entailed, and the women understood that no one would come to their rescue if their lives were endangered. María Escobar, a 1942 graduate of the Institute, who later became Reies Tijerina's first wife, also called such women valientes. "Yes, they could [become missionaries] if they were valiant; they did it under very strict rules," María explained. The records show that neither María nor any of her female classmates were ever authorized to serve as missionaries. For that they needed husbands.[36]

The Assemblies of God spent too much time spouting strict prohibitions against smoking, dancing, drinking, movie attendance, sex, and swearing, rather than doing the Lord's work claimed Reies. He recalled his days at LABI as full of consternation and conflict, constantly seeking God's guidance. "I felt my naked soul caught between powerfull [sic] forces, that were beyond my control or understanding. . . . I had no college education, no elementary education, and the way I was going, I felt that I was sinking more and more in a tunnel without light." Were his interrogations, apprehensions, and interpretations born of his own arrogance? "Should I just keep quiet and join them? . . . I felt my naked soul caught between powerful forces, that were beyond my control or understanding . . . the more I went into the world of religion the harder it seem [sic] to get closer to God. Was the problem in me? Was it the world of society around me? Was it in God himself that he had no use for me?"[37] His troubled mind, body, and soul yearned for definitive answers.

Kenzy Savage, still LABI's superintendent, had a much clearer vision, less vexed answers, and acted quickly to contain what he diagnosed as a continuing disciplinary problem. Reies's LABI transcript notes that in February 1946 he "was again put on probation." Savage described Reies as "a very sincere student," but one who "was fanatical, more peculiar in his thoughts . . . he was not orthodox." On a scale of "good—average—poor," Reies was "average" in leadership, reliability, courtesy, and ability to get along with others. His attendance was "good." His scholastic standing and cooperativeness were "average." And his behavior? Well, that was honestly "poor."[38]

After this probation, things only worsened for Reies. Early that May, on the day before he was to graduate and preach the commencement sermon for which his classmates had elected him, Vicky Rivera returned. Her on-again, off-again relationship with Reies was apparently on again. Both must have had some hope that their romance would bloom anew, for there she was in vivo, vivacious, and no longer mere words in a letter. They had continued corresponding since the previous summer, something the superintendent discovered and also entered into Reies's transcript to justify the probation.

Vicky arrived and invited Reies to lunch in nearby El Paso. He accepted, leaving the campus without permission. On learning of Rivera's return, Savage was furious. Reies had been instructed never to see her again. He had. "You left the premises without a permit. It will cost you your diploma, for you will not be allowed to graduate with the class of 1946." That is how Reies remembered Savage's rebuke. "Reies you are a lost case. You will back slide." With tear-filled eyes Reies replied, "I am not a lost case and I assure you that some day [sic] in the future you will hear my name ringing from coast to coast."39

Reies was barred from graduation the next day, from preaching the commencement sermon, from receiving his diploma, even from being photographed with classmates in their official portrait. So that everyone at the graduation might understand Reies's lapse and punishment, an empty chair was placed on the auditorium's stage. Reies left LABI for good. He remembered himself as a straight A student, an assertion his official transcript does not bear out. He left angry and hurt. This was how Reies's only sustained formal educational experience ended and was recalled.

Several years later, in May 1950, when Kenzy Savage learned that Reies was visiting El Paso, he invited him to that year's graduation for a much belated conferral of his diploma. Reies refused. "I rather have that Diploma here, on the files of this Institution, as a witness to my Rebellion," he retorted. For much of his adult life Reies fumed whenever he was asked about his LABI training and lack of a diploma. The school's official transcript does show that Reies Tijerina completed his two-year course of study in May 1946. Ultimately, it was the credential that authorized him to minister in Assemblies of God.40

CHAPTER 4

Reies Tijerina's Ministry

REIES TIJERINA BEGAN HIS active ministry in May 1946, having been tutored on the Bible, prophecy, homiletics, conversion, and Holy Spirit baptism by his teachers at the Latin American Bible Institute. His evangelistic message was heard by others as a very legalistic and caustic one, articulating a critique of American imperialism and the participation of Protestant churches in a post-war exploitative colonial project around the world. Almost verbatim he echoed the indictment John of Patmos offered of the Roman Empire in Revelation. Lacking a formal diploma but having completed his course of study at the LABI, the Assemblies of God authorized him as a minister. Whatever Reies's foibles and failings as a student, even Kenzy Savage, the director of LABI, who was no fan, admitted that he asked Reies's assistance staging revivals among Hispanos in New Mexico in the late 1940s because he "was a very good speaker, with a lot of spunk and spirit."[1]

On leaving LABI, Reies traveled to Pontiac, Michigan, joining his family already toiling there in its sugar beet fields. Pilar Escobar had also taken his brood there, uniting the Tijerina and Escobar families for another summer of back-breaking work. María Escobar, whom Reies soon married, confessed that she "didn't like to work in the fields," and really did not want to go to Michigan that summer.[2] She had no choice. It was her father's decision.

Reies was now twenty years old but thought himself too young to marry. All his siblings had already wed and fled the familial hearth. Tired of being alone Reies proposed marriage to María Escobar.[3] She had long sought a husband who was an Assemblies of God minister because it was the only way she could possibly become a missionary while raising a family. Marriage made perfect sense for both.

María Escobar

María Escobar's ancestral past was not unlike that of many ethnic Mexicans residing in Texas in the mid-1940s. The family fled Mexico for Texas around the 1880s, caught on the losing side of a local power struggle they remembered as a precursor of the Mexican Revolution. María's great-grandfather Gregorio Escobar, her grandfather Pilar Escobar, and his four brothers were all facing a firing squad. Inexplicably Pilar's life was spared. People surmised that he was deemed too young to die for the crimes of old men, or at least that is how María's mother had told her the story. Spared, Pilar fled to Laredo, Texas, there took a woman named Teresa as his wife, and in 1927 María Escobar was born in San Antonio where the family had settled. María's parents were active members of the Templo Cristiano, an Assemblies of God Pentecostal mission, and it was here that María received her water baptism and was welcomed into this faith community. Teresa Escobar eventually gave birth to fifteen children. María was among the thirteen who survived to adulthood.[4]

María remembers a childhood of poverty, of constant circular migrations between Texas and Michigan to perform grueling, stooped labor tending to sugar beets for much less than a penny on the pound. Like the Tijerinas, the Escobar family worked as a unit, employed on farms owned by Anglos who were never kind, rarely just, and thought of them as herd animals to be driven from field to field. With fifteen mouths to feed, the Escobars remember those days as "very hard." During her childhood María said she found solace in the ecstatic services at the Templo Cristiano, which served as her emotional anchor that helped her endure all the challenges she and her family faced. "This church gave me enormous spiritual power to remain on the path that led to God."[5]

The stories María Escobar and Reies Tijerina independently tell about how they first met diverge. María recalls meeting members of the Tijerina family at the Templo Cristiano. One day in 1939, as María and her siblings walked with Reies's sisters and brothers to choir practice, she saw Reies off in the distance riding a bike. Their initial interactions were exclusively at church. When, in 1944, María's older sister Ester married Reies's older brother Ramón, the two families began socializing more frequently at church services in San Antonio and in Michigan, while toiling on the same farms. Reies's first memories of María date from June 1942, from Deckerville, Michigan, where both families were working. María had just graduated from LABI that May and joined her family to work the rest of that summer.

From a very young age María wanted to be an Assemblies of God missionary. "All I wanted was to . . . work in the cause of God." She chose to study at LABI because its students frequently sang and preached at the Templo Cristiano. "They used to sing so beautifully. I wanted to be just like them . . . a missionary." Her father collected the tuition and in September 1940 she enrolled. The educational training she received was identical to what Reies later experienced, the exception being that she was not plagued by nagging doubts about what she was learning. She joyfully remembered her lessons in prophecy, Christian doctrine, and "how to speak to wayward souls living in sin, calling them to Christ because only Christ was their savior."[6]

Upon finishing her studies María immediately applied to evangelize among ethnic Mexicans. Despite numerous applications she was never picked to lead an assembly or to minister in a foreign mission. Her life-long ambition seemed dashed. If she was to realize that dream, she needed a husband, ideally one trained by the Assemblies of God. While ruminating about her next move, Reies wrote her as a platonic friend, concerned about her soul's well-being, believing that her failure to be assigned to a missionary post might provoke resentment and alienate her from the church. "No, no, I would say. I always go to church on Fridays and Sundays."[7] When I asked María why she did not become a minister, despite all her training and commitment, María offered a stark gendered explanation. "For women . . . it's hard to get into the ministry." Why? "I don't know." She sensed that racism and misogyny were at work but feared that any protestation would only have gotten her shunned, making her goal even more impossible to attain.

When the Assemblies of God first emerged out of the Pentecostal enthusiasm of the early 1900s, women played dominant roles as preachers and pastors. The women dispatched to foreign missions were considered *las muy valientas* (the very valiant ones). By the early 1940s, this had all changed. Now all the leaders were men. The highly trained and biblically literate women had been marginalized and relegated to limited social spaces and subordinated in domestic roles.[8] Where previously the New Testament's injunction that "all souls are equal in the eyes of God" had justified the equal participation of women in church leadership, now women were told, "the head of every man is Christ; and the head of the woman *is* the man; and the head of Christ *is* God" (1 Cor. 11:3). "Let the woman learn in silence with all subjection. But I suffer not a woman to teach, nor to usurp authority over the man, but to be in silence" (1 Tim. 2:11–12). Years later, in 2007, Noah Tijerina, María's fourth child with Reies, confided, "When the Bible stated; wifes [*sic*] 'submit' on to your husbands; she [María] took it literally, and to heart. She had been so conditioned by my father and relegion [*sic*] that looking back I wonder if she ever daired [*sic*] to think for herself."[9]

No matter how excellent their preparation, or invigorating their oratory, women increasingly were limited to bit roles in the Assemblies of God. Those who aspired to missionary lives had two options: (1) to subordinate their ambitions to those of a husband, marrying a pastor and thus being elevated in the community's eyes, or (2) to seek an assignment in a foreign land, facing the isolation and sexual assaults such missionary women routinely experienced, showing how truly "valiant" they were.[10] The explicit message the ethnic Mexican female graduates of LABI got was that marriage was the only avenue they had to serve at the margins of a local assembly as homemakers.

Reies knew that María was an LABI graduate, a deeply religious person, with established familial connections through work and church. Both were equally passionate about spreading the word of God and saving souls. On July 14, 1946, they married in Pontiac, Michigan. Neither ever said that their union was based on physical attraction, love, desire, or erotic passion, though eventually these emotions may have played some role in their relationship. Together they began traveling, staging Pentecostal revivals, casting their evangelistic nets in hopes of rescuing wayward souls and leading them to God.[11]

Reies Tijerina as Evangelist

Late that summer of 1946, Reies was offered his first pastoral job by his old friend Fred Gómez, the pastor who, in 1944, had performed his Holy Spirit baptism and the person responsible for guiding him to the ministry. Gómez was still leading his old assembly nearby in Saginaw, ministering mostly to ethnic Mexican fieldhands, which increasingly included many *braceros*, temporary agricultural guest workers. Fred Gómez hired Reies as his copastor, and by late July he arrived to take up his post.[12] Reies was now educated, biblically literate, capable of holding his own, and thoroughly confident in his ability to lead an Assembly of God congregation without anyone's guidance or paternalistic help.

Little time passed before their long friendship was taxed and the copastoring agreement soured. They quarreled about what the Gospel's message should be for a congregation of poor mexicanos. Gómez thought Reies was too rigid, too legalistic, placing "too much emphasis on the Commandment of God." Gómez fumed, "We are living in a dispensation of Grace, deeds are not the important thing." Dispensationalism was a fundamentalist doctrine articulated in the mid-nineteenth century that divided human history into *dispensations*, or periods specifically ordained by God. Christians in the late 1940s were living in the final dispensation, the premillennial one heralding Christ's imminent return. Premillennialists were certain that Christ would soon return, reign over a thousand years of prosperity, finally judging and destroying the world. Reies's response was that Christ had died for humanity's sins. His life was "rich in good deeds... his life was supposed to be a pattern for our lives." Reies refused to temper the harshness of his sermons or to amend any of his words. After four months, Gómez asked him to leave, ending Reies's first pastoral post. He and María remained in Saginaw, working in the sugar beet fields until the harvest ended, contemplating their next move.[13]

In late November 1946, Reies and María boarded a Grey Hound Bus headed to Dallas. Before they departed Reies gave away most of the couple's moveable goods. "We didn't have much," Reies admitted, "a radio and some chairs, but I gave it . . . to the poor. Because I kept on having a struggle with my conscience, my soul." He frequently gave away all his family's material possessions in emulation of the ancient prophets and to identify with those living at the margins of existence. María, the family's only stable breadwinner, did not particularly relish such charitable acts and repeatedly protested about the hardship this produced for her children.

Reies deemed himself an old-style Mexican patriarch and once he decided something, it was so.[14]

On reaching Dallas, María and Reies separated, each going in different directions. This sort of separation became routine in their marriage. Reies was impulsive, guided mostly by what he said were directives from the Holy Spirit, rarely giving his family's needs much consideration. Whenever he felt the Holy Spirit calling, he bolted. María, on the other hand, was the family's anchor and remained its primary breadwinner both during their marriage and after their 1963 divorce. She was grounded, practical, always trying to assure that her husband and children had food on the table and clean clothes on their backs. Housing was a luxury few migratory farmworkers had and for this María creatively improvised. During summers María often first traveled to Michigan's sugar beet fields with her kin, then migrated back to Texas and westward across the state picking cotton to earn the cash necessary to support her husband's evangelizing. When Reies was on the road during the dead of winter, she returned to San Antonio with her children, working as a typist, shop clerk, and hotel maid, relying on her extended family to help her make ends meet.

After María arrived in San Antonio that November 1946, "without a definite direction," Reies impetuously decided that he was going to Los Angeles, "to look for the living God."[15] He had a longstanding invitation to preach in El Monte, one of that city's suburbs, and had to honor his word. Much more was really on his mind. He had lost his first job as a minister. He had not been allowed to graduate at LABI. He was deeply psychologically bereft, or so Reies said, feeling as if he were "a hypocrite, that I was not doing what I could do." During these moments of doubt, he prayed, meditated, and read the Bible, feeling "that I was way back, way behind, that I had to overcome everything."[16]

Like an Old Testament prophet seeking illumination and mystical union with God, Reies retreated from this world, fasting to purify his body, silencing his mind through meditation, seeking a revelation that would map the course God wanted him to traverse. There, in the foothills of the San Gabriel Mountains, just northeast of Los Angeles, Reies searched for a remote spot, one that would be difficult to find. "If I die in my persuit [sic] of God," he instructed María, "don't tell any body that I died trying to find

God, because that would frighten others."[17] Burrowing into a hill covered by dense scrub brush he dug a cavelike hole, a cocoon of sorts, lining it with cotton upholstery he rummaged from an old car seat he found in a dump. Like a snake entering its nest to morph and shed its skin, so Reies abandoned the world, fasting until his hunger was gone. "If there was a Supreme being, he new [sic] what I wanted and how much I had suffered in trying to find him."[18]

Nights and days passed. Reies lost all sense of time. Delirium followed. "I felt a strange feeling overtaking my hold [sic] body. My mind was reaching out into space." Reies had no memory of the number of days that passed, but clarity soon arrived. "I had great illuminations." He learned that "there was just the two strong powers of good and evil" in the world and that little separated Catholics and Protestants, something he had failed to learn at LABI. Their desires were identical. "They all wanted new automobiles, they were all full of pride and coveted the same things." With this newly found certitude and his doubts gone, his depression turned into mania. Reies returned to El Monte to stage the revival as he had promised. "Now my soul felt a new and very different feeling. A satisfying joy was filling my entire body and spirit." When the El Monte community heard Reies preach, by his own estimation, they were all very, very pleased.[19]

Still in Los Angeles, a telegram arrived from María in early December 1946, informing Reies that he had been offered a post in San Antonio, Texas. Return Immediately! Without explanation Manuel de la Cruz, a local pastor, had to take temporary leave. Reies assumed his post, announcing that he had "a new interpretation of the Bible, just *literally, the way it was*," which had been given clarity and precision during his El Monte mystical retreat. Reies immediately started penning the sermons he eventually gathered and published in 1955, titled ¿*Hallará fe en la tierra* . . . ? (Will He Find Any Faith on Earth . . . ?).

From December 1946 to September 1947, Reies temporarily headed Manuel de la Cruz's Assembly. Here, on July 30, 1947, María's gave birth to their first child, a son they named David (later also known as Reies Jr. and Hugh).[20] When Reies's pastoral contract ended, he floated through a series of short-term assignments between 1947 and 1950. This was not the type of ministry he wanted, but it was all he could find. Reies was a restless soul, most at peace and spiritually nourished as an evangelist going from place to place, visiting congregations, staging revivals, living from hand-to-mouth, emulating Christ, totally bereft of possessions and completely dependent on the charity of others. María sometimes accompanied him on these treks, offering Bible classes to the young and helping however she could and Reies permitted. María, waxing nostalgically, recalled those years as full of joy, "I felt very well doing the work of God." On February 2, 1949, joy again filled their lives. Rose, their second child, was born in Victoria, Texas, while Reies was a pastor there.[21]

Reies remembered his ministry in Victoria fondly because it afforded him the time "to meditate, to pray with a new mentality, to talk to the people without interference from the church leaders." In August 1949, again short of cash, he and María worked their way west across Texas picking cotton. By day they labored plucking cotton bolls. By night Reies's ethnic Mexican coworkers listened to him preach, transporting his audience to a world of justice and mercy, allowing their spirits to soar by listening to the word of God. When the harvest ended, they returned to San Antonio. There Reies began systematically visiting nearby Assemblies, spreading the "new, literal" interpretation of the Bible revealed to him in his El Monte cocoon, embellishing it with his own critiques of American materialism and organized religion. "My target was the pastors, priests, leaders and top 'Church' heads. I new [sic] that the common people were not responsible for the false image of God that the church was presenting to the world. The leaders were misrepresenting the Justice of God. They were strict to demand their share, but they themselves did not render to God, what was due to God." The reactions of church leaders who heard Reies's words, or heard about them, ranged from annoyance to astonishment. Some shunned him, giving him the cold shoulder in public, dismissing him as a lunatic, a fanatic zealot gone amuck and best ignored. Others responded with violence. Reies remembered those days as full of "persecution" akin to what Christ suffered before his crucifixion, ultimately forcing him and his family's flight, fearing for their safety.[22]

Material conditions were stark for the Tijerinas during these years. Reies was committed to an ascetic life devoid of all human comfort, which, as the family's patriarch, he imposed without debate. "I didn't care so much about my belly, as I did for my heart," Reies explained. "I didn't care about the present—my eyes and hope were on the future. The harder the training, the brighter the future."[23] Such rigor toughened Reies, or so he thought. For his wife and children, their bellies mattered, and their hardships were in the present, daring not to think about what the future portended. Living by the anticapitalist words he preached, reviling American materialism, Reies would often take the church collection plate that just had been passed around the congregation to meet his earthly needs and, in dramatic fashion, would stand before his congregants and flatten it with a hammer, leaving the cash strewn about the floor. This is how he demonstrated that he was different. He was not greedy or motivated by money as he claimed most Protestant preachers were.

Reies completely purified himself three more times, while also giving away all of the material possession he and his family had, even their car, to live like Jesus Christ had. In 1952, Reies and his family walked all the way from Michigan to Texas, refusing rides, not accepting payment for his preaching, relying completely on the charity of strangers. They slept in the open under trees, in barns, under bridges, anywhere that offered some semblance of protection from the elements. María Escobar confided that after this third purification she had finally had enough. That was the moment she started thinking of a divorce. "He was endangering the children. They had only the clothes on their backs, rarely enough to eat, and never a stable place to live." It took her more than a decade to finally say *ya basta*, enough![24]

Reies traveled during the next few months without rest, eager to have his new message heard. From San Antonio he went to Austin, where his old friend Alvino Mendoza offered him hospitality and then drove him to Fort Worth. Reies found friendlier churches here, befriending Guillermo Esparza who next drove him to Kansas City, Missouri. In Kansas City, Tomas Reyes, a person who heard Reies preach, purchased him a bus ticket to Chicago. From there he went to Sterling, Colorado, then south to Carlsbad, New Mexico, to Ysleta, Texas, and back to San Antonio. By late 1950 he was back in Eden, Texas, still officially his base, officiating as the pastor of a small assembly there.[25]

When Reies returned, local Assemblies of God pastors had heard of his theatrics, of the alms plates he had smashed with a hammer, and were finally ready to confront him. Many of his peers deemed Reies Tijerina a brash twenty-three-year-old, fire-breathing juvenile who knew very little about the world, less about the church, and was heretical in his interpretation of the Bible, all the factors that historically provoked schism in the Assemblies of God. One Sunday, after Reies's service ended, the local pastors surrounded him in his church. Heated words were exchanged. It ended with his expulsion, the withdrawal of his license to minister in Assemblies of God, and an order that he be shunned. What exactly was said? We do not know. Much later, in 1990, Reies said that the members of his Eden church rallied to his defense, vociferously protesting his expulsion. According to him, what his defenders in Eden said was, "No! No! Reies is not speaking against nobody. He's rebuking. He's exhorting the people. He's advocating reform." When asked about her memories of that day, María said she had not witnessed the confrontation. Her children, David and Rose, were acting up, probably sensing tension and heightened human emotions. She took them home after services. Pastoral assignments and Assemblies of God governance were exclusively the business of churchmen. Their wives had no right to speak up or to protest.

"It was clear," explained María, "that they did not like his message. He used to preach that the churches were collecting money from the poor . . . [and] that there was too much hypocrisy. They would say one thing and do something else. . . . They would ask for offerings from poor people, people who were barely able to live. They would ask for the *diezmo*, the ten percent of what one got. Sometimes one only has for oneself. Well we are trying to collect money to build more churches, the leaders would say. That is why they did not like him."[26] When I interviewed Reies in 2009, asking about his expulsion from the Assemblies of God, he refused to engage the topic, quickly pivoting to his political activism regaining lost Hispano lands.

Shunned, without gainful employment as a minister again, Reies turned to nearby Baptist and Church of the Nazarene congregations, where he found sporadic pastoral work. To eke out a subsistence, the family returned to migratory agricultural work, following the crops between spring and fall like most poor mexicanos in Texas. Winters were always spent in San Antonio, where the Tijerina and Escobar clans could pool the resources they had earned in Michigan. María grimly described the situation they found themselves in with resignation. "That's about it. It was all we could do for a while."[27]

Reies acted as if the expulsion was yet again the type of persecution he relished because it fortified his soul and body. As we will see in the next chapter, his anger was very evident in the sermons he preached admonishing the leadership of the Assemblies of God. Reies interpreted these events as divine signs that it was time to become the itinerant evangelist for which God had given him life and a voice. He proceeded with absolute certitude, never wavering, never modulating his tone, never expressing the slightest doubt about the words he preached, indeed preaching of the ire of the fire of God. Like the migratory farm-labor cycles that extended across the country in the shape of a cross, the vertical axis from Texas north to Michigan, the horizontal from Tennessee west to California, so Reies, María, David, and Rose traversed this topography earning their daily bread. Working by their side were the poor, destitute, and marginalized mexicanos who picked cotton, sugar beets, apples, strawberries, and plums for a pittance so that wealthier Americans could have cheap sugar for their coffee, could bake and eat sweet cakes with strawberry jam for a pittance, never having to imagine the calloused, dirty hands of workers who toiled to put these sweets in their mouths. Preaching to the wretched of the earth was Reies goal, confident that the world's end was near. Then would Christ triumphantly return to rule with mercy and justice for a thousand years. Now was the time for all God-fearing persons to repent. For farmworkers barely existing, short on work, without homes, facing racial discrimination, and Jim Crow segregation wherever they went, hearing Reies's healing words offered hours of repose, imagining a heaven where a loving God would humble the powerful and shower the weak with his love. What a wonderful place this New Jerusalem would be! There they would escape their misery and hunger, relishing better things, if not in life, at least in death.

The years 1947 to 1950 were particularly anxious ones in the United States. America had emerged victorious from World War II. The spoils were being enjoyed by white upper- and middle-class Americans, trickling down slowly and unequally, if at all. In 1949 the Soviet Union exploded its own atomic bomb, sparking an escalating arms race, putting Americans and much of the world on edge. Nervously remembering how Hiroshima and Nagasaki had been incinerated, politicians and scientists tried to calm frayed nerves imagining the possibility that New York, Chicago, or Los Angeles might become targets for Soviet bombs.[28]

In these cold war years, from 1950 to 1956, Reies Tijerina crisscrossed the United States staging evangelistic revivals, sometimes with María and children in tow, most often all alone. Everywhere Tijerina went preaching the word of God, he went as His messenger with a single goal in mind: to draw, captivate, move, and transform the minds, bodies, and souls of his listeners. Those in attendance were mostly poor Mexican Americans and even poorer Mexican temporary guest workers, or braceros. The best they could hope for by attending a Pentecostal revival was finding spiritual comfort in knowing that there was a just God, one who would shower them with his bounty, dignity, and respect, certainly not in this world but hopefully in the next. Toiling many seasons beside these women and men picking cotton, sugar beets, and an assortment of fruits and vegetables, Reies understood their material privations and promised them salvation.

Preaching in homes, in halls, in tents, in parks, virtually anywhere people gathered, he never seemed to tire. His revivals followed a pattern, beginning with singing, followed by prayers, Bible readings, a sermon, Holy Spirit baptisms, and culminating in a call to those needing spiritual and physical healing, asking that they come forward to the center of those assembled for a laying of hands. When the service ended, they broke bread together. This was how María recalled the ritual sequence.[29]

Reies revivals were never short, usually consuming an entire day, and often stretching late into the night. His services were emotionally exuberant events, full of toe-tapping, singing and clapping, praying and swaying, with women and men holding their arms stretched upward, hands wide open ready to welcome the Holy Spirit's arrival. With fits of anger and punching motions into the air to banish evil and Satan from their midst, they shouted, "Hallelujah! Hallelujah! Glory Be! The living God will soon arrive." They sang:

> I await the joyful day when Christ returns,
> Soon he will return to the world to gather us all;

Oh! What joy this thought gives my soul:
That Christ will come to earth again!
Oh! Jesus will come to earth again,
Yes, Jesus will come to earth again;
We will see him atop clouds with the angels of light,
When Christ returns to earth again.
The arrival of Jesus will be a remedy for pain
That always afflicts this poor and sinful world;
Every tear will be washed by our Savior,
When Christ returns to earth again.
The saints of Zion will arrive with eternal joy;
And atop the sacred hill nothing will cause us pain or make us ill,
We will all know God then, then all as equals,
When Christ returns to earth again.
Sin, pain, and death on earth will cease.
Martyrs and saints with Jesus will reign forever,
Every soul will enjoy perfect peace without concern,
When Christ returns to earth again.[30]

Most of the sermons Reies Tijerina preached at these revivals, he wrote by hand in Spanish, collected them, and in 1955 published them as a book for broader distribution. The sermons have a burning urgency to them. Reies heralded to repentance a generation that he believed was lost to the vulgar materialism of modernity. As a person who obeyed the laws of God and who had been destined as a prophetic clarion to gather wayward souls to repentance, Reies was certain that the world was in its "latter days." Already one could "see the dawn," he often said, repeating the words of Revelation. That "dawn," those "latter days" signaled the moment Jesus Christ would return to earth anew to reign triumphantly for a thousand years. On that day God would welcome the righteous and the moral into the New Jerusalem. It would be a day of great rejoicing "for those who loved the Lord with all their heart, for those who obeyed him and did so with patience; [for] those who did not tire of doing what is good, even if it cost them bitterness and many obstacles."[31]

His sermons were simple in form, but brutally stern. They were often lyrical, melodious, delivered with a thunderous cadence, meant as seductive poetry to the ear. Their delivery was equally spellbinding. Eyewitnesses attested that Reies was a mesmerizing orator who could expound extemporaneously for hours without pause. Recall that his LABI classmates selected him as their graduation preacher in 1946 because of this skill. He called out to one's entire body, first exciting the ear with God's words, then illuminate the mind's eye with the many gifts and wonders with which God awaited them in heaven. Then he entered their hearts, pulling them into his, expounding without pause. His call to action was hard to ignore. His sermons were moving. Indeed, that was the point. He wanted his auditors to be moved by what he said.

Reies would modulate the pitch of his voice between whispers and shouts so drawing the congregation into his words. He would animatedly gesticulate with his hands and arms to keep their attention, pacing back and forth across the spaces in which he preached as if possessed by a higher power or as if some turbulent spirit was being channeled through his body. Those gathered before him responded. Sometimes it was with dread and tears, but just as easily, and in a flash, he could flip their emotions to enthusiastic laughter and cheers. His sermons were moving. His call to conversion and redemption was difficult to ignore.[32] In a state of intense animation he promised his listeners salvation, healing, and Holy Spirit baptism, assuring that Christ's apocalyptic return was near. If they accepted Jesus as their savior and lord, they would be raised body and soul into heaven through the rapture before the great tribulation and suffering that would precede the last judgment. Here is a sampling of particularly moving portions of some of Reies's sermons.

> Let us turn the heart to the one who formed it, let us turn our ear to the one who formed it, giving glory to the one who made the heavens and the earth. To him who formed the earth and filled it with beasts, herbs, and fruits; to him who formed the ocean and everything we see and do not see. To him who orders everything with occult wisdom, before he rises to punish earth's inhabitants, let us all return to our God. He is good and Merciful to those who love Him and follow His holy commandments. ("Let Us Return to Our Maker")

My eyes, no matter how blind, can no longer stand seeing so much injustice and hypocrisy. My heart, no matter how hardened, can no longer resist the cry of the oppressed, and the complaints of the abandoned. My ears, no matter how deaf spiritually, hear lies and exaggeration everywhere, this among the children and the adults, among the wise and the foolish. On their lips they profess the truth. From their mouths they say they fear God, and because of this, I have been unable to tolerate the words in my heart. ("The Just One's Clamor")

Our separation must be a separation from the world not from some believers because they have a charming name. If the world abhors, we must love. If the world robs and takes, we must give and serve. If the world delights in seeing, hearing, and speaking evil, we must delight in seeing, hearing, and speaking what is good, that which pleases God, and that which we learned from Christ. ("Where Is Our Benefit?")

Oh, how mercy perished from the earth. Gone are the times when man knew the love of God. Gone are the times when the great were compassionate toward the small. Gone are the times when the man with eyes guided the blind with meekness and patience. Instead, the time has come when the man with eyes shoves the one who has no eyes. The strong man destroys the weak one. In the eyes of the married woman the widow finds no grace. Orphans are not protected by children who have father and mother. All judgment and justice has perished from the earth and it is there we see the pastors of the congregations entertained in vain words, promising people what they themselves do not even have. They are all occupied in chants and dead ceremonies. ("Faith Without Mercy")

Tremble before the Word of God, because if we do not fear now, later we will tremble not before the word of God but before his presence. While the Judgment is delayed, let us all come and do good, banish gossip and anger from our hearts. No one look for the material goods of this earth. These are days for removing from our hearts the things of this world, before we too, like Lot's wife, become an example of rebellion. God loves Justice. Anyone who does Justice will not be shamed. He who says he already has faith, let him prove it with his works in Christ. Christ himself said: "He who believes in me, in the works that I do, will also do them." He who says that he awaits Christ, abandon those things you possess and give them to the poor. He who says he knows Christ, make it manifest with mercy and justice. ("Listen Wise Ones")

Everything has value these days except Christ's name. All pay large sums of money for earthly things except for the name of Christ. Everyone sacrifices for their own whims except for Christ's name. The name of Christ is of little significance these days. And any hypocrite, weighed down by sin, calls himself by Christ's name. Thus the name of Christ comes to be dishonored and abused. Is anyone scandalized because the evil ones are called Christians? ("False Confidence")

The end is near. The end comes. All eyes will cry, and all the strong will tremble. The leaders and the great men who executed the law, they too will place their faces upon the ground. They will scream like women in labor. These greats will flee the riches they once embraced, will curse the luxury and pomp for which once they killed. They will know that God is great and just, and will know that in everything they deceived their poor souls. ("The Yearning of Those Who Adore")

These sermonic words, combined with the program of prayers and songs, punctuated by witnessing testimony and healing hands, and spoken in an atmosphere thick with shouts of "Hallelujah," "Praise the Lord," "Glory Be," and the guttural, other-worldly seeming gibberish of saints speaking in tongues, had the effect of totally dominating the listener's conscious mind. One evangelical revival participant recalled how overwhelmingly total it was.

> I was not passively listening. . . . I was struggling mightily against the grain of my ignorance and incredulity to make sense of what he was saying. His language was so intense and strange, yet deceptively plain and familiar, full of complex nuances and pushes and pulls, that I had no time, no spare inner speech, to interpret him consciously, to rework what he said into my own words as he talked. I just gripped my chair, as it were, and took his words in straight. I was willfully uncritical as well in the sense that I wanted to understand, as best I could, his words from his point of view, to assume his position, to make his speech mine. It was not exactly what [he] said . . . it is that I took it up, merely by listening to him actively and uncritically.[33]

Such active listening was intended to enter and hopefully transform the unconscious mind, to make the religious language of the Bible Tijerina uttered part of the listener's own, ultimately accepting the savior's words into their minds and bodies. To draw his auditors in closer, Reies frequently spoke in the collective "we" and "us." "We have sinned. We have acted in iniquity. We have abandoned good and have twisted every holy path and judgment of God. Let us return to God."[34] This call was reiterated in songs as well. Listen to "You and I."

> So tenderly he is calling us, Christ calls you and me!
> He awaits us with open arms; He calls you and me.
> Come. Come. If you are tired, come; So tenderly he calls
> Oh sinners come.
> Why should we fear his judgment, Christ for you and me?

His benedictions are overflowing, Always for you and me.
Time flies, enjoy what you can, Christ calls you and me;
Coming are the shadows of death, coming; Coming for you and me.[35]

The ritual process of conversion was a dialogue, a conversation between Reies who knew that he had been saved, and his disbelieving listeners who were predisposed to suspend, if only momentarily, their disbelief. Using the New Testament's words, Reies recounted the trials and tribulations of Israel and of the early followers of Jesus who were his church. He told them of the salvation God promised in John's Gospel 3:16: "Yes, God so loved the world that he gave his only Son, that whoever believed in him may not die but may have eternal life."

Reies enjoined those gathered to accept Holy Spirit baptism as described in the Acts of the Apostles 2:4: "All were filled with the Holy Spirit. They began to express themselves in foreign tongues and make bold proclamation as the Spirit prompted them." He promised, as the Apostle James had, that their bodies would be healed of pain and affliction (5:14–15): "Is there anyone sick among you? He should ask for the presbyters of the church. They in turn are to pray over him, anointing him with oil in the Name [of the Lord]." When Christ returned for his millennial reign on earth, the rapture would precede it as prophesied in 1 Thessalonians 4:16–17: "The Lord himself will come down from heaven at the word of command, at the sound of the archangel's voice and God's trumpet; and those who have died in Christ will rise first. Then we the living, the survivors, will be caught up with them in the clouds to meet the Lord in the air. Thenceforth we shall be with the lord unceasingly."[36] Finally, as Revelation 20:14 announced, the Last Judgment would soon arrive: "The sea gave up its dead; then death and the nether world gave up their dead. Each person was judged according to his conduct. Then death and their nether world were hurled into the pool of fire." Martyrs and saints would enjoy eternal bliss in the New Jerusalem, free then of all worldly affliction. These were the rewards sinners would enjoy by accepting God's word.

God's words, combined with prayer and song, Bible readings and preaching, punctuated by witnessing testimony, prepared congregants for the Holy Spirit's arrival. Those who had already been born again through

Holy Spirit baptism offered witness to hasten the conversion of those there for the first time. Reies's revivals gathered a social mix of children and adults, men and women, some neophytes, some saints, with spectators precariously sitting on the fence, uncertain what to make of the event. Some believers entered ecstatic rapture. Others spoke in tongues. Many Pentecostal saints at first believed that Holy Spirit baptism and tongues speech necessarily went hand in hand, that this speech was the physical manifestation of one's total embodiment of the Holy Spirit. Reies, like some of his fellow preachers, eventually became suspicious of tongues speech, downplaying its importance largely because many of those who claimed that the Holy Spirit had entered them had not experienced it. Did the failure to experience glossolalia mean that a less charismatic experience of Holy Spirit baptism existed? Were saints feigning tongues speech to demonstrate their sanctity? In 1955 Reies concluded that glossolalia was a "cult of lips" and never again mentioned it as essential component of Holy Spirit baptism.[37] When María Escobar described her spirit baptism, she said it was "beautiful! It is so different. You can feel the Holy Spirit getting in touch."[38]

Healing through the laying of hands on the bodies of those who came forward seeking succor followed. Reies and those already baptized of the Spirit, healed the physical and psychological ills of those in need through prayer and the Holy Spirit's intercession. Reies and those saints present would lay their hands upon the heads of those who came forward asking that they be healed. Almost instantly they proclaimed relief. "Many would stand up to praise God because they had been healed. Women would shout, 'I got healed.' Others would say I give thanks to God because he cured me of my disease." Antonio Tijerina, Reies's father, recalled being deliriously sick with pneumonia, constantly transfused with blood. "I did not even know who I was." His two sons in the ministry, Reies and Ramón, laid their hands on him, prayed, and he rapidly recuperated. When a person's troubles were financial, the congregants took up a special collection to help.[39]

Those healed expressed enormous joy "for the salvation of God and the Holy Spirit" they had just received. When the healing power of the Holy Spirit entered one's body, it was as if "a current of electricity was being turned on me," said one woman, adding that it felt "like thousands of needles" went through her.[40] Revivals frequently ended with a meal, with communion among those gathered, sharing of themselves and the details of their lives.⁴¹

Reies's revival goal was to get his congregants to leave their old selves behind so that they could be spiritually reborn. Most of the neophytes he called to conversion were ethnic Mexicans. In the vast marketplace of religious and secular ideas that promised reward in the 1940s and 1950s, there were numerous options for mexicanos to choose from. Roman Catholicism's life-cycle rituals at birth, marriage, and burial still had a strong hold on the religious lives of many, but these allowed little individual autonomy or choice, except in marriage. Socialist and syndicalist organizations appealed to the here and now, promising better wages, shorter working days, protection from employer abuses, union representation, and workplace respect. A few professed themselves atheists and agnostics, relying on individual conscience as their guide. What Reies's Pentecostal revivals offered first and foremost was inclusion in a rule-bound, tightly knit, exuberant community of faith vowed to assist widows, orphans, foreigners, the poor, and the oppressed. As you will read in Reies's sermons in the next chapter, he advocated repeatedly for these marginalized groups in mantra-like fashion. It was his raison d'être. Reies's auditors probably found his words appealing precisely because they felt dehumanized and exploited in the racist communities in which they lived and worked.

María Escobar remembered 1950 to 1955 as years of tireless evangelizing. "People would call him [Reies] to give evangelistic campaigns in their churches. . . . It was a peaceful time but was hard because of material things. He did not have stable work because he was paid where he preached."⁴² David Tijerina, María and Reies's eldest son, remembered those years vividly too, but what was most stuck in his mind were not memories of his father's preaching but of the back-breaking farm work he did as a boy. "I remember we were always traveling. Most of the time we were migrant workers. . . . Y siempre we were always going somewhere, following the crops."⁴³

Anthropologist Elman R. Service succinctly notes the problem Reies eventually faced by 1958: without followership there can be no leadership. After years of evangelizing with his fire and brimstone sermons, Reies had gathered very few devotees, something his rival Assemblies of God preachers were doing quite well with full churches.⁴⁴

In this chapter we explored Reies Tijerina's early ministry, his expulsion from the Assemblies of God, and the nature of the revivals he staged throughout the Southwest. He traversed a broad geography spreading the word of God, convinced that the events outlined in Revelation had begun unfolding rapidly after the bombing of Hiroshima and Nagasaki. In the next chapter we turn to the Bible's last book, Revelation. While this may seem like an esoteric expedition, we do so to better understand biblically the text that most influenced Reies preaching and message, and more fundamentally, how he religiously diagnosed the ills of American society and of its Protestant churches.

CHAPTER 5

Of Revelation and Reies

REVELATION, THE BIBLE'S LAST book, has been controversial text since it was written. It was the book that fundamentally shaped the apocalyptic hopes of the Pentecostal movement born in the early twentieth century, and because of the training Reies Tijerina received as an Assemblies of God evangelist, it was the foundation for most of the sermons he preached between 1946 and 1958. Revelation's inclusion in the New Testament was hotly debated by the early church fathers until the fourth century CE, when it entered the New Testament canon, codified shortly after Rome's Emperor Constantine converted to Christianity in 312 CE. The Gospels and Epistles that form the New Testament were addressed to various communities and narrate the details of the life of Jesus, his miracles and parables for virtuous living and salvation. Revelation instead is filled with monsters and satanic creations who God engages in protracted battles, famine, plagues, and curses of the most heinous sort. Revelation ends with Jesus's return to earth for a triumphant thousand-year reign, followed by the last judgment and the earth's destruction. The English word *apocalyptic* comes from the Greek *apokalypsis*, which means a revelation or a disclosure from God announcing his intention to destroy an oppressive age, replacing it with a new emancipatory one, free of the Roman Empire's brutal colonial reign.

Biblical scholars find nothing strange about Revelation's symbolism. Its tropes are antique, taken from an older tradition of Jewish prophetic literature that was then still widely circulating and popularly understood in the first century of the common era. John of Patmos, the author of Revelation, was a second-generation Jesus follower, who was born after the crucifixion of Jesus but was deeply moved by his words and deeds. John's work borrowed extensively from Old Testament prophecies that were familiar to Jewish Jesus followers, taking most of his descriptions and rhetorical frames directly from Isaiah 13–14, 27, Jeremiah 50–52, Ezekiel 26–28, Daniel 7–12, and many other apocalypses then widely circulating, but which never gained sufficient canonic importance for inclusion in the New Testament.

Early leaders of the Jesus movement initially thought that the apostle John, not John of Patmos, had written Revelation, which is why it was so rapidly incorporated into the New Testament. The apostle John had witnessed Jesus's life and teachings. As the presumed author, this John's writings carried considerable importance among members of the burgeoning movement.[1] The book's authorship was questioned as early as the second century CE because it was written in poor Greek, a language the apostle spoke and wrote perfectly, which is what initially generated the search for Revelation's author.

Scholars now agree that a different John, one from Patmos, wrote Revelation. He too was a Jewish Jesus follower, living in exile on the small island of Patmos in the Aegean Sea, some seventy miles south of Ephesus in the final decades of the first century CE. Whether Roman imperial authorities banished him to this island or whether he went there to escape the massacres Jews had suffered in Judah under Roman rule, is not known. As he explained it, "I proclaimed God's word and bore witness to Jesus" (Rev. 1:9), something Roman authorities would have judged seditious. The remote and sparsely populated island offered a certain amount of safety for his clandestine proselytizing and writing.

Revelation was written sometime between 80 and 100 CE, based on the book's internal details indicating that John was living in Asia Minor during the reign of the Roman emperor Domitian (81–96 CE). It was dispatched as a circular letter, intended to be read and then passed among the seven churches of Jesus followers, then composed of Jews and Gentiles (a distinct Christian identity had not yet emerged) living in Ephesus, Smyrna, Pergamum, Thyatira, Sardis, Philadelphia, and Laodicea (Rev. 1:10–11).[2]

Jesus was crucified between 30 and 36 CE. Judea's Roman authorities moved violently to eradicate the movement of this man the Romans mocked as "Jesus of Nazareth, the King of the Jews." Indeed, the plaque Pontius

Pilate had placed at the top of Jesus's cross so that passersby would understand his crime was scornfully inscribed with *INRI* (*Iesvs Nazarenvs Rex Ivdaeorvm*). Jesus had told his followers that he was God's messiah and Israel's future king. He would return to usher in a new kingdom, a promise the Roman state had no intention of allowing in Palestine, given that it was already a hotbed of Jewish resistance to Roman rule.

After Jesus's death, known leaders of his movement were apprehended, forcing many terrified followers into hiding. In short order Peter was crucified. Paul of Tarsus was beheaded. And Jesus's own brother, James, was stoned to death. Weary and resentful of Rome's longstanding colonial oppression, between 66 and 70 CE the Jews of Judah waged a total war against Rome, suffering mass starvation, crucifixions, and enslavement. In 69 CE, Vespasian and his son Titus, both of whom would become Roman emperors, stormed Jerusalem with some sixty thousand mounted soldiers, killing thousands, sacking the city's wealth, desecrating its temple, the physical symbol of the singular relationship between Jews and God, and then burning it to the ground in 70 CE. We as moderns can still see these events triumphantly depicted in sculptural reliefs in Rome on the Arch of Titus, though which visitors then and now enter the Roman Forum. This gate into the empire's administrative and religious center celebrated the victorious return of Titus from Jerusalem flush with gold, booty, slaves, and even with the temple's enormous seven-branched golden lampstand, the menorah, prominently in tow.

John of Patmos was probably born after Jesus and all his apostles were dead. But he most certainly witnessed the Jewish War of 66–70 CE and saw the ashes and rubble where once Jerusalem's temple stood. Most Jewish Jesus followers dispersed to live clandestinely throughout Judea after the war, but by then, few, if any, personally had witnessed Jesus's preaching or miracles. What they knew about Jesus came from secondhand accounts describing events that had occurred forty years earlier. John of Patmos was one of these second-generation devotees. He heard the words of Jesus recounted in secret household churches and gradually began reading accounts in circulating texts, such as the first Gospel written by Matthew around 50 CE. With Jesus and his first disciples dead, how were ordinary persons who believed that Jesus was their messiah to keep their faith in him alive? After the destruction of Jerusalem's temple those Jesus followers who had survived were justifiably terrorized and in hiding. Jesus had not yet returned as their king.

Revelation's goal was to boast morale and calm their nerves by offering them an ugly triumphalist war that Jesus would wage against Rome and win, culminating in his terrestrial millennial reign. John of Patmos was well aware that Jesus followers were rapidly abandoning the movement, subjecting themselves to their colonial oppressors, even openly venerating them as gods.[3] John begins by assuring those who read or heard the content of his circular letter that Jesus was very much alive and would soon return to usher in a new kingdom with a radically distinct sociopolitical order. Believers should not lose hope.

John begins Revelation by explaining that the letter was God's. He was merely its scribe. One day, while fasting and praying, John entered a cave and there, "I was caught up in ecstasy, and I heard a voice behind me . . . which said, 'Write on a scroll what you now see and send it to the seven churches'" (Rev. 1:10–11). John turned to identify the speaker. It was Jesus. His "face shone like the sun at its brightest" (Rev. 1:16) announcing that his father would soon wage a vicious war against the world's evil forces, only slightly disguised as the Roman empire.

John was lifted into heaven, sees God enthroned, surrounded by elders all dressed in white robes. The throne, the very symbol of God's authority, was surrounded by a lion, an ox, an eagle, and an animal with a human face. John attested that while standing next to God, "I saw a Lamb standing, a Lamb that had been slain"; it was the risen Jesus (Rev. 5:6–7). God (referred to as the "One") handed the Lamb seven scrolls and when the seals were broken, from four of the scrolls the Four Horsemen of the Apocalypse emerged. The first rode a white horse and was armed with a bow. The second was mounted atop a fiery red horse, wielding a sword "to rob the earth of peace by allowing men to slaughter one another" (Rev. 6:4). The third horse was black; its rider carrying the scales used for rationing during famine. And the fourth was "a sickly green in color. Its rider was named Death, and the nether world was in his train" (Rev. 6:8). The horsemen punished the earth with war, famine, and plagues. When the fifth seal was broken, dead Christian martyrs began crying out, asking when their deaths would be avenged. The Lamb (Jesus) promised that it would be soon as he gave them the long white robes of martyrs (Rev. 6:10). The sixth seal produced a massive earthquake (Rev. 6:12–17), and from the seventh, came seven angels sounding their trumpets announcing God's approaching reign with hail, fire, blood, and a burning comet crashing into the earth, followed by a scourge of ravenous locusts and scorpions (Rev. 5:1–14).

Revelation here shifts from these earthly punishments back to celestial events, where a pregnant woman is wailing as she births a son (Rev. 12:2–3).[4] A "huge dragon, flaming red, with seven heads and ten horns" attempts to devour the child. This boy is "destined to shepherd all the nations with an iron rod . . . [and] was caught up to God and to his throne" (Rev. 12:3–5). The angel Michael and the dragon who is "the ancient serpent known as the devil or Satan, the seducer of the world" battle (Rev. 12:9). Satan is defeated and expelled from heaven to hell.

Exiled but not vanquished, the devil conjures two ugly beasts. The first has seven heads, ten horns, and a mouth that constantly blasphemes God and his people. The second, whose name is 666, has the horns of a ram and speaks profanities exactly like those of the dragon "to promote its interests by making the world and all its inhabitants worship the first beast" (Rev. 13:12), constructing idols in the beast's honor for everyone to worship, prohibiting the sale of anything not marked with the beast's name (Rev. 13:11–18).

The war between God and the devil intensifies with more plagues as "Armageddon" nears (Rev. 16:16). It arrives as the greatest earthquake yet known. Amid this destruction, an angel lifts John "in spirit" to see how Babylon will be punished. "Come I will show you the judgment in store for the great harlot who sits by the waters of the deep. The kings of the earth have committed fornication with her, and the earth's inhabitants have grown drunk on the wine of her lewdness" (Rev. 17:1–2). John beholds the "woman seated on a scarlet beast which was covered with blasphemous names. This beast had seven heads and ten horns. The woman was dressed in scarlet and adorned with gold and pearls and other jewels. In her hand she held a golden cup filled with the abominable and sordid deed of her lewdness. On her forehead was written, 'Babylon the great mother of harlots and all the world's abominations.' I saw the woman was drunk with the blood of God's holy ones and the blood of those martyred for their faith in Jesus" (Rev. 17:3–7).

The Lamb fights the harlot and wins, proclaiming, "Lord of lords and the King of kings" (Rev. 17:10–19). "Fallen is Babylon the great! She has become a dwelling place for demons. . . . The kings of the earth committed fornication with her and the world's merchants grew rich from her wealth and wantonness." A voice harkens to Babylon's residents: "Depart from her, my people, for fear of sinning with her and sharing the plagues inflicted on her. . . . The merchants of the world will weep and mourn over her too, for there will be no more market for their imports—their cargoes of gold and silver, precious stones and pearls; fine linen and purple garments, silk and scarlet cloth . . . slaves and human lives" (Rev. 18: 1–24).

God then destroys Babylon. Heaven opens anew where John beholds the King of Kings riding atop a white horse. "Justice is his standard in passing judgment and in waging war" (Rev. 19:11). An angel descends "holding the key to the abyss" where Satan is fitfully chained for a thousand years. Those killed for bearing witness to Jesus and refusing to worship the beast now emerge. Together with Jesus they reign for a thousand years, when the last judgment arrives, when all will be judged.

John now beholds the New Jerusalem descend from heaven fully formed, "beautiful as a bride prepared to meet her husband" (Rev. 21:2). The One invites John to behold the bride of the Lamb, or the faithful, his church.[5] The New Jerusalem is as radiant as a diamond, with fortified walls, its gates bear the names of the twelve tribes of Israel, its foundation the names of the Lamb's twelve apostles. The city's gates are always open. A river of life-giving water flows through the New Jerusalem, watering the trees of life, yielding fruit twelve times a year, with the trees' leaves serving as medicine (Rev. 22:3–4).

Several themes unify Revelation, which are both distinct to it and common to older Jewish apocalypses. First, it is a plea to Jesus followers in Asia Minor's seven churches not to abandon Jesus's vision of redemption. John begs the church at Smyrna to persevere in its faith: "I know your tribulation and your poverty . . . the slander you endure from self-styled Jews who are nothing other than members of Satan's assembly" (Rev. 2:9). To the church in Philadelphia, he says much the same: "I know that your strength is limited; yet you have held fast to my word and have not denied my name (Rev. 3:8–9). But for the other five churches imbibing the false words of

"Jezebel—that self-styled prophetess" (Rev. 2:20) and a man named Balaam (Rev. 2:14), John has harsh words. They are encouraging Jesus followers to collaborate with Rome, participate in its pagan blood rituals, and wallow in the blandishment of empire extracted through colonial taxation and predatory trade. To the church at Ephesus John writes, "repent and return to your former deeds" (Rev. 2:5).[6]

Revelation's second major theme, woven into the book's narrative in coded language to escape detection by Roman spies, is a rivalry between two cities, Babylon and the New Jerusalem; between two political economies, Rome's and God's; and two fundamentally different ways of living, greed and inequality versus justice and peace. John radically juxtaposes these two cities to force readers and auditors to understand that if they wish to enter heaven, they must choose the New Jerusalem and God's law, as given to them by Jesus. If they continue living governed by the wicked whore of Babylon (Rome), who seduces men to idolatry with her charms, they will perish from God's punishments.

Through the juxtaposition of Babylon and the New Jerusalem, represented as two women, one a wicked harlot and the other a virginal bride, one evil and the other virtuous, John offers a searing critique of Roman imperialism and the glories of God's kingdom yet to come. The devil himself has empowered two particularly predatory beasts: Rome's emperors and its priests who offer sacrifices to the emperor and to imperial deities. Together they enriched the harlot, authorized her scandalous behavior at the expense of Rome's exploited colonies, creating alliances with client states, while controlling the movement of trade good and peoples to maximize Rome's profits and power. Through its economic prowess Rome had built imposing temples to its gods, forcing the colonized to worship these false deities, demanding they participate in blood sacrifices and idolatry. Choosing the whore guaranteed continued exploitation of the majority for the benefit of a few. "Depart from her, my people, for fear of sinning with her," John writes, "pay her back as she has paid others; pay her double for her deeds . . . repay her in torment and grief" (Rev. 18:4–7). John asks Jesus followers if they have not heard that God soon will destroy Babylon through famine, fire, disease, and plagues? Free yourself. Enter the Kingdom of God. Behold the New Jerusalem's beauty, lushness, and abundant water for all who thirst. Its economy is not governed by exploitation, but by what its residents need. Its wealth is not hoarded in the hands of a few but built into the city's very existence. John asks, which city and which way of living will you choose?

By the fourth century CE, Revelation was incorporated into the New Testament. From that point on Jewish Jesus followers embraced "Christian" as their identity, differentiating themselves from Jews. Revelation became a Christian identatarian text that shaped the hopes and aspirations of a host of revolutionary movements against colonialism, poverty, and class oppression that promised to usher in a new and much more just world.[7] It inspired Dr. Martin Luther King Jr.'s 1963 "Letter from a Birmingham Jail." The South African antiapartheid activist Reverend Allan Boesak often invoked it in his sermons and made it the focus of his 1987 *Comfort and Protest: Reflections on the Apocalypse of John of Patmos*. Liberation theologians drew from Revelation extensively, as did Reies López Tijerina.[8]

Reies Tijerina and Revelation

The introduction to this book opens with Reies Tijerina's 1946 "Grand Vision," in which he describes himself being lifted into the heavens by three angels. During their course of travel, they land in a forest strewn with frozen horses. One comes alive, a white one, and on its back Reies and the angels continue their flight, eventually landing in a celestial kingdom, where he meets "the One," God cloaked in a long white robe who then tells Reies: "You will reign over all of this and above you, only I." He then hands him a key, places him on his throne, and from these heavenly heights, Reies instantly returns to earth.

The sermons Tijerina preached, penned, and ultimately published in 1955 are anchored in Revelation in structure and content. Jesus, the Lamb, struggles against the devil. God punishes the world and asks those who believe in him, will they live by the idolatry of the Roman empire, or will they perish to suffer the pains of hell for all eternity? Will they choose fealty to "the beast," or will they choose the way of the Lamb? Will they live in the New Jerusalem made possible by Jesus's crucifixion and resurrection, or will they wallow in the sinfulness of Babylon made possible through colonial exploitation?

Reies believed that at the end of World War II, Americans were living as Jesus followers had during the first century CE. In fact, as one who had received his Holy Spirit baptism, and as an adept of the Pentecostal movement, Reies wanted Americans to live by the precepts of the primitive church of early Christianity and by the rules of the New Jerusalem God himself had revealed. If they failed to do so, God would unleash his punishments on humanity. What happened to Babylon had happened to Hiroshima and Nagasaki and would soon happen to the United States. Tijerina decried American imperialism, described the presidents of the United States and his handmaidens as the voracious "beast," and "666," the number John of Patmos used to refer to Nero, Reies applied to President Ronald Reagan.[9] American imperialism was deepening the country's class divide between what Reies called *los chicos y los grandes*; what Revelation notes as the "small and the great" (Rev. 19:18). Even the choice one had to make between Babylon's wicked whore and the virginal bride of Christ residing in the New Jerusalem, Tijerina used as a trope to integrate his sermonary.

In the next chapter we turn to an analysis of the sermons Reies Tijerina delivered, penned, and published in 1955 as *Will He Find Any Faith on Earth . . . ?* Here I offered readers an analysis of the Book of Revelation. Without an understanding of the John of Patmos circular letter to the communities of Asia Minor in the second century of the common era, it is impossible to make sense of Reies's sermons that follow in the next chapter. These sermons are a profound critique of American imperialism in the aftermath of World War II. Readers eager to read the original sermons either in English or Spanish, should turn to appendix 1.

CHAPTER 6

Will He Find Any Faith on Earth . . . ?

IN 1955 TIJERINA GATHERED forty-five of his sermons and published them as a book titled, *¿Hallará Fe en La Tierra . . . ?* (Will He Find Any Faith on Earth . . . ?). This is the only extant source that illuminates Reies's religious ideas in the years following his studies at LABI. He boasted constantly during his ministry that he had "a new interpretation for the Bible, just literally, the way it was," given to him in a divine dream.¹ That Reies embraced the Bible as literal truth was nothing particularly unusual as most evangelical Christians did so. It was the first half of the pronouncement, a "new interpretation," that rankled his fellow Assemblies of God ministers. Ultimately, this is what got his license to preach revoked in 1950, with a host of other consequences.

Will He Find Any Faith on Earth . . . ? was published by Imprenta Evangélica de las Asembleas de Dios, an Assemblies of God Spanish-language press in San Antonio, Texas. Despite his earlier doctrinal schism with church leaders, José Cruz, a press employee and old friend, facilitated its production. The book is small in dimension and page length, containing only 119 pages, fashioned as a pamphlet easily tucked into one's pocket or purse. Reies personally paid for the five-hundred copy print run. He dispatched copies to friends and acquaintances near and far announcing his availability as a preacher for hire.²

Successful Pentecostal preachers rarely read their sermons because congregants judged their virtuosity by how extemporaneously they spoke. Those who listened to Reies were simple, largely uneducated women and men, and for them, the preacher's seeming spontaneity suggested that the words were coming directly from God, no matter how scripted or rehearsed they actually were. The political speeches Tijerina delivered a decade later as a land grant activist usually relied on an outline scribbled on a paper scrap to help him organize his thoughts as he spoke.[3]

Reies Tijerina's Sermons

Reies Tijerina's published sermons[4] are uniform in form, reflecting the homiletic formulas he learned at Bible school, based on Alice E. Luce's textbook, *The Messenger and His Message: A Handbook for Young Workers in the Preparation of Gospel Addresses.*[5] I asked Reies if he remembered using this textbook back in 1943–1946. He replied that he and his classmates had learned how to prepare sermons from a book they all used, but he did not recall its title or author. María Escobar Chávez, who finished her studies at LABI in 1941, answered the question identically.

The Messenger and His Message instructed students that effective sermons were organized in four parts: introduction, presentation, application, and culmination. They were urged never to expound on personal themes but instead to pronounce "something received from God and intended for dissemination to all." They should choose topics they knew well, that their audiences would understand, that were of major concern, and that would move them spiritually. A superlative preacher must have "a calling and a definite message," Luce advised. The goal was to relay "the message of God with exactness and fidelity" and never attempt to entertain.[6]

"The Clamor of the Earth," the first sermon in Reies's book, is about society's loss of faith and its increasing secularization and obsession with material goods, which he identifies as the major source of sin. The sermon's presentation and application stages recite the "facts" as the Bible describes them, as Reies saw and interpreted them, and as he and his listeners or as "we" should decry them. The exposition is structured in long, complicated sentences, what a writing teacher might decry as "run-on." Using basic binary oppositions between good and evil, right and wrong, virtue and vice, salvation and damnation, Reies presents listeners and later his readers with a choice: to continue in their sinful ways and risk eternal damnation in hell, or repent, accept the word of God, and enjoy an eternity of celestial bliss.

Time was of the essence, for one could already see the glimmering of the light of the Apocalypse on the horizon approaching. One could feel the earth's surface trembling from the galloping hoofbeats of the approaching Four Horsemen. One could not wait. One could not hesitate. Here was Reies's call to action, what Luce's textbook called the sermon's "culmination."

When Reies López Tijerina began toiling as a Pentecostal preacher in 1946, he deemed America a faithless place and accordingly used the words of the Apostle Luke's Gospel as the title of his book *Will He Find Any Faith on Earth . . . ?* (Luke 18:8). Here Luke recounts Jesus's parable about an unscrupulous judge who lacked respect for God and man. Those who sought justice from him frequently were rebuffed, including a widow who endlessly pleaded her case. Jesus explained that those who pray to God and persevere ultimately enjoy his justice. "I tell you, he will give them swift justice. But when the Son of Man comes, will he find any faith on earth?" Jesus's question was followed by an admonition urging his disciples not to despise others or to act self-righteously.

Jesus's followers answered this question exactly as Reies did. There was no faith on earth and Reies proceeded to elaborate on America's ills. The state, as he saw it, had appropriated the social welfare programs that were church responsibilities. Postwar prosperity had bred vanity, deteriorated the authority of patriarchs, corrupted sexual mores, and led many good Christians to ignore those marginalized in society. All this had to change. It had to change quickly, he fumed, for already one could "see the earth engulfed in flames." The fires that had incinerated Hiroshima and Nagasaki and tens of thousands of its residents in 1945 signaled the rapidly approaching Apocalypse. Soon God would punish America for this murder of innocents.[7]

On the first page of *Will He Find Any Faith on Earth . . . ?*, Reies explains that he had penned this tome "for all who believe that Jesus Christ is the son of God, for all who believe in God, and all who believe that the Bible is God's word. For all of you who gather in churches to adore God, to sing and pray to him. To all those who believe in Jesus Christ's return and await it, to the people who believe in the resurrection of the dead and in the judgment according to our deeds." He apologizes for his use of punitive words, but they were necessary because of humanity's sinfulness, especially that found in the church and its pastors. They had abandoned the poor and the weak, forcing men and women to live like wild animals. "These are without doubt harsh words . . . but remember the days we are in."[8]

In "The Clamor of the Earth," Reies outlines his own Pentecostal reformist dogma and his intended audience. In 1955 Reies was still smarting over his 1950 expulsion from the Assemblies of God. His sermonary had at least two explicit objectives: First, to rebut and admonish his critics and to present his exculpation. In Reies's mind his words and actions had always been beyond reproach. Second, he presents and defends his "new interpretation for the Bible," for anyone willing to read, hear, or consider the evidence.[9] Addressing his critics, Reies begins rhetorically: "Shall I speak with soft words, so as not to offend the believers? Should I use parables so as not to hurt those who worship in the temples of Babylon? The Just Judge of all the land lives, and I shall not stop speaking the truth."[10]

Reies insists that he spoke truth to power and would continue to do so whatever the consequences. "May I be a thorn and a sting to the people of God, even though I may scandalize all. I talk and shall talk. I will accuse the people until the judgment of God comes. I will not stop talking, of denouncing evil and the sin of God's people while days remain, and while God rules and orders that the four angels now tied be released with their world powers."[11] No matter how abhorrent and shrill his words might sound, or how others might seek to defame and shun him, he, Reies Tijerina, was announcing the purification of the church and the day of salvation.[12]

In his sermon "The Lost Justice," Reies elaborates further, likening himself to biblical prophets who despite persecution fearlessly spread the word of God. He describes how John the Baptist proselytized, how he ignored the teachings of the Pharisees, how he had ridiculed the temple's false prayers and fasts, and how he spread the true word of Jesus. "John had the spirit of God and this same spirit illuminated him to discover the evil in them. . . . The Law of God was fallen. . . . God's Justice was twisted." Those culpable in ancient times were the Pharisees; in the 1950s, church leaders were responsible for Christianity's corruption. "All the complaints of the oppressed are against the church and against the heads who occupy the place of princes."[13] What John the Baptist accomplished while Jesus lived, Reies was equally fulfilling. Reies Tijerina describes himself as modernity's John the Baptist offering Holy Spirit baptisms, which were more efficacious than those John performed with water.[14]

God "does not let me be silent or still" Reies insists because he had been filled with the Holy Spirit and anointed from on high.[15] In "The People Without Honor," Tijerina was self-critical, admitting that he felt like a coward for not having decried the church's sins sooner, particularly because God had placed them "in my heart many days ago."[16] He had discussed his concerns with the Assemblies of God leaders, but they fell on deaf ears. Church leaders abhorred God's commandments and had blindly constructed "systems that debilitated simple faith." Reies fully understands "that [my] words will bring [reprimands] . . . from the church."[17] He had already felt that sting. "I will . . . be called . . . Slanderer, I will be called faultfinder, I will be called by others [f]anatic and clumsy. . . . But I know that all the prophets and those who feared and still fear God will so learn and know my spirit."[18] His intention is not to defame the church. Its leaders had already accomplished that splendidly. He simply wants to praise the lord and to herald that his salvation is at hand.

Tijerina's "new interpretation" of Pentecostal theology imagines God as mighty and stern, who swiftly rendered judgment and justice, and demands complete adherence to his laws. Yes, he promises salvation and bliss in the beyond, but he is not effusively generous in showering his faithful with bountiful love or even describing the riches and blessings that awaited the faithful in heaven. Belief produces the virtues necessary to live lives of sanctity. The covenant God promises the faithful in Tijerina's "new interpretation" is to spare his saints from the "Great Tribulation" that would precede the Apocalypse. Then Christ would lift the faithful and those who had died as martyrs fully embodied into heaven in what is still called "the rapture." In two sermons, "Who Will Be Saved?" and "The Enemies of the Cross," Reies explains that there is no way that those who remain sinners will escape the "Great Tribulation" described in Revelation. "Oh for those who expect rapture without keeping God's commandments."[19]

Between 1946 and 1958, Reies traversed the country preaching his gospel. Even his closest friends in the ministry were critical and concerned about of his interpretation. It was too harsh. It was too stern. He was preaching not to the rich and powerful but to ethnic Mexicans who had nothing and who daily suffered a host of abuses from their employers and white supremacists. These wretchedly poor women and men needed a nurturing and loving God. The almighty God had to offer them solace and succor, not punishments that sounded and felt like those their hated field bosses barked daily.

Reies was unmoved. He insisted that he would continue preaching the Bible "the way it was," or at least what he thought it *really* was, fully cognizant that he would continue facing sustained resistance for what many deemed his unorthodox interpretations of it. Reies described the punishments and rebukes he received from Assemblies of God leaders as spilling "the blood of many just men." Turning the tables on his critics, he explains, "Those who rebel against God kill the just."[20] Because he was among the "just," he relished the persecution.

In Reies's theology the faithful obeyed God's commandments because they feared punishment. "When people fear their God, they keep the laws of their God. When the people keep the laws of their God, the lives of those people pleases their God. When the lives of the people are pleasing to God's eyes, even their chants and prayers are heard."[21] Those who love God and delight in his words "keep the commandments of God without complaint."[22] From faith in God's laws flow mercy, love, and justice. "The one who forgives, forgives for faith. The one who loves, loves for faith. The one who works for Justice does so for faith. And the tame and humble are so in faith. Without Faith it is impossible to do right."[23] Christians demonstrate the greatest virtue when they care for society's most despised and oppressed, thereby embodying God's image.[24] The commandments demand concrete actions, which are impossible to achieve simply by listening to the vacuous sermons of corrupt ministers. Nor are temple prayers, fasts, and chanted canticles sufficient. Nay, God's judgment will be measured only by personal sacrifice.

Tijerina's sermons, as a whole, offer a searing indictment of modernity and America's prosperity after World War II. He demands a return to a simpler, purer past, to those days when Jesus lived and preached among his disciples, or what herein I interchangeably call his "primitivist" and "restorationist" goals. Reies rails against unrestrained consumption in America, be it of household items, clothing, appliances, cars, cosmetics, even dancing, elegantly coiffed hair, and alcoholic beverages. Such vulgar materialism was alienating the faithful from their God and undermining the sovereignty of patriarchal authority in households. In equally harsh jeremiads, Reies denounces all Protestant churches for failing their congregants, singling the Assemblies of God for rebuke akin to those he had suffered from them. These Christian churches had developed amnesia, conveniently forgetting their apostolic roots, their biblical obligations. Instead, ministers were groveling for money, building sumptuous churches, surrounding themselves with material goods, wearing expensive clothes and fine leather shoes, living luxuriously as if kings. Recall for a moment the childhood years Reies went about barefoot and how he remembered the dignity he felt when he got his first pair of shoes. Preachers were no longer satisfied with their congregation's weekly collections, demanding higher tithes and even yearly salaries. Who could not see how sinful these developments were?

Tijerina's critiques of American society fall into three broad categories. He condemns first a range of sins wrought by American capitalism, empire, colonialism, and modernity, which were part and parcel of the country's postwar prosperity and displacements quickened by urbanization and immigration. Next, he castigates church leaders for the institutional sins they commit. "The church," by Reies's definition, includes all Christian denominations. Finally, the vulgar consumer-culture capitalism bred results in a host of familial and personal sins: the erosion of domestic patriarchal authority and women's increasing autonomy and participation in the public sphere.

Tijerina articulates these assessments metaphorically, employing language and symbolism taken mostly from Revelation. In the prophecy courses LABI offered, Revelation was the core text. It was to be expected that when Reies began preaching his own version of the Apostolic Faith, he relied extensively on it. At first, he used it only to critique modernity and humanity's sinfulness but later relied on it to denounce the sins of the church. This was precisely what got him expelled from the Assemblies of God.

John of Patmos wrote Revelation carefully deploying allegorical language to befuddle Roman spies and escape persecution. He differentiated the sinfulness of the past from the liberation Jesus promised. Begging people to rise up against their slavery to sin, John metaphorically juxtaposed two cities, Babylon and the New Jerusalem, each personified as women to convey his point. In Reies's sermon "The Captive People—Leave, Leave," he compares Israel's Babylonian captivity to the blandishments American capitalism offers its residents, urging his listeners to flee, seeking liberation as Jews had. Babylon's whore was the symbol of idolatry and sinfulness. "The people of God are captive, prisoners of the passions of Babylon, drunk with the delights of the mother of all earthly fornications and inventions," Reies maintains.[25] Decrying the exploitation American imperialism undertook globally to provide citizens with venal luxuries, Reies critiques this state of affairs with tropes from Revelation. "The commerce of Babylon and the potency of its delights consist of merchandise of gold, of silver, of fine garments and delicate foods. It consists of houses equipped with arrogance, cars that speak of pride, and comforts that delight the flesh of captive Christians."[26]

"Leave! Leave! Leave Babylon!" Reies often remonstrates. "Come out of the city of sin. Flee the great Babylon! Why participate in its sins and in the plagues that will befall it?"[27] If Christians do not repent while they can, God will surprise them as he had Sodom and Gomorrah. "Step away from evil; cleanse your lips of hypocrisy," he commands.[28] "Turn your face to the wall, cast your eyes to the ground," deaden your body's sinfulness.[29] Dress yourselves only "with Christ's love, and take off [y]our clothing of evil, of envy, of ire, of bitterness, of self-importance."[30] Babylon's whore beguiles her children, teaching them hatred, revenge, and selfishness. Her drinks are so potent, her charms so intoxicating that "all peoples, all nations, tribes, and tongues" are ensnared in the "racial egoism, sectarian egoism and nationalist egoism" she breeds.[31]

Babylon's residents had grown "heart[s] of stone for the poor."[32] They ignore the hungry and the oppressed. Those who had been seduced by this mother of all abominations dress, walk, speak, and live lives of complete haughtiness, coveting what others have. "A man with new and expensive clothes is really respected and appreciated. But a man wearing poor and cheap clothes is not esteemed even if he is a man of judgment, even if he is a man of pure actions greatly esteemed before the living God."[33]

Reies repeatedly compares Israel's sins in biblical times with Christian transgressions in the decade following World War II. In nine of his forty-five sermons he implores readers that if they do not repent soon, they too will suffer the punishments Israel experienced during its Babylonian captivity.³⁴ "Israel was a slave of Egypt and the servant of Babylon. And in the shadow of servitude, it had sons and daughters.... In Egypt and Babylon one could not find the Laws of God or the works of the Almighty. But the God of Mercy, remembering His promise, after much time returned them to their homeland." Once free but failing to obey God's commands, he deserted Israel and allowed Rome to punish her mercilessly. "Israel abandoned the paths of God, when it left [Egypt] and ignored Justice and Mercy."³⁵ The Israelites became vain and were punished. God "whipped it, mutilated it, and handed them over to the harshest peoples. He sold them to the cruelest and most merciless government, and completely forgot about them for seventy years."³⁶ Legions of Roman soldiers invaded Jerusalem, starved and crucified its inhabitants, and desecrated and burned their temple, the symbol of God's covenant with the Jews. Israel lost everything.³⁷

"Israel found itself captive in the land of Babylon," as now American Christians are.³⁸ The prayers and songs Israel performed proved worthless after it stopped obeying God. Christian prayers and chants had become rubbish. "Singing or praying has not done anyone good, nor does fasting after leaving the justice and mercy of God."³⁹ Christians are smugly confident that they enjoy God's favor. "Let us lend our ear to the advice the prophet Jeremiah gave to the people of Israel, who also thought it was in good standing before God. The prophet said: 'do not praise the wise for his wisdom or the strong because of his strength, or the rich for his wealth, but if one should praise himself, let it be in this: in knowing me, for I am Jehovah, that I do mercy, judgment and justice on earth, because I want these things, says Jehovah.'"⁴⁰ What evidence do Christians have that they are pleasing God?⁴¹

Why is no one invoking God's name given the corruption at hand? Why is no one plaintively begging to hear God's commandments? "Oh twisted and callous people, open your eyes and see what you have done!"⁴² Leave Babylon. Flee the vanities of modernity, lest they die beside their gluttonous temple ministers who are only concerned about their enormous bellies. These "so-called men of God" continually "bend their knee to the vanities of Babylon." Surely God is more pleased by the ancient hymns of the Pharisees than he is by those who currently preach his word. Their words and deeds are "abomination, dishonor, and corruption."⁴³

"Let us leave [Babylon] the mother who raised us, who taught us to rebel against God and his Justice. Let us abandon the mother who did not teach us Mercy toward anyone. Let us leave the Jerusalem that kills prophets and understand that it was . . . the twisted laws of false teachers who killed the just."[44] These false teachers, like the Pharisees, are Satan's agents. The day of damnation is near. The fire of the ire of God is quickly approaching. It will burn the lecherous whore and her pernicious lovers. "With the whore's end, we will also see the end of Christianity's rebelliousness against God's holy commandments handed to us by Christ."[45]

Reies's message is simple: renounce sin or face damnation. His eschatology, or how he imagines the world's end, again relies on Revelation's descriptions of Armageddon. If Christians hoped to be saved from the punishments God would unleash, one immediately has to break the shackles of slavery to sin, free oneself from egoism and envy, from arrogance and conceit. "Come out of the city of sin. Flee the great Babylon! Why participate in its sins and in the plagues that will befall it?"[46] Tijerina preached, "Step away from evil; cleanse your lips of hypocrisy."[47] "Turn your face to the wall, cast your eyes to the ground," deaden your body's sinfulness.[48] Dress yourselves only "with Christ's love, and take off [y]our clothing of evil, of envy, of ire, of bitterness, of self-importance."[49]

"The fire of the ire of God will burn us. . . . It will be a day of revenge, of fire, smoke, and sulfur. The earth will be emptied of the impious and tyrants will no longer be their owners."[50] On that day God will cleanse the earth, excising the "rotten and healing the sickness that leaders have caused." Tyrants will be humbled. Those who once dressed in sumptuous clothing will be left naked and crying like babies. Gluttons will be left without food, bent over with excruciating hunger pains. "The chalice of the wrath of God Almighty, who fights and judges the land with great justice," will spare no one. Fathers and sons, husbands and wives, men and women, young and old, all soon will face the lord's judgment.[51]

In "Who Will Be Saved?" Reies explains that only those who had "been merciful toward the earth's oppressed" will be spared the pain of the great tribulation.[52] Those who feed the hungry, clothe the poor, care for foreigners, widows, and orphans, and live saintly lives will be "lifted up on the cloud" during the rapture, escaping God's ire. Saints and martyrs have no reason to tremble. Before Christ incinerates the world, the oppressed will be asked to offer testimony about how they had suffered at the hands of so-called Christians. Those who had been callous, those who had been heartless, they will eternally burn in hell. Tijerina urges women and men to banish gossip and anger.[53] Through such abnegation God might show them "mercy in the final days."[54] "Let us open our eyes and see that we ourselves have invited the sword" of God's vengeance. "The end is near, the end comes," Reies thunders. "All eyes will cry, and the strong will tremble. The leaders and the great men who executed the law, they too will place their faces upon the ground. They will scream like women in labor. These greats will flee the riches they once embraced, will curse luxury and pomp for which once they killed. They will know . . . that in everything they deceived their poor souls."[55]

Humanity has one last chance. If it earnestly renounces it sins, it might be welcomed into the New Jerusalem, drinking of its living waters. Christ and his virginal lover and bride, the church, govern this kingdom.[56] Waxing lyrically, Reies explains that the love Christ had for his bride has been long, bitter, and full of suffering, but, nevertheless, enormously rewarding. "No one in the world was happier or more helpful and committed than her."[57] Christ's bride, his pure church, cares for widows and prisoners. She hears the world's cries and responds quickly with compassion. Daily she dresses herself appropriately from head to toe, seeking nothing, desiring nothing, lest the world's material deceits weaken her heart. "This wife of Christ was like a mother for the earth's people. This wife of Christ was the eyes of the blind. This wife of Christ passed her time feeding those who had nothing to eat. She never sought her own good, but instead would spend nights out on the hills and valleys, searching for the needy in dark places, and looking after anyone. This wife of Christ was not at ease until everyone had what they asked for."[58] So holy, so revered was she that the angels in heaven endlessly praised and glorified her name as "she was very loved and esteemed" on earth.[59]

Gradually all this praise began distracting Christ's bride. Men found her attractive. Their adoring declarations befuddled her. Eventually she was seduced. First, her heart and mind weakened. Then she became self-absorbed. She allowed men to serve her rather than showing fidelity to Jesus, her loving master and lord. In time she handed over her authority to powerful men on earth who knew nothing about suffering. "Now she cannot hear the cries of the afflicted, of the poor who walk naked and without bread to eat."[60] The church, Christ's bride, finally is adulterously led astray. This narrative of the church's declension, and the sins of seduction its leaders and ministers committed, dominates many of Tijerina's sermons.

When Reies begins indicting the church for its sinfulness, he refers not only to the Assemblies of God but also to Protestantism as a whole. "Why condemn the Baptist?" he asks. "Why condemn the Pentecostal? Why condemn the Adventist? And why condemn the different organizations?" They are all equally guilty of forsaking the word of God, leading lives of worldliness, and failing to embody Christian virtues.[61] "Open your eyes," Reies demands, "the bad in the Church is neither small nor weak." Using words of mocking contempt, he explains that the church is a sinful wound on Christ's body, but one not easily discussed openly because its leaders easily and quickly take offense. Brooking little criticism, defying correction, the church behaves like a child, delighting in its toys, wasting time glorifying things rather than dedicating themselves to deeds that promise eternal life. "They love everything except justice. They covet everything, except humility. They sacrifice for everything and even to the point of sickness, except for the Cross of Christ."[62]

The wickedness of the church is greater than that of the Pharisees. The true faith of Jesus Christ is not being practiced, only a simulated one. Instead of extending God's mercy, justice, and love to others, these modern-day Pharisees spend their energies in "public worship, chants, prayers, fasts, tithes, and the commandments of men."[63] These "so-called Christian leaders" are heading an apostate church with greater abandon than the "Pharisees who crucified Christ. The difference being that those who crucified Christ only crucified his body, while these have crucified the word of God and the Spiritual life of Christ, and have substituted it for an arrogant life, one full of pride . . . [as] captives of Babylon."[64]

In sermon after sermon, Tijerina mocks church leaders as the so-called men of God. Those who lead the church behave like anointed royalty, adorning their bodies and dressing "their flesh like princes of Sodom."[65] They are haughty and arrogant, wallowing in luxury, and showing no one mercy or charity. In words seething with contempt, Reies explains that he has repeatedly sought the counsel of church leaders, asking them to explain what God's mercy and justice mean, to correct the arrogance of which he stood accused in 1950. What exactly should he preach? He has gotten no answer. The church's leaders are hypocrites. "Those who hold and occupy the pulpits are greedy men, are clumsy men who do not love the truth. They rely on sweet words, and use old examples of saintly men to obtain what they want."[66] They know nothing about suffering, even less about hunger. They are deaf to those who cry in pain. Yet what they relish most are "smoking, drinking liquor, and other vices that men took up after rebelling against God."[67] The law of God is now in the hands of these tyrants.[68]

Such behavior among church leaders afflicts local ministers, too. Reies accuses them of selling God's word for a few shekels of silver. Christ came to earth as a beggar. He was the poorest of the poor, owning nothing. He preached to the oppressed and was intent on leading them to salvation. The only compensation Jesus received for this work was a crown of thorns and crucifixion.[69] Christ was rich, Reies explains, because he had endured humanity's suffering without complaint. But charity can no longer be found among these "so-called men of God," who demand salaries and refuse alms. "If [George] Washington did not want salary to serve an earthly kingdom, why ask for a salary from a spiritual and holy kingdom? If Christ did not do it, why should we?"[70]

Reies never had a salary as a preacher. He believed that those who did were failing to spread Christ's good news. In biblical times prophets preached without concern for their own material needs; such selflessness no longer exists. Salaries signal "the death of the spirit of service towards the meek of the earth."[71] If these alleged teachers preach the word of God accurately, without uttering lies, the faithful will attend to their needs generously, if modestly, with alms. God's good news is not for sale. "Leave salary, each one of you," Reies demands, "and defend the poor, do good toward the oppressed of the earth, let us defend the rights of God."[72]

Charity begins at home. Its effects have to be felt locally and personally, helping those nearby. Reies disliked institutional responses to poverty by the federal government and railed against charitable organizations such as the Salvation Army. If the church obeys God's commandments, there will be no need for government welfare or secular social services.[73] The church is so wealthy that it has no reason to scorn the poor, relying on secular interventions to help the very young and very old. This abhorrent state of affairs reflects the extent to which Christ's church has abandoned its flock. Like the Pharisees who constructed opulent temples and justified them invoking the Law of Moses, so church leaders are similarly parroting ridiculous arguments.[74]

Reies sanctimoniously asserts that he lives as the prophets once had, always relying on charity even to the utter privation of his family. "I speak for God and not for men. My salary is in the heavens. And even if there is no salary for me, it is good for me to speak, because from the beginning we should serve God without any interest whatsoever. My interest is Christ and my salary is eternal life. Oh of those who sell the word of God and substitute judgment and justice for bread that perishes."[75] Reies prays that God will bless the earth with a legion of preachers who, like the apostles, have no interest in monetary compensation whatsoever.

Pastoral salaries are one of the many symptoms of the church's apostasy, evident in the haughtiness of its leaders, in the vanity of its ministers, in their temple constructions, and in their phony rituals. These men are mired in crass consumerism, believing that large, ostentatious churches are expressions of their love of God. "Just as shops for food and shops for clothing grow and become more luxurious to catch the eye of the people and gain customers, likewise pastors dream of large and beautiful temples, disregarding the things God assigned us."[76] Many ministers believe that once they build beautiful temples, full of sonorous chants and public prayers, these are testaments of their faith and love of God. "It is not so."[77] Not even the Pharisees deceived themselves so ludicrously. Every religion, even those worshipping false gods, built grand edifices to mesmerize congregants. Constructing buildings is no demonstration of one's love of God. Instead, it is folly, borrowing money that requires huge mortgage payments, constantly taxing their members, leaving resources for nothing else.[78]

Spending money to build dazzling temples has a purpose: to attract the monied classes. Reies refuses to call these "churches," linking the behavior of Protestant ministers to Jerusalem's Pharisees. These temples are pure distractions. "Who asked for . . . churches from you?" "God wants faithful worshippers. God seeks those who adore him in spirit and in truth. God does not seek empty words and ceremonies. He seeks just actions and acts of repentance."[79] Christ came to earth to feed those spiritually and physically hungry. "The life of Christ produced love, mercy, justice, faith, gentleness and temperance."[80] No matter how melodious their temple chants might sound, no matter the many tears their prayers produce, no matter how long their fasts last, those who do not obey God's commandments will suffer eternally.

The increasing politicization of the church was deeply troubling to Reies, part of an older debate about the separation of church and state. Evangelical Protestants were increasingly being lured into the secular world of politics in which they did not belong. The road to perdition started when radio stations began hosting revival crusades and was followed by television broadcasts for stay-at-home Christians. Starting in 1950, evangelists such as Billy Graham preached by radio to millions of Southern Baptists on his program, *The Hour of Decision*. When Graham began television broadcasts in 1954, the viewership of *Billy Graham Crusades* soared exponentially. Reies has Billy Graham in mind, perhaps even several others, when he reviles nascent televangelists as "The Descendants of the Pharisees."[81]

In the years following World War II, evangelical Protestants were finally beginning to reemerge from the public exile they had suffered since the 1920s, when they were dismissed by an increasing secular society as "fundamentalists," as backward, doctrinaire biblical literalists who denied the value of rationality, science, and modernity.[82] The 1925 Scopes trial over the teaching of evolution in public schools devalued conservative Protestant worldviews, creating a set of binary referents "between supernaturalist and reasoning, backward and progressive, ignorant and educated, rural and cosmopolitan, anti-intellectual and intellectual, superstitious and scientific, duped and skeptical, bigoted and tolerant, dogmatic and thinking, absolutist and questioning, authoritarian and democratic," notes anthropologist Susan Harding.[83] Science and liberal values increasingly gained rhetorical dominance in American life after this, banishing fundamentalists from the corridors of secular political power, at least for a while.

Hoping to regain Protestantism's place in public life, moderate leaders began burnishing the public image of their organizations, establishing the National Association of Evangelicals (NAE) in 1942, announcing themselves "evangelicals," thus hoping to shed their stigmatizing "fundamentalist" cloaks. The Assemblies of God joined the NAE in 1943. By 1950 the NAE had become so visible that it rivaled in stature the National Council of Churches, regularly engaging presidents and congressmen at National Prayer Breakfasts, first convened in 1953.[84] The heads of evangelical churches increasingly took visible roles in national politics, routinely joining US presidents as their spiritual confidants. All of this was collusion with state power, with the "beast," Reies protested. He dismissed these collaborators again and again as "so-called men of God," as evil "princes of Sodom and Gomorrah." That "a preacher of the day is no longer distinguished from the president of a nation" was abhorrent. It fostered a sinful accommodation with American imperialism and its ill-gotten colonial profits drenched in the blood of human exploitation.[85]

Reies's antidote to the politicization of the church and its personnel is a harangue enjoining them not to fornicate with the whore of Babylon or collude with the beast, renouncing their personal investments in the blandishments of modernity corrupted by rationality and science. If they believed in the miracles of modern medicine, those beliefs had to be rejected. The only efficacious healing was the Holy Spirit's. Reies Tijerina's vision of salvation is restorationist, demanding that both the church and society return to a purer and simpler time, to the time when Jesus and his first disciples preached, to the feast of the Pentecost, and to that moment before corruption crept into the Jesus movement through the institutionalization of the church under the Roman emperor Constantine. "Let us return to the ancient laws, to the ancient fear of God, to the ancient forgiveness, to the ancient love, to the ancient justice, to the ancient mercy, to the ancient meekness."[86]

Retreating to the perfection of early Christianity would purify society and the church. This is a recurrent theme Pentecostal Christians have voiced since 1901, believing that little separated first-century Christianity and America in the middle of the twentieth century. It means that evangelical Christians take the Bible as literal truth, never contextualizing the circumstances of its production as if it "dropped from heaven as a sacred meteor" from God.[87] This primitivism is evident in how the Assemblies of God narrate the history of their "Apostolic Faith." It has no history, "the source is from the skies," William Seymour claims.[88] Such an explanation still carried considerable currency in 1961, evident in Carl Brumback's insider history of the Assemblies of God, titled *Suddenly . . . from Heaven*.[89]

Tijerina's demand for a return to a primitive Christianity was his plea to return to local fellowship circles and household churches, eschewing formal governance structures. He wanted egalitarian local assemblies and not the councils, temples, salaries, and rituals that had corrupted the original Apostolic Faith. He wanted individuals to bear witness to Christ personally, imbibing the Bible's truths on their own, without the mediation of trained interlocutors, without tithing, relying only on personal charity. This was the vision of the New Jerusalem he imagined. This is why he cursed his fellow ministers so passionately, calling them corrupt Pharisees, spineless servants of the "beast" seduced by Babylon's cunning and witless whore.

Tijerina's primitivist jeremiads were also his prescription for a set of sins associated with familial life and emergent notions of personal autonomy. These transgressions are anchored in his belief that the authority structure that should govern households is identical to God's, or as the Lord's prayer commands, "on earth as it is in heaven." Children have to honor their fathers and their mothers, wives have to submit to their husbands, and husbands have to protect the shame, the sexual modesty of their womenfolk against verbal and physical assaults. This requires a stern father, a man who rules over the household's members as lawgiver and king, second in authority only to God.

America entry into World War II in 1941 required a labor reorganization that severely disrupted domestic life and established gender roles. Many women left the isolation of the familial hearth to work in factories and in occupations deemed essential to wartime goals. At war's end in 1945, many women gladly returned home to childcare and domestic chores. Other women wanted to remain in the workforce and did. With the country's postwar economy expanding, it became increasingly difficult to restore prewar mores and manners, particularly among young men and women who increasingly relished the independence and material comforts their wages earned. That meant that older agrarian notions of honor as a patriarchal form of familial governance began crumbling in urban and even rural places. Reies thought that personal and familial honor had to be restored not only for personal salvation but also for the continuation of the species. Ironically, while Reies decried church hierarchies as deadening the spirit of Christ among the faithful, he demanded them as essential to familial governance.

In the late 1940s, Reies Tijerina concluded that the ethnic Mexican family was in disarray. "Children have lost respect for their father, have become disobedient, violent, insolent, corrupted in thoughts and words that are dirty and filthy."[90] If parents truly love their children, if husbands honestly love their wives, they first have to teach them how to love God, then how to value justice, and finally how to protect their sexual virtue or honor. Families are unraveling. "Now the father has no power over the son."[91] The behavior of daughters is even more deplorable. Harkening back to his restorationist ideals, Reies insists that the family's collective sense of honor, its social standing and reputation in the world, has to be recovered. For this to occur, one had to return to older, traditional ways, relying on stern patriarchs to correct domestic misdeeds. The family's honor is best displayed when wives obey their husbands and children submit to their father's authority. For honor to arise, for it to remain intact, the *pater familia* has to protect the *vergüenza* or shame of his womenfolk. Shame is gender specific, embodied only by females and displayed through modesty and concern for one's sexual reputation. A woman who embodies vergüenza is a virgin at marriage, sexually faithful to her husband, and decorous in her personal and public behavior, lest others impugn her reputation and, by association, the reputation of her entire family. Women who lose their virtue through seduction, assault, or libertine behavior, and married women who commit adultery, are considered *sin vergüenza* or shameless. Shamelessness dishonors fathers and husbands and significantly lowers the honor of a family. A father concerned for the shame of his womenfolk guards them closely, corrects them constantly to assure that others judge him a man of honor who heads a well-governed family worthy of public respect.[92]

Gender hierarchies in the United States has become so utterly twisted, opines Reies, that "woman has taken the place of the man."[93] Women have lost "their honor, their shame, their decency, their respect [behaving] like women who have never known that there is a God."[94] Their behavior is worse than the women of Babylon. Daughters now "dress and walk and speak like women who do not understand good."[95] Children do not feel indebted to their parents for all the spiritual guidance and the material benefits they receive. Oh, what an intolerable state of affairs, Reies complains. "This generation no longer knows what shame is, nor is it scandalized by the evil upon the land."[96] Reies condemns those women working outside the home and chastises husbands who put "their own women to work."[97] Women are "found in the midst of men working, only to live according to the fashions of the sons of Babylon and to satisfy their carnal appetite for things that burn."[98]

Such words, passionately preached and penned, must have rung hollow to at least one person, María Escobar, then Reies's wife. She toiled outside the home—in the fields as a farmworker, in offices as a typist, in stores as a ribbon clerk, in hotels as a chambermaid—to finance her husband's ministry and to put food in the mouths of her babes. By supporting the family thus, she allowed Reies to pursue his apocalyptic dreams and intensifying belief that he was a prophet, perhaps even a messiah, even though it was not yet apparent to the world. María undertook this work lovingly, cheerfully, and apparently without complaint until much later. That was why Reies so easily and hypocritically condemned minsters who demanded salaries. Yes, he lived as an itinerant evangelist solely by the charity of others only because his wife and his sons and daughters toiled under horrible conditions as agricultural migrant laborers so that he could come and go without any evident concern for their wellbeing. Finally, on March 22, 1963, María divorced Reies. María explained that it was to give her children a more stable, settled life, with predictable daily meals and clean clothes. Lurking unspoken in the background was Reies's adulterous behavior, his desire to take multiple wives, to treat his children immodestly with little concern. Whatever his vaunted words, he did not live by what he demanded of his family, acolytes, Christians, and American society.[99]

Working outside the home was but one of the many ways Reies judged women shameless. It opened the door to a broader array of vices that ultimately weakened the flesh and turned it rancid in God's eyes. Liquor, smoking, movies, dancing, cosmetics, fancy hairdos, all dishonored the family and had to be avoided because they logically led to stealing, adultery, and murder. American capitalism had commercialized "every abomination of the flesh, every filth, lasciviousness, and sensuality," which it marketed mainly to women.[100] Women were obsessed with personal appearance and clothing, which clearly, at least to Reies, was eroding domestic morality and thus was forbidden in his household.

A woman's properly clothed body was "a fruit of honor, a fruit of fear, a fruit of wisdom," while her naked body was "a fruit of the spirit of sensuality and lasciviousness," which signified that "all honor, glory, shame, modesty have perished from the earth."[101] Magazines carried pictures of naked women in seductive coital positions that aroused men's bestial natures. When men went to the barber shop and saw calendars of naked women prominently displayed, would they not return home excited, wanting to treat their wives as whores? Many men undoubtedly committed adultery in their hearts when they saw such images. Women and men should not be forced to see such things in public. While this glorification of promiscuity was not legally prostitution, it provoked adultery, real or imagined, feeding men's lascivious appetites and ultimately corrupting society. Such behavior even scandalized the "daughters of Babylon." "Is there no one who is disgusted by the filth and arrogance of women. . . . Tell the woman that this behavior does not please God."[102]

Such perversity had become so common that some men were even prostituting their own daughters "to pay the debts of their malevolent appetites." These girls were sold on the streets and in houses of prostitution, "passing their most tender years in the lowest and most despicable work there can be for a woman."[103] On judgment day God would punish these fathers and curse the daughters for behaving like the progeny of "the great mother of fornications." In olden times women would have been at home cooking and cleaning, darning and sewing, caring for their husbands and children. Men in the past would have preferred starvation than to see their own women working as prostitutes.[104]

Sexual sin disgusted Reies, or so he proclaimed despite succumbing to adultery several times. As we will see, this concern disappeared after 1958 as he began his land grant activism. Who was to blame? In Revelation John of Patmos identifies two culprits responsible for humanity's alienation from God. First was the imperial Roman state, served by two beasts, the emperor and his local prefects and governors. And second, "the wicked whore of Babylon," the empire's goddess known as Roma who embodied the empire's pagan religious cults and funneled the fruits of Rome's extractive colonialism to its citizens. For Reies, the popular media—radio, newspapers, commercial art—were the whore's modern wiles she had transfused as "poisons into the blood of Christianity."[105] Admittedly, newspapers did report on important world events, but they were mainly advertising tabloids that promoted "the vanities of life," intentionally meant to awaken desires that "irritate the soul." If preachers really care about the salvation of souls, they would teach them how to "resist Satan's art and the forces of darkness."[106] Who other than Reies was doing this? In his mind the church had become a despicable apostate. Even the popular evangelists of Reies's day, like Billy Graham, were "clumsy and vain with their empty speeches."[107]

Tijerina's sermons rarely broached secular political topics as he was taught in Bible school. In only two instances did Tijerina deviate from this norm denouncing current events. The invention, construction, and use of atomic bombs was one, a theme he logically connected to the earth's "latter days." Denouncing modernity in Manichean terms, Reies smoldered over the invention of these weapons of mass destruction. In his sermon "Descendants of the Pharisees," he mocks the stupidity of those who "call atomic energy a blessing" because it had no purpose other than to fill "the earth with violence."[108] The scientists who had unleashed the atom's power were servants "the devil uses to corrupt Christian minds."[109] Day and night, night and day, men toil in Los Alamos, New Mexico, forging steel, inventing instruments, processing plutonium to manufacture weapons of incineration. If Christians do not believe "in killing and in war," why are they "working for the government making atomic bombs, and airplanes with which to drop the bombs"? Government employment was meant to stimulate the capitalist economy, giving workers "money they need to buy their new cars, and improve their earthly homes, despite the fact that they are hastening war and God's ire."[110] Is the destruction of one's enemies so important? Do humans deem themselves more powerful than God? Oh silly, silly man! Tijerina remonstrates. The fire of atomic bombs pale in comparison to fire of the ire of God. Those who seek worldly domination through the invention of such weapons should turn their eyes to God, shed their worldliness, curse the day atomic bombs were born, and purify their sinful souls instead. Throughout the rest of his adult life, Reies remained a strident activist against nuclear proliferation.

Tijerina vehemently denied any connection to the Communist Party of the United States or to communist and socialist ideologies during his pastoral career and later as a land grant activist seeking to recuperate Spanish and Mexican mercedes. He repeatedly asserted that he had never read any communist literature, not even Karl Marx's *Manifesto*, nor had he ever associated with organizations or organizers of this kind. His ideology comes directly from the Bible and from God's commandments. Nothing else. He cannot endorse communist ideas "because these people are not with God."[111] By the same token, capitalism and its titans seem to him more demonically corrupt than the communists. "The devil gave us democracy in which we do as we please."[112] America's capitalist democracy does not produce genuine political freedom, it is a mirage. In reality, Americans enjoy the liberty to consume whatever, whenever, and in the amounts they chose, of course, only if one has cash. Americans praise democracy "not because there is more justice among people, but because there is more gluttony."[113] Is this the kind of democracy Christians should celebrate and demand?

In two of his sermons, "The Provokers of Judgment" and "Good Passes for Evil," Reies praises the social support systems communist states provide their populations. He opines that if such a political system existed in the United States "we would not lose so many people to communism as it grows at a gigantic pace."[114] He expresses dismay about the mocking tone American newspapers report on events and culture in Soviet Russia. It is so full of "hatred and contempt [for] . . . the Red enemy."[115] Christian women, for example, ridicule their counterparts behind the Iron Curtain because they dress in long, loose-fitting dresses with long sleeves, made of dark-colored fabrics, which do not accentuate the body's curves. Russian women dress "humbly and with honor and decency, and many of their customs [are] worthy of imitation by so-called Christians." What ignorant Americans do not understand, Reies lectures, is that "Russia is the only nation that does not praise arrogance or the base ways of the United States."[116] American Christians do not fear God or obey his commandments, consequently they personally are responsible for the emergence of Communism and the Soviet Union's power. "A force like that of the Soviets is born of the rebellious world, we the children of God, have created." Comparing capitalism and communism side by side, Reies concludes, "'communism' has come to do a greater job than our 'love.'"[117]

Reies Tijerina covered a vast geography proselytizing as eight of his sermons indicate where and when they were preached. These are Melvin, Michigan (May 9, 1953); San Antonio, Texas (August 3, 1953); New York (November 27, 1953); Austin, Texas (February 22, 1954); Victoria, Texas (March 12, 1954); El Monte, California (April 15, 1954); El Monte, California (November 22, 1954); and Carlsbad, California (June 30, 1954). His travels were mostly in Texas and California, but he was also crisscrossing the entire country.

The God Reies imagines was primarily a stern, law-giving king, who was due obedience because of his commandments and would judge humanity on whether they obey his dictates. Salvation would be won by living virtuously, demonstrating love, mercy, justice, humility, and honor. Satan and the devil are responsible for estranging women and men from God through arrogance, vanity, selfishness, avarice and greed, adultery, and fornication, drinking and gluttony. Using language directly out of Revelation, he decries the sins of Babylon's inhabitants, the seductions of its lecherous whore, and Jerusalem's Pharisees who colluded with the beast to have Jesus killed. Though Reies does not personally attack leaders of the Assemblies of God and Christian evangelicals, they were clearly his targets.

Over the course of ten years, from 1946 to 1956, his apocalyptic message attracted very few disciples, who left everything to follow him. Ever aware of the approaching world's end, he led some thirty individuals into Arizona's desert where he founded a commune he called the Valle de Paz, the Valley of Peace. In the next chapter, we turn to the agony and ecstasy his Heralds of Peace faced there.

CHAPTER 7

The Valley of Peace

BY 1956, REIES TIJERINA'S orthodox brand of Pentecostal end-time theology seemed jarringly out of sync with American prosperity. He was faced with rising membership in mainstream Protestant churches, but there was no groundswell around his own stern teaching and preaching heralding the apocalypse. "I had fought with the 'church' . . . for ten long years, trying to get it to support the fight of the poor against the rich," Reies surmised. "I failed."[1] He had managed to gather a small group of devotees who relished his sermons and were living their lives by his dictates, prepared to flee the world's corruption at a moment's notice. Reies yearned for a place of "peace and security," far removed from modernity and rapacious "monopoly capitalism," a place far from the reach of the wicked whore of Babylon. There, neither churches nor the state through public schooling would be able to brainwash their children, polluting them with heretical ideas about how family and personal life should be organized. There, Reies imagined that he and his disciples would construct homes, a church, and a school.

Reies dispatched his older brother Ramón to scout throughout the Southwest for such a spot. He found it in Arizona. He purchased a plot of 160 acres for $1,400, located about forty-five miles southeast of Phoenix, between the towns of Casa Grande and Eloy, adjacent to the Tohono O'odham Nation. There were no apparent luxuries to corrupt one's body and soul on this desiccated desert expanse, covered with prickly pear cacti and chaparral as far as the eye could see. Like Moses leading the Israelites through the thickets of the Sinai Desert to escape their oppression, so Reies guided his followers to Arizona to flee the "vanity and corruption of cities." On land Reies described as the "wildest spot I could find so that we wouldn't be bothered," he and his acolytes set out in early January 1956 to build the community on which they would await the apocalypse.[2] They called their refuge the *Valle de Paz*, the Valley of Peace.

Among those who wandered into the desert with Reies was Zebedeo Valdez, who first met Reies at a revival in Salt Lake City, Utah, in the early 1950s. "From the moment he heard me preach, he followed me," noted Reies. Manuel Mata was already an ordained Protestant minister when he too was swept away. María Moreno yearned to become an evangelist and when she heard Reies preach, she followed. Her husband Luis resisted the call for several years, but eventually he too succumbed. Reies met Rodolfo Mares and his wife Celia in 1952, while picking tomatoes in Fruita, Colorado. Three years later when they were again picking tomatoes at the same farm, they decided to become devotees.

By summer of 1955, the families of Reies Tijerina, Manuel Mata, Rodolfo Mares, Juan Reyna, Vicente Martínez, Simón Serna, and Luis Moreno were traveling, living, working, and praying as one. In 1978, by his own patriarchal account, these were the men Reies said were the "valiant ones," the ones who had followed him into the desert. Guadalupe Jáuregui and Zebedeo Valdez were also among the adult men at the Valley of Peace, but Reies never mentioned them. Nor did he name the women or children. María Escobar, Reies's wife, remembered a much larger and more complex community. With Manuel Mata came his father Adrian, wife Alicia (aka Licha), and their children Irene, Jimmy, María, and Elena. Rodolfo Mares, his wife Celia, and their children, Santiago and María Elena, were residents. With Juan Reyna was wife Juanita and their two children. Vicente Martínez and his wife Leonarda were the elders of an extended family that included Luis Moreno, his wife María, their children Abel, Lillian, Tito, and Elida, and Luis's brother Sixto (aka Chito), who was married to María Moreno's sister Celia. Simón Serna (aka *"el ciclón,"* the cyclone) had a particularly large family in tow consisting of Ramón, Sara, Rebecca, Caleb, and Tibor. Francisco Flores and his wife Dorothy came with two small children. If we count Reies, his wife María, and their children at the time, David, Rose, Daniel, and Raquel, the known residents of the Valley of Peace numbered more than thirty, and undoubtedly a few more, as infants were born and adults came and went for short stays.³

On taking possession of the plot, they "elected trustees and called it 'Valle de Paz,' our valley of peace," designating themselves the Heralds of Peace and referred to each other as brothers and sisters. The men sported full, bushy beards and wore long white gowns.⁴ The women completely covered their heads and wore dresses that reached to the floor, something that often provoked laughter and stares among locals in nearby towns.⁵ Rose Tijerina recalled that the women dressed "like Arabian women," because Reies forbade them "to have our hair uncovered."⁶ Working "like ants," they began building homes of an unusual but essential sort. Reies used the Spanish word *fosa* (pit or grave) to describe what they built.⁷ After the United States dropped atomic bombs on Hiroshima and Nagasaki in 1945, Reies constantly preached against the evil of atomic weapons, convinced that their proliferation signaled the world's fiery end as described in Revelation. By the early months of 1956, many Americans clearly were nervous about the escalating arms race between the Soviet Union and the United States and the potential for nuclear war. Reies warned that the United States was building "atomic bombs day and night," and had been continuously since the end of World War II. Nerves became even more frayed when the public learned that the Soviet Union successfully had tested a hydrogen bomb in November 1955.

The cold war fantasy the American government peddled in the 1950s was that if atomic bombs did burst in the air, the blinding light would show that our flag was still there. Nuclear war could be survived. Never mind the slow deaths from cancers and diseases radiation caused. Civil Defense authorities encouraged Americans to protect themselves by constructing makeshift bomb shelters in the basements of their homes. If sirens sounded signaling an approaching bomb, school children were taught to duck and cover under their desks. The Heralds of Peace heard such nightmarish predictions of an approaching nuclear holocaust with joyful anticipation. It signaled Christ's apocalyptic return. When that moment arrived, a time that certainly would be marked by great tribulation, those who had faithfully followed God's laws would be lifted into heaven in what Pentecostal adepts called "the rapture," which would precede Christ's millennial reign. The Heralds of Peace dug large holes into the earth, about six feet deep and roughly four feet by eight, constructing their subterranean homes as bomb shelters. At automobile junkyards they rummaged for car tops to serve as roofs, covering them with several feet of dirt, to produce both cover and coolness in the desert's heat. It took most of the men roughly two months to finish their shelters, but the cost was minimal. If a nuclear attack occurred, it would target America's major cities they hoped. Isolated in Arizona's desert the Heralds of Peace imagined themselves as safe and ready to be lifted in the rapture.

Daily routines at the Valley of Peace were those of a rural agrarian proletariat living from hand-to-mouth. By day, the adult men and women and the older children picked cotton at nearby Anglo farms. By night, the women made whatever clothing was needed, cooked from a collective pantry on stoves fashioned from discarded oil barrels, and tended to their children. It was a "joyful and peaceful place," recalled María Escobar. "We were very happy singing the praises of Jesus day and night" and listening to Reies preach. Reminiscing about the commune's early days too, Reies said, "We felt pampered in that paradise. . . . We built, we worked, we were happy. It really seemed as though we were building a new life of mercy and justice, a real Kingdom of God."[8]

The Gospel messages Reies was preaching to his disciples at the commune quickly became known. Poor souls started flocking to the community with wrenching tales of woe, of injustices by local cotton growers, and of police violence against Mexicans and the poor. They begged Reies for help. He and the Heralds did what they could.

The community's first child was born to María and Reies on April 18, 1956. After Reies delivered his daughter, he noticed a rattlesnake in the room. He quickly killed the viper, interpreting its presence and death as having rid the world of evil. Because that moment seemed so cosmically fraught, Reies decided to name his daughter Ira de Alá (Ire of Allah), invoking the Qur'an's curse for those who refused to believe in God. God was extremely angry with both the church and state. Cursed and reviled they would be by his daughter! As Ira de Alá grew older, she disliked the name, became known as Iradela, and eventually simply as Della or Lita. Reies insisted on serving as the midwife for two of his children's births, despite plenty of experienced midwives nearby María explained: "He was so jealous he didn't want [anyone] seeing you or touching" you down there. For that reason, "I never saw a doctor," eventually resulting in significant medical problems after their divorce.[9]

The bliss the Heralds of Peace enjoyed those initial months soon faded. "At first it went well," Reies explained, "but they didn't like us there, the Anglos up in Casa Grande and over in Toltec."[10] They and others started referring to the community as a pack of dirty Mexicans "living like rats" in a "gypsy camp." Their rhetoric became intensively more derogatory, accusing them of being "Communists," with a capital C, hoping thus to incite state and vigilante violence.[11]

Reies adamantly believed, a belief he articulated to the end of his life, that "the [public] educational system was a lot of lies," organized to twist the minds of ethnic Mexicans, teaching them that their race and culture were inferior, that their history was one of defeat, preparing them only for unskilled manual labor, and destroying the religious lives of families through the secular and individualist ideals they taught. Thus, the first above-ground edifice they built at the Valley of Peace was a one-room school. There the children were instructed collectively, supplemented by parents at home. "I taught them the basics," recalled María Escobar, "starting from the abc's to help them to learn to read." David Tijerina remembered that his father and mother "taught me to read and write . . . by the time I got to school I already knew how to read and write both in Spanish and English." Daily, Reies would sit with his eldest son, David, give him something to read, and then quiz him on what he had learned. "I learned history [from] the Bible," he said. His mother María loved music and taught her children religious hymns, which Reies sometimes accompanied on his guitar.[12]

The home schooling of their children became one of the first challenges the commune faced with the Pinal County School Board. It demanded that the children attend public school; the nearest was three miles away and could only be reached by bus. The elders protested that they dared not send their children to this school by bus because a neighbor's eight-year-old daughter was raped and left for dead while she waited for the transport. The police failed to investigate. The rapist was never identified, though the Heralds of Peace named a group of Anglo teenage boys who had boasted of the crime. The Heralds doggedly resisted sending their children to public school, explained David Tijerina, because his father thought that "the educational system was a lot of lies." They protested all the way to the Arizona State Board of Education but failed to get the exception they sought. They ignored the school board, continued home schooling, and waited to see what the state, "the beast" would do.[13]

The residents of the Valley of Peace were devout Christians, yet nearby white Protestant congregations "never invited us to their churches," but its members insisted on forcing public instruction on their children by Anglo, monolingual English-speaking teachers. What had they done to provoke such animosity? "Why do they dislike us?" Reies repeatedly asked. "From where does the great hate of these magnates come?" Was it their race, their poverty, their belief in God? In the end, rather than allowing tender, uncorrupted young minds to be twisted by public schools, they started planning to move the children from the Valley of Peace.[14]

Next, the same Anglo teenage boys accused of raping one of the commune's girls began vandalizing their homes. Mounted on horseback and brandishing rifles, they began riding their horses over Herald homes at galloping speed, undermining the integrity of their roofs and leaving the children frightened. Reies and his family were in their subterranean shelter one night eating, when suddenly the roof started caving in. The young men were riding their horses over his and other houses. One by one their roofs were caving in. At first the commune's residents ignored the behavior as juvenile pranks. Then, one day, as the men, women, and older children returned from picking cotton, they discovered that two of their above-ground wood buildings had been reduced to ashes and that the roofs of two subterranean houses had been completely torn off.

Reies, Manuel Mata, and Rodolfo Mares traveled to Casa Grande, Arizona, to complain to Sheriff Lawrence White. At first, he appeared sympathetic and interested in hearing the details. But when the Heralds of Peace identified the brands on the horses the teenagers were riding, the sheriff's tone radically shifted. His eyes glazed over. He promised an investigation. Nothing occurred. Nor did Dan Pelton, the local agent of the Federal Bureau of Investigation, want to get involved. It was outside of his jurisdiction.

Shortly after Ira de Alá's birth, toward the end of April 1956, Reies received an invitation to evangelize among a group of Mexican farmworkers in Visalia, California, at the very place Luis and María Moreno, two Heralds of Peace, had first heard Reies years earlier. He routinely accepted such requests because at the end of a revival, the congregants would take up a monetary collection to compensate the preacher. Reies and his Heralds certainly needed the cash. Reies went accompanied by Manuel Mata and Rodolfo Mares. While evangelizing in Visalia, word reached Reies that a springtime monsoon had flooded the Valley of Peace and inundated several homes. Reies's home was underwater, and his wife and children were living huddled under a tarp as their only cover. The news extremely upset Reies. Hundreds of chaotic thoughts raced through his mind that night. About his family without a home, without food, without money, about the other families at the Valley of Peace similarly suffering. It was at that moment that he started to question his life's mission. He reviewed the hardships and failures the commune had faced. He nervously paced. He fervently prayed. He examined his conscience, repenting for previous mistakes. "When will I encounter the mission of my life?" he asked God.[15]

In this tormented state of mind and body, Reies had a dream. For the rest of his life, he called it as his "Grand Vision," or his "Visalia Dream," repeating its narrative thread over and over again to anyone willing to listen, eventually claiming it authorized him as a prophet, his subsequent actions fully ordained by God. In the introduction to this book, Reies describes his dream to Coretta Scott King on May 6, 1968, while offering his condolences to the widow on King's death. For brevity here, I recount the most important elements of the dream, pointing you to the fuller version, if a fuller re-reading is of interest.

On that April night in Visalia, three angels descended from heaven and lifted Reies onto a cloud, transporting him through the heavens until they landed in a dark forest. As Reies explored the forest he stumbled into a cemetery full of frozen horses. One of them instantly came to life. It was a beautiful white horse, which he and the angels mounted and instantly took flight anew, finally landing in a celestial kingdom where Reies was greeted by cheering crowds. There he met "the One," whom he identified as God dressed in long white robes, who gave him a key that would help him solve the world's woes. Finally, God asked Reies to sit on the divine throne. As he did, he was instantly back in Visalia, confused but certain that he had experienced "a revelation, a vision, or a super dream." Reies' descriptions of God, his throne, and white robes, the three angels, and the white horse, the celestial kingdom all closely resembling heaven and the New Jerusalem described in the Book of Revelation. Reies recalled Numbers 12:6 "I the Lord will make myself known unto him in a vision and will speak unto him in a dream."[16]

In the days that followed, Reies said that finally he felt satisfied and safe, seeing things differently, with a depth of understanding he had never felt before. "In my breast I felt vividly the weight of the mission I had just been given. Now my life had a direction and the assurance that I was not alone." Reies constantly affirmed that he believed everything the three angels had shown him.[17]

Reies and his companions returned to the Valley of Peace the next morning. On reaching the commune, he recounted his dream, confessing that he did not fully understand its meaning yet but was confident that God would soon reveal it to him by interrogating his past. He recalled that he had preached in northern New Mexico, which in colonial times enjoyed the status of a kingdom. He had evangelized in Tierra Amarilla, located in the northern-central part of this state in 1945, 1951, and 1952, a land of dense forests. Was this the kingdom and the forests of his dream?

It was early May 1956 by now, and of most immediate communal concern was earning money to feed their brood. They were certain that their old employer Bill Byers would hire them again to plant, tend, and harvest his tomato fields in Fruita, Colorado. Some of the commune's families packed what they needed and indeed Byers hired them. As June approached Reies's Grand Vision came into sharper focus, certain that God was directing him to New Mexico. With five of his valiant ones, he traveled to Tierra Amarilla, leaving behind the older men, women, and children toiling on Byers's farm.

In New Mexico they first visited the home of Zebedeo Martínez in Moreno, where they met the residents living nearby. They all told the valiant ones the history of land tenure in the region, how they had lost their *ejidos*, the communal portions of their merced lands, along with their *propios* (private garden plots), and *sitios* (house lots), which they had been granted by the kings of Spain and the Mexican state as compensation for colonizing this marginal area of the empire considered dangerous and indomitable. The next day Reies and his men went to the villages of Chama, Tierra Amarilla, and Ensenada. In the home of Cristino Lovato, they heard from more elderly men, all of them Hermanos Penitentes, or members of the Confraternity of Our Lord Jesus Nazarene. Their stories were riveting. They were full of "blood, sweat and tears," recounting the long and violent history of how the mercedes and ejidos had been stolen and how personally they had been transformed from honorable landed men of the lower nobility into landless peasants, working as itinerant farmworkers, often for the very Anglos who had swindled them of their lands. Reies was deeply moved by what he heard. He felt as though "my heart had been stabbed." These people clearly had a "holy, just, and sacred cause" that required a savior.[18]

"Do you want justice?" Reies asked. "For more than a hundred years we have been seeking it from Washington and heaven, but no one has yet brought us justice," they replied. Reies later would note in his diary that as he listened, he could see how fearful and intimidated these villagers were of the Anglo power structure. If he was to succeed in helping them, he first had to uproot the "psychic conditioning" of oppression and fear that had been deeply engrained in their personalities over the course of a hundred years. Reies explained that he was a preacher and, until then, only a man of the Bible. But he was willing to study the documents along with the history and law pertaining to their lands to see if he could help. But first they had to help themselves, recuperating their valor, their honor, and sense of self-worth taken from them by Anglos. He promised the villagers that he would soon travel to Mexico to conduct the requisite research but that his most immediate concern was to return to those he left working in Fruita, and then to the few still residing at the Valley of Peace.

Reies was by now was starting to understand the challenge God had given him in the Visalia Dream. The kingdom literally was the Kingdom of New Mexico, the forests were those of northern New Mexico, the frozen horses were the land grants (mercedes), the key God had handed him were treaties and laws that governed land ownership, and the man who sat on God's throne in heaven, well, that was him: Reies the messiah.

By September 1956 all those who still considered themselves Heralds of Peace were back together at their Arizona commune. Some of the married couples were disgusted by Reies's proposal that the commune's men take multiple wives, as the elders in the Church of Jesus Christ Latter-Day Saints (Mormons) did. Hell no! Or so opined those who had been living in monogamous marriages, eschewing adultery, never daring even to lust for others in their hearts. Reies's proposal led Luis and María Moreno, along with their extended family of eight, to pack their goods and return to California, feeling extremely betrayed. They had sold everything they had to join the Valley of Peace, which amounted to the $2,100 they contributed to the community's collective pot. In 2015, I reached several of members of Luis and María Moreno's family by telephone, thinking I would hear rhapsodic memories of their blissful communal years. They all adamantly cursed Reies Tijerina. They were particularly still angry over events that had occurred half a century past because Tijerina had personally pocketed the profits from the resale of the commune's land, refusing to return the Moreno family's substantial initial investment or the entire worth of their property.[19]

In January 1963, a few years after the Valley of Peace was abandoned and sold, Simón Serna, one of the men Reies had long considered his most valiant ones, who signed his letters as "the Cyclone of God," wrote him. Serna had repeatedly loaned Reies money, had assisted him in criminal acts, had committed perjury corroborating Reies's version of events, and still deeply hoped that the Valley of Peace would be rebuilt and restored. Serna finally had had enough. He insisted that he had never succumbed to "the beast" and that he too had been "speaking with the lord through visions," scolding Reies, begging that "for the love of your children turn away from your path of evil." In stinging fundamentalist rhetoric, he urged Reies to obey God's commandments, to forsake concupiscence, to abandon the "carnal knowledge in which the devil ensnared you." He ordered Reies to treat others as God commanded, with honesty and love. "You are no Moses who should say that God orders your acts . . . hypocrite, child of the devil, enemy of God's justice, you who never cease to pervert the righteous paths to God; if you do not repent, his mighty hand will land on you."[20]

With all the conflict that erupted at the Valley of Peace, when it was learned that several of the valiant men had sexually molested Rose Tijerina at the Valley of Peace, including Reies himself, the commune's declensions started. Reies was ready to move on and forget all that had occurred in

Arizona. As he interpreted God's will, his grand dream was a divine sign that he should devote his energies to the recuperation of the Spanish and Mexican land grants in New Mexico and the Greater Southwest. From Arizona, Reies and his family headed back to the clan's San Antonio home, where María and children sheltered while Reies undertook his research on land grants in Mexico City. Before crossing into Mexico, Reies told his brothers Anselmo and Margarito that he was abandoning his vocation as a Pentecostal evangelist for more secular political pursuits. "As of today I'm going to fight for the land of my people. I'm going to strongly challenge the Anglos who robbed us." While his dream certainly quickened his new secular political focus, this decision had been percolating for some time. As a young preacher Reies had met several strangers who admired his oratorical skill and urged him to put it to better use. He recalled an elderly Anglo Methodist who offered him a ride across town and eventually a steak dinner. As they chatted about world affairs, the man said that he had no use for religion. He urged Reies to "study history and law and do more to really help" his people. Ethnic Mexicans in the American Southwest already had too many priests and preachers. What they needed were honest politicians committed to bettering lives. Reies had by then realized that "people are tired of empty religious ceremonies ... [because preachers] are no longer like the hard-feeling, warm-teaching religious leaders of old." Beginning with his expulsion from the Assemblies of God in 1950, Reies had slowly concluded "that there's no mercy in churches, no justice in religious people."[21]

The first step Reies took to address the material needs of Mexican Americans was his research pilgrimage to Mexico City, presenting himself to God as a new person by shaving off all the hair on his head. Reies reached Mexico City late in September 1956. He spent the next three months visiting libraries, archives, and historical sites essential for his education on Mexico's past. He went first to the town of Guadalupe, by then a Mexico City suburb, where in 1531 the Virgin of Guadalupe, the patroness of Mexico, appeared to an Indian named Juan Diego, and where an immense shrine stood honoring her. He prayed there. On February 2, 1848, the Treaty of Guadalupe Hidalgo, which ended the war the United States waged against Mexico, was signed here, spelling out the property rights of those Mexicans who remained on the ancestral lands the United States annexed. Always a propagandist, always an impassioned promoter, Reies sought allies among the city's clergy, politicians, students, and journalists hoping to bring attention to the "forgotten children" Mexico had abandoned and left despoiled of their lands in New Mexico. His publicity campaign worked. Soon Mexican journalists began writing exposés on the poverty and misery of these abandoned children crying for Mexico's help.

He spent days in Mexico's national archives and libraries, learning the country's history, poring over the Laws of the Indies, by which Spain had governed its global empire. He immersed himself in the specifics of the Treaty of Guadalupe Hidalgo. Three times he visited the ancient city of Teotihuacán, ascending the Pyramids of the Sun and Moon to commune with the spirits. There, at the summit of these pyramids, the ancient Teotihuacanos believed that "gods and men unite." Reies felt that presence as "the force of fire and lightening strengthening my determination and valor. . . . I felt the need to return to the old men in New Mexico, to unite them into an enormous force, expunging the fear of Anglos the schools had taught them."[22]

Reies believed that the greatest weakness of American culture was its excessive individualism and celebration of personal freedom. In a well-ordered Christian society, such liberty was unimaginable. Discipline and patriarchal authority were the pillars of familial governance. This was how the families at the Valley were supposed to live. Sermons did not always square with private life, at least for Reies, the self-proclaimed Moses.

By early January 1957, Reies was preparing to return to New Mexico with what he had learned and collected for the land grant heirs. The devil tempted him anew. His flesh weakened, as it had before. In Mexico City he was hosted by Santana Vergara, a fellow Pentecostal preacher. Daily, Reies was guided by María Luisa Barrajas, Vergara's niece, taking him through the sprawling ancient center of the Aztec Empire. Eventually they became intimate. Daily, Reies confessed that he felt as if his heart was being ripped apart by two opposing forces, his love for the oppressed people of New Mexico and his lust for María Luisa, a beautiful young mestiza. Tellingly, María Escobar was not mentioned as a factor in this struggle. Of course, Reies prayed, or so he said. Of course, he tried to purge the young woman from his mind and body. Nothing helped. He left Mexico City promising

María Luisa that he would soon return from the United States to unite again. Had he cooled his passion? Apparently not. Much like his epistolary romance with Vicki Rivera at LABI, he kept exchanging passionate love letters with María Luisa, which María Escobar's commune sisters unsuspectingly retrieved from the post office box the Valle de Paz rented for its mail. They brought the letters to María's attention. She read them. She was devastated. Among other news in the letters, María Luisa had given birth to a baby about whom she crowed "looked so much like Reies." The particularly hurtful sting was that Reies long had accused María of not having been a virgin when they married.[23] How would a young man of God with putatively no sexual experience know how to evaluate such a thing? But he did as he hypocritically proclaimed God's justice and judgment about all sins carnal and venal that corrupted humanity's relationship to the creator.[24]

María confronted Reies about the letters from his mistress in Mexico City. Reies, unaccustomed to being challenged by his wife, flew into a violent rage. As Rose and David Tijerina describe the fight, Reies "wanted to kill her [María] . . . and that's when he tried to burn her face on the stove. David and I were . . . pulling my dad and crying and crying please not to do that. . . . He finally let her go." María packed a suitcase and left her children wailing that night. She did not get far before her anger cooled and realized that Reies was really an absent father. How would her children survive without her? She returned but with a defiant attitude, asking herself, "What am I doing? My children are not in school, my husband tells me he's looking for god but has a mistress."[25]

Rose recalled that as a seven-year-old child she clearly sensed that "my mom feared my father. She never had a voice. Whatever my father said, that was it. No arguments." Whenever the Heralds of Peace gathered as a collective to discuss important matters, if María expressed an opinion, Reies would quickly snap, "Who asked you?" Later came the wallop.[26] Reies physically abused María, something that apparently happened with some frequency at the Valley of Peace. After María read the love letters, "my mom changed. She started talking back to my dad," said Rose.[27]

In 1964, shortly after Reies and María Escobar divorced, María Luisa reentered the picture. Reies "had fallen in love" again. "She came to Albuquerque to marry [me] and I just couldn't go through it," Reies explained. Though he was very upset, even feeling quite ill about the matter, "I took her back, [but] I couldn't marry her."[28] He needed a local wife from a land grant family to cement his credibility as a local New Mexican. Many land grant heirs feared the fast-talking, Texas Protestant outsider who had no real blood ties to New Mexico's land grants.

Reies was back with his extended family in San Antonio by early January 1957. Together they returned to the Valley of Peace, where he found what remained of the commune in utter disarray. Conflicts with Anglo neighbors and nearby constabularies had intensified. The Pinal County Board of Education continued to prohibit home schooling, threatening to jail any household head who did not comply. "We had left our work, we had sacrificed our relatives, and we separated ourselves from the world to find peace." No longer was there much peace. The commune resembled a poorly defended war zone, even a concentration camp, recalled Rose.

The land on which the Valley of Peace was built had been purchased by pooling the personal assets of the commune's members. They bought it for $8.75 an acre, because it did not have a water source for irrigation. Unbeknown to the valiant ones, Paolo Soleri, the internationally renowned Italian modernist architect, rapidly monetized their barren land. Early in 1956, Soleri moved to Scottsdale, searching for a site on which to build a futuristic city that would test his ideas about *arcology*, the marriage between architecture and ecology, to maximize the communal use of resources while minimizing waste. Ironically, this was exactly how the penniless Heralds of Peace were living. Soleri dubbed his utopian idea "Cosanti" (*cosa*=thing, *anti*=anti) or a minimalist place that prohibited the accumulations of things. Soleri's real estate search set off a speculatory real estate frenzy. The Valley of Peace was located right in the middle of Soleri's coveted terrain. Locals quickly calculated how much they stood to profit from the construction of Cosanti. Instantly, land that a year earlier had sold for $8.75 an acre, was commanding $1,200. The estimated value of the Valley of Peace jumped from $1,400 to $192,000. This explains, in part, at least economically, why the local Anglos were intent on driving the "garbage rats" out by any means possible, and perhaps why Reies eventually decided to move on.[29]

A few of the valiant ones remained at the commune to guard the property. The rest boarded a rickety old school bus they purchased in February 1957 and headed to New Mexico. They got as far as Gobernador, in the state's northwest corner, where their bus got stuck in huge snow drifts. With children crying from hunger, the adult men ventured out. By chance Reies and his brother Margarito stumbled onto Manuel Trujillo's farm. He offered them food, help dislodging their bus, and temporary shelter.[30] Reies and Manuel Trujillo soon were fast friends. Eventually he agreed to take Reies to Tierra Amarilla, to reconnect with the land grant heirs Reies first met in June 1956: Cristino Lovato, Enetro Velásquez, José María Martínez (aka Marión). Reies came prepared with the fruits of his Mexican research: a copy of the Spanish Laws of the Indies, the Treaty of Guadalupe Hidalgo, American and Mexican laws governing land, and some of the successful legal briefs Mexican lawyers had used to recoup ejidos.

Cristino Lovato and Reies also became close, the former elaborating more specifically the circumstances of their community's land loss. Reies later addressed another gathering Lovato arranged, explaining in unvarnished terms the legal maneuvers Anglos had used to rob them of their land. If the residents of Tierra Amarilla were to win back their mercedes, they had to organize themselves. They had to unite with all the other dispossessed grantees in common cause. "If we unite all the mercedes, we too will become the giants." They would have to overturn the racist power structure that held Hispanos in frightened submission.[31] Still struggling to feed and shelter their families, in early March 1957, Reies, Margarito, and Zebedeo Valdez returned to the Valley of Peace to work planting cotton that spring, leaving their families behind in New Mexico.

Frank Shedd arrived at the Pinal County, Arizona, sheriff's office to report a crime at about 8 p.m. on March 18, 1957. "Sometime during the night thieves went to the feed pens on the Rodney De Lange Ranch and took four tires and wheels off one feed trailer and two wheels and tires off another. The tires were Gates and Firestone all mounted on eight-hole hub wheels, all painted black." Officers Davis and Kinard immediately investigated. What they found was a distinctive mud-grip tire track from the left rear wheel of a truck that appeared to have hauled the goods. The tracks led to the Valley of Peace, to a truck Margarito Tijerina was working on when the police arrived. It had a left rear tire wheel with the distinctive tread reported as likely to have hauled the stolen goods. Sevedeo Martínez was in the truck's driver's seat. Reies was standing near the truck that seemed to have transported the goods. When the officers looked in a dry well nearby, they found Shedd's tires and wheels. All three men were arrested and booked at the Casa Grande jail on March 19. The police returned the next day with a search warrant and found a large cache—a first aid kit, batteries, tarps, five hats, picks, axes, rope, and much more—most marked "Property of the United States Forest Service." All three protested arrest and claimed innocence. Their accuser, Frank Shedd, hated the Mexicans at the Valley of Peace. His son had torched their school and vandalized their subterranean homes, yet the police refused to investigate these crimes. This was simply another malicious accusation to harass the valiant ones. Whether or not this was true, whether the tires were Shedds', whether the Forest Service property was stolen or scavenged, police records contained no substantive proof. What records did show was that Reies, Sevedeo, and Margarito spent ninety days in jail. Lacking evidence, the charges against Reies and Sevedeo were dismissed. Less than a month later, on April 5, 1957, Reies was charged with illegal possession of Forest Service property. Margarito had remained jailed the entire time because he had violated his parole terms for the murder of Ruperto Rodriguez during a drunken barroom brawl in Kokomo, Indiana in 1947.[32]

Reies posted bail. Margarito remained behind bars awaiting extradition to Indiana to serve the rest of his two-to-twenty-one-year murder sentence. Late on the afternoon of July 7, 1957, G. V. Mecham entered the Pinal County jail to report that one of his "Indian" workers, a man named Gerald Kisto, who had just been released earlier that day, told him that prisoners were planning to escape that night. Sheriff William Ballard amassed additional forces and laid in wait. Sure enough, as soon as it got dark, Norman Wasiikowski, his wife La Verne, John Reina, and Margarito Tijerina sawed off the bars of their cells, crawled out of jail, and were instantly caught. Nearby sat Reies Tijerina in a dark-colored 1949 Ford sedan, ready to whisk Margarito to freedom. Reies was arrested and posted a $1,000 bail bond. When Reies's trial started, his attorney informed him that the Wasiikowskis had been offered a plea deal. If they testified against Reies, falsely claiming that he was the lone mastermind of the jailbreak, charges against them would be dropped. On his attorney's advice, Reies fled, aware that there were many Anglos who wanted to kill him. Rudolfo Mares, one of the last valiant residents at the Valley of Peace, also urged flight, otherwise Reies's newly found cause recuperating land grants would never advance. He was likely to spend several years in jail for the crime.

Reies fled and virtually disappeared.[33] Thus began his fugitive saga, one he boastfully cherished. For now, he faced challenges akin to those Moses had suffered as he fled the Pharaoh's wrath after he tried to stop an Egyptian from publicly beating and murdering Hebrews (Exo. 2:11–22). In Reies's 1978 autobiography, *Mi lucha por la tierra*, he describes his life on the run, the challenges he encountered, the adversities he survived, dodging local and federal authorities for seven years, which he described in a very long, 306-page chapter titled "My Fugitive Life," mapping closely the challenges Moses faced in Exodus. Toughened by these obstacles God had placed before him, Reies emerged ready to struggle to help Hispanos regain their lost lands.

In the next chapter we turn to Reies Tijerina's land grant activism, no longer an evangelist focused on God's commandments but a secular activist who still used his religious theology to judge human treaties and laws with the same restorationist ideals that had structured his sermons. Only now he focused on recuperating land grants and returning to an idyllic time before American imperial expansion.

CHAPTER 8

Restoring New Mexico's Land Grants

REIES TIJERINA RETURNED FROM Mexico with the research he thought necessary to restore the ancestral lands Hispanos had lost in northern New Mexico and the Southwest in the first half of the twentieth century. He concluded that the silver key God had given him in his Visalia Dream was the laws men had created, and thus he returned with the Spanish Laws of the Indies, Mexico's colonization laws, the Treaty of Guadalupe-Hidalgo, and the Constitutions of the United States and of the State of New Mexico. Like the Bible he could quote precisely without prompts, he was now prepared to litigate land rights with the commandments of men, citing law, title, and paragraph numbers without pause. He had learned that after independence much of Spanish America experienced high levels of land alienation that had resulted in agrarian revolts. Among the grievances Mexico's revolution was fought over between 1910 and 1917 was the land concentration that had alienated the ejidos, the village commons that many communities had previously customarily owned. Written into Mexico's 1917 constitution to address this grievance, was the expropriation and redistribution of large, landed estates. Between 1917 and 1945, Mexico redistributed a total of 75.6 million acres dedicated as ejidos, more than half, 45.8 million acres, awarded during Lázaro Cardenas's presidential administration between 1934 and 1940.[1]

With this history and widely hailed model of Mexican land reform in mind, Reies returned to New Mexico with this as his strategy. The original town and community land grants consisted of three parts: sitios, private homes plots; propios, household garden lots; and the *comunes*, the village commons, also known as *tierras realengas*, royal lands that reverted to the sovereign if say gold or some other previous minerals or gems were discovered on them. Reies understood that multigenerational conveyances had transformed sitios and propios into private property that would be difficult to contest. Litigating ownership and use of the commons was the only viable legal strategy possible for the recuperation of these large portions of Spanish and Mexican land grants.

At the end of the Mexican War in 1848, the United States as the conquering sovereign appropriated the commons, transferring their governance to the US Forest Service in 1905. With the creation of the Kit Carson and Santa Fe National Forests in 1908 and 1915 respectively, 60 percent of northern New Mexico's water resources, grazing lands, and forests were placed under Forest Service management. From the Forest Service's point of view, their charge was to oversee these land from a national perspective, "for the public good—for the old lady in Chicago and the businessman in California and the farmer in Iowa—even if it mean[t] limiting their [Hispano] use of the land."[2] Northern New Mexico's Hispanos quickly came to see the Forest Rangers as blood brothers of the Texas Rangers, as an army of occupation that enforced laws on game hunting, animal grazing, and timber and firewood harvesting through the sale of use permits that routinely, as one Hispano put it, "fatten the white man while the brown man starves."[3] Overt and covert forms of racism were endemic to the agency's decisions. The Anglo Rangers "treated us like we were stupid and lazy, like we didn't know anything," said one Hispano. Ranger Allen Peter pretty much confirmed this, marveling: "This is one of the most beautiful of places I have ever seen, how unfortunate that it is populated by the most backward, dirty and brutish people I have ever come across."[4]

In their supervision of these lands, the Forest Service emphasized the capitalization and marketing of natural resources to large corporate interests that were well versed in the nuances of lease contracts, the mobilization of labor, and the massive transport infrastructure necessary to move tons of timber and wool. Small Hispano farmers engaged in subsistence agriculture had neither the money, the expertise, nor command of the English language to participate in these large-scale resource extractions. Unable even to pay for the use permits they needed to feed their animals, to gather firewood, to hunt and fish, gradually they were forced into wage labor to survive, or they simply migrated to Albuquerque, Santa Fe, or Los Alamos to seek work, abandoning the private portions of their increasingly morselized mercedes. By 1960 the transformation of village commons into national forests had produced widespread poverty, malnutrition, hunger, and hopelessness in northern New Mexico and southern Colorado.

Presenting himself as a messianic Moses leading the oppressed Israelites to the promised land, Reies set out to recoup the village commons in personal and community mercedes, which he saw as essential to the economic independence of Hispanos. Recall that the restorationist gospel Tijerina preached from 1946 to 1958 emphasized a return to ancient ways, to ancient governance, to older, purer ways of existence before corruption. The locals were thus primed to understand his rhetoric; indeed, they wanted to return to the older ways of life they remembered so fondly.

Reies Tijerina began championing the land grant cause, fearlessly, loquaciously, as if he were a well-studied expert on land tenure. What he was, was mainly charismatic. His message was compelling, delivered in a language the local villagers understood—Spanish—and with simple stories of the villains and bandits who had robbed them of their daily bread. Tijerina thought of himself as having a moral and ethical compass that always pointed true north in all he said and did. Truth be told, the compass gyrated erratically and unpredictably, morally and ethically, or so confidants, critics, and kin alike recalled. Tijerina was a poor man who had lived by his wits, in poverty like his savior Jesus Christ, but ultimately dependent on the toil of his wife and children for whom he was rarely present, but nevertheless taxed them so that he could follow his dreams. They did not relish his impulsive, dream-ignited crusades. To them they meant itinerancy, all too often hunger, and homelessness under God's heaven and stars. Now he had dedicated himself to a new vision, with wife and kids in tow. He was completely focused on the recuperation of the mercedes, yet with meager resources, like it or not, his family would surely pay economically and psychologically.

In the speeches Reies began delivering first throughout northern New Mexico and southern Colorado, and eventually across the Southwest from Texas to California between 1963 to 1969, he was still very much a Pentecostal preacher. He mixed references on broken treaties, and the US government's failure to protect Mexican American rights as stipulated in the Treaty of Guadalupe-Hidalgo, with biblical exhortations of judgment and justice. The sermonic formulas and revival rituals he had employed as an evangelist continued, but they no longer focused on sin and apocalypses but rather on land alienation and its economic, social, and cultural implications, which undoubtedly would require periods of great tribulation and cataclysmic showdowns. His message toughed raw nerves. He began gathering increasingly large and animated crowds, something he had never achieved preaching only the word of God. His audiences began imagining, if only momentarily, how their lives would change with their lands restored. Some northern New Mexicans even fell to their "knees to kiss his feet, proclaiming him the messiah." Here was the hero of ancient legend, predicting that a man of strength and courage would arrive to drive the invaders out "crying." Foreigners from the east had ridiculed Hispanos long enough, "laughing" at them and forcibly taking their lands.[5]

Reies Tijerina started meeting new people, incessantly speaking to anyone willing to listen, simultaneously preparing to incorporate the Alianza Federal de Mercedes (the Federal Alliance of Land Grant Heirs). In 1963 he sought an attorney's help to review his application papers and to file them. That is how he first met the district attorney of Santa Fe, Rio Arriba, and Los Alamos Counties, Alfonso Sánchez. Reies boasted that the Alianza would "unite the 'raza' against the Anglo and take our land back by force if necessary." Sánchez remembered their first meeting vividly. "I immediately stopped him and asked him if he knew . . . I was the District Attorney . . . if he did anything or threaten anybody to take their land by for[ce] that I would be the one to have to stop him." Sánchez refused to serve as Reies's attorney, and he immediately started investigating who this Reies López Tijerina really was.[6]

The Alianza Federal de Mercedes incorporated as a 501(c)3 nonprofit organization, listing its headquarters in Albuquerque at 1010 Third Street NW, a two-story building it first rented with offices and a large meeting room on the first floor, living quarters on the second, and a multi-use basement. In 1965 the Alliance gained ownership of the building clandestinely, through a trust registered as the Caballeros de Las Indias. The trust swapped the Arizona Valley of Peace parcel for the building, a transaction that enraged several former Heralds of Peace who expected their substantial monetary investments in that land returned from its sale.[7]

The Alliance's stated goal was the recuperation of the "royal land grants" lost after American annexation of Mexico's northern states. They chose to form an alianza, a mutual aid society, because it was an associational form well known and highly respected among the area's Hispanos. Such societies evolved out of Catholic Church confraternities as locally governed and self-funded, of which many existed throughout the Southwest. The Alianza mottos proclaim: *La Tierra es Nuestra Herencia—Y la Justicia Nuestro Credo* (The Land is Our Heritage—Justice Is Our Creed), and that the Alianza was *La Voz de la Justicia* (The Voice of Justice) for Hispanos.[8]

The Alianza's first meeting was held at its Albuquerque headquarters on February 2, 1963, the anniversary of the signing of the Treaty of Guadalupe Hidalgo that ended the Mexican War in 1848. Reies opened the meeting reciting the history of the loss of the royal land grants and how he planned to petition the United States government for their return. To serve as the symbol of their unity he proposed adopting the rainbow as the Alianza's logo, explaining how the rainbow first appeared after the great flood that Noah survived. "It is a symbol of a new social order given by God that demonstrated the promise and pact between man and God. Each color represents a virtue and the spirit of God." On the wall of the Alianza's meeting room was a large mural (five feet by eight feet) depicting the birth of Indo-Hispanos through marriages between Spaniards and Indians made legal in 1514, when the Spanish Crown authorized such unions. Depicted on the mural, too, was a large eagle-like bird, the Secretario Reies remembered perched next to God's throne in his Grand Dream.

Officers were elected. Reies was named the founder and president, Eunice Myrick secretary, and María Escobar the secretary's assistant and scribe. Reies read the Protocol and Article VIII of the Treaty of Guadalupe Hidalgo:

> Mexicans now established in territories previously belonging to Mexico ... shall be free to continue where they now reside ... retaining the property which they possess ... without their being subjected ... to any

contribution, tax, or charge whatever. [P]roperty of every kind, now belonging to Mexicans ... shall be inviolably respected. The present owners, the heirs of these, and all Mexicans who may hereafter acquire said property by contract, shall enjoy with respect to it guarantees equally ample as if the same belonged to citizens of the United States.[9]

Present were representatives from sixteen mercedes reales located in New Mexico, Colorado, and Texas, who expressed interest in cooperating with the Alianza to forge a united front for the restoration of their lands. Eddie Chávez, who would become one of the organization's most faithful members, addressed one of the issues that concerned some of those gathered, affirming that the Alianza was "not an anti-American organization" nor was it founded on communist ideals.[10]

The Federal Alliance of Land Grant Heirs held it first public convention in Albuquerque on September 21, 1963. Copies of its "National Constitution" were circulated, outlining the role and duties of its officers, membership rules, and dues (two dollars monthly). The constitution vowed to "protect and defend all the rights and privileges that the [Spanish] Crown and the Treaty of Guadalupe Hidalgo establish for the protection of royal heirs" (Article IV). Any person who subverted these would be considered a "traitor." The Alliance was necessary because of the "shameful misery" grant heirs were suffering. "Justice for the oppressed was needed; judgement for the oppressors; mercy for the forgotten; and truth for all." Should any member of the Alliance be "suspected of treason" or of "communist affiliation," their membership would be revoked.[11]

In the press releases, newspaper columns, and speeches Tijerina gave in subsequent months, he reminded New Mexicans that the kings of Spain had awarded "sacred, royal land grants" to the colonists who had ventured into New Spain's northern frontier, along with aristocratic titles as hidalgos, as men of honor, with full civic standing as vecinos, free property owners. If this honor and aristocracy was to be restored, they had "to wake up and stand up straight demanding what is yours." For strategic reasons, Reies did not mention the forced indigenous tributary service included in these original royal charters of incorporation. He was trying to forge a new racial identity, one born of racial mixing between "Indios" and "Hispanos," what he called "Indo-Hispano," which did not gain wide currency in Alianza messaging until late in 1965. He assured his auditors the government considered Mexican Americans loyal citizens who had fought in its many wars and deeply respected the constitution.[12] The US government was very interested in solving the land grant problem and "was trying to remedy what it should have done one hundred years ago." Reies assured Alianza members that very soon the federal government and courts would "make good on all of our rights," though he knew nothing of the sort.[13]

Figure 1. Birth of the Indo-Hispano. This is a photograph of the mural that initially graced the main meeting room of the Alianza Federal de Mercedes headquarters in Albuquerque, New Mexico, in 1964. It was destroyed by fire in 1995. Painted by Duke Aragón, the top is adorned with a rainbow and the words Justice/*Justicia*; the tents representing the future. The bottom central quadrant depicts the marriage of a Spaniard and an Indigenous woman; the bride flanked by Native chiefs, the soldier by a priest and soldiers. Right above the marrying couple is a large serpent being killed by an African eagle-like bird that Tijerina referred to as *Secretario*, which had the capacity to kill poisonous snakes. In Reies's Visalia "super dream," he claimed that he had been given this bird by God to help him rule over the terrestrial theocracy he was empowered to form. The Secretario bird appears on many publications of the Alianza almost as a logo. Courtesy Tijerina Pictorial Collection, Special Collections and Center for Southwest Research, University of New Mexico Libraries.

Figure 2. Birth Certificate of the Indo-Hispano. Reies López Tijerina began referring to Indigenous and Hispanic residents of the American Southwest as "Indo-Hispanos" around 1965 as a way of politically unifying two distinct ethnic groups, asserting that their mutual interests were old, going back to colonial times, seemingly erasing the history of ethnic conflict. This birth certificate, issued by the Alianza Federal de Mercedes, announces that Spain's monarchs in 1514 sanctioned marriages between Spaniards and Indians. From such unions the "Indo-Hispanos" were born. In New Spain the children of such mixed marriages are more commonly known as mestizos. Courtesy Tijerina Pictorial Collection, Special Collections and Center for Southwest Research, University of New Mexico Libraries.

Membership grew rapidly. By the end of 1963, the Alianza had registered five thousand members; by the end of 1964 it claimed fifty thousand. In a moment of exaggeration, in 1965 Tijerina claimed the Alianza had eighty thousand members, something membership rolls and bank accounts simply do not confirm.[14] A more accurate tally shows that the Alianza had roughly fifteen thousand members, five thousand from New Mexico, the rest from throughout the country.

Tijerina significantly rethought his diagnosis of the causes and consequences of ethnic Mexican poverty. In the 1950s Reies deemed impoverishment the result of divine design and humanity's failure to obey God's laws commanding Christian charity. By the mid-1960s his analysis was economic and structural, but still morally moored. Poverty was due to land theft, brutally accomplished through collusion among state and federal courts and greedy foreigners (*estranjeros*), eager to advance their monopolistic land and timber cartels, while facilitated by elite Hispanos who participated in this profiteering, lining their own pockets with gold. Reies mockingly referred to them as "Judases," comparing them to the treacherous moneylenders in Jerusalem's temple and to the Sanhedrin's Jewish rabbis who found Jesus's teachings so repugnant that they handed him over to Pontius Pilate for crucifixion for mere shekels. In the Book of Revelation, the Roman emperor and the prefects who executed his dictates were collectively called "the beast." The "beast" in Reies' mind and speeches was the country's presidents and state officials. "We are dealing with a violent government, with the beast, and with a beast you cannot reason" was one of Reies' oft-repeated mantras.[15]

His jeremiads accused the state of "cultural rape." But his comment, "the rape of a culture and the language of a people is a greater crime than the rape of a two-year-old child," tells us much about his own attitudes toward incest and rape.[16] Reies pithily articulated his critique of New Mexico's land tenure in an oft-repeated and easily remembered slogan: "They took your land away and gave you powdered milk.[17] They took your trees and grazing away from you and gave you Smoky the Bear. They took your language away and gave you lies in their own. They took your manhood away and asked you to lie down and be a Good Mexican. They told you [you] were lazy and cowardly and backward, and you believed them."[18] This history of foreign domination was more than a century old. "If we can save the land, we can save the

Figure 3. Justice is Our Creed and the Land is Our Heritage. Reies López Tijerina speaking with a partial poster of Alianza's motto in the background. Courtesy Tijerina Pictorial Collection, Special Collections and Center for Southwest Research, University of New Mexico Libraries.

culture. If we can save the culture, then we can save our families."[19] In Reies's dichotomous racial imaginary of the 1960s, the oppressed and oppressors were nativos versus estranjeros, natives versus foreigners, brown versus white, and Mexicans versus Anglos. As we will see, this, too, changed over time based on "revelations" and dreams, adding Jews to the oppressor side.

The Alianza meetings Reies led between 1963 and 1966 were scripted, following almost exactly the ritual process he had mastered as an evangelist. At Pentecostal revivals he first preached about sin and salvation, read Bible passages and offered his gloss, asking those in anguish to share their troubles, laying hands to heal wounded bodies and troubled souls, followed by singing, communing, and offerings for the preacher's subsistence. Reies led Alianza meetings identically. He started with orations recounting how women and men lost their land and dignity, which he promised to restore. In place of biblical text, he substituted reading from the Laws of the Indies, the Treaty of Guadalupe Hidalgo, and the Constitution of the United States. Personal testimony followed, with stories about how individuals lost their lands and the misery that caused. Reies promised to heal and make them whole again by recuperating their land. Then there was music, food, dancing, and the collection of two-dollar monthly membership dues.[20]

Everywhere Reies went, everywhere he spoke, and every call to action took sermonic form, promising cultural restoration with land as their salvation. Here are portions of two much longer essays Reies published in Albuquerque's *News Chieftain* in 1964, a free Protestant community newspaper, which began carrying his regular column titled "Information from the Alianza Federal de Mercedes" in 1963.

> During the past 100 year[s], or the 5 generations in which American judges have mocked justice and all of our rights to the mercedes has there been born a man capable of uniting all the land grant heirs? No person has shown interest in the sad history and bitter fortune of the heirs; no one raised their voice on behalf of the "Forgotten People," nor sacrificed his life to defend the interests of the land grant heirs. Finally, after 100 years a man has emerged, a brave one who sacrifices all of his life to defend and save the sacred land our forefathers won with their lives.... The treacherous ones are identical to those who robbed the land. They claim to be Christians without any sense of God.... Thus, for the love of our land, do not listen to them.... [They] are trying to defame this grand union of land grant heirs. (*News Chieftain*, July 17, 1964, 3)

> God has turned his Divine eyes upon us, the poor oppressed and robbed, and Justice will no longer be frozen or sabotaged by bad persons. A rain of grace is showering on the land of New Mexico and the sun of justice is starting to shine on the people who for 100 years had been living in the darkness of injustice. But now the mercedes will be returned to their legitimate owners, and the thieves will be confounded by their own machinations: crime does not pay. Arise brave heirs, together as if one

Figure 4. Reies López Tijerina address a church gathering. Courtesy Tijerina Pictorial Collection, Special Collections and Center for Southwest Research, University of New Mexico Libraries.

man, let us treat each other as brothers trying to recuperate the land protected by an international treaty. Brother land grant heir, awaken from your sleep, arise, and come help us. This is about your land. It is about the rights of your children. It is about your HONOR. It is about your citizenship. You cannot let foreigners (estranjeros) trample your sacred rights. (*News Chieftain*, April 3, 1964, 2)

Justice is with us, Justice will speak for us, and Justice will restore our lands. Our cows will have pasturage and water, our livestock will no longer suffer from hunger, as do we; and there will no longer be barbed wire fences limiting and dividing all of our grazing lands. The land will again be free as it was initially; and we will no longer have to drink powered milk. . . . Our union is a holy and just one, free of hypocrisy. Our union is based on our land and our culture, which has been so devalued. We have entered a new age, brilliant and full of hope for our children; because first comes our land and then good education. In this new era and epoch law and justice will reign for the first time in New Mexico, everything will revert to their legitimate owners and no one will rob or oppress the humble as bankers and bad politicians have done thus far. (*News Chieftain*, August 20, 1964, 3)

Reies had a daily radio call-in program—"*La Voz de la Justicia*" (The Voice of Justice)—on Albuquerque's Spanish-language station, KABQ. Here is a portion of his April 23, 1965, program:

The Alianza Federal de Mercedes was born to represent all of our rights in Washington. To revive all of the laws that protect our mercedes and inheritances. It is a sin against our children to keep our mouths shut in the face of so many injustices that foreigners are committing against the heritage of our people. It is a sin to allow false citizens to trample on our constitutional rights. Cultural genocide is being waged against hispanos. Join this sacred crusade [*esta santa cruzada*] for the rights of our children. This is the day of opportunity, that our people were expecting to awaken from our sleep.[21]

Hispano old timers in northern New Mexico were deeply suspicious of outsiders, particularly of Texans who had invaded New Mexico twice in the early nineteenth century. Indeed, as a youngster I recall my maternal grandfather warning me "never trust the Texans." That Reies Tijerina was a Texan and Protestant to boot, married to a Texas Protestant, neither of whom had any connection to a New Mexican merced, created several problems for Reies he resolved quickly. On March 22, 1963, Reies and María divorced. In the weeks that followed Reies underwent a religious conversion. He began life as a baptized Catholic, then became a Baptist, next received his Holy Spirit baptism as a Pentecostal, and finally he was back in the arms of his mother church. To establish a connection to a New Mexican land grant heir, on September 25, 1965, he married Patricia Romero before a justice of the peace in the Alianza's meeting hall. Patricia's ancestors were among the original settlers of the Kingdom of New Mexico. Tomé

Domínguez de Mendoza had arrived in the mid-1630s. He fled, abandoning his land grant, during the 1680 Pueblo Revolt. His descendants returned to New Mexico and managed to have it restored in 1739. Reies and Patricia first met at Albuquerque's Coney Island Restaurant on August 8. Quickly, romance blossomed into marriage between thirty-nine-year-old Reies and his eighteen-year-old bride Patsy whom he often described as "mentally retarded with a low IQ." Both were rather penniless. They moved into a windowless basement room without heating, running water, a kitchen, or bathroom in the Alianza's building, while Reies evicted the residents of his first marriage and family.[22]

From 1963 to 1966, as the Alianza's president, Tijerina wrote letters to the presidents of Mexico and the United States explaining how the Hispanos of the US Southwest had been swindled of their ancestral lands because the American government had failed to honor the Treaty of Guadalupe Hidalgo guaranteeing the protection of life, liberty, and property of Mexicans annexed into the republic. In letter after letter, Reies begged these heads of state for intervention through investigations. The results were minimal, usually short courteous responses, acknowledging receipt and promising to forward his letter to relevant government officers. In many cases the "beast" did not respond. Reies kept writing, shifting targets, addressing government departments and agencies, state governors, local mayors, and human rights organizations with identical pleas.

Ah, then he turned to television! When he saw images of African Americans being beaten in the South, knocked about by powerful water hoses, mauled by vicious police dogs in Alabama in 1965, he quickly understood the medium's power to amplify the impact of the violence aired on screen. Television reporting was changing hearts, minds, and laws, with images that nightly entered the intimate space of American homes. He was already broadcasting daily radio programs, weekly columns in Albuquerque's *News Chieftain*, and issuing press releases to disseminate his message at the speed of light. It was time to start organizing marches and rallies, mass demonstrations to attract television coverage on the evening news. Critics ridiculed his newly found interest, lampooning him "Reies T.V.-rina," because of his habit of chasing television cameramen and departing as soon as the lights and cameras were off.[23]

Tijerina and members of the Alianza undertook a sixty-mile march from Albuquerque to the state capitol in Santa Fe, fashioned after Martin Luther King's Selma-to-Montgomery march on July 2, 1966. They intended to arrive in Santa Fe on July Fourth, Independence Day, a protest that would certainly gain media attention, given that it was routinely a low-news day. More than one hundred participants walked the entire distance, their numbers swelling as they reached Santa Fe and approached the capitol. They carried signs representing "300 ancient Spanish land grants in New Mexico," a list of grievances, and a petition they intended to personally hand Governor Jack M. Campbell. Failing to consult the governor's appointments calendar beforehand, he was in Los Angeles attending the National Governors' Conference. The protesters insisted on waiting until Campbell returned, telling reporters that "a vast conspiracy to deprive Spanish-Americans . . . of their historical lands" existed. Governor Campbell met them on July 11, accepted their petition, promising to forward it to President Lyndon B. Johnson and New Mexico's congressional delegation. Among the grievances the Alianza recited was the lack of good schools and need for bilingual education, Hispano overdependence on welfare for lack of available jobs with living wages, and childhood malnutrition. As the meeting ended, Reies emphasized, "We do not demand anything. We just want a full investigation of the issue."[24] The television coverage he wanted he got.

That same day the Santa Fe's newspaper, the *New Mexican*, published extensive excerpts from a letter Myra Ellen Jenkins, the state's archivist and historian, sent the governor contesting what she deemed the Alianza's propaganda. She insisted that their claims had no legal validity and that the land grant heirs had no proof of lineal descent from original land grantees and were being incited to preposterous demands by "outside influences . . . for pecuniary gain." Land tenure in the Mexican territories the United States annexed in 1848 had been settled by the Office of the US Surveyor General between 1854 and 1890, and by the Court of Private Land Claims in 1890–1900.[25]

Jenkins and Tijerina were known as rabid opponents, something I witnessed many times in 1979 while undertaking research at the State Records Center and Archives. Reies responded. He never passed up an opportunity to brawl with cantankerous Myra Ellen. He was a man of God, not a racketeer or any sort of con man. Jenkins was the one who more justifiably deserved these monikers. She and the owner of the *Albuquerque Journal* newspaper were members of the same Protestant church that owned a large former Spanish land grant. This and other financial interests distorted her research and was why she refused to investigate the Alianza's land claims. As the state's archivist, she had repeatedly legitimized past illegal land seizures by the corrupt lawyers and speculators known as the Santa Fe Ring in the 1870s, including the destruction of the New Mexico's Territorial Archives by Governor William A. Pile. Jenkins's accusations were vile, he protested. Soon she would face the stinging pain of "judgement and justice."[26]

The Alianza held its first three national conventions in Albuquerque in 1963, 1964, and 1965. As the fourth approached, scheduled for September 3–4, 1966, Reies announced that the Alianza was ready for a "showdown," a confrontation to take over a land grant. "We'll just move onto the land and let the United States Government, through the courts, try to get us off. . . . This action will either prove the effectiveness of the Alianza or mean our effort is ended. It'll make us or break us."[27] Days later the Alianza issued a "NEWS BULLETIN—[PRESS] RELEASE." On the morning of October 15, 1966, at 7:00 a.m., a motorcade would leave the Alianza's Albuquerque office "to take over the Pueblo San Joaquín del Rio de Chama, a town established on August 1st, 1806, by [Spain's king] Don Carlos IV. . . . The Alianza does not expect any difficulties."[28] Having garnered little media attention, a second declaration followed, explaining that the organization's patience had reached breaking point. The federal government had yet to address the illegal seizure of land grant village commons. In this "FINAL NOTICE TO THE UNITED STATES OF AMERICA AND TO THE STATE OF NEW MEXICO," Reies explained that "after waiting for more then [sic] a century for justice" the heirs of the royal land grants would "exercise all of their rights and authorities."[29]

William D. Hurst, the Regional US Forester, refused to meet with Reies to discuss the Alianza's threatened "showdown" on October 2, 1966, but replied to his letter. "The property you propose to claim . . . belongs to the United States of America, and I will not, under any condition, allow it to be claimed. . . . The full resources of the U.S. will be used to prevent damage to

Figure 5. Viva la Alianza. Reies López Tijerina routinely gathered those interested in recuperating their land grants and enrolling new dues-paying members in the Alianza Federal de Mercedes by holding outdoor rallies before anyone willing to listen. Here he is with a group of auditors in northern New Mexico circa 1964. Courtesy Tijerina Pictorial Collection, Special Collections and Center for Southwest Research, University of New Mexico Libraries.

Figure 6. Reies López Tijerina Speaking, circa 1966. Tijerina was known as a dynamic and charismatic speaker, capable of rousing crowds.

government property." Reies felt insulted by Hurst's unwillingness to meet. He responded with hundreds of noisy protesters in front of the Forest Service's office in Albuquerque with placards that read: "U.S. Violates International Law," "The Land Belongs to Us Under the Treaty of Guadalupe Hidalgo," "Down with Federal Anarchy," "W. Hurst Insults Spanish Americans," and "We Want Our Land, Not Powered Milk."[30]

Some 350 Alianza members, many of them long-time members of the San Joaquín Town Corporation, which itself had been litigating the ownership of their merced for decades, on October 15, 1966, invaded a portion of the Kit Carson National Forest in northern New Mexico known as the Echo Creek Amphitheatre, a popular campground. Though FBI agents, state and local police officers, and Forest Rangers were ready nearby, they did not stop the takeover, fearing a violent confrontation. The crowd entered the amphitheater, ceremoniously took possession, claiming that they were restoring the original land grant that had been given to Francisco Salazar in 1806 to start the village of San Joaquín del Rio de Chama. They covered the Carson National Forest sign that marked the campground's entrance on both sides with placards that read: "Pueblo República de San Joaquín de Chama, Est[ablished]. 1806." Residents now of their free city-state, they elected a mayor and deputized several marshals to patrol the town. When US Forest Service rangers arrived, the rangers were arrested, tried by the members of the newly established town council, found guilty of trespassing, were roughed up, and released with death threats. For two weeks the Alianza members occupied the campground, arguing that they were the land's legal owners. Tijerina wanted "to force the Federal Government to file Federal charges against us. Now that it is done we will carry the case to the Supreme Court."[31] Though some of the residents of nearby villages were not really fans of Tijerina's tactics, as Jessie Romero put it, "I had never seen such unity among people around here. Even if you did not agree directly with Tijerina, you supported what he was doing." Santiago Juárez assessed these events as "a brown and white case of native versus outsiders. . . . It served to help people remember the injustices they have faced as a community and the rights they have as heirs to the land."[32]

Following the Echo Creek Amphitheatre invasion, the federal government demanded the membership lists of the Alianza Federal de Mercedes. The

Alianza disbanded and incorporated as a new organization, the *Alianza Federal de Pueblos Libres* (Federal Alliance of Free Towns), claiming it had no access to the records of the defunct organization. Almost simultaneously, heirs of distinct land grants began declaring themselves free city-states, presenting themselves before federal, state, and local authorities as the legal representatives of sovereign independent republics. On January 5, 1967, for example, Don Victoriano Chávez, who called himself a "Hidalgo and Caballero de las Indias, Governor of the Pueblo República of San Joaquín del Rio de Chama," demanded that President Lyndon B. Johnson immediately cease "all claims of title, right and interest" in his sovereign city-state. Tijerina wiggled his way into the US State Department in Washington, DC, saying he was there to present his diplomatic credentials to Secretary of State Dean Rusk as the "proctor of the Mission of the Pueblo República de San Joaquín del Rio de Chama." Rusk refused to see him. His assistant politely told Reies that the United States knew of no such republic. Eduardo Chávez, another Alianza militant, went to the mayor's office in Albuquerque's declaring himself "Governor of La Villa de San Felipe de Neri de Albuquerque," authorized by its "Casa de Ayuntamiento" (town council). The *Albuquerque Journal* reported on December 15 that the Alianza's "next goal is to claim land in Albuquerque."[33] By February 24, 1967, J. Edgar Hoover was alarmed. He circulated memos throughout the FBI and Secret Service informing that Reies López Tijerina was "potentially dangerous" perhaps a "communist [or] . . . member of other group or organization inimical to U.S."[34]

In a letter Reies invited Corky Gonzales, his longtime ally in the land grant cause and leader of Denver's Crusade for Justice, to northern New Mexico on March 25, 1967, the day after he was arrested on federal charges for the Echo Amphitheatre invasion:

Corky, This summer the people will take over San Joaquín del Rio de Chama once and for all. The people, or, as I call them, "The Sons of San Joaquín," are aroused and full of ardor and longing not ever seen in the history of New Mexico. The people of New Mexico have moved together in a miraculous manner which causes joy in the soul of the native but great fear and terror in the strangers who arrived in New Mexico but yesterday. The taking of San Joaquín del Rio de Chama will be about the third day of June. And those valiant ones from Denver who wish to be present are invited and can personally see the valor of the "Sons of San Joaquín."[35]

An undercover Santa Fe Police informant got wind of the plan, alerted the FBI on April 17, reporting "rumors to the effect that the Alianza Federal de Mercedes was going to take over Canjilón lakes on April 28, 1967," attaching the following eviction notice then widely circulating as proof.

U.S.A. is trespassing in New Mexico.
U.S.A. has no title for New Mexico.
The Treaty of Guadalupe Hidalgo is a fraud and invalid.
Estados Unidos no tiene jurisdicción en N. Mex.
[The United States has no jurisdiction in New Mexico]
All trespassers must get out of New Mexico Now!
All Pirates go home.
All Spanish and Indian Pueblos are free forever.
All trespassers will be punished by law.
Vivan los pueblos repúblicas libres de Nuevo Mex ...
[Long live the free city states of New Mexico][36]

The eviction notice was followed by a large demonstration in Albuquerque's city center with more than five hundred participants, carrying banners that read: "USA is Trespassing in New Mexico." Winding their way west down Central Avenue, they gathered at the bandstand in Old Town Plaza to hear speeches. "The government is being warned," Reies vaunted, "if anybody is found trespassing on these land grants they will be arrested and punished."[37]

When Alfonso Sánchez, the district attorney for Santa Fe, Rio Arriba, and Los Alamos Counties, heard that Tijerina planned another "major showdown," this time against the State of New Mexico, he took preemptive action. On Friday, June 2, he ordered the state police to blockade all the roads leading into Tierra Amarilla, prohibiting any members of the Alianza to enter the area to attend what publicly was being billed as the Alianza's annual convention that would be held in Canjilón, at Tobias Leyba's ranch.

Sánchez later justified the arrests concerned that more was underway than simply an Alianza convention, which were normally held in Albuquerque, not in northern New Mexico, where the above noted land eviction notices were widely posted. Between 1965 and 1967 large tracts of land had been incinerated in this area. Anglo farms, haystacks, and fences had been torched, livestock had been slaughtered, and farm equipment smashed. A Department of Agriculture field station had been set ablaze. By attacking both symbols of Anglo and federal authority, the Hispanos of northern New Mexico were demonstrating their anger over the alienation of their ancestral lands and the shrinking number of permits for the grazing of their livestock on lands they claimed as their own. Much as African Americans were burning down their ghettos in American cities those same hot summers of urban revolt, so Hispano passions had become particularly incendiary. Of course, the Alianza Federal de Pueblos Libres was not the only group capable of such vandalism. But Sánchez was convinced that the members of Tijerina's Alianza were the culprits. He was determined not to permit any sort of land seizure. Those Alianza members who had reached Tobias Leyba's ranch before the blockade were arrested. Tijerina arrived late to lunch and escaped arrest. The women and children left behind were detained outdoors in cow pens during cold and inclement weather, denied access to sanitary facilities, food, and water. As a result of the trauma, Reies's pregnant wife, Patsy Romero, miscarried, blaming Sánchez for it.[38]

Thirteen Alianza members were arrested by the state police for inciting to riot that Friday and spent the weekend in the Tierra Amarilla Courthouse jail, awaiting arraignment Monday, June 5, 1967. Tijerina and his militants were livid. Their constitutional right to free assembly had been brazenly violated. They had committed no crime. That Monday morning, they gathered at Tobias Leyba's ranch to plan their next move. Believing that District Attorney Sánchez would be at the Tierra Amarilla Courthouse that afternoon to arraign the jailed Alianza members, a contingent of twenty well-armed members arrived at the courthouse eager to execute a citizen's arrest of Sánchez. They arrived angry, and as they searched fruitlessly throughout the courthouse without finding him, their anger exploded into violent rage. Sheriff Benny Naranjo testified that he heard one of the men shouting, "Reies said not to hurt anybody, Reies said not to hurt anybody." But they did.

As the melee in the courthouse unfolded, Juan Valdez apparently panicked and shot State Police Officer Nick Saiz through a lung and upper arm. Jailer Eulogio Salazar was shot through the cheek trying to escape out a window. Reies battered Undersheriff Dan Rivera with a rifle butt. He plaintively asked Reies, "What have I ever done to deserve this from you?" As the sirens of police cars approaching could be heard, the men fled into the mountains, initially with a few hostages they soon released. A major dragnet was launched in northern New Mexico to capture them. Sheriff Benny Naranjo explained that what had just happened was not an attempted jailbreak, as most initial assessments reported. "That's all wrong. They came for Al. . . . The raiders had it in for Alfonso Sánchez."³⁹

The lead story on the front page of the *New York Times* on June 6, 1967, was the start of the Six Day Arab-Israeli War, with pictures of Israeli tanks moving across the Sinai Desert. Further below were pictures of M-42 tanks blazing through northern New Mexico in pursuit of Tijerina and his militants, a comparison Reies took as prophetic, Jews and Hispanos claiming land simultaneously as if by divine design. *Los Angeles Times* reporter Ed Meagher reported that the old Korean War–era tanks dispatched to capture the men were there "more for intimidation than for any other purpose," as they carried no ammunition, moved slowly, and their radios were broken.

Later that day FBI field agents in Albuquerque surveilling the Alianza wired J. Edgar Hoover, informing him of the "courthouse raid," which was how the government linguistically framed the event from the start, not as a "citizen's arrest" which is what it was: "There is no present [FBI] jurisdiction apparent [in this matter] . . . the U.S. Attorney is being kept advised."⁴⁰ Later that same day, District Attorney Alfonso Sánchez called the Albuquerque FBI office asserting that the "Alliance members are communists and pro-Castroites, and he [Sánchez] said he felt strongly that the Federal Government should become involved in this investigation."⁴¹ Hoover hesitated. He believed that he was being used by Alfonso Sánchez to settle a local squabble with New Mexico's Governor David Cargo, who sympathized with the Alianza cause. His wife was a dues-paying member of the Alianza.

The following day, June 6, Hoover asked the US Attorney General's

Internal Security Division Office to conduct a more thorough investigation of the Alianza, given their putative Communist affiliation, large stash of "machine guns," and "a great deal . . . of money." In response to Sánchez's allegations, on June 7 Hoover wired Albuquerque FBI agents: "Close attention must be given any reports of Communist or Pro-Castro influence of leaders or members of captioned group. Such reports must be explored and details obtained through your established sources."[42] The chorus of Communist accusations reaching Washington, DC, intensified when on June 8 US Attorney John Quinn told the Santa Fe *New Mexican* that "although we have no information that his organization is subversive or that Tijerina is a communist, certain of his statements sound that way."[43]

The FBI had been surveilling Tijerina since 1956, when he started the Valle de Paz commune in Arizona. No federal offenses had ever been discovered. Tijerina was so aware that FBI agents were constantly tailing him that every few months Reies or his brother Cristóbal would visit the local FBI office, tell the agent in charge that they were planning a revival, a fast, a pilgrimage, a religious gathering. If they had any questions or concerns, here was their address. Indeed, if they wanted to be saved by Jesus Christ, they should come to one of their Pentecostal revivals.

US Assistant Attorney General William Yaegley finally recommended action on June 9, 1967. Hoover authorized the Alianza's building be searched. By day's end agents wired Hoover. They had found a few books on the history of Latin America and some maps, but "the material examined has no . . . communist or subversive significance . . . no tangible evidence . . . re Communist activity." A few days later Tijerina was captured at a gas station on the outskirts of Albuquerque, asleep in the back seat of a car.[44]

The Mexican American land grant struggle in the Southwest at last became important national news, making the front page of the *New York Times*, with coverage in the *Washington Post*, the *Los Angeles Times*, the *Denver Post*, the *Dallas Morning News*, and a wide assortment of radio and television programs. Finally, "Reies T.V.-rina" had the media attention he craved as a national Mexican American political leader. At least in speeches, interviews, and press releases, he was still fashioning himself a selfless Christ-like messiah for the poor—now with the ire of the fire of God burning in his belly.

Two weeks after the attempted citizen's arrest at the Tierra Amarilla Courthouse, on June 17, George W. Grayson Jr., an economics and political science professor at the University of Virginia, interviewed Reies while he was held at the New Mexico State Penitentiary near Santa Fe awaiting formal criminal charges. Here are some of the questions Grayson asked (marked Q), and how Tijerina answered (A).

> Q [Grayson]: Do you take the Bible literally?
> A [Tijerina]: "Blessed are the meek, for they shall inherit the earth," is what I believe. It wasn't by chance that the Spanish people crossed the Atlantic; it was God that selected them.
> Q: Do you feel that you have been chosen by God?
> A: I guess so. Our people had not a guide, no light, no knowledge. God has chosen me.
> Q: What leader—old or modern—do you consider as a model?
> A: Moses above any other character. Because of the land; he gave the Israelites a place. New Mexico is a promised land too; New Mexico is a very fortunate land. We need a strong faith. God is our father, the earth is our mother.
> Q: What roles does the Church have nowadays?
> A: Religion has been exhausted. Religious leaders are selling the name of truth for pleasure, pride, and money.
> Q: Tell me about the government you will set up when you get your land back.
> A: There will be one city, the head city, named Justicia; it will be pretty hard to become a citizen of Justicia. I bet you.
> Q: What form of government will it have?
> A: Theocratic; the people are thirsty for a theocratic government. The churches have become empty—there's nothing left.
> Q: When do you think you will establish Justicia?
> A: When? By the millennium, the coming of Christ ... when one-third of the people [but no inhabitants of Justicia] will perish.

Q: Has your movement ever considered politics as a means to obtain its goals?
A: I detest politics. Politics is the enemy of God. I have one life to change the rights of the people. In all glory, richness, that is my goal.
Q: I understand the Alianza has been dissolved. Why?
A: Why? Because of persecution. The court persecuted the Alianza as Nero, the emperor of Rome, persecuted the citizens of Christianity.[45]

In other print venues, Reies also interpreted the events at the Tierra Amarilla Courthouse in religious terms. "We don't believe in violence, but we believe in Jesus Christ. The revolution at Tierra Amarilla was like Christ entering the temple and cleaning out the Pharisees."[46]

Many publications supportive of the Mexican American cause started depicting Tijerina as one of America's major civil rights leaders. From his jail cell Reies wanted to shape and control the range of media messaging feeding passions across the political spectrum but could not. The Old and New Left press celebrated Reies as an authentic, salt of the earth national revolutionary akin to Cuba's "Che" Guevara and Mexico's Emiliano Zapata. Elizabeth Martinez and Beverley Axelrod, two women who had long been active in the Student Nonviolence Coordinating Committee, were immediately drawn to Tijerina's "revolution" and moved to northern New Mexico in July 1967 where they started *El Grito del Norte*, a newspaper that publicized the accomplishments of the 1959 Cuban Revolution, its forging of a "new Man," and the necessity to tie local New Mexican struggles over land to Third World national revolutions, particularly the one in Viet Nam. Here was the new Sierra Madre, *El Grito del Norte* announced. That the newspaper's owners chose this name was significant. Mexico's independence movement had begun with *El Grito de Dolores*, the cry or proclamation of independence from the town of Dolores on September 16, 1821. Old Left newspapers covered Tijerina's land grant movement in similar ways, as the quickening of a class struggle that would hasten the proletariat revolution and capitalism's collapse. This was the larger theme of Patricia Bell Blawis's articles for the Communist Party USA's (CPUSA) *The Daily World*.[47]

The burgeoning Chicano student and youth movement that had taken organizational form in the major urban centers of the Southwest by 1969 as MECHA (*Movimiento Estudiantil Chicano de Aztlán*; Chicano Student Movement of Aztlán) hailed Tijerina as the MECHA, the spark that was igniting their liberation. In the eyes of young student radical nationalists, Reies took up arms, violently seizing federal lands, thus emboldening young Chicano men to similar acts, demanding jobs, educational reform, and an end to state violence, laying the foundation for the creation of an independent nation-state they named Aztlán. Aztlán was the mythological homeland of the Aztecs, which at the time no one knew its exact location. The myths simply stated that they had migrated into central Mexico from the North; maybe it was the near north, perhaps the far north, which the was basis for including in this homeland the lands annexed by the United States after 1845.

Newsweek Magazine and the *Militant*, the newspaper of the Student Nonviolence Coordinating Committee, two publications very much at different ideological poles, celebrated Tijerina in 1967 as the "New Malcom X." The *Saturday Evening Post* went further, dehumanizing Tijerina as "King Tiger." The intent was clear. To link Tijerina to the frightening image of the Black Panthers sporting rifles and festooned with ammunition cartridge belts across their chests. The name stuck, fed racial prejudices, and created a caricature of Reies's activism. "Angry Tiger Loose in New Mexico," "Skinning a Tiger," "The Tiger Caught" were but some of the newspaper headlines on Tijerina's activities in 1967 and 1968.[48]

Conservative journalists like Alan Stang, an active member of the John Birch Society, called "King Tiger" a Communist, a gun-toting Castroite, and a "rabble-rousing" (J. Edgar Hoover's term) opportunist in his conspiratorial essay "Reies Tijerina: The Communist Plan to Grab the Southwest," published in *American Opinion*. Stang's tone intensified to a shrill, penning follow-up essays on "Terror Grows: War on Poverty Supports Castroite Terrorists," which argued that funds from the country's War on Poverty, funneled through the Office of Economic Opportunity, were responsible for inciting New Mexico's poor to revolt, terrain Stang further illuminated in "New Mexico: The Coming Guerilla War."[49]

Reies initially hated being called "King Tiger." "They want me to seem like an animal," he said, "I am not proud that I was given this name." Reies wanted national and international attention as the leader of the Mexican American land grant cause, but his political enemies had no intention of allowing millions of acres of prime New Mexican land to be returned. The *Albuquerque Journal* and *Tribune*, co-owned daily newspapers, bedeviled Tijerina until his death. Reflecting on the citizen's arrest twenty years later, he admitted that in 1967 he had not fully understood how the media so profoundly shaped public opinion. "I never knew that [the media] was my principal enemy, because I could not see their hands, could not see their heads or their names. I was punching with gloves . . . at a phantom" whose power and enormity it took him a long time to understand.[50]

While out of jail on bail for the Alianza's Echo Creek Amphitheatre takeover on October 15, 1966, Tijerina was invited to attend the New Left Anti-War National Conference for New Politics, held at Chicago's Palmer House Hotel over the Labor Day weekend, between August 31 and September 4, 1967. The conference goal was "to enable those who work for peace, civil rights, and an end to poverty to register their greatest impact by concentrating money and manpower on direct political action." Approximately three thousand individuals representing hundreds of organizations gathered to unify activists working to end the war in Vietnam and to alleviate racism and poverty. But the main agenda item really was to formulate an electoral strategy to keep Lyndon B. Johnson from winning the presidency again in 1968. Those attending the meeting wanted to build "a different American future . . . to end poverty, fear and despair at home . . . to make our government accountable to us."[51]

Two Mexican American leaders from the Southwest were invited to the conference: Reies López Tijerina, who headed the land grant movement, and Rodolfo "Corky" Gonzales from Denver, of that city's Crusade for Justice. Neither was given much attention nor had much of an impact on the gathering's outcomes, though Tijerina did get a resolution of support for the struggles of Mexican Americans trying to regain their lands. Gonzales and Tijerina left the meeting realizing that national change would require an antiracist coalitional politics between America's blacks and browns who suffered from many identical problems but were divided by geography and race.[52] President Johnson was so unnerved by the conference that he immediately ordered J. Edgar Hoover to surveil all its participants and closely monitor all subsequent conference events. The Chicago Police Department's Intelligence Unit obliged by stealing the conference files, sharing them with the FBI, and ultimately publishing some in the *Congressional Record* as proof of an emergent racial terrorism.[53]

Two additional things happened in Chicago before Tijerina returned to New Mexico. He met for several hours with Elijah Muhammad, the leader of the Nation of Islam. When I asked Reies what he and the imam had discussed, he replied that it was a secret he would never reveal. But conjecturing for a moment, it was probably about the emergence of Black Power, which Malcolm X began articulating as a critique of Martin Luther King Jr.'s peaceful, nonviolent protest around the slogan "Freedom Now." King correctly worried that "the words 'black' and 'power' together give the impression that we are talking about black domination rather than black equality" and would unleash a torrent of white prejudice, which up to that point most whites had been too timid to express openly.[54]

At O'Hare Airport, as King was leaving Chicago and Tijerina was arriving for the conference, they had a chance encounter and short conversation. Weeks later King invited him to lead a Mexican American contingent from the American Southwest to the Poor's Peoples March on Washington, DC, planned by the Southern Christian Leadership Council, to begin on May 12, 1968. Tijerina accepted.

Participation at the National Conference for New Politics and his meeting with Elijah Muhammad quickened government surveillance of Tijerina and the Alianza Federal de Pueblos Libres. In cooperation with Mexico, every movement Reies, his family, and his brothers took was closely monitored. FBI memos reported how Reies was dressed when he entered Albuquerque's airport, what airline and flight numbers he boarded, the make, model, and license number of the automobiles in which he was transported, who he met, where, and how long.

Slightly more than a month after the Chicago Conference for New Politics, the impact of Tijerina's participation on this national stage was apparent when the Alianza held its fifth annual convention in Albuquerque October 19–22, 1967. Among the hundreds who attended were swarms of undercover police from local, state, and federal agencies, monitoring everything said and done. The convention's agenda first moved rapidly through routine Alianza committee reports, followed by some levity. A street-style theatrical performance was billed, a Mexican *lucha libre*, or fighting match, between two wrestlers wearing full-head masks and tight-fitting Speedo trunks. One represented "The Tiger," or Tijerina, who was by then widely referred to as "El Tigre," a name he liked because he associated it with St. Mark, the gospel author often depicted as a lion. His opponent, "The Beast of the North," was President Johnson. Of course, the tiger had to beat the beast.[55]

Though Reies was under a court-imposed gag order on his pending federal court case, at the convention he nevertheless updated the Alianza's members of the fast-approaching trial for the October 1966 reclaiming of the Kit Carson National Forest. FBI agents recorded him saying that he would receive no justice because "the judge has taken the power in his own hands [and] . . . is using the law to take vengeance and drink blood and humiliate our race."[56]

Gathered on the convention stage were a number of Native American, African American, and Chicano militants, most whom Tijerina had met at the Chicago New Politics Conference: Tomas Banyacya, leader of the Free Hopi Indian Nation; Ralph Featherstone, program director of the Student Nonviolence Coordinating Committee (SNCC); Maulana Ron Karenga, cofounder of US Organization (meaning "us black people," an offshoot of the Black Panther Party and the Congress of Racial Equality); Walter Bremond, chair of the Los Angeles Black Congress; James Dennis, director of the Mississippi Congress of Racial Equality (CORE); Eliezer Risco, an editor for the Los Angeles based *La Raza* newspaper; Rodolfo "Corky" Gonzales of Denver's Crusade for Justice; Bert Corona, the head of Mexican American Political Action (MAPA); Anthony Babu of the Black Panther Party; and a few others left unidentified.

Tomas Banyacya of the Hopi Nation spoke first, explaining that the word *Hopi* meant peace and that is why he refused to serve in the Korean War, for which he was punished with six years in jail. Maulana Ron Karenga offered greetings for the podium, affirming racial unity, "*Somos juntos, somos hermanos de color* (We are united, we are brothers of color). Our problems are not different . . . all people of color must fight. Somos hombres, temenos machismo (We are men, we have machismo). Our enemy will not destroy us, we will destroy him. *La tierra es nuestra herencia y la justicia nuestro credo. . . . ¡Viva Tijerina! ¡Vivan los indios! ¡Vivan los hombres de color!*" (The land is our heritage and justice is our creed. . . . Long Live Tijerina! Long live the Indians! Long live men of color!) Ralph Featherstone grabbed the audience's attention by showing them a bumper sticker that read: "Ché is alive and hiding in Tierra Amarilla." It drew thunderous cheers and shouts. "¡Poder Negro! ¡Poder Negro!" (Black Power! Black Power!) Featherstone shouted, his arm straight up and his fist clenched. "We have a common enemy. He is pale-skinned and blue-eyed and blond, and he is a thief. He stole my ancestors from Africa and killed 100 million in the Middle Passage. . . . He raped your culture and robbed you of your language. We cannot allow this man to exist. We must take back what is owed us and what is ours by any means necessary. We can no longer promise nonviolence." With an immense roar, the crowd responded, "Black Power!"[57]

There were several more speeches but what most unsettled state and federal undercover agents present was the convention's culmination: The signing of a "Treaty of Peace, Harmony, and Mutual Assistance" that Reies authored. "In the Name of God Almighty," the treaty began, obliging its signatories to honor it as "a SOLEMN agreement, and subject to the Divine Law of the God of Justice." Each community—Native American, African American, Mexican American—if under siege, would respect each other's faith and culture, and all the rights and liberties "GOD has given to the HUMAN RACE." They promised to remain in constant communication, frequently exchanging emissaries, and if "Nuclear War should erupt," offer mutual aid. The treaty concluded with a promise that they would all collectively denounce the "CRIMES and SINS of the Government of the United States of America."[58]

New Mexico's US Senator Joseph Montoya immediately denounced Tijerina's alliance with Black Power militants and the mutual aid pledge. "Spanish-Americans will make no alliances with black nationalists who hate America. We do not lie down in the gutter with Ron Karenga, Stokely Carmichael, and Rap Brown—who seek to put another wound in America's body." That Senator Montoya appealed to Spanish Americans was significant. This English-language denomination was most often used to buttress a pretentious upper- and middle-class mythology that they were descendants of white Spanish conquerors, not the lowly Indo-Hispano mixes who depended for their subsistence on village commons that no longer existed.[59] Montoya was up for senate re-election in 1970 and needed these votes. He savored every opportunity to curry favor by denigrating Tijerina as a "charlatan, monster, racist and creature of darkness." Montoya had other motives for trying to silence Reies and question his honesty. As a well-connected New Mexican lawyer, he had demanded land from poor clients to cover his fees, rather rapidly ascending from rags to riches.[60]

Words of racial solidarity and mutual aid gained Hoover's attention too, immediately barreling down on Tijerina. Hoover was determined not to allow a Black, Mexican, or Native American messiah to emerge who might forge a much more threatening irredentist movement. Reies had all the makings. To preclude that possibility Hoover used the top secret, unauthorized, and illegal campaign he had created, named COINTELPRO (an acronym for COunter INTELligence PROgram), for the task.

COINTELPRO's goal was to surveil, infiltrate, discredit, and disrupt every social movement committed to racial equality in the United States or an end to the war in Vietnam.[61] From October 1967 on, Tijerina, his family, and the Alianza's leadership became targets, surviving bombs, fires, high-speed car chases, bullets volleys, and sexual assaults. Rank-and-file Alianza members started losing their state and federal jobs without cause, even though they were not active in the organization. Spies and provocateurs infiltrated the Alianza. Soon those committed to the recuperation of their hereditary land grants, language, and culture began to realize the precariousness of their lives and the dangers they faced. Justifiably, they quit the Alianza or drifted away.[62]

After Martin Luther King's assassination on April 4, 1968, the organization and direction of the Poor People's Campaign to be held in Washington, DC, passed to Ralph Abernathy as the new leader of the Southern Christian Leadership Council. Billed as a multiracial coalitional event scheduled from mid-May to mid-June 1968, it promised to bring together Native Americans, blacks, whites, and Mexican Americans to protest the causes and consequences of poverty. Yes, progress toward racial equality was being made through the Civil Rights and Voting Rights Acts of 1964 and 1965, but the "unconditional war on poverty" President Johnson

Figure 7. Reies López Tijerina at the Poor People's March on Washington, May 1968. Before the Rev. Dr. Martin Luther King Jr. was assassinated on April 4, 1968, he invited Reies López Tijerina to lead a Mexican American delegation from the American Southwest to the Poor People's March on Washington. From left to right stand Mad Bear Anderson, Reies López Tijerina, and Ralph Abernathy. Courtesy Tijerina Pictorial Collection, Special Collections and Center for Southwest Research, University of New Mexico Libraries.

declared he would wage in January 1964 to "cure it and . . . prevent it" had not yet been felt. Thousands intended to lobby Congress for an Economic Bill of Rights that guaranteed jobs with living wages, adequate unemployment benefits, access to arable land, loans for the creation of minority businesses, and greater representation in the country's governance.[63]

As the Southwestern delegation made its way toward Washington, conflict emerged between Reies Tijerina and Corky Gonzales, the two major leaders representing the region. They sparred over their relative prominence and stage presence in the larger organization's campaign dominated by African Americans, the importance of rural over urban concerns, how best to alleviate Mexican American poverty, and the nature of their leadership styles. The *Albuquerque Journal* editorialized in early May 1968 that Tijerina was "the wrong choice for [a] leader of the Poor Peoples' March." They were right. Reies was imperiously demanding center stage, expecting honorific deference he felt he was not given, despite his elite accommodations and steak dinners. In short, he acted like a king more than the poor messiah he claimed to be, frequently complaining before impoverished racial minorities and a global press drawn to his verbal pyrotechnics.[64]

Reies Before Federal and State Courts

Reies Tijerina, his brother Cristóbal Tijerina, Jerry Noll, Alfonso Chávez, and Ezekial Domínguez were arrested on March 24, 1967, for violations of federal law stemming from their actions at the Echo Creek Amphitheatre between October 2–24, 1966. They were charged with five counts: assaulting, impeding, and intimidating US Forest Service officers Walter Taylor and Philip Smith, two counts for blocking access to the Forest Ranger's trucks, and conspiracy to commit all of these acts together. The trial held in Las Cruces lasted until mid-December, when the jury declared itself hung on the conspiracy charge. Reies Tijerina was found guilty of assaulting both rangers. Cristóbal Tijerina was guilty of assaulting Ranger Taylor and Ezekial of assaulting Ranger Smith. Jerry Noll and Alfonso Chávez were guilty of assaulting both rangers and impounding their trucks. Reies Tijerina was sentenced to two years on one assault and received a suspended sentence and five years' probation on the second. He was warned that if he or the Alianza announced that they wanted to engage in violent action, his probation would be revoked. The rest of the defendants received lesser sentences and probation. All five appealed their convictions in the 10th Circuit Federal Court of Appeals. All lost. Their request for review by the Supreme Court of the United States was denied.[65]

The state trial on the charges stemming from the failed citizen's arrest at the Tierra Amarilla Courthouse raid began on November 12, 1968. Representing the "Tierra Amarilla Ten," as they became known, was Beverley Axelrod, the SNCC organizer who had come to New Mexico in 1967 to help start the newspaper *El Grito del Norte*, and to whom Eldridge Cleaver had given the original prison letters published as *Soul on Ice* (1968). She was joined by William Higgs who was James Meredith's first lawyer when he tried to gain entry to the University of Mississippi in 1961.

The prosecution was headed by Alfonso Sánchez. The total 584 counts were narrowed to 54 by Judge Paul Larrazolo, soon separating Tijerina's case from the group. The most serious charges against Tijerina were assault on a jail, kidnapping, and false imprisonment of Undersheriff Dan Rivera, a felony that carried the death penalty.

When arguments were about to begin on November 20, Tijerina declared that he would defend himself. The judge allowed it. By all accounts, the defense he mounted had the fire of his Pentecostal revival oratory. His main objective was to get the jury to understand that he and the other nine Alianza members had arrived at the Tierra Amarilla Courthouse to stage a citizen's arrest. Citizens had this right. The first shot had been fired by State Policeman Nick Saiz. Reies and his men were simply defending themselves. Dressed in a simple cotton shirt, no tie, work pants, and scruffy shoes, Tijerina called a slew of witnesses to recount the history of the land grants, the poverty of Hispanos in northern New Mexico, and the Alianza's peaceful goals.

District Attorney Alfonso Sánchez, by contrast, appeared in court every day wearing a black suit, white shirt, tie, and expensive leather polished shoes. His goal was to tie Tijerina to the kidnapping of Undersheriff Dan Rivera, but the connection was difficult to prove because the men who had abducted Rivera were wearing ski masks and dressed in military fatigues. Rivera testified that he knew his abductors only by the sound of their voices and physiques, and so he was not entirely sure Tijerina had been his kidnapper, adding that he did not blame Reies for anything that happened at the courthouse that day.

When Tijerina took the stand, he claimed that he was a weak and powerless David defending himself against the state's Goliath, Alfonso Sánchez, who wielded the instruments of force. He accused Sánchez of a longstanding vendetta, of his constant harassment of the Alianza, and of responsibility for the death of his three-month-old son in the womb of his second wife, Patsy Tijerina. His only goal had been to execute a citizen's arrest. The only crime, if one was committed, was that it went terribly wrong.

The big break occurred when Judge Larrazolo issued jury instructions: "Anyone, including a state police officer, who intentionally interferes with a lawful attempt to make a citizen's arrest does so at his own peril, since the arresting citizens are entitled under the law to use whatever force is reasonably necessary to effect said citizen's arrest and to use whatever force is reasonably necessary to defend themselves in the process of making said citizen's arrest."[66] Four hours later, on December 13, 1968, Tijerina won complete acquittal, although Sánchez retried the case and eventually won conviction on two lesser charges.[67]

Tijerina took his newly found authority for citizen's arrests to Washington, DC, in April 1969. By the authority of the citizens of the free city-state of San Joaquín del Rio de Chama, he tried to arrest Warren Burger, chief justice of the Supreme Court, for refusing to investigate the Alianza's land grant claims. Before a gaggle of television cameras and newspaper reporters, Tijerina theatrically put a lasso around the court's building. Burger did not see the commotion and was shuttled out by guards through a side door. Tijerina next tried to arrest Norris Bradbury, then head of the Atomic Energy Commission's Los Alamos National Laboratories for building atomic bombs. Hacker was out of the country and Tijerina ultimately left a printed arrest warrant in his mailbox.[68]

While Tijerina appealed state charges stemming from the Tierra Amarilla Courthouse, he and Patsy were apprehended setting fire to US Forest Service signs. After repeated appeals all the way to the US Supreme Court, Reies Tijerina was found guilty of two counts of destroying federal property for the sign-burning incident, and one count of assaulting a federal officer while resisting arrest. On October 10, 1969, he was sentenced to three years of imprisonment for each count, sentences that were to run consecutively with each other and with his sentence for assaulting two forest rangers at the Kit Carson National Forest. He began serving his sentences on June 11, 1969, first at the New Mexico State Prison near Santa Fe. Eight months later he was transferred to the Federal Detention Center in Montessa Park, Texas; transferred again to La Tuna Federal Center in Anthony, New Mexico, in July 1970; and finally, to the psychiatric ward of the Medical Center for Federal Prisoners in Springfield, Missouri, on January 14, 1970. There he was diagnosed with schizophrenia and bipolar disorder, marked by frequent episodes of mania and depression. He was released from federal prison on July 26, 1971, with a parole stipulation that he could not hold any future leadership role in the Alianza Federal de

Pueblos Libres and had to undergo regular psychiatric care for five years. For his state sentences he returned to prison on June 29, 1974, and was released on parole on July 29, 1974.[69]

The Chicano Movement

While Tijerina served his prison sentences between October 1969 and July 1971, what mushroomed into the Chicano student movement had its genesis in Denver on March 28, 1969, at the National Youth Conference. Tijerina did not hear about the conference, nor did he see a copy of "El Plan Espiritual de Aztlán," the conference manifesto, until months later. But on hearing that he and the Alianza's land grant struggle was being hailed by Rodolfo "Corky" Gonzales as the beginning of the armed revolution to create the Chicano homeland of Aztlán, Tijerina wrote his followers an angry letter. "I hope he [Corky] doesn't mean it," he penned. "My motto is Justice, not independence, not revolution." But the Plan Espiritual de Aztlán had committed itself to the formation of a nationalist identity-based movement, not unlike New Mexico's Indo-Hispanos trying to regain their lands and livelihoods. Chicanos articulated the plight of urban youth: police harassment, unequal treatment by the courts, residential segregation, educational neglect, poverty, and vulnerability to the draft. Eventually feminist and queer demands for sexual liberation, reproductive rights, and gender equity made their way into the agenda empowering Chicanas, culminating in the National Chicano Moratorium to End the War in Vietnam on August 29, 1970. These were demands of urban young far removed from the issues of land tenure in northern New Mexico.[70]

The history of Mexican American political activism into which Tijerina tapped in the late 1950s was religious, rural, and class based, committed to the poor, the hungry, and the displaced. Such were the appeals of César Chávez, who fought for better wages and working conditions for farm workers of Mexican, Japanese, and Filipino origins. His labor unionization was class based. He was deeply suspicious of young urban Chicano radical nationalists whom he cultivated as allies for staging consumer boycotts of grapes and lettuce, but always at arm's length from his labor organizing. Both Tijerina and Chávez employed religious rhetoric as the foundation for their activism. They were both constantly accused of being Communists, which was simply not true. Neither ever called himself a Chicano.

Tijerina wanted no part of sexual liberation or gender equity. He demanded strict patriarchal domestic order, the sanctification of the body, and abstinence from the blandishments of the evil whore of Babylon—smoking, drinking, dancing, promiscuity. He wanted to restore patriarchal authority and familial honor, not destroy it, ideals he piously preached but failed to obey himself. Such sanctimonious and hypocritical pronouncements quickly put him at odds with Chicana feminists and queer nationalists who dismissed the "old man" who was way too macho in his antediluvian ways.[71]

Tijerina's Prison Release

Reies López Tijerina was a different man when he stepped out of federal prison on July 26, 1971. He seemed broken, chastened, and uncharacteristically cautious. The *Grito del Norte* newspaper speculated in a story titled "Torture of Tijerina" that he had been lobotomized. He clearly was no longer the firebrand he once was. He complained of the psychotropic drugs he had been given at Springfield, which produced demonic hallucinations, of long periods of solitary confinement, of death threats from violent prisoners, and of his inability to receive the proper treatment he needed for a throat tumor that had only grown worse over the years. The throat tumor was surgically removed while he was in the Springfield prison, but he continued to complain about it, though his physicians found no physiological basis for his grumbles.[72]

In his first public speech after prison release, Reies addressed the student body of Eastern New Mexico University in Portales on Mexican Independence Day, September 16, 1971. He reiterated his well-known themes: the need to recuperate the mercedes, to excise "corruption, immorality, envy, jealousy, and hate," and condemning the US government for appropriating the duties "Christ designated for the Church, such as caring for the poor." A new concern was the government's expenditures on studies "of the ocean, the earth, the brain, the blood, the atom," which were accelerating the world's self-destruction through a nuclear holocaust. He ended his speech urging his largely white student audience to help restore the church's importance in society.[73]

Exactly one month after his prison release, he stated a new organization, the Institute for the Research and Study of Justice, on August 27, 1971. Its goal was "to study from a scientific point of approach all aspects of the question of justice." The documents Reies filed with the New Mexico State Corporation Commission named him the organization's president, his wife, Patsy Romero, and attorney William Higgs as officers, and listed 1010 Street NW in Albuquerque, the Alianza's building, as their address. He needed a new formal organization to advance his causes because one of the conditions of his federal parole barred him from any participation in the Alianza for five years. While Reies was incarcerated, the Alianza had lost most of its members. The loyalist core had devolved into warring factions, with sparing among Reies's brothers, his children, and longtime Alianza officers over fiscal problems, competition for the Alianza's leadership while Reies was in prison, and romantic entanglements that proved quite rancorous. Several of Reies's valiant ones had sexual relations with Patsy Romero. No one denied the fact, just finger pointing as to why sex occurred and whether it had been consensual or coerced. Reies's vengeance followed.

If Reies wanted to remain a public figure, he needed to rehabilitate his reputation as a political leader and important voice addressing racial and class inequalities in New Mexico and the greater Southwest. After the Echo Creek Amphitheatre takeover and the failed citizen's arrest at the Tierra Amarilla Courthouse, his reputation sank to its lowest point. No longer hailed as a savior, New Mexicans of different classes, races, and political persuasions mostly deemed him a criminal, a renegade, a violent man, and a communist. He wanted to return to his public persona as a man of God, as a herald of peace who had always been committed to racial reconciliation. Of course, that was far from true. One only had to recall his speeches about the means he would use to expropriate Anglo lands. Now, as he put it, he needed to contest the "campaign of defamation that the *Albuquerque Journal* had unleashed against the head of the Alianza." New Mexico's attorney general, David Norvell, was still calling him an "Anglo hater." US Senator Joseph Montoya continued to denounce him as "a beast from the darkness." Many still thought he had murdered or ordered Eulogio Salazar's assassination, even though those responsible had already been identified as part of a state police–funded plot to discredit Tijerina. "I was fighting to survive!" Reies explained. "I didn't know how to defend myself or how to protect—survive from the barrage of attacks. . . . I was fighting against all odds, and my only defense was to trust in God."[74]

Through his newly established Institute for the Research and Study of Justice, on April 8–9, 1972, Reies convened the first of several yearly "Brotherhood Awareness" conferences devoted to the idea and practice that all persons were "Brothers Under God w/o regard to race, color or creed to avoid confrontations and promote harmony." In the initial press release Reies issued inviting political and faith leaders to the event, he asked that "Warring Minorities Call a Cease-Fire," urging racial reconciliation by burying "the hatchet of self-interest." Writing in the third person about himself, something he frequently did after his release from prison, Reies assured invited dignitaries of his profound personal transformation:

> Tijerina, who spent 775 days in federal prison for leading an armed insurrection in the New Mexico hills, has put down his gun and taken up the battle cry of love and peace. We have Black Power and Brown Power. We need to build a human basis where a more realistic justice can grow. Justice has always been the aim of Tijerina. Some of his methods have been unorthodox but he has probably done more than any other Mexican American in New Mexico to bring attention to the inequities in our society. His life is the stuff films are made of and could well be material for a documentary.[75]

Tellingly, there was no mention of white power, which was the source of many of his problems. He dared not name it.

In his keynote speech inaugurating the first Brotherhood Awareness Conference, Reies expounded: "For six thousand years our planet experienced hate and war. We have now reached the peak of danger, hate and distrust, by building nuclear weapons to destroy our entire civilization many times over—But also, our education, research and discovery has reached a peak; a state of awareness." This first of several yearly conferences was well attended, drawing hundreds of civic, religious, educational, and cultural leaders from throughout the nation.

New Mexico's elected politicians participated by yearly declaring

"Brotherhood Awareness Week." New Mexico's Republican Congressman Manuel Lujan enjoined the US House of Representatives to issue Joint Resolution No. 1049, declaring the first Saturday of every April as "National Brotherhood Day." He did so on June 5, 1974, perhaps unaware that June 5 was the anniversary of the failed citizen's arrest at Tierra Amarilla Courthouse, which Tijerina loyalists celebrated yearly as a way of renewing their cause and restructuring their memories of their heroic struggles for land. To avoid any possible symbolic association with June 5, New Mexico's US Senators Joseph Montoya and Pete Domenici had their identical joint US Senate Resolution No. 215 not issued until June 17.[76]

Despite the wide range of detractors, Reies Tijerina still thought himself as Moses, still striving to lead Indo-Hispanos to their lost lands. To symbolize this prophetic quest, he commissioned the sculpting of a 430-pound rock that would serve as an eternal monument to his life and cause. The rock weighed exactly 430 pounds because Francisco Vásquez de Coronado "had come here 430 years ago" leading the first expedition of discovery into New Mexico, initiating the union of Indians and Spaniards, thus birthing the Indo-Hispano race. The idea of a stone monument had come to him in a dream, recalling how Jacob and his father-in-law Laban had reconciled their long-festering recriminations, symbolizing their covenant of peace with a stone (Gen. 31:45–48).[77] He named the rock *Armonía Fraternal*, Brotherhood Harmony, because on April 8, 1972, just as he was about to inaugurate the first Brotherhood Awareness Conference, his wife Patsy gave birth to a baby girl. Impulsively he named her "Harmony" because it was the "spirit of the conference, trying to develop harmony among different groups." Chiseled into the Armonía Fraternal stone's surface were the names of the leaders who supported Brotherhood Awareness.[78]

Brotherhood Awareness proved well intentioned, but it largely failed. Reies's critics did not cease or desist. In public, audience members would brazenly shout, "Who is he trying to deceive with his Brotherhood Awareness camouflage?" "The blood of Salazar, the murderer of Salazar, Tijerina, how can you now be speaking about Brotherhood Awareness?" Impervious to criticism, Reies dismissed the taunts as "poisonous propaganda," but the result was clear as attendance shrank at Brotherhood events. When, in 1977, he drew only forty attendees, he stopped convening the conferences.[79]

Figure 8. Brotherhood Awareness / Harmonia Fraternal Rock, 1973. After Reies Tijerina was released from prison in 1971, he attempted to rehabilitate his legacy in New Mexico as a man deeply committed to peace and reconciliation. From 1973 to 1976 he organized yearly Brotherhood Awareness Conferences, bringing together local civic and political leaders to discuss ways of eradicating racial hatred. He was still deeming himself a prophetic Moses. To commemorate the first Awareness meeting in 1973, he had this rock sculpted, ordering that it weigh exactly 430 pounds because it had been 430 years since Spain first explored New Mexico through the expedition of Francisco Vásquez de Coronado in 1540. Courtesy Tijerina Pictorial Collection, Special Collections and Center for Southwest Research, University of New Mexico Libraries.

Reies's federal parole conditions ended in 1976. He returned to the land grant issue anew as president still of the Institute for the Research and Study of Justice. Records for the Institute exist until 1981, when he submitted a grant request for $240,360 to the Campaign for Human Development of the United States Catholic Conference on January 15, 1981. The proposal's goal was to sue the federal government so that the residents of the Pueblo de San Joaquín del Rio de Chama could regain their land.[80] No documentary evidence remains about the application's funding or if the Institute ceased to operate after this date. What is known is that during it ten years of existence, the institute regularly offered student and teacher antiracism courses and week-long workshops.[81]

As Reies López Tijerina attempted to reshape his public persona, morphing from a violent insurrectionist to a peaceful mediator, his rhetoric of racial harmony and religious reconciliation went radically askew, precipitated again by dreams. His Manichean understanding of race relations as simply dichotomous, pitting oppressors against oppressed, foreigners against natives, Anglos against Indo-Hispanos, by 1980 included Jew against Christians but with caveats. He did not declare all the tribes of Israel enemies, just those infamous for killing their messiahs. To Reies's new thinking, to his genealogical investigations documenting his Jewish origins, which intensified his complex messianic confabulations, we turn.

CHAPTER 9

Of Prophets, Ancestors, and Tijerinas

Jesus was praying and his disciples asked him how they should pray. This was the prayer he gave them: "Our Father in heaven, hallowed be your name, your Kingdom come, your will be done, on earth as it is in heaven ... and lead us not into temptation."

—MATTHEW 6: 9–13

SITTING IN JAIL, SIXTY-FIVE days into his incarceration, Reies Tijerina penned a letter to his supporters fashioned after Martin Luther King Jr.'s 1963 "Letter from a Birmingham Jail." Widely circulated in Mexican American, leftist, and radical student-movement newspapers, "My Letter from Prison: August 15–17, 1969," detailed his struggles against the federal government. "I feel very, very proud and happy, to be in jail" for attempting to recuperate the land, language, and culture that were stolen from Indo-Hispanos. "I pray to God that all the Indo-Hispano people will awake to the need for unity, and to our heavenly and constitutional responsibility for fighting peacefully to win our rights. . . . The Jewish people accused the Pope of Rome for keeping silent while Hitler and machine persecuted the Jews in Germany and other countries. . . . By the same token, I denounce those in New Mexico who have never opened their mouths at any time to defend or support the thousands who have been killed, robbed, raped of their culture." Indo-Hispanos had to stand firm, united in their pursuit of justice. Reies was driven only by his desire for "the happiness of my people." That was his "divine dream."[1]

As the days and months in a prison cell agonizingly passed, and his appeals to higher courts were denied, "The weight of [possibly] facing twenty-six years in prison began to press on my mental faculties. I lost my faith and lost my feelings.... I began to lose contact with my reality." Reies felt as if time was standing still. It was a horrific time. Caged, the Tiger felt powerless, surrounded by guards with appetites for brutality, dodging the criminally insane, fearing rape, and placed with cell mates he was sure were there to kill him. Reies said he was surviving in his prison maze only by stepping "softly like a cat."[2]

On January 14, 1970, Reies was transferred from La Tuna Federal Prison in Anthony, New Mexico, because the warden felt that this low security institution, which mainly warehoused ethnic Mexican prisoners, lacked sufficient resources to protect the notorious Tijerina. Two days later, he arrived at the Medical Center for Federal Prisoners in Springfield, Missouri, coincidentally the headquarters of the Assemblies of God Reies so detested because they had expelled him as a preacher. First, he underwent several intake exams. A Stanford Achievement Aptitude Test established that his English vocabulary was at the level of a tenth grader, had the English language proficiency of an eighth grader, the math skill of a sixth grader, and accordingly was assigned to janitorial duties in the prison kitchen. A physical exam found no major medical problems save that he frequently sighed and cleared his throat, complaining of pain in a "somewhat histrionic manner." "Globus hystericus," the sensation of having a lump in the throat when nothing is there, was the initial diagnosis, exacerbated by a "hysterical personality." He was referred to a psychiatrist. Esophagostomy surgery removed the mass suspected as the source of his throat pain on May 18, 1970. Two weeks later a Penrose drain was inserted into the incision to drain an accumulation of fluids doctors feared might cause an infection. A hernia operation followed on July 21, 1970. From this, too, he recuperated well.[3]

Reies's first psychiatric exam concluded, "The man's defenses are rigid and internally felt... he appears psychotic... the patient is basically schizophrenic and probably has been for some time." By July 7, his condition had worsened. "The diagnostic impression should be changed to schizophrenia, essentially paranoid with grandiose and persecutory ideation. A major component also includes [somatic] delusions. The patient functions on borderline psychotic status," a conclusion four different psychiatrists confirmed.[4]

The drugs Reies received at the Springfield prison between January 14, 1970, and July 26, 1971, included common over-the-counter medications, from cherry cough syrup to Maalox, Mylanta, Tylenol, and Sudafed. A much larger list of more highly controlled drugs was listed on his medical record. When I consulted a psychiatrist about this list, his response was, "What craziness. I hope they didn't prescribe all of these over a short period of time. Back then the first-generation anti-psychotic drugs often had extensive adverse effects. They still do, just not as much. Thorazine (clorpromazina), Stelazine (trifluoperazina), Mellaril (tioridazina), and Haldol (haloperidol) are now the most commonly prescribed for severe mood disorders."[5] Thorazine is used to treat schizophrenia, particularly the manic phase of bipolar disorder, reducing aggressive behaviors such as the desire to hurt oneself. Stelazine tempers nonpsychotic anxieties. Mellaril is prescribed for schizophrenic patients who fail to respond to less potent antipsychotic medication but can cause heart arrhythmias and death. Haldol decreases suicidal thoughts, hallucinations, and hyperactivity.

Reies Jr., Tijerina's eldest child, visited his father in Springfield in early July and was startled by his father's mental deterioration. On July 31, 1970, he consulted Dr. Leonardo García-Buñuel, a professor of psychiatry at the University of New Mexico who had examined Reies several times in 1969. "At no time did I feel he was psychotic," García-Buñuel explained to Reies Jr. "He was, indeed, extremely depressed and, I thought even suicidal as the idea of taking his own life had occurred to him a few times. I did feel that he might become psychotic if his incarceration were to continue much longer." It now seemed as if Reies López Tijerina had "progressive and deepening psychotic disorganization."[6]

Days later, on December 6, 1970, Dr. García-Buñuel wrote Judge Howard C. Bratton of the US District Court passionately urging him to release Reies Tijerina or incarcerate him closer to his family, which might temper his worsening state. He was severely depressed, crying "easily while trying to laugh away his 'weakness.'" He complained of his solitary confinement for almost six months, that his "soul just shivering most of the time," with a feeling of disintegration. On many sleepless nights he had contemplated suicide. During these moments of desperation, he would read "the Bible or thinking about its teaching so that he will not fall apart and take his own life." Reies fully understood that he had "unwittingly hurt" others. "He is not exactly sorry for what he did . . . he did not want to hurt anybody." Indeed, Reies already was thinking of how to create a World Harmony project as penance.[7]

Further aggravating Reies's mental state was learning that his wife, Patsy Romero, was drinking heavily, having extramarital affairs, and barely supporting their children on welfare. He loved his wife very much and if imprisoned closer to home, with more frequent visits, he might be able to save his marriage and curtail Patsy's stress-induced behaviors.[8] Bratt was not moved by Dr. García-Buñuel's letter, nor those that followed with similar pleas from Governor David Cargo and Dr. Max Pepper of the National Institute of Mental Health.[9] The prison's visitor log showed that Patsy visited Reies thirty-four times during his eighteen months, or twice monthly, as had several of his children, despite the 827-mile distance from Albuquerque.[10] Friends and family wrote Reies often and warmly, telling him how much they loved and missed him. "I miss you very much and less so what we used to do for justice," wrote Rachel in June 1970. She continued:

> I know that you are a very smart man, I am very proud that you are my father. I know that you have a mind inspired by God, even if others say you are a communist. Your mind is inspired by God for the only thing you think about is helping the poor who are suffering because they were victimized by bandits who stole the lands God gave Indo-Hispanos. . . . God permitted his son Jesus to suffer on the cross to help his people, so too you have suffered. God has a good reason for allowing you to suffer as you have. . . . Since I was a young girl, I remember all the suffering we experienced. We never had the material things other families, we were always on the road, stopping only where we found work picking crops. All of our sweat was devoted to the cause of God's justice. . . . I think we have waited a long time for God's throne and for that reason I know I must keep the faith and continue to wait.[11]

In his 1978 autobiography, *Mi lucha por la tierra*, Reies Tijerina devoted twenty-three pages to his confinement in the psychiatric ward of the Springfield Federal Prison Hospital. He understood that he was there as a political prisoner on orders of the imperialist beast in the White House, President Richard Nixon, who intended "to destroy me" by surrounding him with crazy people because "I was an incorrigible schizophrenic . . . and thought myself a god." Nixon "hated me because I had questioned his right to govern. I abhorred him because he had destroyed our human rights, had trampled on the Constitution. He was a complex psychopath." Nixon and his rich Anglo cronies were using the psychiatrists at the Springfield prison "to destroy my mind," angry that Tijerina had demanded the restoration of Indo-Hispano lands and rights. Reies actively resisted these forces while in prison, not allowing himself to be lured into their mental traps, not eating food he suspected poisoned, not sleeping when new cell mates arrived sure that they were there to kill him, even refusing his drugs. To understand for himself how Nixon's cabal operated, Reies started reading books on psychiatry from the prison library, intent on turning the tables on his tormentors, intending to interrogate psychiatrists as handmaidens of a political class. During and after Tijerina's incarceration, he often spoke and wrote about himself in the third person, as a disembodied intellect, observing and describing a distinct self: Reies the physical body, present only as a corporeality.

"I discovered that the Anglo race suffered from the mental disease of psychopathy," a neuropsychiatric disorder marked by the lack of empathy, which often produces criminal behavior. "This is how I learned of the enormous hate [Anglos had] for anything regarding the historical rights to the lands on this continent discovered by [Christopher Columbus, who was] a Jew." Through these readings on psychiatry, Reies felt he totally understood the Anglo mentality: why they had exterminated the buffalo, assassinated Indians, propagated the Black Legend, drafted a constitution that restricted liberty but promoted licentiousness, swore on the Bible and signed treaties "In the name of Almighty God" yet separated church from state, why the Liberty Bell had cracked, why the government had built atomic bombs, and why Americans were so addicted to sex and drugs. "This grand psychopath had me in a mental ward trying to declare me the psychopath." It was the other way around. Nixon, the White House, and his psychiatrists were "the beast John saw with seven heads and ten horns" in Revelation 13.[12]

Reies complained that from the moment he arrived at the Springfield prison, psychiatrists surrounded him morning, noon, and night. They pestered him endlessly. Some were "faggots" (*maricones*), perverting their own patients yet had the temerity to inform the White House that he, Reies Tijerina was a psychopath with delusions of grandeur. These therapeutic sessions focused primarily on his childhood. Did he harbor anger toward the rich? they asked, seeking to confirm that his adult rebelliousness was rooted in childhood resentments toward rich Anglos. No. That simply was not true. When Indo-Hispanos lost their lands, they lost their livelihoods and were left impoverished at the margins of survival. This was what produced his protestations, not some idiocy that Reies had scavenged through the garbage cans of rich Anglos seeking food and consequently hated them. Was he afraid of the dark? No. He relished thunder, tempests, and hurricanes. They "excited me and gave me a great amount of joy," recounting the exuberance he felt during several Texas hurricanes and the rumbling and shaking of a Mexico City earthquake. Throughout all of these "interrogations," as he called them, he never revealed his true thoughts because he often felt as if he were in a trance. The drugs he was taking were probably doing just that, inhibiting manic outbursts and suicidal thoughts.[13]

Reies Tijerina was released from prison on July 26, 1971. As he worked to rehabilitate his public persona, hoping to morph from a violent insurrectionist to a peaceful mediator, he also delved deeply into his ancestral routes in the broadest sense possible, digging deeply into the Old Testament to map his lineage and prophetic origins in the Old Testament, and then more proximally through his family roots. In his mind this involved understanding his Jewish ancestry, but it also seems to have been the moment in his life when he went from comparing the land grant struggles in the American Southwest to Israel's struggle for a homeland. Jews went from being allies suffering similar historical displacements to being enemies in a worldwide conspiracy almost two thousand years old against Indo-Hispanos. To understand Reies's ruminations, let us first turned to Jewish history to illuminate some of his neuroses and what he analyzed as those that afflicted Jews.

Of Psychopaths and Psychiatrists

Reies Tijerina emerged from the Springfield prison deeming himself a sagacious psychiatrist on the basis of his slim prison readings. Addressing the valiant ones who gathered on June 5, 1987, to commemorate the "20th Anniversary of the Revolution in Tierra Amarilla," Reies explained: "If the Jews have admitted to me that they are psychopaths, they are schizophrenics, and I'm a psychiatrist, how can I hate them? No, no, I can't. I'm just speaking the truth. And I'm speaking about a patient, a patient that made the atomic bomb in self-defense. . . . How can a psychiatrist become the enemy of a psychopath?"[14]

Having just excoriated his Jewish enemies, denounced Jews as the anti-Christ, and expounded on the Jewish conspiracies that had thwarted the Alianza's recuperation of Indo-Hispano lands, many in the audience protested his remarks as unacceptably anti-Semitic. He retorted just as vehemently. "Don't give me any shit that Reies is anti-Semitic. No sir, that's shit. Because I didn't read book [sic] or literatures of enemies of the Jews. Every book I have is Jewish books [sic] written by Jewish authors." He fully knew the history of Israel's twelve tribes, their traditions, their struggles. As a long-time promoter of Brotherhood Awareness and racial and religious reconciliation, how could anyone possibly call him a Jewish hater? He was a descendant of Jews himself and as their "psychiatrist," it was his duty to expose their pathologies.[15]

Having anointed himself the psychiatrist of the Hebrews, his primary goal was to expose the psychopathic ideations that had led them to betray their messiah Jesus, persecute him, and have him crucified for thirty pieces of silver. To pursue this goal, he purchased a complete sixteen-volume, first edition set of the *Encyclopaedia Judaica*. Reading many of its entries expanded Reies's ideas. The research results of his years of study are spelled out in two large but still unpublished book manuscripts titled *La Historia de la Casa de Israel* (The History of the House of Israel) (1984) and *My Life, Juda-ism, and the Nuclear Age* (1986). Since much of what Reies Tijerina wrote in *La Historia de la Casa de Israel* maps rather closely with *My Life, Juda-ism, and the Nuclear Age*, below I rely primarily on this latter tome to illuminate the arguments he advanced.

My Life, Juda-ism, and the Nuclear Age offers readers what Reies called a "legal" history of Judaism in which he sweepingly connects the ancient Tribes of Israel, early modern European imperial expansion, land grabs after the annexation of the American Southwest, the production and use of atomic bombs against Japan in 1945, and his attempts to recuperate Indo-Hispanos lands. This manuscript is a very personal and total autobiographical text recounting the persecution he had selflessly suffered at the hands of many visible and invisible enemies. Organized as a diary, with sequential, chronically dated two-to-three-page entries, the end result is a series of unconnected historical fragments spread over 387 pages. Imagine for a moment the narrator in Marcel Proust's novel *In Search of Remembrance of Things Past*. When he bites into a madeleine and savors its flavors, out rush a torrent of memories, a jumble of sensations, described in kaleidoscopic streams of consciousness. Reies Tijerina was no Marcel Proust. I draw this comparison only to give you a sense of how a man who had suffered from undiagnosed and untreated schizophrenia probably since adolescence wrote himself backward into Christianity's long history and then forward, predicting the world's destruction he expected was very close, or as he would always put it, just beyond the horizon. The text is riddled with large temporal gaps, with neck-breaking flashbacks, and biblical misreadings and misquotations. The only sustained formal study of the Bible Reies ever took occurred in the mid-1940s as a student at the Latin American Bible Institute. His gaffes are explicable, as I hope are mine, as I have tried to make sense of *My Life, Juda-ism, and the Nuclear Age* for you, dear readers.

A search for a deeper understanding of Jewish history propelled Reies to undertake decades of research, which started with his own family tree. In the mid-1960s many Hispanos in New Mexico and Texas were discovering ancestral roots as conversos, those Jews who in 1492 had been forced to convert to Christianity or face exile. As the discovery and conquests of Hispaniola, Cuba, and the Aztec and Inca Empires advanced, many conversos fled to the New World, seeking lordship, opportunities, and safe havens for their clandestine observation of the Law of Moses. The fruits of Tijerina's genealogical research suggested a Jewish diaspora that led his ancestral kin from Spain to Hispaniola, and from there to north-central Mexico and Texas, chronicled in chapter 1. There I incorporated Reies

Tijerina's verified genealogical discoveries, carefully nuancing my own text where there were major documentary gaps and exuberant flights of fancy. Reies stated that the Indo-Hispanos of the American Southwest were "Christians by faith and Jews by Blood." How did he know this? "I felt it," he wrote. Something he thought he "proved" by digging through archives and genealogical records.[16]

That his Spanish ancestors were conversos is certainly quite plausible, given the many who left Spain as part of larger Sephardic diasporas hastened by the religious orthodoxy Spain's monarchs imposed after their reconquest of the peninsula from the Moors in 1492. Escaping religious persecution, living secretly as crypto-Jews, and centuries later rediscovering this ancestry in the American Southwest are experiences well documented in several scholarly tomes. This seems to have been the impulse and curiosity that led Reies to historical archives in Spain, Mexico, and Texas.[17]

Reies's in-depth research for ancient roots and routes produced an argument that his ancestors first made their way out of Assyria in biblical times, migrating across North Africa and into the Iberian Peninsula. It was certainly possible but was based on no evidence. A Diego Texerina and María Hernández in 1510 embarked at Cádiz for Santo Domingo. Whether Reies Tijerina's family tree emerged from these passengers to the Indies is another big leap of faith. This discovery was, of course, more purposeful than possible, enhancing Reies's self-representation, claiming that he hailed from an antique lineage of biblical prophets that in descending order connected Reies to Jesus, Joseph, Jacob, and Abraham, and to the religions that emerged therefrom as Judaism, Christianity, and Islam.

Most of what Reies wrote about his connection to Old Testament prophets and the false messiahs killed by Jews was based on essays in the *Encyclopaedia Judaica*.[18] Reies maintained that "Juda-ism"[19] and Israel were two different categories that should not be conflated. His spelling of "Juda-ism" points to this argument, connecting the members of this religion to *Judá*, which is the Spanish spelling of Judah. This division between Judah and Israel began as a brotherly conflict Reies explained:

> [Judah and Joseph] were [the] sons of Jacob. The conflict extended from two persons to two tribes; and later on, it extended from two tribes to

two kingdoms, and finally: it extended from two kingdoms into two world-wide religions: Judaism and 'Christianity.'... The great conflict between [the House of Judah] and the House of Joseph can be traced and documented through-out the five books of Moses. The Kingdom of Israel, was never the kingdom of Juda[h]. The kingdom of the House of Israel never killed its profets [*sic*]; while the kingdom of Juda[h] killed all its profets.[20]

The killings of which Tijerina writes are described in 1 Thessalonians 2:14: "You suffered from your own people the same things those churches suffered from the Jews who killed the Lord Jesus and the prophets and also drove us out." The larger point Tijerina starts to advance here is that he too is a messiah and that is why agents of the American state tried to assassinate him several times.

Tijerina proceeds to describe the division of King Solomon's state into two: the Kingdom of Judah and the Kingdom of Israel, collapsing Judah and Judaism as one category, in opposition to Joseph and the Israelites. As noted above, the House of Israel/Joseph morphed over time into "Christianity" and, according to Reies, connects Indo-Hispanos in New Mexico to Old Testament lineages through Christianization. One early sixteenth-century Franciscan theory of Native American origins was that they were one of the lost tribes of Israel; others have since similarly speculated about this connection including Joseph Smith, founder of Mormonism and the Church of Christ of Latter Day Saints.[21] Tijerina used quotation marks around a number of known identities, which he believed were incorrect, among them "Christianity," "Gentiles," "Samaritans," "Marranos," and "Anti-Semites." Judaism had propagated these names to breed confusion, "creating more and more false-impression name against their eternal foe: the House of Joseph."[22]

The conflicts between the House of Judah and the House of Joseph were political and geographic. "When God unleashed his wrath against the Joseph/House of Israel, he sent them to Assyria the sit [site] of Sem [Shem], and West to Spain. But 120 years later he sent the house of Juda to Babylon, the site of Ham."[23] The Babylon of Judaism was a cursed land as its name meant "confusion" (Gen. 11:9). God removed Abraham from this land, but nevertheless it remained the "birth-place of Juda-ism ... the birth-place of

Levite-Judaism 'grandiose' mentality." It was a "melting-pot of ideas, religions and demons," the place where the Babylonian Talmud and Kabbalah originated. It was in Babylon that Judaism developed its demonic beliefs that made them "the closest thing to Satan, the enemy of Jesus."[24]

Why was Babylon cursed? Noah cursed it because his sons Shem and Japheth saw him naked and drunk, and it became the "the play-ground of Satan and all his demons."[25] This was the foundation for Reies's claim that Judaism was born in a cursed land. As he saw it, Jews were the descendants of Ham, not Shem, and had been mistakenly identified as Semites. Nimrod, the grandson of Ham, established Babylon. He died in the flood Noah survived. Nimrod, by Reies's reckoning should be considered Judaism's founder primarily because of his rebellious spirit.[26]

Based on his theory of a rivalry between two houses, Tijerina moved back and forth, sideways and back, historically, from the earliest figures in the Old Testament, from Cain and Abel, Adam and Eve's sons, to the 1980s, based on a logic apparent only to him. Chart 1 below, is intended to help readers follow some of these sophistries of descent connecting Reies Tijerina and Indo-Hispanos to the Old Testament as a chosen people. The chart orders the sequence of conflicts between Good (Israel) and Evil (Judaism). Here is how Reies explained it:

> My research took me back into biblical history. Back to Cain -v- Abel. To Sam [Shem] -v- Ham. To Jacob -v- Esau. To Joseph -v- Juda. To the House of Israel -v- The House of Juda and the House of Levy; to the true Messiah -v- Leviticual Judaism, etc. The deeper I reached ... the better I understood the Atomic Age and its mentors. I learned that my fight was not really with the Anglos, but with the Haskalah Jews. They were the legal-responsables [sic] for the raping of our Pueblo-Towns. The Haskalah had learned how to hide his true identity.[27]

Abraham was a direct descendant of Shem (Gen. 11:10–32), who originated in Assyria. But God did not want him to live there among the Canaanites and led him to Babylon where his descendants were given lands between Egypt and the Euphrates, as God had promised (Gen. 15:18). This fact seemed evident to Reies because Muslims, also the children of

THE HOUSE OF JUDA / JUDA-ISM	THE HOUSE OF ISRAEL / JOSEPH
Juda	Joseph (also Jacob)
	Israel, Israelites
	"Christianity," Jesus
Juda-ism	Indo-Hispanos, New Mexico
	Tijerina
Followers of Satan	Followers of God
Cain	Abel
Ham (also Canaan)	Sem / Shem (also Noah)
Babylon, the site of Ham	Assyria, the site of Sem / Shem
Nimrod, a Hamite	Abraham, a Semite
Talmud	
Kabbalah	
Demonology, "Demon Jews"	
Killed their prophets	Did not kill their prophets
False Messiahs	Jesus
The House of David	(Nathan's curse)
Solomon's Temple	
Jewish mentality, grandiose, chosen	
Schizophrenia	
The Levites (also John Hyrcanus)	Jesus, Samaritans, Karaites
Haskalah Jews	
"Chameleons"	
Atomic Age / Nuclear Holocaust	
Zionism ("Jewish Messianism")	
The "Jewish State"	Palestinians; Lebanon (Sabra and Shatila)
England (also Henry VIII, Charles II); the United States	Spain
The Anglo-Juda-ism League	The New World
	Christopher Columbus / Cristóbal Colón

Table 1. In his unpublished manuscript, *My Life, Juda-ism, and the Nuclear Age*, Reies Tijerina offers a sweeping, partial, and highly idiosyncratic theory of Jewish history that begins by differentiating between the House of Juda and the House of Israel. He also sequentially outlines the oppositional historical evolution of these houses, inscribing himself as a descendant of Joseph and Jesus.

Abraham, primarily reside now in the Middle East between the Nile and Euphrates.[28]

Joseph, the great-grandson of Abraham (who descended from Jacob, Isaac, and Abraham) was especially blessed by his father. "The blessings of thy father have prevailed above the blessings of my progenitors unto the utmost bound of the everlasting hills; they shall be on the head of Joseph, and on the crown of the head of him that was separate from his brethren" (Gen. 49:26–27, as quoted by Tijerina). The seed of Joseph, as Tijerina postulated, had inherited the New World, "the land between two great oceans: the Atlantic and the Pacific." But the Jews and Protestants jointly colluded to "drive Spain out of the New World, outlaw Spanish and Catholic law [and] neutralized every political municipality created by Catholic-Spain." As Reies explained it, "From this illegal act, the Anglo-Jewish league continued to undo everything that Spain and the Church had legally created; down to the religious and property rights of all the Indo-Hispanos of the 'Southwest.'"[29]

Judaism's patriarch Judah committed two crimes motivated by jealousy. The first by kidnapping and selling his brother Joseph into slavery among the Ishmaelites, and the second by marrying a Canaanite, the daughter of Shuah (Gen. 38:1–2). For as Deuteronomy 7:1–6 commands, "When the Lord your God brings you into the land that you are entering to take possession of it and clears away many nations before you. . . . You shall not intermarry with them." Judah disobeyed God's command, turning him into "a legal renegade against the true and legal House of Israel."[30]

"Moses said this about the tribe of Judah: 'O Lord, hear the cry of Judah and bring them together as a people. Give them strength to defend their cause; help them against their enemies!'" This prophetic Song of Moses, which appears in Deuteronomy 32, Reies claimed was the "key to all the prophecies in regard to the true AND LEGAL House of Israel [and] . . . all the major profests [prophets], in their prophesies, stayed with-in the legal boundaries of Moses prophetic Song." The words "They turned to demons and not to God, Deut. 32:17, so he sold them 32:30, and spoke of the nucliar [sic] age, 32:43." This nuclear age, which Deuteronomy predicted would be "a fire . . . kindled by my wrath, one that burns down to the realm of the dead below. It will devour the earth and its harvests and set afire the foundations of the mountains."[31]

Reies next charted the history of the children of Joseph from their origins in the House of Israel to their contemporary geographic distribution in Palestine, Spain, and the New World. How they got to these places is explained in a manner akin to the conflict between Cain and Abel, and between Judah and Joseph. A war waged on the Iberian Peninsula for more than seven hundred years pitted Assyrian invaders against Spain's residents. Christian Spain emerged victorious. In 1492 Spain not only subordinated Islam in its realm, but Christopher Columbus discovered the New World. In 1494 the pope in Rome granted Spain and Portugal exclusive control over the Americas through the Treaty of Tordesillas. England responded with anger, refused to respect "the rights of the [Catholic] church or the political rights of Spain." From 1532 on, England was in cahoots with Judaism, constantly attacking Rome and Spain. To weaken Spain, Protestant England legalized piracy, encouraging the murder of Spanish missionaries and the burning of their churches, and in 1665, enacted the Surinam Act. This legislation birthed the "Anglo-Jewish League." It granted members of the "Hebrew nation . . . every liberty and privilege possessed by and granted to the citizens . . . and shall be considered as English-born."[32] This alliance eventually created the conditions for a "nuclear Holocaust" that one day will destroy Judaism. This is how the demonic goals of the Jews leapt from Babylon to England, and from there to the United States. The evil of this Alliance was physically evident in the fact that the "'Liberty Bell' [cracked] three times." That is why America's largest city was named "Jew York" and the country as a whole was the "Jew-nited States" of America.[33]

For Reies Tijerina the Anglo-Jewish alliance manifested its religious and racial hatreds in the United States through a group of secular, assimilated "court Jews" that he identified as the "Haskalah Jews," who had infiltrated the highest levels of power in politics, science, and medicine. *Haskalah* was the Hebrew term for an Enlightenment movement that began in the 1770s and extended into the 1880s. It promoted Jewish assimilation in language, dress, and manners, fostering loyalty and integration as citizens in the modern nation-state, considering this as the antidote for feelings of isolation and alienation among many Jews.[34] Tijerina, who was often very haphazard with his periodization and how history unfolded temporally, claimed that "the Haskalah-Jews were behind the anti-Catholic and anti-Hispanic

American hate. These chameleon-Jews have been exploiting the Spanish-English friction since 1532, when King Henry VIII broke away from the church." If the Haskalah first emerged in the 1770s, how could they have been at work since 1532?[35] But let us not quibble.

Watergate, the FBI, and the Nuclear Holocaust

On June 17, 1972, the Democratic National Committee headquarters in the Watergate Office Building in Washington, DC, was broken into by burglars connected to President Richard M. Nixon's re-election campaign. Aggressive reporting by the *Washington Post*, the creation of a Senate Select Committee on Presidential Campaign Activities, and the revelation of a steady stream of dirty tricks forced Nixon to resign the presidency on August 8, 1974. As these events unfolded, Reies confides in this autobiography that "Watergate forced me and gave me the green light to ask for my FBI files." He had long suspected that "the Beast" Nixon was his grand tormentor who worked through others. J. Edgar Hoover, whom Reies abhorred as a known homosexual, was one of Nixon's enforcers. He had ordered Tijerina surveilled. But in Reies's mind there had to be much more to the story that secretly unfolded. Reies suspected that a major conspiracy against him existed, which originated in the White House as an "Anglo-Jewish Alliance" with its tentacles and horns extending everywhere. The FBI had been spying on Tijerina's activities since the founding of the Valley of Peace in Arizona, and particularly as he and the Alianza attempted to liberate the free city-state of San Joaquín del Rio de Chama. It was after this event that Hoover's counterintelligence program agents set out to infiltrate, disrupt, and silence nationalist leaders who had the potential to become prophets. About these covert actions Tijerina was justifiably paranoid.

On December 17, 1979, seventeen months after he had requested it, Reies's FBI file arrived. Flipping through those 5,500 pages, "I found the footprints of an invisible force, an invisible force. . . . We were barking up the wrong tree. We were fighting the wrong enemy. The real enemy was invisible. The real enemy had complete control of the media, money, medicine." Reies previously had thought that the culprits were Anglo "capitalists, the rich, and that [they] had legislated against our towns." Now, he understood that the "same heirs who killed Christ, who crucified Christ . . . they put me with crazy people in prison." Here, at last, was proof perfect of the terrorist conspiracy waged against him, his family, the Alianza leaders and members, indeed, of the entire Indo-Hispano race.

In the pages of Reies's FBI file, "the real mentor and engineers of the terrorist conspiracy began to unfold before my eyes." The name "Rosen" kept appearing throughout those pages, authorizing actions against Reies and the Indo-Hispano towns, even signing the federal court documents that sent him to prison. "This Rosen tipped me off. This was a shocker for me. For the first time in my life I learned without a doubt, that Jews, not Anglos were after my head. This Rosen, an Haskalah, no doubt, was the missing link to Sutin (Satan)." Elaine Pagels, a historian of early Christianity, argues that the histories of Satan's origin and power that appeared shortly after the crucifixion of Jesus blamed the emergence of the devil on Jews and soon after were identified as the anti-Christ.[36] It took little to convince Reies to see clearly, though quite erroneously, that those who had robbed Indo-Hispanos of their land grants "were the magnates, the creator of the atomic bomb." Priding himself a learned student of "the nuclear age, the nuclear power, the nuclear terror," behind everything "nuclear," he found Jews. With this knowledge, Tijerina claimed he now better understood "the Atomic Age of terror. Haskalah Jews call this Nuclear Age, the age of 'light,' 'illumination,' and 'science,' but my investigation tells me otherwise."[37] What his research uncovered was that the "Authors of the Atomic Age," the scientists who had gathered in Los Alamos, New Mexico, to construct atomic bombs were Jews. "Robert Oppenheimer, Jew," even the man who unleased the potential for the construction of such a bomb, "Albert Einstien [sic], a Jew."[38]

Since his early days of Pentecostal evangelizing, Reies Tijerina had divided human behavior dichotomously, as good and bad, friend and foe, oppressed and oppressor, virtuous and evil, Mexican and Anglo, periodically revising these oppositional forces in history as his understanding of events evolved. In 1963, for example, the enemies of Indo-Hispanos and the Alianza were race-hating, land-hungry, Anglo capitalist invaders who took control of the Southwest in the decades after the Mexican War. As he sat in prison between June 1969 and January 1971, suffering from a long-undiagnosed case of schizophrenia, his enemies were Anglos. After his genealogical research into his ancestral roots and receipt of his FBI file, evil was now the result of an Anglo-Jewish alliance seeking world domination, which soon would end in a fiery nuclear apocalypse, prefigured as a showdown between God and Satan and, of course, as described in Revelation. All of this Reies finally understood and now could clearly see perhaps because of his hallucinations.

He asked himself: Would his testimony, based on his extensive research, and his suffering detailed in this manuscript, *My Life, Juda-ism, and the Nuclear Age* ever be known?

> I still don't know if I will have the time and will to publish this book. I am surrounded with Juda-ism controled [*sic*] power and terror; and my family is tired of so many acts of violence. Again, this book might serve the House of Israel and the surviving nations of the world, after the fire world baptism [*sic*]. At the moment, the agents of Juda-ism are keeping a very close watch of all my movements. I have done my best to keep a temporary silence, until I'm ready and my family in a safer place. But, hopefully, the world will get my life story and the truth about Juda-ism, before it is to [*sic*] late.[39]

Tijerina believed that for more than two millennia, the House of Judah had murdered men popularly acclaimed as messiahs. They killed Jesus in 34 CE, Simon Bar Kokhba in 135 CE, Menahem ben Salomon around 1160 CE, Shabbetai Zevi in 1676 CE, Jacob Frank in 1791 CE, John Fitzgerald Kennedy on November 22, 1963, Martin Luther King Jr. on April 4, 1968, and Robert Kennedy on June 6, 1968.[40] Reies Tijerina feared he was next.

Of Kinship and Kingship

In the final chapters of Genesis, the patriarch Jacob is described as having four wives, twelve sons, and one daughter. With three wives, ten children, and thirty-five grandchildren, Reies Tijerina would have been deemed Jacob's equal. He may not have had the prowess of King Solomon who had "seven hundred wives of royal birth and three hundred concubines" (1 Kings 11:3), but Reies Tijerina's patriarchal reins were second to none, easily rivaling any antediluvian biblical king. He was stern in the exercise of the laws of Moses, demanding the strict subordination of his wives and children to his impulsive, unexplained commands and mood swings. As we saw in chapter 7 on the Valley of Peace commune, Reies admired the multiple wives of the ancient prophets, especially the forty-nine plural marriages of Joseph Smith. The community fractured when Reies encouraged the senior men to consider polyamory. Quoting Isaiah 4:1 as his biblical authority, "And in that day seven women shall take hold of one man, saying, We will eat our own bread, and wear our own apparel: only let us be called by thy name, to take away our reproach." Instantly the Heralds of Peace split into factions. What amity they once shared toward each other dissolved into hostility and recriminations.[41]

Reies's first marriage was to María Escobar, a fellow Assemblies of God trained preacher, on July 14, 1946. They both attended the same Pentecostal church in San Antonio and knew each other because their extended families worked side-by-side in Michigan's sugar beet fields several summers. During their seventeen years of marriage, Reies and María sired six children, three sons and three daughters: Reies Hugh, also known as David (1947), Rose (1949), Daniel (1952), Rachel (1954), Ira de Ala, or "The Wrath of God," also known as Lita and Della (1956), and Noah (1959).

In the weeks following the inauguration of the Alianza Federal de Mercedes on February 2, 1963, María demanded more stability for her children, determined at last to enroll them in school fulltime. She begged her husband to find a job with sufficient pay to support eight. María was tired of their peripatetic life. Their yearly treks between Texas and Michigan as agricultural farmworkers following crop cycles, toiling under the broiling sun in back-breaking work from dawn to dusk, physically and psychologically cost the family more than the recompense they got. They rarely knew where they would sleep, if they would have enough to eat, and by what means they would move about, hopefully not on foot. Things had to change. All good and well, or so Reies must have thought. He had other things on his mind. He had just formed the Alianza. It was time to hit the road again, to traipse throughout New and Old Mexico organizing Indo-Hispanos who had lost their land grants, which he vowed to regain. Divorce followed on March 22, 1963.[42] The divorce decree declared the "parties are incompatible to such an extent it is no longer possible for them to live together as husband and wife . . . due to the fact that he would spend most of the family's income on his land grant issues which she considered a losing cause."[43]

Eighteen months later Reies married Patricia Romero on September 25, 1965. Their courtship was two weeks long. Reies confided that to make sure that this union was God's will, that he was not acting too impulsively, he consulted the angels who had lifted him into heaven during his Visalia dream. "Whenever I fear that I am about to do something inappropriate, the angels and spirits bother me." They did not.[44] Their union produced four children: Isabel (1966), Carlos (1968), Harmony (1972), and Danitha (God is Judge), also known as Donna (1973). These children were rarely mentioned by Reies in any of his subsequent writings or interviews. They were born between the height of the Alianza's attempted land seizures and after Reies served his prison sentences. Patsy's children were too young to remember much or to have participated in any of these events. María Escobar's children, on the other hand, were born in the thick of the Alianza's activism, the take-over of the merced of San Joaquín del Río de Chama, participated in the attempted citizen's arrest at the Tierra Amarilla Courthouse, and David and Rose were jailed on lesser charges. Subsequently they had much to say about their childhood at the Valley of Peace, their migration to Albuquerque, the history of the Alianza Federal de Mercedes, and their father's patriarchal rule.

Reies married a third time on July 19, 1994, to a Mexican woman named Esperanza García Valladares who resided in Uruapán, Michoacán, where they made their home until 2006. They relocated to Ciudad Juárez, Chihuahua, that year, which borders El Paso, Texas, moving because of Reies's deteriorating health from diabetes and a stroke. He required the attention of more specialized medical providers in El Paso through his Medicare benefits.[45] During one of their temporary separations, Reies wrote complaining about his lack of energy, how his eyes were irritated and burning, and that he had not been able to hold down any of his food. "My dearest love," he closed, "my heart beats with yours. . . . I long to be in your arms and know how unhappy I am with so far away. I feel exactly as you feel."[46]

Family Life in the Escobar-Tijerina Household

By all accounts from various vantage points, María Escobar suffered enormously as Reies's wife. When he announced that he had to travel to Mexico City for an extended period in February 1963, she concluded it was time to untie the knot and walk away. Reies had to undertake research on the legal origins of Spanish and Mexican land grants, or so he said. María knew better. She was no fool, though her husband often treated her as one, in an age when misogyny was sanctioned in ethnic Mexican families and submissive wives were the expected norm. Reies had a mistress in Mexico City named María Luisa Barrajas, with whom he had fathered a son he never recognized. "He took off and I filed for a divorce . . . he couldn't support us from over there," explained María. Reies said nothing to his children about his mistress or son, only his rationale for the breakup. It was entirely strategic. He needed a wife who was an heir of a New Mexican merced. María was not. Many locals were suspicious of Reies as a Protestant, Tejano, fast-talking outsider with no vested rights in land. Reies urged his children not to fear about what the divorce meant. "In the eyes of the Lord they were still one [family]."[47]

David Tijerina (Reies Jr.), their eldest and the one closest to his father, parroted that his parents divorced "under pressure from the U.S. government," an explanation that sounded as if it could have come directly from Reies's mouth. It was government persecution, pure and simple, he opined. After Reies traveled to Mexico, his mother was left without financial support. María applied for welfare but initially was denied because she was married. Her husband was legally responsible for their support. "So they divorced under pressure from the U.S. government," swore David. "And once they got divorced, my mother she felt free. . . . And slowly they became further and further apart." Rose Tijerina's narrative about the divorce echoed David's; it was for the advancement of the Alianza "cause . . . so that the [government] could support the family cause he [Reies] could not."[48]

Noah remembered the initial years after his parent's divorce as extremely difficult for his mother, brothers, and sisters. "The denial of any help for his first children was just a [source of] pride" for Reies. "Suffering for the [land grant] cause is the only way to win. 'After all it's a Godly cause,' my father said. My father said it. We believed it. That ended it. It was our father speaking. He controlled us with just his eyes. If we had objected to his orders and denial of help [he wanted] we were labeled enemies of the cause. The cause, our land, our people, and what's right is right."[49]

María undoubtedly needed more help housing, feeding, and clothing her six children than her $200 monthly welfare check provided.[50] Yet Reies was impervious to his children's basic needs. Noah recalled that one day he and his older sister Della (Ira de Alá) went to ask his father for some money to buy food. "He wasn't home, so we took some silver change that was in his desk." María quickly returned the money, knowing how angry Reies would become. "The next day my father took both of us out of school. My sister peed in the back seat from fear. He really beat us bad that day. All we wanted was food."[51]

Noah never forgot this episode nor the time he went to see his father at the Alianza's building when he was around ten. Noah desperately needed a new pair of shoes as his toes were sticking out of the ones he had. Recall how proud Reies felt when he got his first pair of shoes. "Son, you can't be bothering me anymore," he recalled his father's scolding. "I belong to another family now." Noah was stunned. "My hunger couldn't be seen but my anger could." Noah was four years old when his parents divorced. He missed his father, wanted to be near him, and yearned for his attention and affection. As Noah recalled these memories, he recounted how deeply he had "a desire to be accepted, approved of and loved by my father," something he carried throughout his childhood and adolescence into adulthood. He remembered how Reies would tell him that "I was going to make a good soldier in our people's army. He would pat me on the back and encourage me to resist, what he called brainwashing by the system. . . . [I had] to listen, learn and obey his word as law." Though Noah tired of these oft repeated maxims, he felt he had not and dared not protest.[52]

Four years passed. It was now 1974 and Noah was fifteen years old. Reies went to María's apartment in an agitated state and forbade Noah from visiting him at the Alianza building. His wife Patsy "had told him I had tried to make love to her." What? That was all a total lie. After that, for years Noah made no attempt to see his always absent, always manipulative, always commanding father. He began suffering extensive bouts of depression, frequently was in trouble with the law, living as a fugitive, much as his father had. What remained deeply embedded in Noah's memory was his constant childhood hunger, never having enough to eat, never even a morsel of love from his father to satisfy that desperate need.[53]

For Rose, Reies's eldest daughter whom he always called his "Rosita," his little rose, and she fondly called him her "papi," or daddy, their relation was equally fraught, vacillating between attraction and repugnance. Reies started sexually abusing her as a child, something that continued into her early adulthood. From the moment Reies began his Pentecostal evangelizing in 1946, preaching fire-and-brimstone sermons about sexual sin, lambasting those who succumbed to the lecherous wiles of Babylon's wicked whore, he indulged in what he most abhorred. I had heard many whispers and not-so-well-kept secrets about Reies's libidinous proclivities, his numerous extramarital affairs, the condoms he routinely carried should his charisma, his good looks result in comforting moments away from his matrimonial bed. I asked Reies point blank one day if he had ever sexually molested his daughters as was widely rumored. He looked at me intensely, eyes wide open, not even a blink. He smirked and without a word acted as if cradling an infant in his left arm close to his chest, while with his right middle finger pretended to touch the infant. That pantomime spoke a thousand words.

From reports on the implosion of the Valley of Peace commune, more than murmurs surfaced about the sexual abuse of young girls there by some of the older male Heralds of Peace. In an interview recorded in 2000, Rose admitted that when she was seven years old residing at the commune, "I suffered from bad experiences." She did not elaborate but became very upset, asking José Angel Gutiérrez, who was conducting the interview, to stop the tape recorder. He did. Nothing more was said. She needed a break to regain her composure.[54] In a subsequent 2007 interview, she spoke candidly about the "sexual abuse by her father . . . when she was a child and while at the Valle de Paz."[55]

Rose traveled with her father to Mexico City shortly after the Alianza Federal de Mercedes was formed in February 1963. The goal was to publicize the organization's formation and to plan a car caravan from Albuquerque to Mexico City that he hoped would bring media attention to the land grant cause both in the United States and Mexico. Reies was secretly playing matchmaker, trying to arrange a marriage between fourteen-year-old Rose and a young Mexican named Mauricio, who was nineteen. After Rose met Mauricio, Reies had a conversation with her, explaining that he had to prepare her for sexual intercourse because God had revealed to him that she would be the *vaso de la alianza*, the "cup of sacrifice from which the cause would drink." Rose recounted what later occurred. "He started molesting me. Every night . . . but I fought him off by crying and crying." Reies and Rose were being hosted by Dolores Rebelde and her husband, fellow Pentecostals, in their single bedroom apartment in Mexico City. Aware of what was going on the other side of the curtain that divided the room's beds, Dolores telephoned María Escobar, insisting, "Send for Rosita. Send for Rosita. She needs to be back with you, [sister]."[56]

What exactly did Reies mean when he told Rose that she would become the "cup" of the Alianza, or "el vaso de la alianza"? That was a question Rose asked herself but could not answer until she was much older. Biblically, Reies was referring to Christ's Last Supper, when Jesus and the apostles shared bread and wine, drinking from a shared cup, currently recreated during the Eucharistic portion of the Mass by drinking wine from a chalice and eating bread in the form of a host, but when consecrated, transubstantiated, and ingested becomes Christ's body and blood. "He took a cup and when He had given thanks He gave it to them saying 'Drink this, all of you; for this is My blood of the covenant, which is poured out for many for the forgiveness of sins,'" (Matt. 26:27–28). In Spanish *vaso* literally means "cup" or "vessel," but it is also the word used to describe a woman's vulva (*el vaso de la vagina*) through which semen must pass for the perpetuation of bloodlines and the marital creation of affines. This, I suspect, was the deeper meaning Reies had in mind.

Rose Tijerina was a very beautiful young woman. Men swooned in her presence. Reies observed that and soon started using his daughter's charms to attract powerful men to his cause, imbibing of the Alianza's "cup" laid before them. Mexican President Luís Echeverría Álvarez was mesmerized by Rose in 1975. Reies took her along with an all-male delegation to meet the president to discuss the lost mercedes, seeking the assistance of the Mexican state to help the Alianza litigate violations of the Treaty of Guadalupe Hidalgo. Echeverría diplomatically listened to Reies. Promised nothing. Echeverría's real focus was on Rose. He engaged her in extended conversation about a possible career as a Mexican movie star and showered her with gifts before she departed for Albuquerque, urging her to return soon.[57]

New Mexico's former governor David Cargo was so taken by Rose that he proposed marriage in 1985. "He wanted us to get married on June 5th at the Courthouse in Tierra Amarilla," claimed Rose. The proposal was retracted a year later, after the press lampooned what they deemed a poorly conceived unequal romance. Cargo acknowledged that he had dated Rose but never promised marriage. Rose displayed the engagement and wedding rings on her hands as her proof. Cargo did not want them back.[58]

To ritualize and honor the role Reies expected Rose to play in the Alianza Federal de Mercedes, at one of its yearly conventions Rose was ceremoniously presented a specially designed certificate proclaiming her "El Vaso de la Alianza." Reflecting on that event, Rose quizzically wondered in 2000 what exactly it *really* meant. She stated it in Spanish thus:

> "*Que yo iba ser el vaso de donde la Alianza, de la causa, iba tomar de mi.*"
> That I was the glass [*vaso*] *for la cause.* The *causa* (cause) was gonna serve itself from me, of my services. I guess that's what he [Reies] meant. And that I was gonna have to make a lot of sacrifices. There are sacrifices that I cannot mention here. That I will not mention yet. Someday when I'm an old woman I will. When some people are gone and dead.[59]

The crucial word in Spanish is *tomar*, which means both "to take" and "to drink."

That moment of revelation arrived on June 5, 1992, the twenty-fifth anniversary of the Tierra Amarilla Courthouse attempted citizen's arrest. The *Albuquerque Journal* published an interview with Rose where she confided that she had been diagnosed with "depression disorder and post-traumatic disorder," from which she had suffered since the 1967 courthouse fracas in Tierra Amarilla. "When I learned a lot of my reasons for my depression I decided my father is a lot of harm to me." Rose was under psychiatric care, taking medications for her depression, and "undergoing shock treatments."[60]

Rose was not the only victim of Reies's sexual impulses. It also destroyed Rose's younger brother Daniel. We know very little about him except for a few historical glimpses. In April 1968, Rachel, his younger sister, led a student "BROWN AND BROWN JUNTOS Walk Out," at Washington Junior High, in which David was also prominently involved. The first of their nineteen demands was that corporal punishment at their school be stopped. They wanted a higher number of Mexican American teachers, "REAL" bi-lingual, bi-cultural education, the firing of teachers who discriminated against Mexican Americans and Negroes, textbooks that reflected their participation in American history positively, the creation of a student council, an end to racist IQ tests, and a student lounge with a jukebox and staff, among other things. Rachel and Daniel were expelled, even though their final demand on the list was that no one get expelled for the Walk Out.[61]

In April 1971, David Tijerina was invited to attend and present at the White House Conference on Children and Youth, held in Washington, DC. There, addressing President Nixon and representatives from across the nation, he described the conditions in which the Indo-Hispano people lived.

> We have had it rough all of our lives and never had a home of our own. Ever since my father started this fight for justice here in New Mexico, it is very difficult for us to get a job. Our lives have been threatened. Our headquarters . . . has been bombed. The police and National Forest Service men have persecuted us and locked us up. I have also had to drop out of school twice because of my name. You see, the teachers don't like it very well. . . . We have not been brainwashed or whitewashed in the schools. . . . We need justice here in the United States, not in Vietnam. At the age of eighteen we have to go to Vietnam to die like animals or go to jail if we won't. . . . If all countries can't unite in peace, why don't you try to get peace here by satisfying your own people, not Koreans or Vietnamese.[62]

One year later, in 1971, at the age of nineteen, Daniel was drafted into military service, leaving behind the land grant wars in northern New Mexico for those in the jungles of Vietnam.[63] On his returned to New Mexico, he died from what many suspected as a suicide. On May 2, 1974, after a night of heavy drinking, he was involved in a high-speed, head-on automobile collision near Zuni, New Mexico, thought to have been fueled by rage on allegedly learning that his father had had sexual relations with his wife. The mortuary receipt for his burial on May 5 indicated that Reies Tijerina paid those costs.[64]

Rose confided in an extended 2000 interview that her mother had suffered enormously as Reies's wife because he "was like a wild horse." He "didn't want to settle for what little the establishment or the system has to offer. He didn't want a day-to-day job. . . . He always had this little [group of followers] with him. . . . But he didn't know for what. He just knew that there was so much injustice. . . . He wanted justice. He wanted to fight for something, but he just hadn't . . . pinpointed it."[65] Despite the many hours of work Rose devoted to the Alianza over the years, even going to jail for her participation in 1967 events at the Tierra Amarilla Courthouse, she always felt marginalized and infantilized by her father. Why? "I'm a girl." The real work of the Alianza was conducted by macho men.[66]

Noah recalled that his mother María never spoke ill publicly of the familial effects of her husband's choices. "She was a firm believer in the family, and she demonstrated unbelievable faith." But later, when the government, the media, politicians, and white supremacists began attacking anyone with a Tijerina surname, María "was left alone except for her kids. . . . My mother talked so much about the lord and obedience to him that it made me hate, because anything connected to God in our house, involved hunger. Worse yet, it required leaving any hostility, for whatever reason in God's hands." All they heard from their father were stale beatitudes and biblical refrains; "Jesus Christ had suffered for us, so it was only right that we should suffer for his cause." Noah lamented that his father "didn't teach us how to fight." He often felt like a chained-up dog constantly taunted and provoked by societal inequalities and injustices, but not allowed to fight back. "This was worse than being castrated."[67]

Della recounted that when she would ask her mother María to tell her stories about her childhood, María "often broke down in tears, recounting all the suffering she, David, Danny and Rose experienced while they migrated picking cotton, how [Reies] had given away the family's car, forced them to hitchhike long distances, and suffered even more in the Alianza." Writing her father on March 4, 1970, then incarcerated in Springfield, she begged, "Papie, forget about the past. . . . I [*sic*] sure God will pay us by some way."[68]

María Escobar suffered Reies's public humiliations silently, but in private she did not. She had worked tirelessly giving her six children the education God commanded. She wrote Reies in 1971, shortly after his release from

Springfield prison, complaining that he had failed in his paternal duties by not providing the child support the children were due ever since their divorce in 1963. How could he still possibly insist on María managing on her monthly welfare checks? What hurt María most, as she expressed it in this letter, was "when you ordered the children to give Patsy $10 a month to support her. Did I raise them so that they can support their step-mother? I . . . have a larger family to support than Patsy . . . and my health is ruined."[69] Reies continually failed to give María any child support. On March 29, 1974, she sued Reies in Bernalillo County District Court for the money she was owed for Noah's basic needs. He was then only fifteen years old and not yet emancipated.[70]

When Rose was asked about her childhood memories, she said, "I don't remember having a really neat, enjoyable childhood." Her family was always moving. "We were always in fear." As a young girl she did not exactly understand why her life was in perpetual locomotion, but as she grew older, she understood that they earned their daily bread as agricultural migrant laborers. "It was very hard work for children." David, Rose, and Daniel all concurred in almost identical words that their memories of childhood agricultural work were harsh, marked by hunger, limited food and water, and living quarters that were dumps. The only reward they received for their work, according to David, came on Sundays when Reies "would give me $1. He would give my sister Rose 50 cents, my brother Danny 25 cents, and my sister Rachel 10 cents," to spend as they wished. It was usually on candy.[71]

Then came the collateral damage associated with the Alianza. María Escobar believed that after she divorced Reies, with sole custody of their six children, they would no longer have to fear for their lives. She was wrong. "They were still coming after her too. It made no difference," recalled Noah. The hate and violence Reies Tijerina's land grant activism generated throughout the southwest had lethal consequences for the family because Reies had left them unprotected. Before Reies evicted them from the Alianza's living quarters to make room for Patsy, they had guards stationed outside the building, had bricked windows and metal doors, and they were relatively safe. All that changed. María Tijerina reverted to her maiden name Escobar because no one would hire a Tijerina and did not want herself or her children easily located and targeted. In 1968, while living with her children in a small apartment in Albuquerque, a bomb was thrown through her bedroom window. Maria's two-year-old niece was asleep on the bed by it and "flew all the way to the kitchen."[72]

Both Rachel and her younger brother Noah felt completely humiliated in 1969 when their middle school screened the NBC television documentary *Reies Tijerina: The Most Hated Man in New Mexico* before the entire student body. Soon the white girls at Washington Junior High started harassing Rachel, pulling her hair, throwing her to the ground, and kicking her, which ended in her expulsion. Noah remembered being ridiculed and harassed because of his father's radical rhetoric and confrontational actions. His classmates accused him of carrying a chip on his shoulder. "In reality what I wanted was to be left alone."[73] His father's criminal activities only led to fights at school and a sexual assault.

In *A Cause to Die For*, the autobiography Noah Tijerina penned in 2007, he narrated the years of violence and harassment his family experienced because of his father's land grant activism. Born in 1959, Noah was only four years old in 1963 when the Alianza was formed and his parents divorced. By the time he was eleven he had experienced death threats, unwarranted arrests, beatings, and home bombings. He and his siblings remembered how their mother protected them fearlessly. They were simply considered the collateral damage for his father's actions, the sad but necessary "casualties of that war."[74]

Despite the spartan public assistance on which María and the children survived, Reies still insisted that they had to pay their monthly Alianza membership dues. The Alianza "was and always would be god's and la familia's 'causa,'" he would tell them. From her monthly welfare checks María financed Reies's research trips to Mexico City. She undertook much of the bureaucratic work to forge the Alianza as a mutual aid society, serving informally as its corresponding secretary, office manager, and meeting note-taker with little appreciation or thanks.[75]

Shortly after Reies's release from the Springfield prison in 1971, while attending a national civil rights conference in Washington, DC, he publicly demanded an investigation into the vicious rape of his wife Patsy by a New Mexico state policeman and some nine other men while he was in prison. Rose had already informed her father in a very explicit letter of her stepmother's very public behavior. Patsy was having extramarital affairs with several different men. Reies refused to acknowledge the facts and instead launched a media campaign to get himself and the Alianza back into the news. In the final report issued by New Mexico's Attorney General David L. Norvell, who investigated Reies's accusations, the conclusion was:

> It is the firm opinion of this office that the allegations made by Reis [*sic*] Lopez Tijerina are patently spurious and unfounded, appear to be maliciously derogatory to the State of New Mexico and its State Police. In short, the allegations made by Tijerina appear to be calculated lies generated as a sop to his obviously bruised ego ... if Patsy Tijerina has been a victim of any wrong, it's that of her husband in his insatiable quest for publicity, power and recognition. She has been violated only by his, and his organization's callous disregard for her well-being and that of her family.[76]

Norvell had only contempt for Reies and would probably have accepted as true the account of the state police over anything Patsy Tijerina might say. Reies had several times spoken of Patsy as being mentally retarded based on an intelligence test she was given in high school. One, thus, has to read Norvell's report and conclusions with a grain, better, a cup of salt.

While Patsy's alleged rapes were being investigated by the attorney general and Reies was "bombarding the police" daily in newspapers and on television, Rose received a telephone call one night from a man who said he was Ray Otero, an Alianza member she knew only in passing. She had never had a conversation with him so the fact that his voice did not sound familiar did not alarm her. Otero said that the Alianza's vice president, Santiago Anaya, had asked him to pick up Rose to attend a meeting at the University of New Mexico that night. It was already dark outside when the designated car pulled up. As she entered, she did not recognize the driver. It was not Ray Otero. When she asked the driver who he was, and who was the man in the back seat, he replied that it really did not matter. "See those cameras back there in the back seat? ... Those are for you.... We need to send pictures to your dad to show him what rape really is." She was so terrified by what these strangers threatened that as the driver slowed the car to turn onto a different street, she jumped out. She called her mother, who picked her up badly shaken and black-and-blue. Rose recounted the details of the attempted rape to Reies and the Alianza's attorney William Higgs, but they decided not to take any legal action or to demand any sort of investigation. Reies's publicity stunt not only shamed Patsy Romero, publicizing her alcohol consumption, drug use, and sexual behavior, but Rose too was left badly bruised physically and psychologically.[77]

One day in 1973, "My daughter Lita (Ira de Alá), 17, came to me crying," Reies recalled. The owner of the Albuquerque jewelry shop at which she worked tried to rape her. "Why resist?" Jack Laduke asked her. "You're only the daughter of a murderer?"[78] Noah recounted a similar tale of horror, but this time a rape did occur. It all began one snowy winter night in 1974, as he was leaving Albuquerque's Dog House Drive-in, where he liked to hang because it had a jukebox and pinball machines. As he exited, he heard a car's horn repeatedly honking to gain his attention. It was police officer Albert Vega in a dark Plymouth Fury II sedan. He asked Noah, "Do you know where Fuchon lives?" He did and gave Vega driving instructions. Vega insisted that Noah get into the car and guide him. *"Y yo como pendejito* [And I, like a little stupid kid], you know, real stupid, real innocent got in the car and within minutes he was tearing my pants off. . . . I guess that's when God gave me the strength to turn around and start kicking the hell out of him. . . . I fought for my manhood." Noah broke free and exited the car, desperately pulling his pants up from his ankles. The rest of the night he remembers only as a fog until Reies reached the emergency room yelling, *"Te la metió? Te la metió?* [Did he stick it in you?] That's what I remember of my dad. The doctor turned around and said, 'No.' . . . That's what I remember of my loving father. 'Te la metió?'"[79]

Noah wanted Vega prosecuted. He was a known pedophile with a long record of sexual crimes in northern New Mexico. He allegedly had been recruited by the police to target Tijerina's family, or so Noah maintained. Reies again refused to file a legal complaint, explaining that the state police promised Reies quick parole on a pending state sentence and $1,000, to make all of this disappear. Reies indeed was paroled after a month in jail.[80]

"Every one of the kids had been raised to believe in 'la cause' but we were all still kids," writes Noah. "Hell, the way I saw it, my father was already married to another woman, and already had other kids. Why target me? My father didn't pay much attention to me anyway, so why would the police? But, I was young, and naive. I was about to find out the hard way. The New Mexico State Police didn't care about their targets' age or sex, when they were ordered to neutralize and discredit the Tijerina's, they did a very thorough job."[81]

Noah was given no say in the negotiated rape settlement and ultimately only got $500 of the $1,000 promised. Reies pocketed the other $500. Noah felt wounded and betrayed. Those feelings only intensified the next day when the *Albuquerque Journal* reported that Reies Tijerina's son Noah had been raped. The rape had not been so quietly resolved. Vega was eventually charged, pled guilty, and sentenced to two years of probation. From that point on "I was a loner. Nobody hung around with me then. All my friend's parents [would say], 'don't hang around with that Tijerina kid.' ... So, I grew up mean and alone."[82] María Escobar attested that these events took a major toll on Noah's mental health and resulted in three failed marriages. "He's a very sick man ... He has many problems. Psychological. Nervous. Irritable."[83] Noah admitted that through all of his trials and tribulations he tried to get his "strength from God. Because for a long time I tried to draw it from my dad. ... And it wasn't working." Noah ultimately fathered a son and a daughter. He named his son Reies López Tijerina and his daughter, Israel Tijerina. What greater tribute could a son give his loveless father?[84]

Four years later, in 1977, an Anglo man sporting his hair in a crew cut tried to abduct Reies's eight-year-old son Carlos, from his marriage to Patsy. The Alianza's large building in Albuquerque had a boxing ring where young boys and men were taught self-defense. Reies heard strange noises coming from the area. When he rushed to see what the commotion was all about. "I caught this strange looking Anglo leading my son into his car. I pulled my son, while holding my gun pointing at the Anglo stranger. I got so angry I almost pulled the trigger."[85]

These were the trials and tribulations Reies Tijerina and his family faced from his entry into the ministry in 1946. His imprisonment from 1969 to 1971 brought his schizophrenia to light. His reading of his FBI file in 1979 finally allowed him to understand how extensively the federal government surveilled him and tried to silence him. He had been justifiably paranoid. In moments of depression or anxiety, or when he sought divine inspiration for actions, he turned to his Bible. In all his written work and public speaking, Reies always extensively quoted the Bible to illuminate and legitimatize his actions. Imagine, for a moment, a person who lived his life governed by the Bible's alpha and omega. It begins with the Pentateuch, the first five books of Moses (Genesis, Exodus, Leviticus, Numbers, and Deuteronomy), which describe the world's creation, Moses leading the Israelites to Canaan, their promised land, and ends with the commandments God handed Moses' before his death. These were the genealogical roots Reies claimed for his clan. According to his own mental maps, his enemies had been perusing him for millennia. He confidently asserted that a route from Assyria had led him to New Mexico to recuperate Indo-Hispano land grants. Turn next to the Bible's last book, Revelation, which describes the punishments God promised to inflict on the sinful. As the apocalypse approached, it would be marked by great tribulation, rapture, and end in the world's incineration. Factor in the psychiatric diagnoses of schizophrenia and his medication, with grandiose ideations accompanied by intense paranoia, and one begins to enter Reies López Tijerina's mental universe more deeply. This is what made the lives of his wives and children so difficult, or in Noah Tijerina's view, the collateral damage they experienced.

EPILOGUE

Reies López Tijerina was a complex person as a preacher and social activist, as a husband, father, and leader. He died on January 19, 2015. He lived to the age of eighty-one and was an eyewitness to enormous societal changes wrought by the Great Depression, America's entry into World War II, and all of its subsequent wars as an evangelist offering redemption to the sinful. Reies was a social activist who helped shape the long civil rights movement for racial justice that resulted in major but short-lived reforms of the 1960s. He was born into an ancestral lineage who colonized Texas in the 1740s, which deemed itself noble and prosperous until they lost the lands the kings of Spain gave them for colonizing the frontier. With the loss of these lands, they were forced into wage work and share cropping to survive, quickly descending into poverty that reproduced itself generationally. Reies's mother, Herlinda, died when he was four years old, leaving his father Antonio with seven children to raise on his own. To survive they followed the crops they planted, tended, and harvested. Constantly on the move, poorly paid, the childhood memories of Reies's brothers and sisters and those of his sons and daughters were of chronic hunger and homelessness. Reies matured bristling under the mores and manners of white racial supremacy in Jim Crow Texas, barred from hotels, restaurants, bathrooms, water fountains, swimming pools, even cemeteries. Understandably he talked back to those in power as a young man. By the time he was an adult he was courageous. He rarely looked away or walked away when others faced adversity. When others were in desperate need, he gave away everything he owned to alleviate their suffering. Whether picking cotton in Texas, planting sugar beets in Michigan, or plucking tomatoes in Colorado, he selflessly spoke up for those too powerless to protest, demanding just wages, better work conditions, and a decent place to rest one head. He was drawn to an evangelistic ministry in 1943 largely because a preacher gave him a copy of the Bible, and later in 1958, he turned to civil rights politics, believing that God had chosen him as Moses to rescue American society from a sinfulness born of prosperity and to protest the injustices America's mid-nineteenth-century imperial expansion had wreaked on the communal lands in the Southwest Indo-Hispanos once owned.

As a Pentecostal preacher Reies Tijerina called sinners to an apostolic faith that would free them of their worldly woes through Holy Spirit baptism and the laying of hands, promising those with few comforts in life an afterlife of abundance. His message to land grant heirs was identical. It too was restorationist, certain that he would recuperate their stolen land grants. When that day arrived, Hispanos would prosper planting verdant fields of plenty as they had in past times, on which they and their livestock would fatten. What followed was the formation of the Alianza Federal de Mercedes in 1963, endless petitions begging the US government to honor the property provisions of the 1848 Treaty of Guadalupe Hidalgo. When that failed, the Alianza and its supporters took over a small portion of the Kit Carson National Forest, declaring it the free city-state of San Joaquín del Rio de Chama. The state and federal governments, along with New Mexico's rich and powerful, had no intention of letting such fantasies become reality. What finally led to the manhunt and arrest for Tijerina and twenty of his valiant Alianza loyalists was a now-famous or infamous Tierra Amarilla Courthouse fracas on June 5, 1967.

How should this event in Tijerina's land-grant struggle be framed? Several years ago, after a talk I gave at the University of Michigan on Reies Tijerina's religious critique of American imperialism in the 1960s, I mentioned the Tierra Amarilla Courthouse Raid. María Varela, who also presented on her work on participatory democracy, thanked me for the talk but told me I was wrong.[1] It was not a "courthouse raid," it was a failed "citizen's arrest." As I reread the trial records, to determine if Reies was guilty of first-degree kidnapping and pistol-whipping the jail's deputy sheriff Dan Rivera, María was absolutely right. I asked myself how did that language of the "courthouse raid" get so deeply implanted in my brain? As the trial transcript showed, in his own defense Reies insisted that he and the Alianza members who arrived at the courthouse on June 5 were there to make a citizen's arrest of District Attorney Alfonso Sánchez for illegally depriving them of their constitutional right to assembly. Tierra Amarilla Sheriff Benny Naranjo confirmed this, saying that what had transpired was not an attempted jailbreak or courthouse raid. "That's all wrong. They came for Al. . . . The raiders had it in for Alfonso Sánchez."[2] When Dan Rivera testified for the prosecution, he, too, testified that he did not blame Reies for anything that happened at the courthouse that day. Before the jury began its deliberations, the state's prosecution lawyers, headed by District Attorney Sánchez, maintained that the Alianza members had been arrested preemptively, to forestall another rumored land invasion. Judge Paul Larrazolo, who presided over the trial, instructed jurors on what constituted a citizen's arrest and that they were legal. Tijerina was found not guilty, sparing him a sentence of life in prison or death.

Framing June 5 as an armed "courthouse raid" was an attempt by the state to take one life. By using this language, Tijerina's opponents vilified him as a violent, radical, nationalist revolutionary. Such language rapidly made him a conservative bête noire, caricatured as "King Tiger" (aping the Black Panthers), and as the Mexican American Malcolm X. The dominant narrative of the events at the Tierra Amarilla Courthouse on June 5, 1967, were forged initially by District Attorney Alfonso Sánchez who, since 1964, had been asserting that Reies was a communist. The Albuquerque *Journal* and *Tribune* newspapers repeated this "raid" language, as did US Senator Joseph Montoya, J. Edgar Hoover and the FBI, and other powerful interests in the Southwest determined to depict it as an illegal act and Reies Tijerina as a criminal. That narrative has not changed even in the most recent publications on Tijerina's actions during the Alianza period, reminding us of the enormous power of the state, its elected officials, and the media to shape dominant narratives of history, and our need to resist and contest how these forces easily distort memories and bias how history is told and taught.

One of the themes in this book has been to offer readers entry points into Reies Tijerina's mental universe. He mystically transported himself to ancient Palestine, engaged the Bible's prophets, was lifted by angels into celestial kingdoms, and anointed by the "One" to rule over the world. He often recounted a dream he had when he was five years old, of his death and resurrection, walking hand in hand with Jesus Christ, which he called his "little death." I puzzled and agonized over what to make of this when first I read it. He repeated it so many times throughout his life. Initially, I suspected that perhaps it originated as a song, a prayer, a story, or a religious picture of Jesus walking hand in hand with a child that adorned his house and that for some reason was deeply imprinted in his memory. I read it as his parable of invincibility. Even if he died, he would be resurrected victoriously to battle evil just as Jesus Christ had. As Reies aged, he continued mentioning dreams, visions, the little death, hallucinations, and deep depression, which prompted me to wonder about his mental health since his adolescence. Physicians who treat manic depression and schizophrenia maintain that these mood disorders usually emerge in late adolescence, around the age of seventeen. Antonio Tijerina, Reies's father, had minimal access to medical care, relying mainly on the communal laying of hands at Pentecostal revivals to quell demons. Late in my archival research, I chanced on the assessments of several psychiatrists, who treated Reies before and after he entered prison in 1969. While incarcerated at Springfield, he was diagnosed as suffering from bipolar disorders, acute paranoia with grandiose and persecutory ideations, and schizophrenia they suspected had been present for a long time. Working backward through the documentary traces that chronicle Tijerina's life, those symptoms are present in his own self-descriptions and also comments by others.

The first signs of manic depression occurred when he left home to attend the Latin American Bible Institute in 1943. Reies sank into a sullen state almost instantly. He had expected angelic visitations there, but when they did not occur, he isolated himself, judged his classmates harshly, and was combative with his teachers. His official student record at LABI described his behavior as "poor," noting that he was twice suspended and forbidden to graduate with his classmates, even though he had completed his course of studies. Back with his family during these suspensions in 1944 and 1945, at the height of World War II, whenever letters from his brothers arrived describing the atrocities they were witnessing as soldiers on the European front, the family gathered to read them out loud. Reies would instantly panic and hide under a bed for hours until he calmed.

After he lost his first post as an Assemblies of God evangelist in November 1946, he went to Los Angeles to seek God. He was deeply psychologically bereft, or so Reies himself said, feeling as if he was "a hypocrite" without direction, "that I was way back, way behind, that I had to overcome everything."³ There in the foothills of the San Gabriel Mountains, at the age of twenty-one, he dug a cave-like hole and crawled into it. After fasting for days and entering a delirious state, he described his mind as "out into space."⁴ He instructed his wife María, "If I die in my persuit [sic] of God don't tell any body that I died trying to find god."⁵ In that cocoon he lost track of time. When he emerged, he wrote that he finally understood that "there was just the two strong powers of good and evil" in the world, something he should have known already from Bible school.⁶

In *Mi lucha por la tierra*, Reies's 1978 autobiography, he described the creation of the Valley of Peace commune in the wilds of Arizona as an escape from the world. Previously he had burrowed himself under a bed at home, dug himself into a cave in Los Angeles, and now at the Arizona commune, he and his valiant ones lived underground in makeshift bomb shelters awaiting the nuclear holocaust, which according to Reies, he could see rapidly approaching, just beyond the horizon. When the commune fractured over his desire to live as the prophets of the Talmud and the Mormons with multiple brides and incestuous relations, he again bolted to California where he had his super dream, the one at Visalia. This time he was carried by angels on a cloud to the kingdom of heaven, there "the One" authorized only him to rule over the earth as God reigned in heaven, or, as the Lord's Prayer says, terrestrial relations should mirror the celestial order. After that revelation he abandoned his ministry for the recuperation of land grants, probably based on his own ancestral experiences in Texas and from what he learned about New Mexico's land grants while staging revivals there in the late 1940s and early 1950s. How Reies connected the dots among the thick forests, frozen horses, ancient kingdom, and cheering throngs remains one of the puzzles he never really explained. Nevertheless, by 1963 he was now convinced that he was Moses incarnate.

There were many more dreams, feelings of being unjustly persecuted, flights of grandiosity, suicidal moments, dramatic mode swings, manic sermons and speeches that went on all day and into the night, violent confrontations he called "showdowns" invoking the tribulation that Revelation predicted would accompany the Apocalypse. He generated such "showdowns" by invading and appropriating a section of Kit Carson National

Forest to reestablish San Joaquín del Río de Chama in October 1966, and announcing another "showdown" planned for June 1967, which prompted Alfonso Sánchez to arrest Alianza members preemptively.

When he entered prison in 1969, Reies Tijerina was clinically paranoid and delusional. His physicians there, mainly psychiatrists, concluded that he suffered from schizophrenia. When he finally received his redacted FBI file in 1979, he learned that his paranoia was justified. J. Edgar Hoover, the FBI, and the New Mexico State Police were responsible for the targeted violence he and his family had suffered to silence him. Those were not ideations. These were documented facts. That documentation generated a whole new set of conspiratorial theories, dark forces lurking everywhere, all denying him the terrestrial rule God authorized in his Grand Dream.

This was when he became openly anti-Semitic. Having personally interacted with Reies many times from 1978 on and hearing him publicly speak, that hatred began being publicly enunciated in the 1980s. When Reies began his Pentecostal ministry, he often described Jews as an old, historical people and placed them in biblical history positively as a group who had spent millennia seeking God. He focused on Moses leading them out of their Egyptian captivity, living by the commandments God gave Moses. In *Will He Find Any Faith on Earth . . . ?* (1955) Reies's sermons mention Jews many times but only their suffering and resistance under Roman imperial rule, how devastated they were on seeing their temple in Jerusalem destroyed by Roman soldiers in 70 CE. Through all this tribulation Jews persevered, keeping their faith in God and rejecting all the blandishments Rome's colonial exploitation offered.

After Reies started the Federal Alliance of Land Grant Heirs, he compared the desire of Indo-Hispanos to recuperate their own lost land grants to the creation of a Jewish homeland in Israel. When the *New York Times*, on June 6, 1967, reported on the Arab-Israeli Six Day War that began the very same day of the failed citizen's arrest in Tierra Amarilla, Reies found the media coverage and the convergence of these two events as of divine design. God had brought these two land struggles to the world's attention for resolution.

In *Mi lucha por la tierra*, Reies's 1978 autobiography, the most critical thing he wrote about Jews was still anchored in the side-by-side stories in the June 6, 1967, issue of the *New York Times*. He highlighted the fact that Jews had abandoned their lands in Palestine for two thousand years, yet the Western powers had given them Israel as a homeland. Why, then, was the United States so unwilling to restore the ancient Indo-Hispanos lands? Unlike the Jews, Indo-Hispanos had never abandoned their homeland. They had legal titles and had been petitioning for their return for a century. Reies compared the "true sons of the Southwest" to the "Jews who now reside in the ancient towns of Palestine." He even acknowledged that Jews had joined his Brotherhood Awareness movement. There was nothing approaching anti-Semitism in this tome.[7]

Reies's receipt of his FBI file in 1979 seems to have precipitated a break in his thinking and reordering of his demonology. In 1986, he claimed that Indo-Hispanos were Jewish by blood. What followed from his intensive genealogical studies was his own lineal descent as a messiah from Abraham, Jacob, Joseph, and Jesus. His anti-Semitism vacillated between a generalized hatred of all Jews in the present, but a more targeted one in biblical times against the descendants of the House of Judah because they had routinely killed those men who emerged as messiahs. This is why they had tried and continued to try taking his life. These Jews detested his messages. All this was unfolding during the Ronald Reagan presidency, between 1981 and 1989. He was part of an alliance between Haskalah-assimilated Jews and "the Beast," or the president of the United States, to kill Tijerina. His proof perfect was in numerology. The name Ronald had six letters. Reagan had six too. He was the devil incarnate referred to in Revelation as 666.

Reies Tijerina's unvarnished anti-Semitism appears in his 1986 *My Life, Juda-ism, and the Nuclear Age*. He writes:

> Never in the history of human civilization had one people raised a standard of hate and vengeance, as the Jew and Juda-ism has done it against another people. This Jewish war-cry, helped me to create consciousness of my own Indo-Hispano people's persecutions, massacres and real holocausts, in Texas, New Mexico and California. With the great legal differences, that the Indo-Hispano people were not guest of the butchers, like the jew were in Germany. Where is the legal monument to the holocausts in Texas, California and New Mexico? Where

are the holocaust monument to the true legal Indians of the United States?"[8]

This was the extent of what I found in Tijerina's writings, though in person I heard more strident denunciations of Jews in 2012, when I heard him speak in Los Angeles. By then his speech was garbled by a stroke he had suffered, and he was in a wheelchair unable to walk. He was no longer the psychiatrist to Jews. He was the one who suffered from psychopathy, the lack of empathy for others.

Reies Tijerina, both as a preacher and political activist, always behaved in condescending, demeaning, and dismissive ways toward women. He surrounded himself with men, particularly aggressive macho men. They were his most "Valiant Ones" fighting evil. Four strong-minded women who intersected with Reies Tijerina in major and minor ways assessed his ideals and actions bluntly but truthfully. Myra Ellen Jenkins, New Mexico's State Historian and Archivist, recited facts about which Reies continually sparred with her. These included the fact that land tenure in the Mexican territories the United States annexed in 1848 had been settled by the Office of the US Surveyor General between 1854 and 1890, by the Court of Private Land Claims from 1890 to 1900, and shortly after was ratified by Congress. Also, whatever injustices, fraud, illegal land seizures, and the destruction of deeds had occurred in the remote past. Jenkins believed those grievances were almost impossible to reverse. Powerful federal, state, and corporate interests were determined to forestall any change to property rights. New Mexico was governed by the rich who were not particularly concerned about poor, landless Hispanos; they were only a source of cheap labor and little else.[9] María Escobar, Reies's wife of seventeen years, reached a very similar conclusion. She divorced Reies because she was tired of him spending "most of the family's income on his land grant issues [which she deemed] a losing cause." What María failed to note in her petition to end their marriage was that she was the family's only wage earner supporting eight, while funding Reies's "research trips" to Mexico, which included the comforts of a mistress.[10]

Rose Tijerina, Reies's eldest daughter offered a longer perspective in 2000. Her father behaved "like a wild horse.... He didn't want a day-to-day job.... He just knew that there was so much injustice.... He wanted justice. He wanted to fight for something, but he just hadn't ... pinpointed it."¹¹ When he finally identified and focused on the recuperation of Indo-Hispano stolen land grants, he lacked the organizational skills to accomplish it. Aware of the media attention African American protest gained, which he concluded had resulted in President Johnson signing into law the Civil Rights Act of 1964 and the Voting Rights Act of 1965, he sought to learn from their organizational tactics, thus seeking alliances with Dr. Martin Luther King, Elijah Muhammad, and a number of Black nationalists. Perhaps through osmosis and some coaching he might emulate their media savvy in shaping news. Toward that end Reies Tijerina met María Varela, a seasoned activist in SNCC, in Chicago during the National Conference for a New Politics in early September 1967. A week later Tijerina wrote Varela, extending an invitation to visit New Mexico to help the Alianza improve its media strategy. He needed "a true fighter and a very brave girl ... to spend some time among our people."¹² She accepted but in less than a year ended her association with Tijerina and the Alianza, disillusioned by what others had caricatured as "Reies T.V.rina." His forte was his ability to mesmerize a crowd with his oratorical skills and incendiary pleas for justice. These tactics easily grabbed the media's gaze. "For him," explained Varela, "any media attention was one more block in the wall or stepping stones to build power. ... That's what he thought his job was. He wasn't an organizer. He was a preacher. And preachers need an audience."¹³

In early 1968, on the eve of his April 4 assassination, at the very moment the Rev. Dr. Martin Luther King Jr. was himself becoming more radical around issues of economic justice, he was profoundly unsettled by the language of Black Power. For decades he had rallied a wide range of allies around the Freedom Now slogan. Early in 1968 King confronted Stokely Carmichael, explaining that "the words 'black' and 'power' together give the impression that we are talking about black domination rather than black equality," correctly predicting that this rhetoric would unleash a torrent of white prejudice, which up to that point most whites had been too timid to express openly.¹⁴ When Reies and the Alianza's members gathered for their fifth annual convention in Albuquerque with leaders of the Black Power Party, the Free Hopi Indian Nation, and Chicanos advocating the revolutionary formation and succession of Aztlán to sign a "Treaty of Peace, Harmony, and Mutual Assistance," the power of the federal government barreled down on Tijerina. The legal criminal webs that ensnared Reies landed him in prison, led to the unravelling of the Alianza, and delegitimized him as a civil rights leader. He was now a convicted criminal, a stigmatizing status he failed to rehabilitate.

Every history book is rooted in the concerns of its moment, looking backward critically at the past to project forward into the future stories of alternative possibilities, failed experiments, and paths that proved successful for change. In 2006, Tarana Burke, an African American woman who as a child and teen was raped and sexually assaulted, was credited with starting the #MeToo movement of empathy, to draw attention to the patriarchal form of domination that in the past silenced women, particularly the poor, the young, and the most vulnerable. Since 2006, women and men have stepped forward to expose, shame, and indict the perpetrator of sexual abuse and assault, and to recognize the human dignity women and men, young and old, and all members of racialized and stigmatized ethnic groups deserve. This is a theme that has emerged in recent demythologizing accounts of Mexican American leaders of the civil rights era. Recent work on César Chávez's behavior as the president of the United Farmworkers of America, chronicles his extramarital affairs, his demeaning treatment of women, and the routinely crude sexual language he used to denigrate his closest associates and staff. This from what many venerated as Saint Cesar, the Mexican American Mahatma Gandhi.[15] Here I have delved into Reies Tijerina physical and mental abuse of his wives and children. As a religious and secular leader, he toiled tirelessly to offer spiritual rejuvenation to the sick and powerless, hoping that through the collective actions of the mutual aid society he founded as the Alianza Federal de Merced, he would recuperate the land grants the Spanish and Mexican colonizers of the Southwest lost after 1848. He failed winning back that land. He failed, too, to resist the wiles of the wicked whore of Babylon, succumbing to the sexual sins he said he most abhorred.

My contention here has been that if one hopes to understand the explicitly articulated logic of Reies Tijerina's words and actions both as an evangelical preacher and as a land-grant activist, one has to focus on the dimension of his education as an evangelist, particularly on the New Testament's Book of Revelation, which profoundly shaped his theology, eschatology, and ultimately served as the lexical and symbolic arsenal he deployed repeatedly in his rhetoric. With this excursion through the longer arc of Reies's biography, we saw his desire to be reborn of the Holy Spirit, which laid the path to his training as a Pentecostal evangelist. The "beast" was always at work, leading a voracious and racist American imperialist state. It had to be crushed, chained, and condemned to hell exactly as God proscribed in the Book of Revelation. God had chosen Reies for this task. Had his mother not prophetically named him *Reies* (king), after the King of Kings? Had his daughter Rose not been born on February 2, 1949, the anniversary of the Treaty of Guadalupe-Hidalgo signed that day in 1848? Had he not been imprisoned in Springfield, Missouri, the organizational headquarters of the Assemblies of God, against which he had rebelled in 1950? Had Robert F. Kennedy not been assassinated on June 5, 1968, the first anniversary of the Tierra Amarilla Courthouse confrontation? Had the daughter he named *Armonia* (Harmony) not been born on April 8, 1972, the very day he convened his first Brotherhood Awareness Conference? Had his arch enemy US Senator Joseph Montoya not died on June 5, 1978?[16] Perhaps. Perhaps. Perhaps. For Reies, everything happened according to God's larger divine plan. Unless one had a "Grand Vision," the unfolding of history was unknown to humanity until after it occurred.

NOTE ON TRANSLATION

Reies López Tijerina's sermon in "Hallará Fe en La Tierra . . . ?" posed a number of translation challenges. His original sentences in the Spanish language are often very long, connected by multiple semicolons. I have broken up such sentences when it seemed appropriate and when it did not too substantively change the meaning of the text. My goal was not to lose anything in translation but also to make for clearer meaning and smoother reading. Many of Reies's sentences started with "and," "because," and "but." Some of those I slightly altered, where appropriate, beginning them with the article "The." To translate quotations Reies took directly from the Bible, I used *The New American Bible* (New York: World Publishers, 1970), and substituted Reies's abbreviations for the Bible's various books with the full name. There are a few passages where Reies's biblical citations were wrong. Those I have corrected and noted the fact in an endnote. I also corrected erroneous information about scientific discoveries in atomic weapons.

APPENDIX I
¿Hallará Fe en La Tierra . . . ? /
Will He Find Any Faith on Earth . . . ?

The Church that currently guides people once preached law and salvation. It once cherished knowledge of God. It once had eyes to see what was good and what was bad. But now its eyes are closed and no longer has the privilege of seeing what comes before it. Its eyes cannot see what awaits it. Now the things that are coming are hidden. You fell into the hands of tyrants, oh people of God. They deceived you with great deceit and they covered your eyes so that you will not see your sad end. Oh, people, you fell into error and until now you have not been able to stand up, for to this day you lay prostrate on the ground. Your days are over, and your opportunity has passed; and your recompense, to whom will you pass it to? Those who have taught you and those who have indoctrinated you, have hidden from you the right to salvation. They have invalidated God's eternal commandments, which were revealed to us by His Son. Oh, if only people knew, the evil that awaits them, and the end of time.

Will He Find Any Faith on Earth . . . ?

—LUKE 18:8.

Kindness and truth shall meet; justice and peace shall kiss. Truth shall spring out of the earth, and justice shall look down from heaven.

—PS. 85: 10–11

1. The Clamor of the Earth

Every eye that reads these words, do not fear or be scandalized; temper your heart, as you read these words. The ear that can hear these words, do not be irritated. These are without doubt harsh words, and somewhat strange; but remember the days we are in and see what is to come over all the men that inhabit the land.

The land complains and cries against its inhabitants because faith and love has left those who adored; and the just who remains is oppressed and abused. The one who hears, do not mock these words; and those who believe, to fear God: do not become uncomfortable; because these words are not aimed at one person, nor emerge because of any group. Before all together left law; and because of vanity have strayed from justice.

I speak to those who profess to believe in God, and who admit his existence. In such bad times, in days so gloomy like the ones that surround us: is reprehension bad; will this word divert the just? Will the wise be irritated as they hear or read these words? Isn't it the wise one who sees evil and hides, while the stubborn trusts his stubbornness and stumbles?

Days of vanity surround us, and the just clamor for correction. Because Love is gone for those who adored, and mercy is not found in those who invoke the name of God; before all abhor justice and mock the works of the just. Let's not deceive our souls as Israel did, nor trust in the works of Jacob's rebelliousness. Wasn't "Samaria" the fruit of Jacob's rebelliousness? (Micah 1:5) And what is the fruit of the rebelliousness of the church? Isn't the Earth divided in names, and the Bible divided into 538 names of sects? But just as the Israelites inhabited Jerusalem in vain, likewise now in vain they have and possess the Bible, those called Christians. These are bad times when children do not obey their parents; parents do not correct their children. These are times when the young come to be heads of households: without reaching the proper age or having knowledge of God. Now the Earth is full of murmurs, and each aims at his brother; men are violent for everything. They walk the streets like storms, and like lightening they shine in the vanity of their arrogance. Each seeks his own good and takes food without chewing it: because of the violence within them. And with all the land sunk in evil and corruption: Will we stop speaking the Truth? Shall I speak with soft words, so as not to offend the believers? Should I use parables so as not to hurt those who worship in the temples of Babylon? The Just Judge of all the land lives, and I shall not stop speaking the truth; because this generation no longer knows what shame is, nor is it scandalized by the evil upon the land; each who worships: opens the door of the vanity of the day and find amusement in the fruit of arrogance. And who confesses his evil?

Evil is done in secret and everybody avoids his brother: but no one can hide from his Creator because they lost faith. No one fears and walks straight before his Creator. In these bad days, in which faith and love have disappeared. Will we speak with weak and soft words? Everyone will open his eyes and see that the bad in the Church is neither small nor weak. Oh to those who are scandalized by these words, and oh, to those who try to diminish the evil found in the people of God because many are those who say: "God is among us, and we have not left his justice." But hear that the clamor of the poor rises up against them.

These words will stir up the just, but will make the stubborn stumble; he, who is clean, will be cleaner, but the filthy will become filthier.

He who fears will listen, and the arrogant will hide and die in his throne. Are worshippers lacking to praise the Church? Will I also praise the people who have rebelled against their God? How will I speak what I do not know? How will I say what I have not seen? My eyes do not see good for these people; my ears do not hear good news for this generation. Because—what is the reward of a people who lost Justice and Mercy—Judgment without Mercy will be made with this generation. Vengeance and death await the people. Oh for the prophets who see peace for these people who have abandoned Love, because confusion will surprise them. And on the last day the lie will leave their mouths.

Because the Church treats the poor of the land without Mercy she also will be treated without Mercy (James 2:13). And if someone wants to reach God's mercy, step away from evil; cleanse your lips of hypocrisy and use Mercy for all those afflicted. Because by the same measure we use to measure, they in turn will measure us. And oh for those who expect to gain God's mercy when they never acted Mercifully. Earthly leaders have invented laws to satisfy their cravings, but oh for them. Because of them widows and the oppressed of the land were neglected. The laws they establish laws for believers serve their own benefit. They impose yokes to enlarge their nests since their glory lies in embellished temples.

But what about the poor of the land? Which law have they established in favor of the poor? Where is the law that defends widows?

Just as shops for food and shops for clothing grow and become more luxurious to catch the eye of the people and gain customers, likewise pastors dream of large and beautiful temples, disregarding the things God assigned us. Oh, for these men because wisdom was put on earth for them, and because of these men rented by the Church the commandments of God have become the commandments of least esteem. Of course, according to them they have not abandoned the commandments of God, but their lives are moved by commandments of men. The judgment of God is nearing, when everyone will know if we have committed a small sin by abandoning the Justice of God and his sacred commandments. With the very eyes they see justice on earth and do not care about anything, with these same eyes they shall see the earth engulfed in flames.

On that day all will know that man behaved worse than the beasts of the countryside; then they will seek correction, but they will not find it.

Oh, for those who say, "We are wealthy, and God has blessed us greatly." Because they do not know that the reward for their rebelliousness awaits them; do not know that they are poor and naked before the justice of God.

There has not been in the history of man a generation so awkward and given to vanity like the present generation which wants to cleanse evil from their lives by visiting the temples. Silence now pastors and prophets, before the day arrives and the hour nears when with your hands over your mouths, you will roll about upon the land. Those who have a clean mouth and the eyes to see, tell people what is coming. Do not spend your time pleading for bread. Instead, each one should care for their life and tremble at God's word.

---

2. The Lost Image

Mercy and truth for everyone who fears God and acts in Justice; may judgment and justice be the image of those who await in God. But the stubborn do not accept advice or use wisdom. What advice will attract the attention of this generation? Well that the same revelation of God, manifested in the life of Christ, has been ignored, and his sacred commandments which are for life have been disdained (John 12:47–50). The image of God has been erased from man and now there only remains the image of man as animal. The Image of God is neither in flesh nor form, but it is Spirit. When man lost Justice and Mercy, was when he lost the Image of God. The Image of God is Justice and Judgment, Mercy and Truth. The man who works for Justice and dispenses makes Mercy: this person embodies the Image of his Creator. Because of this, Christ asked us to be as Merciful as our Celestial Father is Merciful; that we do good to those who do us harm, because our Father does all these things for those who do wrong: giving them good days, with rain and sun and the enjoyment of their land. When God made man, He also gave him His image; that is, man was invested with Mercy, with natural affects, with clemency, kindness, Justice and Judgment. But gradually man began losing this Image of the Spirit of God, and now man lies prostrate on the land, full of murmurs, of rebelliousness, of envy; ingrates, traitors, without natural affect, implacably without Mercy.

The Pharisees had the image of the flesh and the form, which is law, but they lacked the Image of God, which is the Spirit that carries out Justice and Judgment. For this reason, Christ accused them of abandoning Justice, Mercy, and Faith: things in which one sees the Image of God. He who has these things enacts the will of God and does good for everyone, including his enemies. Christ promised that everyone who guarded his sacred commandments would receive the Spirit of God, which would guide them to all truth and all Justice. The fruit of the Spirit is charity, joy, peace, tolerance, goodness, benevolence, faith, meekness, and temperance. When these things went missing, the land was divided by the false opinion of rented men. The Pharisees were men-animals, thus, they were unable to perceive the things that were of the Spirit of God. But they, as is the case with this present generation, thought they possessed right and the Spirit of God. What is horrible these days is that not even the animal image is visible in man. When sons give orders to their parents, as is among this present generation, it is because we carry the image of Cain. Here is man against his Creator; the masters have risen against the master of creation. Where is the good that the commandments of men have brought to the so-called Christian home?

God will accuse the masters who have mutilated the sacred commandments that Christ himself ordered and fulfilled. God will reclaim this from the hands of those who teach congregations. The Image of God is not visible in figure, or in flesh. Its Image is seen in Spirit. He who enacts the works of the Spirit, that person carries the image of the almighty.

Now no one defends or speaks for the Justice of God. Everyone carries their own idea of Justice. And because of this, the land is full of hatred and arrogance. No one takes pleasure in the Justice or in the Judgment of God, no one finds pleasure in upholding the commandments of God. Everyone loves what perishes and presents their flesh in vivid sacrifice for what perishes.

The honor of a woman has no price. Children no longer feel indebted to their parents. Even parents have lost modesty. Everybody has languished. They cannot satiate the hunger for the things of life and their thirst for vanities cannot be controlled. Not contented with this, they subject their daughters to the flames of Babylon. And to pay the debts of their malevolent appetites, they put their daughters in the public market; tender daughters, who in times past were in the kitchen or sewing. Now they lie in shops, passing their most tender years in the lowest and most despicable work there can be for a woman. Even when one sees all this, where are those who should speak from the pulpit? Why don't they stop this evil? There is no one who gives advice, no one who abhors the evil spells of the whore of Babylon, mother of all earthly fornications. BEFORE, when man worked alone and was content to gain his bread and to cover his body even if with humble clothes, now, because of the glow of envy that runs through his veins, they put even their own women to work, and this for what they themselves have chosen; and not to be content with what God sent.

The man of yesteryear preferred to die of hunger before seeing his wife working in traffic of men, serving a greedy generation.

But now, where is the wisdom of the man and where are the wise men who teach for money? Aren't they receiving a salary to teach and to avoid evil? The Pharisees in their clumsiness avoided evil better than this generation of teachers. Because in their times, women had a better position, and tender young women were not involved in the traffic of the market. Let us open our eyes and see that we ourselves have invited the sword. And for our rebelliousness the fire of the ire of God will burn us. Why hide behind prayer, and why cover ourselves with public worship? Why abominate the commandments of Christ, subjecting our souls to the commandments of men? If I do not find life in the commandments of God, which Christ revealed to us, then I will turn to the commandments of men. All those who find meaning in the commandments of men, do so because the light of the Spirit has not dawned on them. The commandments that God has revealed to us do the soul good, but not the body. This generation loves the body more than the soul, that is why it has rebelled against the holy commandments of God. Oh, for those who say: "We are in other times" and twist the commandments of God to fit the times. But fortunate are those who remain faithful to all the commandments to the end. They will be saved. The Pharisees and the Sadducees will rise against this generation and condemn it because even as they killed the body of Christ, this generation has killed the Spirit of Christ from within the Church of Christ and has taken away the Image of God from among those who adored it. And the Pharisees ignored Mercy and Justice as much as this generation of rented teachers.

The widow has been discharged empty handed and they have dedicated themselves to building temples. So great is the arrogance that moves the heart of these people that they have held on to damnation for love of the temples to the point that they have asked for loaned money to carry out the work of their spirit.

God is not against temples, if in them Justice is preached. The present generation does not know what the Justice of God is. Because they have trampled what makes up the Justice of God: the commandments of God, given through Jesus Christ.

3. The Day of God

The day of God has begun. The day of the great God to suffer painfully. Illustrious day announced by all of God's prophets. It will be a day of revenge, of fire, smoke, and sulfur. The earth will be emptied of the impious and tyrants will no longer be their owners.

The ire of the Lamb of God, as described in Revelation and written by John, the Apostle of Jesus Christ, will be emptied over the land and its rebels. God, like a giant, will purge the earth with strong fire, doing his job. It will be strange work and difficult to endure because in it neither Mercy nor compassion will be found. The day has arrived, and sin has matured. Faith has ceased and those who prayed are corrupted. All lips have turned to lying; all eyes are given to coveting; all ears listening to twisted advice and lies. God saw from above that the earth lacked wise people and that in it the just were about to perish. The heart of man was allied with the world and the worst and wickedest machinations are found in those who offered others advice. Hypocrisy came out of heads that defended the work of the whore mother of all the fornications on earth.

It is day of rage and jealousy; a day of ire and vengeance; a day of purging and cleaning the earth; day of removing the rotten and healing the sickness that leaders have caused on earth.

Those who worship, like those who curse; those who pray, like those who commit blasphemy; those who fast, like those who get drunk; those who build temples, like those who build taverns; fathers like sons, man like woman; all will drink from the chalice of the wrath of God Almighty, who fights and judges the land with great justice.

There has not been another day, nor will there be one after this, because man will be purified, and no longer devoted to the work they now do. The great cities of the earth and all the pride of mankind will be forgotten because everything will be consumed by flames. Through fire everything small and large will be consumed; the beautiful and the ugly; everything that deceived mankind will be incinerated through fire.

Woman will be left without their jars of ointments, and perfume will cease to exist. Fine cloth, all ornaments and adornments will no longer exist as will those who seek such things. Oh, for those who have eyes to see. Oh, for those who will listen on that day because what has never been seen before will be seen, and what has never been heard before will be heard. The brave shall fall to the ground without strength in their hearts. Women will fall on their backs. Who will be able to stand on that day? It is the day of God. It is the day in which God, the Creator of everything, will take revenge; revenge against those who lead others; revenge against those who teach; revenge against those who have twisted his holy commandments and rendered null the commandments of the New Testament. The anger of the Lamb of God is like the fire that melts wax, and since his love was extensive and ample for all, so will his ire be vast and terrifying for all the rebels.

Is this the time to be disputing the dogmas of men? Is it time to give into those accords of men that only benefit men? Has any of the advice mankind pronounces ever brought peace to a household? Has any of this advice ever restored a woman's honor? What advice has led children to honor their parents? They teach people to murmurs all over the land. Because of this the earth is consumed by jealousy and infamy. And they have pitted those who believe in God, against others who also believe in God. They have brought infamy upon the land because of the evil they create. Is it not enough for them to spread over their land? They now also want to spread it across the seas.

Stop singing sweet melodies and each of you show Mercy and Justice toward your peers because the great and terrible Day has arrived. Return what you have taken from the widow, shelter the orphan, host the pilgrim, and make the foreigner feel at home. The time to sing and pray has passed. The time of cleanse your lips is over. The time of prayer is over because the time of clean hearts has passed. This is not the moment to ask for gifts and blessings from above because these are only for those who listened to the cry of the widow, attended to the needy and oppressed; and instead of these fantasies return to the old paths, give away what you possess. Instead of all this, Love your enemy. Do good before the day of God falls upon us. Kiss the Son of God by humbling our souls doing what he ordered. Embrace him, giving what you possess to the poor.

Shed tears, each in one's room and turn your faces toward the wall. Turn your back on all the whore's evil spells, which are gold, silver, fine and colorful clothes, perfumes, ointments, hairstyles, outfits, fine glasses, cars, homes, and everything made in Babylon. Oh, for those who mock by embracing all of this because on the day of the ire of God, all this will be an affront and source of pain; all this will bring bitterness and great heaviness to the soul. Because all these earthly things are the nourishment of arrogance and envy. As mankind grows in possessions, his arrogance and envy also grow. If there are wise people on earth, leave all this behind. Do not remove your ears or your heart from these words. Be mindful of the punishment and correction of the Holy Spirit.

4. The Faith of Our Times

El Monte, California (November 22, 1954)

He who knows the times, he who showed us how to reach Salvation, he not only knew what was in the heart of the men who surrounded him in his time, but he also knew what would come to pass in the generations after His departure. To this we owe the great question, that even the wiser tremble as they hear; is it true that nothing is offered to the disobedient? He said: "But when the son of man arrives, will He find FAITH on earth?" All who have the spirit of God know what this question entails. All who fear God know what this question means coming from Christ's lips.

Christ, who knew the value of FAITH, and who knew that his people depend on the FAITH in God. On many occasions he warned the chosen of latter days and explained the faith of the last generations. Many of the ones who understand also ask: "Will he find faith on earth?" If Christ comes in these days, will he find faith on earth?

Christ knew that the last generations would worship without FAITH, when he said, "And the charity of many will grow cold." Because without faith it is impossible for love to be in our hearts. Faith is the substance of all that is good, and in faith every good work is manifest.

Because of this no one can please God without faith. Faith is the origin and beginning of Love, of Justice, of Mercy, of Wisdom. Where there is no faith there is no Love, where there is no faith there is no Justice, and who will be able to please God without Justice and without Love? John the Apostle said: "Whoever does not practice Justice is not of God."

Truly the Pharisees also had the type of faith found these days in those who adore, but Christ denounced the faith of the Pharisees. The Faith of the Pharisees was a faith that did not have Love or Justice. It was a simulated faith that did not have true Faith. It is true that the Pharisees had abodes and thought they had a good and lively faith only because in it they had public worship, chants, prayers, fasts, tithes, and the commandments of men. But Christ rejected this simulated faith because within it there was no Mercy for the afflicted of the earth. In it there was no Justice or Love of God.

Like the feigned faith of the Pharisees is the faith that deceives worshippers of these last days. No one has faith to serve, to give the destitute like Lazarus, to do Justice and right. There is no one who has the faith to keep the commandments that Christ gave us. All have faith to sing, to pray in public like the Pharisees, to tithe like the Pharisees did, even if reluctantly, since it is demanded in the flesh and not in the Love that suffers everything. But, what about the Faith of the prophets, of Abraham, of the apostles? All abominate the customs of our ancient fathers and there is no one to imitate the faith of the ancient vanquishers. The faith of this generation looks for its own good. The faith of these people is divided according to the names and opinions of men. Will Christ find FAITH when he comes? Will he find faith on earth? The men who offer counsel have suppressed the little faith there was in those who worshipped because they are men who only love themselves. They are men who do not hear the cry of the afflicted. These are the ones who the devil has used to remove the faith from the humble of the earth. Everyone humiliates the poor and mocks the one who wants to be humble because for them it is a shameful and fastidious thing to have a humble person before their eyes. Where then is the faith that Christ looks for? Where will he find it? The works of those who carry one name are similar to the works of those who carry another name. And what about faith? The sons of those who worship dishonor their parents because there is no faith. The woman has taken the place of the man because there is no faith. Faith then is the substance of Love, the substance of Justice.

Without faith we cannot act in Love and Justice. Because of this, Love is gone and Justice has disappeared, because Faith has drained from us. And now we shall be cast like discarded silver and vomited because there is no flavor in our salt. Paul too spoke with the same Spirit as Christ when he said: "God sends operations of error, so you can believe lies"; "So all who did not believe truth may be condemned." Here are the people who do not believe in truth. They believe like the Pharisees, only in things that are convenient to them, and also in the commandments of those who lead. But they do not believe in the commandments of Christ. Christ commanded us to love our enemies, yet this generation does not even love its own peers or brothers (be they in flesh or faith), much less their enemies. This generation does not have the faith to obey God in what He commands, but they do want to discover faith performing false miracles. They succeed in their purpose, stealing the faith of the sick, to gain glory for themselves. But those who act by using the error of arrogance will be surprised when God judges them according to their evil deeds. Because those moved by the same greed that moved Simon the magician, ignore Justice and Mercy, because they do everything for vulgar gains.

Christ on his return shall find many temples, many preachers, and many worshippers. But will he find faith on earth? Goodwill to the Merciful because they shall reach mercy. The Merciful are not men without faith, because Mercy comes after faith. Without faith Mercy is impossible. Oh, for the worshippers who do not know Mercy, because they will be counted among the rotten trees, and tendrils without fruit. In all good works living Faith is manifest, but this generation is very poor on works, and miserable in Mercy because it does not have faith.

The one who forgives, forgives for faith. The one who loves, loves for faith. The one who works for Justice does so for faith. And the tame and humble are so in faith. Without Faith it is impossible to do right.

This generation does not know what is right because it has lost faith. This generation in all its desires shows its greed and its clumsiness. In everything it does it manifests its arrogance and its egoism because all are quick to judge with twisted and materialist judgment.

There is no one who ignores the weakness of his peers and the entire earth was consumed by gossip. Each adores without shame for his iniquity. Each published his hypocrisy, and they adore without faith and without shame.

The widow whom Christ places in the parable of the unjust judge, asked with a plea, for she suffered because of her adversary. But this generation was ordered not to place their eyes on things that perish and not to search for things that perish. Now each is mired and indebted because of the things Babylon makes every day. The people of God have no reason to have faith. No one needs faith. Everyone is content and well served with the powerful delights of the great whore Mother of all the fornications of the earth. No one suffers because even the women, wives of those who worship, are found in the midst of men working, only to live according to the fashions of the sons of Babylon and to satisfy their carnal appetite for things that burn.

What has God done with the land when its inhabitants lose their Faith?

History teaches us, and the Judgments that God has made between nations warn us. The earth no longer bears its inhabitants because each acts without faith. Salary has taken the place of Faith. Those who worship try to please man. Those who lead, search for the present (bread of the widow) that did not belong to them. Christ did not ask if he would find beautiful temples, or chants, or worshippers who fight for places like the ignorant Samaritan woman did. Instead, he asked if he would find living Faith on the land.

The widow in the parable clamored for Justice. But in these days, Who clamors for Justice? Israel also lost everything, except for its vain adornments and public adorations. No one should trust what they see or think that God has asked from an unfaithful and hypocritical people, chants, and public ceremonies. Now he who has faith shows it through his Justice because the just for his Faith shall live.

What, then, will Christ find on Earth when he comes? Divisions? Arrogance? Vanity? It is true that temples have taken the place of God and the adoration that should be about obeying the commandments of God, in making Mercy, in working for Justice and right, now have subordinated in the temple, but the poor of the earth gained nothing from that adoration. Content are those who lead and this adoration of vain lips satisfies the taste of those who shape advice, but are not aware that the land is now faithless. Thus, in the day of God the temples will be unable to defend those who worship. Nor will the false things of this generation save them from the hand of God.

Because it is God who is irritated and not men, it is God who has been offended. Who is it that does not know that the commandments of God are on earth? Which is the commandment of God that this generation is obeying? No wonder the beast and the false prophet have found their worshippers in the temples, and all who bend their knee at altars, also bend their knee to the vanities of Babylon. Who does not admire the vanities that now adorn the streets of the towns?

Who is the wise man who refuses to gaze at the vanities offered in store windows? The people of God lost their sense and faith left them. They found their home in Babylon and denied their Creator.

Oh for those who profess faith in promises without keeping a single commandment. Let us leave the religion of Cain. No one should be content with the faith of the Pharisees, because these are days of ire, and the creator is against its creation because all of us have rebelled and no one kept the faith. All just and wise, let us return to the faith of our fathers; and let us leave those who follow faith without works.

---

5. The Lost Wise Man

El Monte, California (April 15, 1954)

Wise thoughts came out of their heads. Evil visited earth and in the hearts of the elders, death found its nest. Wise men strengthened the hand of the one who destroys and with the multitude of oppressive laws invited he who kills. The wisdom of the wise man will kill him because only the eye and the flesh are nourished by all of their inventions which is the nourishment for arrogance. The evil of the earth took the place of Justice. The wise man's science of the wise and the work of the inventor shall stir ire, and with their very works will bring about their own end. They prepared, filling the earth with violence and they accomplished their immoral thoughts. For this reason, God will also end their strange and horrible work.

God saw, and no one could escape evil, or stand against it. Everyone fought and cared for their own womb, feeding off the thoughts of strangers. Those who taught good also gave in to vanity, and for a salary instructed the multitude.

The paths that the son of God brought us were abandoned by the greatest men. Those who were wise mocked humility. The gentleness of Christ perished among those who pray. Love is not found among those who fast because each fast is undertaken to gain a place greater than that of his peer. In pursuit of worldly interests, they pray and fast.

Will any of this be worth much after leaving and mutilating the commandments God sent through his son Jesus Christ? Is it time to ask for strength against the demons? Is it time to ask and demand promises from the Just God? Is it not time, instead, to return to the paths of Justice and walk in fear, to search for forgiveness, to give mercy to those who clamor for it? If in these days one believes himself dignified and thinks himself noble enough to ask God for the things that belong to the just and to saints, well, let him. Those who want life, turn your face to the wall, cast your eyes to the ground, do not look at the wife of your neighbor (do not look for the good of the body.) Let us look for Mercy from above, which is Forgiveness. But it is necessary that everyone do good for their peer, that each one look after the widow, the orphan, the needy.

So-called Christians are those who mock the obedient, the humble. If this is not so, one of you leave your delicate garments and dress in discarded rags. He will be criticized and condemned, not by sinners, or by drunks, or by those who kill and steal. On the contrary, he will be condemned and criticized by those who attend Churches and sing. He will be criticized by those who call themselves Christians. Here you have the instruments of the whore; these are the sons and citizens of Babylon, who defend the clothes of Babylon. So-called Christians (with the exception of the Just) empower the inventions of Babylon, or what they call "fashion" and "style." The Just God calls all this abomination, dishonor, and corruption. God sees that those who call themselves by his name everywhere are those who are most captive, and the closest to the works of today. Who dresses like the people of God? Who among the people of God eat delicate things? Only the princes of Babylon and those in the homes of presidents and kings. For this reason, God calls them senseless people, and clumsy people. All Christians finds themselves as Israel found itself, captive in the land of Babylon. The people of God are captive, prisoners of the passions of Babylon, drunk with the delights of the mother of all earthly fornications and inventions. Who follows such colors and figures as if they were the people of God?

All who fear God, come. Let us turn to the one who formed us, search for the one who gave the message to our Lord. Let us show mercy to all the afflicted of the earth and console those who cry and clamor at the oppressor's hand. Let us come together in the good of God and walk together along ancient paths. No one should search for an alliance of men or for a union of human commandments. It is because of these men called wise and leaders that wisdom has disappeared from the earth. Because of them the Holy Spirit has been cast outside the "Holy Place." Let us unite in the Spirit of God and be moved by the Faith of our ancient fathers.

Let us walk in the Light of the Justice of God, and we will not stumble on the day of God's ire. Leave behind the people who want to be purified by chants. Do not associate with the people who anoint themselves with long public prayers only to be seen and heard by all. The times of the just are over and now man must bow his head, humiliate his soul because law has been taken from earth. Those who pray, do not think that God can be fooled. Those who sing should not think that God is adored by those who are liars and merciless, who leave the orphan and the widow to the mercy of the government and the state. Is it not the Church that should receive those who lack food, be they good or bad? Those who ask in the spirit of Simon, the magician, for selfish evil, clean your garments, cleanse your souls, before the day of God arrives and surprises you like Sodom and Gomorrah.

---

6. The Captive People—Leave, Leave

Israel was a slave of Egypt and the servant of Babylon. And in the shadow of servitude, it had sons and daughters. Children were born but not in freedom; they were born wrapped in pagan customs and serving the flag of tyrants. Their days were lived under the yoke of injustice within an arrogant nation.

In Egypt and Babylon, one could not find the Laws of God or the works of the Almighty. But the God of Mercy, remembering His promise, after much time returned them to their homeland. Those who returned were a new generation born in the cradle of slavery.

The people of God lacked wisdom, and because they lacked fear of God, they were taken captive. And likewise, the sons of the Church now serve in the land of strangers and are born under the flag of the same and ancient mystical Babylon. The Christians who now are being born once again, are born under the flag of error and serve God with pagan practices.

The Church of Christ, the people of God are not free, nor do they serve God with knowledge of the fear of God. For many years the Church has been producing sons and daughters, but this under the reign of a strange kingdom unknown to God. This is why the sons of the Church do not know wisdom, nor do they even understand right. All are born with entrails that have no Mercy, in the shadow of the kingdom of darkness that surrounds them. Christ spoke of the captivity of the Church and predicted that the people of God were to pass through this great servitude and slavery.

The Holy Spirit spoke and said that because of this captivity of Christian souls the Church would remain naked, blind, poor, unfortunate, and miserable. The fact is that the church and people of God now find themselves without the garments of Justice because those who teach the people of God do not know Justice. These people are blind. Despite their lack of love, mercy, faith, justice, or fear of God, they say they do have all these things; thus, they are blind. It is miserable because despite its claims to be rich, it is very poor when it comes to the works of God. Thus, the poor of the earth and widows cannot find a single piece of bread in the people of God.

Oh, people of God and sons of the Almighty, note that your birth was not in a land of freedom and justice, but instead were born in a stranger's land and in a city of sinners.

The Lord asks us to leave this evil and twisted generation because our souls are slaves of error. Our entrails are moved by the voice of arrogance and ire because our lords are envy and egoism. The sons and daughters born daily to the church, born in a land of slavery, are enveloped by the spirit of division and hatred. And the mother of all the earth's fornications has raised us in hatred, in revenge. Due to this everyone hates each other because of names.

The mother of the Christian people is Babylon. Because they are brought up in arrogance, nourished in selfishness, wrath runs through their veins. Each is happy and rejoices in the ruin of his brother, if such was known by another name.

Among the people of God there is no one who procures the good of his brother because they have inherited this from the Mother who raised them. The people were conceived by one spirit and raised by another. No one should ask or say, Why is there no love among the people of God? Why is there no joy, like there was in past days? Every Christian (so-called) should understand that we have been born in the kingdom of Babylon and all our teachers are salaried. This is why the Almighty calls us to leave their midst. Leave arrogance, lies, egoism; leave the vanities of life, ire, and vengeance. Because this is the fruit of Babylon. We were created in these bad spirits. Leave, all who understand and love life, leave quickly. Sever communication with the vanities of life. And let us learn from Christ, let us fear God before the wrath of the Lamb falls on us. It is time to separate ourselves from arrogance. The day is quite advanced and there is only time for those who really want to liberate their lives. Each of you open your ears to the truth; the just should not resist repression, no one should fear the laws imposed by men. No one should listen to the accords of men, because these accords are against the widow and the needy. They enact laws for their own good.

Let us leave the mother who raised us, who taught us to rebel against God and his Justice. Let us abandon the mother who did not teach us Mercy toward anyone. Let us leave the Jerusalem that kills prophets and understand that it was not the buildings and homes of Jerusalem, but the twisted laws of false teachers who killed the just. Therefore, leave false laws and the teachings of councils that kill rights and ignore justice. Councils where you cannot find bread for the hungry or clothing for the naked. No one among these false teachers advocates for justice or judgment because they are agents of Babylon and paid by the great whore. These are the ones who capture the small of the earth and twist the rights of the just.

Oh, for these evil men, who do not disguise arrogance. Even in public they dress like princes of Sodom, and their words travel and surround the earth. The ire of the Lamb will fall on these, surprising them more than Hiroshima and Nagasaki.

Our mother who raised us (Babylon) taught us to sing and worship in public but did not teach us Mercy and Justice; she taught us to pay tribute to its teachers, but did not teach us to show compassion for the oppressed and the needy. Of this she never gave us an example through its hired teachers.

In these days of captivity, of yoke, of servitude, there is no one who can learn humility and gentleness, because the business and commerce of Babylon do not permit it. The commerce of Babylon and the potency of its delights consist of merchandise of gold, of silver, of fine garments and delicate foods. It consists of houses equipped with arrogance, cars that speak of pride, and comforts that delight the flesh of captive Christians. Let us leave. Why should we die along with the false hired ones who teach for the love of their bellies? What is the drink of this whore, which everyone has drunk from? What is its flavor, that everyone, all peoples, all nations, tribes, and tongues enjoy?

What, then, is the thing in which everyone has participated? Is it not gold? Is it not pomp? Is it not earthly possessions? And this, is it not the nourishment of arrogance? Is it not the nourishment of selfishness? And arrogance and selfishness, is this not what has divided the entire earth, like all the homes and nations? Is there no one who desires to leave slavery? Is there no one who loves the freedom of the soul? Behold what our daughters lost in Babylon: their honor, their shame, their decency, their respect. And now they dress and walk and speak like women who do not understand good, and like women who have never known that there is a God. Because in Babylon they have learned practices that are furthest from truth, and of the most lascivious customs. And to teachers, what is given? They do not care that our daughters are objects of greed and lust. All who are tired of the yoke of Babylon and the slavery of Egypt, leave and rest your souls working in faith and mercy.

Let us care for the poor, advocate for the defenseless, open our mouths to speak for the mute, place our eyes at the disposition of the heavens. Let us do good for it is no longer the moment to sing to the air or pray to the altars of Babel.

Let us adore in spirit because God is Spirit. God is pleased more by actions than by words, and he is honored by the just, abhorring those of lying lips. Let us leave the customs of Babylon that the agents of Satan taught us. And all those who love life, do not allow your eyes to focus on terrestrial life.

It is the works we have done without love or Mercy that have brought ignominy to our prayers.

It is our rebelliousness against the commandments of Jesus Christ what has made all our ceremonies and rites repugnant to the ears of God. It is not for lack of melody or notes that God abhors our chants, but because our heart does not know mercy and we have not done well by the oppressed. No one should be fooled that the worship of the Pharisees is better; it is not for lack of worship but for lack of sanctity. The reason God left Israel, for that same reason, he has left us. Israel abandoned the paths of God when it left and ignored Justice and Mercy. Now there is no mercy even among sons for their parents, much less for the orphan and the foreigner. All our Prayers are no longer heard by God: when we closed our ear to the one who shouted and did not respond to the need of the oppressed. And each one deceives himself, believing and testifying that his petition has been received. Will God forgive the unforgiving? Will God have Mercy for the Merciless? Will God bless those who curse? Does God not condemn those who condemn their peers? On the other hand: will the merciful receive mercy? Will he who forgives be forgiven? Will he who gives not receive? Who gives without learning about Christ? Who forgives without learning about Christ? Who can act mercifully without first learning about Christ?

Without Christ we can do nothing. For this reason, we cannot do good; because we have deserted Christ. And all our worship has come to be abominable to the eyes of God. He cannot suffer our prayers any longer.

No one should trust public prayers and chants. It is true that in chants as in prayers there is nothing wrong. The wrong is in our lives, which displease God our Creator. Let us cleanse our hearts and then we shall elevate our songs. Everyone repent and show Mercy. Then your Prayer also will be heard.

The time to present petitions has passed, nor is it time to build temples. Raise your eyes and behold the fire that comes across the entire land. The land clamors to be purged because of our great rebelliousness. No one deceive their heart. The heart is deceitful and vain in appearances, but the stubborn do not understand this. The wise man builds his home on Justice, and with his works builds it on God. The stubborn are confident and bring harm, but the God-fearing know the times.

---

7. The Lost Love

The Love of God perished from human hearts. We no longer see the Love of God among Christians. And how do we know there is no longer Love? What is the fruit of Love? What is the strength and virtue of Love? What signs and manifestations are there, where Love exists? Can one see Love so we can talk about it? We speak of the Love of God, not of the love of men. The Love of God is spirit, is life, is virtue, and is strength. He who knows God knows God's Love. But what is it to know God? Love is as profound as wisdom itself. Love is as profound as any other force that God formed. Just as any science has its depth, its height, its width, and its length. So too the Love of God has its depth and height. Many play music, but few really know it. Many use numbers in arithmetic and depend on numbers to make accounts, but few really know arithmetic. Many talk about history, but few really know it. Many cite the Bible, but few really know it. Many speak of botany, but few really know it deeply. Well, the Love of God is like that. Many speak of it, but very few partake of God's Love. The Love of God is the spirit that binds all things as one. It is the spirit that interconnects all of God's creation. The Love of God is not a thing that is learned or acquired in a year or even two. Like all other science, it is a matter of a lifetime, but differs in much to other sciences, and overpowers all knowledge. He who knows the Love of God, understands all things. He who has or knows the Love of God does not get irritated, does not think negatively, does not look only for himself, does not look for the worldly or glories in the wealth of this world. He who has the Love of God does not rebel against the commandments of God nor causes prejudice to persons or opinions like the whole world does these days. He who has the Love of God places no trust in chants and ceremonies but fears God and does good for everyone. He who has Love advances justice, shows mercy to everyone, gives and does not refuse those who ask. He who has Love of God delights in the word of God and keeps the commandments of God without complaint. But what a pity and what a great disgrace. These days the Love of God is identified with one word. All disdain the Love of God. Christ said: "He who has my commandments and keeps them, he is the one who really loves" (John 14:21–23). But who is the one who keeps the commandments of Christ these days? All speak of loving God, but in their hearts they abhor the things of God. Here we have a world without love of God. Here we have the people who will be put in flames for leaving the love of God. Here we have the people who deserted the widow and the orphan and still says "We Love God."

These people are selfish, dissolute, and daring. Without love for anyone they want God to love them. Since hatred has its symptoms, its signs and fruits, so too the Love of God has its proof and evidence. And all we can see in these people who inhabit the earth are signs of hatred, evidence of arrogance, manifestations of selfishness. But what signs or evidence is there that the Love of God is in these people? All the poor complain about these people. These same Christians accuse one another and cannot demonstrate to each other the Love of God. Some fear and distrust others and this is why they address each other courteously. But they do not do this out of love. They fear not greeting each other because they know each other as gossips, easily insulted, and capable of bearing false witness. It is so that one's brother does not feel hurt that they greet each other; and the brother replies so that the other will not speak ill of him. Let the prophet or preacher proclaim that these people have Love of God. Such a man is the most false and deceptive prophet of all the men now on earth, who all do what they do, for useless gain and vain glory. Even those who seek power these days by gaining attention with signals and marvels, do not teach the Love of Jesus Christ. All covet the power to perform miracles and healings but why do they not covet doing good and showing mercy? Why do they not teach people what to do for the good of their souls? Why do they not tell the people of the destruction that we ourselves are racing toward?

For this reason, no one keeps the commandments of God. Because teachers of the Love of God have disappeared. Christ himself said: "He who does not love does not keep my commandments" (John 14:24). And this is why we do not obey the commandments of Christ. These are rebels, not those of Moses, nor those of Christ. What pact are we under, then? What are the laws that must govern us? No wonder no one knows sin, for the law of Spirit has disappeared, and without law, well, where is sin? Because of this no one is contradicted, no one is reprimanded. Law is lost (2 Kings 22:8). Who is guilty that the law of Christ is buried in oblivion? In a few days peoples will miss the Law of Christ and will lament the loss of the Law of the Spirit. Then everyone will look for it but will not find it. They will find this very lost Law, but they will find it on the last day, when by this same law they shall be judged and condemned for disdaining and abusing it. Who can minimize the word of God and escape alive? Oh, for the disobedient. Oh, for those who mock the commandments of God. On that day they will search for places and caves to hide from the wrath of God. They will flee, like one flees at the sight of a lion, but without success.

---

8. The Arrogant of This Generation

Austin, Texas (February 22, 1954)
The world, nations, and their leaders are founded on sand. The work of man and his best projects, both national and religious, are founded on sand.

Nations are built on earth. Peoples are built on sand. Homes are also built on sand. And in these last days, what is built on secure rock? Who has taken the advice of the Prince of Peace? Churches are not sure of their congregations. Parents are not sure about their children. Nations are not sure about their leaders. And the consequence of building on sand is large and evil.

Christ said: "Anyone, then, who hears these words and heeds them, I will compare to a prudent man who built his house on the rock." Christ, like at any time, was clear on these words, to explain the true wisdom, the true salvation of the soul. That is: not merely salvation from vices, not only salvation from liqueur or cigarettes, or adultery or theft or murder. But He spoke of the salvation from eternal death, of the salvation of the soul in all aspects. That is: save us from pride, from arrogance, from envy, from ire, from egoism because these are what have destroyed all the earth. Arrogance is what has deceived even the wisest men such as Solomon, King of Israel. Even men who followed Christ have been humiliated by arrogance. Arrogance has caused men to divide the body of Christ into concept and opinion. Arrogance has placed woman as object of greed, of lasciviousness, and adultery. Arrogance has made and inspired the men of God (or the so-called men of God) to visit like princes of Sodom and Gomorrah. A preacher of the day is no longer distinguished from the president of a nation. Arrogance is what has made the Church forget and neglect the widows of the earth, the poor and orphans, as well as the foreigners. Arrogance is what has split the earth, peoples, homes, marriages. He who hears the word of Christ and puts it into practice, who lives in them is freed from all this. Those who nowadays call themselves saved do not even know what they are saved from, unless they know that they are victims and captives of Babylon, of the potency of delights, of racial egoism, sectarian egoism, and nationalist egoism. They trust in what their blind teachers have shown them.

Christ said that he who puts his word as deed and did the things he commanded, he was free of the things that come to life and enslave the man with spirits of arrogance, egoism, and ire. Now, in these last days remaining for mankind, all are moved by any lie. That is, they are moved to ire, to arrogance, and to speak what they speak or think what they think with ire, with arrogance, with egoism.

Why can we not do and live according to the words of Christ? There is no faith in good things. There is no faith in the word of God. And there is no faith in God and his holy words.

Christ told his disciples: "You are now cleansed by the word I have spoken" (John 15:3). Those apostles had faith in the word Christ gave them. They had faith that those words were from God and could save the soul from ire, from envy, from arrogance, from error, from hatred, from narcissism. In short, they saw that the word of Christ, if applied to their own lives, could put an end to all the evil there is in the heart of man. Faith is what we need these days. It is always faith that has been needed to walk the paths of life, the very paths of God, which Christ brought in his holy life. Faith. Without faith no one can live according to the words that Christ spoke in what they now call "SERMON OF THE MOUNT." What were the words Christ spoke? To what words did he refer when he said: "He who hears my words?" Which words? We all know he referred to the gospel he brought and is found in Matthew chapters 5, 6, 7. What words did he speak? In these words, Christ made forgiveness clear to us when he said: "If you do not forgive men for their trespasses, neither will my celestial Father forgive you your trespasses." There is no one to intercede for us if we do not forgive, not even the blood of Christ himself is valid to pardon our offenses or sins if we do not forgive our peers the offenses they cause us. The gospel the Pharisees (enemies of Christ) preached and taught also cleansed from drunkenness, from murder, from stealing, and adultery (Luke 18:11). But this is not what really causes the rebelliousness of the earth and the evil there is throughout earth. Because all this is only the result. There is an evil behind drunkenness, adultery. There is an evil behind and before robbing, killing, and bad habits, and this is envy, ire, arrogance. Arrogance stops the contest (Prov. 13:10). And before any rupture is arrogance (Prov. 16:18). What the preachers call evil and sin is nothing but the result and fruit of the real sin that they themselves cannot know or discover, because they themselves are tied and are servants of the same Sins.

By stopping murder one does not remove or kill arrogance. By quitting drinking or some bad vices, arrogance does not end. Arrogance is a spirit, and it is a power that governs the life of man. It is a force under which he thinks and talks and acts as well. It is this spirit and evil power which makes enemies and causes resentments.

This present generation, with the path it follows, and with the spiritual weapons it possesses will never be able to free itself from arrogance. Let us understand that it is arrogance that sends men to hell, and it is this malignant power that has put Christians on such a base level that now they themselves do not recognize the marks of Christ and the true form of saintly life. Because of arrogance, Christians are scandalized by the saintly, the humble, and the meek. It is only humility that resists arrogance. It is the humility of Christ in our lives that allows us to resist what has divided the world—arrogance. Many know liquor, murder, theft, adultery, and some other things that come off the sensuality of the flesh. But how many know arrogance? Who can distinguish arrogance? Who knows the fruit of arrogance?

As true humility bears fruit, so too arrogance bears fruit. As arrogance creates enemies, so humility brings friends. As arrogance creates evil, humility produces good. Arrogance is what kills the living faith in the hearts of Christians.

He who put an end to arrogance, ends all his vice and bad habits. In addition to that, his tree of life bears fruit and in the shade of its love and mercy the earthly poor find happiness and the widows do not leave embarrassed or empty-handed. No one now has an appetite for the fruit of those who now call themselves Christians. Even if they have abandoned some of the vices preachers condemn as sins, overall, they have not been cleansed of arrogance. He who quits bad vices has done well, but only for his own flesh and not for the poor and oppressed of the earth. The dwellers of the earth have become more arrogant than in the past because the church has forsaken humility and give no attention to its works. The biggest disgrace and the most powerful deceit is that the church in its rebelliousness does everything in the name of God.

Who then can counsel the people of God? The Pharisees cleaned the external, but not the internal. But this generation does not even clean the external. We have not brought any good to the world, nor have we done any healing. Certainly, we have remained like the People of Israel; for they did no good on earth (Isa. 26:18).

Let us search for the faith of our fathers. Let's turn our souls to the Love of Christ. If we keep his sacred commandments we will be in his love, just as Christ kept his Father's commandments and was in his saintly love (John 15:10). Men have disdained Christ's commandments and have established all kinds of accords, human commandments, and laws by which no one will be able to escape arrogance or ire, much less from egoism. Because of this the people and the Church of Christ itself have been divided.

What human Law or organization will be able to liberate us from the ire that will come? For if they do not teach people how to escape envy, egoism, arrogance, can they teach us the path to escape the ire of God? No one trusts in his brother, not even in his friend, because now the greatest enemies of man are those in his own house.

Everyone should deny themselves just as our fathers denied themselves. Each person who loves life, place your eyes on the things from above. Which are the things from above? Love is not from above? Mercy is not from above? Humility and tenderness, peace and Justice are from above. Place your sight on these things. All currently keep their eyes set on faults, in stories, in clothes, in good food, in a good appearance. But this is nothing more than the fruit of the mother of all the fornications of the earth, which is the Spirit of error. It is Babylon with all the witchcraft of its last days. It should be enough that the nations are also about to receive the ire and reward for their evil excesses. Oh, for those who have conformed to the rites of the church and do not act with Mercy toward others. Oh, for those who sing to God and do not obey even their own parents. Oh, for those who do not chastise this bad generation, which is about to experience the judgment of God. Oh, for those who glorify themselves because they do not kill, because they do not steal, because they are not adulterous, because in this they are no different than the sons of the devil. In earlier times, as it is written, "Whoever does not act in Justice and does not love his brother, is not of God" (1 John 3:10). Oh, for the present generation, because the works of the Pharisees were greater than the works of these people. Nineveh[1] received God's advice, but these so-called wise people do not receive advice. This generation will not be accused and condemned because it does not sing. Nor will it be judged because it does not pray, or because it does not go to the temples or because it has no temple rites. It will be condemned because within it one cannot find mercy nor love of God. One does not find Justice from above. Instead of God's justice, there is man's justice, which shelters the arrogant, and mutilates the humble.

9. The Ignored Sacrifice

New York City (November 27, 1953: 2 p.m.)
Oh, for those who believe in the SACRIFICE of Christ, and do not keep his sacred commandments! Oh, for those who profess to believe in the blood of Christ and ignore the PACT, by which Christ's blood was spilled! The commandment of life was ignored because Faith was lacking (John 12:50). And without faith it is impossible to please God because it is our faith that conquers the world (1 John 5:3–4). Many are those who believe in Christ's sacrifice, that is, that Christ suffers. But they do not believe that they too must suffer for Justice. This is why everyone searches for their own wellbeing, some in one way and others in another. But they have been unwilling to offer their bodies in living Sacrifice in ways that are pleasing to God. Paul, the Apostle, also believed in Christ's sacrifice of Christ. Yet this did not keep him or inhibit him from presenting his own body in sacrifice, placing it "in servitude" (1 Cor. 9:27). And in what way did the apostle place his body in servitude? In this same chapter he speaks to the Corinthians and says to them that he refuses to receive salary from them, so as not to interfere with Christ's Gospel. And in 1 Corinthians 4:9–13 he also tells us something about the way in which he placed his body under servitude, when he said, "Until this hour we fast and have thirst, and we are naked and wounded from blows and we wander as vagabonds. We work with our hands; they curse and we bless; we face persecution and suffering . . . we are the waste of all until now." This was part of the suffering of the apostle. And why did the apostle suffer from nakedness and hunger? Would his brothers not help him? Did the apostle give incorrect church testimony when he spoke in this manner? For who would supply his needs? The Apostle, like his Master, who did not have a fox's cave, suffered with delight, and at the same time left a good example for his brothers, as he also denied opportunity and entry to the wolves and false workers who through unmerited gains spoke the word of the kingdom without knowing the Spirit of God. How do we know that Paul was one of those who knew the value of the Sacrifice of Christ better than anyone else? When he said, "I bring in my body the marks of Christ"

and, what marks did he bring on his body? Marks of affliction, of tribulation, of anguishes, of hungers, of thirsts, of all kinds of needs. Did Paul also have to give his life for all of us? Why, then, did Christ not stop the blows that Paul, his servant, received? Know that this was the example that Christ left for all of us. Christ himself said that in the world we would have tribulation. And why in these days do all flee from tribulation, and necessities, and poverty? All seek their own good. And again, the earth was left without wise men. Who will stand as example for Christian people? This is why everyone searches for their own good. Because no one in the kingdom works for free, instead they search for what comes from the womb. Because of this no one wants to crucify his flesh. All believe that Christ had to crucify his body, but no one in these last days wants to crucify his own flesh. Do not forget that if we want to inherit the kingdom that is close at hand, we must be born again. The faith and the Love of God have been absent from those who believe in the sacrifice of Christ. Why punish a people who do not believe in the Sacrifice of Christ? Many believe it, but very few understand it well; and those who understand it do not demonstrate it in their lives.

If Christians understood the sacrifice of Christ and his holy gospel, it would be another thing. The Christian children would honor their parents with help. Some would carry the burdens of others. The world itself would give testimony in favor of Christians. Because where there is Justice and Faith, Mercy and love, there is found good testimony that the weak of the earth will not be mocked as they now are. The Sacrifice of Christ does not require handmade temples, nor does it ask for ceremonial sacrifices. The Sacrifice of Christ demands from our lives Mercy and Judgment, Faith and Justice, Humility and calmness. It demands that we raise those who have fallen, that we feed the hungry, and that we give rest to the afflicted and tired. Let us stop the vain worship of lips and begin the worship of deeds and of spirit, or it is already late, and it is no longer time to be celebrating cults of lips.[2] For what humility, what mercy or love do we see in the cults of lips? What good do the hungry and naked receive from our gatherings? Let us do good on the streets, in homes, giving what we have, and not offering the things that not even we have experienced. All promise what they do not have, and what they really have, this they deny to the needy and afflicted. Mercy and truth is what God asks of us, and not a cult of lips. Because even the cult of the Pharisees was better than the one offered to God in temples nowadays. And if our Justice does not surpass the justice of the Pharisees who crucified Christ, then we are among those who killed Christ. Where is the glory of those find joy in the sacrifice of Christ without fearing God or doing mercy on earth? Certainly, the blood of Christ will fall over those who do not follow his saintly will. Oh, to those who carry this sacrifice of their lips, but in their hearts carry arrogance and envy, burdened with things that perish, forgetful of the needy. They too will be forgotten on the final day.

Christ did not say that during the final days we would lack temples in which to adore him. He did not say that during the final days people would refuse to sing and pray, because this has abounded at all times; both before he came as after.

What, then, did Christ say would be lacking on earth and among its inhabitants? Faith and Love. These are the things that Christ said would be missing during the final days. Neither did he say that faith and love would be missing among the sons of darkness in comparison to those of light. Because what faith or love can be expected from those who do not know God?

To build temples one does not need faith in God, not even love of God. This is why all religions have built grand temples no matter how false the religion. The Pharisees, even if they were (as Christ said) sons of the devil, deceived people and built temples, grand synagogues. Many believe that once there exist temples, ministers, beautiful chants, public prayers, and fasts, like all sorts of activity found in the temples today, that all of this is proof that there is Love and Faith. It is not so. Although the Pharisees did not have faith, or mercy, or Justice, they had grand temples, great preachers (and teachers too) and prayers like all sweet deeds resembling benediction. According to the Spirit of God testimony, the Pharisees although they had less light than today's so-called Christians, were better and closer to the kingdom than we are.

The Pharisees cared for widows better than did the Roman government. Today, the government looks after the widows better than the so-called church.

Through faith all the ancients triumphed and because of faith they obeyed the ancient pact. But these people want to justify themselves only through ceremonies. More is required than the belief in the Sacrifice of Christ. It is necessary that we also walk in faith on the new path that the Sacrifice of Christ has marked. So Peter was able to expel demons when Christ asked him to. He was also able to perform many miracles without Christ increasing his faith. But when Christ urged him to forgive his brother up to seventy times seven, Peter said: "Lord, increase my faith." Why did he now lack faith? Faith is necessary to forgive, to love, to give, and to serve. When living faith perishes, all perishes along with faith: love perishes, forgiveness, service. When faith perish so too justice and mercy, fear of God and wisdom. Without faith there is nothing we can do. We cannot please God in any way. Neither with chants nor even with prayers can we please God. Without faith even the most solemn ceremonies are an abomination to God. No one can please God with faithless acts. Because everything pertaining to ceremonies and rites can be done without faith. Otherwise there would be no false religion. Nothing regarding true life and nothing of love and of justice can be carried out without Faith. It is faith, thus, that has perished and been absent from earth.

If there was faith, the government would not be providing for the widows and orphans. If there was faith, there would be Love, justice, and mercy among believers. Faith is what straightens things that are crooked, and faith is what we need.

Let us turn our hearts to he who died because of our fault. If he died for our sins and faults, shall we continue repeating them? He who says that Christ died for his faults and sins and yet continues to live in faults and sins, that person brings unto himself judgment and boiling ire of the final day. Why do envy, arrogance, evil thoughts, lies, selfishness, feuds, fights, jealousies, anger, and rivalries continue, all works that have caused hundreds of divisions in the body of Christ?

Therefore, if anyone believes that Christ died for him, then that person must also be dead to evil and the flesh, and live in justice and in Christ. No one should be fooled in these evil times. Ire comes because the people of God have strayed from the path of justice. Anyone who awaits Christ's return, move away from all that perishes and place your life in the hands of God, with living faith, revive in your life all the words that Christ spoke to his followers. It is time not even to believe those who are closest because everyone speaks without meaning too. In these days the just will hear and will be greatly affirmed. Because reprimand works on the wise but not on the stubborn. Although the stubborn needs it, he does not receive it. But the wise one, although he may rejoice, humbles himself and receives a strong reprimand. The wise knows what makes one grow, yet the stubborn trusts and carries evil.

---

10. What Is Humility?

Those who despise Humility are not free of arrogance. The men who stop to mock humility are not wise. Arrogance in life appears when Humility is lost. Arrogance becomes strong in the heart of man when Humility weakens. It is the spirit of arrogance that mocks true Humility.

Not even Solomon, with all his wisdom, dared to speak against Humility. Now there is no one who praises Humility because those who took time to worship, and speak, and explain true Humility have perished. Christ not only took time to speak of Humility, but always taught Humility in his life. When he was invited to eat, he always took the last chair or seat at the table. Christ showed his Humility in his life, in his speech, in his eating as in his dress, in his thoughts as in his actions. Humility has perished from earth, because love and living faith also perished, hypocrisy and the humility of the modern Pharisees can never replace true Humility, because true Humility has large and rich fruits. Humility bears the fruit of Mercy, the fruits of Justice, the fruits of Love, the Fruits of fear of God, the fruits of Faith. Where would feigned humility get these fruits of the Spirit?

When men ignore Humility, they are blind and lost in the drunkenness of life.

There is only one kind of true Humility, and it is to this Humility that I refer. Christ is the true Humility. As he said: "Learn from ME, for I am calm and HUMBLE at heart" (spirit). Men have lost Humility because they no longer learn from Christ. All learn from the world how to speak and think, how to eat and dress, how to buy and sell, who to ask and respond. All have the same spirit of error, of which Christ said: they would have for forsaking the Love of truth. Humility is not enjoyed by being waited on, but by serving. Humility is not enjoyed by receiving, but by giving. The Spirit of Humility finds no joy in the comforts of life, or in the things that so-called Christians enjoy. Instead, humility is enjoyed by suffering for Christ. It is enjoyed by being mocked. Within the obscurity of arrogance, of envy, of egoism, and of ire, Humility shines and manifests itself. In Humility there is no ire, there is no revenge, there is no egoism, there is no lie, there is no bad thought. Because Humility came from above. Humility is spirit and not word. Humility is found by he who fears God, but the arrogant, and those who trust too many letters, will never speak well of Humility. Because for them Humility is a heavy and abhorrent thing. Before the complete ire of God appears, I hope many will be able to read these small words, before God turns against the inhabitants of the earth. Even the small of the earth have forgotten Humility because the great of the earth do not teach Humility. All fruit of Humility and all splendor and vigor of Humility have perished because of the greats. All that remains are only empty and dead words. This is why no one wants to hear these words, it is because they are dead. No one takes the time to speak of Humility, much less to live in the spirit that Christ lived, which is calm and humble. God have Mercy on us, otherwise who will be able to remain standing, when God appears with just judgment? The time approaches when the arrogant who disdained and mutilated Humility will be tormented and in great confusion. Yes, that time is coming, when men will want to rid themselves of arrogance and tyranny, but without success. They will not be able to achieve salvation. They did not even understand the opportunity God gave them in Jesus Christ. Oh, for those who do not find pleasure in the humility of Christ because they will lack the strength to cry as much as they would like. Oh, for those who now mock and disdain the Humble of the earth. And oh, for those who rule and have the governance of the church in their hands. Because they will be guilty that the Humility of Christ disappeared from the Christians. These will be guilty that arrogance has taken the place of Humility.

Humility is the fruit of the Spirit of God. When Humility disappears from man, this is a sign that the Love of God and the Spirit of God no longer exist in that man.

No one disdains arrogance. All receive it with compliments and with great interest. No one abhors arrogance nor wars against it, no one denounces it, and if they do, this man is harassed and treated as a fanatic. Oh, for those who praise Christ with lip service, yet abhor the Humility of Christ. Oh, for those who call themselves Christians and abominate the Humility of Christ, abhor the true Cross of Christ, which is lived in Humility. I know and am conscious that these words are lifeless for many. But the day approaches when these same words will be sought by the same rebels and the prideful one, but they will not find them but for their condemnation. Because, what grace is there in trembling for fear of death? The demons also tremble when their hour approaches. And also those who mock Humility will tremble. I exhort you, in the name of the Lord of all the earth, and with fear and humility, for you to turn, and learn from Christ the true Humility and calm. Why mock the same Spirit of God? Did not God reveal himself in Christ with Humility and calm, to serve everyone? Let us search, then, for the Spirit of God, which powerfully exhibited through Christ, as it can manifest itself in us if only we deny our arrogance and pride.

---

11. To Whom Does Justice Belong?

Victoria, Texas (March 12, 1954)
"We will have JUSTICE," said Moses, servant of God, "when we are careful to place before Jehovah our God, all these commandments as he has ordered." (Deut. 6:25). And, how will we find justice without the will of God? God "does JUSTICE to the orphan and the widow; and also loves the foreigner and provides him bread and clothing" (Deut. 10:18).

The principle of God's justice is discovered when he does good for the oppressed and the earth's afflicted. Who are the afflicted besides the widow, the poor, the orphan, and the foreigner? For this very reason God gives testimony in favor of his servant Job. And Job described his own work when he said: "I dressed in JUSTICE and it dressed me like a mantle" (Job 29:14). Later he explains his work of Justice when he said: "Because I liberated the poor who screamed, and the orphan who lacked aid." To the heart of the widow, he gave joy. I was the eyes of the blind, and feet of the lame. This is ancient wisdom, this is the true work of Job. Let us take note that after Job talked about his justice and Mercy for the oppressed of the Earth, his three friends Eliphaz, Bildad, and Zophar remained quiet. While Job spoke of the greatness of God and of his fidelity, his friends had a chance to reply. When he spoke, as we see in 31:16[–18], he said: "If I have denied anything to the poor, or allowed the eyes of the widow to languish while I ate my portion alone, with no share in it for the fatherless, though like a father God has reared me from my youth, guiding me even from my mother's womb." This is why the apostle James says: "Mercy triumphs over judgment" (James 2:13). In truth Job's justice put an end to the argument and accusation of his three friends. Because the seat of God's throne is JUSTICE and JUDGMENT, and Mercy and truth come before it (Ps. 89:14). This is why blessed is the man who fears Jehovah and greatly delights in His commandments. His seed will be powerful on earth. The progeny of the upright will be blessed. Abundance and riches are in his house and his Justice will prevail forever. He has clemency, is merciful and just. He governs his things with judgment (Ps. 112: 1–5). Where are the blessings for today's men? Who are the ones who have today gained these blessings? They are gone from the earth. Gone are the ones who followed Justice and Mercy. This is why life remains hidden from the eyes of this bad and twisted generation (Prov. 21:21). In the time of the prophets, justice also had disappeared and he said: "Listen to me, those who seek Justice, those who search for Jehovah. Look at the rock from which you were carved" (Prov. 51:1). The rock from which they were carved was Abraham, a man of faith and Justice. Justice, judgment, and mercy are the things that God requests and wants (Jer. 9:23–24). But the things in which we can see Justice and Mercy have disappeared, and because of man-made laws, Justice cannot be seen. Because the forms of Justice that the children of God should undertake are now done by the children of darkness. Because the widow's bread and clothing are provided by the children of darkness. Who defends the poor of the earth? These seek asylum and refuge in the public courts of the world, because the church has rejected them. Let us listen still to the voice of the prophet Hosea: "Sow for yourselves Justice, reap the fruit of piety" (10:12). Blessed are those who hunger and thirst for Justice in these last days. Because now they have tired of vanities. As for the things that the prostitute is offering the church's children, they have mutilated the Justice of God and ignored all commandment of God for those of men.

Everyone justifies themselves by the laws and accords of their own religious group. And the meaning of justice that their leaders pronounce has led to the loss of Christ's peace. Now that peace cannot even be found in homes, much less within religious groups. No one yet has discovered that ignoring the widow and the orphan, is fruit and evidence that we have abandoned God. Because he who oppresses the poor affronts God. The poor and the widow have been oppressed because the Levites have eaten the part that belonged to them (Deut. 14:28–29; 26:12–13). Barbarous are the wolves that now watch over the cattle. And these, as the prophet Isaiah said, "are dumb dogs, they cannot bark, dreaming as they lie there, loving their sleep. They are relentless dogs, they know not when they have enough" ([Isa.] 56:10–11). The justice of God is discovered in Christ, from faith in faith (Rom. 1:17). But, where is the Church's Justice? Who will justify the church in its state of apostasy? Man, in his justice, will live, but where is the justice of those who are now called the children of God? Those who are not servants of justice, are servants of sin (Rom. 6:18).

We were chosen for God's justice and to do good here on earth. God is not served in temples nor is he adored by the words of rebels "for what you did to the smallest thing, you did to me." He showed this when he said: "when you have a reception, invite beggars and the crippled, the lame and the blind. You should be pleased that they cannot replay you, for you will be repaid in the resurrection of the just" (Luke 14:13–14). When Paul spoke to Felix in prison, Felix was not frightened by the ceremonies Paul showed him, or by the prayer, fasting, and tithes. What scared him was the Justice, the judgment, and the continence Paul spoke about. Let us not resist the Justice of the Holy Spirit.

All who love justice and fear God, return to God. Search in sacred archives for the wholesome word of God. Those who tremble at God's word, these are the ones who will not suffer the wrath of the great Almighty God. I urge you to fear God. Those who love life and want to relish good days, work for justice, do not buy or sell simply to live as vain and false Christians, who spend their days buying and selling vain things, becoming rich on earth, but poor in God. It is time for those who fear God, lift up your eyes. The time to disbelieve even those closest to us has arrived, because all tell lies without intending to. All are vain and liars. These are the days when all who speak, say they speak in the name of Christ, but nevertheless sell the word of God and are not moved by the justice they see on earth. I do not sell this word because it is not mine. Were it mine I would probably sell it like all false merchants who have dedicated themselves to selling the word of God do. I cannot sell the words I speak, because my body was not lifted up, nor does the world revolve because of all its intensely colored things. What life-giving thing could I buy in the world? Everything in the world are objects made by men who do not fear God. Why would I allow my soul to be tricked by what has no wisdom? All the things that the bad and vain man is inventing are things that distance us from humility and obedience to Christ. Why focus our eye and heart on these things that are not so? Around the world, the Church of Christ has descended to this level, calling mud and manure "gold," calling the good "bad" and the bad "good." Can there be a people more senseless than this, who leave the justice of God, for the justice of men? Who leave love and mercy, for arrogance and vengeance? And worst still, is that each claims to be better off than his peer simply because his beliefs are different than those of his peer, but all are equal in spirit. All abhor the spirit, the Commandments of God, and rebel against God's judgment resisting the Spirit of God. Oh, for these people because they have behaved like the ostrich, which abandons its eggs, the fruit of its womb, as if it cost nothing. Likewise, these people have abandoned Christ's path as if it cost Christ nothing. But await Christ's return when all will discover how wrong they were, and how twisted their souls were. All, like people without reason, like a crazy people, pursue vanities and pay highly for things that turn them away from God. Like people without understanding, all covet the same things. What is it they covet? Love? Mercy? Justice? Judgment? Faith? Obedience? No, none of this—instead they will kill for earthly things and lose even their closest friendships. Has there existed a people more impious and sinful? History does not register one more given to vanity than these who claim to have a love of God, but without even loving their own carnal relatives. I am surprised and perplexed at leaders in whom I expected to find something good. I said in my heart: Without a doubt these great men of the earth who direct the people in the word of God, must know the law of God. Without a doubt they could help know what Mercy is. But in all this I was deceived because I found that what emerged from them was the greatest hypocrisy; that they were the guiltiest that justice was dirt. But I noted that they gave great value to the commandments that they themselves established on their own whims. This scandalizes me. There is no poor person on earth who gives testimony on behalf of the church. Those who hold and occupy the pulpits, are greedy men, are clumsy men who do not love the truth. They rely on sweet words and use old examples of saintly men to obtain what they want. They may well speak the words of Paul—this they do because they do not have their own words—they lack even words. To deceive they use the words of the ancient wise men. Why do they not live the lives those saints lived? If they love Paul so much, why don't they imitate him? If they loved God and loved the lives of those saints, they would not abhor these words, nor would they disdain the love of Christ. But now, in what do we see the love of Christ? One devours the other, and how many have been felled by the same fights and divisions that are so common these days. This group and that, who profess to know Christ, cannot stand each other. And of this, on the great day, God will testify when there will be vengeance for all those who were evil and unjust, resisted correction, and made war on the law of God.

12. The Real Salary

It is here that everyone's God approaches and brings with him the salary of all, those who call him God and those who do not call him God. All will see their own salary, and each will see the result of their life, the fruit of their conduct. The so-called wise will discover if they really were wise, or if they were stubborn and senseless. The real salary of all will appear and evident to the eyes of all. Those who showed mercy likewise, with their own eyes, will see the mercy and Justice of God.

The salary of our thoughts has arrived, the salary of our words, the salary of our deeds. And where will those who now justify themselves in a vain faith hide? All who carry in their lives a Christ without work and without justice, what will become of them?

Nothing will remain without being a wage earner. This I say to those who follow the flesh and the vain desires of life. The just is not a wage earner, not on this earth, not even in the kingdom of Christ. Before the reward of the just is a gift of God. Eternal life is free. Its reward is not counted in salary, but as a great award from God. Oh, for those who receive salary for speaking with their tongues and not with their lives. Oh, for those who demand salaries for establishing laws that support the unjust and the hypocrite. With the measure they measured, they too shall be measured. For they did everything for salary, and with salary they corrupted the earth, because even the lowly demanded salary, and no one attended the works of mercy. Each of the great learned to work for money and from the great learned to charge and demand.

Each one bent themselves toward the earth and toward things that nourish arrogance. They sacrificed their lives. Salary even made the eye of the wise man gloomy. Even if during its youth [salary] was disdained, in its old age it is worshipped. Those who preach Christ without attending to the widow will also be paid with the Judgment of God. Oh, for those who call themselves "preachers" without knowing what "Mercy" is. Oh, for those who show the path, without knowing it themselves. Oh, for those who promoted salaries on Earth and by them captivated innocents.

Because of salary, all became alienated from mercy, but the compassionate and obedient do not know a salary, because it is an affront. Teachers are paid a salary when the merciful are missing. When the earth lacks wise men—those who need salary multiply. But when the wise lead, those who need salary cannot find bread.

When those who dominate need a salary, the widow finds no aid. Oh earth, evil will soon be removed and the just will possess you once again!

Shame the evil one and confuse those who need a salary because he did not learn this from Jesus Christ. The salaried do not know mercy, but the Merciful do. In giving, he receives, and by pardoning, he also is pardoned. The compassionate cannot be rented, nor can the wise be obtained through salary. Salary attracts the stubborn and the evil seek salary.

Each of you, look at your maker and tremble at the voice of the one who formed you. It is to this place that Justice comes, and no one shall escape the word of God; each will behold his own deeds, and no one will escape from his salary. No one should attend to the voice of those who out of clumsy interest, teach lies, and for vain glory, pursue public careers. Let us turn our souls to the one who formed them and heed the advice of he who wants to save us from the ire that is coming. God has been offended because of our rebelliousness and is irritated because of our many sins.

Our forefathers who came from afar to live on these lands, were they paid to speak the word of God? Certainly not even the heads of nations received such thing. George Washington, first president of the United States, did not accept such a thing as a salary. Much less the workers who preached the word of God. But, what now? Workers do nothing for free. They are even paid to speak lies. If what they spoke were true, there the fruits of Justice and of Judgment would exist. There also would be Mercy, but none of this has resulted. Today, the presidents of the Nation have learned from the workers of the kingdom to receive salary. George Washington gave to public service the large sum of money the government paid him for serving in the war.

And when he served as president, he never accepted a salary. This was a great example for the Nation. George also came out of the Christian home and in him we can see that the gospel that was preached in those days was cleaner. He learned from workers to refuse a salary for serving humanity. But in these days, all demand a salary because they have learned this from the heads of the Church, who have sold themselves to error. This was the death of the spirit of service toward the meek of the earth. A paid person is not valiant because salary twists the heart of the wisest. Valiant ones, those who love rights, remove yourselves, leave examples for the young and mark paths of Mercy. All who fear hunger and nakedness, get off this path and do not interfere. Do not bring infamy to the kingdom of Christ because the Kingdom's servants are not made up of paid people, but of parents who treasure their children. If Washington did not want salary to serve an earthly kingdom, why ask for a salary from a spiritual and holy kingdom? If Christ did not do it, why should we?

All of you who pray, contemplate the poor. Those of you who sing in congregations, bear the afflictions of those who suffer. Those who fast and sacrifice food for their stomachs, subject your tongue to a fast so that it will not speak about your peer, so it will not probe the earth in vain talk. He who empties his stomach of nourishment, also empty the heart of evil thoughts. He who subjects his body to fast, force your eye also to fast so he will not covet the neighbor's wife. It is time that the people of God present their body in vivid sacrifice, and no longer serve the eye, or even their own body. Those who perform and offer worship and prayers in public, display Mercy and truth in public. Because, oh, for those who pray in public and lie in secret. Oh, for those who sing in public and abhor in secret. Oh, for those who speak well in public but in private speak with a crooked tongue. Oh, for those who give in public gatherings, but in secret do no good toward anyone. He who thinks of God, think of your peer. He who asks of God, give to others before expecting. He who does not want to be judged, stop judging. He who does not want to be condemned, stop condemning others. He who does not want to be gossiped about, stop gossiping. He who wants to be forgiven, first forgive your peer. From the beginning Christ taught us this, he said: "Do not judge and you will not be judged. Do not condemn, and you will not be condemned. Pardon and you shall be pardoned. Give, and it shall be given to you" (Luke 6:37). Those who await Christ and His return, leave all the bad deeds that you commit in secret, purify each action that you undertake secretly. All those devoted to the temples, tremble at the word of God. Those who imagine liberation, give others liberty, because he who does not lend an ear to the clamor of the poor, he too will clamor and not be heard. He who bends his knee to ask the Almighty, extend your hand to give to the needy and oppressed. He who closes his eyes to pray, close your eyes to coveting. He who opens his mouth to ask of the living and just Judge, open your mouth too to defend the afflicted and the orphan. He who is not ashamed of singing in the congregations, do not be ashamed of forgiving before he who reprehends. To he who asks, give, and he who receives, do not deny. He who does not want to be condemned, close your mouth. And he who does not want to be judged, do acts of mercy, because mercy is glorified against judgment. All who want to receive from God, do not dismiss the poor with "welfare." He who waits to be lifted, lift those already fallen. And he who loves long days, search for the peace of the poor. He who understands that we are in the last days, do not speak. And he who knows that the end is near, do justice and mercy. Those who teach the people how to ask, teach also how to share. Because in every labor there is fruit, but in lip service there is only poverty. He who speaks, think, and he who thinks, obey. He who obeys, share your lot with those who cry out because those who share are torches, and the generous are heard from above. He who is offended, do not be irritated because ire is not man's and those who are silent cause no arguments.

The blind man does not covet, the mute does not cause arguments, and the deaf does not collect lies. He who has eyes to see, his deeds are also seen. He who has mouth to speak, will have to answer many questions on the day of Judgment. He who has ears, has no excuse. The enemies of the poor, like those who do not care for widows, are not worthy of teaching congregations. Because any teacher who is internally hardened will only produce cruel disciples. All who do not delight in doing good, the tears they shed on the altar are also in vain. He who does not show mercy is not a disciple of Christ; and he who does not share with the poor, does not know Christ. He who does not show mercy and justice is a stranger and unknown in the Kingdom of Jesus Christ. Those who trust only in what is done within temples are friends of the Pharisees, and those who neglect sanctity in the home are captives of Babylon.

Those who fast in order to receive, should also fast to be able to give and serve others. Those who fast only when they are afflicted are just like others, so do not point with an accusatory finger. Because to the children of God work for mercy and truth. Mercy is not the fruit of the flesh, nor is it a product of the earth.

Those who walk along ancient paths will not be surprised. Yet those who invent accords and rules about the people who worship, they shall account for everything, and life's author will condemn them in the presence of all his holy angels. Thus, let us do good without demanding salary, and work without charging tribute of men because he who charges will also have to pay. He who spares a favor, is like the one who does not do it. All that belongs to God is free: yet he, who negotiates with the word of God will lose his life. The merciful are called wise, but those who dress like princes bring a curse unto themselves.

13. Let Us Return to Our Maker

San Antonio, Texas (August 3, 1953)
God be my judge and the one who judges me, if in me there is deceit or egoism as I speak these words. Let it be God who will stand against me, if

my lips do not speak truth and equity, because I have learned what I speak from God. If I speak against good and if my words are not of God, let it be God who reprehends me. If I speak in the flesh and if I have written these words to gain earthly glory, judge me God, and make judgment with me he who does not make sense to people.

My eyes have seen evil in all the churches and in the place of Justice; there I have seen injustice. In the place of mercy, there I have seen ingratitude and only the work of the flesh. All this forces me to ask, Why does part of me abhor the bad actions and evil deeds seen among the church? Why does my soul reject and deny being in accord with what now passes as the word of God? Who am I to speak and rise up against bad actions and all injustice? Why is it that I cannot stop speaking? Why do I not keep silent? The Spirit in me does not let me rest. What God placed in my heart and the anointment that came from high does not let me be silent or still. I speak for the good of those who fear God. I speak for the good of those who make peace. He who fears God, open your ears and attend to these words. Oh, for those who think they are well with God, because the greatest of the earth are those who have done the greatest evil. God is angry at them. The Judgment and Justice God will envelop the earth and all the people who occupy it.

Some are so far from mercy as others. And no one loves mercy. Some are so far from God's love as others. All claim to know God yet do not know justice, even though God is Justice. He who knows God is also supposed to know justice. He who knows God also knows mercy. But in these days, all run away from the justice of God; all abhor doing good. The poor and unsheltered of the earth can testify and confirm these words. Oh, for those who have left the judgment of God, because in the latter days they will be surprised with the same judgment they disdained. Oh, for those who view God's commandments with contempt. Because of Him they will soon tremble and cry for mercy and wisdom, but no one will take pity on them. They will cry but not receive anyone's mercy because they had no compassion for anyone. All have grown and become lords of the earth and even of souls, yet all rule and accept no advice from anyone. Oh, for all of these because during the final days they will cry and lament abusing the things of the Spirit of God, when on their lips they professed to possess the Spirit of God. This has brought great evil upon the earth and has mutilated the things of God. Oh, for those who do not have compassion toward the oppressed, because on that day who will be compassionate toward them? Oh, for those who mock obedience and humility, because on that day their own derisiveness will kill them, and they will rot in their own wealth. Because the men who directed the word of God looked toward the earthly, all have lost the hunger and thirst for justice, and instead of this, all pursue the earthly. All look for luxuries and brightly colored things, even if they do not leave a single piece of bread for the poor and the orphan. God is angry and the very Lamb of God will throw his great and terrible ire over those who profess his name without even knowing what mercy is. Oh, for those who say they fear God and do not keep his holy commandments. Oh, for those who say they are saved and do not obey even their own parents. Oh, to those who trust the words of men and commandments of the salaried, because great will be the ire of God over these people who only confessed to him with lips but gave their hearts to the devil and deeds of iniquity. God have mercy on humanity, because many innocents are guilty of nothing, but have been deceived through the cunning of bad men. Holy God! Liberate the small of the earth. Make us see that we live in times when there is no love or faith with which to understand the times and to repent with wise hearts. Some of you like others, those who share this or that name, all pursue what perishes. All of you close your heart's doors to the mercy of God as well as justice and judgment. What will we do in these days of War and ire? Loosen the lips of the earth, men of reason speak, what good have we done on earth? Have we not robbed women of their honor? Have we not made sons abhor their fathers and disobey them? Is it not our fault that the earth is divided? For not preaching the word of God as he commanded, and for not living according to the commands he gave leaders, because of this the entire earth is divided and arguing. Oh, for those who have caused this evil over the earth. I look everywhere to see if men and women demonstrate shame. But I do not find it. All are corrupted. Everyone, men and women, children and the elderly, have been corrupted by greed. The church has lost its sanctity. The church has left God's path and lost its appeal. Who will rise up as a shining example for us? From where will light emerge to light the ways for our souls and those of others? For we have left the will of God and mocked his every good and holy commandment, which were handed to man so that he would live according to God's will of God and not falter.

Those who mock humility and obedience disdain Christ and hand down a sentence on their own lives. Those who belittle Justice belittle Christ because Christ is Justice. He who dresses in fine clothes will stumble on them. He who searches for delicious bread will be confounded by it. On that day teachers will understand why all the prophets were poor, and why our teacher never even experienced a fox's cave. The prophets were not poor not because God did not bless them or because they lacked for bread. They voluntarily avoided all these things that have always been the obstacle and cause for the fall of the greedy. Because of the Spirit they had received, they knew and understood that all these things are vanity of vanities. I am certain that none of the prophets would covet the wisdom offered by the teachers of our day. Because in the eyes of a just and truly wise man, these men by force resemble sodomites (for they do not cover their filthiness). And like the most stubborn of the world, they covet with zeal. The greed that moves them is like the wind that moves the sea's great waves. There is no colorful thing or figure they do not covet. Now, why do I say this; will I be judged for speaking so? Am I, as Jeremiah was also accused, seeking the bad acts of the people? Am I the scandalous one, while nothing is wrong with the people who claim to be of God? Am I so blind that I imagine all of this evil, when in truth none of it exists? Could it be that there are some faults in the people of God, but much good can also be found among them? What is the good that the church has done on earth? Let the wise men meet and dispense advice, defending the people of God and their justification. If I am alone in these words, if I speak only from my very brain, and if God is too remote from these alien words, each of you justify yourself and defend the good that can be found in the Church. Evil would be upon me, if I were alone in speaking these words. He who defends Justice and fights for rights is above all others. He is the holder of the truth, he is the one who lays claims to all of this.

Who am I to claim such right and justice on behalf of the people of God? What has been given to me? Above, in the heavens, is the one who asks this of his people. Each of you, desert greed, do good as our fathers did in the beginning, let us lift the paths that our fathers drew, and let us lift up what is on earth.

Let us turn the heart to the one who formed it, let us turn our ear to the one who formed it, giving glory to the one who made the heavens and the earth. To him who formed the earth and filled it with beasts, herbs, and fruits; to him who formed the ocean and everything we see and do not see. To him who orders everything with occult wisdom, before he rises to punish earth's inhabitants, let us all return to our God. He is good and Merciful to those who love Him and follow His holy commandments. Why should we be ashamed before the holy and Just God? Who can stand with arrogance before him? God is worthy of our fear. His force and wisdom cannot be measured or spoken. Man cannot see his awesome force with the naked eye nor bear the effect of his words. The earth, with all its great mountains and vast seas, trembles like a drunk when He speaks. On seeing him irate, the hills smoke and the hardest rocks break. His ire is terrible, and with it He cleanses the earth and liberates it from tyrannical worms because man is nothing more. His love perfects things and through His love gives life to all things. In His ire he destroys everything that corrupts and snuffs life so that it will not sin. The wise men the world praises and teachers who are considered great in the eyes of congregations are like fleas in the presence of God. As with everything, our great God does not underestimate anyone, nor did he burden mankind with more than was just. He speaks and a million things tremble. He orders and all obey. His holy works are put to action when he issues commandments. The clouds, the wind, the earth, the animals in the fields, the birds in the skies, and the men of earth all wait in him. And he, like a compassionate father, gives nourishment to all. The great and wise men have never comprehended his work, nor can the illustrious estimate his creation. Solomon made the effort, but soon tired. He proposed to know the work of God and understand his wisdom but had little success. The wind that we cannot see, the wind that cannot be touched or felt, the wind that has no shape or color, the wind that does not bother even an insect, well, God orders it. When he becomes angry, he orders it, and the wind becomes strong. God gains force and demands more of the wind, and then this wind that before did not move even an insect, now moves through the mountains, hurls across the deserts, envelops the entire world. With its great force it tears the great sea. With its ire it breaks even the most ancient cliffs, humiliates even the strongest work of man. And this wind, which before did not even stir a hair, now the strongest fear it and the most stable disappears. No one can stop its course. Let us consider, then, who spoke to Moses, who lifted Jesus Christ as judge of the living and the dead. Let us leave the work of man and not trip on the wisdom of man, which leads to death if we follow it to the end. But the wisdom that belongs to God, first of all, it is life, then strength, wealth, and endless peace. Let us return our heart to its owner. Peace be with all who fear when they hear or read these words. And may God bless all who receive the wisdom's guidance.

---

14. The Unfaithful Spouse

Melvin, Michigan (May 9, 1953)
The true wife of Christ loves her Lord. The Church of Christ has experienced only bitterness throughout its long journey on this earth. Her husband, who was Christ, taught her to suffer. He was the first to learn of suffering, to bear and suffer the mockery of people. He had no house of his own, and for this they called him a beggar. He had no treasures. He was truly the poorest of the poor. He carried nothing in his pockets, for he did not even have pockets. This prince of the poor knew of all sorts of poverty. That is, he was poor according to our standards, according to what the world says. But according to God he was not poor. He did not feel poor. He felt satisfied because there was peace in his heart. Because of the sin that existed in the world, he suffered very much. His whole life was full of contempt and strikes from bad people. The Church that followed him also knew all sorts of suffering, and this Church loved suffering. This wife of Christ was like a mother for the earth's people. This wife of Christ was the eyes of the blind. This wife of Christ passed her time feeding those who had nothing to eat. She never sought her own good, but instead would spend nights out on the hills and valleys, searching for the needy in dark places, and looking after anyone. This wife of Christ was not at ease until everyone had what they asked for. She stayed up during the night. She was the last to eat so everyone else would be able to eat. She really obeyed her holy husband in every way and pleased her husband in everything he ordered.

Christ removed this Church from a kingdom of darkness, from a place of servility. And because of this, this Church felt very grateful and indebted. It served out of pure love. It did it with all of its heart and with much joy in its soul. No one in the world was happier or more helpful and committed than her. Really, in everything she was a model. Everyone searched for her and cried out to her because she helped widows, visited prisoners, and advocated for those imprisoned until they were freed. The energy of this saintly woman was never deterred. It seemed as if the more she served the world's laments, the more strength she received. Even the angels adored her. Christ was not ashamed to call her his beloved wife. The glory of Christ was reflected in how his wife comported herself amid all. All the other women envied her very much, because she was very loved and esteemed by all of the poor, widows, foreigners, and orphans. Her garments were clean from head to toe. Her heart was not deceived, nor did her eyes seek out vanities, for she was content with her possession. She sought nothing because she had everything that makes a faithful wife happy and content. This faithful wife behaved like this for a long time. But her fame and glory grew so much that soon she began to focus on her own garments and saw that she really was beautiful and good looking. Her heart therefore began to slip, and her mind began to focus on her own beauty. When she noticed that many other men had fixed their eyes on her, it moved her heart and stirred her soul. Her ears began to listen to what they said and told her. They gave her many offers of happiness and joy, which she did not consider dangerous, sinful, or adulterous. She was only going to participate in those things that are necessary for life. There were many admirers who offered to serve and attend her well so that she would not have to bother about anything. She saw that there was nothing wrong with resting and letting others serve her. Well, she thought, she had already suffered enough for others and had already done so for a long time; there was nothing wrong that now others attended to her. This was how this beautiful woman tasted the respite the world gives. She saw nothing wrong in it. She began to have many servants who attended her with great reverence and fear. All she ordered was done quickly and happily. This began to delight her soul, and she began to forget about her sufferings, about her great works for the poor. The rich of the earth also began to offer her free services, to revere her, something that did not disgust her. Soon the rich and the great who served her were given the authority to rule over others from her. And she rejoiced in giving orders to many greats because, in reality, her soul felt pleased. She did not lack, she said, and seemed to be experiencing her best success and triumph. From all parts of the earth came the great, offering their services free. Seeing that great and powerful men humiliated themselves before her, she began to be filled with such joy and pride that she forgot about her days in captivity. She forgot about the days she spent in iron chains serving like a slave. When they had her with a band around her eyes so she could not see the Sun of Justice; when her feet were bound so she could not escape. She forgot about all the tears she shed in that dark prison. She also forgot about who took her out of that disgusting place. The happiness of all those who served her and administered to her was so great that even she began to be intoxicated with joy by those who loved her and gave her great service, and because of the yells and merrymaking that surrounded her. Now she cannot hear the cries of the afflicted, of the poor who walk naked and without bread to eat. She completely forgot about those who are still in prison. Later she began to listen to the powerful that served her and she began to give them authority to administer what she once did. These men had never known affliction and suffering, for they had never aided the fallen, fed the hungry, or sheltered the orphan and the widow. They had no gratitude because they had never served anyone and did not know about true suffering of those who suffer. The great began to exert themselves over her, began to twist her heart, and took away the mercy that she once had.

Next, the men who had never experienced sadness and bitterness in jail began to give her new ideas and laws that she had never known. Those who currently govern the Church of Christ are men who have never known suffering. They do not have gratitude because all they have are the vices of the world, like smoking, drinking liquor, and other vices that men pick up after rebelling against God. And because of this, those who now lead as representatives of the real church do so without mercy. They do not have the love of God. They do not have accomplishments deserving of repentance. They do not have the humility of Christ, who lifted the Church from its state of slavery. These servants are ungrateful men, who have abandoned the poor, orphans, and the needy, and only seek their own good. Hundreds of afflicted, because of the prisons that torment them, cry and scream. And these men who deceived the true Church do not care that the world is on fire, just as long as they are not. Who will save us now from these wolves, from these shepherds who appease themselves, and give the sheep only dry grass? These great men who look at the mercy of the earth, but do not care. But do fight for and defend their own name; this is what the rebel church searched for. God calls us, and says, my children, return to what I have taught you and I will shower my Spirit unto you.

We, the Church of Christ, must feed the hungry. Give rest to the tired and take the orphan into our home. But we have not done any of this. The earthly government has had to feed the hungry because the Church has no time to feed them, is too busy buying the many things it needs. This is quite embarrassing. God have mercy on us.

Let us return to the one who liberated us from the yoke of servitude. Let us turn to God who liberated us from the hand of the devil. It is not late, let us rise and turn our heart to God who is slow to ire, and quick in Mercy.

15. Confusion and Shame

Christians with scandal and with pride describe what they call sin.

They are scared because liquor is more broadly consumed, and because murder, stealing, and adultery also have also multiplied. But they do not notice that these things have multiplied because we do the will of God; we should see and lose his light.

God is not scared by the evil that multiplies among the children of darkness, but he is surprised by the evil that grows among the children of light. Instead of seeing the evil of the children of darkness we should focus on what we ourselves have caused by separating the word of God and the body of Christ. And the worst of it is that no one has lost the taste of salt, and our lamp must shine light on how the chosen men mined jealousy and arrogance. We should be scandalized of how our daughters and our own wives dress. We should be scared and muzzle our mouths because our children order us around. Now the father has no power over the son. Much harm is caused by the vices of liquor, smoking, movies, dancing. But we know that this is not fruit from a good tree. And those who do such things do not profess to fear God.

Even children know that these things are bad. And I think that none of this was found in the Pharisees, but did it save them? Were they justified because they were or called themselves the children of Abraham? Did they escape God's ire in the taking of Jerusalem only because they gave or paid tithes, because they sang, prayed, and fasted? Was any of this worth it? Let us not deceive our souls. I think that in these final days we find more fear of God among the peoples of Asia, which we call pagan, than in ourselves. There is more humility and a spirit of service in those, than in the ones who call themselves Christians.

We must use our reason and see that the love of God is no longer found among us. We should be ashamed, all cover our mouths, because judgment and justice of God is not found in us. Justice and judgment once belonged to us. But none of this is found among Christians. As I say this, I am ashamed, for it is against the people of God that I speak. I feel sad and confused as I see our condition in such a state.

What will we tell the sinner? What good is in us when it comes to justice, Mercy, love for the sinner, in exchange for the liquor and the vices he carries? Let us take away the rites. Let us not deceive our hearts with chants and vain prayers. Singing or praying has not done anyone good, nor does fasting after leaving the justice and mercy of God. Israel also did it, even after leaving good and the God's commandments. But God sent the Prophet Isaiah so he would speak to them about the vanity of their dead works (Isa. 58:1–10).

We should be ashamed to see the widow begging for bread from the state and the children of darkness instead of the children of light. It should cause us shame and terror to see our children doing as they wish and acting dissolutely.

Because the God to whom we address our petitions looks from above and considers from that place that we should receive nothing when he sees the earthly poor suffering for want of everything.

For he too shall seek revenge and for this reason he has shut his ear to our petitions, for he sees that we have shut our ear to the orphan and foreigner. And God, as the judge who advocates the cause of the widow and orphan, and who rewards us according to each person's works, he too will give us according to our conduct toward the oppressed. All the complaints of the oppressed are against the church and against the heads who occupy the place of princes.

May I be a thorn and a sting to the people of God even though I may scandalize all. I talk and shall talk. I will accuse the people until the judgment of God comes. I will not stop talking, of denouncing evil and the sin of God's people while days remain, and while God rules and orders that the four angels now tied be released with their world powers. They will do the will of God over earth at their exact hour. The wise ones of the earth, those who hunger and thirst for Justice, satisfy yourselves making justice and judgment for all. Sow in mercy, because it is not time to complain, for we all have failed God. Soon his son, the King of Kings, will ask our souls. And with what will we respond to the son of God? Let me offer my testimony that God may hear my words. I have not stopped denouncing your evils and through letters make our iniquities notorious, because they are not to be overlooked. Otherwise, by no other way would we reach the burning of peoples and towns. The people of God are the only ones who can avoid the ire of God and stop destruction. When the ire comes, it will be because the people of God have lost their sense of life. What awakens the ire of God over the earth is the rebelliousness of its own people. Because if its people are well, its own people will save the earth.

---

16. The Weapons of Babylon

Carlsbad, California (June 30, 1954)

Error covered the earth, evil overtook strong places, and transgression and rebellion developed in man's heart. This is how apostasy overtook the earth and justice lost its place in men's hearts.

Error and evil cannot be reconciled, iniquity and filth do not respect MOVEMENTS. For rebelliousness to advance there can be no grounds for agreement, nor can the power of the antichrist be reduced to a single movement. Evil finds its home in the heart of men and the whore mother of all the fornications on earth has intoxicated everyone from this chalice. Because lies, egoism, and arrogance are not found only in one Nation, or in one religion.

The chalice from which Babylon (the whore) has given to all peoples and languages consists of ERROR, REBELLIOUSNESS, and EVIL in the lives of men. This evil is seen in the words of the present generation, in their thoughts, in their egotistical actions, and in their lives, which are full of greed and arrogance. Each person looks for their own benefit. Who can say that this evil is only seen in a council?

The Spirit of God finds home in the heart that fears and works Justice. In the same manner the spirit of the whore finds a home in the heart that calls itself of God yet is rebellious and selfish. Who has escaped from the chalice of the whore? Blessed is the one who has not known the whore's depths.

Those who knew good, left it. Those who understood law, abandoned it. And all who were wise, left justice and mutilated mercy. Each was intoxicated with arrogance and stumbled on the stone of life (Christ) not obeying the sacred commandment.

Like children without faith, they revealed themselves, demanding promises from on high. They trample the rights of the Spirit and do not attend to the commandment of Christ. The whore kills. The Antichrist kills. And Jerusalem over which Christ wept also kills. The whore's ministers are not only drunks and adulterers, but they did not kill Christ, rather, those who called themselves by God's name. The whore's ministers are workers who despise the cross, but not of the ceremonies or of traditions invented for public adoration. The enemies of Christ's life, of his humility, of his obedience, of his mercy, these lead lives full of arrogance of life, caused by what they possess. They declare themselves before the eyes of God as the greatest enemies of Christ's cross. The whore's agents propagate arrogance. Which council can resist arrogance? All condemn the drunk, the thief, and the adulterer, because they cannot find anything else to condemn. But, what about the arrogance of life seen in the clothes princes wear, the pleasure-filled homes they possess, their ointments, their egotistical words of boast, and rebellion against the Holy Spirit's commandments? The commandments of Christ do not form peoples or councils but one sole kingdom, saintly and ruled in Justice. Thus no one should try to sanctify themselves in these days of error and rebellion with chanting ceremonies and public prayers. Because although the flesh is weak to undertake the good and justice of God, the flesh is not weak enough to sing and pray. The Pharisees although they were of weak (the flesh) could still sing, pray, and tithe. The flesh consciously was weak when it required forgiving, loving the enemy, looking after the widow and the orphan during their tribulations. Accordingly, he who is in the flesh cannot do the things that are in the Spirit and in the kingdom of Justice. Because of this the whore and the Antichrist like the "Jerusalem of below." It does not deny or burden us with ceremonial laws. But this whore is against all work of Justice and Mercy. Because of this, the mother of all the fornications on the earth keeps us occupied during times that should be devoted to the widows and the earth's poor. She has us all intoxicated with the delights of life, delighted in the foods of princes, in garments of presidents, in homes without humility, and in crafty work.

When the whore is burned and kings eat their own flesh, the arrogance of life will also pass. With the whore's death, the ministers who taught the Christianity of the latter days will also pass. With the whore's end, we will also see the end of Christianity's rebelliousness against God's holy commandments handed to us by Christ. Because even when people are divided in opinion and in ceremonies, in spirit they are not. Because all have the same spirit of greed, of rebellion against the commandments of Christ, all have the same spirit of arrogance, and a same spirit has taught them to speak with lies against their own brother. The arrogance of life can be seen in all when they speak, in their dress, in their thoughts, in their deeds. Because their deeds are not of mercy and forgiveness, their words are not of peace and union, their thoughts are not clean but instead focused on the wife of their peer. This is why evil has engulfed the earth. Even though men have attempted to sanctify themselves by separating themselves from their groups and from each other, this does not change their lives. Because they do not heed the Holy Spirit's advice and the division simply is fruit of sin and rebellion against God.

Blessed is he who understands which is the whore's chalice and its drunkenness so he will not participate in the delights that have corrupted the entire earth. The chalice and the whore are not, as many suspect, in some sort of agreement akin to those used to accuse the Catholic Church. Nor does it consist in the sin we see among thieves, the earth's criminals, and in those who smoke. It consists in the errors that have driven everyone to the drunkenness of life, to crimes of the womb. It consists of man's craziness and thoughtlessness which result from abandoning the Holy Spirit's laws and the creating those of his own whims and invention, explaining that it is so that work will expand and for the kingdoms' (councils) good. This is the error that leads man to death and to become an enemy of Christ's kingdom.

Listen all you wise men, all who love life, all who fear God and await his return, seek the paths to God anew, which are all of humility and obedience. The paths of life consist of love and mercy. Everyone doing good for his brother and his enemy, without looking at your brother's circumstances nor your enemy's evil. Because in times as bad as ours, even the wise one closes his mouth to avoid speaking against anyone. No one should raise their hand against anyone. Each feels miserable and leaves laughter for tears. Leave receiving for giving, stop speaking to hear the voice of the Holy Spirit, which calls us to his reprimand. Clean your hand, close your mouth, there is no more time to justify ourselves, because all have drunk from the great whore's chalice and with its deceits, we all have rebelled against our God's commandments. No one buy, no one sell, leave commerce and search for the one who gives life. Return to the one we have offended. Why deny our souls life? Leave Babylon, all who loves life. Leave the arrogance evident in your speaking, dress, and behavior. Leave behind the confidence you place in ceremonies, because those who sang from their hearts are gone, and those who prayed with all their hearts no longer live. The merciful were heard in their prayers, but where are the merciful now? Oh, for those who know good yet do not do it. Oh, for those who know Christ's commandments but do not obey them. Oh, for those who invite the Holy Spirit but resist love. Love is fruit of the Holy Spirit. All who wail because of all the evil in the people of God, leave Babylon. The people of God are captive in Babylon, and those who teach, feed on the intoxication of the mother of all the fornications of the earth. Therefore, no one should trust his teacher. Those who cry, raise up your eyes, for here comes the one who will judge the great whore and will destroy the works and laws of vain men.

17. What Is Mercy?

What thing is mercy? The world these days is not a place to contemplate or investigate what sort of thing MERCY is. But for the good of those who fear

God and want to know what mercy is, I will speak of this fruit of God, of this vital force that exists in the spirit of God, like any other who carries the spirit of God. Mercy is important because where there is mercy, one finds the spirit of God, or God's. Where there is mercy there is liberty, so that all can gain their share or opportunity.

Mercy is a virtue moved by the Spirit of God. He who has the spirit of God demonstrates mercy. Mercy is that force and work that we see between two persons; two persons are necessary to see mercy. Mercy is demonstrated by the man who has eyes and guides the one who does not. For mercy to become visible and manifest, it requires two persons, one capable and the other not. It requires a wealthy man and a poor one, a strong one and a weak one, a healthy one and sick one, a blind one and one with eyes, one great and one small, one wise and the other ignorant. When these different persons extend their hand to each other in a clean and just way, without avarice or interest, then Mercy becomes visible and manifest to the world. When the rich provides for the poor, when the one who sees guides the one who cannot, when the wise teaches with love for the ignorant, when the strong supports and lifts the skinny and weak, that is when God is present in human hearts. When we do such things and work with mercy that is when we also reach God's MERCY. James the apostle tells us "Merciless is the judgment on the man who has not shown mercy" (James 2:13). And in a parable, Christ told the story of the two debtors who owed a king or great and wealthy lord ten thousand talents. Through his mercy the king pardoned the debt. Later the debtors confronted one of their servants who owed them one hundred dinars. But the men whose entire debt had been pardoned did not want to forgive their servant's debt of one hundred dinars and took him before the king for judgment. And the angry king handed these men to the executioners so that they could pay all the previously forgiven debt. Through this example Christ speaks to us and says that God too will hand us over to executioners if we do not forget our debtors. Everywhere God speaks to us about mercy. "Blest are they who show mercy; mercy shall be theirs," says Christ (Mat. 5:7). But what a pity it is to see what mercy is on earth. The rich disdain the poor, the strong make fun of the scrawny and weak, and the one who has eyes or thinks he has eyes cast the blind to an even deeper abyss. Like the Pharisees when they converted a gentile, they would throw that person into the abyss, making him a child of hell worst in habits than they. The healthy do not visit or console the sick. He who deems himself wise does not advise the ignorant. The proof of all this is that our children are being devoured by the arrogance and concupiscence of the world. This happens in homes and in schools, and in churches too, which are full of dead and weak advice. Where can we see mercy? He who comes to do good, does not do so unless he has personal interest or has something to gain. Like the interests of the "Salvation Army," "welfare," and many organizations that for clumsy gains create orphanages or homes to place the needy. The men who do this certainly do some good, but why don't they teach and preach that everyone must do these works? On the contrary, instead of teaching this they trick people by saying that it is for the poor. I am certain that if they preached and taught that each of us has the obligation to help the poor, they would soon fail in their endeavors. People would not give money to these organizations. Instead of giving it to a public fund, each person would give it more personally to their poor and needy neighbor, which they each have. This is how it was taught even by the Law of Moses.

The mercy of God is visible in as much as he is strong and we are weak. He is compassionate toward us when we attempt to walk in his will. God is rich and we are poor, which is evident in his mercy when he shares the riches in his glory. But instead, we have shown a preference for earthly riches instead of Christ's. I see that very few really love and are thankful for God's mercy, which is Christ by whom (if we are loyal and obedient) have all the things we want and request, provided that they will foster eternal life and do us good. True mercy without dents or stain was revealed through Christ's life. If we love Christ we will receive the spirit of Christ, assured by the words of John the apostle: "The man who claims, 'I have known him,' without keeping his commandments, is a liar; in such a one there is no truth" (1 John 2:4).[3] So it is settled that we will do as Christ did when he said: "If you love me and obey the command I give you, I will ask the Father and he will give you another Paraclete to be with you always" (John 14:15). God in his mercy sent his son. Christ in his mercy by the same Spirit gave us the gospel that cost him his life. Whoever shows mercy will never be able to rebel against God's commandments nor to ignore the condition of the widow and the orphan. He who has mercy is not affirmed by arrogance as is so common these days. God gives us from his mercy. Let us hope that we walk in the fear of God and try to elevate mercy on earth, from the depths that infidels and the arrogant have placed it. I want Mercy said the lord of all the earth.

18. The Yearning of Those Who Adore

Day and night the men of war were heard. By day and night weapons are made, everyone working hard, everyone active in the great work. Factories and plants moved by great electric motors all cooperating toward the great goal. In the great cities all over the world, industry is booming. Men hurry, bosses rush, raw iron is thrown into fiery ovens with one goal. Even women work day and night in the factories, in the plants, making great instruments, powerful appliances. The men of science are occupied in their laboratories, thinking even in their beds at night, and making advances, inventing great appliances and projectiles, working in their minds like man has never before worked. Miners are extracting metal from the earth, and coal to melt the raw metal. Pilots are practicing day and night for the big day, flying at a terrible speed. What is the purpose of all this? What has God said about this great day? All these men of war who prepare day and night, look and wait for the day in which they will fly through the wind, will climb over the clouds, loaded with destruction and death for all the earth's inhabitants. These men will reach the peoples, crush the glory of the rebels, one against the others. Towns will burn. Summer homes and the winter homes equipped with all class of pomp and finery will no longer remain on earth. The glory of man will perish, his inventions will perish. Its big and powerful machines will cease to exist. Men and women, and everything that has a name on the earth, will suffer the consequence. Fine food and fine clothes will lose their great value and man will discover that, in reality, he was deceived by what he was not. Let us lift our eyes and no longer sacrifice for our mortal bodies. Let us immediately sacrifice for our souls. Let us cure our souls.

Many are the things that man seeks for the good of his own body, and in this way has neglected doing good and obeying its Creator. Man is doing nothing for its own soul. In these days man's soul is sterile, dry, and without fruit of God.

Fathers, mothers who fear God, look out for your children, care for their souls. Why do you leave your children to perish? Are your children not worth more than the earthly? Are your children not of more value than diamonds and pearls? Take your children out of hell before it is too late. Speak to your children about the end that approaches. Speak to them about God's love and works of justice before them so they will learn how to do good. Give to the poor from your possessions before the enemy seizes them. Listen to Christ: "What I say to you is this: Make friends for yourselves through your use of this world's goods, so that when they fail you, a lasting reception will be yours" (Luke 16:9). Why do we wait for the ire of God to come in the hand of the Antichrist and take our goods? Let us make treasures in the heavens before it is too late. Look for someone to do good to. Those who mock this advice, which Christ gave, one day will lament and wail, seeing their own riches rotten and burned. Then they will say: we should have been kind to the poor with our riches; we should have made justice and mercy with our peers. But they will be able to do this when it is too late, because the restless one and dreamers are deceived by evil's riches. They go along with things that are convenient, but the most important things of God's kingdom they have mutilated, which are justice, judgment, and mercy. Unfeigned faith, like the love of Christ, is good for all, including enemies. These do no good and also keep others from doing it. They are corrupted in everything and have been taken over by the spirit of error, which is why they do not want the love of truth.

Let us raise our eyes and behold the repentance of "Nineveh's" men, which is why they received mercy and forgiveness. Their repentance was from the heart, not only among the greatest sinners, but even the greatest priest and prophet found among them. I am certain that if someone would repent with the same spirit that Nineveh repented, he would be thrown out of the temples, called crazy and eccentric. Oh, for the obedient of the earth. Oh, for those who want to repent from their heart because they will be scorned by the citizens of great Babylon. Oh brothers, those who want to connect with your God must suffer the mockery. Let them make fun of you. This only will be for a short time because very soon they too will rid themselves of what they have and will cry bitterly. The end is near. The end comes. All eyes will cry, and all the strong will tremble. The leaders and the great men who executed the law, they too will place their faces upon the ground. They will scream like women in labor. These greats will flee the riches they once embraced, will curse the luxury and pomp for which once they killed. They will know that God is great and just and will know that in everything they deceived their poor souls.

Oh, for those who rule. Oh, for those who establish accords and unjust laws. On that day God will make them responsible for all the evil the people did. Oh, for those who change Christ's commandments, enacting commandments in councils and by vain men who did not even know how to love their own children and who did not attend to the rights of the just and the small. Where will they hide? To where will they escape? Who will support them? Because this will be a day of judgment when everything that was once hidden will be brought into the light of all. This will be a day of great confusion for the great.

19. The Holy Commandment

"He who has my commandments and keeps them, he is the one who loves me; and he who loves me, will be loved by my Father, and I will love him, and will manifest to him."[4] With these words Christ teaches to his disciples the difference between Christians who love him and those who do not. "He who has my commandments and keeps them, he is the one who loves me," which means that he who does not keep his commandments does not love him. Many want to love God but do not know why they cannot love him in a way that pleases the Lord. God does not connect with many Christians because they do not love him. Although they deny this and say that they do love him, God knows they do not because they fail to keep his commandments. Christ did not reveal what God did not want us to know, nor explain or command what God does not want us to do. Instead, all that Christ spoke and commanded was ordered and commanded by his father for our good. It is the will of God that we love one another, and for this reason he gave his son this commandment so that his son would give it to us, enjoining us to love one another. We know the words of Christ more extensively because of what he preached. And it was in these words that we can see the will of God and in the words of Jesus Christ we see the complete "Gospel." Christ, knowing that he had to undertake the will of his father, also ordered us to keep God's will. For the Lord says: "He who loves me, will keep my word; and my father shall love him, and we will come to Him, and make our home with him." Here Christ promises us the presence of the Father we so desire and promises that He and his Father will dwell in everyone who keeps their word. We see that Christ does not compromise the will of his father in any way, because as he explains: "He who has more commandments and keeps them" this is the condition that he places on us that the Son and the Father can be with us. If we refuse them by not keeping their commandments, we automatically refuse the Holy Spirit even when we are inviting him with our very lips. What Christ speaks is final. He received this commandment from His Father. I do not doubt that there are many persons who are quite sincere and want to please the Lord and would also like to love him over all other things. I say too that my heart is with those people. But the apostle St. John clarifies this good thing when, in his third letter, he tells an old woman and her children: "And this is love, that we walk according to his commandments."[5] But someone will certainly ask: well, which commandments my brother, and how many? The Lord Jesus Christ distinguished the Holy Spirit's commandments from those of Moses in a very distinct manner when he said: "You heard that it was said to the ancients you shall love your neighbor and abhor your enemy." I tell you. Love your enemies. Bless those who curse you, do good to those who abhor you, and pray for those who insult and persecute you." Later on, Christ did not retreat from these commandments, nor did he annul them. Instead, he fulfilled them by praying for his enemies. Every word that came out of Christ's mouth was spoken by the Spirit, and God did not disavow any of the words Christ spoke. As John said (John 17:18): "As you have sent me into the world, so I have sent them into the world" and in chapter 14:24 he also makes us realize that Christ spoke nothing or ordered anything without the will of God, saying: "The word you have heard is not mine, but of the father who sent me." Christ taught us that the

Christians would be judged by his word, as when he told us in John 12:48: "Whoever rejects me and does not accept my words already has his judge, namely, the word I have spoken—it is that which will condemn him on the last day." In verse 49 of John chapter 12, the Lord continues: For I have not spoken on my own; no, the Father who sent me has commanded me what to say and how to speak." Through these words we understand that the Word Christ spoke was of great importance to help us understand how we must love God and how we must obey him. It is Christ who on this occasion tells us who loves him and who does not. "He who has my commandments and keeps them, he is the one who loves me." How many will love God in these final days? In plainer words I ask, how many are obeying God in the words that his son spoke, whose words were sealed with his own blood? Speaking to his disciples Christ told them: "You are clean already, thanks to the word I have spoken to you" (John 15:3). In verse seven of the same chapter, he adds: "If you live in me and my words stay part of you, you may ask what you will—it will be done for you." He is clear on this, if you are in me and my words are in you.

20. Who Will Be Saved?

Who are the ones who expect to be lifted up on the cloud and escape the ire that approaches the entire earth? Where are these who have not transgressed God's commandments and are in Jesus Christ? These will be lifted and escape all the evil that God will do toward the rebellious inhabitants of the earth. How were they purified? How was it that they found grace before God thus allowing him to free them? What good did they do deserving of treatment with such distinct glory and with such elevated mercy? Those who say that they will see no evil and that their God will protect them from all the evil that will overtake all: How is it that they gained such grace before God's eyes? Why will they be treated so differently than the rest? Have those who have not transgressed God's commandments to be treated with unequaled mercy and sheltered? These were the ones who acted as the arms of the handicapped, the eyes of the blind, the mouth of the mute, the legs of the lame, and they fed the hungry. Was Christ's love in them? Or how was it that these gained such prize and such distinct privilege of being taken at such a strange hour? Did they sing better than the rest? Did they pray secretly and better than the rest? How did they distinguish their works to receive such great honor? Were these original in their works, not following the traditions and ceremonies of the other people? Did they love their enemies? Did they bless those who cursed them, do well toward those who abhorred them, and pray for those who harmed them?

Surely, these who will experience rapture always had their heavenly defender and never needed earthly defenders. Without a doubt they always lost and left their spoils in the hands of their adversaries for always having God on their side.

These who hope to escape the ire of God, do they ever fight for temples or enter the courts of the impious to defend their glory? Do they work like their master and Christ did, for free and without salary? All they did for love to the cause, which they did without doubt. How many miles did their heads travel without charging? These will escape such a bitter hour, surely all were volunteers in the labor of God and carried it out without avarice or salary because they wanted to imitate their Christ exactly. Even in their garments they showed their humility and were not ashamed to be naked because of the foreigner or love of the needy. Oh, for those who await the rapture to escape God's ire without having shown justice on earth! Can God lie? Will the entire earth not be judged according to the Gospel of Jesus Christ? Can the ones who did no good receive good? Can those who never exhibited mercy receive mercy? Can man receive tribute for what he did not do?

Is there confusion in God's work? Will we be able to harvest wheat from trees or fruit from stones? Neither can the impious and hypocrites receive good without first sowing it. Oh, for those who expect to be spared of the tempest if they have not been merciful toward the earth's oppressed. On that day, the testimony of orphans, of widows, of the oppressed and unsheltered will rise against those who call themselves "Christians" without having or doing Christ's works. Christ said: "He who believes in me, the works I do, will also do them." In these days everyone performs Christ's works expecting miracles, but no one wants to perform these "WORKS" for mercy, for meekness, for justice, for humility, for obedience. Do not deceive yourselves. Why do you deceive your own souls? Leave vanity, leave what perishes. Each of you surrender to good actions, to obedience, to working in love and mercy because so maybe we will also enjoy God's mercy in the final days. The Just by their faith shall live and by their faith stand tall. The Just by their faith love, forgive, obey every commandment, and by their faith undertake works in justice and mercy. The just by their faith avert their gaze from things that perish, and by faith refuse to offer their sweat and strength (like other so-called Christians do) for things that the great whore is inventing daily. The just lives by faith in his Lord and Savior, Jesus Christ. But where is the faith of the one who has no mercy? Where is the faith of the one who does not love his enemies? Where is the faith of the one who does not shelter the widow, the orphan, as he should the foreigner and the poor? Where is the faith of the son who does not honor and help his father?

Who of those who await Christ can justify himself and say that he is worthy of escaping the approaching ire? Who has his hands clean of the poor, the widow, and of all commandments of God capable of saying that he is not worthy of the punishment that will come? If somebody knows what mercy and fear of God are, speak and say these words. But if one does not know what Mercy and Justice are, close your mouth. Perhaps, thus, you will be better off and will not accumulate so much judgment and ire against yourself. Therefore, I say: He who awaits his Lord and King, begin to work in mercy and justice according to God and not according to the men who have formed assemblies for their own glory. Attend to the clamor of the needy, if you want to escape what is coming because surely, according to our deeds, that is how we will reach the just Judge. Suspend all ceremony, rites of song and prayer, and attend to justice and mercy, with fear and faith in God. Open every door of justice and truth so that good may flow over all the earth. Let us loosen all ties that limit judgment and justice. Fear God with great fear. Let us give glory and honor with all our being to the one who lives and reigns forever.

21. The Evil in the Seat of the Good

I know the evil that these words will provoke from the Church. I am conscious of the torment that these words will cause in the hearts of those who are deceiving the people. But what dishonor can I bring to the Church?

Is it not your own children who bring dishonor not only to the church, but even to homes? Where is the son who in these days obeys according to God? Why should we be scandalized when the parents themselves take their children through the flames of ancient Babylon? Arrogance has grown in children, and who is the child who does not act according to his whim? Call him. Applaud him. As soon as you find him say: Here is the child who honors his father with aid. I look, seek, and ask, and according to the answers that the so-called Christians offer, all disdain and abhor the commandments that our Lord Jesus Christ left us. Why has the word of God become so cheap? Where is reason? Let the intelligent respond. Let the wise speak. Why do even the small abhor humility and right to pursue arrogance and vanity? From whom have they learned to flee humility? Who was their teacher? I sought right and humility in the greats but instead of this, found that they had sealed and blindly authorized to all the human methods and systems that debilitated simple faith. Any humble example that Christ left us has been mocked and abandoned. All love the present and abhor the commandment. Why ask people if they believe in Christ? I know that all believe, but do not obey. This is the stone on which rebels stumble and fall. The men study the word of God, but not to learn humility and meekness from it, not to learn judgment, justice, and mercy as well, but instead they study it to divide (without knowing, of course), to acquire glory from the people, to become masters of innocent souls. This is why love disappeared from hearts as Christ anticipated, and faith disappeared from the earth. This is why even children have rebelled against parents, because children have inherited their parent's arrogance. I only ask that they give me liberty to speak, to say the things that I in my clumsiness I see. My eyes are not clean like those of my God. And if my eyes are scandalized and cannot stand to see the great abomination in the so-called Church of Christ, how much more are God's eyes. If it were not for the world's wisdom, which the Church has inherited, Christians would not be courteous. I know that even the Pharisees would feel insulted if we tried to compare ourselves to them, for their works were greater that those of this so-called Christian generation. Even the beasts would feel insulted if we wanted to resemble them, for they have remained subject to the laws restraining themselves from establishing better laws than those God gave them, and which he clearly left us in his

Holy Son. The church in these days shows greater fear of the laws of men than the laws of God and tries to be more at peace with man's laws than God's will. Why is this so? Who has scared the people? Have they not told the people about God's terrible ire? Have they not been told about how God took revenge with the people who did not listen to the words of Noah; about how God fought those people? Is it possible God has changed? Can he make sense of persons? Have they not discussed the justice of God shown Sodom and Gomorrah? Does God not demand more justice of this generation than of Sodom and Gomorrah? Was their gospel better than the one we received?

If Christ called the Pharisees "the devil's sons" (not because they did not believe in him, but because of their evil works) for the lives they lived, what will he call us? Or are our works better? Do we give to the widow with the publicity of a trumpet? Do we fast twice a week? Who is wise enough to understand these words? Who is wise enough not to anger at the sound of these words? The wise ones have nothing to lose hearing these words, but the foolish are only irritated. The blind and foolish do not benefit from this word. Yet the wise, if he is bad and twisted, soon recovers, for he knows the time and the word's spirit. God stands with the humble, which I know so clearly in these times, are badly tormented, because in such bad times the humble suffer bitterness. In the bad days, the bad rule the earth and as a consequence the small who possess no human authority suffer bitterness and unjust yokes. The just has been tossed from his place. The meek have been mocked. Evil men and those who are blind relish these times in a position of power. Oh, humble of the earth who fear God! Close your mouth. Do not contend anymore with those who serve as judges. It is their time. They rule now. Soon their time will pass. Have a good spirit and do not lose strength. Suffer like our King suffered and yet was gentle. More than ever imitate the suffering of Christ and ignore the force of vanity. Befriend the ancient prophets in their suffering. Love correction and walk with fear in these final days. Only the wise at heart can see clearly in these days. The greats deem everything good. But Christ came to purge filth and all vanity, teaching us to live content with what he gives us and orders. Therefore, let us not call good what is evil.

22. The Merciful One Was Missing

The merciful people of the earth are missing. No longer do we have meek ones on earth. No one delights in doing God's good works. There is no one who cries or complains because of so many iniquities. All are content and satisfied with the dead rituals. What has become of the wise one of the earth? Where are those who understand law? Why do they not declare justice and judgment? Even the small and weak have been nourished with vain and false promises. But no good has been done with these vain and false promises because they only have divided people and made them err. Everyone pursues the world and its riches; each covets vanities and ephemeral things that make the soul of loved ones err. The voices of those who profess loving God, speak lies and even deceit to their own brother. They do not speak truth, nor can they, because they were weened in lies and exaggeration. The consciences of these promotors of vanities are dead to judgment. Who then will be able to contradict this generation? They proclaim that they are prospering and rich, not knowing that they are poor and very blind. The just judgment of God approaches and reaps rewards hastily. But nothing about this moves them because they believe they are ready. Oh, blind one, where your house is built. Your house is not on stone. Your confidence is anchored on sand and on the pagan traditions of men who never feared God. Note that your temples have deceived you. Your long prayers and phony chants have made you err. Why do they trust these deceitful words? Who asked for chants, prayers, and temples from you? God wants faithful worshippers. God seeks those who adore him in spirit and in truth. God does not seek empty words and ceremonies. Instead, he seeks just actions and acts of repentance.

God seeks men and women who will obey his command. God loves those who obey him above any obedience to men. This is why we lost the love of God, because we abandoned the commandments that his holy son left us. Christ spoke and said: "If you will live in my love, if you keep my commandments, even as I have kept my Father's commandments and live in his love" (John 15:10). We are not living in his love because we do not keep his commandments. We have also made ourselves content with the world because we abandoned his laws and resisted the Holy Spirit. For these reasons our children have also rebelled against us. Our women become dissolute. Your daughters have become objects of desire because you yourselves have humiliated them into nakedness and shamelessness. Every abomination of the flesh, every filth, lasciviousness, and sensuality has been called the latest style and fashion. When did God speak of style or of fashion? When did God give us permission to pursue worldly things for a garment? We are not even clean inside or outside. And if the just wants to reprimand these people for their sensuality, quickly they attack him, and make war against him. How can God speak to these people? They do not admit judgment, do not admit correction. Who then will free these people of their terrible fate? No one turns his face from luxury. No one abhors vanity. Their heads and leaders are the masters and the ones who advance greed because each wants the best and rejects [Christ's] manger and the path of God's prophets. The clothes they wear declare them as haughty and that they swell in vanity. They adorn their bodies and dress their flesh like princes of Sodom. They defend the payment of salary and ignore justice. Oh, for these evil and rebellious people. How will they escape the ire that will come? Who will intercede for them? They all will crowd to hide in caves and will try to save their skins and heads from the ire and furor with which the entire earth will be burned.

These who now mock God's commandments will scream and gnash their teeth at seeing and discovering that they themselves were the enemies of the cross. Oh, for those who expect to be raised up into the skies and escape the ire of God despite their corrupt understanding, dead conscience, and lazy wombs. Do you expect to be raised in this way? Against which commandment have you not rebelled, you rebels at heart? You of lascivious hands, adultery-filled eyes, mouths full of lies, do you expect to go to Heaven like this? Is there no one who will tell you and teach you that liars will not inherit life? Your mouths do not know how to speak truth. Your eyes do not pursue humility, your entrails are not moved by the sight of the poor. Instead, your viscera move at the sight of new things, as well as the woman of your own brother and neighbor. It is time to close the mouth. Time to humble our souls. It is time to rid our bodies of all vanity and all arrogance. Let us search for justice and judgment, asking with our humiliated souls for that ancient path, which is Christ. The damage you have committed is not small. Against whom have you rebelled? Against a council of men? No. You have rebelled against the son of God. Where will you hide so you cannot be found? He who rebels against a council of men is expelled but remains alive. Yet he who has rebelled against the holy commandment would be better off throwing himself to the sea. The rebels will not remain alive but will pay for all the evil they did on earth, deceiving many innocent souls who wanted and sought life, yet erred because their salaried leaders took from the very nourishment of widows. The word of God will rise against these liars who fed their own bellies and weakened the law.

23. Faith Without Mercy

I will not ignore the many names that I will be called for speaking out, denouncing the behavior of the final days. Slanderer I will be called. Faultfinder I will be called by others. Fanatic and clumsy others will label me. But I know that all the prophets and those who feared and still fear God will so learn and know my spirit. I speak for the good of all. But let us leave the foolish to perish in foolishness because it is no longer the time to try to persuade the foolish. Let he who is dirty become dirtier; but he who fears God take succor in that fear.

I know the ancient ones will not call me a fanatic, nor slanderer; and I never want to take part in hypocrisy because I know that God will subject all actions to Judgment. Nothing will remain hidden.

Who will be able to rise and declare to woman her shame and honor? Who will be able to show man what his duty is, and how he must correct a home? All invent laws that only serve temples and the people who attend them, but none of this has effect in the home. Therein all become more hypocrites and pretend to have more without having anything. Oh, for those who mock other councils and movements when they themselves have the same pride, the same arrogance and selfishness, the same ire and rebelliousness against God's holy commandments. Arrogance, clashes, the mundane dwells in all. Why then criticize when we are all prisoners of the same thing? Instead let us look to see from where we have fallen and admit that we have all abandoned the love of God and we have become vain in all works of men. We have spent our money to wallow in the flesh and to banish humility from our homes. Is this not so? All are full of ire and revenge. All travel the streets in their cars, and one cannot even honk at them for they become enraged. Everyone looks at others scornfully and no one is clear in his sincerity; they are but pretenders. To avoid mockery, no one wants to go to the city public square dressed in dull and cheap clothes. All travel the same path. They fear one another. That is why each dresses in the best and most expensive suits and dresses they have to raise their value before others. A man with new and expensive clothes is really respected and appreciated. But a man wearing poor and cheap clothes is not esteemed even if he is a man of judgment, even if he is a man of pure actions greatly esteemed before the living God. This shows that we are citizens of the great Babylon. The same temples are full of arrogance, even if the people contradict me and deny it. But one day they will know, and God will be my witness that I speak the truth. I know that none of this moves consciences. Hopefully from the many who read these words one wise and sensible person will receive correction and will place his life in safety to escape from what will come. The sun and the moon, the earth and the heavens have always been witnesses to the words that prophets spoke to save those enveloped in rebelliousness and death. I, too, speak before these same witnesses and say: we have sinned. We have acted in iniquity. We have abandoned good and have twisted every holy path and judgment of God. Let us return to God. Do not wait for God to arrive for no one will escape his terrible presence. When God visits many will finally appreciate these words. Will we admit then that we were wrong? Why wait until that day? Man has become vain and no longer speaks truth, not even with his own wife. Men have lost their worth already, and in the temples, where they were supposed to learn the truth, they only go to hear fables and words that do not move one to the judgment of God. Such words do not rebut the hypocrite, gossip, and vanity. We hear all this instead of the advice of the spirit. Oh, how mercy perished from the earth. Gone are the times when man knew the love of God. Gone are the times when the great were compassionate toward the small. Gone are the times when the man with eyes guided the blind with meekness and patience. Instead, the time has come when the man with eyes shoves the one who has no eyes. The strong man destroys the weak one. In the eyes of the married woman the widow finds no grace. Orphans are not protected by children who have father and mother. All judgment and justice have perished from the earth and it is there we see the pastors of the congregations entertained in vain words, promising people what they themselves do not even have. They are all occupied in chants and dead ceremonies. Is God glorified with chants? Is God pleased by the empty speeches of men who do not have mercy and do not defend the small of the earth? It is most unlikely that God believes in these men full of lies, who to make their keep use sweet words of blessing. These will soon get what they deserve. Who will tell the woman about all her arrogance? Who will tell the woman how she has sinned? No one sees sin in the immoral life of the men and the women. All are satisfied. They fill their eyes with the nakedness of women, and here I speak of the best there are in churches. I do not speak of the world because the world does not know what it does. It was our duty to teach the straight and holy, in words as well as in deeds and dress, through which we see the honor and wisdom of a people. Just as nakedness is a fruit of the spirit of sensuality and lasciviousness, the covered and decent body is a fruit of honor, a fruit of fear, a fruit of wisdom. But in these days, what do we have? What do we glory in? All honor, glory, shame, modesty have perished from the earth. We have remained as a people without walls and without weapons, exposed to the attack of an evil and cruel enemy. Who will escape without weapons and without wisdom? God help us.

24. Listen Wise Ones

The holy proceeds from the holy, and evil proceeds from evil. And Mercy and justice are not without fruit.

Daniel advised King Nebuchadnezzar telling him: "Therefore oh king, accept my advice, and redeem your sins with Justice and your iniquities with Mercy toward the poor."

And again, the Holy Spirit says: "By kindness and piety guilty is expiated, and by the fear of the LORD man avoids evil" (Prov. 16:6). And again: "He sins who despises the hungry; but happy is he who is kind to the poor!"

(Prov. 14:21). Again: "He who oppresses the poor blasphemes his Maker, but he who is kind to the needy glorifies him" (Prov. 14:31). And he says once again: "He who has compassion on the poor lend to the LORD, and he will repay him for his good deed" (Prov. 19:17). And he goes on to say: "The dread of the king is as when a lion roars; he who incurs his anger forfeits his life" (Prov. 20:2). Where, then, is the mercy that sustains the Christian of these days? Respond, he who knows the use of mercy. Where is the honor of the Christian? And where is his Justice? Because of this the Holy Spirit spoke, when it said: "He who pursues justice and kindness will find life and honor" (Prov. 21:21).

Christ our Lord spoke these same things when he said: "Blest are they who show mercy; mercy shall be theirs" (Matt. 5:7). Before this the Holy Spirit advised, saying: "Let not kindness and fidelity leave you; bind them around your neck" (Prov. 3:3). He adds: "He who shuts his ear to the cry of the poor will himself also call and not be heard" (Prov. 21:13).[6]

He also speaks for the Apostle James, saying: "Merciless is the judgment on the man who has not shown mercy; but mercy triumphs over judgment" (James 2:13). This is what the Lord accused the Pharisees of when he said to them: "Justice and mercy and good faith. It is these you should have practiced, without neglecting the others" (Matt. 23:23). And who can find glory against these things? What sacrifice can take the place of mercy? None, because of the very sacrifice Christ made. It is mercy and truth, and this is because, when he exhorted us saying: "Be merciful, as your Father is merciful" (Luke 6:36). It is understood, then, that the merciful are God's children. But where is the mercy of the church? What good have we done in the world? There is a fund for the pastor, fund for the missionary, fund for temples, and funds for all kinds of interests of councils. But where is the fund for the widow? Where is the fund for the poor, for the needy, for the foreigners, and for orphans?

The children who live in the shadows do better in that respect because earthly government, administered by men who do not pretend to be men of God, have looked after the elderly, widows, the poor, and orphans. Even though it is true that they charge people taxes, from these they reserve a part for the poor and needy. But the churches, what do they reserve for the needy? They even demand it from the poor, from the little they have. How then will we stop the ire that comes? Or how will we escape?

The rich man, of whom Christ spoke, was not sent to hell because he smoked, or because he only had vices. He was not thrown to hell because he did not pay his tithe, or because he did not sing and pray. Instead, he was thrown or put in hell because he did not show mercy. What use does God have for ingrates, who aside from having no mercy also establish laws and accords that weaken mercy and inhibit those who want to practice it? Because of their evil desires and whims, many have been deceived and stumbled because of the liberty noted in the gospel and grace of Jesus Christ. Because they say: "By grace we are saved, and not by works" and with these words have weakened good and mercy.

They have stumbled of their own free will. Saint Paul the apostle, speaking to the Ephesians, explained: "We are his handiwork, created in Christ Jesus to lead the life of good deeds which God prepared for us in advance" (Eph. 2:10). And by the same Spirit he spoke on another occasion exhorting the Philippians to work for all that is true, all that is honest, all that is Just, all that is pure, all that is respectful and of good name; that is, if in one's actions there was some virtue or praise. To think about these things.

To make what he was trying to teach clearer and simpler, he added: "Live according to what you have learned and accepted, what why have heard me say and seen me do. Then will the God of peace be with you" (Phil. 4:9).[7]

The same Apostle exhorted the Colossians to dress with "heartfelt mercy, with kindness, humility, meekness, and patience" (Col. 3:12). And to the Ephesians he also says: "Be kind to one another, compassionate" (Eph. 4:32). Can love and mercy exist without good works? When the poor, the widow, and the needy are abandoned to the mercy of shady government, can we say there is love and mercy? Was Paul trying to save the Ephesians, the Colossians, and the Philippians through good works? Why then did he speak to them of this? Like he also tells Titus, explaining that Christ gave himself for us, to redeem us of all iniquity, and cleanse for himself a people, eager for good works. Does he also tell them to learn to govern in good works? (Titus 2:14 and 3:14).

Everyone now mocks his neighbor because teachers have taught that no one should set their eyes on good works and have demeaned its value. But soon they will notice the great error they have caused on earth. Then they will notice that they are guilty of mercy and love perishing from the hearts.

If there is no good in good works, neither is there evil in evil works.

Teachers have failed, abandoning the most important aspects of Christ's Kingdom. They failed became they became infatuated of gold, calling it what it was not. They forgot that Christ said: "He who hears these words and does them, I will compare to a prudent man." Now they want to become wise, but they cannot because they have become foolish rebelling against the only thing that could give them life. The Proverb says: "For a fool, to be silent is wisdom" (Prov. 24:7). And elsewhere it says: "The senseless man seeks in vain for wisdom" (Prov. 14:6). But the intelligent man finds it easily. This is why the Just thinks before he speaks, because he seeks peace and fears his God. Yet the stubborn spews ire from his mouth and divides people.

Nebuchadnezzar was thrown to the beasts for not taking the advice Daniel gave him. He ignored mercy and mocked justice. But after the beating, he recovered and acted with wisdom. But this present generation does not receive correction or accept good advice. One day they will seek advice, but they will not find it. Israel also left mercy and knowledge of God (Hosea 6:6). In these days not even children show mercy toward their own parents. Such behavior is even lower level than that displayed by the beasts of the earth who teach their offspring to obey their mothers.

Never before had this earth had such arrogant and ignorant inhabitants. When has history recorded a people as blind as this one? Men have set their eyes upon their own work. Even the temples where they worship are works that not even King Nebuchadnezzar could accomplish. The arrogance of Nebuchadnezzar was small in comparison to the arrogance of those who now lead God's people. And the eyes of the smallest pursue the work of the great. No one seeks true humility. All seek honor, but do not find it, nor will they find it because true honor comes upon showing true humility (Prov. 15:33). Who knows what true humility is without stopping to search it?

Those who want to escape the ire that will come. Those who love their lives and do not want to be surprised by the fire of the wrath of God, empty your hearts of all evil. Pour out your souls for the oppressed. Serve the tired. Do the good that Christ told us about. Why let the last day of salvation pass? Let us wash our hands of all evil, banish evil thought from our heart, and dress our interior with mercy. These are days of seeking God once more. Oh, for those who say they are saved and are not free of arrogance or lies. Oh, for those who say they know salvation and do not know what mercy and justice are. Oh, for those who await the return of Christ without undertaking works of love and mercy. Many are those who believe they are on the path of life and rectitude without knowing that the end of the path they traverse is a path of death. And just as the wealthy man who refused to notice the beggar Lazarus tricked himself, so many others these days are tricking themselves and will be very surprised on that day when God reveals all works to the Light of His Loved Son.

Tremble before the Word of God, because if we do not fear now, later we will tremble not before the word of God but before his presence. While the Judgment is delayed, let us all come and do good, banish gossip and anger from our hearts. No one look for the material goods of this earth. These are days for removing from our hearts the things of this world, before we too, like Lot's wife, become an example of rebellion. God loves Justice. Anyone who does Justice will not be shamed. He who says he already has faith, let him prove it with his works in Christ. Christ himself said: "He who believes in me, in the works that I do, will also do them." He who says that he awaits Christ, abandon those things you possess and give them to the poor. He who says he knows Christ, make it manifest with mercy and justice.

Oh, for those who are faithful to men and faithful men's accords and do not make mercy and justice. Oh, for those who fear men and do not fear God. Because who will defend rebels before God? Who will be the one who advocates for those who disobeyed Christ's commandments? All who are just and those who fear God, leave the places God abominates. Leave the great Babylon because the place that once belonged to the holy has been taken over and occupied by abomination and completely false religion. Therefore: ALL MUST REMEMBER, THAT ACCORDING TO OUR DEEDS, we will be judged. No one should deceive himself believing that God will justify him as men have justified him. To the contrary, what workers now deem as clean, God will find filthy and abominable. Blessed be God now and forever. All who work for Justice, do not be ashamed. God be for the Just . . .

25. The Provocateurs of Judgment

A strong and embarrassing curse is decreed against those who rebel against God. Humanity is not innocent of this because God announced it through all his holy prophets, making it well known through the centuries. To declare the truths of the future it has cost God the blood of many just men. The just were abhorred and mistreated because they announced the ruin and destruction of the rebels. Those who rebel against God killed the just. Unfortunately, the rebellious ones have always been God's people. Blind and ignorant people cannot rebel against anything because they do not know any of God's laws. It is God's people who know good and his will who rebel, leaving God's Law for the law of men, who deceive them using cunning. To win glory and riches they establish unjust laws in which one cannot find good or justice, not even for the poor, much less shelter for widows and the oppressed.

The people of Israel, who God so loved, were taken out of Egypt by the power of his strong arms, with miracles and marvels. For these people he toiled and suffered, tolerating their imprudence and craziness as well as their rebelliousness. These people, to whom he gave so many beautiful and great promises, he distinguished from all others. God humiliated many other nations for the love of Israel. His best promises were for these people, and he even spoke in voice and thunder with these people who God loved and esteemed so much. God called Israel a chosen treasure and cared for it, just as a man cares for the girl who is the apple of his eye. Despite his great love and all he had done, when these people rebelled against him, God punished it, whipped it, mutilated it, and handed them over to the harshest peoples. He sold them to the cruelest and most merciless government, and completely forgot about them for seventy years. The hardest and cruelest curse known in history fell over them. When the enemies of Israel (once called "The Chosen Treasure") fell upon Jerusalem, a city that before had been one of peace and blessing, they killed the men, ravished their women, and their children still nursing were crashed over the rocks. The king's children were killed before his very eyes, and he took out his own eyes. Thus, he died blind in a strange land, fed with the crumbs of a king that God had roused to humiliate his people, Israel. God is the same yesterday, today, and through the centuries. History makes us see that God takes care of this planet. He is vigilante and through his guardians knows of the activities of the men who guide the people. By the great and terrible commandment that we have received from God, we know that we have rebelled to the extreme. Not only against God but against our peer, coveting his woman. Even the children have rebelled against their parents, the women against the word of their husbands, the rich against the poor, the sheltered against the helpless, the strong against the weak, the ingrate against the merciful, the married woman against the widow, the wise against the ignorant, the one who has eyes against the blind, the one who has ears against the deaf, the one who has feet against the maimed. The earth has filled with dishonor and sin because of the people who supposedly knew the paths of God that, through Christ, were written and established.

The most shameful curse, the most terrifying ruin, the saddest end, is decreed on this adulterous and rebellious generation. It calls "black," "white," calls and eats absinthe like honey, calls honor dishonor, and all of this similarly in speaking as in dress, in eating as in actions. He who works in fear of God they call rebel and fanatic, this only because he does not humiliate himself to their twisted and divisive laws.

Everything points to the fact that we are a rebellious, gluttonous, dishonorable, blind, and despotic people. Our people say so. Our clothing and food stores are witness to this. The paths and streets we walk on publicize our violence and stupidity. In sum, our homes are engulfed in flames of discord and fights, disputes and arguments. It is publicly known that no dweller of the earth can learn anything about honor or decency, humility or fear of God from us because sons have robbed their fathers' honor, women stole their husbands' honor, and man has become worse than beasts because in beasts there is no such thing as dishonor, or that children rise against their elders. Egoism in man has reached a peak, has developed as never before in history. Egoism has given man a twisted and crazy sense, to the extreme of glorifying in his craziness, glorifying in his own works, which will do nothing more than give him over to the slaughterhouse. Because God, who abhors the arrogance of man and abominates the pride of these final days, has raised one man up and has prepared an instrument that shall carry out his will on his people, decapitating them.

As we can see, communism has come to do a larger job. People buy the cheapest things and seek the greatest liberty. If we had these, we would not lose so many people to communism as it grows at a gigantic pace. Although Jeremiah did not love the Chaldeans, to please God he took their side. He always proclaimed that the Chaldeans would take the land of the Jews, and while people did not believe it, so it was so because God had determined it. I do not say that communism can replace God's government or that it offers a lasting peace. Much less, Christ is not evident in their government. But because we have left God, and because God has raised a great enemy against this nation, although I trust that we would come out well, it does not mean that we will be well. Our sin has marked our end. Our rebelliousness has raised the great enemy of Peace. I cannot be with these people because these people are not with God. All have left the path of life and now are captives of Babylon, the mother of all of life's sorcery. All are victims of gluttony, of wealth, of arrogant clothes. No one sees, no one accepts advice, all have become lords of the earth. And everywhere we see boards or signs that read posted KEEP OUT. This is how they publicize malice and testify that the earth is full of evil people. There is no one who trusts his peer. This too is proof that there is nothing good in people. We are a people without heart, a generation that knows no mercy. If this is not so, why is it that socialization in the United States is so useless? Christians would rather all work together to make the atomic bomb, to make airplanes to fortify their war defenses. Who among them protests? Who finds useful the ends such preparation will bring? Everyone, weakened and blind, like beasts are led into the deceit and abyss, which is the end of our rebelliousness. There is no one who protests or rebels against the mortal work in which all the people are occupied, even though they profess to fear God. Fathers and sons, mothers and daughters, husbands and wives, old and young, good and bad, all are occupied with a single end. This end is to fulfill the will of God which will harm us. Because we have left him, he too has left us. Where are the earth's wise ones? Where are the ministers who will teach these people? There is no one to give relief to the heart, no one to win souls. Those who form councils, those who organize groups of peoples who every day establish laws for the good all, those who rescue fishermen, where are they? Why do they not stop these people who are advancing like blind cattle toward the holocaust? Long ago God has sentenced judgment against those who would take the path these people have taken. No wise, strong, or rich person can discover weapons or shields against the just Judgment that comes. If he did not forgive Israel, how will he forgive our evil, which is greater? We have infected the entire earth with works and arts that have taken the honor of man and the sanctity of woman. Because of our deeds, the humble have also erred, and no one has discovered what mercy and justice are in our days. What they have manufactured is the things seen inside the temples. In the vast temple (the universe) full of the poor, widows, oppressed, orphans, and needy foreigners, what good have they done? False worshippers believe that if they are not in temple they cannot worship. The worship that our Christ taught us, was on earth, adoring God through the poor, oppressed, and afflicted of the earth. He taught us to adore God in Spirit and not in temples. Temples have little value when people fear God. But when they lose their fear of God and withdraw from his love, they all become busy building temples, only to bring glory to their earthly lives. Because of this God comes to leave his people.

Since God has determined the Judgment against us, since he has turned his face against us, let us humble our souls, leave behind the pride that is vanity and death. We have left God's commandments, which give true life to our souls.

Those who fear God, those who have been unwillingly deceived by men with heads full of pride, leave the life of such tricks, leave Babylon, leave the power of delights, shake your souls of all pride and all egoism. Do not drink from the chalice of Babylon, which is a drunkenness that does not care for life, or drink of the vanities that separate us from God. When the earth is about to be burnt by our own rebelliousness, leave behind your commitment to the world, cleanse your hands of all that now occupies humanity, of all eating and drinking, buying and selling, sleeping like princes in peace. All see mercy and justice all around, but no one is interested in it. Each looked after their own interest, and so man has lost the sense that Christ left us. Let us leave the inhabited towns, leave the streets of traffic and greed. Cease to buy and sell and instead see God in the small, who are disgusted and abhor evil and vanity. Eat little, mend your clothes, and give to the needy from the few goods that we have, and in that way remove judgment from your head.

God long ago announced that he will make use of a strong man, so the wise who fear can flee and escape the parching ire. The arrogance of these people has reached such extremes that they call atomic energy a blessing. The world has not known it for long. But long before the world knew it, invincible agents by the will of God had deposited the secret in the mind of a man called MENDELEEV; and to the surprise of many arrogant men of the west, this man was RUSSIAN, this was in 1869. Mendeleev constructed the first fundamental table of natural elements, arranged by atomic weights. The first machine to smash the atom was formed in Moscow in 1937.[8]

But this was not the beginning of a blessing, because if it were a great blessing, the one worthy of it would be our first fathers who walked straighter than we did. But God permitted this in the latter days. Therefore, the stench of our iniquities has risen to the heights, and in these last times, the maturity of our major abomination has arrived.

The women of these nations, called Christian nations, mock that women behind the (so-called) iron curtain simply because they wear their dresses too long and loose, and mock them because their dresses are loose and wide in the waist and in the arms. Because they wear long sleeves, because they use only sad and somber colors, our women jeer at all this. This is fruit and testimony that the arrogance of our women is everywhere. The church and the state are separated in opinion, but not in spirit. The appetites of the nation's leaders are identical to the appetites of the church's leaders. Although these are two distinct careers, the same spirit moves them: arrogance, envy, selfishness, and vain glory.

For the good of those who doubt the information of how people live in Russia, their ways of dressing so humbly and with honor and decency, and many of their customs worthy of imitation by so-called Christians, I say: because in it there is more shame and honor (even if it is only human or moral honor). This news was published in a magazine called the *Ladies Home Journal*. And they were sent from Russia [to the United States] by Mrs. Lidia Kirk, wife of the ex-ambassador, Mr. Alan G. Kirk. Although this news had as its goal humiliating these poor women, nevertheless there are some wise people on earth who can understand what this indicates. Because if the naked body testifies to one's dishonor, then the covered body testifies to a woman's honor. History, according to God's word, as well as profane history prove that dress and the manner in which people dress, is a fruit of their hearts, and a fruit of their lives, for good or evil.

Russia is the only nation that does not praise arrogance or the base ways of the United States. All the nations model themselves on the United States, in the way they dress, in the way they eat, in the way they speak with arrogance, as in the way of living. According to Mrs. Kirk's testimony,

Russian mothers do not permit their children to learn the ways of our children, because there are many children born to men who represent this nation who have to play separately. In Russia we are accused of being the most hypocritical people because they are informed by the New Testament of the life of Christ and of the lives of those who followed Christ. They compare all this with our way of life and find, as our Lord concluded: a people without faith and without love of God. Calling themselves wise, they have become foolish and become abhorrent to everyone.

The day the Lord arrives with the fire and ire of God is upon us. All the arrogant will be surprised. But the humble and oppressed of the earth, what arrogance can they lose? He who is not arrogant, why does he fear?

"Wait" the Lord has said for the day when your homes will not have agreeable paint, when our furniture will not have the luster to see our faces are reflected on them, when we will not be able to walk on our streets because of violence, our bodies will not be dressed with fine fabrics, the creams and perfumes we wear will not please anyone's noses. Those who sing in choirs, like those who adore with music (to the ear) will cease. The haughty woman's face, like the man's shaved face, all of this will cloud their own eyes. Now all are blind and see nothing wrong in the adornments that have come from Babylon. But on that day, man and woman will be purified of all this. If we have lost the fear of God, what do we expect of Russia? A force like that of the Soviets is born of the rebellious world, we the children of God, have created. And "communism" has come to do a greater job than our "love."

26. The Just One's Clamor

With fear and humility, I commit these words to writing for all who believe that Jesus Christ is the son of God, for all who believe in God, and all who believe that the Bible is God's word. For all of you who gather in temples to adore God, to sing and pray to him. To all those who believe in Jesus Christ's return and await it, to the people who believe in the resurrection of the dead and in the judgment according to our deeds, to the people who believe all this, to them I speak.

They are not people who have not known the word of God either; they are the people who admit and know they are sinners; nor are they the people who publicly declare themselves sinners. Nor are they those who kill, drink, steal, or any public sinner. . . . These sinful people want nothing to do with the things of God and because of this I will not speak to them.

Instead, I speak to the people who knowing that they must do good do not do so, knowing they must love, do not. I speak to the people who, knowing that they must forgive, do not, knowing that they must be humble and obedient, are not. Having gone to many places on foot, after talking with many peoples, and after searching for the good and for the wise of the earth, only after all this, I have been moved to speak.

The many sins, the many injustices, the many hypocrisies, and arrogance have made me speak. The church's iniquity has forced me to speak. As I see justice and judgment on the ground, my inner being has been moved to speak words that will irritate many, words that for some may be too harsh, as some who first followed Christ said (John 6:60). But these words will be for the good and health of the souls of those with wise hearts.

My eyes, no matter how blind, can no longer stand seeing so much injustice and hypocrisy. My heart, no matter how hardened, can no longer resist the cry of the oppressed, and the complaints of the abandoned. My ears, no matter how deaf spiritually, hear lies and exaggeration everywhere, this among the children and the adults, among the wise and the foolish. On their lips they profess the truth. From their mouths they say they fear God, and because of this, I have been unable to tolerate the words in my heart. I do not see obedience in children, do not see the hand of parents offering them correction, do not see respect in temples, do not see a fear of God in those who speak God's word. I do not see men who search for the good of God, nor see anyone who delights in defending the orphan, the widow, the maimed, the poor, the blind, and the mute. He who makes a banquet, does it for his relatives, but not for the poor as Christ ordered (Luke 14:13, 14). He who loans, only loans things to his friends and relatives (if he does), but not to the poor. Nor does he request loans, much less give them as God commanded (Deut. 15:10, 11; Luke 6:30). I seek good, worthy of praise, so that I can keep my mouth shut, but I do not see it. They have not stopped singing, not stopped praying, not stopped preaching, nor have they stopped building temples. No, they have not stopped any of this. Instead, all of this abounds, but what they have cast aside (God is witness) is mercy, the love of God, the justice of God, and the fear of God, relying instead on the fear of men. What they have cast aside are humility and obedience. What makes me speak is not the sort of love or justice that I see among people. What makes me speak are the arrogance and greed that exists among the people. The abomination that resides in a sacred place is what makes me speak; and it is this abomination that has ignited God's fury. Hypocrisy has replaced the saintly and the genuine, hatred has replaced love, and lies have replaced the truth. The evil are in the place of the good. The haughty and arrogant occupy the place that belongs to the humble. The law of God is in the hands of salaried men and in the hands of tyrants. The Christian no longer imitates the humble in dress, no longer imitates the humble in what they eat, no longer imitates how the humble live; no longer imitates how the humble sing or pray. No one imitates the humble man from Galilee in anything. Instead, all are swollen with pride and despotism. Is this evil of small dimensions? Can it be that the evil we have done to our souls is small? Now all the earth is consumed by the same spirit of error. It is the same spirit that exists among all the people, apparent both in temples as in life, in song as in prayer. It is the same spirit that makes us covet a single thing. It is the same spirit that makes us tell lies and makes everyone search for the worldly. Christ said: "Be on guard lest your spirits become bloated with indulgence and drunkenness and worldly cares" (Luke 21:34). This is precisely what is ruining the entire Christian world. Because of the cares of life, Christians have forsaken love and have cast all of God's commandments aside. Instead of imitating the one who told us, "Learn from me for I am gentle and humble of heart." We would rather imitate the world's impious and arrogant in our speech as well as in living, in our dress, eating, and in our sight. Where do our daughters find examples, if not from the worst women? Our sons, by force, must attend schools where the same hell is present. Where, then, is the sovereignty of the church? Where is the zeal of God? Because of all this the Church is about to be burned in God's fire and ire. It has lost its flavor, sanctity, and zeal. It will be thrown out. How can the world imitate us so it leads to Christ? What can one find in the church about love? What humility is there in the Church? What meekness is there in the church? What justice and judgment is there in the church? There is nothing of this in the church. Instead of any of this, there is hatred, pride, injustice, and all works of division. Who can deny this? Raise your hand and justify the church.

27. The People Without Honor

This generation will be surprised more than any other generation. There has not been, nor will there be, a people more surprised than this. There will not be a writer, there will not be a reporter that will be able to describe the things that will surprise this evil generation. No brave man will remain standing on that day; the brave will walk like the very drunk, and pride-filled men will not find a place where they can find peace. God has been provoked by the inhabitants of the earth, having twisted all the right that his beloved son brought to the earth. Who can contemplate with his own eyes the ire and all the fire that God will bring on his day, and continue standing? Many speak now, but on that day, who will be able to open his mouth? Men will tremble, as they have never before trembled. They will shout in a way that has never been heard before. And this twisted generation that has irritated its God will be bitterly sorry on that day. It will regret its disdain for the holy commandment, which even Christ himself obeyed. This generation has never before seen the burning ire of its God, nor have they learned from the pages of history. Did God pardon the women in the flood? Did the all-seeing God pardon the children when he sent the flood over that evil generation? Let us open our eyes and recognize God even in his ire. Why let that day surprise us as it surprised the ancient rebels? Let us not be like Israel, which always thought things were all right and that it kept its God happy. What evidence do we have that we have a contented God? Well, the poor are not content, nor are the widows, or even our own brothers, much less God who sealed his holy commandment with the holy life of his Sacred Son. How will we escape that day of which we can already see the dawn?

The great Babylon is the only one that commands and rules in these days, evident as feigned faith, self-esteem, the spirit of error that has always cauterized the consciences of men who have become vain. These men who have been lovers of salary and gifts. The humble of the earth do not give orders, do not rule over anyone. What now dominates is the great Babylon, which establishes laws that contradict the Spirit of God and produces rebels against God's holy commandments. These are the agents of the great Babylon. Why do you think that the great Babylon is a certain sect, or movement? If there is no mercy, justice, judgment, meekness, or love of God in you, well you are part of the great Babylon. The widow herself, the orphan, the foreigner, the poor and all the oppressed, they can tell you that. What is the great Babylon? In the great Babylon there is no place for the poor and for the oppressed of heart. For the great Babylon does not know anything, except how to oppress, deceive, and insult God.

Whoever has Christ in his heart, is identified by his love of God, by his mercy, like he reached mercy. He is identified by the works of God and His beloved son. These works are with love, in peace, in benevolence, in gentleness, in mercy, in justice, in true faith, in the Holy Spirit, because all these works come from a single Spirit, which is Christ's. I pray, fearing God, for all those who do not possess the works of the Spirit of Christ. Let him leave the great Babylon and with fear in his heart for the one who made all things, and not set his sight on things that perish. Nor should he spend the sweat of his life pursuing the worldly and vain things everyone loves. Abhor what Christ abhorred and love what Christ enjoyed doing. Although in the beginning it may seem hard and a difficult thing, later, in the earth's final days, they will be coveted. Oh, what terrible judgment awaits the people who denied shelter to the righteous, the people who cast aside God's love, the people who stopped enlightening others, and the people who lost their flavor. We are guilty and God will deem us guilty of everything that has occurred in the church. Search for decency, search for shame, search for honor in the people of God. But in vain, for I do not find it. The Church of God, that is, all who call themselves Christians, and know the name of Christ, should sit on ashes and dress in mourning, for losing what they lost. Not only did they lose their first love, but are now blind, naked, miserable. The church lost its honor. No one respects her because she has filled herself with earthly wealth. All the lovers who praise her and serve her, never mentioned her great and terrible defect. For this God will wreak vengeance. Who will be able to restrain God's hand when it is raised? I feel like a coward for not denouncing these things sooner, because God put them in my heart many days ago. I know that I am not revealing or declaring, as I should, the great evil that the church is doing over the earth. Because I see that the earth will receive great blows from its God and mortal whiplashes because the church was incapable of speaking the truth or defending God's law.

The world and all its inhabitants are tied up and occupied in its divisions and fights that they have brought upon themselves. All are confident in opinions and caprices, like all kinds of human ideas, while laws and mercy are becoming history. Oh, if only the church raised its head and listened to the real laws of God, whose law does good for the oppressed, domestic life, relations between man and woman. But now all this is hidden from him because of man's own rebelliousness and tenacious caprices. The Pharisees and the Sadducees will rise up in judgment against this twisted generation and will condemn it. Later, believing that they behaved as well as they could, this generation cannot even display worldly courtesy. Who will affirm this rebellious generation? Let us look for its lovers.

28. Justice That Does Not Perish

God's justice does not sting. The love of God does not burn. He who does well and trusts in God will not be shamed in any way. Instead, he who obeys God and works for the good of all, stands firm and nothing can move him. Not so with the incredulous and disobedient one because all the rebels will be confused and shamed. The confidence of the present Christians will be incinerated. All the glory of false Christians will be enveloped by the flames of justice because the just and saints are the judgment of God. The confidence of hypocrite Christians will be unable to resist the coming judgment. With what confidence do these now profess to know God? Your confidence is in temples and ceremonies, is it not? Who in these days has placed his confidence in a fear of God and in the mercy of the Almighty? Who delights in doing and working well for all? Who is he who gives without expecting acclaim from people? Who pardons without expecting acclaim? Those who fear God and those who delight in doing the will of God, these are the ones who can do this without expecting acclaim. For they are sons of the Almighty, who does good and gives breath to all. He who really knows God, knows him in love, in justice, in mercy, in judgment, in goodness, in gentleness, in faith, in all good works, and not only in name as they now admit. God is known in spirit, not simply by name and ceremonies, as is now done.

Oh, for the confidence of these people because they will be engulfed in flames and will be unable to resist God's judgment. He who fears God, works for his justice obeying his word, he does not fear the end, or trembles at seeing the world set on fire because his hope is spirit and life. The man who does good that pleases God's eyes, he has his home and his life founded on rock; nothing scandalizes him. All the confidence of the rebels will not pass the judgment of God, nor will their avowed firm love protect them from the ire that comes. As wax melts under the heat of the sun, so will false love and faith melt before God's judgment of God. On that day false preachers will not find words with which to speak. What now passes for Christianity, in a few days will no longer firmly stand. On that day all the heads and leaders of the people will know what "the word of God" is and what is the "Commandment of God."

The justice that now exists will be consumed and burn. Likewise, the love that now exists will be engulfed in flames because it is not really a love of God. Temples and ceremonies are now the only things that now take the place of justice. But who receives the benefit human glory? The widow and the orphan do not receive benefits when there are so many temples. All focus their charity by giving only to temples, and the more temples multiply in number, the more neglected is the widow. And all this because they receive orders from their grand leaders. Will God keep silence on seeing all this evil? Does God look favorably on these rebellious and arrogant children? As eyes abhor smoke, so God abhors the works of these arrogant and hypocritical people. They only do good when it is in their self-interest. But this too is common in the world and among the children of the shadows, but in better and more sagacious ways. Christ taught us to love even our enemies. But now a brother does not even love his own brother, much less his enemy. A brother in Christ, like a brother in faith, fight in the same way, while no one does good for his peer. Who is the son that aids his own father? All customarily lend money, but few give it, not even a cent. Were it not for the preachers who threaten people with the judgment of God, not even they would earn their bread or receive the tithe that they have imposed as tribute. I say "as tribute" because the people do not give it as a fruit of love, or voluntarily, instead they see it as tribute for belonging to the church. In the presence of God, this smells horrible and is a shameful thing; because all defend their own property, but no one intercedes for the mute and for the ignorant. Even arrogant and dissolute children, who are disobedient toward their parents are heralded as ambassadors of Christ. I am certain that if the leaders of these groups were kings on earth, they would not like such hypocritical and dissolute ambassadors. The preachers who now take the word of God in their mouths are full of lies, and clearly were prematurely born. These are greedy men who now teach the people. What can these men possibly teach? If they passed an exam administered at the hands of God, the earth would open its mouth to swallow them as it did and his following.[9] For this reason, God's justice has lost its potency in the land of the valiant because blind men replaced judges and salaried men now interpret God's law.

Men who have never known God's love or mercy; men who do not know what judgment and justice are; these are the ones who have been charged to teach the life of God as was revealed through Jesus Christ. Because of this even the young on earth do as much evil as they do good, drinking evil as if drinking water. All have twisted the law, because of the false teachers who now appear everywhere. If all this is true, who will be able to deny these words and emerge favorably before God? Come closer and come to judgment with God. I speak for God and not for men. My salary is in the heavens. And even if there is no salary for me, it is good for me to speak, because from the beginning we should serve God without any interest whatsoever. My interest is Christ, and my salary is eternal life. Oh, for those who sell the word of God and substitute judgment and justice for bread that perishes.

---

29. Do We Lack Teachers?

The number of teachers has multiplied. Prophets abound on earth. The earth is full of teachers who all guarantee eternal life and promise lasting peace.

Earth has been surprised by the greatest plague, a plague that not only has made the earth rotten but its inhabitants as well. The plague consists of salaried prophets, teachers who contend purely with history, and who are divided in vain opinion. This plague has harmed the earth. God expected sweet grapes from his people, and good fruit. Instead came bad fruit and bitter and wild grapes. These teachers spend time fighting about the past, while ignoring the word of the Spirit, which is God's commandment of God. Physicians concern themselves for the living, not for the dead. Today's prophets concern themselves for the dead, on what has already passed, narrating the historical past by painting multicolored portraits so as to maintain the attention of their listeners. The commandment of the Spirit, God's sacred will, has been totally ignored and mocked. They procure to cure the soul of the fishermen with vain words and promises that are not fulfilled. All say: "Do not sin anymore." "Do not sin anymore!" Yet they never find sin, nor call it by its name so that sinners can know what sin is. Who knows sin and can distinguish it in these dark days? Everyone is at once filled with malice, with arrogance, everyone searching for the same thing. Everyone seeks riches and have closed off their inner selves to the poor and the orphan. Law is not history. The will of God has not been fulfilled. Let us discuss this and occupy our souls in doing the will of our God, which is to love not only our brothers, but even our enemies. If we do not do good toward our brothers, will we be able to do good toward our enemies? People have abandoned the holy commandments because salaried teachers all resist the Spirit of God because they have been led to treacherous paths. They refer to holy Law of God as the "sermon of the mount." Where did that name come from? The apostles did not give it this name. Why have the people ignored the word of God? All mock the commandments of God and want to live and progress in goodness without executing the will of God.

People everywhere confess, but despite all of this motion they are not carrying out the will of God nor are they obeying God according to his commandments. Why is it that the people's prophets and the teachers say just the opposite, that they are obeying God?

Oh! My brothers, do you not see how the people fight? Do you not see everyone in dispute and divided by words and opinions? What distinguishes one from the other? Do they not all dress with elegance and arrogance? Do they not all eat on the tables of the rich? Do they not all, some as much as others, go after body figure and color? Do they not all display their arrogance even by the heels of their shoes? Do they not all make sure to show their own body figure, their own face? Who does not adorn his face to attract the gaze of his peer's wife? Ignorant people, listen to the voice of your God, who tells you: "Leave, my people." Do not touch what is filthy. The entire world will be put to flames and is in complete confusion and desolation because of us. We have allowed the Law of God to perish. Our bodies were supposed to be temples of the Holy Spirit and the Almighty's dwelling. Our bodies were supposed to be homes and dwellings of love, of mercy, of justice, of God's holy judgments of God. But now, what lives in the heart of men? Malice, envy, egoism, arrogance, clumsy words, gossip, and all sorts of repugnant deeds.

Why condemn the Baptist? Why condemn the Pentecostal? Why condemn the Adventist? And why condemn different organizations? Who can raise their hand in opposition against any creed or movement? Do they not all try to please God? Do they not all read the Bible? Behold the spirit that has ruined the entire world: self-love, arrogance, which everyone has, envy, disobedience to God our creator. Because we abandoned justice and mercy, this is what ruined us. If we do not obey God, are not all the world's inhabitants sentenced to death? Who is he that has not broken the will of God? Where is he who is obeying God in all his holy commandments?

Will you shelter the widow or the orphan? Do you give of your bread to the hungry and distribute the many clothes you have to the needy? Is your mind clean? Do you covet your peer's wife? Respond, and raise your hand. Oh, people covered in rebelliousness! Humble your soul. Close your mouth. Lift up your head and behold the repentance of the people of Nineveh. Do you want forgiveness? Pardon your enemy first and talk no more against your brother who with difficulty searches for the same door you seek. Is there not but one judge of all the earth? Who then are you to judge another? Do you have greater love than he? Do you do better works than he? What do you boast of if you do not yet know what God's love is? Do you keep the commandments of God? Otherwise, you are a liar and there is no truth in you.

My brothers, let us consider these times. The life of men is already becoming shorter. Time will soon be over. Let us be wise at heart and consider our sad condition. We need God. Do we not all need the same water to live? Do we not all eat the earth's same food in order to live? Why not feed our souls from the same fountain of wisdom, of the love of God, of mercy. Let us dress ourselves with the heart of mercy.

---

30. For Whom Is Mercy?

It is certainly true that God promised to keep his "pact of mercy" with his people. But he specified it saying: "With those who love me and keep my commandments." God never has promised to keep his pact with those who do not love him or keep his commandments.

The disciples kept God's word that Christ explained. Because of this he told them: "Now you are cleansed by the word I have spoken." These men and women really had obeyed the word of God as Christ explained it. The word that Christ always preached was his Father's, as he himself said: "The word you have heard is not mine, but of the Father who sent me." The word of God these days is scorned by the people's leaders and pastors. This is why the word does not cleanse us or bring us knowledge. Those who had faith in the word of God, the word was enough. Just as we are satisfied by listening to the word alone when something is false, or words that are uttered about us so that we can believe them, so should the word of God alone should be enough for us to believe it.

God cannot sanctify us by his word, as Christ tells us in John 17:17, because we do not believe in the word. Nevertheless, people truly think that they believe in God, but their deeds contradict them. This is the reason why God cannot keep his pact or show mercy toward us. We do not fear him, nor do we do keep his Commandments. God not only said this in the Old Testament, but Christ also said it (John 14:21–24): "He who obeys the commandments he has from me is the man who loves me and keeps them, he loves me; and he who loves me will be loved by my Father. I too will love him and reveal myself to him." And this same apostle John said: "If someone says they have known him and do not keep his commandments: he is a liar and there is no truth in him." How can we be in his love without keeping his commandments? When Christ himself said, "If you keep my commandments, you will be in my love, like I have kept the commandments of my Father and am in his love!"

This is why these days the word only cleans us from vices and habits. But evil thoughts, arrogant and vain words, like the bad and disagreeable deeds, are not only against God. They also are actions that do not shelter the widow or the orphan, nor can they benefit the poor or the foreigner. It does not cleanse all this. Why? Because the commandments that people keep and obey are men's commandments and accords who love their bellies and what pleasures the eye. They sacrifice much for their positions and titles, authored by the hands of men worse than they. If the people of God kept the Word of God, the widow would not be scorned by the church and fed by the government and "welfare." If we kept the commandments of God that Christ told us, Christian children would not dishonor their parents. If we obeyed God's advice, our eyes would not be focused on great temples, on new cars, on spacious houses, on princely clothes, and on all vain things. The poor, the foreigner, and the orphan would testify something in our favor if we were keeping the commandment of God. If we do not even know what mercy is, how will we display mercy? To whom have we shown mercy? We have not even acted well toward our own parents, much less to those who abhor us. Christ said that the merciful would reach mercy but did not say that the hypocrites would. Mercy is not seen in the temples. Mercy is not demonstrated in chants or in prayers. Nor is mercy displayed in the vain ceremonies of men, or in fasts and preaching. Instead, mercy is demonstrated in good deeds toward the poor without means, to the widow and the orphan. Mercy is seen in forgiveness, in giving, in serving our peers. Mercy is seen when giving to the sick and the needy which requires a sacrifice, rather than giving what are leftovers.

All this has vanished from the land of the living because of those that have taken over the control of law. These who serve as examples of the people act without mercy. And these same people are so habituated and accustomed that they do not even see it. This is why it is written. Judgment without mercy will be done with he who does not show mercy. Whoever knows mercy and does it has nothing to fear because mercy is gloried against judgment and against the Law. There are no words or Law of God that condemns mercy; this is mercy according to God. Because there can be no mercy in men without first knowing God and his son who revealed his Father's truth to us. There is such a thing as knowing the gospel of these days and the conversion of these days, and not showing mercy. The earth is full of these people. The poor of the earth, like the widows and the orphans testify against what is now called the "church of Christ." Mercy and truth are not shown even to the kings of the earth. And if with clemency they sustain their own thrones, how much longer will the Christian live if he remains in it (Prov. 20:28)? This is why Christ also said that the one who listens to the word and executes it will build on firm rock. Even David says that God is good with the good, pure with the pure, honest with the honest. God becomes strict with the perverse (2 Sam. 22:26). And who will be able to justify himself now that the ire of God comes? Who thinks that he is not worthy of the ire that comes? Stand up.

31. This Generation's Justice

Oh, for those who ally themselves with the strong nation. Oh, for those who trust atomic energy. This nation has left its God. Oh, for the prophets who did not correct it. God himself created mankind and raised prophets to humble it with words of wisdom, but instead of announcing God's justice they made it into a business. Because of this the nation has withdrawn into iniquity and violence. Stronger were the men of the shadows than the men of light. The blind were more powerful than those who said they had eyes.

The sons of evil persons were more powerful than the sons of good ones, a reputation that became known throughout the earth. This ruination and the defeat of Christians was divulged across the earth. Zealousness for justice perished. The vigor of hearts died, and all pursued the beauty of this great Nation. If from such people—hypocrites, ingrates, unjust, without good fruit, and without testimony—God constructed his church, I abhor the day I met these people. Let it not be that God justifies a people who received a truth so great and precious, and who now behave with such a great despotism, and with a heart so arrogant. Oh, great of the earth, who deter the truth and forbid justice from becoming manifest. What evil am I doing?

Your justice has no color or form. Not even the most miserable can benefit from your mercy. Who benefits from your love? Certainly, not even your own relatives offer testimony in your favor, much less your enemies. Has the widow received any good from you? Has the world benefited from your examples? Have you taught the world how to dress with honor and decency? Has any believer changed with your words of wisdom and humility? Do they not all speak with arrogance because of you? People have learned to place all their heart, all their strength, and all their understanding to achieve carnal cravings, because they have learned this from the rented Prophets. Oh, rented prophets! If you are of God, suffer this injury for you will lose nothing. Salaried teachers, have patience and bear this reproach that I in my craziness speak, because this name is given to all who scold. Why do they condemn Jeremiah's enemies simply because they received salary? Is your salary not greater than theirs? Certainly, those false prophets did not walk with the pomp you do. Nor were their stomachs as full as yours. They showed more courtesy (since courtesy is a disguise of hypocrisy) than you.

Suffer this lecture teachers and prophets because the jealousy of God has entered my blood and what I did not want has overwhelmed my heart. You teach that your Christ did not open his mouth when he was accused. Why then do you open it against this false teaching? Is salary not your motive? Would you teach, even without salary, the love toward Christ who did not receive salary, only a crown of thorns? Oh, elder prophets, can you not see all the younger prophets running after your fixed salary? This is why mercy was abandoned and love lost its strength in the hearts of peoples.

Of what substance were we cut, from a Lamb or from a wolf? Who is our example, a humble one or an arrogant one? Search your hearts according to the word of God and you shall find a great sin enveloped within you. Certainly, it was in vain that Bible versions multiplied, producing a throng of prophets, but that hardly mattered as they were all formed by the same word seeking the same things: fame, glory, property.

Oh, of those who have accumulated here on earth. Great will be your loss. Many will be your tears. Search for fine gold and give it to the poor. Open your eyes to deny the things of the world. Why do you mutilate your lives in what is not? Why do you throw your days away for things that quickly will pass? Do you see not the example that you will leave to your followers?

Soon power will be given to the beast. Where will the arrogance with which you mock the commandments of Christ remain? What will happen to your thrones and great titles when the will of God appears in that humble man from Galilee? See how your positions and titles have rotted and ransacked your hearts. Humility and mercy disappeared when men invented grand thrones on which they sat so that other men would fear them. And people thus fear men not because of the righteous lives they live, but because of the place and throne they occupy.

Blessed are those who also in these days hunger and thirst for justice. Few merciful people remain on earth but blessed are they because they will attain mercy. There is no assurance that hypocrites and the unjust will reach mercy. Instead, as the apostle James said: "Judgment without mercy will be done to those who do not use mercy." For a long time, we have talked of the love of God. The people have not wanted to live in this love of God. Now the people will taste the ire of God. And because they did not want love, they will receive the ire of God.

32. Sinners Stand at the Forefront

The state had to concoct an idea to feed the elderly, who were living on earth without food. The state realized that elderly parents were without food or anyone to feed them, and thus was moved to mercy, giving food to parents who were left abandoned with no one to provide them with food. These parents were all elderly, the parents of strong children, of healthy Christians, but they were too busy in their own affairs, so they could not help their own elderly.

The state would not have established such a plan had it not seen the many elderly abandoned by the church of Jesus Christ. The state was required to look after the elderly because the church was too busy building temples to please God. The people of God should shroud its face in shame. If the state did not feed the elderly, if the children of darkness had not invented this plan to feed the elderly and the widows, what would the church have done? Would it be moved to show mercy? No. In the homes we hear curses because the children who call themselves Christians, instead of helping their parents and giving them what they need, only loan them money as if their parents were strangers. They do not give a single cent to their parents. Is this not hideous? Do we have a right to go before God and ask for mercy? Instead, God has been generous because he has not taken the earth away from us. We are a people unworthy of inhabiting this good planet. We are not a proper people to inhabit this earth. We have corrupted all creation. In my ignorance I search for testimony that can vouch for the church, but in vain. I have been unable to find it. No one dares to stand up to defend the church from its great abominations. Who will justify this generation? Even the blind of the world do not dare to give good testimony on her behalf. You just ones of the earth, do not fear, do not let your own souls be scandalized when you hear or read this word. But I do advise the young and weak to make an effort to be worthy of escaping the ire that will burn the entire earth, and to stand without trembling in the presence of Christ the king of the entire earth. If the just, with much difficulty can save themselves, where will those who do not love stand, those who have no mercy, those who feed on evil thoughts? Let us tell the just that because of their justice they will live. But the hypocrite should not fool himself because all the things done in secrecy, God will bring to the light of all, and he will give to each according to his own deeds.

    The blood of Christ was spilled in vain by this evil generation. Many in the past obtained forgiveness, gratefully walking in the fear of Christ and the wonder of life. But these people have not been cleansed. Instead, they devalued Christ's blood so that others would also trample the blood.

    The just stand firm and nothing can move them; the just are not scandalized by these words. He is confident in his fear of God. His deeds are clean and worthy of praise, like the deeds of Dorcas, like the works of Cornelius. But who covets the deeds of present Christians? What intercession can God hear in favor of this generation? The intercession of Moses? Of Daniel? Of Abraham? No. God has been stirred from his holy place because of us; we have provoked him. The end will come, and no one can hold it back. Prayers are worthless because the lips of those who pray utter lies against their own brother. Prayers are now worthless, because they are vain prayers, prayers without the fear of God.

    The ingrate who does not show mercy toward orphans and widows, will he reach the mercy of God? Never has such a thing been heard on earth, because God is just and defends the widow and the orphan. Let us turn toward the one who informed us. Leave our rebelliousness. Strip ourselves of all arrogance and we will find grace before God. Let us open our heart to the word of God and leave the profits of the world behind. All of this will disappear in a few days. Why deny our souls salvation? In the time of our Lord, there were also struggles appropriate to those days, over elegant clothes and some meals better than others. But our master left the best for the worst; he left wealth and chose the manger. Or was it accidental that Christ was born in a manger? Could it be due to God's carelessness that Christ was born in a manger? No. What for mankind is wealth, for God is filth and clumsiness. If riches are good, why then did Christ deny them? Why did Paul call them "manure"? Oh, blind one, do you not see the end of all these things? Take what remains and do not deceive your souls with illusory things. Love justice, do good, in the morning nourish your souls by doing merciful deeds. Why fill your hearts with sweet but empty names? Let the spirit of God live in you and fructify you to eternal life. Humble your will before the arrival of the day when you will have to give it up by force.

Look. What has God asked of us? Some difficult deed? Has he demanded of us a deed like the ones he undertook in the six days of creation? No, he only asks of us what we are capable of doing. Can we not forgive? Can we not love our peer? Surely we can, but what hinders us is the pride that has overpowered our souls. Leave behind, then, that which ruins our soul. Say goodbye to greed, ire, malice.

33. Where Is the Wise Man?

Who should we imitate to learn justice? Who will teach us how to love? Who on earth is worthy of being imitated? Who among leaders? Is there a man of intelligence who can teach us good sense? Search the streets, search towns, enter the temples and ask for wise men. Ask for a man who is concerned about God's judgment.

Search for a man who does not sell the word of God; a man who looks after the oppressed, for one who is not salaried. Raise a flag on the place where you find him. Shout and spread the news so that we can all learn from him what we need for God. The day has become dark. The sun of justice has fallen. Who will take our hand to guide us in this darkness? Search for eyes that do not seek reward. Search for lips that do not speak treachery or exaggeration. Search for ears that are not inclined toward vanity. From these clean eyes we will learn good, from these truthful lips we will hear the judgments of God, which are clean and healthy for the mind. Where is the school of justice? Where is the school of mercy? Take us there. Where is a man who is not moved by earthly affairs? Where is the man who is not moved by popular opinion, like the one who is about to be consumed by the ire of his maker? Seek the man who does not have his eyes on things that the foolish man is inventing. Seek a man that is not scandalized by the commandments of God and his son. We want a man that does not seek things for his own benefit. This man will not emerge until the King of Kings appears, who will rule the earth with a steel rod. And on that day, where will those who get colic from these written words be? Do not fear these simple words. Leave your fright and fear for the day when you will see face to face your own sins and injustices. God has risen from his holy place because the great ones of the earth have resisted justice; have made the just stumble, have not given a place to mercy, but like black clouds, they rise menacing all those who want to act in justice and judgment. They have made the small stumble, even in prayer, because they have taught prayer in public. The unjust have contrived and saddened those who wanted to live in fear [of God], and later ask: How have we harmed the just? With your own laws and your bad conduct, you bind the soul of the innocent. On your face there is nothing but pure mockery and sarcasm. You speak the truth with mockery and jokes but speak your lies with seriousness.

How would it be possible for the blind, starting on their path, not fall? Who that begins life will escape? With your curses that have so much power? Blessed is the one who escapes and works for justice because God will place him on a high pedestal. Joyful is the man who frees himself of ancient Babylon's many tricks. Tell the just, who will soon rule, that in truth he will work for justice. Tell him that those earning salaries will no longer rule. Soon, very soon, the earthy kingdoms of royals will become the kingdoms of our Lord and Savior Christ the King.

Oh, for the women who have been placed as nets on earth for the ruination of men. Oh, for those who adorn themselves with all sorts of ornaments. What perfume, what ointments, what ornament do women not use? Our women were adorned like the daughters of Babylon. The man's eyes are humbled by the beauty and composure of the women. Who is the man that escapes the powerful figure with which the woman has been adorned? Are there no wise men among their leaders? Is there no one who is disgusted by the filth and arrogance of women? Tell the woman that this behavior does not please God. Tell her that God will put her to shame and in great humiliation. The adornment of women has provided and greatly opened the door of adultery. Are men so clean of heart that they cannot be harmed by the figure and appearance of women? Are they so clean that they are not bothered by the nakedness of women? No, of course not, instead they feed their corrupt appetites, and their eyes do not tire of seeing what is not theirs, do not disrupt this great evil. I speak this not about the sinners who know and admit this happens among the daughters of Babylon. I say all this to stop evil, establish justice and honor on earth. But these blind guards do not know how to stop evil. Instead of attacking evil, they attack good, and give free passage to the evil that develops among the daughters of Babylon. They do all of this while embracing the word of God. They say, God is not against the arrogance of women, nor does God abhor the aromas and ointments with which woman is adorned. Nor does God abhor the sheer clothes that our daughters wear. Sin has multiplied on earth! Women's decency and honor have perished. Gone is shame and respect for another man's wife.

The mind of men was dulled. Who will tell women the evil they are causing on earth?

34. Where Is Our Benefit?

The elders chose the commandment of the Holy Spirit, but this generation has chosen the promises with a heart full of avarice. The elders chose to serve humanity, but these people have chosen to be served. Because of this demand, justice perished from the earth and can no longer be seen. This displaced God from his place on seeing that the greats became masters and mistreated the weak. From his dwelling God saw that the wise had lost their sense, and pursued vanity. Because of this, God will burn the work of man. Man has fooled himself with his own work and neglected life and the correct path because of the things that concern the belly and the body. Is this not what occurs among the senseless? To this we owe so many human sectarian divisions because no one has fractured so to become more gentle or humble. No one has divided to be more merciful, or for the sake of more and better justice. Before, each of those that has divided, did so for the glory and for earthly thrones. Nothing has improved as a result of so much division. The world has not received any benefit. Not even believers have improved as a result of the many schisms. All this is fruit of our rebelliousness. This we did not learn from Christ. Our schism must be in spirit and not based on human opinions in words and names. And to separate, our separation must be a separation from the world not from some believers because they have a charming name. If the world abhors, we must love. If the world robs and takes, we must give and serve. If the world delights in seeing, hearing, and speaking evil, we must delight in seeing, hearing, and speaking what is good, that which pleases God, and that which we learned from Christ.

Did Christ speak without the will of God? Did Christ transgress and ignore the words of his father? What about us? This is why Christ said to the father: "Consecrate them by means of truth—Your word is truth" (John 17:17). In another place the Lord said, "In this my father is glorified, in that you take much benefit." Where is our benefit? And what kind of benefit does the Lord ask of us? Ceremonies? Sweet chants from lips? Vain and lengthy prayers? Grand and fine temples? No, this was not the benefit that the son of God had before. The benefit of Christ's life was feeding the hungry, spiritually and materially. The life of Christ produced love, mercy, justice, faith, gentleness, and temperance. These fruits pleased the father. Do they please our fathers? Not even our own brothers crave the benefits we are giving. Release us God. Force us to see our misery which is poor, blind, naked, and very miserable. Holy God, open our eyes before you arrive with the consuming fire, because who will be able to stand firmly with such rebelliousness against you?

I do not have money and riches, much less fame and an important name, because my name is trampled by many. This sermon is the only one in my heart. If it does not reach you, I have nothing else to offer. But this sermon will be strong testimony against all the rebels who in the last days will try to excuse themselves before My God. There will be no stranger's blood on my hands because I saw the end approach and warned all the people. Who will be able to say he was innocent, after reading the words of this book? I speak truth in God and do not lie, even though others speak lies, each even with their peer. A husband listens to many things from his wife, as does a wife from her husband. Things they should conceal are not. I do not lie when I say that man has been perverted by evil thoughts. His heart does not stop thinking of evil and everyone's eyes are swollen by adultery. There is no beautiful and poised woman they do not covet. Can all this behavior be sustained? Will the one who assesses thoughts allow such things? Will these men's prayers be accepted by the one with clean eye who sees and assesses all of his creation? How can we call ourselves good when we are bad? How can we call ourselves new creatures, without new works that please God? This is what has lit the furor of God. Cry, wail, for your miseries will reach you. Erase your name from the human race before we are confused and surprised by God's justice. Those who pray in public and seek the Lord tearfully, yet without working justice or doing mercy, why do you so trick your souls?

Do good, search for justice, love as Christ commanded and taught us. Tolerate the ignorant so that God will see us with compassionate eyes. Love all. It is no longer appropriate for man to walk with his eyes raised and with his mouth open.

Behold the world, which is trembling before its creator, even the mountains already feel the great visit from their Maker. Let us experience this great visit from the north.

35. The Enemies of the Cross

I do not speak of the laws that make the sun perfect because the sun has never left the laws God set for it to follow. The sun has no need for anyone to show it anything, because God showed it his way and he has kept it to this day. Nor do I speak of the laws that govern the earth, the wind, the clouds, and all the things God formed with his powerful and terrible hand. All of these things sustain God's will and from the beginning of time have done as they were ordered. All these things would perish in a moment without the laws God prepared for them, causing a vast and terrible disorder in all of God's creation. Since all of these things remain ordered according to God's will, there is no need to speak of them, or of the laws that govern and sustain them. Instead, I speak to men and not beasts. I speak with animated people and not inanimate things. I speak with people who were made according to the image and resemblance of God. And because all things received the laws that mark each of their paths, so mankind also received a holy Law. Man received a new life, allowing him to walk according to the importance of his new life. Christ was the font of this new life by which man must control those who have faith in God and who love him. Without faith it is impossible to please God. Whoever does not love does not know God. He who does not keep his commandments does not love him (John 14: 21–24). On the contrary, he who keeps his commandments is in his love: "You will live in my love if you keep my commandments, even as I have kept my Father's commandments, and live in his love" (John 15:10).

Here then is the reason for the downfall and ruin of the entire world. Man failed when he wanted to save himself without obeying God. Egoism itself twisted him. Men seek temples in which to do good, thinking that love itself grows simply by going to temple and being devout in its rituals. All of these efforts are really man-made activities, which God never ordered. Men have obtained a bewitched salvation made within these temples because they do not bear the fruit of love, of mercy, of gentleness, of justice. The salvation God and the work of the Holy Spirit offers us a new life not composed simply of chants and prayers, but of saintly fruits, saintly works, saintly judgments, saintly love. We have fallen from these heights because we have abandoned the saintly path God marked out for man. All the things that God birthed and formed, keep the order and the commandment of God, their creator, except man. Every day man invents new laws, trying to curtail the evil that he has brought himself by forsaking God's commandment.

Everywhere men struggle to invent laws so that people can improve themselves. But as far as I can see, these laws only bring benefits to those who invent them. None of these laws protect the widow or the orphan. These laws do not shelter nor help the earth's young. Instead, the just are oppressed and mistreated by the laws that emerge every day. GOD spoke of these things, which were once very popular. The apostles did not ignore the holy commandments that Christ preached and commanded in them. As we can see, these were given to everyone, forever, until Christ returns. Let me remind you that these commandments were not disdained by our parents. In this same path of which God speaks, our forefathers found peace. Indeed, they delighted in these laws. Not only did they enjoy calling Christ "Lord, Lord" and profess it as is done nowadays, but they obeyed Christ and kept all the commandments they received from him.

I want to be clean before God and for this reason I preach of the fear of God, of the violence the church undertakes in these final days. I will be culpable if I do not say and speak of what my eyes see and what my ears hear. Let it be known, and perhaps someday confessed, that someone who spoke to them, telling them that they were acting badly and were very far from God. Hypocrites have multiplied on earth, and these are the very ones who attack God's laws. These bad and salaried people are the ones who wage war on the true Cross of Christ. These men abhor the life of Christ. If you do not abhor the life of Christ, why do you not live the life that Christ asks of us? Leave salary, each one of you, and defend the poor, do good toward the oppressed of the earth, let us defend the rights of God. If someone loves life and wants to see good days in what is about to occur, fear God with all your heart and do the good of God. Each one of those who wants to undertake good works and to save your life, if you already believe in Christ and love God, seek the commandments God gave us so we would have life. Insist with all your heart to enter by the narrow door. In these days the door is narrower than ever because there is greater evil. Rush our souls to purity before the ire of God appears. Then, there will be no one to defend us or anyone who can escape. The days of vengeance are near. The day of ire is what we can now see. All the rebels will be removed. And those who substituted God's laws for human commandments will also receive a terrible punishment. Each should attempt to escape, doing mercy and justice toward the oppressed of the earth to redeem ourselves. Oh, to those who mock and disdain these words for I speak in bad days. The wise will consume these words and set their souls free. God be with those of humble heart and broken spirit.

I do not speak of abundant things nor with soft words that deceive the soul. Therefore, I say that we will be surprised by God's great judgment. God will show vengeance for all holy words we ignored, which he himself promised would bring salvation or condemnation.

I speak to those who await the day of the Lord. I address those who take the name of God and call themselves children of God. If you have not maintained a fear of God and if you have not obeyed the Lord in anything, why do you await the day of the Lord? Oh, for those who await good without showing mercy toward anyone. Oh, for those who expect rapture without keeping God's commandments. Oh, of those who expect to see Christ face-to-face without demonstrating love for their peers in the ways Christ ordered us to love one another. Oh, for those who say: "I cannot keep the commandments of God." Because on that day they shall tremble like Babylonian King Belshazzar trembled. Each of us struggles to reach the things we want. But no one gets upset by the matters of the soul. Everyone, pursue what is earthly. Oh, for those who say: "No to good work so that no one shall be glorified." Because on that final day, it will weigh heavily on them that they did not work for justice and mercy toward their peers. On that day they will discover that they themselves chose death. They themselves made a pact with death as Israel did. Because you had the word of God in your homes and did not put it to work. When people fear their God, they keep the laws of their God. When people keep the laws of their God, the lives of those people pleases their God. When the lives of the people are pleasing to God's eyes, even their chants and prayers are heard. But when the people close their ears to avoid hearing the holy commandment: even their prayers and solemnities are an abomination in the presence of God (Prov. 28:9).

Everyone speaks lies. Each person exaggerates when it is convenient. No one believes in the truth. If there are still inhabitants on earth who have ears with which to hear, all of you, turn to God and do good works. To rebel sons, to your fathers, to your violent daughters, to their mothers, and to the woman who now speaks as much as a man: keep your mouth closed and return to the honor women should display. Because each has lost their honor, and no one orients their paths by following the eyes of God.

Ordered notes govern sounds and so come to form music that is sweet to the ear. The man who likewise orders his paths by the commandments of God, his deeds are governed by the Spirit of the Law of Christ, which form a sweet and pleasant note to the eyes of God. But oh, to those who want to live the life of Christ without fearing the commandment of God. That is like seeking fruit in a dry tree. I tell the wise of the earth, tolerate me a bit and suffer my words, because this is why I remained on earth. I know that the man who reprimands on earth is not appreciated. And these words are heard by few. Of this I am not ignorant, because the one who placed the words in my mouth, he permitted my eyes to see the condition of his people. He made me see that more would abhor these words, and that very few would receive them to correct their lives. Why be so rebellious? Will we also perish by Israel's same error? Israel also thought that it was in good standing, so too thought the Pharisees. Did Nineveh not also repent upon hearing God's advice? Why let the people of Nineveh arise against us on the great day of God? We have done no good on earth. What then shall we glory in? Let us lend our ear to the advice the prophet Jeremiah gave to the people of Israel, who also thought it was in good standing before God. The prophet said: "Do not praise the wise for his wisdom or the strong because of his strength, or the rich for his wealth, but if one should praise himself, let it be in this: in knowing me, for I am Jehovah, that I do mercy, judgment, and justice on earth, because I want these things, says Jehovah."

Days will come when all our bravery will perish, as well as all our wisdom. On that day our riches will also vanish. And what will be our refuge and our shelter? What works will be to our credit? We have not fulfilled what we were put here on earth to do. Instead, we have abandoned the good that belonged to us, deeming the commandments Christ gave us as useless. The words for which Christ died were in vain.

For this generation the new pact Christ enacted was in vain. God's advice has brought no advantages to this slow and rebellious people. They, like Israel in their rebelliousness, formed their own commandments, in which there is no life, only division and contention. All differ in their creed and opinion, but in their deeds and spirit, they are all alike. They all love the vanities of this world. All are irate, violent when they respond. Each feeds on evil thoughts and opens his eyes to someone else's wife. And who is ashamed of this? Certainly no one is scandalized by this. Everyone feels it proper to engage in evil and covet what is not theirs.

With what medicine will cure these people? Is there no remedy? The campaigns men have undertaken to enliven these people have not worked well. Instead, they make these people give up and vacillate with their step toward death. Why not search for the best medicine for your souls? Let us open our ears to the word of the Almighty, who to this day has kept with his word on all things. Can he not cleanse us with his word like he cleaned the apostles who united their faith with his word (John 15:3)? Israel did not combine faith with the word God gave them (Heb. 4:2). This is why the word did not sustain them. Let us have faith in the word of God and work for justice in the few days that remain for us. Let it not be that God visits the earth and no one escapes.

36. The Vanquished People

The darkness of evil and violence have become more intense. Evil has become stronger than ever. And the weapons of the devil and Satan's kingdom are more powerful than ever. Who will be able to resist the evil of these in these days with such a weak gospel that is being preached? Sinners are becoming stronger, and Christians are becoming weaker than ever. The weapons of Satan are stronger in these days than those of Christians. This is why there is no love, why there is no meekness and humility, why Christians cannot offer others the benefits of the Holy Spirit, because they are very weak, and have forsaken Wisdom.

Christians are more concerned with worldly matters and their bellies than with their souls. They care more about the flesh than the spirit, more about the body than the soul. What strength is there among the Christians in these days? Everywhere the world has vanquished the Christian and defeated him. The men of greatest importance and those most advanced in human science are the ones the devil uses to corrupt Christian minds. The spirit of confusion has penetrated the heart of Christians, turning all of them into the clients and merchants of the great Babylon. Christians are drunk from the delights of the great Babylon, and all of the design of life's vain arts has produced profit among Christians. The inventors of ointments, perfumes, clothing, and fine fabrics; the inventors of delicious and vain foods, sugary drinks; the inventors of appliances that transmit deceit, pastimes, noise, and music and every sound pleasant to the flesh; all these inventors have enriched themselves with the great Babylon, in which Christians without faith and without love of God also are included. Who is the Christian who does not delight in the vanities of life? Who is the Christian who is not indebted because of vain things? The strength of the Christian is invested in pure vanities. If in these things I just mentioned there is no evil, why does God condemn them in the great mother of fornications (Rev. 18:12) (Isa. 3:16–24)? If these things tricked the ancients, will they not also trick our souls? If God condemned these things in the lives of those who did not yet have the high understanding that we have, will he not condemn them even more in our lives? Certainly, he will.

The devil has Christians completely occupied in vain art. He has them occupied in things that destroy the soul and dull minds. For example, we have newspaper reporters but what kind of reports do they give us daily? One or two good reports; the rest simply announce the vanities of life; announcements about delights and things that Christians should not even know. These reporters have become more like women who come and go to irritate the peaceful soul. These reporters fill newspaper pages with incidents and events that are most unnecessary. The worst of it is that Christians occupy themselves daily talking about the things published in the newspaper, vain things, which offer no edification. These reporters could very well relate important events, things that are true, but instead they report such vain things because they have found that Christians hunger for vain things and things that do not enhance wisdom. Radio and periodicals are the largest media with which the most insensate teachers can instruct and transmit their poisons into the blood of Christianity. Of course, Christians see nothing evil in the radio and periodicals. When the Lord appears, then they will know the great evil that these instruments of Satan did to the heart of Christians. The smartest architects of evil have been chosen to paint naked women, to draw human figures, and the most powerful images. And who is not disturbed by these figures? If Christians relied on the ancient Gospel, with holy and jealous teachers, if the preachers of the word were wise, and smart, then there would be Christians who could resist Satan's art and the forces of darkness. But with this dull and weak Christianity, who will confront the forces of darkness? Artists draw women's faces that are more beautiful than those that exist so as to disturb the minds and poison intentions. What sort of resistance to this are the earth's wise undertaking? They are victims of these arts themselves and feed on these evil figures. Teachers and the so-called men of God go to barber shops to cut their hair and there see completely naked women on calendars and compare these naked women with their own wives. Will they say, certainly my wife is well-dressed and maintains her shame. But they do not understand that in the eyes of God and true Christians, their wives behave and walk like evil and shameless women. During apostolic times loose women and whores dressed better than the so-called Christian women of our days. Is this a coincidence? Will this pass soon? Does God ignore our ways of dressing? Am I the first to speak about the nakedness of women? Am I the only fanatic who has denounced sin? Certainly, the evil that the church is causing on earth will not be overlooked. Because of this a great ire will sweep throughout the inhabited earth. The eyes of teachers are evil and accustomed to see dishonor in the people. Because of this they do not care at all about the state of women. Oh, what a great ruin! What terrible disaster the church has brought upon itself. Because of this misery and hunger that will come over the earth, death and cries, anguish and difficulty, terror and clamor, will overtake all those who mock the holy life.

37. False Confidence

The name of Christ has been defamed everywhere. The name of Christ has reached such a low level that even the very sons of the devil call themselves by that name. The sons of perdition call themselves Christians. No one else is guilty of this great worldwide dishonor against God but the men who are charged with the word of God. What is the mark that distinguishes the true Christian from the hypocrite Christian? There is no mark to distinguish one from the other, only that some have some vices that others have not. Some, like others, lack the mercy of God. Some as much as others abhor humility and the love of God, which is the Cross of Christ. Evil men are those who call themselves Christian in these latter days. But those same people who call themselves Christians are worse than the Pharisees who crucified Christ. The difference being that those who crucified Christ only crucified his body, while these have crucified the word of God and the Spiritual life of Christ, and have substituted it for an arrogant life, one full of pride. In present day Christianity, there is a place for all kinds of people; men who are arrogant, evil, and full of perjury. Sons who are rebellious against their parents pass as Christians. Ingrate women and men, without natural affect, without fear of God, adults and the young who are implacable and without mercy, who abhor the good and the holy. Malicious, filthy in word and thought, cruel with the young and orphans, a generation of badmouths, of bad deeds, of bad thoughts. They do not know what fear of God is because not even their leaders know it. Gossipy people, that is what now replaces Christians. People of bad thoughts and adultery are what now fill the pulpits that once belonged to holy and zealous men. These are the ones who have brought infamy to the word of God and to the holy name of Christ, because now all profess belief in the name of Christ. These are the ones who have nullified the sacrifice of Christ. These are the ones who have devalued the blood of Christ and have used it only to authorize their liberty to sin. Is it not shameful that sons have become more important than parents? And is it not our fault? Blasphemous men are the ones who now preach the word of God for a salary. These are also the ones who have heightened the ire of God, provoking and irritating him. Everything has value these days except Christ's name. All pay large sums of money for earthly things except for the name of Christ. Everyone sacrifices for their own whims except for Christ's name.[10] The name of Christ is of little significance these days. And any hypocrite, weighed down by sin, calls himself by Christ's name. Thus, the name of Christ comes to be dishonored and abused. Is anyone scandalized because the evil ones are called Christians? Surely, no one is because all are equally weighed down by sins and malice. All are nourished on the same kind of thought; each gossip murmurs against his brother. For having abandoned the living God and for nullifying Christ's Great Sacrifice, the world will be engulfed in flames, and

Christians will be handed over into the devil's hands. God will bring just judgment upon this nation, as he also does over other things that occupy the earth. The false church (Christianity without fear of God) will be put to flames because of its confidence and pride. The church believes that this nation is strong and that no one can do anything to it. But this confidence will turn to ashes. God himself will give the beast special permission (as he gave to Nebuchadnezzar). Because those who now are called Christians do not have a Love of God, or know what mercy is, the antichrist will rule over them. And where will those who call themselves Christians appear? Will the ones who now direct people to a precipice with all sorts of deceit stand firm? Will these be able to stand before God's just judgment, which will come with great ire? Who will stand clean before the presence of God? Certainly, those of clean heart will fear nothing, nor will those who were sanctified by the blood of Christ and his Holy Word be confounded. They will be able to stand without fear as Christ approaches, but not so those who mocked Christ's commandments. Then will these hypocrites know and see that they left the true life for a life empty and dead.

38. The Servants of Babylon

Who is the great Babylon? Who are the citizens of the great Babylon? How do its citizens speak? How do they see? How do they hear and what do they hear? How do they sing? How do they pray? These citizens honor God with their lips, but these people of Babylon are covetous and have a heart of stone for the poor. All the people of this great Babylon seek their own benefit. Each goes after vanity. This is how they were taught by the great whore to dress with haughtiness, to walk with haughtiness, to speak with haughtiness, and to live in haughtiness.

These people, erroneously instructed, do not know how to speak truth, do not love truth, do not think in the truth. Nothing is given to these people to see the truth on earth. Because of the great whore, mother of fornications, all the people learned to pray in vain, to sing with lips, and to read the Bible without understanding anything nor obeying the God's commandments.

From this great Babylon everyone learned to do things in public, because she herself is a public woman.

What things do Christians do in secret? Their bad deeds they do in secret but their ceremonies they conduct in public to be observed. Oh, for this generation because they overdid even the works of the Pharisees. This generation praises the ancient prophets with their lips, they praise Abraham, Moses, Daniel, Christ, John the Baptist, Paul, and their suffering. But their deeds show that they abhor the prophets, and with bad works born of envy and arrogance they declare that they are enemies of all those who suffered. They are enemies of Christ's Cross and do not let anyone live as the ancients did. But the ire of God will soon be manifest. It will contradict them and will shame them. They all endorse the commercial activities of the great Babylon, and they have made evil prosper. No one is apparently guilty, only the apostate church. She apparently has filled the earth with hypocrisy and with deceitful works of every sort. Why blame a single movement and make it responsible of all the evil there is on earth? Is the same Spirit not in everyone? Do they not all seek the same things? Money, glory, name, honor, and all the things that perish. Not satisfied with this, all seek and covet their brother's wife, the wife of his peer. Is this not shameful?

No one denies himself but offers lip service that they behave differently. Nothing is denied to the eye, nothing is denied to the ear, and nothing is denied to the tongue. All speak, hear, and see what is most convenient for them. Their haughty and greedy eyes are denied nothing. What, then, has this bad generation denied itself? Who shelters the poor? Who delights in doing good toward their brothers or toward their enemies? Will the mother be able to forget the fruit of her womb? Well, these people who were educated in the great Babylon have forgotten God's commandment. No one cries for the word of God. No one weeps to see his commandments on earth. All are busy buying the best, eating the best, dressed in the best, with living in the best house. Oh, twisted and callous people, open your eyes and see what you have done! Do you not see that you are deprived of love? Can you not tell that you now stand much poorer in the presence of God? Can you not tell that mercy does not accompany you, that justice is not with you? Who, then, is by your side?

You have left Christ's holy commandment. So, who will be your advocate?

If someone says they have known Christ and does not keep his commandments, that person is a liar and there is no truth in him (1 John 2:4).

Let us understand that we have behaved very badly, violating God's good. How do the poor benefit with all our chants and prayers? All our chants and prayers. Can we be reconciled with God though all our chants and prayers? What benefit does God receive from our vain praise?

Blind man, open your eyes to behold that you are dressed in arrogance. Stop your walk and meditate on the holy path, and you will discover that you live in envy and that there is no love in your heart.

No one should identify himself by name and vain words anymore. If someone wants to announce or reveal his Christianity, reveal it and identify it as God is revealed and identified. How is God revealed? Christ told us how: "Be merciful as your celestial father is merciful." God is identified through deed, not just word. How is God identified through the sun and rain? Giving it to all without the people's assent.

Do we behave as his children? No. Instead, everyone seeks their own benefit, and no one imitates Christ in forgiving, in serving, in giving, in overcoming, in loving, in what makes peace.

In order to be seen, everyone has become vain through their public chants and ceremonies. Is this not the spirit of the great whore, the mother of all abominations? From the very same mother (the great Babylon) the Pharisees also learned to undertake their deeds in public.

Illnesses have multiplied in physical bodies as medical science has also greatly increased the medicines to combat disease. As Christ said, now sin in the church has multiplied too. In what sense has wisdom in the words of the prophets multiplied to combat this augmented level of sin? Not at all. All have become vain and have adapted to these heightened levels of sin. The prophets have become clumsy and vain with their empty speeches. What good has this done on earth? Nothing. Woman has lost her shame, her honor, her respect, her decency. What have children learned from these vacuous speeches? Nothing. Children have lost respect for their father, have become disobedient, violent, insolent, corrupted in thoughts and words that are dirty and filthy. From a young age, in secret, they enact bad deeds and thus have lost their glory as children.

What is secret is done publicly and what is public is done secretly. I speak to teachers. I speak to wise men. What is wisdom? What is a wise man? How does a wise man live? How does a wise man speak and think? What is the fruit of wisdom? What are its symptoms? Does the wise man lack love, justice, mercy, humility? These things are the gifts of a wise man or a son of God. The man who does not have mercy, love, justice, and fear of God, this man is a dry tree that bears no fruit. Will we be wise? "A wise man heeds commands, but a prating fool will be overthrown" (Prov. 10:8). Here, then, was our downfall. Our ruination began when we left God's commandments. The wise accepts correction. The wise love mercy. The wise is not salaried, nor can they be rented. Search history. What wise man was salaried? Did Moses receive a salary for liberating the people of Egypt? Not even Socrates, the ancient Greek, received a salary, nor did he want one. The wise are not discovered through money. They have God in their heart. God himself is wisdom and because of this, these wise men give up their lives for people who love God. Let us seek wise men to speak to these people, telling them that they have abandoned their God.

On the day that God visits the earth, all things shall be burned by his ire.

39. Where Is Faith?

The days of which Christ spoke have arrived. Faith on earth has disappeared. The virtue of the faith is depleted. Love has come to be something abhorrent, love is very hidden for the people of these days; Christians have become alienated, they have become strangers to love.

In faith there is no virtue, in the virtue there is no science, in the science there is no temperance, and in what little temperance there is, there is no fear of God, and in the little fear there is, there is no fraternal love, and in the little fraternal love there is, there is no charity. Without faith it is impossible to please God. Why is it impossible to please God? What thing, then, pleases God? We know his son pleased him. Why did Jesus Christ please his Father? He pleased because he lived by the will of the father, and always did what pleases the father. What things please the father? Life in true and pure love; life full of mercy as Christ lived it. Whoever loves as Christ loved, he pleases

God. Whoever forgives as Christ forgave, he pleases God. What will we say about these days? Do we forgive? Do we love? Christ loved his enemies, but we do not love even our own brothers. Here is the evidence that there is no faith; whoever has faith in God, obeys God. Whoever obeys God in his holy will and commandments, he has faith. This is why without faith it is impossible to please God. For faith we must obey all that God commands. For faith we must keep ourselves clean. For faith we must love our enemies. Faith is what moves all our being, or should move it because God is not in person among us. That is to say we do not see him with our carnal eyes. Faith is what we need to believe in him. Faith is what we need to forgive, to love, to suffer. Without faith we cannot please God because without faith we do not do as he commands, and in not doing what he commands, well, how will we please him? This is why we have ignored and left the will of God, the commandments he gave us through his son, because we have no faith. We are an incredulous people and we do not obey. We pretend to have faith, but only in those things we want, such as when we are sick. Then we do want to believe. But God cannot be fooled. God knows well that this generation does not love him.

This present generation does not care for the poor, widows, for the oppressed. It has no faith to shelter the oppressed, has no faith to love its brother, much less to love its enemies. It has no faith to visit the needy, no faith to stop the evil eye from focusing on his peer's wife. These people have no faith to keep their hearts from evil thoughts, have no faith to obey any of the commandments of God in Christ. Yet, when they are bedridden, or when they are dying, they quickly do what the people of Israel did in ancient times. Quickly they cry out to God and quickly ask to pray for him. And the men Christ prophesized would do many miracles in his name deceive these rebellious and evil people, telling them that they must only believe that they can be healthy, and they will be.

The promises that were given to God's humble and obedient people, they confiscate for themselves, as if they were not very rebellious, as if they were fundamental to their will.

The hypocrisy of these people has appeared all over the world, far away from the truth. There is no nation that it has not corrupted with its lies. They have taken women's glory and shame. They have taught their children how to rebel against their parents. What good have they done in the world? All the miracles that in the last days will occur, will occur in the name of Christ. It is easy to know that the workers of these last days are the children of error because they are taking great advantage of the word of God and deceive many.

Do these men live the life of Christ? Do they have humility in their lives? Do they love the needy? Do they care for and teach people to do good deeds? No. The benefits they receive for themselves. They started off well, as many do, but the devil soon puts them under his feet. Soon the devil made them bend their knee to mammon. Soon it darkened their eyes. Let us pray, all you just ones and children, I beg you to pray to God for his love, for love to this poor generation. Send them a few men who are not salaried, a few to teach the path to God without reservation or hiding place as men now do without a fear of God.

God seeks men who abhor the darkness, men who do not love gifts or presents. Men who understand the times and denounce the sin found in the church.

It is no longer appropriate to be satisfied with ceremonies, with feigned cries and tears, with all the pagan traditions with which we have resisted the Spirit of God. When the Spirit of God is absent in a people, they do not have love for their peers, do not do what is right or show justice. This is the reason why this generation does not have justice or even love of God. Sons without faith are those who adore God these days. They all speak much, all say much. In the temples they talk a lot, in the temples they sing a lot, in the temples they profess to love God, but on the street, in their home, in the world, they are children without faith. They are rebellious children.

Oh, for these bad people. Who will liberate them from the ire that approaches? Who will intercede for them? All will be surprised when God's holy judgments appear. It should come as no surprise that the world is corrupted and grows in evil. What is surprising is that a people, like the ones who now call themselves Christians, who, having known the path of justice, which is Christ, turn to violence, evil, to all sorts of filthy deeds in secrecy. Oh, for these people. Great will be the judgments against them. And who will liberate them in that hour?

In what will God praise us? For what does he thank us? Have we obeyed his holy words so that he might be pleased with us? Instead, we have bartered his saintly glory, we have given him less honor than to a man. All fear man more than God and believe man more than God.

The false man, the deceitful prophet says that there is peace and security for Christians, but this is a lie. In these words, there is no truth. God is unhappy and angry with those who pretend to act in his name because in nothing do they obey him. They have neglected all he commanded of them.

Our violence has provoked nations against each other because pure love was missing, justice on earth was missing. We abandoned the prince of peace and all of us have become divided, one against the other, even among family members. But the worst is that we are divided, not because of love or for a cause of justice and law, but for caprices and strong opinions.

This has dishonored the word of God and, because of this, law and justice have ceased on earth. Let us leave the great Babylon. Those who fear God, do well, humble your souls, do not gossip, do not judge anyone for we are in horrible days, ones in which all of us have failed and offended God. Do not condemn or display prejudice. Forgive and love with all your heart. Let us return to the ancient laws, to the ancient fear of God, to the ancient forgiveness, to the ancient love, to the ancient justice, to the ancient mercy, to the ancient meekness. Let us do good toward those people Christ sent us and implored us saying: "When you prepare a dinner or banquet, do not invite your brothers, or your wealthy neighbors, or your friends, because they will return the favor and you will have nothing on that day. When you prepare banquet or dinner invite the poor, the blind, the maimed, the needy because these do not have anything to reward you with, but you will be rewarded in the resurrection of the just." Let us lift up the fallen paths and walk standing straight. It is time to turn to God who gave us his beloved Son.

Why do you place your eyes on what will be destroyed by the ire of God? Why waste our strength on riches that do not last? Let us not waste our time. Let us not deceive our poor souls. It is time to restore what has been harmed. It is time to free the oppressed, giving him what we love, serving him as we ourselves like to be served.

It is time to do the will of God with care. It is time to ignore the world with all its beautiful and vain offerings. It is time to disdain the things that have deceived us. Why throw our money and waste our strength and time only to revel in the world and those who like pomp? Were we not created to walk in humility in all our things and deeds? Why go dressed, with foods and homes like the citizens of the great Babylon? Each of you, close your eyes to the things that your neighbor owns. Do not covet them anymore. If your brother pursues pomp and luxury, let him. Why imitate the arrogant? Why imitate the vain? Imitate, instead, the humble and the meek. Why seek arrogant and frivolous company? Instead, why not seek the company of those who have suffered and been disdained, of humble and God-fearing company?

The just by his faith and justice shall live. Who will lift a hand against him? Yet these words are to a false people, a lying people, people that have left life in favor of death. Blessed be the one who receives these words with fear and humility. Blessed by God are all who are not scandalized in these words.

Sons and daughters of Babylon: why do you not obey your legitimate father? Leave the one you now call mother, because she is not your mother. By living with her you have learned every way of spreading lies and deceit. By living with her you have learned how not to have mercy because she is a woman who is hard and evil-hearted. She does not pity anyone because she spends time adorning her house and seeking valuable things to display before her lovers.

She has no mercy for the orphan or for the oppressed, but instead she robs everyone she can to celebrate her festivities with pomp and luxury. In these days all have become drunk with her hardened heart and because of this we can no longer find just people on earth. This evil woman has banished every just person who clamors for justice. Egoism, arrogance, envy, ire, and all sorts of lies are the virtues of this evil woman who has deceived the entire world. This is why our own children rise up against us, why daughters are raped by so-called Christians, why our wives are desired by all, because we have dressed them with the adornments of greed, given them to the lascivious eye. Is this not so? This is what we have learned from the great whore. Parents lost interest in instructing their children about the holy paths. I place as my witness the very word of God. I do not lie. I speak words of truth, words that are not invoked to undertake commercial transactions or to sell them. They are uttered so that the just can exit this apostate church, not in opinion, but in actions.

These are words that help man emerge from avarice, from arrogance, from envy, and from all egoism. Words that are sold carry no mercy. Words sold for money serve no good purpose. A man who buys words usually sells them later on, but the man who is given words, he will also give them. I have not purchased these words, and thus I do not sell them either. Some might say, what is given has no value, but what is purchased does. Always understand that these purchased words are those of false merchants, blunt men, disciples of the great whore. All you just ones, beware of the merchants, citizens of the great whore. Do well by starting in your home.

40. The Scorned Works

Christ came to do good for humanity. He came to teach love, not only in words but in deeds and in Spirit. He came to teach us what "Mercy" is and to make manifest the judgment and justice of God's kingdom. For this reason, for this reason alone, the Lord gave us commandments, underscoring for us all words and works of love and mercy (Eph. 2:10).

The Apostle Paul was referring to this when he said: "We are truly his handiwork, created in Christ Jesus to lead the life of good deeds which God prepared for us in advance."

It is very true that no one is saved by acts and our good works will never erase our bad deeds of the past. But for this reason, we were saved, and by the Blood of Christ we were reconciled, to walk along the paths and works the Father has prepared for us to walk. Christ, the Son of God, partook in these holy works. He lived by the paths that the father marked out for him, and in nothing did he offended God. Why do we not walk along the same paths? He who says that he was saved by grace and does not walk in the paths God marked, it is because it has not yet dawned on him. He is still in the darkness. Maybe he will attain salvation, but not the one God offers. Perhaps this person has received the salvation men offer, but not that of God.

In these last days, all excuse themselves. So as not to walk in the paths of God, they say that good works do not save. Who says that the good works save? No one has said such a thing. Instead, good works are fruit of those who really are saved. He who thinks he loves in these days, look at Christ's love and at the way Christ loved the world. Be ashamed, confused, because love is the cheapest thing one finds these days. He who says he loves and has no mercy for orphans, widows, foreigners, and all the needy and afflicted is a liar. There is no truth in him. He deceives his poor soul. He who says he loves and does not live in peace with his relatives, he is a liar. Who is the person who lives in peace with his parents or with his relatives? For this reason, the end of the world and of all rebels is inevitable. We have corrupted the entire earth, we have forsaken God's holy commandments, and instead we have obeyed the commandments of men who have no understanding of the living God. All these men who have given us the commandments we now have, are men who love worldly things and do not speak truth. Instead, they lie to each other like faithless children. Everyone says, "By grace we are saved and not by actions so that no one will glory in themselves." Late in understanding the truth, the same one who said these words, did he not also urge us to "clothe yourselves with heartfelt mercy, with kindness, humility, meekness, and patience" (Col. 3:12)?

Was the blood of Christ not spilled to form a people zealous for good works? Where then are these people zealous for good works? Did the apostle Paul himself not tell Titus: "In everything show yourself as example of good deeds"? Why then do all avoid good deeds? Each seeks his own benefit, and all have neglected the love of Christ which benefits one's peer, whatever love, for divisions. What people have been as divided as this generation, professing and complaining of the same Christ? If everyone shared the same love of Christ, not as many groups and people would be divided. Instead, as we are urged, all would be one, forming one single body. Thus, we must be moved and taught by one single Spirit. What is happening these days? All are teachers, all are cluttered instructors who have twisted the law of God. First, care for those who are weak and thin, and then for the strong and old. The law of God first looks after widows, after the earth's poor, and then after the children of God. We have all irritated God by becoming enemies of the "Cross." Who fights in defense of Christ's commandments? Everyone forms his own caprices and establishes his convictions in historical words, but these do not contain the holy commandment of God spoken by Christ himself. Does the very apostle of Christ not say, "Put to death whaever in your nature is rooted in earth:

fornication, uncleanliness, passion, evil desires, and that lust which is idolatry. These are the sins that provoke God's wrath" (Col. 3:5–6) Let us look, then, for the things that have led us to fall from true grace. Everyone is worried about the things of life. This led us to gluttony, and to works of filth and concupiscence. We are called a dead people and one without faith because of this, because we do not have works. We say we are rich and that we do not need anyone's advice, but we do not know that we are blind and naked when it comes to God's justice and mercy. In the Book of Revelation God speaks to the seven churches of Asia, which represent a single church in a continuous process. He speaks to these seven churches, he says, "I know your works." And to them he also says, "Whom shall I vanquish?" And to the seven he says, "He who has ears to hear, listen." All this means that, first of all, he judges us and weighs us, condemns or justifies us, by our own works. Second, the condition he announces to all is, "whom I shall vanquish"; that is, he who vanquishes the world, who vanquishes true Egoism, who vanquishes the true old man, who vanquishes envy, arrogance, sin. Can someone vanquish the world without keeping God's commandments? Can someone vanquish the world with all the concupiscence of life without walking in the love of God that is Christ himself? Finally, "He who has ears to hear, hear." In other words, the commandment of God and his paths are for all those who have ears. Only the one who has no ears can be excused for not keeping the will of God that is formed of all his holy commandments his son gave us.

Oh, for the children of light, for they will be surprised. Oh, for those who expect blessing, because a great and awful curse will come to you. Oh, for those who have the law in your hands because by the same law you shall be uprooted. The law and the doctrine of the spirit lost their value in the hearts of men because of those who did not want to suffer. The arrogant snatched up the law and ground up the flesh of the just. The evil ones are many, but if anyone who is salaried fears God and loves justice, do not rise up against this word lest he be seized by the fire of God's ire. All who fear God, suffer these words and turn to God. I advise those who await the return of the son of God, to humble their souls, and elevate the law. Do not trust in the words of men who do not fear God or keep his commandments. Instead, each of you trust God, and with fear and trembling, obey God in all his holy commandments that he conveyed through his holy son, Jesus. Each of you be merciful, speak truth with few words, avert your eyes from vanity, humble your heart to the justice of God, each delight in the laws of God. In the midst of this evil generation, let us imitate Christ. Reconcile our souls with God our creator before he exposes his arm of vengeance, from which no one will be free. And you, oh, heads and leaders, speak of the law of God without any reservations. Do not fool the humble of the earth any longer. Work for law and justice and not for salary. Await God for he gives us a better salary. Give an example to those who want life and do not seek feasting attire. Those who dress in fine clothes are presumed in the homes of kings. It is not for you to dress in costly clothes, or to walk like lit torches along the paths. Because of this behavior, greed, humility, and meekness are in short supply on earth. Learn from Nineveh, who repented with great fear and turned to God. Do not be hard on the nape of your neck or resist God's correction. Why receive the same salary as the Pharisees? Why will we perish like Sodom and Gomorrah? Is there no way to escape? God has lain out a path, let us walk along it. The skies and the earth, which have always testified against rebels, will be witnesses once again, that I have spoken to you and have denounced you, your great evil and rebelliousness. Christ spoke of these times, but why not escape them? So that the prophecy not be fulfilled among us, let us escape the ire of God. What does God ask of us? Only that we not seek our own benefit and that we do judgment and justice. Is mercy a burdensome thing? These are the things God asks of us. Why resist? The world has deceived us, and we have employed all our money in vanity. Large houses are what we covet, new and costly cars, meals of kings and clothes of princes, thus taking our sight off of Christ's cross. Because of these things we have erred. Let us return to the old paths. Let us open our eyes to the light of God and loan our ears to his commandments. Each of you plot a way forward in fear of God and not gossip against anyone. We all share the same situation, all of us have irritated God because we have not acted according to his holy will. No one wants to be considered unimportant, each loves to be the first, esteemed by all. Great is the evil we have done on earth, and because of our fault we lost our flavor as salt of the earth. The evil one multiplied on earth and evil increased.

How will we respond to God? What argument will we use? We are evil and courtesy is the only thing we still have. But courtesy does not nourish the widow, nor does the orphan receive any good from courtesy. Let us strip this cloak of hypocrisy and dress in clothes of justice. Oh, deceivers. When will you finally distinguish truth from lies? When will you finally receive healthy correction? I am ignorant about many things, but the great rebelliousness of the church has made me speak. I fear all of you, and in my heart there is fear because of your arrogance. But who, on seeing what my eyes see, would be able to stop speaking? You may try to empty the blood from my veins, but your rebelliousness shall remain. The fire comes for you.

---

41. The Fallen

What is conquered with the sword, with the sword must be cared for and protected; what is conquered with love, with love must be cared for and protected. What is conquered with the sword, cannot be protected [only] with the sword.

If the love of Christ brought us to God, it is necessary that we stay in the love of God. If by human means and ceremonies they brought us to Christ, with these same things they may keep us, but not in God, only in the love of men. Every heart moved by the Spirit of God, every heart moved by Christ's Gospel, this heart does not rebel against the laws of the Holy Spirit. But everyone who was persuaded by human forces and human interests, these are not much interested, or even at all, in the will of God while he is carrying out men's will. The born-again person who has been reborn according to God, this person delights in the things that belong to the kingdom of God. For this child of God, service and love are not tedious things because the love of God is perfectly in him. Brothers, it is necessary not to mock the virtues of the Holy Spirit, which will guide us to all justice and all truth if we give it a chance by humbling ourselves. The devil's evils and the forces of darkness become stronger each day. We must give God a place from which to govern our souls, even if it is difficult to pass near places like "Gethsemane," for by this God is glorified. If God was glorified when his son endured these bitter hours, will we not also be glorified when we suffer these ourselves? Let us humble our souls so that God will be served and glorified in the tabernacle of his Spirit, which is our mortal body. With all our heart, then, let us lift up the love of God, the humility of the spirit, the meekness of the soul, which are fallen. God is with those who in their heart want to do what is right before his eyes. Do not feel ashamed of doing good for the souls of those who do not feel shamed by the example Christ left us, and who are not ashamed of obeying his holy commandments. Why be ashamed of the holy commandments that Christ gave us by the same Spirit? Did the apostles ignore the commandments of Christ and of the Holy Spirit? Did Paul not love his enemies as Christ commanded his followers? Did Paul not suffer together with the prophets who went before him? It is important that we ignore the forces of the world and the human methods the devil offers us. He who trusts the hand of man reaches a curse, and sooner or later will fall, and will discover that he is powerless against evil thoughts, against envy, against arrogance, against the lies of lips, against the crazy and vain passions. In these days we know that the whole world goes after the works and marvels that man has made with his own hands and God's marvels are ignored. Is this not something worrisome to the eyes of God? This is a hard thing, and great is the evil that we the people of God have done. God wants us to return to the first works and to give him honor with our lives, humbling our souls to the God and father of our spirits. Brothers and dear companions in pilgrimage, why not sacrifice what we have left for the things and riches of the soul? The man that God formed is a marvel and a miracle. God gave us a heart to be able to understand and strength to be able to decide. Why use these strengths and this heart to gain the earthly things our flesh seeks? Do these things not end? Where is what our parents possessed? And what we possessed in the past, where is it? Everything passed. Yes, everything passed. Could we not fill these hearts, which God has given us, with celestial riches? Then, let us dress our souls and our lives with the love of God and with the humility of Christ to be able to serve our God. Love is not seen in words or chants, love is seen in works of justice. Love is seen and felt. Love is not heard. Why speak love? If we possess it, the brother, the widow, and the orphan will give testimony of it and God will also be found in our petitions. For he has said: "Blessed are the merciful. Because they will reach mercy." And he also says through the same Spirit: "Judgment without mercy will be done with he who does not use mercy." Brothers, beloved ones, and God's desired, let us realize that this is not the time to spend our last days in the works and traditions of men. God is against men's traditions because due to them they stray from God's true path and cease to fear because they forget His Holy Commandments in which man finds nothing but good. Have we by chance found fault in the commandments that Christ left us? The commandments of Christ, are they not for the sons of God, as Christ was? Did he not also fulfill them with all fear and reverence? Leaving behind all malice and bitterness born of competition, let us serve God, obeying his holy word, which as all his saints have said, as well as his holy son, that this his Holy Word will make us wise and saved. Let us not mock the word of God with our conduct because Christ told us that by this very word we would be judged. Christ came to save us, not only from the vices that men have invented now; he came to save us from things that are as old as the very devil, such as envy and arrogance. We must flee from these things. In these days many are taught to flee from vices, but not much else. Christ wants to free us with his truth: from lies, from ire. These are the things that destroy entire nations. These things are what wage battle within our flesh. Let us raise our hearts in search of this liberty, a complete liberty. In the Salvation men offer each other these days, one cannot find the good that God wants from his children. Because they manage to extract tithes from the people, only they find salvation. This is not wrong, but they have stopped offering a salvation through which not only they but also the widow, the orphan, and God would reach goodness in truth. God hears all who cry for real Salvation, like the one the holy apostles preached and offered to souls that were hungry for the justice of God. But now it cannot be offered by a man who does not know it himself. Who offers what he does not have? Only the devil because he was a liar from the beginning. Brothers, I beg you on these last days, I tell you with fear in my heart that you must embrace the salvation that the son of God has brought us. I know that many are already content with what you have, but this does not mean you are happy. There are many hearts that are not happy with what they have. If they obey him, these few who are not happy will be satiated by God's love.

Christ himself told us: "Whoever has my commandments and keeps them, he is the one who loves me, and whoever loves me will be loved by my Father, and I will love him and will manifest in him." In these days, what a great disgrace and what a great evil it is that people do not possess or understand Christ's commandments, not even from memory, much less in their lives. This is a great evil. What can we expect after we have left the holy commandment of the holy God? This is why the world is full of ire and confusion, and of division, which was begun by the so-called Christians. The Jews were far from God when Christ appeared for the first time, but they were not as divided as we are. Why? Is this a coincidence? Does the very word of God not say that because of the rebelliousness on earth, princes multiply? Many leaders are made by this very sin. The Jews were not called children of God, they were only called the children of Abraham. But in these days, all of us who pass as Christians are called children of God. This is more significant than calling ourselves children of Abraham as the Jews did. But was this worth anything for them when they stood before Christ? Did Christ not call them children of the devil whom the devil had converted with human traditions? Let us look, then, to see on what our souls are dependent these days. There is not much time to go around giving our souls up. Oh, for those who know that God's commandments are for God's children and do not embrace them or live in fear. I remind you, brothers, that you remember the advice that Christ gave us when he said, "Learn from me, for I am meek and humble of heart." The greatest evil in our way to understanding our poor standing and seeing our own evil, is what Christ tells us when he said, "You say, I am rich, and have no need of anything; but you do not know that you are blind, and naked, and poor."

The Holy Spirit says that we do not know we are blind. This is the same evil that existed among the Pharisees. The Pharisees did not know they were blind either. The spirit says that we believe that we are rich in our relationship to God. This is what we believe. Throughout the world everyone believes that this relationship is good. That is because everyone has the name of God in their mouths, and no one admits the need for correction. God corrects the one who accepts correction and does not correct rebels until the final time when he will snare all the arrogant ones into the fire of his ire. My brothers, let us accept God's correction. Is it not true that we are full of avarice, of arrogance, of ire, of vengeance, of malice, of dirty thoughts, of lies in our lips? Is this not so? Will we still deny it? We see that the evil that we have brought upon ourselves is near, yet we do not want to admit it. Why, my brothers? Let us not trust in the hand of man nor in our own heart. Because our heart will deny us if we trust it. If God tells us we are far from him and that we are blind and naked and poor, will we believe this? Will we still continue to trust in our own lying heart? No. Let us forsake this false confidence. Let us search for God with tears and fasts. Why deny our poor souls? Everyone sacrifices for their own self interests. Everyone daring undertakes acts of great dangers for earthly things. Why not sacrifice in the same way for our souls, for the well-being of eternal life? Our children follow in our footsteps and accordingly become inebriated by the same advice we have grasped from the world. Why throw our children off such a lugubrious precipice, to a twilight as uncertain as the false Christianity that currently exists? Which God will throw to his left.

42. The Prudent Will Understand

I advise the small of the earth, those who believe that they need advice, for I know that to the greats of the earth I cannot give advice. Not even Christ himself could advise them. I cannot advise those who govern the world and those who care over souls. I have nothing good for them. But to the weak of the earth, to those who fear God, I do want to offer advice because they know the voice of the good shepherd. They know when it is word of God, and on hearing it, they obey it, because they fear God. And they are ready to do all that the almighty commands. Let us believe as the scriptures say and listen to what the Holy Spirit advises: "that we do not know more than what is written." Let us care for the poor before Christ comes and finds us in the evil he warned us about. Let us struggle to be found doing the things he commanded us to occupy ourselves in. Let us feed the needy without searching for advantages and our own self-interest. It is no longer time to decide who we should help. Let us throw ire out of our home, throw vengeance out too. Do not let bad thoughts and lying mouths reign in our homes. Expel all that God abominates and in turn the peace of God will come to reside in our home, and in it we will find the perfect love of Jesus Christ.

The malice we have ignored so long has made a home for itself in our hearts. Let us open the door of our heart and throw it out forever. It does no good in the temple of the Holy Spirit, which is our body and through which God is glorified.

I advise those who fear God and those lacking advice that God is with all the humble of heart and grants grace to those who have compassion for the poor. God sees that we no longer delight in aiding the needy. This is a great evil in the eyes of the just Judge of all the earth, who does good toward all. He wants all men to be saved and to have green pastures, food for their little ones, which he gives them himself. I beg you my brothers, let us see this and fear God. Let us see what great love Christ brought to the world. Let us embrace this love; dress ourselves with Christ's love, and take off our clothing of evil, of envy, of ire, of bitterness, of self-importance. I am certain that God does not dismiss those who make an effort to find God's justice because Christ himself said: "First look for the kingdom of God and his justice." We already have the justice of men, but what good has it done to us? We have learned to look after our own good and ignore the needs of our peers, whom Christ taught us to love as ourselves. All the energy we are using to search the whole world for the things and comforts of life are efforts thrown to the wind, for all this is vanity of vanities. Let us do good for everyone and employ all our energy and understanding for the things of heaven. The obedient of heart shall inherit God's abodes, but the rebels who ignored God's advice will have no right to these homes prepared for the obedient of heart, for those who loved their brothers more than their own souls. These are the ones who will be first on that day. Let us not allow God's word to remain where men have left it. All you humble of the earth, together let us elevate the word of God in our own lives. This will please God, as the life of his son, in whom He found contentment, pleased him. Let us tear out our haughty eyes, our lying lips, the arrogance in our heart, and let us not trust in lies, calling ourselves what we are not. God will send our souls help by humbling ourselves through tears and fasts. He will comfort our spirit through his Holy Spirit. Let us be courageous and fear not the injuries of the arrogant. Our Lord and all the prophets who loved the kingdom that will come also suffered because of justice. Always the humble are mocked. Fear not. The one who loved us and gave himself for us suffered more. Forward, then, ignoring what can be seen, not feeling intimidated by the devil's threats, who himself has no way to enter the kingdom of our God. Let us love the gift of God and the coming life. Let's not dismiss God's advice, which is in the word of God; this advice the arrogant have forgotten and only learned God's promises. These do not belong to them, but to the meek of the earth. The devil has dulled the senses of those who love material things and has given them scriptures that to him seem appropriate to deny all those who feel the earthly.

Let us ignore those who speak to us, but instead fear God's word. God lives in the one who fears his holy word. Thus, we should not fear obedience to the holy commandments and not resist the spirit that wants to guide us to all of God's truth and toward all justice.

43. Words to the Last Generation

Why try to cover up and hide the evil that exists? There is nothing to cover it with. The daughter is against her mother, the mother against her daughter. The son is against his father and the father against his son. The daughter-in-law and her mother-in-law cannot live in peace for three days. Shepherds and their sheep do not love each other with God's love. Why try to cover up all this evil when the world itself is not distinguished from the ones who today call themselves Christians? The church is a big wound. What can we talk about so as not to offend it? It does not appreciate correction. It does not love the Creator's punishment. With what will we cure it so that we do not hurt it? The wounds of Jesus Christ, which cure if we invest ourselves in them, are not wanted by them. They prefer to suffer for their own caprices and for their cravings of earthly delight. They pay even with their life. Like a child, it is corrupted with too many toys. The time it should use doing the will of his parents, it spends playing. This is the church. It spends time that it should use to follow the will of God and spends it instead on the things that only deceive and robs the time one needs to gain eternal life. What machine, what invention, what toy, what vanity does not entertain and rob the time from so-called Christians? They love everything except justice. They covet everything, except humility. They sacrifice for everything and even to the point of sickness, except for the Cross of Christ. Rise up and testify against these words. Who will be able to condemn these words? Do I by any chance see better than my God? Am I more scrupulous than my God? If, with a small portion of his Spirit that was deposited in me, I can look out and am able to see so many things, such as the bitterness of violence that not even I would live with, how much more my God, who is holy. He cannot tolerate the hypocrite or find the guilty innocent. The eyes of this generation do not tire of seeing. The eye of each is placed on the neighbor's wife. The mouth of this generation speaks of everything, except of love and mercy. It does not speak of these things because they abominate them and can live their lives without needing these things. When the great day of ire comes, all will seek God's mercy, but will not find it because they themselves once mocked it, when it was opportune and unique. Brothers, to all who fear the name of God, I speak in the love of God. For your own good come out of the deceits of darkness. Why waste that good time God has blessed us with? Why place the heart in things that will pass in the ire of God? If the things in which God's people are spending their soul and their money were worth it, God would not burn them. Why aggrandize our name and dress our life with things that even Solomon abominated? Why not get pure gold from God and solid wisdom from above? It is time to discard our bread to the waters, for soon we will find it in a good time and place. It is time that we rightfully be called crazy. But who is that who in these days does not flee mockery and the scoffing of the blind and clumsy?

These are times of error, of mocking, of vanity, of greed, of craziness. Everyone wants the best and yet possesses the worst that has been registered in history. Those who claim the Spirit of God, abhor all that is of God's spirit. Why is this? Everything is easily found except charity, the delight of the Spirit, the peace of Christ which is because of the same Spirit, tolerance, goodness, kindness, faith, meekness, and temperance. Is it by chance that these things are not found among the people of God? Should this not be our vestment? Will we find these things in this world? If on the world they do not exist, well where will we seek them? Or is it not time to produce such thing? Is it that we have the spirit of God? Is God to blame that we do not have these things? Or, better yet, are we not the ones who should be blamed? The reason is that the world has robbed our soul, and our heart has been filled with all sorts of carnal craving, and envy and greed for the things that are worth a lot of money. We do not covet the things that are of the spirit, which are free. The earth has corrupted exactly as Christ said it would. Blessed is the one who believes what Christ said. All seek money and many are using God's word to earn their bread and purchase vanities simply to live more comfortably. Never in history has the word of God been so profitable to the men who use it to earn their bread. This is why the word of God has lost its value in the hands of the impious, and the small are left without shelter, since the word of God is the only one that relieves and nourishes them. Who do we see imitating the humility and meekness of Christ, as he instructed, urging us to pursue the things he loved? When did Christ speak saying that the people of the last days would be well in love and in FAITH? Why then do men teach and tell the people that eternal peace will come to them? When in fact, what will surprise them will be darkness and confusion from here in a few days. I know these words hurt. They wound the hearts of many who lead the people. Where, then, is humility? Where are patience and meekness? Should the people of God not have to suffer these words in order to heal? If someone becomes angry, you would do well to be ashamed. I do not speak of the property of anyone in particular. If I speak ill, I speak against God, because he is in the owner, and not those who lead the people. I am not mocking anyone's dress, nor the house or car. Why then do you become angry? The dress, the house, the car, is your importance, but of that I do not speak. Instead, I speak of the things of God. What has been forgotten.

Against whom are these words directed? The spirit of God is not against those who love Justice, nor against the one who forgives his brother, nor against the one who does good toward his peer, the poor, the needy, the orphan. This word is not against the meek of the earth, nor against the humble of heart. Against whom are these words addressed? Are they addressed against a movement? Against an organization or sect? Far from it. God is irritated against those who irritate him, against those who break his laws, against those who support evil among those who act evilly. Is arrogance not upon the entire earth? Does egoism not swell the hearts of believers these days? Is the heart of man not full of malice these days? Does this occur only in a movement or a religious organization? No. Greed has the world in flames of antagonism and hatred. Because of this same spirit of error, the people are divided. Who has love? Who shows mercy on those who perish?

Approach God and he will teach you justice and truth. Malice in our heart, and egoism and arrogance have distanced us from God. With these words I speak against those who abhor, against those who do understand people, against those who do not forgive, against those who gossip, against those who do not obey their parents. Is it a coincidence that God is irritated with the living? Is God unjust because he intends to destroy the earth with its rebels? Are drunkards the ones who have irritated God? Are the nonconverts the ones who have made God angry? Who then has irritated God? The rebels of the earth. Those who have discarded their commandments on the ground. Let us understand that we have discarded the law of the Creator. We have strayed from the path of the one who made the sun, the earth, and everything that breathes. Who has spread love, the fear of God? Who is the one who upon seeing justice on earth can approach the light of God?

For us who have known the name of Christ and the love of God, it is convenient to stop the law of God. But because of us his law fell to the ground and later evil multiplied, entering even the hearts of the small. For this God will hold us culpable.

We are prisoners, guilty of great crimes because having been taught by the son of God, we turned away from the paths of life, and as a result, nothing came to us when evil entered the church.

These days the wise of heart places his hand over his mouth. The one who fears God covers his ears because of so much evil that one hears. The humble of heart close their eyes because of the powerful evil in the deeds of men. But, what about this generation? Do they close their eyes and ears to evil? Do they cover their mouths? No. Instead the eyes of this present generation even are wide open to evil. Their mouth speaks the abominable thoughts that their hearts think. Evil they call good and good they abhor. Who delights in doing good works? Who finds delight in using mercy? For this very reason the word of God lost its value in the heart of man. Carrying out God's will was Christ's very nourishment. But now all mock the will of God, which is for our own good. All flee from the cross of Christ. Because of this the heart of this generation has been darkened and turned to stone, and no one has compassion for the afflicted. Everyone feeds themselves of the world. Each sees and covets what God abhors. He abhors and abominates the covetous eye. God cannot stand the heart that schemes evil thoughts. Why are all the people in material debt? Have we become indebted because of the widow? Because of the poor, the afflicted, or because of mercy? No. Instead, we are indebted because of our cravings. It is greed, the world, and arrogance that have made us fall into such great debts. Does history not itself speak? Before us, was there a generation as indebted as this one? Are our debts due to the great necessity and poverty on earth? No. Instead, by going after the world and the rich, by not being less than our enemy, whom we call brother, that is why we are in debt. Because of this we kill ourselves. For this reason, we have forgotten love and mercy.

This generation in nothing imitate Christ. All want to possess the things "Simon the magician" has. Let us not deceive our souls any longer. Let us not trust our heart. Turn to God. Why leave the advice of God? Why crush wisdom? Why resist the spirit? Let us abhor prejudice and cease gossip. We are all equal before God because we have all absorbed justice and mercy, a faith that is not feigned, and a fear of God. Let us not make obscene hand gestures. Is not the end near? Oh, blind and clumsy people! Do you not see that your days have become shorter? Gather your fingers, close your mouth, close your eyes and ears to evil. Do you not see that the end is near for you? Did Christ the king not say: "By your words you will be acquitted, and by your words you will be condemned" (Matt. 12:37)?

For the little love of God that remains in your hearts, I beg you to close your mouths. Why increase the condemnation? Let us humble our souls and loan our ears to the ancient advice by which our forefathers were saved. Let us not help propagate the vanities of the world, buying and selling all that forms pride in our hearts. Do you not know that all these vain things have made our souls stumble? Our hearts do not retain God's gifts because we have allowed that which God abominates to enter.

Why then call Christ LORD, if we do not obey him? These words will be used against us on judgment day.

44. Descendants of the Pharisees

We have nurtured sin on earth with our ignorance, with our arrogance, with our jealousy for possessing and buying, we have hastened evil. Seeing the time mature and opportune, the devil gave us democracy in which we do as we please, and in which the hunger to possess was born and developed further. With democracy more jobs opened up, there was more money, more expenses, more ambition, more food, and all craved to improve their earthly lives. The belly grew and became more ample. Inventors, on seeing people hungry for vain things, hungry for curiosities, took to inventing. This is why everyone praises democracy. They praise it not because there is more justice among people, but because there is more gluttony. People do not become more merciful by being under a democratic president. Instead, the more there is the more the hearts of those who call themselves the children of God close up. And now that they are a people protected by such a great and strong nation as "the United States," this is why the church is confident that no one can scare it. This is a bad thing. Because of this, people do not seek their God because they are equipped with everything that is necessary, even if they do not have God's love or know God's judgment. Nothing worries them. To tear down the arrogance of the church, God will punish this nation. When did we previously see the mistrust that now exists? When did a woman speak of her husband as she now speaks? When in history had mankind loved earthly gold as it does in these days? The so-called Christians walk along roads lit like torches, walking along these paths at great speed as if someone is dying in their homes. But when they get home, they lie on their beds. The sons of darkness have nothing to learn from the children of light. On the contrary, the children of light follow after the children of darkness. Christians who do not believe in killing and in war are working for the government, occupied in making atomic bombs, and airplanes with which to drop the bombs. Christians are working for the government intent on earning the money they need to buy their new cars and improve their earthly homes, despite the fact that they are hastening war and God's ire. But about this Christians are not worried. What a child of God sees in these latter days is a difficult thing. In truth only the very brave and the truly wise of heart can escape from the final great and mortal deceits.

I do not speak here to the children of the shadows who are sinners or nonconverts. I speak instead to the ones who pretend to be Christians. These are days for humbling the soul. Days for renouncing the things that have so long deceived us before the ire of God arrives. Why wait like Lot? Brothers, let us return to our father who formed us. Ask for forgiveness. Let us be wise of heart and walk in the ancient paths. Why be ashamed of those paths? All the prophets walked along those holy paths. Why trust in the deeds of men, which God never asked of us? The confidence of this generation is in chants and ceremonies that God never demanded. He ordered Justice from us and said, "If your justice were not greater than the justice of the scribes and Pharisees, you will not enter the kingdom of Heaven." They also sang, they also prayed, they also fasted, they also paid their tithe, but all of this was worthless when Christ came. How will we get out? I have one thing that marvels my eyes, and it is that in those days the women and children had more shame. In those days there was more devotion toward the things of God. In those days more alms were given, with or without fanfare. But now not even with fanfare, much less without are alms given. The writing of these days is in vain. People do not believe what they read nor do those who speak it obey it. From what were we cleansed by the blood of Christ? Which sins did the forgiveness of God free us from? Does envy, arrogance, injustice, and all evil thought continue in us. Will God be pleased by a people without the fruit of justice?

Not even the pagan people believed in leaving the widow and the orphan without shelter. Even the beasts in the field are more easily moved to display mercy than the present generation. I speak to the people who have known the law of their God. I speak to those who say that they have been cleansed by the blood of Jesus Christ. God placed me here to mock. Who will be able to remove me from this seat? My flesh trembles somewhat at the thought of the people to whom I speak because I know that they do not understand the reason of God. I am not innocent. I know what will come of this because the enemies of the cross are stronger than ever. I do not ignore what these words will bring upon me, for it will not be from drunkards or from the thieves of this world, but of the so-called Christians. But soon my witness will come who will shed light on what I now speak in words. Leaders and elders, why not lend your ear? Are the humble of heart not greatest in the presence of God? Did David not humble himself? Did Solomon not humble himself? Or are your heads wiser than King Josiah's, and other saintly men of God who humbled themselves with all their heart? Did God not lift the heads of these men because they humbled themselves? Let us return to the voice of justice. What is our present justice? Where are our good works so that men will glorify God? Not even the blind testify in our favor. Let us suffer this word and seek shelter before it is too late. Is it not God who comes with great destruction? Well, why has God become irritated? Have the drunkards irritated God? Is it not his people who call themselves by his holy name? We are not carrying out the works of our God. Did Christ speak against John the Baptist simply because John did not walk with him? Or did John speak against Christ? Did Paul not speak against divisions? Did the prophets not speak of the justice Christ would bring? Has God contradicted himself at any time? God has always tried to unite his children and has tried to establish good will among them. Because of this he gave his beloved son so that people would learn from his son how to live in communion with each other. God never has wanted humanity, which come from a single blood, to live in disputes, debates, and disagreements, which eventually grow into divisions of word, later divisions of spirit, and later become great wars between equals. Why, then, do the children of God who have known his holy word, not see this? Why do they not love each other or help each other? Is this not the result of arrogance? Is it not that arrogance is the result of abandoning humility and meekness of Christ? Let us return to Christ and learn from him. Let us not deceive ourselves anymore. Let us speak the truth. So-called Christian homes are full of hate, fights, and envy. The son lends money to his father, the daughter to her mother, but no one gives money to their father or mother. No one does good. And if by chance someone among the people does good, others mock and insult him. Because of this the earth is against its inhabitants and does not stand its stinky winds.

Everywhere the earth resists the farmer and denies him blessing, but not even because of this does the inhabitant open his eyes or return to his senses. How can God speak with the inhabitant of the earth? If he sends them punishment, they attribute it to the devil. If the devil gives them riches, like the ones he offered Christ on the mount of temptation, then they attribute these to God. In this way these people do not allow the correction of the soul.

Take note of how evil has grown among us, how we cooperate so that it grows even more. Just as we see earthly things grow, we cannot see the growth of spiritual things, but they nevertheless cause more harm than the ones we see. The man who formed one of the earth's things—the automobile—is now dead. The automobile remained, as did other men who added to its shape and color. The woman who designed the dress that brought dishonor is dead now too, but the dress remained as did women who added to its shape and color.

So are the evil laws that have been introduced by evil men. The man who invented many of the accords that deny Christ and the Holy Spirit is now dead, but those pronouncements remained, with human laws augmented and expanded. Thus, arrogance has equally grown and augmented. Each generation has added to the heritage of its elders, and in this way sin has multiplied in such way that now very few can escape from it. Come out valiant ones. Come out of the city of sin. Flee the great Babylon! Why participate in its sins and in the plagues that will befall it?

Our evil deeds have made even our chants and prayers abominable to the presence of God. Our egoism has separated us from the humility of Christ. We are no longer capable of suffering. We defend ourselves from everything and suffer nothing. What is this? Did God command us to defend ourselves from his word? It is time to hush up, time to keep silent? It is not wise to speak up these days. He who is clean should remain clean, and if he can, cleanse himself even more. But he who is filthy, leave him to dirty himself even more. The time to cleanse others has passed. No one should be deceived, placing his eyes on others or on the sinners, believing that he is already clean and can therefore cleanse another. Remove your sin first. Sweep away sin within yourself and then to cleansing another. But do not deceive yourself, because you harbor arrogance and great iniquity. Attend to justice and look after those in your home, placing your children first. For if you have no passion for those who are bone of your bones, and flesh of your flesh, how will you have piety for those who are not related to you? Work for justice and truth and your children will enter life seeing and knowing true justice.

The publication of books has multiplied, and their sales have grown in a great way. Who has brought about the ire that approaches? Have the books not been cleaned? Have we good benefits from so many books? Could this be the science to which the Angel referred? The day is passing. The great judgment approaches. The elements of the earth are ready. Nations no longer support the business of the church. The ire of God has reached its limit. The Lamb of God can no longer tolerate the cries of the oppressed and the complaints of the very weak. The Lamb who manifested all his love by spilling his holy and innocent blood, this same one will manifest his terrible ire. Who will be able to stand firm or justify himself before him? Will all the temples and their ceremonies appease his ire? Will those who cover themselves in vain chants and prayers escape?

---

45. The Lost Justice

"The kingdoms of the world have come to be the kingdoms of Jesus Christ."

These were the words that the angel spoke. This is what the humble of the earth await with all their heart. The poor in spirit are wailing about this event. And all those who love justice long for this great event and prodigious change in which the great of the earth will be humbled and the small of the earth will be placed in high places. This will be the day when the might of man will no longer rule, nor will man's works be admired over those of God. The dawn of this great day is already visible. It will be a day of rejoicing for those who loved the Lord with all their heart, for those who obeyed him, and did so with patience. Those who did not tire of doing what is good, even if it cost them bitterness and many obstacles because of the infidels who did not love the Lord or feared him in their hearts.

This day will confound many and they will leave quite shamed. On this day many will discover that the words Christ spoke to us, which they had been ignoring, giving instead more attention to the lessons of men taught, fearing more what men commanded than what God ordered. This kingdom, which will never end, nor will it admit rebellious citizens or will those who were ashamed of humility, of poverty, of life, of the orphan, which Christ taught us. Into this kingdom no investors will enter.

Christ, who was the prince of the poor, the friend of the very small, the one who did not have a place to rest his head, this very Christ will be king in this realm in which justice shall reign. This will not be the justice that men now call justice, but real justice in which there are no great or small, but all are equal. When Christ came to earth the first time, all the earth's great did not receive him, but instead were confused by him. Their arrogance made them reject Christ's life and refused to accept Christ as an example of liberty, as a life that pleases God. They did not even want to acknowledge him as Lord. Without even demonstrating any love, they thought they had what pleased God. They vanished into the nothingness they possessed. When Christ came for the first time, he knew he was coming to a blind world, to a people burdened with evil. He knew they had sinned, and upon seeing that there was great evil in the world, he was not scandalized. He expected that this would be their condition. He came to forgive them, showing it to those who received him, to those who admitted they were in need, and to those who were not content with what they had received from men. He pardoned all the sinners and offered them a new path on which to walk. But now that he returns again, he will not tolerate rebels. He will not pardon those who did not obey him and those who nullified all of his commandments, those who tried to justify themselves with a false profession, which does not bear the fruits of justice. In this return of our Lord, many will be surprised by God's terrible justice.

John, a man sent by God, spoke to those who came to be baptized by him and told them: "Undertake acts worthy of repentance." John had not been in Jewish temples. He had not imbibed the spirit of the Pharisees. He was not raised to be moved by the same spirit as the Pharisees. God did not want him to be drenched in the teachings of those men who had nullified God's advice, replacing them with the established traditions and commandments of men in which there was no love or God's justice. If John had been brought up in their teachings, he would not have seen the evil among them. He would have conformed as others conformed. A man moved by human teachings would not have spoken what John spoke. John was not deceived as are the men of these days. Nor did he focus on their worship, their prayers, their fasts, their temples. He saw that the great ruled on the back of the small and saw that there was no mercy among the people. It was so because those who taught did not teach the love of God nor did they possess it. Now in these final days, temples and the ceremonies celebrated in them are performed in a dead and jealous spirit, without love. They delight us and we are satisfied because temples are full of people. But this did not fool John. John was a man of God. John knew that those were not acts of repentance. He knew that the temples and their ceremonies were but a great show, full of deceit if it were not done in Spirit and with the fear of God. John spoke with the Pharisees and the scribes who came out to be baptized by him. Can you imagine that John told them that they are children of Abraham? This spirit that deceived the Pharisees, making them believe they were children of Abraham, is identical to the one in the hearts of the men in these final days, making them believe they are children of God. No, said John. The axe is already placed on the root of the tree and any trees that do not bear good fruit will be chopped down and thrown into the fire. Yes, when it comes to fruit, the giving good fruit, every heart trembles and has fear. All flee this word. Why is it that the Christians do not want to hear about good fruit and bad fruit? Could it be a coincidence? Christ said, "In this my father is glorified, in that you carry much fruit, and be my disciples in this way." I find that people everywhere do not want to hear about such fruit. This surprised the people who heard John the Baptist, when he spoke about fruit, they found themselves in anguish, and soon said: what will we do? John spoke to them about something they did not even think about, "whoever has two tunics, give one to the one who does not have any." This seems curious and without much value. The truth is that we have forgotten love, which has disappeared from Christian hearts. We have left behind what was best. It was forgotten because they mock the teachings of the men of God. Christ did not contradict what John said on that occasion. He spoke and said: "Do good toward those who abhor you." "Be merciful like your celestial Father is merciful."

It takes love to fulfill and carry out what John preached and what Christ confirmed. The arrogant of the earth mocked the advice God gave them through John's lips. John did not tell them to believe in God because they thought they already believed, but instead he spoke to them about the things that the children of God should do. This love had disappeared from the earth and for this reason Christ came to free those oppressed by the devil, and to denounce the so-called children of God. These so-called children of God did not have the works of God. Therefore, Christ denounced them as children of the devil. This of course did not seem right to the Pharisees because they thought they were the best of all the land. In truth it seemed that they were the best because they were the ones who constructed the temples, and they were the ones who spoke of the Law of Moses. They were the ones who sang, who offered the longest prayers, who fasted, who paid their tithe. For them then to receive this reproach from a humble man like Christ, well, this, in truth, seemed quite ridiculous. But since that had already been recorded in history, we all believe it. But what about our own condition? We are in very poor condition, without fruits of repentance. The only fruits that can now be manifest are the vices we abandon. John spoke to them, about fruits, that is, about good deeds. He did not preach to them of vices because already they had left those behind. This we now know was true. John was not nor could he be easily fooled, because he did not seek his own benefit, as people now do. John had the spirit of God and this same spirit illuminated him to discover the evil in them. He told them: "Lift the fallen, straighten out the twisted." What had fallen? What was twisted? The Law of God was the fallen and God's Justice was twisted. Who had twisted God's Justice? The Pharisees had twisted it. Yes, it is not the drunk or the thief who twists the Justice of God, because they do not teach it, or call themselves by the name of God, nor do they defame the name of God. Those who have the Law of God are precisely the ones who can lift it or can humiliate it.

Christ preached and said that in these last days there would be much evil. Everyone would come in his name and, in reality, who does not come in the name of Christ in these days? Who freely admits to being false or a hypocrite?

46. Good Passes for Evil

The world has rebelled against the Son of God. Men have forsaken Christ's advice who died and gave himself for them. Each has forgotten the commandment of life and there is no one who appreciates or fears God's advice. We, our teachers, our princes, and our presidents have acted with iniquity. We have sinned. We have rebelled, leaving the holy commandment and the path of justice. There is no one who clamors or complains because of so much evil. We have mutilated the example of the saint, which Christ's life revealed to us. All abhor the saintly, the decent, the humble, the just, and instead everyone seeks harm for their neighbor. Each delights in the ruin of their brother, the son of the same mother. The true Christ, the one who died on the cross on Calvary in the city of Jerusalem, this is the one who has been abandoned, and against this, all have revolted, each doing what Christ abominates. Now, what remains is only the historical Christ. They speak his name on their lips to deceive the earth's poor. All together they form a single spirit of error, and together all love evil and following the wrong path. There is no one who shows mercy toward his peer. To the eyes of this Christ and of God, there can be no reconciliation or movement. All are children of perdition. All love evil. All grasp evil and swallow it as if it were something beneficial. All covet. All grab. All think only of evil in their hearts. There is no one who thinks of justice, of judgment, of mercy. Now over earth there is no one to care for the fallen or the afflicted. Each person has become a capitalist, a prince, a dictator, but no one looks after the invalid. Nothing but the works of Satan exist and each excuses himself with the "Red Cross," with the "Salvation Army," with "welfare," but all these entities are schemes and deceits to rob people. They dispatch the poor empty-handed. The money they collect, they spend on the most modern and vain appliances. They use the money they collect with deceit in vain offices and the most luxurious furniture. For this reason, the church has fallen asleep, and its workers do not teach the people good and mercy. All excuse themselves through these deceitful groups. God is witness to all of this because he also has eyes like we do and sees throughout the earth.

All the nations have left him, each ignores the son of God, and no one turns to God to walk along straight. Each seeks God's aid, but only to walk more easily and to rob his brother. Because of this the ire of the Lamb and the fury of God have come to their end, and there is no one who can stop God's arm from destroying the earth with its false inhabitants. The ire of the lamb will consume all the liars and will burn all the violent people who lived in vanity, trusting in temples and in vain words. Know that the son of God is extremely irate. No one is innocent. The furor of God will put to an end all of the unjust who used the word of God to teach and to rob the afflicted using Christ's teachings. The end is upon us. Each will discover that God cannot be mocked. Because God will begin his holy and just judgment by the holy house, by those who go by his name. God will show his retribution on those who taught congregations how to rebel against God's holy commandments, which were given by his son Jesus. And what will happened to the gold and the silver that the unjust deceitfully collect from the poor? Where will appear the one who travels in a car fit for princes? Those who dress gallantly and construct tall houses with the money of the poor? No commandment of Christ is being executed by the people who call themselves by God's name; not a large commandment or a small one. All of you who lead others, respond to this.

Which is the commandment that the worshippers are enacting? Where is the wise, to answer this question? If they were executing a single commandment, mercy would not be on the ground, justice would not be ignored.

All have become vain, preaching pure promises to a rebellious and unjust people. Certainly, this generation is not worthy, nor does it offer even the smallest potential. If it did God would not allow the holy judgment to reach his people. But it is his people who day and night worship him only on their lips, but their heart is full of evil thoughts, full of avarice. The heart of these people who sing and pray in public to be seen by others, feeds on alien and abominable thoughts. It does not fear coveting the wife of his closest peer. Where, then, are the wise who will tell this evil and twisted generation that its end has arrived? Because God has said so by his holy prophets who came before us. Who will be able to justify this evil generation that eats the flesh of its peers? Every leader says, "The work is growing, and God is blessing our activity." In this way they believe they are rich and without need. Yet these blind ones do not understand that they are poor and very miserable in all that belongs to the kingdom of God. Blind like the Pharisees were, each one looks at the number of his followers, and each trusts and depends on the number of believers. They do not realize that they do not yet even know what mercy is, much less know what Justice is.

What teaching of Christ does this generation have? Does it know mercy, justice, love, humility, meekness, wisdom, fear of God, or judgment? Certainly, this bad and disobedient people have none of this. Because of this the earth became full of iniquity and all sorts of evil deeds. Gone are the ones who knew justice and mercy. Gone too are the men of faith. This is why the truth was twisted and judgment was not correctly shown. Justice did not develop and the man who feared God was placed in prison by councils of unjust men. This great evil has irritated the Lamb, and within a few days, even the great and rich will scream and discard money and everything in which they trusted. They will cry like children. They will careen throughout the hills like angry bulls. There will be no one to defend them because they did not defend the oppressed from the hands of the oppressor, consenting to all evil and then disguising its appearance in religious chants and long prayers.

The day of God approaches, and the hypocrites will come out of their hiding places. Then they will recognize that the work of their hands was heavier and more evil than the work of the Pharisees. Without a doubt those of Sodom and Gomorrah will condemn this generation because they did not have the knowledge that these people had. Oh, for those who now cry out and jump for joy because the day will turn into darkness and their laughter will turn into the weeping of the first-born. Oh, for those who now have everything they need but fail to look after their peer. On the day of God, they will lack everything and with the same measure they used to judge others, they too shall be measured. Judgment without mercy is undertaken with all who do not show mercy. The earth is full of gossip, and each has become an enemy of his brother. Gossip is on the lips of the mother, in the mouths of the sons, in the daughter-in-law, the father, grandchildren, grandparents, uncles, nephews, friends, neighbors, wife, and son-in-law. No one exists who has escaped this plague on earth, which is full of it, because of the false and those who are salaried. All mock like children who are stubborn and without education. When they speak of their enemy, their blind hatred is so enormous that they do not leave any part of their body without description. They speak of their eyes, speak of their mouth, speak of their nose, and with disdain describe their enemy as if describing a true beast. Through this we see the stubbornness and clumsiness to which false and clumsy teachers have thrown us.

Even daily newspaper reporters contemptuously describe in minute detail what they think of their Red enemy. And they do not leave anything at face value, describing their enemy with hatred and contempt. Why do the wise behave this way? Does history speak of any wise man who has described the face of his enemy with such hatred and contempt? Never!

This nation of preachers mocks the poverty of other nations, and insults the customs of their neighbor nations, despite the fact that the customs of the other nations are cleaner and more decent. Is there a nation more immoral than this one? Oh, arrogant people, you who have constructed your home on clouds, you who boast because you think that someday you will know other planets, from above you will be thrown down and your fall will be greater than Germany's. You will be more humiliated than Japan because the one who will throw you to the ground is the one who is almighty. It is your Creator, the same one who put you on this earth, he will be the same one to cast you to the ground.

Reies L. Tijerina

¿Hallará Fe en La Tierra....?

LUC. 18: 8.

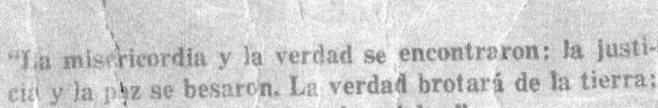

"La misericordia y la verdad se encontraron: la justicia y la paz se besaron. La verdad brotará de la tierra; y la justicia mirará desde los cielos."

Salmo 85:10, 11.

La Iglesia que ahora rige a las gentes, en un tiempo poseía el derecho y la salvación; en un tiempo abrigaba sabiduría de Dios; en un tiempo tenía ojos para ver el bien y el mal.

Mas ahora, sus ojos están cerrados, y no tiene el privilegio de ver lo que le viene; sus ojos no pueden ver el mal que le espera. Ahora le están ocultas las cosas que le vienen. Caíste en manos de tiranos, oh pueblo de Dios; te engañaron con grande engaño, y taparon tus ojos para que no veas tu fin tan triste; Caíste en error oh pueblo, y hasta ahora no te has levantado, hasta este día permaneces postrado en tierra. Tus días han terminado, y tu oportunidad se ha pasado; y tu recompensa ¿a quién la pasarás? Los que te enseñan y te doctrinan: han escondido el derecho de la Salvación; han invalidado los mandamientos del Dios eterno, los cuales nos reveló por Su Hijo; ¡oh, si solo supiera la gente, el mal que le espera, y el fin de los días.

EL CLAMOR DE LA TIERRA

Todo ojo que lea estas palabras, no se asuste ni se escandalice; tiemple su corazón, al leer estas palabras. El oído que alcance oír estas palabras, no se irrite. Son sin duda palabras duras, y algo extrañas; pero recuerden los días en los cuales estamos, y miren lo que está ya para venir sobre todos los hombres que habitan en la tierra.

La tierra se queja y gime contra sus moradores, porque la fe y el amor se fué de los que adoraban; y el justo que queda: es oprimido y ultrajado. El que oye de oídos, no escarnezca estas palabras; y los que creen estar temiendo a Dios: no se desincomoden; porque estas palabras no son a una persona, ni salieron a causa de algún grupo. Antes todos a una, dejaron el derecho; y por la vanidad se apartaron de la justicia.

Hablo a los que profesan creen en Dios, y que admiten su existencia. En tiempos tan malos, en días tan tenebrosos como los que nos rodean: ¿hará mal la reprensión; desviará esta palabra al justo? ¿Se irritará el sabio al oír o leer estas palabras? ¿No es el Sabio que ve el mal y se esconde, y el necio confía en su necedad y tropieza?

Días de vanidad son los que nos rodean, y los justos claman por corrección. Porque el Amor se fué de los que adoraban, y la misericordia ya no se encuentra en los que invocan el nombre de Dios; antes todos aborrecen la justicia, y escarnecen las obras del justo. Ya no engañemos nuestras almas como lo hizo Israel, ni confiemos en la obra de la rebeldía de Jacob. ¿No fué "Samaria" el fruto de la rebeldía de Jacob? Miqueas 1:5? ¿Y cuál es el fruto de la rebeldía de la Iglesia? ¿No es la tierra partida en nombres, y la Biblia divida en 538 nombres de sectas? Pero como en vano habitaron los Israelitas en Jerusaelm: así también ahora en vano tienen y poseen la Biblia, los que se llaman Cristianos. Ahora son tiempos malos en los cuales los hijos no obedecen a sus padres; los padres no corrigen a sus hijos. Son tiempos en los cuales los jóvenes vienen a ser padres de hogares: sin tener edad ni conocimiento de Dios. Ahora la tierra está llena de murmuración, y cada uno apunta a su hermano; los hombres son violentos para todo; caminan por las calles como chuvascos, y como relámpagos brillan en la vanidad de su soberbia. Cada uno mira por su propio bien, y la comida la pasan sin masticar: por la violencia que en ellos hay. Y con toda la tierra hundida en mal y corrupción: ¿Dejaremos de hablar Verdad? ¿Deberé yo hablar con palabras blandas, para no ofender a los creyentes? ¿Usaré de parábolas, para no lastimar, a los que adoran en los templos de Babilonia? Vive el Justo Juez de toda la tierra, y yo no dejaré de hablar verdad; porque esta generación ya no conoce lo que es vergüenza, ni se escandalizan por la maldad que cubre la tierra; antes cada uno de los que adoran: abren la puerta de la vanidad del día, y en el fruto de la soberbia se recrean. ¿Y quién es el que confiesa su maldad?

El mal lo hacen en secreto, y cada uno se cuida de su hermano: pero no hay quien se esconda de su Creador, porque perdieron la fe. No hay quien tema y ande derecho delante de su Creador. En estos días malos, en los cuales: la fe y el amor han faltado: ¿Hablaremos con palabras débiles y blandas? Cada uno habrá sus ojos, y mire que el mal que hay en la Iglesia no es poco ni débil. Ay del que se escandalice en estas palabras, y ay de aquél que trata de hacer pequeña la maldad que en el pueblo de Dios se haya: porque muchos son los que dicen: "Dios está entre nosotros, y su justicia no hemos dejado." Pero he aquí, que el clamor del pobre se levanta contra ellos.

Estas palabras levantaran al justo, más al necio, de tropiezo servirán; el que está limpio, se limpiará más, mas el sucio, se ensuciará más.

Oirá el que teme, y se esconderá mas el soberbio en su trono perecerá. ¿Faltan alagadores para que alaguen a la Iglesia? ¿Alagaré también yo al pueblo que se ha rebelado contra su Dios? ¿Cómo hablaré lo que no sé, como diré lo que no hé visto? Mis ojos no ven bien para este pueblo, mis oídos no oyen buenas nuevas para esta generación. Porque ¿Cuál es la recompensa de un pueblo que perdió la Justicia y la Misericordia-Juicio sin Misericordia será hecho con esta generación; y venganza y mortandad le espera a este pueblo. Ay de los profetas que miran paz para este pueblo que dejó el Amor; porque confusión les sorprenderá; y en el último día la mentira se les irá de su boca.

Como la iglesia trata a los pobres de la tierra sin Misericordia así también ella será tratada sin Misericordia (Santiago 2:13). Y si alguién quiere alcanzar misericordia de Dios: pues apártese del mal; limpie sus labios de hipocrecia, y use de Misericordia para con todos los afligidos: Porque con la misma medida que medimos; nos volverán a medir. Y ay de los que esperan alcanzar misericordia de Dios: cuando ellos nunca obraron con Misericordia. Los cabezas de la tierra, han inventado leyes para alcanzar sus antojos; pero ay de ellos: porque por ellos las viudas y los oprimidos de la tierra fueron descuidados. Establecen leyes sobre los creyentes, para provecho de ellos mismos; e impoenn yugos para engrandecer sus nidos; ya que la gloria de ellos está en los templos enbellecidos.

¿Pero qué de los pobres de la tierra? ¿cuál ley han establecido a favor de los pobres? ¿Dónde está la ley que defiende a las viudas?

Así como las tiendas de comida y las tiendas de ropa van creciendo y haciéndose lujosas a fin de ganar el ojo de las gentes y reunir clientela; así también los pastores, sueñan templos grandes y bellos: sin importarles las cosas que Dios nos encargó. Ay de estos hombres, porque por ellos la sabiduría fué puesta en tierra; y a causa de estos hombres alquilados por la Iglesia: los mandamientos de Dios han venido a ser, los mandamientos de

2

menos estima. Por supuesto que según ellos, no han dejado los mandamientos de Dios: pero sus vidas son movidas por mandamientos de hombres. Ya se acerca el juicio de Dios, en el cual sabrán todos: si es poco el mal que hemos cometido con abandonar la Justicia de Dios y sus santos mandamientos. Con los ojos que ven la Justicia en tierra y nada les importa: con estos mismos ojos verán la tierra toda envuelta en llamas.

En aquél día sabrán todos, que el hombre se portó peor que las bestias del campo; entonces buscarán la corrección, pero no la hallarán.

Ay de los que dicen: "Estamos ricos, y Dios nos ha bendecido en gran manera." Porque no saben, que la recompensa de su rebeldía les espera; no saben que están pobres y desnudos en cuanto a la justicia de Dios.

No ha habido en la historia del hombre: una generación tan torpe y dada a la vanidad, como la presente generación; la cual quiere limpiar la maldad de sus vidas con ir a los templos. Callen ya, los pastores y profetas: antes de que llegue el día, y se acerque la hora, en la cual: con sus manos sobre sus bocas, se revolcarán en tierra. Los que tienen boca limpia y ojos para ver: digan a las gentes lo que viene; y no pasen su tiempo alagando al pueblo por interés del pan. Antes, cada uno mire por su vida, y tiemble a la paalbra de Dios.

LA IMAGEN PERDIDA

Misericordia y verdad, para con todos los que temen a Dios y obran Justicia; juicio y justicia sea la imagen de los que esperan en Dios. Pero el necio no advierte consejo, ni ocupa la sabiduría.

¿Qué consejo llamará la atención de esta generación? Pues que la misma revelación de Dios manifestada en la vida de Cristo, ha sido ignorada, y sus santos mandamientos que son para vida han sido despreciados. (Juan 12:47-50). La Imagen de Dios, ha sido borrada del hombre, y ahora solo queda la imagen del hombre animal. La Imagen de Dios no es en carne ni en figura, sino que es Espíritu; Cuando el hombre perdió la Justicia y la Misericordia, fué cuando perdió la Imagen de Dios. La Imagen de Dios es Justicia y Juicio, Misericordia y verdad; y el hombre que obra Justicia y hace Misericordia: este tal tiene la Imagen de su Creador. Por esto mismo, Cristo nos pidió, que fueramos Misericordiosos como nuestro Padre Celestial es Misericordioso; que hicieramos bien a los que nos hacen mal, porque nuestro Padre hace todas estas cosas para con los malos: dándoles buenos tiempos, con lluvias y sol y el provecho de su tierra. Cuando Dios hizo al hombre, también le dió su imagen; es decir, lo invistió de entrañas de Misericordias, con afectos naturales, con clemencia, bondad, Justicia y Juicio. Pero gradualmente el hombre fué perdiendo esta Imagen del Espíritu de Dios; y ahora el hombre yace postrado en tierra, lleno de murmuración, de rebeldía, de envidias; ingratos, desleales, sin afecto natural, implacables sin Misericordias.

Los fariseos tenían la imagen de la carne y en figura: la cual es letra; pero no tenían la Imagen de Dios, la cual es Espíritu que obra Justicia y Juicio. Por esto Cristo los acusó, que habían dejado la Justicia y la Misericordia y la Fé: en las cuales cosas se ve la Imagen de Dios; y el que tiene estas cosas obra la voluntad de Dios, y hace bien a todos, incluyendo a sus enemigos. Cristo prometió que todos los que guardaran sus santos mandamientos, iban a recibir el Espíritu de Dios el cual les guiaría a toda verdad y a toda Justicia. El Espíritu cuyo fruto es caridad, gozo, paz, tolerancia, benignidad, bondad, fe, mansedumbre, y templanza. Cuando estas cosas faltaron, la tierra fué dividida por la falsa opinión de los hombres alquilados. Los fariseos eran hombres animales, y por eso no pudieron percebir las cosas que eran del Espíritu de Dios; Pero ellos como esta presente generación, pensaban que tenían el derecho y el Espíritu de Dios. Cosa horrible se ve en estos días, porque ni la imagen animal se ve en el hombre; cuando los hijos mandan a los padres como lo es en esta presente generación, es que llevamos la imagen de Caín. He ahí el hombre contra su Creador; los maestros se han levantado contra el maestro de la creación; ¿y dónde está el bien que los mandamientos de los hombres ha traído al hogar llamado cristiano?

Dios acusará a los maestros que han mutilado los santos mandamientos que mismo Cristo mandó y cumplió; Dios reclamará esto de manos de los que enseñan a las congregaciones. La Imagen de Dios no se ve en figura, ni en carne; sino que su Imagen se ve en Espíritu; y el que obra las obras de su Espíritu: este tal lleva la Imagen del altísimo.

Ahora nadie defiende ni habla por la Justicia de Dios, todos llevan su propia Justicia; y debido a esto: la tierra se ha llenado de odio y soberbia. No hay quien se deleite en la Justicia o en el Juicio de Dios, no hay quien halle placer en perpetuar los mandamientos de Dios; cada quien ama lo que perece, y presentan sus carnes en sacrificio vivo por lo que perece.

La honra de la mujer no tiene precio, y los hijos no sienten la deuda a sus padres; y los padres perdieron el celo. Todos se han entorpecido, no pueden sasiar el hambre por las cosas de la vida, y la sed por las vanidades no la pueden controlar; No contentos con esto: pasan sus hijos por las llamas de Babilonia; y para pagar sus deudas de sus malvados apetitos: ponen sus hijas en el mercado público; hijas tiernas, que en tiempos pasados estaban en la cocina y en la costura: ahora yacen en los kreses y en las boticas, pasando lo más tierno de su edad en el trabajo más bajo y más detestable que pueda haber para una mujer. Aun con todo esto, ¿Dónde están los que hablan trás el púlpito? ¿Por qué no detienen este mal? No hay quién dé consejo, no hay quién aborrezca las hechicerías de la ramera, Babilonia madre de todas las fornicaciones de la tierra. ANTES el hombre trabajaba solo, y se contentaba con ganar para el pan y para cubrir su cuerpo aunque fuera con ropa humilde; Pero ahora, por la lumbre de la envidia que corre por sus venas, ponen aun a sus propias mujeres a trabajar, y esto por las cuantas que ellos mismos han buscado; y por no estar contentos con lo que Dios mandó.

El varón antiguo, prefería morir de hambre, antes de ver a su mujer trabajando en tráfico de hombres, y sirviendo a una generación codiciosa.

Pero ahora, ¿Dónde está la sabiduría del Varón, y dónde están los sabios que enseñan por dinero? ¿Acaso no están recibiendo salario para que enseñan y para que atajen el mal? Los fariseos en su torpesa atajaban el mal mejor que esta generación de maestros. Porque en sus tiempos, la mujer tenía mejor lugar, y las jóvenes tiernas no andaban en el tráfico de mercadería. Abramos los ojos, y veamos que nosotros mismos hemos invitado la espada. Y por nuestra rebeldía, el fuego de la ira de Dios nos va a abrazar. ¿Para que escondernos detrás de la oración, y para que cubrirnos con alabanzas en público? ¿Para que abominar los mandamientos de Cristo, sujetando a nuestras almas a mandamientos de hombres? Si yo no hallo vida en los mandamientos de Dios que Cristo nos reveló: entonces me tornaré a los mandamientos de los hombres; y todos los que hallan sabor en los mandamientos de los hombres, es porque la luz del Espíritu no les ha amanecido. Los mandamientos que Cristo nos reveló, hacen bien al alma, pero al cuerpo no hacen bien; y como esta generación ama el cuerpo más que el alma, por eso se han rebelado contra los santos mandamientos de Dios. Ay de los que dicen: "Estamos en otros tiempos" y sujetan los mandamientos de Dios a los tiempos; más bienaventurados los que permanecen fiel en todos los mandamientos hasta el fin: porque estos seran salvos. Los fariseos y los saduceos se levantarán contra esta generación y la condenarán, porque bien que aquellos mataron el cuerpo de Cristo: esta generación ha matado el Espíritu de Cristo de entre la Iglesia de Dios, y han quitado la Imagen de Dios de entre los que adoran. Y tanto ignoraban los fariseos la misericordia y la Justicia, como esta generación de maestros alquilados.

A la viuda la han enviado vacía, y a edificar templos se han dedicado; y tanta así es la soberbia que mueve el corazón de esta gente, que se han sujetado a la maldición por amor a los templos; a grado que han pedido dinero prestado para llevar acabo la obra de su espíritu.

Dios no es contra templos, si es que en ellos se pregona la Justicia; pero esta presente genración ya no sabe lo que es Justicia de Dios. Porque han pisoteado lo que compone la Justicia de Dios: que son los mandamientos de Dios, dados en Cristo Jesús.

EL DIA DE DIOS

El día de Dios ha principiado, el día de Dios grande y penosos para sufrirse. Día ilustre y anunciado por todos los profetas de Dios; día de venganza será; de fuego humo y de azufre; la tierra será vaciada de los impíos, y los tiranos ya no serán sus dueños.

La ira del cordero, vista en revelación y escrita por Juan, el Apóstol de Jesucristo, será vaciada sobre la tierra y sus rebeldes; Dios cual gigante, purgará la tierra, y con fuego fuerte hará la obra; obra extraña y grave de sufrirse, porque en ella no se hallará Misericordia ni compasión. Llegó el día, y se maduró el pecado; se acabó la fe y se corrompieron los que adoraban; todos los labios se tornaron a la mentira, todo ojo se dió a codiciar, los oídos de todos se inclinaron a oír el consejo torcido y de mentira. Y de arriba miró Dios que la tierra carecía de sabios, y que en ella los justos estaban para perecer; El corazón del hombre estaba ligado al mundo, y las maquinaciones más malas y pesadas se hallaban en los que formaban el consejo; la hipocrecía salía de los cabezas, y eran ellos los que defendían la obra de la ramera madre de todas las fornicacions de la tierra.

Es día de enojo y saña, día de ira y de venganza; día de purgar y limpiar la tierra, día de quitar la podridumbre y sanar la enfermedad que los líderes causaron en la tierra.

Los que adoran, como los que maldicen; los que oran, como los que blasfeman; los que ayunan, como los que se embriagan; los que edifican templos, como los que edifican tabernas; los padres como los hijos, el hombre como la mujer; todos beberán del caliz de la ira del Dios Todopoderoso, el cual pelea y juzga la tierra con grande justicia.

No hubo otro día, pero ni habrá después de este; porque el hombre quedará purificado, y no se dará a la obra que ahora fabrican; Las ciudades grandes de la tierra, y todo el orgullo del hombre quedará en olvido, porque todo será dado a las llamas; y por el fuego pasará lo grande y lo pequeño, lo bello y lo feo; por el fuego pasarán todo lo que engañó al hombre.

La mujer quedará sin pomitos, y el perfume pasará para ya no ser; las telas finas, y todo ornato y compostura pasarán junto con los que lo buscan; Ay de los que tienen ojos para ver, y ay de los que oyeren en aquel día: porque se verá lo que nunca se vió, y se oirá lo que nunca se había oído antes. Los valientes caerán a tierra sin fuerza en sus corazones, las mujeres caerán de espaldas; ¿y quién podrá estar en pie en este día? Es el día de Dios, es el día en el cual el Dios y Creador de todo tomará venganza; venganza contra los que dirigen, venganza contra los que enseñan, venganza contra los que torcieron sus santos mandamientos y dieron por nulos los mandamientos de Nuevo Testamento. El enojo del cordero es como el fuego que derrite a la cera, y como su amor fué ancho y amplio para con todos, así será su ira grande y espantosa para con todos los rebeldes.

6

¿Es acaso tiemp de estar en dipustas por dogmas de hombres? ¿Es tiempo de claudicar en los acuerdos de los hombres, que solo son a su provecho? ¿Cuál de todos los consejos de los hombres han traído paz a algún hogar? ¿Cuál de todos ellos ha devuelto la honra a la mujer? ¿Cuál de todos ellos ha devuelto la honra de los hijos para con los padres? Enseñan a las gentes a traer mumuración sobre toda la tierra, porque por causa de esto la tierra se ha dado a la envidia e infamia. Y estos mismos han puesto a los unos que creen en Dios, contra otros que también creen en Dios; y han traído infamia sobre toda la tierra, porque el mal que ellos fabrican, no se conforman con efectuarlo en su propia tierra, sino que lo llevan más allá de los mares.

Dejad de cantar las dulces melodías, y haced Misericordia y Justicia cada cual con su prójimo, porque el Día grande y terrible ha llegado; devolved a la viuda su parte, y amparad al huérfano, meted en casa al peregrino, y haced que el extranjero se sienta en casa. Ya pasaron los tiempos de cantar y de orar; porque ya pasaron los de labios limpios; se acabaron los tiempos de orar: porque ya pasaron los de limpio corazón; Ya no es tiempo de pedir de arriba dones y bendiciones: porque esto era para los que oían el grito de la vuda, y atendían a la necesidad del menesteroso y oprimido; y en vez de todos estos simulacros: volved a las sendas antiguas, dad lo que poseeis; en vez de todo esto, Amad al enemigo; haced bien antes de que caiga sobre nosotros el día de Dios. Besad el Hijo de Dios humillando nuestras almas, y haciendo lo que él nos mandó; Besadlo, dando al pobre lo que poseeis.

Derramad lágrimas, cada uno en su recámara; y vuelvan sus rostros a la pared. Dada la espalda a todas las hechicerías de la ramera, que son: el oro, la plata, las vestiduras finas y de colores, los perfumes, los pomitos, los peinados, las composturas, los vasos finos, los carros, las casas compuestas, y toda obra hecha en Babilonia. Ay de los que se burlan, y abrazan todo esto; porque en el día de la ira de Dios, todo esto les será afrenta y dolor, todo esto les traerá amargura en el alma, y mucho pesar en el corazón. Porque todas estas cosas de la tierra, son el alimento de la soberbia y de la envidia. A medida que el hombre crece en posesiones, crece también su soberbia y su envidia; dejad todo esto, si hay sabios en la tierra: no retire sus oídos ni su corazón de estas palabras. Atended el castigo y la corrección del Espíritu Santo.

LA FE DE NUESTROS DIAS
Nov. 22, 1954
El Monte

El que conoce los tiempos, el que reveló el consejo de Salvación: no solo sabía lo que había en el corazón de los hombres que le rodeaban en su tiempo, sino que también sabía lo que iba a haber en las generaciones después de Su partida. A esto se debe la gran pregunta, que aun más sabios tiemblan al oírla; es cierto que a los necios nada se les da. Dijo: "Empero cuando el hijo del hombre viniere, ¿hallará FE en la tierra?" Todo aquél que tiene espíritu de Dios, sabe lo que envuelve esta pregunta; y todo el que teme a Dios sabe qué significa el salir tal pregunta de los labios de Cristo.

Cristo, que conocía el valor de la FE, y que sabía que su pueblo depende de la FE en Dios: en muchas ocasiones advirtió a los escogidos de los últimos tiempos, y les explicó la fe que habría en las últimas generaciones. Muchos de los entendidos, también preguntan: ¿hallará fe en la tierra? Si Cristo viene en estos días, ¿hallará fe en la tierra?

Cristo sabía que las últimas generaciones iban a adorar sin FE, Cuando dijo: "y la caridad de Muchos se resfriará." Porque sin fe es imposible que haya Amor en nuestros corazones. La fe es la substancia de todo lo bueno, y en la fe se manifiesta toda buena obra.

Por esto mismo nadie puede agradar a Dios sin fe: Porque la fe es el origen y el principio del Amor, de la Justicia, y de la Misericordia, de la Sabiduría. Donde no hay fe no hay Amor, donde no hay fé no hay Justicia; y ¿quién podrá agradar a Dios sin Justicia y sin Amor? Juan el Apostol dijo: "cualquiera que no hace Justicia no es de Dios."

Cierto es que también los fariseos tenían de la clase de fe que hay en estos días en los que adoran; pero Cristo denuncio la fe de los fariseos. La Fe de los fariseos, era una fe que no tenía Amor ni Justicia; en fin, era una fe fingida que no tenía Fe verdadera. Cierto es que los fariseos tenían en qué holgarse, y pensaban tener una buena y viva fe solo porque en ella había adoración pública, cantos, oraciones, ayunos, diezmos y mandamientos de hombres. Pero Cristo repudió esta fe fingida, porque en ella no había Misericordia para con los afligidos de la tierra; en ella no había Justicia ni Amor de Dios.

Semejante a la fe fingida de los fariseos, es la fé que engaña a los adoradores de estos últimos días. No hay quien tenga fe para servir, dar a los méndigos como Lázaro, para hacer Justicia y derecho; no hay quien tenga fe para guardar los mandamientos que Cristo nos dió. Todos tienen fe para cantar, para orar en público como los fariseos, para dar el diezmo como también los fariseos lo hacían; aunque de mala gana a causa de que lo demandan en la carne y no en el Amor que todo lo sufre. Pero ¿qué de la Fe de los profetas, de Abraham, de los apóstoles? Todos abominan las costumbres de nuestros antiguos padres, y no hay quien imite la fe de los antiguos vencedores. La fe de esta generación, busca su propio bien; la fe de este pueblo está dividida en nombres y opiniones de hombres. ¿Hallará FE Cristo al venir? ¿Hallará fe en la tierra? Los hombres que dirigen el consejo, han oprimido la poca fe que había en los que adoraban; porque son hombres amadores de sí mismos; son hombres que no oyen el grito del afligido. Estos son los que ha usado el diablo para retirar la fe de los humildes de la tierra. Todos humillan al pobre, y escarnecen al que quiere ser humilde, por-

8

que les es cosa penosa y fastidiosa, el tener un humilde delante de sus ojos. ¿Dónde pues está la Fe que Cristo busca? ¿Dónde la hallará? Las obras de los que llevan un nombre, son semejante a las obras de los que llevan otro nombre; y ¿qué es de la fe? Los hijos de los que adoran, deshonran a sus padres porque no hay fe, y la mujer ha tomado el lugar del varón porque no hay fe. Es pues la fe, la substancia del Amor, la substancia de la Jutsicia.

Y sin fe no podemos obrar en Amor y Justicia; por esto se fué el Amor y desapareció la Justicia: porque la Fe se escurrió de nosotros. Y ahora seremos arrojados como plata desechada, y seremos vomitados porque no hay sabor en nuestra sal. Pablo también hablo por el mismo Espíritu que Cristo habló cuando dijo: "Dios les envía operación de error, para que crean a la mentira;" "Para que sean condenados todos los que no creyeron a la verdad." Aquí está el pueblo que no cree a la verdad; creen como los fariseos, solo a las cosas que a ellos les conviene, y también a los manadmientos de los que dirigen; pero no creen a los mandamiento de Cristo. Cristo mandó que amaramos a nuestros enemigos: pero esta generación no ama ni a su propio prójimo o hermano (sea en la carne o sea en la fe), menos a sus enemigos. Esta generación no tiene fe para obedecer a Dios en lo que él manda; pero sí quieren descubrir fe para obrar milagros mentirosos: y logran sus propósitos, robando la fe del enfermo, ganan gloria para sí. Pero estos que obran por la operación del error de soberbia, serán sorprendidos cuando Dios los juzgue según sus malvadas obras. Porque estos movidos por la misma codicia que movió a Simón el mago, ignoran la Justicia y la Misericordia, porque todo lo hacen por torpe ganancia.

Cristo en su regreso, hallará muchos templos, muchos predicadores, muchos adoradores; pero ¿hallará fe en la tierra? Bienaventurados los Misericordiosos, porque ellos alcanzarán Misericordia. Y los Misericordiosos no son hombres sin fe, porque la Misericordia viene después de la fe: y sin fe es imposible la Misericordia: Ay de los adoradores que no conocen Misericordia, porque serán contados entre los árboles marchitos, y pámpanos sin fruto. En toda obra buena se manifiesta la Fe viva, pero esta generación está bien pobre en las obras, y miserable en la Misericordia: porque no tiene fe.

Por fe perdona el que perdona, por fe ama el que ama, por fe hace Justicia el que la hace, y fe es manso y humilde el que lo es; y sin Fe es imposible obrar derecho.

Y esta generación no conoce el derechco, porque perdió la fe. Y esta generación en todos sus deseos enseña su codicia y su torpesa; en todo lo que hace manifiesta su soberbia y su egoismo: porque todos son ligeros para juzgar con juicio torcido y carnal.

No hay quien ignore la flaqueza del prójimo, y la tierra entera se dió a la murmuración; y así cada uno adora sin tener vergüenza de su iniquidad; cada uno publica su hipocrecía, y adoran sin fe y sin vergüenza.

La viuda que Cristo pone en la parábola del juez injusto, pedía con ruego, porque sufría a causa de su adversario; Pero esta generación que se le mandó que no pusiera los ojos en las cosas que perecen, y que no buscarán las cosas que perecen: ahora cada uno está undido y endeudado por las cosas que Babilonia fábrica cada día. El pueblo de Dios ya no tienen porque tener fe, no hay quien necesite la fe; todos están contentos y bien servidos con los deleites poderosos de la gran ramera Madre de todas las fornicaciones de la tierra. No hay quien sufra, porque aun las mujeres esposas de los que adoran, se hallan en medio de los hombres trabajando, solo para vivir según la corriente de los hijos de babilonia, y para saciar el apetito carnal de las cosas que se queman.

¿Qué ha hecho Dios con la tierra, cuando sus moradores pierden la Fe? La historia nos enseña, y los Juicios que Dios ha hecho entre las naciones nos advierten. La tierra ya no soporta a sus moradores, porque cada uno obra sin fe: y el salario tomó el lugar de la Fe. Los que adoran, tratan de agradar al hombre; y los que dirigen, buscan el presente (pan de la viuda) que no les pertenecía a ellos. Cristo no preguntó que si hallaría templos hermosos, o cantos, o adoradores que pelean lugares como lo hizo la mujer samaritana en su ignorancia: antes preguntó que si hallaría Fe viva en la tierra.

La viuda en la parábola, clamaba por Justicia, pero en estos días: ¿Quién clama por Justicia? También Israel, todo perdió menos los simularos y adoraciones vanas y en público; así que nadie ponga su confianza en lo que se ve, ni piense que Dios haya pedido de un pueblo infiel e hipócrita, cantos y ceremonias públicas. Ahora el que tiene fe, manifiestela con su Justicia; porque el Justo por su Fe vivirá.

¿Qué pues hallará Cristo en la tierra al venir? ¿Divisiones? soberbia? ¿vanidad? Verdad es, que los templos han tomado el lugar de Dios, y la adoración que debe de ser en Obedecer a los mandamientos de Dios, en hacer Misericordia, en obrar Justicia y derecho: ahora la han rendido en templo; pero el pobre de la tierra nada ha alcanzado de esa adoración. Contentos se encuentran los que dirigen, y esta adoración de labios vanos satisface el gusto de los que forman el consejo; pero no descubren que la tierra ya quedó sin Fe. He aquí, que en el día de Dios, los templos no podrán defender a los que adoran, ni los falsos simulacros de esta generación podrán salvarles de la mano de Dios.

Porque es Dios el que está irritado y no los hombres; es a Dios al que han ofendido. ¿Y quién es el que no sabe, que los mandamientos de Dios están en tierra? ¿Cuál es el Mandamiento de Dios que esta generación esta cumpliendo? Con razón la bestia y el falso profeta, hallaron sus adoradores en los templos; y todos los que doban su rodilla en los altares, también doblan su rodilla a las vanidades de babilonia; y ¿quién no admira las vanidades que ahora adornan las calles de los pueblos? ¿Y quién es el sabio que le rehusa a su ojo las vanidades que se ofrecen en los aparadores? El pueblo de Dios perdió el sentido, y se le fué la fe; halló su morada en babilonia, y negó a su Creador.

Ay de los que profesan tener fé en las promesas, sin guardar ni un solo mandamiento. Dejemos la religión de caín, y ya nadie se contente con la fe de los fariseos, porque son días de ira, y el creador está contra su creación; porque todos nos hemos rebelado y nadie guardó la fe. Todos los justos y sabios, volvamos a la fe de nuestros padres; y dejemos a los que van tras la fe sin obras.

EL SABIO PERDIDO
Abril 15, 1954
El Monte

Los pensamientos sabios, salieron y se fueron de los cabezas. El mal visitó a la tierra, y en los corazones de los mayores, la muerte halló su nido; los sabios hicieron fuerte la mano del que destruye, y con la multitud de sus leyes opresoras invitaron al que mata. La sabiduría del sabio le matará, porque solo el ojo y la carne se alimentan y con todas sus invenciones formaron el alimento de la soberbia; los malos de la tierra tomaron el lugar de la Justicia; La ciencia del sabio, y la obra del inventor, moverá la ira; y con sus mismas obras, traerán su propio fin. Prepararon, llenaron la tierra de violencia, cumplieron sus inicuos pensamientos; por esto Dios también acabará su obra extraña y horrible.

Dios miró, y no hubo quien atajara el mal, ni quien se pusiera contra la maldad; cada uno peleaba y miraba por su propio vientre, y se alimentaba con pensamientos ajenos. Los que enseñaban el bien, también se dieron a la vanidad, y por salario enseñaban a la multitud.

Los caminos que el hijo de Dios nos trajo, estos fueron abandonados por los más grandes, y los sabios hicieron burla de la humildad; la mansedumbre de Cristo pereció de los que oran, y el Amor ya no se halla en los que ayunan; porque cada uno ayuna para conseguir silla más alta que la de su propjimo, y por interes terrenales se dan a la oración y al ayuno.

Pero ¿valdrá todo esto después de haber dejado y mutilado los mandamientos que el alto Dios nos mandó por su hijo Jesucristo? ¿Son tiempos de pedir poder contra los demonio? ¿Es tiempo de pedir y demandar promesas al Justo Dios? ¿No es antes tiempo de volvernos a los caminos de Justicia y andar en temor, de buscar perdón, de hacer misericordia para con los que claman? Si alguno se conciente digno en estos días, y piensa ser noble en pedir de Dios las cosas que a los santos y justos les pertenecen: pues dejadlo; los que quieren vida, tornen su rostro a la pared, pongan sus ojos en tierra, ya no miren a la mujer de su prójimo (ya no busquen el bien del cuerpo.) Busquemos Misericordia de arriba, Perdón; pero es menester que cada uno haga bien a su prójimo, cada uno mire por la viuda, por el huérfano, por el necesitado.

11

Los llamados cristianos, son los que escarnecen al manso, al humilde; y si esto no es así: Deje alguno sus vestidos delicados, y vistase con trapos despreciados, y será criticado y condenado: no por los pecadores, ni por los borrachos, ni por los que matan y roban; pero todo al contrario, será condenado y murmurado por los que van a las Iglesias y cantan, será criticado por los que se llaman cristianos. Así que estos son los instrumentos de la ramera, estos son los hijos y ciudadanos de babilonia que defienden el vestido de babilonia. Los llamados cristianos (con excepción del Justo) son los que dan fuerza a las invenciones de babilonia, lo que ellos llaman "Moda" y "Estilo". Pero el Justo Dios, llama a todo esto: abominación, deshonra y corrupción. Dios ve, que los que se llaman de su nombre por todas partes: son los que están más cautivos, y los más allegados a las obras del día actual; ¿quién viste como el pueblo de Dios? ¿Quién come como el pueblo de Dios, cosas delicadas? Solamente los príncipes de babilonia, y los que están en las casas de los presidentes y de los reyes. Por esto Dios les llama gente insensata, y pueblo torpe; todo el pueblo cristiano se halla como se encontraba Israel en tierra de babilonia cautivo. El pueblo de Dios está cautivo, y es preso por las pasiones de babilonia, y esta embriagado con los deleites de la madre de todas las fornicaciones de la tierra y de las invenciones. ¿Quién va tras el color y la figura, como el pueblo de Dios?

Todos los que temen a Dios, venid, volvamonos al que nos formó; busquemos al que dió el mensaje a nuestro Señor; hagamos misericordia para con todos los afligidos de la tierra, y consolemos a los que lloran y que claman por la mano del opresor. Juntémonos en el bien de Dios, y juntos andemos en los caminos antiguos. Nadie busque alianza de hombres, ni unión de mandamientos de hombres; porque por estos hombres llamados sabios y directores: ha sido quitado la sabiduría de la tierra; y por causa de ellos el Espíritu Santo ha sido puesto fuera del "Lugar Santo". Unamos el Espíritu de Dios, y muévanos la Fe de nuestros antiguos padres.

Andemos a la Luz de la Justicia de Dios, y no tropezaremos en el día de la ira de Dios; Dejad al pueblo que se quiere purificar en cantos, ni se alleguen al pueblo que se unge con oraciones largas en publico para ser vistos y oídos de todos; se acabaron los tiempos del justo, y ahora el varon le pertenece bajar su rostro, humillar su alma porque el derecho ha sido quitado de la tierra. Los que oran, no piensen que Dios puede ser engañado ni los que cantan piensen que Dios es adorado por mentirosos y crueles, que dejan al huérfano y a la viuda a la misericordia del gobierno y del estado. ¿No es el ceno de la Iglesia la que recibe a todos los que carecen de alimento, ora sean buenos o sean malo? —Los que piden con el espíritu de Simón el mago, por codicias malas, limpien sus vestidos, laven sus almas, antes de que llegue el día de Dios, y les sorprenda como a Sodoma y Gomorra.

12

EL PUEBLO CAUTIVO — SALID, SALID

Israel fué esclavo de Egipto, y siervo de Babilonia; y en sombra de servidumbre, tuvo hijos e hijas; hijos nacían pero no en libertad; nacían envueltos en costumbres paganas, y sirviendo a una banedra de tiranos. Bajo el yugo de injusticia, y dentro de una nación soberbia fueron sus días.

En egipto y babilonia, no se hallaban las Leyes de Dios, ni las obras del Todopoderoso; pero el Dios de Misericordia acordándose de su promesa, después de mucho tiempo los volvió a sus tierras nativas; todos los que volvieron eran una generación nueva que habían nacido en cuna de esclavitud.

Al pueblo de Dios le faltó sabiduría, y por falta de temor de Dios, fué llevado cautivo. Y de igual manera, los hijos de la Iglesia ahora sirven en tierra de extraños, y nacen bajo la bandera de la misma y antigua Mística Babilonia. Los Cristianos que ahora están naciendo de nuevo, nacen bajo la bandera de error, y sirven a Dios con prácticas paganas.

La Iglesia de Cristo, el pueblo de Dios no está en libertad, ni sirve a Dios con Sabiduría en el temor de Dios. Por muchos años, la Iglesia ha estado engendrando hijos e hijas, pero esto bajo un reino extraño y desconocido a Dios; y a esto se debe que los hijos de la Iglesia, no conocen sabiduría, pero ni entienden derecho; todos nacen con entrañas sin Misericordia, por la sombra del reino de tinieblas que les rodea. Cristo habló sobre la cautividad de la Iglesia, y predijo que el pueblo de Dios iba a pasar por esta grande servidumbre y esclavitud.

El Espíritu Santo habló y dijo que a causa de este cautiverio del alma de los cristianos: la Iglesia iba a quedar: desnuda, ciega, pobre, cuitada y miserable. Es un hecho, que la iglesia y pueblo de Dios ahora se encuentra sin vestiduras de Justicia; porque no conocen Justicia los que enseñan al pueblo de Dios; este pueblo se encuentra ciego: porque a pesar de no tener amor, misericordia, fe, justicia ni temor de Dios. Dice que sí lo tiene, pero esto se debe a que está ciego. Y es un miserable porque a pesar de que dice que está rico: está bien pobre en cuanto a obras de Dios; y los pobres de la tierra, y las viudas, no hallan ningún pedazo de pan en el pueblo de Dios.

¡Oh pueblo de Dios, e hijos del Altísimo: notad que vuestro nacimiento no ha sido en tierra de libertad y de justicia; antes en tierra ajena y en ciudad de pecadores hemos nacido.

El Señor nos pide que salgamos de entre esta mala y torcida generación; Porque nuestras almas son esclavas del error; las entrañas nuestras se mueven a la voz de la soberbia y de la ira; porque nuestros señores son: la envidia y el egoísmo. Los hijos e hijas que cada día nacen a la iglesia: en tierra de esclavitud nacen; envueltos por el espíritu de división y odio. Y la madre de todas las fornicaciones de la tierra: nos ha criado en odio, en venganza; y a esto se debe que todos se aborrecen los unos a los otros, por razón de nombres.

La madre de la crianza, del pueblo cristiano, es babilonia.

Porque en la soberbia se crian, con el egoismo se alimentan, y venganza corre por sus venas. Cada uno se alegra y se regocija en la ruina de su hermano, si este llevaba otro nombre.

Entre el pueblo de Dios no hay quien procure el bien de su hermano, porque esto heredaron de su Madre de crianza; este pueblo, por un espíritu fué engendrado, y por otro espíritu fué criado. Ya nadie pregunte: ni diga: ¿por qué no habrá Amor entre el pueblo de Dios? ¿por qué no habrá el gozo que había en los días pasados? Entienda todo Cristiano, (llamado así) que en el reino de babilonia hemos nacido, y todos nuestros enseñadores son asalariados. Por esto nos llama el Altísimo a que salgamos de entre ellos. Salgamos de la soberbia, de la mentira, del egoismo; salgamos de las vanidades de la vida, de la ira y venganza. Porque esto es el fruto de babilonia, y en estos malos espíritus nosotros fuimos creados. Salid, todo el que entiende y ama la vida, salga pronto. Corte la comunicación con las vanidades de la vida. Y aprendamos de Cristo; temamos a Dios antes de que caiga sobre nosotros la ira del Cordero. Es tiempo de separarnos de la soberbia; el día está muy avanzado, y solo hay tiempo para los que quieran de verdad poner sus vidas en libertad.

Abrá cada uno su oído a la verdad; no resista el justo a la reprensión, ni tema nadie a las leyes puestas por hombres. Nadie dé oído a los acuerdos de los hombres; porque estos acuerdos son contra la viuda y el menesteroos; para provecho de ellos acuerdan leyes.

Dejemos la madre de crianza, la cual nos enseñó a rebelarnos contra Dios y su Justicia; abandonemos la madre que no nos enseñó Misericordia para con nadie. Saglamos de la Jerusalem que mata a los profetas; y entended que no eran los edificios y casas de Jerusalem: sino las leyes torcidas de los falsos maestros, los cuales mataban a los justos. Por lo tanto, salgamos de las falsas leyes y enseñanzas de concilios que matan el derecho e ignoran la justicia. Concilios en los cuales no se halla pan para el hambriento, ni vestido para el desnudo. No hay quien advierta juicio ni justicia a dentro de estos falsos maestros, los cuales son agentes de babilonia, y asalariados de la grande ramera. Estos son los que cautivan a los pequeños de la tierra, y tuercen el derecho del justo.

Ay de estos malos hombres, que no encubren la soberbia; aun por fuera visten como príncipes de Sodoma, y sus lenguas pasean y rodean la tierra. Sobre estos caerá la ira del Cordero, y más sorprendidos serán, que Hirochima y Nagasaki.

Nuestra madre de crianza (Babilonia) nos enseñó a cantar y orar en público, pero no nos enseñó Misericordia y Justicia; nos enseñó a pagar el tributo a sus maestros: pero no nos enseñó a compadecernos de los oprimidos y menesterosos; de esto nunca nos dió ejemplo por sus asalariados.

En estos días de cautividad, de yugo, de servidumbre: no hay quien pueda aprender humildad y mansedumbre; porque el negocio y tráfico de babilonia no lo permite; el comercio de babilonia y la potencia de sus deleites consiste en mercadería de oro, de plata, de vestiduras finas y comidas delicadas; consiste en casas equipadas con soberbia, carros que predican el orgullo, y comodidades que deleitan la carne de los cristianos cautivos. Salgamos, y ¿por qué vamos a perecer juntamente con los falsos asalariados que enseñan por amor al vientre? ¿Cuál es el caliz de esta ramera, que todos han tomado de él? ¿En qué consiste su sabor que a todos les agrada, a todos los pueblos, a todas las naciones, tribus, y lenguas?

¿Cuál pues es la cosa de la cuál todos han participado? ¿No es el oro? ¿no es la pompa? ¿no son los bienes terrenales? ¿Y esto, que no es el alimento de la soberbia? ¿No es el alimento del egoismo? ¿Y la soberbia y el egoismo, que no es lo que ha dividido a toda la tierra, como también a todos los hogares y naciones? ¿No hay quien desee salir de la esclavitud? ¿No hay quien ame la libertad del alma? Ved, lo que nuestras hijas perdieron en babilonia: su honra, su vergüenza, su decencia, su respeto; y ahora visten y andan y hablan como mujeres que no entienden el bien, y como mujeres que nunca han sabido que hay un Dios; porque en babilonia han aprendido de las practicas más ajenas a la verdad, y de las costumbres más lasciviosas; ¿Y a los maestros, qué se les da? Nada les importa a los enseñadores que nuestras hijas sean objeto de codicia y de lascivia. Todos los que estén cansados ya del yugo de babilonia y de la esclavitud de Egipto. Salgan y descansen sus almas ejercitándose en la fe y en la misericordia.

Miremos por los pobres, abogemos por los que están sin defensor; abramos la boca por el mudo, pongamos nuestros ojos, a la disposición de los cielos; hagamos bien, que ya no es tiempo de cantarle al aire, ni de orarle a los altares de Babel.

Adoremos en espíritu, porque Dios es Espíritu; Dios se agrada de obras, más bien que de palabras; y es honrado por los justos más a los de labios mentirosos, aborrece. Dejemos las costumbres de Babilonia, que los agentes de Satanás nos enseñaron; y todo aquel que ama la vida: quite sus ojos de las cosas de la vida terrenal.

Son nuestros hechos sin amor ni Misericordia, los que han traído ignominia a nuestras alabanzas.

Es nuestra rebeldía, contra los mandamientos de Jesucristo: la que ha hecho repugnante a los oídos de Dios, todas nuestras ceremonias y ritos; No es por falta de melodía o por falta de nota, que Dios aborrece nuestros cantos; sino por que nuestro corazón no conoce misericordia, y al oprimido no hemos hecho bien. Nadie se engañe, que mejor alababan los fariseos; y no es por falta de alabanza, sino por falta de santidad. Por la razón que Dios dejó a Israel: por esa misma razón, nos ha dejado a nosotros. Israel abandonó los caminos de Dios, cuando dejó e ignoró la Justicia y la Misericordia; y ahora, no hay Misericordia ni entre los hijos para con los padres; menos para el huérfano y el extranjero. Todas nuestras Oraciones dejaron de ser oídas por Dios: cuando nosotros le cerramos el oído al que gritaba, y no respondimos a la necesidad del oprimido. Y cada uno se engaña solo, creyendo y testificando que ha recibido su petición. ¿Perdonará Dios al que no perdona? Tendrá Dios Misericordia del que no tiene Misericordia? ¿Bendecirá Dios al que maldice? ¿No condena Dios al que condena su prójimo? Por otra parte: ¿No alcanzará misericordia el misericordioso? ¿El que perdona, no alcanzará Perdón? ¿El que da no recibe? y ¿quién da sin aprender de Cristo, quien perdona sin aprender de Cristo? ¿Quién puede obrar con misericordia sin haber antes aprendido de Cristo?

Sin Cristo no podemos hacer nada; y es por esto que no podemos hacer bien: porque hemos dejado a Cristo. Y todas nuestras alabanzas han venido a ser abominables a los ojos de Dios: y nuestras oraciones ya no las puede sufrir.

Nadie confíe en cantos y oraciones públicas. Es cierto que en los cantos como en las oraciones nada malo hay; sino que el mal está en nuestras vidas, que desagradan a Dios nuestro Creador. Limpiemos nuestros corazones, y luego elevaremos cantos. Arrepiéntase cada uno, y obre Misericordia, y luego su Oración también será oída.

No es tiempo ya de presentar peticiones, ni es tiempo de levantar templos; levante cada uno sus ojos y mire el fuego que viene por toda la tierra; la tierra clama por ser purgada, a causa de nuestra mucha rebeldía; nadie engañe su corazón. Engañoso es el corazón y vana la apariencia, pero esto, el necio no lo entiende; mas el sabio sobre Justicia pone su casa, y con sus hechos en Dios la edifica. Los necios confían, y llevan el daño; mas el que teme a Dios, conoce los tiempos.

EL AMOR PERDIDO

El Amor de Dios, pereció del corazón de los hombres; ya no se ve el Amor de Cristo en los cristianos. Y ¿cómo sabemos que ya no hay Amor? ¿Cuál es el fruto del Amor? ¿Cuál es la potencia y virtud del Amor? ¿Qué señas y manifestaciones hay, donde el Amor existe? ¿Se vé el Amor, para que hablemos de él? Hablamos del Amor de Dios, no del amor de los hombres; El Amor de Dios es espíritu, es vida, es virtud, es potencia. El que conoce a Dios conoce el Amor de Dios: pero ¿qué es conocer a Dios? El Amor es profundo como la misma sabiduría, el Amor es profundo como lo es cualquier otra potencia que Dios formó. Así como cualquier ciencia tiene su profundidad, su altura, su anchura y su longitud. Así también el Amor de Dios tiene su profundidad y su altura. Muchos manejan la música, pero pocos en verdad la conocen y la saben. Muchos usan los números de la arithmética, y se valen de los números para arreglar cuentas; pero pocos en verdad conocen la arithmética. Muchos hablan de historia, pero pocos en verdad la conocen; muchos citan la Biblia, pero pocos en verdad la conocen. Muchos hablan de botánica; pero pocos en verdad la conocen a fondo. Pues así es en el Amor de Dios; muchos hablan de él, pero bien pocos tienen parte del Amor de Dios. El Amor de Dios, es el espíritu que une a todas las cosas en una; es el espíritu que interpenetra en toda la creación de Dios. El Amor de Dios no es una cosa que se aprende o se adquiere en un año ni en dos; como toda otra ciencia, es asunto de toda la vida, pero difiere en mucho a las otras ciencias: y sobrepuja a todo conocimiento. El que conoce el Amor de Dios, entiende todas las cosas. El que tiene o conoce el Amor de Dios: no se irrita en nada, no piensa lo malo, no busca lo suyo propio, no busca lo terrenal ni se gloria en las riquezas de esta tierra. El que tiene el Amor de Dios, no se rebela contra los mandamientos de Dios. ni tampoco hace prejuiciosa causa de nombres y opiniones como lo hace el mundo entero en estos días. El que tiene el Amor de Dios no confía en cantos y ceremonias, sino que teme a Dios y hace bien a todos. El que tiene Amor obra justicia, hace misericordia con todos, da y no rehusa al que le pide, el que tiene Amor de Dios se deleita en la palabra de Dios y guarda los mandamientos de Dios sin renegar. Pero que lástima y que desgracia tan grande: que en estos días el Amor de Dios lo identifiquen con una palabra; todos desprecian el Amor de Dios. Cristo dijo: "El que tiene mis mandamientos y los guarda, aquél es el que me Ama" (Juan 14:21-23). Pero ¿quién es aquel que guarda los mandamientos de Cristo en estos días? Todos aman a Dios de labios, pero de corazón aborrecen las cosas de Dios. He aquí, un mundo sin Amor de Dios, he aquí el pueblo que será puesto en llamas por haber dejado el amor de Dios; He aquí el pueblo que dejó a la viuda y al huérfano: y todavía dice "Amamos a Dios."

Este pueblo es egoísta, disoluto, y atrevido; sin amor a nadie, quiere que Dios le ame; Como el odio tiene sus síntomas, sus señas y frutos: así también el Amor de Dios tiene sus pruebas y evidencias. Y lo único que se ve en este pueblo que habita la tierra son señas de odio, evidencia de soberbia, manifestación de egoísmo. Pero ¿qué señas o evidencia hay de que el Amor de Dios esté en este pueblo? Los pobres todos se quejan contra este pueblo; los mismos cristianos, los unos acusan a los otros, y no se pueden ver con Amor de Dios; Los unos a los otros se tienen miedo y desconfianza, y por eso es que usan cortesía para saludarse lo uno a lo otro: pero esto no lo hacen porque le amen; tienen miedo de no saludarse los unos a los otros, porque ya se conocen los unos a los otros que son murmuradores y sentimentosos; como también levanta falsos. Es porque no se sienta el hermano: que se saludan los unos a los otros; y el hermano saluda, por tal de que no le refieran. El profeta o predicador que diga que este pueblo tiene Amor de Dios: este hombre es el profeta más falso y mentiroso que todos los hombres que están ahora sobre la tierra; todos hacen lo que hacen, por ganancia torpe y vanagloria. Aun los que buscan en estos días el poder hacer señales y maravillas, no enseñan el Amor de Jesucristo; Todos codician el poder para hacer milagros y sanidades: pero ¿por qué es que no codician el hacer bien y misericordia? ¿Por

\qué no enseñan a la gente lo que deben de hacer para el bien de sus almas? ¿Por qué no le dicen al pueblo de la destrucción que nosotros mismos nos vamos a carrera?

Por esta razón nadie guarda los mandamientos de Dios; por que a causa de los enseñadores el Amor de Dios desapareció. Cristo mismo dijo: "El que no me ama no guarda mis mandamientos" (Juan 14:24). Y esta es la razón porque nosotros no guardamos los mandamientos de Cristo; Rebeldes, ni los de Moisés, pero ni los de Cristo. ¿Bajo qué pacto estamos pues? ¿Cuáles son las leyes que deben de gobernarnos? Con razón ya nadie conoce pecado, pues ya desapareció la Ley del Espíritu; y sin Ley, pues ¿dónde está el pecado? Es por esto, que ya nadie es redargüido, ya nadie es reprendido: pues se perdió la Ley (IIReyes 22:8). ¿Y quién es culpable porque la Ley de Cristo esté sepultada en olvido? De aquí en pocos días las gentes le echarán menos a la Ley de Cristo, y lamentarán la pérdida de la Ley del Espíritu. Entonces todos la buscarán, pero no la hallarán; hallarán esta misma Ley perdida, pero la hallarán en el último día: cuando por esta misma Ley serán juzgados y condenados por haberla desdeñado y ultrajado. ¿Quién podrá tener en poco la palabra de Dios, y escapar con vida? Ay de los desobedientes, hay de los que se mofan de los mandamiento de Cristo; estos buscarán en aquel día, lugares y cuevas para esconderse de la ira de Dios; huirán, como el que huye al ver un león, pero esto sin ningún éxito.

LOS SOBERBIOS DE ESTA GENERACION
Austin, Texas
Feb. 22, 1954

El mundo, las naciones y sus cabezas están fundados en arena; la obra del hombre y sus mejores proyectos, tantos nacionales como religiosos están fundados en arena.

Las naciones están fundadas en tierra; los pueblos están fundados en arena; los hogares también están fundados en arena. Y en estos últimos días ¿qué cosa está fundada en piedra segura? ¿Quién ha tomado el consejo del Príncipe de Paz? Las iglesias no están seguras de sus congregaciones, los padres no están seguros de sus hijos, las naciones no están seguras de sus líderes. Y la conecuencia de fundar en arena es grande y mala.

Cristo dijo:: 'Cualquiera, pues, que me oye estas palabras y las hace, le compararé a un hombre prudente, que edificó su casa sobre la peña;" Cristo como en todo tiempo, aquí en esta palabra fué claro, para explicar la verdadera sabiduría, la verdadera salvación del alma. Es decir: no salvación de vicios meramente, no salvación del licor o del cigarrillo nada más, o de adulterio como robo o matar. Sino que él habló de la salvación de la muerte eterna, de la salvación del alma en todo aspecto; es decir: salvarnos del orgullo, de la soberbia, de la envidia, de la soberbia, de la envidia, de la ira, de egoismo; porque estas cosas son las que han destruido toda la tierra. La soberbia es la que ha engañado aun a los hombres más sabios: tales como Salomón, Rey de Israel, aun hombres de los que siguieron a Cristo también fueron humillados por la soberbia. La soberbia ha causado que los hombres dividan el cuerpo de Cristo en concepto y opinión; la soberbia ha puesto a la mujer como objeto de codicia, de lascivia de concupiscencia, y de adulterio. La soberbia ha hecho e inspirado a los hombres de Dios (o que son llamados hombres de Dios) a que se visitan como príncipes de Sodoma y de Gomorra. Un predicador del día ya no se distingue de un presidente de una nación; La soberbia es la que ha hecho que la Iglesia olvide y descuide a las viudas de la tierra, a los pobres y huérfanos, como también a los extranjeros. La soberbia es la que ha partido a la tierra, a los pueblos, a los hogares, a los matrimonios. De esto se libra el que oye las palabras de Cristo y que las pone por obra, que vive en ellas. Los que hoy en día se llaman salvos, no saben ni de qué son salvos; sin saber que son víctimas y cautivos de babilonia, de la potencia de los deleites, del egoísmo racial, egoísmo sectario y egoísmo nacional: confían en lo que los ciegos enseñadores les ha enseñado.

Cristo dijo, que el que pusiera su palabra por obra y que hiciera las cosas que el mandaba: este estaba libre de las cosas que vienen a la vida y esclavizan al hombre con espíritus de soberbia egoísmo e ira. Ahora en estos últimos días que al hombre le quedan: todos son movidos por cualquier mentira, es decir: son movidos a la ira, a la soberbia, y hablan lo que hablan lo que piensan con ira, con soberbia, con egoísmo.

Y ¿Por qué no podemos hacer y vivir según las palabras de Cristo? No hay fe en las cosas buenas, no hay fe en la palabra de Dios, no hay fe en Dios y sus santas palabras.

Cristo les dijo a sus discípulos: "Ya vosotros sois limpios por la palabra que os he hablado." Juan 15:3. Pero aquellos apóstoles tuvieron fe en la palabra que Cristo les entregó. Tuvieron fe que aquellas palabras eran de Dios y podían salvar el alma de la ira, de la envidia, de la soberbia, del error, del odio, del amor propio. En fin ellos vieron que la palabra de Cristo si se ponía en efecto en sus propias vidas: pondrían fin a todo lo malo que hay en el corazón del hombre. Es la fe la que necesitamos en estos días; y siempre es la fe la que se ha necesitado para andar en los caminos de la vida: que son los caminos de Dios, los cuales Cristo trajo en su vida santa. Fe, y sin fe nadie puede hacer según las palabras que Cristo nos habló en lo que ahora llaman: "SERMON DEL MONTE" porque ¿cuáles fueron las palabras que Cristo nos habló? ¿A qué palabras se refirió cuando dijo: "El que oye estas mis palabra? ¿Cuáles palabras? Todos sabemos que se refirió al evangelio que el trajo, y que es halla en Mateo capítulos 5, 6, 7; y ¿Qué palabras habló? En estas palabras Cristo nos hizo claro el perdón cuando dijo: "Si no perdonaréis a los hombres sus onfensas, tampoco mi padre celestial os perdonará a vosotros vuestras ofensas." No hay quien interceda por nosotros si no perdonamos; ni aun la sangre de Cristo mismo es válida para perdonar nuestras ofensas o pecados si es que no perdonamos a nuestros semejantes las ofensas que ellos nos hacen. El evangelio que los fariseos (enemigos de Cristo) predicaban y enseñaban, también limpiaba de la borrachera, del matar, robar, adulterar (Luc. 18:11). Pero no es esto lo que en verdad causa la rebeldía de la tierra y el mal que hay por toda la tierra. Porque todo esto solo es resultado. Hay un mal detrás de la borrachera, del adulterio, hay un mal detrás y que es primero que el robar, matar y las malas costumbres: y este es: la envidia, la ira, la soberbia. La soberbia pare la contienda Prov. 13:10. Y antes del Quebrantamiento es la soberbia Prov. 16:18. Lo que los predicadores llaman mal y pecado: es nada más el resultado y el fruto del verdadero pecado que ellos mismos no conocen ni pueden descubrir, porque ellos mismos están atados y son siervos de los mismos Pecados.

Con dejar de matar, no se quita ni muere la soberbia; con dejar el licor o algunos malos vicios no se acaba la soberbia. La soberbia es un espíritu, y es un poder que gobierna la vida del hombre; es una fuerza, bajo la influencia de la cual piensa y habla, como también obra. Es este espíritu y poder malo el cual hace los enemigos y despierta rencillas.

Y esta presente generación, con el curso que lleva, y con las armas espirituales que posee: nunca podrá despojarse de la soberbia. Y entendamos que es la soberbia la cual manda a los hombres hasta el infierno, y es este maligno poder el cual ha puesto a los Cristianos en un nivel tan bajo, que ahora, estos mismos desconocen las marcas de Cristo y la verdadera forma de la vida. santa. A causa de la soberbia, los cristianos se escandalizan de lo santo, de lo humilde y manso. Cuando es la humildad, lo único que resiste a la soberbia. Es la humildad de Cristo en nuestras vidas la cual puede darle resistencia a lo que ha dividido al mundo, que es la soberbia. Muchos conocen el licor, el matar, el hurto, el adulterio, y algunas otras cosas que se desprenden de la concupiscencia de la carne: ¿Pero cuántos conocen la soberbia? ¿Quién puede distinguir la soberbia? ¿Quién conoce el fruto de la soberbia?

Como la verdadera humildad tiene fruto, así también la soberbia tiene fruto. Como la soberbia acarrea enemigos, así también la humildad acarrea amigos. Como la soberbia hace mal, así la humildad hace bien. Es la soberbia, lo que mata la fe viva del corazón de los cristianos.

El que acaba con la soberbia, acaba con todo vicio y malas costumbres: pero aparte de esto, su fruto es árbol de vida; y a la sombre de su amor y misericordia se recrean los pobres de la tierra y las viudas no salen avergonzadas ni con sus manos vacías. El fruto de los que ahora se llaman cristianos, nadie lo apetese: Aunque hay dejado algunos vicios que los predicadores condenan como pecado, con todo, de la soberbia no se han limpiado. El que deja los malos vicios, ha hecho un bien, pero esto solo a su propia carne y no a los pobres y oprimidos de la tierra. Los moradores de la tierra se ha ensoberbecido más

20

que los pasados, porque la iglesia dejo la humidlad y no tiene luz en sus obras. La desgracia más grande, y el engaño más poderoso es que la iglesia en su rebeldía hace todo en el nombre de Dios.

¿Quién pues podrá aconsejar al pueblo de Dios? Los fariseos limpiaban lo de fuera, pero no lo de adentro: pero esta generación ni lo que de afuera limpia. Ningún bien hemos acerreado al mundo, ni hemos hecho salud alguna ciertamente que hemos quedado como el Pueblo de Israel; porque ellos ningún bien hicieron en la tierra Isa. 26:18.

Busquemos pues la fe de nuestros padres; volvamos nuestras almas al Amor de Cristo. Si guardamos sus santos mandamientos estaremos en su amor, como Cristo guardo los mandamientos de su Padre y estuvo en su santo Amor. Juan 15:10. Los hombres han despreciado los mandamientos de Cristo y han establecido un montón de acuerdos y mandamientos humanos y ordenes por las cuales nadie podrá escapar de la soberbia ni de la ira; mucho menos del egoismo, pues que por este que han dividido los pueblos y la misma Iglesia de Cristo.

¿Qué Orden de hombres, o qué organización nos podrá librar de la ira que viene? Pues si no enseñan a la gente a escapar de la envidia del egoismo de la soberbia: ¿podrán enseñarnos el camino para escapara de la ira de Dios? Nadie confie en hermano, pero ni en amigo; porque ahora los mayores enemigos del hombre son los de su propia casa.

Cada uno, niégese como nuestros padres se negaron; cada cual que ama la vida, ponga sus ojos en las cosas de arriba; y ¿cuáles son las cosas de arriba? ¿El Amor no es de arriba? La misericordia ¿No es de arriba? La humildad y la mansedumbre, la paz y la Justicia son de Arriba. Pues en estas cosas poned los ojos. Todos ahora guardan los ojos en las faltas, en los cuentos, en la ropa, en la buena comida, en la buena apariencia. Pero todo esto no es más que el fruto de la madre de todas las fornicaciones de la tierra que es el Espíritu de error, Babilonia con todas sus hechicerías de los últimos días. Nos debe de bastar que las naciones ya están para recibir también la ira y la recompensa de sus malvadas sobras. Ay de los que se han conformado con los ritos de la iglesia y no obran Misericordia para co nnadie; ay de los que cantan a Dios y no obedecen ni aún a sus propios padres. Ay de los que no reprenden a esta mala generación, la cual ya está para pasar al juicio de Dios. Ay de los que se glorian porque no matan, porque no roban, porque no adulteran; porque en esto no se distinguen los hijos del diablo: Antes como está escrito, "Cualquiera que no hace Justicia y que no ama a su hermano: no es de Dios." 1 Juan 3:10. Ay de esta presente generación: porque mayores eran las obras de los fariseos, que las obras de este pueblo. Nínive, recibió el consejo de Dios, pero este pueblo llamado sabio no recibe consejo. Esta generación no será acusada y condenada porque no canta ni será juzgada porque no ora, o porque no va a los templos o porque no tiene ritos en el templo: mas será condenada porque en ella no se halla misericordia, ni amor de Dios; no se halla Justicia de arriba; antes en lugar de la justicia de Dios, está la justicia de los hombres, la cual ampara al soberbio, y mutila al humilde.

EL SACRIFICIO IGNORADO

Nov. 27, 1953 2 p. m.
New York City

¡Ay de los que creen en el SACRIFICIO de Cristo, y no guardan sus santos mandamientos! ¡Ay de los que profesan creer en la sangre de Cristo e ignoran el PACTO, por el cual la sangre de Cristo fué derramada! El Mandamiento de vida fué ignorado, porque faltó la Fe; (Juan 12:50) y sin fe es imposible agradar a Dios; porque es nuestra fe la que vence al mundo. (1 de Juan 5:3, 4). Muchos son los que creen en el Sacrificio de Cristo: es decir, que Cristo sufra: pero ellos no creen en que ellos deben de sufrir por la Justicia. Por esto es que todos buscan su propio bien, unos de una manera y otros de otra; pero han negado el presentar sus cuerpos en Sacrificio vivo y agradable a Dios. Pablo el Apostol, también creía en el Sacrificio de Cristo: pero esto no quitaba ni le impedía que él presentara su cuerpo en sacrificio, y que lo pusiera "bajo de servidumbre" (1 Cor. 9:27). Y ¿En qué sentido ponía el apostol su cuerpo bajo de servidumbre? En este mismo Captíulo a los corintios les habla y les dice que el negaba el recibir salario de ellos: por tal de no poner tropiezo al Evangelio de Cristo. Y En el capítulo 4 de primera de Corintios, y versículos del nueve al trece: nos dice también algo de la manera que él ponía su cuerpo bajo de servidumbre: cuando desea: "Hasta esta hora hambreamos y tenemos sed, y estamos desnudos y somos heridos de golpes y andamos vagabundos. Trabajamos obrando con nuestras manos; nos maldicen y bendecimos; padecemos persecución y sufrimos.... somos el desecho de todos hasta ahora." Esto era parte de los sufrimientos del apostol; ¿y por que el apostol padecía desnudez y hambre? ¿No lo ayudarían los hermanos? ¿Daba el apostol mal testimonio de las iglesias al testificar de esta manera? ¿Pues quién debería de suplir sus necesidades? Antes el Apóstol, igual que su Maestro que no tenía una cueva de Zorra sufría con gusto, y a la misma vez dejaba un buen dechado a los hermanos; como también cerraba la ocasión y la puerta a los lobos y falsos obreros que por torpes ganancias hablaban la palabra del reino sin conocer el Espíritu de Dios. ¿Cómo sabemos que Pablo era uno de los que conocía el valor del Sacrificio de Cristo mejor que ninguno otro? Cuando dijo él: "Traigo en mi cuerpo las marcas de Cristo" y ¿Cuáles marcas traía en su cuerpo? Marcas de aflicción, de tribulación, de angustias, de hambres, de sed, de toda clase de necesidad. ¿Qué también Pablo tenía que dar su vida por los pecados de nosotros? entonces ¿por que Cristo no detenía los azotes que sobre Pablo su siervo venían? Sabed que este fué el dechado que Cristo nos dejó a todos. Cristo mismo dijo que en el mundo tendríamos tribulación. Y ¿por qué en estos días todos le huyen a la tribulación, a las necesidades y pobrezas? Todos buscan su propio bien. Y otra vez volvió a quedar la tierra sin sabios. ¿Quién se pondrá como ejemplo de la gente Cristiana? Por eso todos buscan su propio bien: porque nadie trabaja en el reino, de balde; antes buscan lo que pertenece al vientre. A esto se debe que nadie quiere crucificar su carne, todos creen en que Cristo debía de crucificar su cuerpo; pero nadie quiere en estos últimos días crucificar su propia carne. No se olviden que si queremos heredar el rieno que ya está para venir: debemos de nacer otra vez; La fe y el Amor de Dios ha faltado de los que creen en el sacrificio de Cristo. ¿Para qué reprender a un pueblo que no cree en el Sacrificio de Cristo? Muchos lo creen, pero bien pocos lo entienden; y los que lo entienden no lo llevan en sus vidas.

Si los cristianos entendieran el Sacrificio de Cristo y su santo Evangelio: otra cosa fuera; los hijos de los cristianos, honrarían a sus padres con socorro; los unos llevarían las cargas de los otros. El mundo mismo daría testimonio a favor de los cristianos; porque donde hay Justicia y Fe, Misericordia y amor: ahí hay buen testimonio, y los flacos de la tierra no serían escarnecidos como ahora lo son. Al Sacrificio de Cristo no pide templos hechos de manos, ni tampoco pide sacrificios cremoniales. El Sacrificio de Cristo demanda de nuestras vidas: Misericordia y Juicio, y Fe y Justicia; Humildad y mansedumbre; demanda que levantemos al caído, que demos de comer al hambriento; y que demos descanso al afligido y cansado. Paremos la alabanza vana de labios, y comenzemos la alabanza de hechos y de espíritu; pues que ya es tarde, y ya no es tiempo de estar celebrando cultos de labios; Porque ¿qué humildad qué misericordia o amor se ve en los cultos de labios? ¿Qué bien recibe el hambriento y desnudo, de nuestras reuniones? Obremos el bien por la calles, en los hogares; dando lo que tenemos, y no ofreciendo las cosas que ni nosotros hemos experimentado; porque todos prometen lo que no tienen, y lo que en verdad tienen, esto lo niegan al necesitado y afligido. Misericordia y verdad pide Dios de nosotros: y no culto de labios. Porque mejor era el culto que los fariseos rendían, que el que ahora se rinde a Dios en los templos. Y si nuestra Justicia no sobrepuja a la justicia de los fariseos que crucificaron a Cristo: entonces nosotros estaremos en el número de los que mataron a Cristo. ¿Y dónde está la gloria de aquellos que se holgan en el sacrificio de Cristo sin temer a Dios ni obrar misericordia en la tierra? Ciertamente que en verdad caerá la sangre de Cristo sobre todos los que no hacen su santa voluntad; y ay de los que teniendo el sacrificio de sus labios: en sus corazones guardan toda soberbia y envidia, cargados con las cosas que perecen, olvidados de los menesterosos. También ellos serán olvidados en el último día.

Cristo no dijo que en los últimos días iban a faltar templos para adorarle; tampoco dijo que la gente en los últimos días no iba a querer cantar y orar; Porque esto siempre ha abun-

dado en todo tiempo; antes de que él viniera, como después.
 Qué fué pues, lo que Cristo dijo que iba a faltar en la tierra, o en los moradores? La fe y el Amor: estas son las cosas que Cristo dijo que iban a faltar en los últimos días. Tampoco dijo que la fe y el Amor íban a faltar en los hijos de las tinieblas; antes en los hijos de la luz; porque ¿qué fe o qué amor se espera de aquellos que no conocen a Dios?
 Para edificar templos no se necesita ni fe en Dios, pero ni Amor de Dios; por eso es que todas las religiones han levantado templos grandes: por falsa que sea la religión. Los fariseos aunque eran (como dijo Cristo) hijos del diablo: ellos engagañaban a las gentes, y levantaban templos grandes sinagogas. Muchos creen, que al haber templos, ministros, cantos hermosos, Oraciones en público, y ayunos, como toda clase de obra que ahora hay en los templos: que todo esto es prueba de que hay Amor y Fe. Pero no es así. Porque los fariseos aunque no tenían fe ni Misericordia ni justicia: tenían grandes templos, grandes predicadores (y catedráticos también) y Oraciones como toda obra dulce y que parecía de Bendición; y segun el testimonio que el Espíritu de Dios da: los fariseos a pesar de tener menos luz que los llamados cristianos de estos días, estaban mejor y más cerca del reino que nosotros.
 Los fariseos miraban mejor por las viudas que el gobierno romano; pero en estos días, el gobierno mira mejor por las viudas que la llamada iglesia.
 Por la fé vencieron todos los antiguos, y por la fe obedecieron el antiguo pacto; pero este pueblo, con puras ceremonias se quiere justificar. Se necesita más que creer en el Sacrificio de Cristo; es menester que nosotros también, por fe andemos en el nuevo Camino que el Sacrificio de Cristo nos marcó Pedro pudo echar fuera demonios, cuando Cristo lo mandó; también pudo hacer muchos milagros, sin que Cristo le aumentara la fe; pero cuando Cristo le habló sobre el perdonar al hermano hasta setenta veces siete. Pedro dijo: "Señor, auméntame la fe. ¿Por qué es que ahora si le faltaba fe? Es la fe, la que se necesita para perdonar, para amar, para dar y servir. Cuando la fe viva perece: todo perece juntamente con la fe: perece el amor, el perdón, el servir; también juntamente con la fe perece la justicia y la misericordia el temor de Dios y la sabiduría; porque sin fe nada podemos hacer; por eso en nada podemos agradar a Dios. Ni en cantos pero ni en las oraciones podemos agradar a Dios; y sin fe, aun las ceremonias más solemnes son abominación a Dios, y no hay quien agrade a Dios en obras sin fe. Porque todo lo que respecto a ceremonia y rito, se puede hacer sin fé; de otra manera no hubiera falsa religión; pero nada de la verdadera vida, y nada del amor y de la justicia se puede hacer sin Fe. Es pues la fe la que ha perecido y faltado de la tierra.
 Porque si hubiera fe, el gobierno no estuviera manteniendo a las viudas y huérfanos; Si hubiera fe, hubiera Amor, justicia y misericordia en los creyentes. Es pues la fe la que endereza lo torcido, y es fe la que nosotros necesitamos.

24

Volvamos nuestros corazones a aquél que murió por nuestra culpa; ¿y si murió por nuestros pecados y culpas, permaneceremos en ellos? El que dice que Cristo murió por sus culpas y pecados: /y sigue viviendo en culpas y pecados: el tal se acarrea juicio y hervor de ira para el último día. ¿Cómo pues permanece la envidia, la soberbia, los malos pensamientos, la mentira, el amor propio, las enemistades, los pleitos, celos, iras, contiendas y toda obra que ha causado centenares de divisiones en el cuerpo de Cristo?

Por lo tanto, si alguno cree que Cristo murió por él, también la tal persona debe de estar muerta al mal y a la carne, y vivir en justicia y en Cristo. Nadie se engañe en estos malos tiempos, la ira viene porque el pueblo de Dios ha dejado los caminos de justicia; y todo aquel que espera el regreso de Cristo: apártese de todo lo que perece y ponga su vida en las manos de Dios; y con fe viva, reviva en su vida todas las palabras que Cristo le habló a sus seguidores. Es tiempo de no creerle ni al más cercano: porque todos sin querer hablan. En estos días, oirá el justo, y se afirmará más. Porque la reprensión es para el sabio y no para el necio; porque el necio aunque la necesita, no la recibe; pero el sabio, aunque tiene de que holgarse, se humilla y recibe toda fuerte reprensión. El sabio sabe lo que hace crecer, mas el necio, confía y lleva el mal.

¿QUE ES HUMILDAD?

Los que desprecian la Humildad, no están libres de la soberbia; los hombres que se detienen para escarnecer la humildad, estos no son sabios. La soberbia de la vida aparece cuando la Humildad se pierde; la soberbia se hace fuerte en el corazón del hombre: cuando la Humildad se hace débil; Porque es el espíritu de soberbia, el que escarnece a la verdadera Humildad.

Ni aun Salomón, con toda su sabiduría se atrevió a hablar mal de la Humildad. Ya no hay quien alabe a la Humildad, porque perecieron los que tomaban tiempo en alabar y hablar y explicar la verdadera Humildad; Cristo no solo tomó tiempo en hablar de la Humildad, sino que en su vida siempre enseñaba la Humildad. Cuando lo invitaba a comer, siempre tomaba la última silla o asiento. Cristo enseñó su Humildad: tanto en su vivir, como en el hablar; tanto en el comer, como en el vestir; tanto en el pensar, como en el obrar. La Humildad pereció de la tierra, porque el amor y la fe viva también perecieron; la hipocrecía y la humildad de los fariseos modernos, nunca pueden tomar el lugar de la verdadera Humildad; porque la verdadera Humildad tiene grandes y ricos frutos; la Humildad tiene fruto de Misericordia, fruto de Justicia, frutos de Amor, frutos de temor de Dios, frutos de Fe; ¿De dónde consigue la humildad fingida, estos frutos del Espíritu?

Cuando los hombres ignoran la Humildad, están ciegos y perdidos en la embriaguez de la vida.

Solo una clase de Humildad verdadera hay, y a esta Humildad

me refiero yo. La verdadera Humildad es Cristo: como lo dijo: "Aprended de MI, que soy Manso y HUMILDE de corazón" (espíritu). Los hombres han perdido la Humildad, porque ya no aprenden de Cristo. Todos aprenden del mundo: tanto para hablar, como para pensar; tanto para comer, como para vestir; tanto para vender, como para comprar; tanto para preguntar como para responder: Todos tienen el mismo espíritu de error, el cual Cristo dijo: que recibirían por haber dejado el Amor de la verdad. La Humildad no se goza en el ser servida, sino en el servir. La Humildad no se goza en el recibir, sino en el dar. El Espíritu de la Humildad no encuentra ningún gozo en las comodidades de la vida, o en las cosas que los llamados cristianos se gozan; antes la Humildad se goza en el sufrir por Cristo se goza en el ser escarnecido. Entre la obscuridad de la soberbia, de la envidia, del egoismo, y de la ira: la Humildad resplandece y se manifiesta; En la Humildad no hay ira, no hay venganza, no hay egoismo, no hay mentira, no hay mal pensamiento. Porque la Humildad vino de arriba, la Humildad es espíritu y no palabra. La Humildad la halla el que teme a Dios; pero los soberbios, y los hombres que confían en muchas letras, nunca hablarán bien de la Humildad. Porque les es cosa pesada y aborrecible la Humildad. Antes de que aparezca la ira completa de Dios, y espero que muchos alcancen leer estas palabras pequeñas, antes de que Dios se voltee y se ponga contra los habitantes de la tierra. Aún los pequeños de la tierra se han olvidado de la Humildad, a causa de que los grandes de la tierra no enseñan la Humildad. Todo fruto de la Humildad, y todo resplandor y vigor de la Humildad ha perecido a causa de los grandes: y solo queda la pura palabra vacía y muerta. Por eso es que nadie quiere oír esta palabra, porque está muerta; nadie toma tiempo para hablar de la Humildad, menos para vivir en el espíritu que Cristo vivió: el cual es Manso y Humilde. Dios tenga Misericordia de nosotros, de otra manera ¿quién podrá permanecer de pie, cuando Dios aparezca con justo Juicio? Tiempo viene, cuando los soberbios que con arrogancia despreciaron y mutilaron a la Humildad: serán puestos en apriete, y grande confusión. Sí, viene tiempo, en el cual los hombres querrán despojarse de su soberbia y tiranía: pero esto sin ningún éxito; pero no supieron lograr la salvación, ni conocieron al oportunidad que Dios les dió en Cristo Jesús. Ay de los que no hallan placer en la Humildad de Cristo; porque fuerza les faltará, para llorar tanto como ellos quisieran. Ay de los que ahora se mofan y desprecian a los Humildes de la tierra. Y ay de los que mandan y tienen el gobierno de la Iglesia en sus manos; porque estos serán culpables de que la Humildad de Cristo desapareciera de los Cristianos; estos serán culpables, de que la soberbia haya tomado el lugar de la Humildad.

La Humildad es fruto del Espíritu de Dios; cuando la Humildad perece del hombre: esto es seña de que ya no existe el Amor de Dios y el Espíritu de Dios en aquél hombre.

Nadie desprecia la soberbia; todos la reciben con alagos y

con grande interés; no hay quien aborrezca la soberbia y le haga guerra, y no hay quien la denuncie; y si alguien la denuncia: este pobre es ultrajado y le tratan de fanático. Ay de los que alagan a Cristo de labios, mas aborrecen la Humildad de Cristo. Ay de los que se llaman Cristianos y abominan la Humildad de Cristo, aborrecen la verdadera Cruz de Cristo: la cual se vive en Humildad. Yo sé, y estoy consciente, de que estas palabras para muchos no tienen vida; pero día viene, cuando estas mismas palabras serán buscadas por los mismos rebeldes y orgullosos, pero no las hallarán, sino para condenación. Porque, ¿qué gracia hay en el temblar por miedo a la muerte? También los demonios tiemblan cuando se les acerca su hora. Y también los que escarnecen la Humildad, temblarán. Os exhorto, en el nombre del Señor de toda la tierra, y con temor y humildad a que os volváis, y aprendáis de Cristo la verdadera Humildad y mansedumbre. ¿Por qué escarneced al mismo Espíritu de Dios? ¿No se reveló Dios en Cristo con Humildad y mansedumbre, para poder servir a todos? Busquemos pues, el Espíritu de Dios; el cual obró en Cristo poderosamente; como tambien en nosotros obrar si negamos nuestra arrogancia y soberbia.

¿A QUIEN PERTENECE LA JUSTICIA?

Mar. 12, 1954
Victoria, Texas

"Tendremos JUSTICIA," dijo Moisés siervo de Dios, "Cuando cuidaremos de poner por obra todos estos mandamientos delante de Jehová nuestro Dios, como él nos ha mandado." (Deut. 6:25).
Y ¿cómo hallaremos la justicia fuera de la voluntad de Dios? Dios "hace JUSTICIA al huérfano y a la viuda; y ama también al extranjero dándole pan y vestido" (Deut. 10:18).
El principio de la Justicia de Dios se descubre cuando él hace bien a los oprimidos y a los afligidos de la tierra; y ¿quiénes son los afligidos fuera de la viuda, del pobre del huérfano, y del extranjero? Por esto mismo, da Dios testimonio a favor de su Siervo Job. Y Job declara su misma obra cuando dijo: "Vestíame de JUSTICIA y ella me vestía como un manto" (Job 29:14). Y más delante explica él su Justicia cuando dijo: "Porque libraba al pobre que gritaba, y al huérfano que carecía de ayudador"—al corazón de la viuda daba alegría—Yo era ojos al ciego, y pies al cojo. Esta es la sabiduría antigua, este es el verdadero fruto de Job. Notemos que después que Job habló sobre su justicia y Misericordia para con los oprimidos de la tierra: sus tres amigos Eliphas, Bildad y Sophar quedaron con sus bocas cerradas. Mientras Job hablaba de la grandeza de Dios y de su fidelidad, los amigos tenían lugar y con que contestarle: pero cuando él habló, como se ve en 31:16: "Si estorbé el contento de los los pobres, e hice desfallecer los ojos de la viuda: y si comí mi bocado solo, y no comió de él el huérfano (Porque desde mi mocedad creció conmigo como con padre, y desde el vientre de mi Madre fuí guía de la viuda"). Con razón Santiago dice, que:

"La misericordia se gloría contra el juicio" Sant. 2:13). Y en verdad que la justicia de Job puso fin al argumento y acusación de sus tres amigos. Porque el asiento del trono de Dios es: JUSTICIA Y JUICIO, y Misericordia y verdad van delante de él. (Salmo 89:14). Por esto es "Bienaventurado el hombre que teme a Jehová y en sus mandamientos se deleita en gran manera. Su simiente será poderosa en la tierra: la generación de los rectos será bendita. Hacienda y riquezas hay en su casa y su Justicia permanece para siempre. —Es clemente, Misericordioso y justo—Gobierna sus cosas con juicio. (Salmo 112:1-5). ¿Dónde está la bienaventuranza para los hombres de ahora? Y ¿quiénes son los que ahora han ganado esta bienaventuranza? Se fueron de la tierra. Se acabaron los que seguían la Justicia y la Misericordia. Por esta razón la vida está escondida a los ojos de esta mala y torcida generación. Prov. 21:21). En los tiempos del profeta Isaías, también había perecido la Justicia: y les decía: "Oídme, los que seguís Justicia, los que buscáis a Jehová: Mirad a la piedra de donde fuisteis cortados." 51:1. La piedra de donde ellos fueron cortados era Abraham, hombre de fe y de Justicia. La Justicia y el juicio y la Misericordia, son las cosas que Dios pide y quiere. (Jer. 9:23, 24). Pero las cosas en las cuales se puede ver la Justicia y la Misericordia han perecido; y a causa de las leyes de los hombres, la Justicia no se puede ver. Porque las Justicias que los hijos de Dios deberían de hacer: ahora son hechas por los hijos de las tinieblas. Porque el pan y el vestido de la viuda lo proveen los hijos de las tinieblas. ¿Y quién defiende a los pobres de la tierra? Estos buscan asilo y refugio en las cortes públicas del mundo, porque la Iglesia los ha rechazado. Escuchemos todavía la voz del profeta Oseas: "Sembrad para vosotros en Justicia, segad para vosotros en misericordia (10:12)." Bienaventurados los que tienen hambre y sed de Justicia en estos últimos días. Porque ahora todos se hartan de las vanidades. Y por las cosas que la ramear está ofreciendo a los hijos de la Iglesia, han mutilado la Justicia de Dios y han ignorado todo mandamiento de Dios por mandamientos de hombres. Cada uno se justifica por las leyes y acuerdos de su propio grupo religioso; y la justicia que los cabezas ofrecen ha sido causa que la paz de Cristo se pierda. Y ahora esta paz no se halla ni en los hogares, menos en los grupos religiosos. Y nadie ha descubierto que el dejar la viuda y el huérfano, es fruto y evidencia que hemos dejado a Dios; Porque el que oprime al pobre, afrenta a Dios. Y el pobre y la viuda han sido oprimidos porque los levitas se han comido la parte que les correspondía a ellos. (Deut. 14:28, 29; 26:12, 13). Son barbaros los lobos que ahora miran por el ganado. Y estos como dijo el profeta Isaías: "son perros mudos que no saben ladrar, y estos perros mudos aman el dormir echados, y lo peor es que no conocen hartura (56:10, 11). La Justicia de Dios se descubre en Cristo, de fe en fe, Rom. 1:17. Pero ¿dónde está la Justicia de la Iglesia? ¿Quién justificará la Iglesia en su estado de apóstacia? El hombre en su Justicia vivirá, pero

28

¿Dónde está la justicia de los que ahora se llaman hijos de Dios? Los que no son siervos de la justicia, son siervos del pecado. Rom. 6:18.

Nosotros fuimos apartados para la justicia de Dios y para obrar el bien aquí en esta tierra. Dios no es servido en templos, ni es adorado por labios de rebeldes—"Por cuanto lo hiciste a uno de estos pequeñitos, a mí lo hiciste." Esto enseñó cuando dijo: "Mas cuando haces banquete, llama a los pobres, a los mancos, los cojos, los ciegos; y serás bienaventurados; porque no te pueden retribuir; mas serás recompensado en la resurrección de los justos." (Lucas 14:13, 14). Cuando Pablo en la prisión le hablaba a Felix, no se espantó Felix, por las ceremonias que Pablo enseñaba, ni por la oración, ayunos, y diezmos. Lo que le espantó fué, la Justicia el juicio y la continencia de la cual Pablo le hablaba. No resistamos a la Justicia del Espíritu Santo.

Todos los que aman justicia y temen a Dios, vuelvan a Dios; busquen en los archivos sagrados cual sea la sana palabra de Dios. Los que tiemblan a la palabra de Dios, estos serán librados de la ira del gran Dios Todopoderoso. Aconsejo en el temor de Dios, a todos los que aman la vida y quieren ver buenos días; que obren justicia, ya no compren ni vendan simplemente por vivir como los cristianos vanos y falsos, que están gastando sus días en comprar y en vender cosas vanas, enriqueciendo aquí en la tierra, pero pobre en Dios. Y es tiempo que los que temen a Dios, levanten sus ojos; llegaron los tiempos en los cuales no podemos creer ni a nuestros más cercanos; porque todos hablan mentira sin querer; todos son vanos y mentirosos; Son los días en los cuales, todos los que hablan, hablan en nombre de Cristo, pero todos venden la palabra de Dios, y nada se les da por la justicia que miran en tierra. Esta palabra no la vendo, porque no es mía, si fuera mía tal vez si la vendiera como todos los falsos mercaderes, que se han dedicado a vender la palabra de Dios. Yo no puedo vender las palabras que hablo, porque no fuí levantado por la carne, ni tampoco se mueve el mundo con todas sus obras de colores chillantes. ¿Qué cosa que me dé vida pudiera yo comprar en el mundo? antes todo lo que hay en el mundo son obras hechas por hombres que no temen a Dios. ¿Por qué dejaré que mi alma se engañe en lo que no tiene sabiduría? Todas las cosas que el hombre malo y vano está inventando, son cosas que nos alejan de la humildad y mansedumbre de Cristo. ¿Porque poner nuestro ojo y corazón en estas cosas que no son? A este nivel ha llegado la Iglesia de Cristo por todo el mundo; a llamarle oro al lodo y estiércol; a llamarle bueno a lo malo, y malo a lo bueno. ¿Habrá un pueblo más insensato que este—que deja la justicia de Dios, por la justicia de los hombres? ¿Qué deja el amor y la misericordia, por la soberbia y la venganza? Y lo peor, que cada uno reclama estar mejor que su prójimo: simplemente porque la creencia de su cabeza es diferente en letra, a la de su prójimo; mas en espíritu, todos están iguales; todos aborrecen en espíritu, a los mandamientos de Dios, y se rebelan contra el juicio de Dios; haciendo resistencia al Espíritu de Dios. Ay de este pueblo, porque se ha mostrado como el avestrus: el cual abandona sus huevos, el fruto de su vientre, como si nada le hubiera costado; Así también este pueblo, ha abandonado el camino de Cristo, como si nada le hubiera costado a Cristo; pero esperen el regreso de Cristo, en el cual todos descubrirán lo errado que estaban, y lo muy desviado que estaba el alma de ellos. Todos, como pueblo sin razón, como pueblo loco: se van tras las vanidades; y pagan altos precios por cosas que los desvían más de Dios. Como pueblo sin entendimiento, todos codician las mismas cosas; ¿Y que cosas son las que codician? ¿Amor? ¿Misericordia? justicia? ¿Juicio? ¿Fe? ¿Mansedumbre? NO, nada de esto, antes por lo terrenal se matan y pierden hasta las amistades más cercanas. ¿Había existido pueblo más impío y torpe? La historia no registra pueblo más dado a la vanidad que este presente pueblo que reclama tener el amor de Dios, sin amar ni a sus propios parientes en la carne. Estoy sorprendido yo, estoy perplejo de los líderes, en los cuales yo esperaba hallar algo bueno; Dije yo en mi corazón: sin duda que los grandes de la tierra los cuales dirigen a las gentes con la palabra de Dios, han de saber el derecho de Dios: y ellos sin duda me pueden ayudar para que yo conozca lo que es Misericordia; pero en todo esto fuí engañado: porque hallé que de ellos salía la mayor hipocresía; y que ellos eran los más culpables de que la justicia estuviera en tierra. Pero noté que ellos daban mucho valor a los mandamientos que ellos mismos establecían de sus propios antojos; esto me escandaliza. No hay pobre en la tierra, que dé testimonio a favor de la Iglesia. Los hombres que tienen y ocupan los púlpitos, son hombres avarientos, son hombres torpes que no aman la verdad; se valen de palabras dulces, y usan de labio los ejemplos antiguos, de hombres santos, para poder sacar el provecho que ellos quieren. Si bien hablan las palabras de Pablo: esto lo hacen porque ellos mismos no tienen palabras de ellos mismos; carecen hasta de palabras, y para engañar usan las palabras de los antiguos sabios. Pero ¿por qué no viven las vidas que aquellos santos vivieron? Si tanto aman a Pablo ¿por qué no lo imitan? Si ellos amaran a Dios y amaran las vidas de aqeullos santos: no aborrecieran estas palabras; ni tampoco tuvieran en poco el amor de Cristo. Pero ahora, ¿en qué se ve el amor de Cristo? Unos con otros se devoran, y cuántos no han caído por los mismos pleitos y divisiones que en estos días se hacen. Unos y otros que profesan conocer a Cristo, no se pueden ver; y de esto, mismo Dios dará testimonio en el día grande: en el cual hará venganza contar todos los malos e injustos que resistieron la corrección, y le hicieron guerra al derecho de Dios.

EL VERDADERO SALARIO

He aquí el Dios de todos se acerca, y consigo trae el salario de todos; los que le llaman Dios y los que no le llaman Dios, todos verán su propio salario; y cada uno verá el resultado de

30

su vida, el fruto de su conducta; los llamados sabios, descubrirán si en verdad fueron sabios, o si fueron necios e insensatos. El verdadero salario de todos los asalariados, aparecerá a la vista y a la luz de todo ojo; los que hicieron misericordia de igual manera, con sus propios ojos verán la misericordia y la Justicia de Dios.

Llego el salario de nuestros pensamientos, el salario de nuestras palabras, el salario de nuestras obras. ¿Y dónde se esconderán los que ahora se justifican en una fe vana? Todos los que llevan en sus vidas un cristo sin obra y sin justicia: ¿Qué será de ellos?

Nada quedará sin ser asalariado, esto, los que andan según la carne y los deseos vanos de la vida; porque el justo no es asalariado, ni en esta tierra, pero ni en el reino de Cristo; antes la recompensa del justo es Don de Dios, y es gratuita la vida eterna; su recompensa no se cuenta como salario, sino galardón de Dios. Ay de los que reciben salario por hablar con sus lenguas y no con sus vidas; ay de los que demandan salarios por establecer leyes que apoyan al injusto e hipócrita. Con la medida que midieron, también serán medidos; ya que todo lo hicieron por salario, y con el salario corrompieron la tierra; porque aun los pequeños demandaron salario, y nadie atendió las obras de misericordia; cada uno, de los grandes aprendieron a trabajar por dineros; y por los grandes fueron enseñados a cobrar y demandar.

Cada uno, a la tierra se inclinó, y por las cosas que alimentan a la sobrebia: sacrificaron sus vidas; aun el ojo del sabio, por el salario fué hecho tenebroso; aunque en su mocedad lo desdeñaba: en su vejez lo alabo. Los que predican a Cristo sin atender a la viuda, también serán asalariados con Juicio de Dios; ay de los que se llaman "predicadores" sin conocer lo que es "Misericordia," ay de los que enseñan el camino, sin conocerlo ellos mismos; y ay de los que asalariaron la tierra, y cautivaron a los inocentes.

A causa del salario, todos se mostraron ajenos de la Misericordia; pero el compasivo y manso no conoce salario, porque le es cosa afrentosa. Los maestros asalariados salen, cuando los misericordiosos faltan; cuando la tierra carece de sabios: lo asalariados se multiplican. Pero cuando los sabios dirigen, los asalariados no encuentran pan.

Cuando el asalariado domina, la viuda carece de ayudador; ¡Oh tierra, ya pronto será quitado el malo, y el justo volverá a poseerte!

Avergüencese el malo, y confundase el asalariado: porque esto no aprendió de Jesucristo; El asalariado no conoce misericordia, pero el Misericordioso: dando, recibe; y perdonando, también él es perdonado. El compasivo no es alquilado, ni el sabio se consigue por salario; pero el salario acarrea necios, y los maols corresponden al salario.

Cada uno mire a su hacedor, y tiemble a la voz del que lo formó. He aquí viene la Justicia, y nadie escapará de la palabra de Dios; cada uno mirará su propia obra, y nadie escapará de su salario. Nadie atienda a la voz de los que por interés torpe, enseñan mentiras, y por vana gloria, llevan carreras públicas. Volvamos nuestras almas al que la formó, y atendamos el consejo del que nos quiere salvar de la ira que viene; Dios ha sido ofendido, por nuestra rebeldía, y está irritado, por nuestros muchos pecados.

Nuestros padres que vinieron de lejos para habitar en estas tierras, ¿acaso eran asalariados por hablar la palabra de Dios? Por cierto que ni los cabezas de la nación, recibían tal cosa. George Washington, primer presidente de los Estados Unidos, no aceptó tal cosa como salario. Menos los obreros que predicaban la palabra de Dios. Pero, ¿qué ahora? los obreros nada hacen de valde; y aun se les paga por hablar mentira: porque si fuera verdad lo que hablan, habría fruto de Justicia y de Juicio; también habría Misericordia; pero nada de esto ha resultado. También ahora, los presidentes de la Nación han aprendido de los obreros del reino a recibir salario. George Washington, entregó una gran suma de dinero (que el gobierno le pagaba por haber servido en la guerra para el servicio público.

Y cuando estuvo sirviendo como presidente, nunca aceptó salario; y este era un grande ejemplo para la Nación; también George salió de hogar cristiano, y en él se ve que el evangelio que se predicaba entonces, estaba más limipo, y él aprendió de los obreros: a rehusar salario por servir a la humanidad. Pero en estos días, todos demandan salario, porque lo han aprendido de los cabezas de la Iglesia, que se han vendido al error; así vino a perecer el espíritu de servir a los pequeños de la tierra. Un asalariado no es un valiente, porque el salario tuerce el corazón del más sabio. Salid valientes, los que amáis el derecho; dejad ejemplos a los pequeños, y marcad huellas de Misericordia; pero todo el que teme al hambre y a la desnudes, quítese del camino y no estorbe; no traiga infamia al reino de Cristo: porque los servidores del reino, no se componen de asalariados; sino como padres que atesoran para los hijos. Si Washington no quiso salario por servir a un reino terrenal. ¿Por qué pedir salario de un reino espiritual y santo? ¿Si Cristo no lo hizo, porque nosotros?

Todos los que oran, piensen en los pobres; los que cantan en las congregaciones, lleven las aflicciones de los que padecen necesidad. Los que ayunan, y sacrifcan el vientre de alimento: pongan también la lengua en ayuno, para que no hable del prójimo, para que no sondeé la tierra en pláticas vanas; el que vacía el vientre de alimento, también vacíe el corazon de los pensamientos malos; el que pone su cuerpo en ayuno también ponga su ojo en ayuno para que ya no codicie la mujer de su prójimo. Es tiempo de que el pueblo de Dios, presente su cuerpo en sacrificio vivo, y ya no sirva al ojo, pero ni a su propio cuerpo. Los que performan y hacen las alabanzas y oraciones en público, también hagan Misericordia y verdad en público. Porque, ay de los que oran en público y mienten en secreto; ay

32

de los que cantan en público, y en secreto aborrecen; ay de los que hablan bien en público pero en secreto hablan con una lengua torcida. Ay de los que dan, en públicas congregaciones, pero en secreto no hacen bien a nadie; el que piense en Dios, piense en su prójimo; el que pide a Dios, dé antes de esperar; el que no quiere ser juzgado, pare de juzgar; el que no quiere ser condenado, deje de condenar a otros; el que no quiere ser murmurado, deje de murmurar; el que quiere ser perdonado perdona antes a su prójimo; porque Cristo lo enseñó desde el principio cuando dijo: "No juzgueis, y no sereis juzgados; no condenéis y no seréis condenados; dada y se os dará perdonad y seréis perdonados." (Lucas 6:37). Los que esperan a Cristo y su regreso, dejen todas las malas obras que en secreto cometen; purifíquese cada uno de sus obras que en secreto ejerce. Todos los devotos a los templos, tiemblen a la palabra de Dios; los que piensan ser librados: pongan a otros en libertad; porque el que no da oído al clamor del pobre: también él clamará y no será oído. El que dobla la rodilla para pedir al Altísimo: doble su mano para repartir al necesitado y oprimido; el que cierra sus ojos para orar: cierre sus ojos para no codiciar; el que abre su boca para pedir al viviente y justo Juez: también abra su boca para defender al afligidio y al huérfano. El que no se avergüenza de cantar en las congregaciones: no se avergüence de perdonar delante del que reprende; el que pide, regale, y el que recibe, no niegue. El que no quiere ser condenado, cierre su boca; y el que no quiere ser juzgado, haga misericordia: porque la misericordia se gloría contra el juicio Todos los que de Dios quieren recibir: no despachen al pobre con el "well-fare". El que espera ser levantado, levante al caído; y el que ama largos días: busque la paz del pobre. El que entiende que estamos en los últimos días: no habrá su boca; y el que sabe que ya viene el fin, haga justicia y misericordia. Los que enseñan al pueblo como pedir: también enseñen cómo repartir. Porque en toda labor hay fruto, mas en las palabras solas de labios: existe la pobreza. El que habla piense, y el que piense, obedezca; el que obedece, reparta su parte con los que lloran; porque los que reparten son antorchas, y los liberales, de arriba son oídos. El que es ofendido, no se irrite, porque la ira no es del hombre; y el de boca cerrada, no causa contiendas.

El ciego no codicia, el mudo no provoca contiendas, ni el sordo recoge mentiras. El que tiene ojos para ver, también sus obras son vistas; el que tiene boca para hablar, también en el Juicio a muchas preguntas tendrá que contestar; el que tiene oído, no tiene excusa. Los enemigos de los pobres, como el que no mira por las viudas: no es digno que enseñe a las congregaciones; porque todo maestro de entrañas duras, también sus discípulos salen crueles; y todo lo que no se deleita en hacer el bien: también sus lágrimas sobre el altar osn en vano. El que no hace misericordia, no es discípulo de Cristo; y el que no distribuye a pobres, no conoce a Cristo; porque el que no hace misericordia y justicia, es un extraño y desconocido al reino de Jesucristo. Los que confían, solo en lo que dentro de templos se hace: amigos son de los fariseos; y los que negligen la santidad en el hogar, cautivos son de Babilonia.

Los que ayunan para poder recibir, también ayunen para poder dar y servir. Los que ayunan cuando están en aflicción, también correspondan con las de otros, y no apunten con el dedo. Porque a los hijos de Dios pertenece el hacer misericordia y verdad; y la misericordia no es fruto de la carne, ni tampoco producto de la tierra.

Los que andan por las sendas antiguas no serán sorprendidos; mas los que inventan acuerdos y reglamentos sobre las gentes que adoran: de todo darán cuenta, y el autor de la vida los condenara en presencia de todos sus santos ángeles. Hagamos pues bien sin demandar salario, y sirvamos sin cobrad tributo de hombres; porque el que cobra, tendrá que pagar también; y el que sobra un favor, es como el que no lo hace. Lo de Dios todo es gratuito: mas el que negosea con la palabra de Dios, perderá la vida. Los misericordiosos son llamados entendidos, mas los que visten como príncipes, ganan para sí Maldición.

VOLVAMONOS AL QUE NOS FORMO
Agosto 3, 1953
San Antonio, Texas

Dios, sea mi juez, y él me juzgue, si en mí hay engaño o egoismo al hablar estas palabras. Sea Dios el que se ponga contra mí, si mis labios no hablan verdad y equidad: porque de Dios he aprendido lo que hablo. Si hablo contra el bien, y si mis palabras no son de Dios: sea Dios el que me reprenda; si yo hablo en la carne, y si por ganar gloria terrenal he escrito estas palabras, júzgueme Dios, y haga juicio conmigo el que no hace acepción de personas.

Mis ojos han visto el mal en todas las Iglesias, y en el lugar de la Justicia, ahí he visto injusticia; en el lugar de la misericordia, ahí he visto ingratitud y toda obra de la carne; esto me hace hablar, ¿y qué parte de mí, aborrece los malos hechos y las malvadas obras que entre la Iglesia se ven? ¿Por qué mi alma repugan y niega el estar de acuerdo con lo que ahora pasa por el nombre de Dios? ¿Quién soy yo para que hable y me levante contra las malas obras, y contra toda injusticia? ¿Por qué es que no puedo resistir el hablar? ¿Por qué no guardo silencio? El Espíritu que en mí hay, no me da descanso; lo que Dios puso en mi corazón y la unción de lo alto no me deja estar silencio ni callado. Hablo para el bien de los que temen a Dios, hablo a favor de lo que hace la paz; el que teme a Dios, abra sus oídos, y atienda a estas palabras. Ay de los que creen que están bien con Dios; porque los más grandes de la tierra son los que han hecho los males más grandes, y contra ellos está Dios enojado; Juicio y Justicia hará Dios sobre la tierra y

sobre todos los habitantes que ocupan la tierra.
Tan lejos están unos de la misericordia, como los otros; y nadie ama la misericordia. Tan lejos están los unos del amor de Dios como lo están los otros; todos reclaman conocer a Dios pero no conocen la justicia, siendo que Dios es Justicia; el que conoce a Dios también sopone conocer la justicia, el que conoce a Dios, también conoce la misericordia. Pero en estos días, todos le huyen a la justicia de Dios, todos aborrecen el hacer el bien. Los mismos pobres y desamparados de la tierra pueden dar testimonio y confirmar estas palabras; ay de los que lo han dejado el juicio de Dios, porque en los últimos días serán sorprendidos con el mismo juico que ellos escarnecieron. Ay de los que miran los mandamientos de Dios con desprecio, porque de aquél a poco tiempo temblarán y gritarán a la misericordia y a la sabiduría, pero no habrá quien se compadezca de ellos. Llorarán pero de nadie alcanzarán misericordia, porque ellos mismos de nadie se compadecieron. Todos han crecido y es han hecho señores de la tierra y aun de las almas; todos mandan y de nadie reciben consejo; ay de estos porque en los últimos días, llorarán y se lamentarán por haber ultrajado a las cosas del Espíritu de Dios, cuando de labios profesaban tener el Espíritu de Dios; esto ha traido grande mal sobre la tierra, y ha mutilado a las cosas de Dios. Ay de los que no se compadecen de los oprimidos, porque en aquel día ¿quién se compadecerá de ellos? Hay de los que escarnecen a la mansedumbre y a la humildad, porque en aquel día la soberbia misma los matará, y la riqueza de ellos los pudrirá. A causa de que los hombres que dirigían la palabra de Dios buscaron lo terrenal; todos han perdido el hambre y la sed por la justicia: y en vez de esto, todos van tras lo terrenal. Todos buscan las cosas de colores brillantes, y cosas de lujo, aunque no dejen ni un pedazo de pan para el pobre y el huérfano. Dios está enojado, y el mismo Cordero de Dios va a arrojar su grande y terrible ira sobre los que profesan su nombre sin conocer ni lo que es misericordia. Ay de los que dicen que temen a Dios y no guardan sus santos mandamientos; ay de los que dicen que son salvos y no obedecen ni a sus propios padres; ay de los que confían en palabras de hombres y mandamientos de asalariados: porque grande será la ira de Dios sobre este pueblo que de labios le confesó, mas su corazón lo entregó al diablo y a toda obra de iniquidad. Dios tenga misericordia de la humanidad, porque muchos inocentes nada deben, pero con astucia de los hombres malos han sido engañados. ¡Dios santo! libra tú a los pequeños de la tierra; haznos ver que estamos en los tiempos que no hay ni amor pero ni fe: para poder entender los tiempos, y arrepntirnos con sabiduría de corazón. Tanto los unos, como los otros; tanto los llamados de este nombre, como los llamados de aquél nombre: todos van tras lo que perece, todos cierran las puertas del corazón a la misericordia de Dios como a la justicia y al juicio; ¿qué haremos en estos días de Guerra y de ira? Salgan los sabios de

la tierra, hablen los hombres de seso; ¿Qué bien hemos hecho en la tierra? ¿No hemos quitado la honra a la mujer? ¿No hemos hecho que el hijo aborrezca al padre y no le obedezca? ¿NO es por nuestra culpa, que la tierra está dividida? Por no haber dado la palabra de Dios como él la mandó, y por no vivir las vidas que el mandó a los cabezas: por esto mismo, toda la tierra está dividida y peleada y ay de los que han causado este mal sobre la tierra.. Miro por todas partes por ver si hay vergüenza en el hombre como en la mujer: pero no la hallo. Todos se han corrompido, todos van tras la codicia, hombres y mujeres, niños y viejos. La Iglesia ha perdido su santidad, la Iglesia ha dejado el camino de Dios y ha perdido su sabor. ¿Quién se levantará a brillar por nosotros? ¿De dónde tomaremos luz, para conducir nuestras almas y las de otros? Pues hemos dejado la voluntad de Dios y hemos escarnecido a todo buen y santo mandamiento, los cuales fueron dados para que el hombre viviera en la voluntad de Dios y para que no callera.......
Los que escarnecen a la humildad y a la mansedumbre: a Cristo escarnecen, y contra sus propias vidas declaran sentencias; los que tienen en poco a la Justicia, a Cristo tienen en poco: porque Cristo es Justicia. El que viste con vestiduras delicadas, en ellas tropezará; el que busca pan delicado, en él saldrá confundido; en aquel día sabrán los maestros por qué todos los profetas fueron pobres, y por qué nuestro maestro nunca tuvo ni siquiera una cueva de zorras. Los profetas no fueron pobres porque les faltaba, ni carecieron de pan porque Dios no los bendecía; antes, se guardaron voluntariamente ajenos de todas estas cosas que siempre han sido el tropiezo y la caída de los codiciosos: porque sabían y entendían por el Espíritu que habían recibido, que todas esas cosas son vanidad de vanidades. Estoy cierto que ninguno de los profetas codiciaria la sabiduría de los maestros de nuestros días. Porque a los ojos de un justo y de un verdadero sabio: estos maestros parecen: aun por fuerza (puesto que no encubren su inmundicia) a sodomitas, y como los más necios que el mundo ha tenido: codician con ardor, y la codicia de ellos les mueve: como el viento que mueve las grandes ondas de la mar. No hay color ni figura que no codicien; y ahora: ¿Por qué digo esto, seré juzgado; porque hablo así, busco el mal del pueblo como también Jeremías fué acusado? ¿Seré yo el escandaloso, y nada de mal hay en el pueblo que se llama de Dios; estaré tan ciego que me figuro toda esta maldad, pero en verdad nada de ello existe? ¿Serán nada más faltas las que hay en el pueblo de Dios, pero mucho bien también se halla entre ellos? ¿Cuál es el bien que la Iglesia ha hecho en la tierra? Reúnanse los sabios, y dada consejo, defended al pueblo de Dios y justificarlo; si yo estoy solo en estas palabras, y si de mi propio ceso hablo, y si Dios esta ajeno de estas palabras: cada uno presente su justicia, y defienda el bien que en la Iglesia se halla. Para mí sería el mal, si estoy solo en estas palabras. El que reclama la Justicia, y pelea por el derecho esta arriba; el dueño de la verdad es el que reclama todo esto.

36

Porque ¿quién soy yo para que reclamara tal derecho y justicia del pueblo de Dios? ¿Qué se me da a mí? Arriba esta el que pide esto de su pueblo. Deje cada uno la codicia, hagamos bien como nuestros padres al principio, levantemos las sendas que nuestros padres arrojaron, levantemos lo que está en tierra.

Volvamos el corazón al que lo formó, tornemos el oído al que lo formo, demos gloria al que hizo los cielos y la tierra. Al que formó la tierra y la hinchió de bestias, de hierbas y frutas, al que formó la mar y todo lo que vemos como lo que no vemos. Al que lo orden todo con oculta sabiduría; antes de que se levante para castigar al morador de la tierra; vamos todos volvamos a nuestro Dios, el es bueno y Misericordioso, para los que le aman y guardan sus santos mandamientos. ¿Por qué avergonzarnos delante del santo y Justo Dios? ¿Quién podrá pararse con soberbia delante de él. Digno es Dios de que se le tema; Su potencia y su sabiduría no se puede medir ni platicar; su obra terrible no la puede ver el hombre con su ojo desnudo, y el efecto de sus palabras no las puede soportar el hombre; la tierra con todas sus grandes montañas y con su basta Mar, tiembla como un borracho cuando él habla. Humean los montes, y se quiebran las rocas más fuertes, tan solo al verlo airado. Su ira es terrible, y con ella limpia la tierra, y la libra de los gusanos tiranos, porque el hombre no es más. Su amor perfecciona las cosas, y en su amor da vida a todas las cosas; también en su ira, destruye todas las cosas que le corrompen y les quita la vida para que no pequen. Los sabios que el mundo alaba, y los maestros que son grandes a los ojos de las congregaciones: son como pulgas a la presencia de Dios. Y con todo, nuestro gran Dios no desestima a nadie; tampoco cargó él al hombre más de lo justo; El habla, y un millón de cosas tiemblan, él ordena y todos obedecen, su santa obra se pone en acción cuando de él salen mandamientos. Las nubes, el viento, la tierra, las fierras del campo, las aves de los cielos, los hombres de la tierra: todos esperan en él. Y él como un Padre compasivo, a todos da alimento. Los grandes sabios nunca han comprendido su obra, ni los ilustres han podido sondear su creación. Salomón, se esforzó, pero pronto se cansó; propuso conocer la obra de Dios y entender su sabiduría, pero esto sin ningún éxito. El viento, que no se vé, el viento que no se puede tocar ni palpar, el viento que no tiene ni figura pero ni color; el viento el aire que no molesta ni a un insecto: pues Dios, le manda, y se enfurece; le ordena y el viento se hace fuerte. Dios se esfuerce y exige más del viento, y entonces este viento que antes no movía ni a un insecto: ahora se mueve por las montañas, se lanza por los desiertos; envuelve al mundo entero, rompe con su fuerza a la gran mar; quiebra con su ira a los peñacos más antiguos; humilla a la obra más fuerte del hombre; y ante este viento que antes no movía un cabello: los más fuertes temen, y lo más estable desaparece; y no hay quien se le pare en su carrera. Temamos pues, al que habló a Moisés, al que levantó a Jesucristo para ponerlo por Juez de vivos y muertos. Dejemos la obra del hombre, y no tropecemos en la sabiduría del hombre la cual es muerte si la seguimos hasta el fin. Pero la sabiduría que es de Dios, primeramente es vida, luego fortaleza, riqueza, y no tiene fin de paz. Regresemos el corazón a su dueño; Paz sea con todos los que teman al oir o leer estas palabras; y benditos de Dios sean todos los que reciben la corrección de la sabiduría.

LA ESPOSA INFIEL

Mayo 9, 1953
Melvin, Mich.

La verdadera Esposa de Cristo, ama a su Señor; La Iglesia de Cristo, toda su larga jornada en esta tierra, ha sido de tragos amargos. Su Esposo que fue Cristo, la enseñó a sufrir; el fué el primero en aprender el sufrimiento; en llevar y sufrir los escarnios de la gente; él no tuvo casa propia, y por esto le llamaban méndigo; no tuvo tesoros cual ningunos. Fué en verdad el pobre de pobres. Nada cargaba en sus bolsas, por que ni bolsas tenía; este príncipe de los pobres supo de toda clase de pobreza. Es decir fué pobre según onsotros, según lo que el mundo dice; pero según Dios no fué pobre; él no se sentía pobre; él se sentía satisfecho, porque en su corazón había paz, a causa del pecado que había en el mundo, él sufrió mucho; toda su vida fué llena de desprecios y aventones de la gente mala; y la Iglesia que le siguió a él, pues también conoció de toda clase de sufrimiento, y esta Iglesia amaba el sufrimiento. Esta esposa de Cristo era como una madre para las gentes de la tierra. Esta esposa de Cristo era ojos para el ciego; esta esposa de Cristo pasaba el tiempo dando de comer a los que no tenían qué comer; nunca buscaba su propio bien, antes sus noches las pasaban por los montes, por los vallados, por los lugares lóbrigos buscando un cesitado, y mirando a quien pudiera ayudar; no estaba agusto esta esposa de Cristo hasta que todos tuvieran lo que perdían. Ella se desvelaba; ella era al última en comer, por tal que todos alcanzaran de comer; en verdad que ella obedecía en todo a su santo esposo; le agradaba todo lo que su esposo el mandaba.

Esta Iglesia, Cristo la había sacado de un reino de tinieblas, de un lugar de servidumbre; y por eso, esta Iglesia se sentía muy agradecida y endeudada; servía de puro amor. Lo hacía con todo el corazón, y con mucho gusto en su alma. Nadie se hallaba en este mundo más contenta que ella, ni más servidora y acomedida que ella. En verdad que en todo era ella un modelo; todos la buscaban, y la lloraban porque ella atendía a las viudas, visitaba a los encarcelados, y entercedía por los presos hasta tanto no verlos libres. Nunca se agitaban las fuerzas de esta mujer santa; parecía que entre más servía al mundo en sus lamentos más fuerzas recibía; aun los ángeles la alababan. Cristo no se avergonzaba de llamarla Esposa amada; era la Gloria de Cristo ver a su esposa como se portaba en medio de todos;

38

Todas las demás mujeres la envidiaban mucho, porque ella era muy amada y estimada por todos los pobres, las viudas, los extranjeros, los huérfanos; sus vestiduras de ella eran limpias de arriba a abajo; El corazón de ella no estaba engañado, ni sus ojos se iban en pos de las vanidades; porque ella estaba contenta con su posesión; nada buscaba ella, porque tenía todo lo que hace feliz y contenta a una Esposa fiel. Así siguió esta fiel esposa por largo tiempo; pero creció tanta su gloria y su fama, que ella comenzó a mirar y a poner sus ojos en sus propias vestiduras; y miró que en verdad era ella bella y de hermoso parecer. Su corazón por tanto se comenzó a resbalar, y su mente comenzó a pensar en la hermosura de ella. Cuando ella miró que muchos otros hombres tenían puestos los ojos en ella, esto le movió el corazón; y su alma se estremeció; sus oídos se abrieron para oír lo que estos le hablaban y le decían.. Muchas ofertas de alegría y de felecidad le daban; ella miró que las ofertas no eran peligrosas, y que no era pecado, por cuanto ella no iba a adulterar; solamente iba a participar de cosas necesarias para la vida); hubo muchos servidores que le ofrecían servirla y atenderla bien, para que ella no tuviese que molestarse para nada; ella miró que no había mal en descansar y dejar que otros la sirvieran; pues, pensaba ella que ya había sufrido mucho ella por otros, y que ya había servido ella por mucho tiempo, y que nada mal había en que ahora la atendiesen a ella. De esta manera probó esta hermosa mujer el descanso que el mundo da. Nada de mal le pareció en ello; ella comenzó a tener muchos siervos y siervas que la atendían con mucha reverencia y temor; todo lo que ella mandaba se hacía pronto y con buena gana; esto comenzó a deleitar a su alma, y comenzó a olvidarse de sus sufrimientos, de sus grandes obras para con los pobres. Los ricos de la tierra también comenzaron a darle servicio gratis, y a reverenciarle; cosa que a ella no le disgustó; pronto los ricos y los grandes que le servían a ella, comenzaron a recibir autoridad de ella para mandar a los demás; y ella se gozaba en dar ordenes a muchos grandes, porque en verdad que su alma ella la sentía bastante alegre; nada le faltaba, ella decía; y le parecía estar en su mejor éxito y triunfo; de todas partes de la tierra venían a ella los grandes ofreciéndole su servicio gratis; pero ella viendo que hombres grandes y poderosos estaban humillándose a ella, se comenzó a llenar de tanta alegría y orgullo, que se olvidó de sus días de cautividad, se olvidó de los días que pasó en grillos de hierro sirviendo como esclava. Cuando la tenían con una banda en sus ojos para que no mirara el Sol de Justicia; cuando la tenía natada de sus pies para que no se huyera. Se olvidó ella de todas las lágrimas que derramaba en aquella negra prisión; también se olvidó un tanto del que la había sacado de aquél lugar tan asqueroso. Las alegrías de todos los que la servían y le administraban eran tan grandes que hasta ella comenzó también a embriagarse de gozo juntamente con aquellos que la amaban y que le rendían grande servicio; y a causa de los gritos y alegrías que la rodeaban, ella ya no podía oír los gritos de los afligidos, y de los pobres que andaban desnudos y sin pan para comer; ella del todo se olvidó de los que todavía estaban en prisión. Ella luego comenzó a prestar oído a los grandes que le servían y ella les comenzó a dar autoridad para que ellos administraran lo que ella antes administraba y aquellos hombres que nunca habían sabido de aflicción y de sufrimiento, pues no ayudaban al caído, ni daban de comer al hambriento, al huérfano y a la viuda no los amparaban. Pues ellos no tenían agradecimiento, porque ellos nunca habían servido a nadie, y no sabían los verdaderos sufrimientos de los que sufren. .Los grandes comenzaron a crecer sobre ella, comenzaron a torcer el corazón de ella; y le quitaron la misericordia que ella antes tenía.

Luego los hombres que nunca habían pasado experiencia en las cárceles de tristeza y amargura, comenzaron a darle a ella nuevas ideas y leyes que lla nunca había conocido.

Los que en estos días gobiernan a la Iglesia de Cristo son hombres que nunca han sabido de sufrimientos; no tienen agradecimiento; porque todo lo que ellos han dejado, son los vicios del mundo, tales como fumar, tomar licor, y otros vicios que los hombres levantan mucho después que se rebelan contra Dios. Y por eso, estos que ahora administran como representantes de la Iglesia verdadera, lo hacen sin misericordia; no tienen amor de Dios. No tienen frutos dignos de arrepentimiento; no tienen mansedumbre como Cristo, él que levantó a la Iglesia de su estado de esclavitud. Estos servidores son hombres ingratos. Que han dejado a los pobres a los huérfanos, a los necesitados; y solo buscan el bien de ellos mismos. Centenares de afligidos lloran y gritan por las prisiones que les atormentan; y estos hombres que engañaron a la verdadera Iglesia no se les da nada que el mundo entero esté en lumbre, solo que ellos no estén; ¿Quién nos salvará ahora de estos lobos, de estos pastores que se apacientan ellos mismos, y que a las ovejas solo les dan zacate seco. Estos hombres grandes que miran a la misericordia de la tierra, y no les importa; pero el propio nombre de ellos si lo pelean y lo defienden; esto buscó la rebelde Iglesia. Dios nos llama, y nos dice Hijos míos, volveos a mi corrección, y yo derramaré de mi Espíritu sobre vosotros."

Nosotros como Iglesia de Cristo nos correspondía dar de comer al hambriento. Dar descanso al cansado; meter en casa al huérfano. Pero nada de esto hemos hecho. El gobierno terrenal ha tenido que dar de comer al hambriento, porque la Iglesia no tiene tiempo de dar de comer a los hambrientos, está muy ocupada comprando muchas cosas que ella necesita. Esto es bastante vergonzoso. Dios tenga misericordia de nosotros.

Regresémonos a aquél que nos sacó del yugo de servidumbre; volvámonos a Dios que nos libró de la mano del diablo; no es tarde, levantémosnos y volvamos el corazón a Dios el cual es lento en la ira, y pronto en la Misericordia.

40

CONFUSION Y VERGUENZA

El pueblo Cristiano con escándalo, y con alarde, describe lo que ellos llaman pecado.

Se asustan porque el licor se ha multiplicado, porque el matar el robar y el adulterio también se han multiplicado. Pero no echan de ver que estas cosas se han multiplicado, porque nosotros hacemos la voluntad de Dios; debieramos de ver y hacer perdido su luz.

Dios no se susta por el mal que se multiplica en los hijos de las tinieblas, sino que a él le sorprende que el mal se multiplique en los hijos de la luz. Nosotros en vez de ver el mal que hay en los hijos de las tinieblas, debieramos de ver lo que nosotros mismos hemos causado, dividiendo la palabra de Dios y el cuerpo de Cristo. Y lo peor es que ni unos pero ni otros hemos perdido el sabor de la sal, y nuestra lámpara ha de ver la envidia y la soberbia como ha minado a los hombres más escogidos. Más bien debieramos de escandalizarnos de cómo se visten nuestras hijas, nuestras mismas eposas. Debieramos de asustarnos y tapar nuestras bocas porque nuestros hijos nos mandan. Ya el padre no tiene mando sobre el hijo. Mucho mal hace el vicio de licor, de fumar, el cine, el baile. Pero esto sabemos que no es fruto de un buen árbol. Y lo que hacen tales cosas no profesan temer a Dios.

Aun los niños saben y conocen que estas cosas son malas. Y creo que nada de esto se hallaba en los fariseos; pero ¿a caso les salvo? ¿Salieron justificados porque eran o se llamaban hijos de Abraham? ¿Escaparon de la ira de Dios en la toma de Jerusalem, nada más porque daban o pagaban el diezmo, porque cantaban oraban y ayunaban? Les valió todo esto? No engañemos a nuestras almas. Creo que en estos últimos días se halla más temor de Dios en las gentes del Asia a las cuales nosotros llamamos paganas, que en nosotros.

Hay más humildad y espíritu servidor en aquellos, que en los que pasan por el nombre de cristianos.

Debemos de razonar, y ver que el amor de Dios ya no se halla en nosotros. debiéramos de avergonzarnos, y tapar nuestras bocas todas; porque el juicio y la justicia de Dios no se halla en nosotros. A nosotros nos pertenecía el juicio y la justicia. Pero nada de esto se halla en los cristianos. Me averguenzo al decir esto, por ser contra el pueblo de Dios que hablo. Me siento triste y confundido al ver nuestra condición en tal estado.

¿Qué le diremos al pecador? ¿Qué hay de bueno en nosotros en cuanto a justicia, a Misericordia, amor para darle al pecador, en cambio por el licor y los vicios que el lleva? Quitemos ya los ritos. No engañemos nuestros corazones con cantos y oraciones vanas. A nadie le ha valido el cantar u orar, ni el ayunar después de dejar la justicia y la misericordia de Dios. Israel también lo hacía, aun después de haber dejado el bien y el mandamiento de Dios; pero Dios mandó al Profeta Isaías, para que les hablara sobre la vanidad de sus obras muertas. Isa. 58:1-10.

Debiéramos de avergonzarnos al ver a la viuda pidiendo su pan al estado y a los hijos de las tinieblas en vez de ir a los hijos de la luz. Nos debiera de causar verguenza y terror al ver nuestros hijos tomando el derecho y haciendo disolutamente.

Porque Dios al cual pedimos nuestras peticiones, mira desde lo alto, y considera de su lugar que nada se nos da al ver a los pobres de la tierra sufriendo necesidad de todo.

Pues el también se vengara y por esto mismo ha cerrado su oído para no oir nuestras peticiones; pero el mira que nosotros hemos cerrado el oído al huérfano y al extranjero. Y Dios siendo el juez que aboga la causa de la viuda y del huérfano, y que da el pago según la obra de cada uno: él también nos dará según nuestra conducta para con el oprimido.

Todas las quejas de los oprimidos son contra la iglesia y contra los cabezas que ocupan el lugar de príncipes.

Sea yo una espina, y un aguijón al pueblo de Dios; sea yo el escándalo de todos: pero hablo y hablará; acusaré al pueblo, hasta que se desprenda el juicio de Dios; no dejaré de hablar, de denunciar el mal y el pecado del pueblo de Dios, mientras quedan días, y mientras Dios manda y ordena a los cuatro ángeles que están atados, que suelten a los cuatro potencias mundiales; las cuales en su hora exacta harán la voluntad de Dios sobre la tierra. Los sabios de la tierra, los que tienen hambre y sed de Justicia, hartaos haciendo justicia y juicio para con todos. Sembrad en Misericordia; porque no es tiempo de reclamar, pues que todos hemos faltado a Dios. De aquí a poco, el hijo, el Rey de Reyes preguntará a nuestras almas: y ¿con qué responderemos al hijo de Dios? Sirva yo de testimonio, y oiga Dios mis palabras: que no he dejado de denunciar vuestras maldades; y por carta hago notorio vuestras iniquidades; porque no son de pasarse: de otra manera no llegaría lo que está para quemar los pueblos. Porque el pueblo de Dios es el único que puede evitar la ira de Dios y detener la destrucción. Pero cuando la ira llega: es porque el pueblo de Dios ha perdido el sentido de la vida. Los que despierta la ira de Dios sobre la tierra, es la rebeldía de su mismo pueblo. Porque si su pueblo está bien: pues su mismo pueblo guardará la tierra.

LAS ARMAS DE BABILONIA
Junio 30, 1954
Carlsbad, Calif.

El error cubrió la tierra, la maldad se apoderó de los lugares fuertes, la transgresión y la rebeldía se desarrolló en el corazón del hombre; así fué que la apostasía se apoderó de la tierra, y la justicia perdió su lugar del corazón de los hombres.

El error y la maldad no conoce concilios, la iniquidad y la inmundicia no respeta MOVIMIENTOS; porque para la rebeldía no existen paredes de concilios, ni la fuerza del anticristo se reduce a un solo movimiento. La maldad halla su morada en el corazón de los hombres, y la ramera Madre de todas las fornicaciones de la tierra, a todos ha embriagado del mismo cáliz;

porque la mentira el egoismo y la soberbia: no se hallan solo en una Nación, o en una secta.

El caliz del cual Babilonia (la ramera) ha dado a todas las gentes pueblo y lenguas, consiste de ERROR, REBELDIA, MALDAD en las vidas de los hombres; y esta maldad se ve en las palabras de la presente generación, en sus pensamientos, en sus hechos egoístas, en sus vidas llenas de codicia y de soberbia. Cada uno buscando su propio bien; ¿quién puede decir que esta maldad se ve solo en un concilio?

El Espíritu de Dios haya morada en el corazón que le teme y obra Justicia; de igual manera el espíritu de la ramera haya morada en el corazón que llamándose de Dios, es rebelde y egoista. ¿Quién ha escapado del caliz de la ramera? Bienaventurado aquél que no ha conocido las profundidades de la ramera.

Los que sabían el bien, lo dejaron; los que entendían el derecho, lo abandonaron; y todos los sabios dejaron la Justicia y mutilaron la misericordia; y cada uno se embriago de soberbia, y tropezaron en la piedra de vida (Cristo) no Obedeciendo al Santo mandamiento.

Como hijos sin fe se mostraron todos, demandando promesas de arriba: pisotean los derechos del Espíritu, y no atienden al Mandamiento de Cristo. La Ramera mata, el Anticristo mata, y Jerusalem sobre la cual Cristo lloró también mata; Los ministros de la ramera no son borrachos ni adúlteros nada más: porque los borrachos no mataron a Cristo: sino los que se llamaban del nombre de Dios. Los ministros de la ramera son obreros enemigos de la cruz; no enemigos de ceremonias ni de tradiciones compuesta de adoración pública; sino que enemigos de la vida de Cristo, de su humildad, de su mansedumbre, de su misericordia; estos obreros con sus vidas llenas de soberbia de la vida, a causa de lo que poseen: se declaran a los ojos de Dios como los más grandes enemigos de la cruz de Cristo. Los agentes de la ramera propagan la soberbia, ¿y cuál es el concilio que resiste la soberbia? Todos condenan al borracho, al ladrón, al adúltero; porque no hallan más qué condenar. Pero ¿qué de la soberbia de la vida: esto en el vestido de príncipes que visten; en las casas de placeres que poseen; en pomitos, en palabras en hechos egoistas; y la rebeldía contra todo mandamiento del Espíritu Santo? Los mandamientos de Cristo no forman pueblos ni concilios: antes forma un reino solo, santo y regido en Justicia. Por lo tanto nadie trate de santificarse en estos días de error y rebeldía con ceremonias de cantos y oraciones públicas. Porque aunque la carne es flaca para obrar el bien y la justicia de Dios: para cantar y orar, la carne no es débil. Porque los fariseos aunque estaban en la carne y que estaban en lo flaco (la carne) podían hacer todas estas cosas de cantar y orar y dar el Diezmo. La carne se conciente flaca: cuando se trata de perdonar, de amar al enemigo, de mirar por la viuda y el huérfano en sus tribulaciones; por lo tanto el que está en la carne no puede hacer las cosas que son del Espíritu y del reino de Justicia. Por eso la ramera y el Anticristo como "Jerusalem de abajo." No nos evita ni nos estorba en leyes ceremoniales. Pero esta ramera es contra toda obra de Justicia y de Misericordia. A esto se debe que la Madre de todas las fornicaciones de la tierra, nos guarda ocupados en tiempos hechos con la parte que les correspondía a las viudas y a los pobres de la tierra. A todos nos tiene embriagados de los deleites de la vida; deleites en comidas de príncips, en vestidos de presidentes, en casas ajenas de humildad; y en toda obra de artífice.

Cuando la ramera sea quemada, y los reyes coman su carne: la soberbia de la vida también pasará; con la muerte de la ramera, también pasarán los ministros que enseñaron el cristianismo de los últimos días; con el fin de la ramera: también tendrá su fin la rebeldía del cristianismo contra los santos mandamientos de Dios que nos fueron dados por Cristo. Por que aunque las gentes estén divididas en opinión y en ceremonias: en espiritu no lo están; porque todos tienen el mismo espíritu de codicia, de rebeldía contra los mandamientos de Cristo; todos tienen el mismo espíritu de soberbia, y un mismo espíritu los ha enseñado a hablar con mentiras contra su mismo hermano. La soberbia de la vida a todos se les ve en su hablar, en su vestir, en su pensar, en su obrar. Porque sus obras no son de misericorida y perdón, sus palabras no son de paz y de unión, sus pensamientos no son limpios ni ajenos de la mujer de su prójimo. Por eso la maldad ha hundido la tierra, y aunque los hombres se han querido santificar dividiéndose de los grupos y unos de otros: con todo sus vidas no cambian, porque no acatan al consejo del Espíritu Santo; y la división simplemente es fruto del pecado y de la rebeldía contra Dios.

Bienaventurado el que entiende cual es el caliz y la emgriages de la ramera: a fin de que no participe de los deleites de la ramera; con los cuales ha corrumpido a toda la tierra. El caliz y la ramera no consiste como muchos creen: en algún concilio como algunos acusan a la iglesia católica; ni consiste en el pecado que se ve en los ladrones, en los criminales de la tierra, ni en los que fuman. Consiste en el Error que a todos los ha conducido a la embriaguez de la vida, a los deleites del vientre; consiste en la locura e incensates del hombre cuando quita las leyes del Espíritu Santo y establece sus propios caprichos e invenciones: dizque para que la obra crezca, y para bien de sus reinos (concilios). Este es el error que conduce al hombre a la muerte y a constituirse enemigo del reino de Cristo.

Por lo tanto: todo Sabio, todo aquél que ama su vida, todo aquél que teme a Dios y espera su regreso: Vuélvase a los caminos de Dios, que son en toda humildad y mansedumbre; los caminos de la vida, los cuales son en Amor y en Misericorida. Cada uno haciendo bien a su hermano y a su enemigo. No mirando ya la paja del hermano, ni el mal de su enemigo. Porque en tiempos tan malos como los nuestros: aun el sabio cierra su boca para no hablar contra nadie. Nadie alce su mano contra nadie. Cada uno siéntase Miserable, y deje la risa por el llanto. Deje el recibir por el dar, deje el hablar por el oír la voz del Espíritu Santo, el cual nos llama a su reprensión. Limpie su mano, cierre su boca; ya no hay tiempo de justificarnos: porque todos han bebido del caliz de la gran ramera; y con sus engaños todos nos hemos rebelado contra los mandamientos de Nuestro Dios. Nadie compre, nadie venda, deje el comercio; busquemos al que da la vida; volvámonos al que hemos ofendido; ¿por qué negarle la vida a nuestras almas? Salid de Babilonia; todo el que ama la vida: deje la soberbia, la cual se ve en su hablar, en su vestido, en su camino. Deje la confianza en ceremonias; porque ya se acabaron los que cantaban de corazón y ya no viven los que Oraban de Todo Corazón. Los misericordiosos eran oídos en sus Oraciones: ¿Pero donde están ahora los Misericordiosos? Ay de los que saben el bien y no lo hacen. Ay de los que conocen los mandamientos de Cristo y no los Obedecen. Ay de los que invitan al Espíritu Santo y Resisten al Amor: porque el Amor es fruto del Espíritu Santo. Todos los que gimen a causa de tanta maldad que hay en el pueblo de Dios: salgan de Babilonia; porque el pueblo de Dios es cautivo de Babilonia; y los que enseñan, se alimentan con la embriaguez de la madre de todas las fornicaciones de la tierra. Por lo tanto, nadie confie a su maestro. Los que lloran, levanten sus ojos, que ya viene el que juzgara a la gran ramera y quitara las obras vanas de los hombres y sus Leyes.

¿QUE ES MISERICORDIA?

¿Qué cosa es Misericordia? el mundo en estos días, no es para considerar o a investigar qué cosa es MISERICORDIA. Pero para bien de los que temen a Dios y quieran saber lo que es Misericordia: hablaré de este fruto de Dios, o de esta fuerza vital que existe en el Espritu de Dios, como en todo aquél que tiene el Espíritu de Dios. La misericordia es importante, porque donde hay misericordia: ahí hay Espíritu de Dios, ahí hay amor de Dios. Donde hay misericordia hay libertad, y todos alcanzan la misma porción u oportunidad.

Misericordia es una virtud movida por el Espíritu de Dios. El que tiene el Espíritu de Dios, es movido a usar de misericordia. Misericordia es aquella fuerza y obra que se vé entre dos personas; es menester que haya dos personas para que se vea la misericordia. La misericordia se vé en aquél hombre que teniendo ojos, guía al que no tiene ojos. Es menester que haya dos personas, la una posibilitada, y la otra imposibilitada: para que la misericordia sea vista y manifestada. Un rico y un pobre, un fuerte y un débil, un sano y uno enfermo, un ciego y uno con ojos; un grande y un pequeño, un sabio y un ignorante; y cuando estos diferentes personajes se dan la mano el uno al otro, de una manera limpia y justa, de una manera sin avaricia ni interés: entonces la Misericordia comienza a verse y a manifestarse al mundo. Cuando el rico suple al pobre, cuando el que vé guía al que no ve, cuando el sabio enseña con amor al ignorante, cuando el fuerte sobre lleva y levanta al flaco y débil, entonces es cuando Dios está en el corazón del pueblo; cuando nosotros hacemos y obramos con misericordia, es entonces cuando nosotros también alcanzamos MISERICORDIA de Dios. Pero mismo Santiago el apóstol nos dice que "Juicio sin misericordia será hecho con aquel que no usare de misericordia" (Santiago 2:13). Y también Cristo nos habló en la parábola de los dos deudores, que debían aun rey o señor grande y rico; el uno debía diez mil talentos; y este habiendo recibido perdón o habiéndole sido borrada la cuenta por misericordia que usaron con él: fué más tarde a un consiervo de él, el cual le debía cien denarios: pero al que le habían perdonado toda la suma, no quiso perdonarle a su consiervo cien denarios; y los hombres entregaron a este al rey para que hicieran con él juicio. Y el rey enojado le entregó a los verdugos para que pagara toda la deuda que antes le debía. Ahora, y en seguida nos habla Cristo a nosotros y nos dice, que también Dios nos entregara a los verdugos, si no perdonamos a nuestros deudores. Por todas partes nos habla Dios de la misericordia; y Cristo dijo: "Bienaventurados los misericordiosos, porque ellos alcanzaran MISERICORDIA." (Mat. 5:7). Pero, que lastima es el ver la misericordia por tierra. El rico desdeña al pobre, el fuerte se burla del flaco y débil, el que tiene ojos o que cree que tiene ojos arroja al ciego a una cima más profunda: como los fariseos cuando hacían un prosélito, lo arrojaban y lo hacían hijo del infierno doble más que ellos mismos. El sano no visita ni consuela al enfermo, el que piensa ser sabio, no aconseja al ignorante; y la prueba está en que nuestros hijos están siendo devorados por la soberbia y la concupiscencia del mundo, tanto en los hogares, como en las escuelas, y también en las Iglesias con consejos muertos y débiles. ¿Dónde se ve la Misericordia? El que llega hacer el bien, no lo hace: a menos que tenga interes propio, o que le deje ganancia; como el interés del "Salvación Army" el "Wellfare" y muchas organizaciones que por torpe ganancia levantan orfanatorios, o casas para poner a la gente necesitada. Estos hombres que hacen esto, ciertamente hacen un bien, pero ¿Cómo no enseñan y predican a la gente que cada uno debe de hacer estas obras? Al contrario, en lugar de enseñar esto: piden a la gente con el achaque de que es para los pobres. Estoy cierto que si ellos predicaran a las gentes y enseñaran al pueblo de que cada uno tiene la obligación de ayudar al necesitado: pronto se quebrarían ellos; y ya la gente no daría dinero a esas organizaciones, sino que cada uno en lugar de darlo para un fondo público, cada uno lo daría en particular a su vecino pobre y necesitado; y cada uno tendría vecinos pobres a quien ayudar. Y así lo enseñó hasta la misma ley de Moisés.

La misericordia de Dios, se ve: en que siendo él fuerte y nosotros débiles, se compadece de nosotros: es decir, cuando nosotros nos esforzamos por andar en su voluntad. Dios es rico y nosotros pobres, y otra vez se ve su misericordia cuando nos reparte de sus riquezas en gloria, mas nosotros hemos preferido las riquezas terrenales en vez de las riquezas de Cristo. Yo veo que muy pocos aman en verdad y agradecen la misericordia de Dios: la cual es Cristo, en quien tenemos (si es que somos fieles y obedientes) todas las cosas que queramos y que pidamos; siempre que sean cosas que pertenecen a la vida eterna, y que nos hagan bien. La verdadera Misericordia, sin tacha y sin mancha: fué revelada en la vida de Cristo; si amamos a Cristo, recibiremos el Espíritu de Cristo; siempre teniendo en cuenta lo que Juan el apostol dijo: "Si alguno dice que conoce a Cristo y no guarda sus mandamientos: el tal es mentiroso y no hay verdad en él." (Juan 2:4). Así que queda por sentado que haremos como Cristo mismo lo dijo: "Si me amáis, guardad mis mandamientos; y yo rogará al padre, y os dará otro consolador." (Juan 14:15). Dios en su misericordia envió a su hijo. Cristo en su misericordia por el mismo Espíritu nos dió el evangelio que le costó la misma vida. Y quien tenga misericordia, nunca se podrá rebelar contra los mandamientos de Dios, ni tampoco podrá ver a la viuda y al huérfano en la condición en que se encuentran. Tampoco el que tiene misericordia no se afirma en soberbia como lo hacen todos en estos días. Dios nos dé de su Misericordia, y ojalá que andemos con temor de Dios, y tratemos de levantar la misericordia de la tierra, de dónde los infieles y soberbios la han puesto. Misericordia Quiero dijo el Señor de toda la tierra.

EL AFAN DE LOS QUE ADORAN

De día y de noche, se aperciben los hombres de guerra; de día y de noche se hacen las armas; todos trabajando duro, todos activos en la gran obra, fábricas y plantas movidas por grandes motores eléctricos; todo cooperando para el gran fin. En los grandes pueblos por todas partes del mundo la industria se mueve, los hombres se apuran; los jefes dan priesa, el hierro crudo es echado en hornos de lumbre, todo hecho para un solo fin; aun las mujeres de día y de noche trabajan en las fábricas en las plantas, haciendo grandes instrumentos, poderosos aparatos; los hombres de ciencia ocupados en sus laboratorios, pensando aun en sus camas de noche, y haciendo adelantos; inventando grandes aparatos y projectiles, trabajando a sus mentes como nunca jamás la ha trabajado el hombre antes. Los mineros sacando de la tierra el metal, el carbón para coser el metal crudo; los pilotos ensayando día y noche, para el gran día, volando a una terrible velocidad; ¿y cuál es el fin de todo esto? ¿Qué ha dicho Dios de este gran día? Todos estos hombres de guerra que día y noche es aperciben, miran y esperan el día en el cual volarán por el viento, subirán sobre las nubes, cargados con destrucción y muerte para todos los habitantes de la tierra. Estos hombres llegarán a los pueblos, pisarán la gloria de los rebeldes, unos contra otros; los pueblos arderán, las casas de verano y las casas de invierno equipadas con toda clase de pompa y finura ya no estarán sobre la tierra; la gloria del hombre perecerá, sus invenciones perecerán. Sus maquinarias grandes y portentosas dejarán de existir, los hombres las mujeres, y todo lo que tiene nombre sobre la tierra sufrirá la consecuencia de nadie. La comida fina, la ropa de gala, perderá su gran valor, y el hombre descubrirá que en verdad, fue engañado por lo que no era. Levantemos nuestros ojos ya no sacrifiquemos por nuestros cuerpos mortales; antes sacrifiquemos por nuestras almas, hagamos bien a nuestras almas.

Mucho es lo que el hombre está buscando por el bien de su propio cuerpo, y así ha descuidado el hacer el bien, y el obedecer a su Criador, Nada está haciendo el hombre por su propia alma; el alma del hombre en estos días, está estéril, está seca y sin fruto de Dios.

Padres, Madres que temeis a Dios, mirad por vuestros hijos, velad por el alma de ellos; ¿por qué dejáis a vuestros hijos que perezcan? ¿No valen vuestros hijos más que lo terrenal? ¿No son vuestros hijos de más valor que diamantes y perlas? Sacad vuestros hijos del infierno, antes que sea tarde; hablar a vuestros hijos del fin que se acerca; habladles del amor de Dios y obrad justicia delante de ellos para que también ellos aprendan el bien. Dad a los pobres de vuestros bienes, antes que el enemigo se apodere de ello; Oíd a Cristo "Hacéos amigos de las riquezas de maldad (por medio de las riquezas) para que cuando faltareis, os reciban en las moradas eternas." (Luc. 16:9). ¿Por qué esperaremos que venga la ira de Dios, en la mano del Anticristo, y tome nuestros bienes? Hagamos tesoros en los cielos antes de que sea tarde; busquemos a quien hacer el bien. Los que se burlan de este consejo que Cristo dió, un día lamentarán, y gimirán, viendo sus propias riquezas podridas y quemadas: Entonces dirán: Hubieramos hecho bien a los pobres con nuestras riquezas, o que hubieramos hechos justicia y misericordia con nuestros semejantes. Pero esto lo harán ya cuando sea muy tarde, porque estos querellosos y soñadores, están siendo engañados por las riquezas de maldad; cumplen con cosas que les convienen, pero lo más grave del reino de Dios lo han mutilado, que es la justicia el juicio y la misericordia, como lo es la fe no fingida y el amor de Cristo el cual hace bien a todos, incluyendo a los enemigos. Y estos no hacen el bien, pero ni dejan a otros que lo hagan; se han corrompido del todo, y han sido entregados a espíritu de error, por cuanto no quisieron el amor de la verdad.

Levantemos nuestros ojos, y miremos el arrepentimiento de los hombres de "Nínive" por eso alcanzaron misericordia y perdón, porque el arrepentimiento de ellos fué de todo corazón, y esto no solo entre los más pecadores, sino hasta el más grande sacerdote y profeta que entre ellos se hallaba; estoy cierto que si alguien se arrepiente con el mismo espíritu que Nínive se arrepintió, lo echan fuera de los templos, llamándole loco y ecéntrico; ay de los mansos de la tierra, ay de los que se quieran arrepentir de todo el corazón: porque tendrán que ser escarnecidos por los ciudadanos de la gran Babilonia; Oh hermanitos, los que os quereis allegar a vuestro Dios: sufrid el escarnio, dejadlos que es burlen de vosotros, esto será solo por un corto tiempo;

porque ellos un día ya muy cerca también se despojaran de lo que tienen, y lloraran con llanto amargo. ¡El fin se acerca, el fin viene, todo ojo llorará, y todos los fuertes temblarán; los cabezas y los grandes que llevaban la ley, también pondrán su cara en tierra; gritarán como la mujer que da a luz: estos grandes le huirán a las riquezas que antes abrazaron; maldicirán al lujo y a la pompa, por la cual antes se mataban. Conocerán que Dios es grande y justo, y sabrán que en todo engañaron a sus pobres almas.

Ay de los que mandan, ay de los que ponen acuerdos y leyes injustas; porque en aquel día, Dios los hará responsables de todo el mal que las gentes hicieron; ay de los que cambian mandamientos de Cristo, por mandamientos de concilios y de hombres vanos que no sabían ni amar a sus propios hijos y que no sabían oír en derecho al justo y pequeño. ¿En dónde se meterán estos? y ¿a dónde escaparán, y quién los apoyará? Porque día de juicio será este, en el cual todo lo oculto será puesto a luz de todos. De grande confusión será este día para todos los grandes.

EL SANTO MANDAMIENTO

"El que tiene mis mandamientos, y los guarda, aquél es el que me ama: y "el que me ama, será amado de mi Padre, y yo le amaré, y me manifestaré a él." Cristo enseña con estas palabras a sus discípulos, la diferencia de los Cristianos que le aman, y de los cristianos que no le aman; "el que tiene mis mandamientos y los guarda, "Aquél es el que me ama" y da por sentado, que, él que no guarda sus mandamientos, no le ama; muchos quieren amar a Dios, pero no saben, el por qué no pueden amarle de una manera que agrade al Señor. Dios no trata con muchos Cristianos, porque ellos no le aman, y aunque se nieguen y digan que si le aman, Dios sabe que no le aman, porque no guardan sus mandamientos. Cristo no habló lo que Dios no quería que supiesemos, ni habló o mandó lo que Dios no quiere que hagamos, antes, todo lo que Cristo habló y mandó, es porque el Padre se lo ordenó y se lo mandó para nuestro bien; es la voluntad de Dios de que nosotros nos amemos, y por eso le dió el mandamiento a su hijo para que su hijo nos lo diera a nosotros de que nos amemos unos a otros. A Cristo lo conocemos más bien por lo que él habló, y en lo que él habló, se deja ver la voluntad de Dios, y el completo "Evangelio" también se deja ver en las palabras de Jesucristo. Cristo sabiendo que era menester que el cumpliese la voluntad de sus padres, también a nosotros mandó que guardaramos la voluntad de Dios. Dice luego el Señor—"El que me ama, mi palabra guardará; y mi padre le amará, y vendremos a El, y haremos con él morada." Aquí Cristo nos promete la presencia del Padre que tanto deseamos, y nos promete que El y su Padre, harán morada en cada uno de los que guarden su palabra; Se ve que Cristo no compromete al padre en ninguna manera, porque dice— "El que tiene mis mandamientos y los guarda" esta es la condición que nos pone para que el Hijo y el Padre estén con nosotros, y si rehusamos al Hijo y al Padre con no guardar sus mandamientos, automáticamente rehusamos al Espíritu Santo, y esto aunque lo estemos invitando con nuestros labios. Porque lo que Cristo habla, es final, y este mandamiento recibió de Su Padre. No dudo que hay muchos que son bastante sinceros y quieren agradar al Señor, y también quisieran amarle sobre todas las cosas, y también digo que mi corazón es con el de tales personas; pero el apóstol San Juan, nos aclara esta buena cosa, cuando en su tercera Epístola les dice a una anciana, y a sus hijos: "Y este es Amor, que andemos según sus mandamientos". Pero alguien dirá: pues cuales mandamientos hermano, y cuántos. El Señor Jesucristo distinguió los mandamientos del Espíritu Santo, de los mandamientos de Moisés, de una manera muy notable; cuando él decía: "Oiste que fue dicho a los antiguos amarás a tu prójimo, y aborrecerás a tu enemigo," mas yo os digo, Amad a vuestros enemigos, Bendecid a los que os maldicen, haced bien a los que os aborrecen, y orad por los que os ultrajan y os persiguen." Cristo no se retractó de estos mandamientos más tarde, ni los hizo nulos, antes los cumplió orando por sus enemigos; toda palabra que salió de la boca de Cristo, fué hablada por el Espíritu, y Dios no desaprobó ninguna de las palabras que Cristo habló: Antes como dijo (Juan 17:8). "Las palabras que me diste les he dado; y ellos las recibieron" y en el capítulo 14:24b. También nos hace ver que nada habló Cristo ni mandó sin que fuese la voluntad de Dios, diciendo: "La palabra que habies oído, no es mía, sino del Padre que me envió" Y Cristo nos enseñó que los Cristianos iban a ser juzgados por la palabra de él, cuando en Juan 12:48, nos dijo "El que me desecha y no recibe mis palabras, tiene quien le juzgue: la palabra que he hablado, ella le juzgará en el día postrero" y el versículo 49 del mismo capítulo, dice el Señor continuando: "Porque yo no he hablado de mi mismo; mas el Padre que me envió, me dió mandamiento de lo que he de decir y de lo que he de hablar." Así que por estas palabras entendemos que la Palabra que Cristo habló, es de suma importancia, para que nosotros entendamos como debemos de amar a Dios, y cómo debemos de obedecerle. Porque es Cristo quien en esta ocasión nos dice, y él es el que escoge o nos dice quien le ama y quien no le ama: "El que tiene mis mandamientos y los guarda, aquél es el que me ama." ¿Cuántos amarán a Dios en estos últimos días? Pero en palabras más sencillas, ¿Cuántos estarán obedeciendo a Dios en las palabras que nos habló su hijo, cuyas palabras fueron selladas con su propia sangre? Cristo hablando con sus discípulos, les dijo: "Ya vosotros sois limpios por la palabra que os he hablado" Juan 15:3. Y añade en el verículo 7, del mismo capítulo: "Si estuviereis en mí y mis palabras estuvieren en vosotros, pedid todo lo que quisiereis y os será hecho." Bien lo aclara, si estuvieres en mí, y mis palabras estuvieren en vosotros.

50

¿QUIENES SERAN SALVOS?

¿Quiénes son los que esperan ser levantados en las nubes, y escapar de la ira que viene sobre toda la tierra? ¿Dónde están estos, que no han transgredido los mandamientos de Dios que son en Cristo Jesús? Estos que serán levantados, y escaparán de todo el mal que Dios hará a los rebeldes habitantes de la tierra: ¿Cómo fueron purificados? ¿Cómo es que hallaron gracia delante de Dios para que él los libre? ¿Cuál es el bien que ellos hicieron, que serán tratados con tan distinta gloria, y con tan elevada misericordia? Estos que dicen que no verán mal, y que su Dios los esconderá de todo el mal que viene sobre todos: ¿Cómo fué que ganaron tal gracia a los ojos de Dios? ¿Por qué serán tratados tan diferente a los demás? ¿Ampararon estos, que no han transgresado los mandamientos de Dios que son serán tratados con sin igual misericordia? Fueron estos el brazo de los imposibilitados, ojos para el ciego, boca para el mudo, piernas al cojo, y dieron de comer al hambriento, y había el amor de Cristo en ellos? O ¿cómo fué que estos ganaron tal premio y tan distinto privilegio de ser arrebatados a una hora tan rara? ¿Cantaban mejor que los demás? ¿Oraba en secreto y mejor que los demás? ¿En que se distinguieron sus obras que recibieron tan grande honor? ¿Eran estos Originales en sus obras, y no seguían las tradiciones y ceremonias de las otras gentes? ¿Amaban estos a sus enemigos? ¿Bendecían a los que les maldecían, hacían bien a los que les aborrecían, y oraban por los que les hacían mal?

Seguramente, estos que serán raptados siempre tenían su abogado en los cielos, y nunca se defendían aquí en la tierra por abogados de este mundo; sin duda que siempre perdían y dejaban el despojo en manos de sus adversarios por tal de tener a su Dios siempre a su lado.

Estos que esperan escapar de la ira de Dios, ¿nunca pelean por templos, ni andan en las cortes de los impíos para defender su gloria? ¿Trabajaron como su maestro y Cristo, de balde sin recibir salario? Todo lo hicieron por amor a la causa, y esto sin duda; ¿cuántas millas andaban sus cabezas sin cobrarlas? Estos que escaparán de tan amarga hora, sin duda que todos eran voluntarios en la labor de Dios y lo hacían: ajenos de avaricia y de salario, porque querían ser cual su Cristo. Estos aun en sus vestidos enseñaban su humildad, y no se avergonzaban de quedarse desnudos a causa de extranjero o por amor a los menesterosos. ¡Ay de los que esperan el rapto y escapar de la ira de Dios sin haber hecho justicia en la tierra! ¿Podrá Dios mentir? ¿No será toda la tierra juzgada según el Evangelio de Jesucristo? ¿Podrán recibir bien los que no hicieron bien? ¿Podrán alcanzar Misericordia los que nunca hicieron misericordia? ¿Podrá el hombre recibir galardón por lo que no perpetuo?

¿Hay confusión en la obra de Dios? ¿Podremos cosechar trigo de los árboles, o fruta de las piedras? Tampoco los impíos e hipócritas podrán recibir bien sin haberlo sembrado antes. ¡Ay de los que esperan ser librados de la tempestad, sin haber ellos hecho misericordia con los oprimidos de la tierra. En aquel día, el testimonio de los huérfanos, de las viudas, de los oprimidos y desamparados, se levantará contra los que se llaman "cristianos" sin tener ni hacer las Obras de Cristo. Cristo dijo: "El que cree en mí, las obras que yo hago: también él las hará." Pero en estos días todos quieren hacer las obras de Cristo en orden a milagros: pero nadie quiere hacer las "OBRAS" en orden a misericordia, en orden a mansedumbre, en orden a justicia, en orden a humildad, en orden a obediencia. No os engañéis; ¿por qué engañáis a vuestras mismas almas? Dejad la vanidad, dejad lo que perece; y entrégese cada uno al bien hacer, al obedecer, a obrar con amor y misericordia, quizás alcanzamos también misericordia de Dios en los últimos días. El Justo por su fé vivirá y por fé está en pie. El Justo por fe ama, perdona, y por fe obedece a todo mandamiento y por fe el justo obra justicia y misericordia; el justo por la fe quita sus ojos de las cosas que perecen, y por la fe niega a dar su sudor y su fuerza (como lo hacen los llamados "cristianos") por cosas que la gran ramera esta inventando todos los días; El justo vive por fe en su Señor y Salvador: Jesucristo. Pero ¿dónde está la fe del que no hace misericordia? ¿Dónde está la fe del que no ama a sus enemigos? ¿Dónde está la fe del que no ampara a la viuda, al huérfano, como al extranjero y al pobre? ¿Dónde está la fe del hijo que no honra con socorro a su padre?

¿O quién pues de los que esperan a Cristo podrá justificarse y decir que es digno de escapar de la ira que viene? ¿Quién tiene sus manos limpias del pobre, de la viuda, y de todo mandamiento de Dios; para que diga que él no es digno del castigo que viene? Si alguno sabe lo que es misericordia y temor de Dios: hable y diga las mismas palabras; pero si no sabe lo que es Misericordia y Justicia: cierre su boca, que quizas le vaya mejor y no amontone tanto juicio e ira contra sí mismo. Por lo tanto, yo digo: El que espera a su Señor y Rey, comience a obrar misericordia y justicia según Dios y no según los hombres que para propia gloria han formado concilios. Atended el clamor de los menesterosos, Si es que querráis escapar de lo que viene: porque de seguro que según nuestras obras, así alcanzaremos del justo Juez. Sospended toda ceremonia y rito de canto y oración: y atended a la justicia y a la misericordia, con temor y fé en Dios, abrid toda puerta de justicia y verdad, para que corra el bien por toda la tierra. Soltemos toda ligadura que detiene el juicio y la justicia. Temed a Dios con grande temor. Demos gloria y honra con toda nuestra vida al que vive y reina para Siempre.

EL MALO EN LA SILLA DEL BUENO

Yo conozco el mal que estas palabras me acarrearán de parte de la Iglesia; yo soy conciente del tormento que estas palabras causarán en los corazones de aquellos que están engañando al pueblo. Pero, ¿qué deshonra podré traer yo a la Iglesia? ¿No son vuestros propios hijos los que traen deshonra, no solo a las iglesias, sino que aun a los hogares? ¿Dónde está el hijo que en estos días obedece según Dios? ¿Por qué escandalizarnos? cuando los mismos padres pasan a sus hijos por las llamas de la antigua babilonia; la soberbia ha crecido en los hijos; y ¿quién es el hijo que no hace según su antojo? Llamadlo, aplaudidlo, tan pronto como lo hallen decir: He aquí el hijo que honra a su padre con socorro. Miro, busco y pregunto, y según las respuestas que los llamados cristianos dan, todos desdeñan y aborrecen los mandamientos que nuestro Señor Jesucristo nos dejó; ¿por qué se ha hecho tan barata la palabra de Dios? ¿Dónde está la razón? que respondan los inteligentes, que hablen los sabios; ¿Por qué aun hasta los pequeños aborrecen la humildad y el derecho, y van tras la soberbia y la vanidad? ¿De dónde han aprendido ellos a huirle a la humildad? ¿Quién fue el maestro de ellos? Yo buscaba el derecho y la humildad en los grandes, pero en vez de esto, hallé que ellos habían sellado y autorizado ciegamente a todos los métodos humanos y sistemas que debelitan a la fe sencilla; todo ejemplo humilde que Cristo nos dejó, ha sido escarnecido y abandonado; todos aman el presete y aborrece el madamiento. ¿Para qué preguntar a la gente que si cree en Cristo, pues yo sé que todos creen; pero no obedecen. Esta es la piedra en la cual los rebeldes caen y tropiezan. Los hombres estudian la palabra de Dios, pero no para aprender de ella humildad y mansedumbre, no para aprender de ella juicio y justicia como misericordia; sino antes la estudian (sin saber porsupuesto) para dividir, para adquirir gloria de las gentes, para hacerse amos de las almas inocentes. Por eso pereció el amor de los corazones como Cristo lo anticipó; y la fe desapareció de la tierra. Por eso aun los hijos se han rebelado contra los padres, porque los hijos han heredado la soberbia de los padres. Solo pido yo, que me den libertad para hablar, para decir las cosas que yo en mi torpeza veo; mis ojos no son limpios como los de mi Dios; y si mis ojos se escandalizan y no pueden soportar el ver la grande abominación que hay en la llamada Iglesia de Cristo: Cuanto mas los ojos de mi Dios. Si no fuera por la sagacidad del mundo, que le ha heredado a la Iglesia, no cortesía usarían los cristianos; sé, que aun los fariseos se llamarían insultados, si nosotros quisiesemos compararnos a ellos; por cuanto la obra de ellos eran mayores que las de esta generación llamada Cristiana. Aun las bestias se llamarían insultadas si nos quisieramos asemejar a ellas; por cuanto ellas han permanecido sujetas a las leyes riendo establecer leyes mejores que las que Dios les señalo;

y claramente nos dejó en Su Santo Hijo. La Iglesia en estos días teme más a las leyes de los hombres que a las leyes de Dios; y procura estar más en paz con las leyes de los hombres que con la voluntad de Dios. ¿Por qué es esto así? ¿Quién ha asustado al pueblo? ¿Acaso no han dicho al pueblo de la terrible ira de Dios? ¿No han contado como Dios se airó con la gente que no dió oído a las palabras de Noé, y como Dios arrancó a aquella gente? ¿Habrá cambiado Dios? ¿Hará acepción de personas? ¿Qué no han hablado de la justicia de Dios, sobre Sodoma y Gomorra? ¿No reclama más justicia Dios de esta generación que de Sodoma y de Gomorra? ¿Era mejor el evangelio que aquellos tenían, que el que a nosotros se nos entregó?

Si Cristo llamó a los fariseos "hijos del diablo" (no porque no creían en él, sino por sus malvadas obras) por las vidas que vivían como nos llamará a nosotros? ¿O son nuestras obras mejores? ¿Damos a la viuda aunque sea con trompeta? ¿Ayunamos dos veces a la semana? ¿Quién es sabio, para que entienda estas palabras? ¿Quién es sabio para que no se enfurezca al oír estas palabras? El sabio no tiene qué perder, al oír estas palabras; pero el insensato, solo se irrita; el ciego e insensato no saca beneficio en esta palabra; mas el sabio si está mal y torcido, pronto se endereza, por cuanto él conoce el tiempo, y el espíritu de la palabra. Dios esta con los humildes, los cuales yo sé que mas que nunca en estos días, son malamente atormentados; porque en los días malos los humildes sufren amarguras. En los días malos los malos rigen la tierra, y como consecuencia los pequeños que no tienen autoridad humana sufren amarguras, y yugos injustos. El justo ha sido aventado de su lugar, los mansos fueron escarnecidos. Los malos hombres y ciegos, conformados con el tiempo están en el lugar de la potestad. ¡Oh humildes de la tierra que temeis a Dios! Cerrad vuestra boca, no contendáis mas con los que tienen el lugar de jueces; es el tiempo de ellos; ellos mandan ahorita; pronto pasará el tiempo de ellos; tened buen ánimo, no desmayeis; sed sufridos como nuestro Rey fué sufrido y manso. Imitad más que nunca el sufrimiento de Cristo, y no miréis la fuerza de la vanidad; haceos amigos de los profetas antiguos en cuanto a sufrimiento; amad la corrección, y andad con gran temor en estos últimos días. Solo los sabios de Corazón pueden ver bien en estos días. Los grandes a todo llaman bueno; siendo que Cristo vino a quitar la inmundicia, y toda la vanidad enseñándonos a vivir contentos con lo que él nos da y nos manda. Por lo tanto no llamemos bueno a lo que es malo.

FALTO EL MISERICORDIOSO

Faltaron los misericordiosos de la tierra; se acabaron los mansos de la tierra; y no hay quien se deleite en hacer el bien de Dios. Ya no hay quien llore y se queje a causa de la mucha iniquidad: todos están contentos y conformes con los ritos muertos. ¿Qué es de los sabios de la tierra? ¿Dónde están los que entienden el derecho? ¿Por qué no declarán justicia y juicio? Aun los pequeños y flacos han sido alimentados con promesas falsas y vanas; pero ningún bien han hecho con estas débiles promesas, porque han dividido a las gentes; y las han hecho errar. Todos van tras el mundo y sus riquezas; cada uno codicia vanidades y cosas que no duran, y hacen errar el alma de sus amantes; Las bocas de los que profesan conocer a Dios, hablan mentira y engaño cada uno con su hermano; no hablan verdad, ni tampoco pueden; porque en la mentira y en la exageración fueron desarrollados. Las conciencias de estos habladores de vanidades, están muertas al juicio. ¿Quién pues podrá redarguir a esta generación? Pues ellos dicen que van prosperando, y que están ricos. No sabiendo que están pobres, y muy ciegos. El juicio justo de Dios se acerca a ellos, y viene apresurada su recompensa; pero nada de esto les mueve, porque ellos creen que están ya listos. Oh ciegos, mirad donde está vuestra casa fundada; vuestra casa no está en piedra, vuestra confianza está fundada en arena y en tradiciones paganas de hombres que nunca temieron a Dios. Mirad que vuestros templos os han engañado; vuestras largas oraciones y cantos finguidos os han hecho errar. ¿Por qué confían en palabra de mentira? ¿Quién pidió cantos, oraciones y templos de vosotros? Dios quiere adoradores fieles; Dios busca quien le adore en espíritu y en verdad. Dios no busca palabras y ceremonias, antes: él busca obras justas, y obras de arrepentimiento.

Dios busca hombres y mujeres que obedezcan a sus mandamiento; Dios ama a los que le obedecen a él antes que a los hombres. Por eso perdimos el amor de Dios, porque dejamos los mandamientos que su santo hijo nos dejó; Cristo habló y dijo: "Si guardareis mis mandamientos, estareis en mi amor; así como yo he guardado los mandamientos de mi padre y estoy en su amor." (Juan 15:10). No estamos en su amor, porque no guardamos sus mandamientos. También nos hemos contentado con el mundo, porque dejamos sus derechos e hicimos resistencia al Espíritu Santo; Por eso también nuestros hijos se nos han rebelado; nuestras mujeres hacen disolutamente; vuestras hijas han sido hechas objetos de codicia, porque vosotros mismos las habéis humillado a la desnudes y desverguenza. Ya toda abominación de carne, a toda inmundicia, lascivia y concupiscencia le han llamado estilo y moda. ¿Cuándo habló Dios de estilo o de moda? ¿O cuándo nos dió Dios permiso de ir tras el mundo en cuanto a vestidura? Ni por dentro estamos limpios, pero ni por fuera; y si el justo les quiere reprender su concupiscencia: pronto arremeten contra él, y le hacen guerra. ¿Cómo podrá hablar Dios a este pueblo? No admiten juicio, no admiten corrección. ¿Quién pues podrá librar a este pueblo de su terrible fin? No hay quien vuelva su rostro del lujo, ni quien aborrezca la vanidad. Sus cabezas y líderes son los factores, y los principales en la codicia; porque cada uno quiere lo mejor y le huye al pesebre, y al camino de los profetas de Dios. La ropa que visten los declara que son soberbios y que se hinchen de lo vano; Adornan sus cuerpos y visten sus carnes como príncipes de Sodoma; defienden el salario, e ignoran la justicia. Ay de este pueblo malo y rebelde, porque ¿cómo escaparán de la ira que vendrá? y ¿quién abogará por ellos? Todos en montones se meteran en cuevas, y tratarán de librar sus pieles y sus cabezas de la ira y del furor con el cual será abrasada toda la tierra.

Estos que ahora tienen en poco los mandamientos de Dios, gritarán, y crujirán los dientes al ver y descubrir que ellos mismos eran los enemigos de la cruz. Ay de aquellos que esperan ser levantados en los aires y escapar de la ira de Dios; corruptos de entendimiento, conciencia muerta, vientres perezosos; ¿Así esperáis ser levantados? Rebeldes de corazón, ¿contra cuál mandamiento no habéis sido rebeldes? Manos lasciviosas, ojos llenos de adulterio, bocas mentirosas: ¿Así pensáis ir al cielo? ¿Qué no hay quien os diga y enseñe que los mentirosos no heredarán la vida? Vuestras bocas no saben hablar verdad; vuestros ojos no van tras la humildad, vuestras entrañas no se mueven al ver al pobre; antes todas vuestras entrañas se mueven al ver las cosas nuevas, como también al ver la mujer de vuestro propio hermano y prójimo. Tiempo es de cerrar la boca, tiempo es de humillar nuestras almas; es tiempo que despojemos nuestros cuerpos de toda vanidad y de toda soberbia. Busquemos justicia y juicio; preguntemos con nuestras almas humilladas por el camino antiguo el cual es Cristo. No es pequeño el daño que habéis cometido. ¿Contra quién os habéis rebelado? ¿Contra algún concilio de hombres? No, antes os habéis rebelado contra el hijo de Dios: ¿Dónde se meterán que no sean hallados? El que se rebela contra un concilio de hombres, es expulsado: pero queda con vida; mas ay de aquél que se ha rebelado contra el santo mandamiento: mejor le fuera que se arrojara en el mar. Los rebeldes no quedarán con vida, antes pagarán por todo el mal que hicieron en la tierra: engañando a muchas almas inocentes, que querían y buscaban la vida, mas erraron a causa de los cabezas que recibieron salario del mismo alimento de las viudas. La palabra de Dios se levantará contra estos mentirosos que alimentaron sus vientres, y debilitaron el derecho.

LA FE SIN MISERICORDIA

No ignoro los muchos nombres que se me darán por hablar y ponerme contra las obras de los últimos días. Murmurador, se me llamará; criticón seré llamado por otros, y fanático y torpe me llamarán otros; pero sé que todos los profetas y los que temieron y temen a Dios sabrán y conocerán mi espíritu. Hablo para el bien de todos: pero dejemos al insensato que perezca en su insensatez, porque ya no es tiempo de estar tratando de persuadir al insensato; el que esté sucio que se ensucie más; mas el que teme a Dios guardese en el temor de Dios.

Sé que los antiguos no me llamarán fanático, ni tampoco murmurador; y parte con la hipocresía nunca quiero tomar; por-

56

que sé que Dios traerá toda obra a Juicio, y nada quedará oculto.

¿Quién se podrá levantar y declararle a la mujer su verguenza y su honra? ¿Quién podrá enseñarle al hombre cual es su deber, y como debe de corregir un hogar? Todos inventan leyes que solo sirven para los templos, y para la gente que asiste a los templos, pero nada de esto tiene efecto en el hogar; antes todos se hacen más hipocritas, y pretenden tener más sin tener nada. Ay de los que escarnecen a otros concilios y movimientos, cuando ellos mismos tienen el mismo orgullo, la misma soberbia y egoismo, la misma ira y rebeldía contra los santos mandamientos de Dios. La soberbia, la contienda, la mundanalidad tanto está en unos como en otros, ¿por qué pues criticar, cuando todos somos réos de la misma cosa? Miremos más bien de donde hemos caído, y admitamos todos que ya hemos dejado el amor de Dios y nos hemos envanecido en toda obra de los hombres; hemos gastado nuestro dinero para crecer en la carne, y para retirar la humildad de nuestras casas; ¿no es esto así? Todos están llenos de ira y de venganza. Van todos por las calles en sus carros: y no se les puede ni pitar, sino que se enfurezcan; todos se ven de reójo, y nadie es claro en su sinceridad, antes son fingidos. Nadie quiere ir a la plaza de la ciudad con ropa triste y barata, por no ser escarnecido, antes todos van por un mismo camino; se tienen miedo los unos a los otros, es por esto que cada una se viste de sus mejores y más caros trajes y vestidos para aparecer con valor ante la gente. Un hombre de vestidos nuevos y de valor, es en verdad respetado y apreciado; pero un hombre de ropa pobre y barata no es estimado aunque sea un hombre de juicio, aunque sea un hombre de limpios hechos y de gran estima delante del Dios vivo. Esto enseña que somos ciudadanos de la grande babilonia. Los mismos templos están llenos de soberbia, aunque la gente me desmienta y se niegue; pero un día sabrán; y Dios será mi testigo de que hablo verdad; pero todo esto yo sé que no mueve a las conciencias; ojalá que de muchos que lean estas palabras algún sabio y sensato reciba corrección y ponga su vida en salvo para que escape de lo que viene. El sol y la luna, la tierra y los cielos: siempre han sido testigos de las palabras que los profetas hablan para salvar a los que están envueltos en rebeldía y muerte. Yo también, hablo delante de estos mismos testigos, y digo: nosotros hemos pecado, hemos obrado inicuamente; el bien lo hemos dejado; y hemos trastornado todo santo camino y juicio de Dios; volvamos a Dios; no sea que Dios llegue y nadie escape en su presencia terrible; muchos cuando Dios nos visite, hasta entonces apreciarán estas palabras; y hasta entonces admitirán que estábamos mal; pero ¿para qué esperar hasta aquel día? El hombre se ha hecho vano, y ya no habla verdad, ni con su propia esposa; el hombre ya perdió su valor; y en los templos donde suponían aprender la verdad, ahí van solo para oir fábulas, y palabras que no mueven a hacer el juicio de Dios, palabras que no redarguyen ni a un hipócrita; parlería, y vanidad, esto se oye en el lugar del consejo del Espíritu. Ay cómo pereció la misericordia de sobre la tierra, se fueron los tiempos cuando el hombre conocía el amor de Dios, se pasaron los días cuando el grande se compadecía del pequeño; se acabaron los tiempos cuando el hombre de ojos conducía al ciego con mansedumbre y paciencia. Y en cambio han llegado a los tiempos cuando el hombre de ojos avienta al que no tiene ojos, el hombre de fuerza, destruye al que no tiene fuerza. La viuda no halla gracia a los ojos de la mujer casada; los huérfanos no son protegidos por los hijos que tienen padre y madre. Antes todo juicio y justicia ha perecido de sobre la tierra; y he ahí los pastores de las congregaciones entretenidos en palabras vanas, prometiendo al pueblo lo que ni ellos mismos tienen. Todos ocupados en cantos y ceremonias muertas. ¿Es glorificado Dios con cantos? ¿Le agradan a Dios los discursos vacíos de hombres que no tienen misericordia y que no defienden a los pequeños de la tierra? Lejos sea, que Dios se crea de hombres mentirosos, que para sacar la vida usan palabras dulces y de bendición; estos ya pronto tendrán su recompensa. ¿Quién le dirá a la mujer, toda su soberbia? ¿Quién le dirá a la mujer en qué ha pecado? No hay quien vea pecado en la vida disoluta del hombre y de la mujer; todos están conformes, hartan sus ojos con la desnudez de la mujer hablo de lo mejor que hay en las Iglesias, y no hablo del mundo, por que el mundo no sabe lo que hace; a nosotros nos correspondía el enseñar lo recto y lo santo, tanto en palabras como en hecho y en vestido, en el cual se ve la honra y la sabiduría de un pueblo. Así como la desnudez es un fruto del espíritu de concupiscencia y lascivia: así también el cuerpo cubierto y decente, es un fruto de honra, un fruto de temor, un fruto de sabiduría; Pero en estos días; ¿qué tenemos, de qué gloriarnos? Toda la honra, la gloria, la vergüenza, la modestia ha perecido de sobre la tierra; y hemos quedado como un pueblo sin muro y sin armas, expuesto al ataque de un enemigo malo y cruel. ¿Quién escapará sin armas, y sin sabiduría? Dios nos libre.

OID SABIOS

Lo santo procede de lo santo; y lo malo, procede de lo malo. Y la Misericordia y la justicia no son sin fruto.
Daniel aconsejó al Rey Nabucodonosor diciéndole: "Por tanto oh rey, aprueba mi consejo, y redime tus pecados con Justicia, y tus iniquidades con Misericordia para con los pobres."
Y otra vez dice el Espíritu Santo (Prov. 16:6). "Con Misericordia y verdad se corrige el pecado; y con el Temor de Jehová se apartan del mal los hombres." Y otra vez: "El que tiene Misericordia de los pobres, es Bienaventurado" (Prov. 14:21). Otra vez: "El que tiene misericordia del pobre, honra a Dios." (Prov. 14:31). Y vuelve a decir: "A Jehová empresta, el que da al pobre" (Prov. 19:17). Y pasa a decir: "Misericordia y verdad

guardan al Rey; y con clemencia sustenta su trono" (Prov. 20: 2). Pero ¿Dónde está la misericordia que sustenta al cristiano de estos días? Responda el que sabe usar de Misericordia. ¿Dónde está la honra del cristiano? y ¿Dónde está su Justicia? Por esto habló el Espíritu Santo, cuando dijo: "El que sigue la Justicia y la Misericordia: hallará la vida, la Justicia, y la honra." (Prov. 21:21).

Lo mismo habló Cristo nuestro Señor cuando dijo: "Bienaventurados los misericordiosos, porque ellos alcanzarán Misericordia" Mat. 5:7. Y antes de esto aconseja el Espíritu Santo diciendo: "Misericordia y verdad, no te desamparen; átalas a tu cuello, escríbelas en las tablas de tu corazón: Y hallarás gracia y buena opinión en los ojos de Dios y de los hombres" Prov. 3:3.

Añade: "El que cierra su oído al clamor del pobre: también él clamará, y no será oído" Prov. 21:12.

Y también habla por el apóstol Santiago, diciendo: "Juicio sin misericordia será hecho con aquel que no hiciere Misericordia" Sant. 2:13. De esto acusó el Señor a los fariseos; cuando les dijo: "Lo más grave de la Ley lo habéis pasado por alto, a saber: La justicia la Misericordia y la fe. Mat. 23:23. Y ¿quién se podrá gloriar contra estas cosas? ¿Qué sacrificio podrá tomar el lugar de la misericordia? Ninguno, porque aun el mismo sacrificio que Cristo hizo: Es Misericordia y verdad, y a esto se debe, cuando el nos exhortó diciendo: "Sed Misericordiosos, como vuestro Padre celestial es Misericordioso" Lucas 6:36. Queda pues, por entendido, que: los Misericordiosos son hijos de Dios. Pero ¿Dónde está la Misericordia de la iglesia? ¿Qué bien hemos hecho en el mundo? Hay fondo para el pastor, fondo para el misionero, fondo para templos, y fondos para todos los intereses de los concilios. Pero ¿dónde está el fondo de la viuda? ¿Dónde está el fondo para los pobres, para los menestrosos, para los extranjeros y huérfanos?

Mas bien hacen los hijos de las tinieblas en este respecto: porque el gobierno terrenal, que es administrado por hombres que no pretenden ser hombres de Dios: han mirado por los ancianos, por las viudas, por los pobres y huérfanos. Y aun que es verdad que ellos cobran tributos de las gentes: pero de estos tributos, sacan ellos la parte para los pobres y necesitados. Pero las iglesias: ¿qué parte sacan para los necesitados? Antes le exigen aun a los pobres, de lo poco que ellos tienen. ¿Cómo pue detendremos la ira que viene? o ¿cómo escaparemos?

El hombre Rico, del cual Cristo habló: no fué puesto en el infierno porque fumaba, o porque tenía nada más que vicios; ni fué arrojado al infierno porque no pagaba sus diezmos, o porque no cantaba y oraba. Antes, fué arrojado o puesto en el tormento, porque no usó de misericordia.. ¿Qué uso tiene Dios para los hombres ingratos, que aparte de no tener misericordia establecen leyes y acuerdos que debilitan a la misericordia y detienen el bien de aquellos que lo quieren hacer? Muchos, por sus malvados deseos y antojos: han sido engañados y han tropezado en la misma libertad que hay en el evangelio y gracia de

Jesucristo. Porque dicen ellos: "Por gracia somos salvos, y no por obras" y con esta palabra debilitan el bien y la misericordia.

Voluntariamente han tropezado. Porque el mismo apostol San Pablo hablando a los mismos Efesios les añade: "Porque somos hechura suya, criados en Cristo Jesús; para buenas obra las cuales Dios preparó para que anduviesemos en ellas." Efesios 2:10. Y por el mismo Espíritu habla en otra ocasión diciendo y exhortando a los Filipenses, a que se ocuparán en todo lo verdadero, en todo lo honesto, en todo lo Justo, en todo lo Puro, en todo lo amable y que fuera de buen nombre. Esto es, si en ello había alguna Virtud, alguna alabanza; y que pensarán en estas cosas.

Y para hacer más claro y sencillo lo que trataba de enseñar, les añade: "Lo que aprendisteis de mí, lo que recibisteis de mi, lo que oisteis de mí, y lo que visteis en mí: ESTO HACED." Fil. 4:8, 9.

Y el mismo Apóstol exhortó a los colosenses a que se vistieran de "Entrañas de Misericordia, de benignidad, de humildad, de mansedumbre y tolerancia. (Col. 3:12). Y a los Efesios también les dice: "Sed los unos con los otros benignos y misericordiosos" Efe. 4:32. ¿Podrá existir el Amor y la Misericordia sin obras buenas? Ya cuando el pobre, la viuda y los menesterosos son abandonados a la misericordia del gobierno de las tinieblas; ¿se podrá decir que hay Amor y Misericordia? ¿Trataba Pablo de salvar a los Efesios y a los colosenses como a los filipenses por medio de buenas obras? ¿Por qué pues les hablaba de esto? como también le dice a Tito, diciéndole que Cristo es entregó por nosotros, para redimirnos de toda iniquidad, y limpiar para Sí un pueblo propio, Celoso de buenas obras. También les dice que aprendan a gobernarse en buenas obras? (Tito 2:14 y 3:14).

Por esta razón cada uno escarnece a su prójimo; porque los enseñadores han enseñado que nadie ponga sus ojos en las buenas obras, y han quitado el valor de las buenas obras. Pero pronto van a echar de ver el error tan grande que causaron en la tierra; entonces echarán de ver que ellos fueron los culpables de que la misericordia y el amor pereciera de los corazones.

Si no hay bien en las buenas obras; tampoco hay mal en las malas obras. Por ver abandonado lo más grave del reino de Jesucristo, los enseñadores han fracasado; se hicieron fatuos llamando oro a lo que no era. Se olvidaron que Cristo dijo: "El que oye estas mis palabras y las hace, le compararé a un hombre Prudente" y ahora ellos quieren hacerse sabios, pero no pueden porque se han hecho insensatos rebelándose contra lo único que les podía dar vida. Y el Proverbio dice: "Alta está para el insensato la sabiduría." Prov. 24:7. Y en otro lugar dice: "El escarnecedor busca la sabiduría, mas no la halla." Prov. 14:6. Pero el hombre entendido la halla con facilidad. Por esto es que el Justo piensa para hablar, porque él busca la paz y teme a su Dios; mas el necio con sus labios derrama la ira, y divide al pueblo.

Nabucodonosor fué echado con las bestias, por no haber

tomado el consejo que Daniel le dió; ignoró la misericordia y escarneció la justicia; pero después del azote, recuperó y obró con sabiduría; pero está presente generación no recibe corrección; ni admite el buen consejo. Un día buscarán el consejo, pero no lo hallarán. Israel también dejó la misericordia y el conocimiento de Dios (Oseas 6:6). En estos días, ni aun en los hijos hay Misericordia para con sus propios padres; esto es ya un nivel más bajo que las bestias de la tierra; porque las bestias enseñan que sus hijos obedecen a sus madres.

Nunca antes había tenido esta tierra, habitantes tan soberbios e ignorantes; ¿cuándo registra la historia a un pueblo tan ciego como este? Los hombres han puesto sus ojos en la obra que llos mismos han hecho. Aun sus templos donde adoran, sin obras que ni el Rey Nabucodonsor pudo lograr; y la soberbia de Nabucodonosor era pequeña, comparada a la soberbia de los que ahora dirigen al pueblo de Dios. Y los ojos de los más pequeños, van tras la obra de los más grandes; y nadie busca la verdadera humildad. Todos buscan honra, pero no la hallan ni la hallarán; porque la honra verdadera, viene después de la humildad verdadera. Prov. 15:33. Pero ¿quién sabe lo que es verdadera humildad sin pararse a escudriñarla?

Los que quieran escapar de la ira que viene; los que amen sus vidas y no quieran ser sorprendidos por el fuego de la ira de Dios: vacíen sus corazones de todo mal; derramen sus almas por el oprimido; servid a los cansados; hagamos el bien del cual Cristo nos habló. ¿Por qué dejar que se pase el último día de Salvación? Limpiemos nuestras manos del mal; echemos el pensamiento malo de nuestro corazón y vistamos nuestras entrañas de Misericordia. Son días de buscar de Nuevo a Dios. Ay de los que dicen que son salvos, y no están libres de la soberbia ni de la mentira. Ay de los que dicen que conocen la salvación y no saben lo que es Misericordia y Justicia. Ay de los que esperan el regreso de Cristo sin haber hecho obras de amor y Misericordia. Muchos son los que creen ir en camino de vida y recto, sin saber que el fin del camino que ellos llevan son caminos de muerte. Y como se engañó el rico que cerró sus entrañas para con el mendigo de Lázaro, así muchos son los que en estos días se están engañando y muy sorprendidos serán en aquel día cuando Dios saque toda obra a la Luz de Su Hijo Amado.

Temblemos a la Palabra de Dios, porque si no tememos ahora: mas tarde temblaremos no a la palabra sino a la presencia de Dios. Mientras se detiene el Juicio, vengamos todos y hagamos bien, echemos la Murmuración y el enojo de nuestros corazones. Nadie mire por los bienes de esta tierra. Son días de sacar las cosas del mundo, de nuestro corazón, antes de que quedemos por ejemplo de los rebeldes como lo fué la mujer de Lot. Dios ama la Justicia, y todo aquel que hace Justicia no será avergonzado. El que dice que ya tiene Fe, que lo pruebe con sus obras de Cristo; pues que Cristo mismo dijo: "El que cree en mí, las obras que yo hago, también él las hará." El que dice que espera a Cristo, abandone las cosas que posee y dé las a los pobres; El que dice que conoce a Cristo, hágalo manifiesto con misericordia y justicia.

Ay de los que son fieles a los hombres, y fieles a los acuerdos de los hombres: y que no hacen misericordia y justicia; ay de los que temen a los hombres y que no temen a Dios. Porque ¿quién se pondrá por los rebeldes delante de Dios? ¿Quién será aquel que abogara por los que no obedecieron a los mandamientos de Cristo? Todos los justos y que temen a Dios salgan de los lugares que Dios abomina; salgan de la gran Babilonia; porque el lugar que pertenecía a lo santo, ha sido tomado y ocupado por la abominación y toda religión falsa; por lo tanto: RECORDAD TODOS, QUE SEGUN NUESTRAS OBRAS, así seremos juzgados. Y nadie se engañe solo, creyendo que Dios le justificará, según los hombres le han justificado. Al contrario: lo que los obreros pasan ahora por limpio. Dios lo pasará por inmundo y abominable. Y sea Dios Bendito ahora y siempre; y todo el que obra Justicia, no se avergüence. Sea Dios por el Justo. ... ...

LOS PROVOCADORES DEL JUICIO

Una fuerte y penosa maldición, está decretada contra los que se rebelan contra Dios; la humanidad no está inocente de esto, porque Dios lo ha notificado por todos sus santos profetas, y lo ha hecho notorio atravès de los siglos. A Dios le ha costado la sangre de muchos hombres justos, para declarar las verdades del futuro; los justos fueron aborrecidos y maltratados, porque anunciaban la ruina y la destrucción de los rebeldes, que contra Dios se rebelan; y estos mismos les dieron muerte. Por desgracia el pueblo rebelde siempre ha sido el pueblo de Dios. Porque el pueblo ciego e ignorante, de nada se puede rebeldar, por cuanto no conoce ninguna ley de Dios. Pero es el pueblo de Dios que habiendo conocido el bien y la voluntad de Dios: mas tarde se rebela dejando la Ley de Dios y siguiendo la ley de los hombres que para engañar usan cautela, y para ganar gloria y riqueza establecen leyes injustas: en las cuales no se halla bien ni justicia, ni aun para los pobres, menos amparo para las viudas y oprimidos.

El pueblo de Israel que Dios tanto amó, aquél pueblo que sacó de Egipto con brazo fuerte, con milagros y maravillas; el pueblo por el cual tanto se afano y sufrió, tolerando sus imprudencias y locuras como también muchas rebeldías. Este pueblo al cual dió tantas hermosas y grandes promesas; pueblo distinguido de todos los demás, Dios humilló muchas otras naciones por amor de Israel, las mejores promesas estaban determinadas para este pueblo, y aun habló en voz y truenos con este pueblo el cual Dios amaba y estimaba tanto. Dios le llamó tesoro escogido, y lo cuido: como el hombre cuida la niña de su ojo mismo. Con todo esto, y a pesar de amarles con tan grande amor: Cuando este pueblo que Dios tanto amaba se rebeló contra él: Dios lo castigo y lo azotó y lo mutilo y lo entregó en las manos de las gentes más duras, los vendió en manos del gobieron más cruel y más sin misericordia; se olvidó de ellos por completo por espacio de 70 años. Calló sobre ellos la más dura y cruel maldición que en la historia se conoce. Cuando los enemigos de este pueblo (una vez llamado "Tesoro Escogido") calleron sobre Jerusalem, Ciudad que antes había sido ciudad de Paz y bendición: Mataron los hombres, forzaron a sus mujeres, y a sus niños de pecho los estrellaron sobre las piedras, al rey le mataron sus hijos delante de sus propios ojos, y a él le sacaron sus ojos, y así murió ciego en tierra extraña, alimentado con las migajas de un Rey que Dios había levantado para que humillara a su pueblo Israel. Dios es el mismo ayer hoy y por los siglos. La historia nos hace ver que Dios no se descuida de este planeta; y el vela y tiene guardianes quienes están al tanto de los procederes de los hombres que dirigen a las gentes. Y por el grande y terrible Mandamiento que de Dios hemos recibido, sabemos que hemos rebelado hasta el extremo. No solo contra Dios, sino que contra nuestro prójimo, codiciando su mujer. Y aun los hijos se han rebelado contra sus Padres, las mujeres contra la palabra de sus maridos, el rico contra el pobre, el amparado contra el desamparado, el fuerte contra el débil, el ingrato contra el Misericordioso, la casada contra la viuda, el sabio contra el ignorante, el que tiene ojos contra el ciego, el que tiene oídos contra el sordo, el que tiene pies contra el manco; y la tierra se ha llenado de deshonra y de pecado por el pueblo que soponía conocer los caminos de Dios que en Cristo fueron apuntados y establecidos.

La maldición más penosa, la ruina más aterrorizadora, el fin más triste, está decretado sobre esta generación adulterina y rebelde: que a lo negro llama blanco, al ajenjo llama y lo come como miel, a la honra deshonra; y esto tanto en el hablar como en el vestir, tanto en el comer como en el obrar. Y al que obra con temor de Dios: le llaman rebelde y fanático; esto solo porque no se humilla a sus leyes torcidas y no acarrean más que división.

Todo da testimonio que somos un pueblo rebelde, glotón, deshonrador, ciego y déspota. Nuestros pueblos lo dicen, nuestras tiendas de ropa y de comida lo testifican. Los caminos y las calles por donde caminamos publican nuestra violencia y estupidez. En fin nuestros hogares encendidos en llamas de discordias y contiendas, disputas y pleitos: lo publica, que ningún morador de la tierra puede aprender en nosotros algunas cosas de honra o decencia, de humildad o de temor de Dios; Porque los hijos robaron la **honra de los padres, las mujeres** robaron la honra de los esposos, y el hombre se ha tornado peor que bestias por cuanto en las bestias no hay tal deshonra, que se levanten los hijos contra los padres. El Egoismo en el hombre, ha llegado a su cúspide, se ha desarrollado como nunca en la historia, y el Egoismo ha entregado al hombre a un sentido torcido y loco, al extremo de gloriarse en su locura, a gloriarse en sus obras las cuales no harán más que entregarle al degolladero. Porque Dios el cual aborrece la arrogancia del hombre, y abomina la soberbia de los últimos días: ha levantado un hombre, y há preparado un instrumento que hará su voluntad en su pueblo degollandolo.

El comunismo ha venido hacer mayor obra por lo que se ve. La gente compra lo más barato, y busca la mejor libertad. Si nosotros la tuvieramos, no perdieramos tantas gentes; y el comunismo va creciendo a pasos gigantezcos. Aunque Jeremías no amaba a los caldeos: por agradar a Dios se puso al lado de los caldeos; y siempre hablaba que los caldeos tomarían la tierra de los judíos; y aunque la gente no lo creía: así fué, esto, porque Dios así lo había determinado. Y yo no digo que el comunismo puede tomar el lugar del gobierno de Dios, ni que ofrece una paz duradera. Mucho menos que Cristo se vea en el gobierno de ellos. Pero porque hemos dejado a Dios, y porque Dios ha levantado un grande enemigo contra esta Nación; aunque yo dijera que saldríamos con bien, no por eso nos iría bien. Nuestro pecado ha marcado nuestro fin. Nuestra rebeldía ha levantado al grande enemigo de la Paz. Yo no puedo estar con este pueblo, porque este pueblo no está Con Dios; antes todos han dejado el camino de la vida, y ahora todos son cautivos de babilonia la madre de toda hechicería de la vida. Todos son víctimas de la glotonería, del lujo, del vestido de soberbia. Nadie ve, nadie recibe consejo, todos se han hecho señores de la tierra. Y por todas partes se ven cartulinas o tablas que leen POSTED KEEP OUT. Y así publican la malicia y testifican que la tierra está llena de gente mala. No hay quien confie al prójimo, esto también es prueba que nada bueno hay en la gente. Somos un pueblo sin entrañas, una generación que no conoce misericordia; si esto no es así, ¿por qué a nadie le puede la preparación de los estados unidos? Antes los cristianos todos juntos cooperan para hacer la bomba Atómica, para hacer aviones, para fortificar la defensa de guerra. Y ¿Quién de todos exclama? ¿a quién le puede el fin de lo que nos acarreará la preparación? Todos embotados y ciegos como bestias son llevados en el engaño y abismo del fin de nuestra rebeldía. No hay quien exclame y se rebelde contra la obra mortal en la cual se ocupa todo el pueblo que profesa temor de Dios. Padres e hijos, madres e hijas, esposos y esposas, ancianos y jóvenes, buenos y malos, todos se ocupan para un solo fin; este fin es: para cumplir la voluntad de Dios la cual es para nuestro mal. Porque lo hemos dejado, él también nos ha dejado. Y ¿Dónde están los sabios de la tierra? ¿Dónde están los consejeros para que enseñen a este pueblo? No hay quien dé alivio al corazón, no hay quien gane almas. Los que forman consejo, los que organizan grupos de gentes los que cada día establecen leyes para el bien; los que resgatan a los pecadores: ¿Dónde están? ¿por qué no detienen a este pueblo que como vacas ciegas van al holocáusto? Dios ha sentenciado juicio desde mucho tiempo atrás, contra los que tomaran el camino que está gente ha tomado; Y no hay sabio ni fuerte o rico, que descubra armas o escudos contra el Juicio Justo que viene. Sino perdonó a Israel, ¿cómo perdonará nuestra maldad que es más grande? porque nosotros hemos inficcionado toda la tierra de obras y artes que han quitado la honra del hombre y la santidad de la mujer. A causa de nuestra obra, los humildes erraron también; y nadie ha descubierto lo que es misericordia y justicia en nuestros días. Lo que ha fabricado es la apariencia que se ve dentro de los templos. Pero en el vasto templo (el Universo) lleno de pobres, viudas, oprimidos, huérfanos y necesitados extranjeros: ¿Qué bien ha hecho? Adoradores falsos, si no están en templos no pueden adorar. La adoración que nuestro Cristo nos enseñó, fué en la tierra, adorando a Dios através de los pobres oprimidos y afligidos de la tierra. Nos enseñó a adorar a Dios en Espíritu y no en templos. Los templos tienen poco valor cuando el pueblo está en el temor de Dios. Pero cuando el pueblo pierde el temor de Dios, y que se aparta del amor de Dios: Todos se ocupan en levantar templos, solo para acarrear gloria a sus vidas terrenales; por esta causa Dios viene a dejar a su pueblo.

Ya que Dios ha determinado Juicio contra nosotros, ya que ha tornado su rostro contra nosotros: humillemos nuestras almas, dejemos la soberbia que es vanidad y muerte. Nosotros hemos dejado los mandamientos de Dios, los cuales dan vida verdadera a nuestras almas.

Los que temen a Dios, los que habéis sido engañado contra de vuestra voluntad por los cabezas de soberbia: salid de la vida de engaño, salid de babilonia, dejad la potencia de los deleites, sacudid vuestras almas de toda soberbia y de todo egoismo. Ya no tomen del caliz de Babilonia: el cual es embriaguez de los cuidados de la vida, y de las vanidades que nos apartan de Dios. Dejad el compromiso del mundo, sacudid vuestras manos de lo que ahora ocupa a toda la humanidad; todos comen y beben, compran y venden, y duermen como príncipes en paz: Cuando la tierra ya está para ser quemada por nuestra misma rebeldía. Todos ven la misericordia y la justicia en tierra y a nadie le interesa; cada uno miró por su propio interés, y así el hombre ha venido a perder el sentido que Cristo nos dejó. Salgamos de los pueblo habitados, dejemos las calles de tráfico y codicia; mire Dios en los pequeños, que están disgustados. aborrezcamos el mal y la vanidad, dejemos de comprar y vender. Comed poco, parchad vuestras ropas y repartid al menesteroso de nuestro poco bien, y así retirad el juicio, de vuestra cabeza.

Dios se va a valer, de un fuerte, al cual desde mucho antes lo había anunciado: para que los sabios que temen huyan y escapen de la ira asoladora. La arrogancia de este pueblo ha llegado a tal extremo, que llamen Bendición, a la energía Atómica, la cual hace poco que el mundo la conoció. Pero mucho antes de que el mundo lo supiera, Agentes invincibles por la voluntad de Dios: lo habían depositado el secreto en la mente de Un hombre llamado MENDELEEV; y para la sorpresa de muchos arrogantes del poniente, este hombre era RUSO, esto fué en el Año 1869. A este hombre se le entregó la primer tabla fundamental de elementos naturales; ordenados según el peso de cada átomo. Y la primer máquina para desintergrar o quebrar el átomo fué formada en Moscow el año 1937.

Pero esto no fué el principio de una bendición, porque si fuera una bendición grande, los dignos serían nuestros primeros padres los cuales anduvieron más derecho que nosotros. Pero esto fué permitido por Dios en los últimos días, por cuanto el hedor de nuestras iniquidades han subido a lo alto, y en estos postreros tiempos vino la madurez de la abominación mayor.

Las mujeres de estas naciones llamadas naciones cristianas, escarnezcen a las mujeres que están tras la cortina de hierro (así llamada) simplemente, porque aquellas visten muy largo y sus vestidos sueltos; y escarnecen porque sus vestidos están sueltos y anchos de la cintura como lo está en sus hombros. Porque que aquellas usan mangas largas, porque aquellos usan puros colores tristes y oscuros: de todo esto nuestras mujeres se burlan. Esto es fruto y testimonio de que la arrogancia de nuestras mujeres está en todo. La iglesia y el estado están separados en opinión, pero en espíritu no. Porque los apetitos de los líderes de la Nación, son los mismos que los apetitos de los líderes de la Iglesia. Porque aunque son dos distintas carreras, el mismo espíritu los mueve: que es arrogancia, envidia, egoismo y vana gloria.

Para bien de Aquellos que dudan. Las informaciones de como se vive en rusia, sus maneras de vestir tan humilde y con honra y decencia; y muchas de las costumbres dignas de que los llamados cristianos las imiten: digo esto porque en ello hay mayor vergüenza y honra (aunque sea honra solamente humana o moral) estas informaciones salieron en un magazín llamado "Ladies Home Journal." Y fueron enviadas de Rusia por la señora Lidia Kirk, esposa del ex-embajador Alan G. Kirk. Y aunque estas informaciones han sido con el fin de humillar a esas pobres mujeres, no obstante: hay algunos sabios en la tierra que pueden entender lo que esto indica. Porque si el cuerpo desnudo testifica por la dshonra, luego también el cuerpo cubierto testifica por la honra de la mujer. Y la historia en la palabra de Dios como también la historia profana prueban que la vestidura y la manera como la gente se vista es un fruto de su corazón, y un fruto de su vida o para bien o para mal.

La única Nación que no alaba la soberbia y los modos tan bajos de los estados unidos es Rusia; todas las naciones han recibido ejemplos de los estados unidos, tanto en la manera de vestir, como en la manera de comer; tanto en la manera de hablar con soberbia, como en la manera de vivir. Y según el testimonio de la señora Kirk, Las madres rusas, no dejan que sus niños aprendan los modos de nuestros hijos, esto es porque allá hay muchos niños de hombres que representan a esta nación, y estos tienen que jugar separados. En Rusia se nos acusa de ser la gente mas Hipócrita, porque ellos estando informados por el nuevo testamento de la vida de Cristo y de las vidas de aquellos que seguían a Cristo: comparan todo esto con nuestra manera de vivir; y hallan, como también nuestro Señor lo dijo: un pueblo sin fe y sin Amor de Dios. Llamándose sabios, se han hecho fatuos y con todos se dan aborrecer.

Pero he aquí que el día del Señor viene con fuego e ira de Dios; y todos los soberbios serán sorprendidos. Pero los humildes y los oprimidos de la tierra, ¿qué soberbia pueden perder? ¿El que no tiene soberbia, por qué teme?

Por lo tanto, "esperad" ha dicho el Señor, el día cuando nuestras casas no tendrán pintura agradable, nuestros muebles no tendrán lustre donde el rostro se ve, nuestras calles no serán para caminar con violencia; nuestros cuerpos no serán adornados con telas finas; Los pomitos y perfumes no agradarán a la nariz de nadie. Los que cantan en corros como los que adoran con música (al oído) cesarán; el rostro altivo de la mujer, como el rostro afeitado del varón: todo esto será tropiezo al ojo de los mismos. Ahora todos están ciegos, y nada mal ven en las composturas que de babilonia han salido. Pero en aquel día, de todo esto será el varón y la mujer refinado. Si nosotros hemos perdido el temor de Dios, ¿qué esperamos de Rusia? Una fuerza como la fuerza soviética, nace de un mundo rebelde como nosotros los hijos de Dios lo hemos hecho. Y el "comunismo" ha venido hacer mayor obra que nuestro "amor"

EL CLAMOR DEL JUSTO

Con temor y humildad pongo estas palabras por escrito; a todos los que creen que Jesucristo es el hijo de Dios; a todos los que creen a Dios, y todos los que creen que la Biblia es la palabra de Dios. A todos los que se reunen en templos para adorar a Dios; a todos los que cantan a Dios, y que también oran. Al pueblo que espera y cree en el regreso de Jesucristo, al pueblo que cree en la resurrección de los muertos y en el juicio según nuestras obras; al pueblo que en esto crea: a él hablo.

No son gente que no haya conocido la palabra de Dios tampoco al pueblo que admite y sabe que es pecador; tampoco a la gente que en público se declara pecadora, No a los que matan, a los que toman, a los ladrones: ni a ningún pecador público.... Esta gente pecadora no quiere nada con las cosas de Dios, y por eso no hablaré a ellos.

Mas bien hablo al pueblo que sabiendo hacer el bien no lo hace, que sabiendo que debe amar no ama; hablo al pueblo que, sabiendo que debe de perdonar, no perdona, sabiendo que debe ser humilde y manso: no lo es. Andando y caminando por muchos lugares, después de hablar con muchas gentes, y después de haber buscado el bien y a los sabios de la tierra; es después de todo esto que he sido impulsado a hablar.

El mucho pecado, la mucha injusticia, la mucha hipocrecía y soberbia me ha hecho hablar. La iniquidad en la Iglesia, me ha forzado a hablar; al ver la justicia y el juicio por tierra, mis entrañas se han movido a hablar palabras que a muchos los irritará, palabras que para algunos serán demasiado duras: como dijeron algunos de los que al principio siguieron a Cristo; (Juan 6:60). Pero estas palabras para otros sabios de corazón, serán para bien y salud del alma.

Mis ojos por ciegos que estén: ya no soportan el ver tanta injusticia e hipocresía; Mis entrañas por duras que estén, ya no pueden resistir el grito de los oprimidos, y las quejas de los desamparados; mis oídos, por sordos que están en lo espiritual: oyen mentira y exageración por todos lados; y esto en pequeños como en grandes, en sabios como en insensatos. De labios profesan la verdad, de boca temen a Dios: y por esto mismo, yo mismo no he podido soportar las palabras que en mi corazón hay. No veo obediencia en los hijos, no veo corrección en la mano de los padres no veo respeto en los templos, no veo temor de Dios en los que hablan la palabra de Dios; No veo hombre que busque el bien de Dios, no veo quien se deleite en hacer y defender al huérfano, a la viuda, al manco, al pobre, al ciego, al mudo. El que hace banquete, a sus parientes lo hace, pero no al pobre como Cristo lo mandó. (Lucas 14:13, 14). El que empresta, solo a sus amigos y parientes empresta, (cuando mucho) pero no al pobre; no le emprestan, mucho menos dado como Dios lo mandó. (Deut. 15:10, 11). (Luc. 6:30). Busco algún bien digno de ser alabado, para guardar mi boca cerrada; pero no lo veo. El cantar no han dejado, el orar no han dejado, el predicar no han dejado, tampoco han dejado de levantar templos. No nada de esto han dejado, antes en todo esto abundan; pero lo que han dejado (Dios es testigo es la misericordia, el amor de Dios, la justicia de Dios, el temor de Dios por el temor de los hombres; lo que han dejado es la humildad y la mansedumbre. No es el Amor o la justicia que veo entre el pueblo lo que me hace hablar; sino que es la soberbia y el egoísmo que hay entre el pueblo, lo que me hace hablar. La abominación que está en el lugar santo, es la que me hace hablar; y es esta abominación, la qu ha encendido el furor de Dios. La hipocrecía está en el lugar de lo santo y lo genuino; el odio está en el lugar del amor; La mentira está en el lugar de la verdad. Los malos están en el lugar de los buenos. Los altivos y soberbios están en el lugar que le correspondía a los humildes. La Ley de Dios está en manos de asalariados y en manos de tiranos. El cristiano, ya no imita al humilde para vestir, ya no imita al humilde para comer, ya no imita al humilde para vivir; ya no imita al humilde para cantar u para orar; ya nadie imita al humilde Glileo para nada, antes todos están hinchados de soberbia y despotismo. ¿Es pequeño este mal? ¿será poco el mal que hemos hecho contra nuestras almas? Ya toda la tierra está llena del mismo espíritu de error; es el mismo espíritu que hay en todas las gentes: tanto en los templos, como en el vivir; tanto en el cantar como en el orar. Es un mismo espíritu él que los hace codiciar una misma cosa, es un mismo espíritu el que hace que todos hablen mentira, el que hace que todos busquen lo terrenal. Cristo dijo: "Mirad por vosotros, que vuestros corazones no sean cargados de glotonería y de los cuidados de la vida" (Luc. 21:34). Y es precisamente esto lo que esta arruinando a todo el mundo cristiano. A causa de los cuidados de la vida, los cristianos han dejado el amor, y han dejado todo mandamiento de Dios. En vez de imitar aquél que nos dijo: "Aprended de mí que soy manso y humilde de corazón." Mejor imitamos al impío y al soberbio del mundo, tanto para hablar como para vivir, tanto para vestir, como para comer; tanto para pensar como para ver. ¿De dónde toman el ejemplo nuestras hijas, si no es de las mujeres más malas? Nuestros hijos tienen que asistir por la fuerza, a escuelas donde está el mismo infierno. ¿Dónde está pues la soberanía de la Iglesia? ¿Dónde el celo de Dios? Por esto mismo la Iglesia ya está para ser quemada en fuego e ira de Dios; porque ha perdido su sabor, ha perdido su santidad y su celo. Fuera será arrojada. En qué nos puede imitar el mundo para que le conduzca a Cristo, ¿Qué hay en la Iglesia de amor? ¿Qué hay en la Iglesia de humildad? ¿Qué hay en la Iglesia de mansedumbre? ¿Qué hay en la Iglesia de Justicia y Juicio? Nada de esto hay en la Iglesia; en lugar de esto, hay odio, soberbia, injusticia y toda obra de división. ¿Y quién podrá desmentir esto? Levante la mano, y justifique a la iglesia.

EL PUEBLO SIN HONRA

Esta generación será sorprendida más que ninguna otra generación; no ha habido pero ni habrá gente que sea más sorprendida que esta. No habrá escríbano, no habrá reportero que pueda describir las cosas que van a sorprender a esta mala generación; no habrá valiente que quede en pie en aquél día; los valientes andarán como los más borrachos, y los hombres de soberbia no hallarán lugar en el cual hallen paz. Dios ha sido provocado por los habitantes de la tierra, por cuanto han torcido todo el derecho que su hijo amado trajo a la tierra. ¿Quién podrá contemplar con sus propios ojos la ira, y todo el incendió que Dios hará en su día, y continuar de pie? Muchos hablan ahora, pero en aquel día ¿quién podrá abrir su boca?; los hombres temblarán, como nunca han temblado jamás; gritarán como nunca se han oido gritos; y esta torcida generación la cual ha irritado a su Dios, le va a pesar amargamente en aquel día; se va a arrepentir de haber desdeñado el santo mandamiento que aun mismo Cristo obedecio. Esta generación nunca ha visto a su Dios encendido en ira; y no han aprendido en las páginas de la historia. ¿Acaso perdonó Dios a las mujeres en el diluvio? ¿Perdonó el ojo de Dios a los niños cuando trajo el diluvio sobre aquella mala generación? Abramos los ojos y reconozcamos a Dios aun en su ira. ¿Por qué dejar que ese día nos sobrecoja como sobrecogió a los antiguos rebeldes? No seamos como Israel, que siempre creía que estaba bien, y que tenía contento a su Dios. ¿Cuáles son las evidencias que nosotros tenemos contento a Dios? Pues no tenemos contentos ni a los pobres, a las viudas, a nuestros propios hermanos, cuanto menos a Dios el cual selló su santo mandamiento con la vida santa de su Santo Hijo. ¿Cómo escaparemos de ese día, cuya aurora ya se ve?

La grande babilonia es la única que manda y rige en estos días; ésta es: la fe fingida, el amor propio, el espíritu de error que siempre ha cauterizado a las consciencias de los hombres que se han hecho vanos; de los hombres que han sido amadores de salario y de presentes; los humildes de la tierra no mandan, no rigen a nadie; Lo que ahora domina, esla grande babilonia; quien establece leyes que desmienten al Espíritu de Dios y que se rebelan contra los santos mandamientos de Dios, estos son los agentes de la grande babilonia. ¿Para qué cree que la grande Babilonia es cierta secta, o movimiento? Si en ti no hay misericordia, justicia, juicio, mansedumbre, amor de Dios, pues tu compones parte de la grande babilonia. La misma viuda, el huérfano, el extranjero, el pobre y todos los oprimidos, ellos pueden decirte a ti. Quien es la grande babilonia; porque en la grande babilonia no hay lugar para los pobres y para los oprimidos de corazón. Pues que la grande babilonia no sabe, más que oprimir, engañar, insultar a Dios.

Quien tenga a Cristo en su corazón, se identifica por su amor de Dios, por su Misericordia, como él alcanzo misericordia; se identifica por las obras de Dios y de Su amado hijo, las cuales obras son en amor en paz, en bondad, en mansedumbre, en misericordia, en justicia, en fe, no fingida, en Espíritu Santo; porque todas estas obras proceden de un mismo Espíritu, cual es de Cristo. Y yo ruego en el temor de Dios, a todo aquel que no posee estas obras del Espíritu de Cristo: que salga de la grande Babilonia, y tema de todo corazón a aquel que hizo todas las cosas; y ya no ponga sus ojos en las cosas que perecen; ni gaste el sudor de su vida por ir tras las cosas del mundo y las cosas vanas las cuales todos aman; aborrezca lo que Cristo aborreció, y ame aquello que Crito se gozó en hacerlo, aunque al principio parece duro y cosa difícil, pero más tarde el fruto que todos codiciarán en los últimos días. ¡Oh que terrible juicio le espera al pueblo que desamparo el derecho, el pueblo que dejó el amor de Dios, el pueblo que djó de dar luz, el pueblo que perdió su sabor. Somos culpables, y Dios nos hará culpables de todo lo que ha entrado a la Iglesia. Buscó decencia, buscó vergüenza, buscó honra en el pueblo de Dios, pero en vano, porque no la veo: La Iglesia de Dios, es decir todo aquel que se llama Cristiano, y que ha conocido el nombre de Cristo, debiera de sentarse en ceniza, y vestirse de duelo, por haber perdido lo que perdió; no solo perdió su primer amor, sino que quedó ciego, desnudo, miserable. La iglesia perdió su honra; nadie la respeta, porque se ha llenado de lucro terrenal; y todos sus amantes que la alagan y que le sirven, nunca le dijeron su grande y terrible defecto. De esto hará Dios venganza. ¿Quién podrá detener la mano de Dios cuando se levante? Yo me siento como un cobarde, por no haber denunciado estas cosas más pronto, porque Dios las puso en mi corazón muchos días pasados; sé que no estoy desnudando ni declarando el mal grande que la iglesia está haciendo sobre la tierra, de la manera que lo debiera de hacer. Porque veo que la tierra va a recibir de su Dios grandes golpes, y mortales azotes, por cuanto la iglesia no supo hablar verdad, ni detener el derecho de Su Dios.

El mundo con todos sus habitantes están enlazados y ocupados en las divisiones y pleitos que ellos mismos han hecho; todos confiados en opiniones y caprichos, como toda clase de ideas humanas; mientras el derecho y la misericordia están pasando a la historia. Oh si solo la iglesia levantara su cabeza y escuchara el verdadero derecho de Dios, el cual derecho hace bien a los oprimidos, a los hogares, al hombre y a la mujer; pero ahora le está encubierto todo esto, por su propia rebeldía y sus tenaces caprichos. Los fariseos y los saduceos se levantarán en el juicio contra esta torcida generación y la condenarán, por cuanto ellos creyeron más tarde, e hicieron el bien que sabían mas esta generación ni la cortesía del mundo sabe usar. ¿quién hablará a favor de esta generación rebelde? Busquemos a sus amantes.

LA JUSTICIA QUE NO PERECE

La justicia de Dios no arde; ni se quema el amor de Dios. El que haciendo el bien confía en Dios, de ninguna manera será avergonzado; antes el que obedece a Dios y obra el bien para con todos; este esta firme y nada lo puede mover; pero no así, con la incrédulos y desobedientes, porque todos los rebeldes serán confundidos y avergonzados. La confianza de los cristianos presentes será quemada; toda la gloria de los cristianos falsos será puesta y abrazada en llamas de justicia: porque justos y santos son los juicios de Dios. La confianza de los cristianos hipócritas no podrá resistir el juicio que viene: porque ¿cuál es la confianza de los que ahora profesan conocer a Dios? ¿No está vuestra confianza en Templos, en ceremonias? Y ¿quién en estos días ha puesto su confianza en el temor de Dios, y en la misericordia del Altísimo? ¿Quién se deleita en hacer y obrar el bien para con todos. ¿Quién es aquel que dá sin hacer acepción de personas? ¿Quién es el que perdona sin hacer acepción de personas? Los que temen a Dios y los que se gozan en hacer la voluntad de Dios: estos son los que lo pueden hacer sin hacer acepción de personas: por cuanto ellos son hijos del Altísimo, el cual hace bien y da respiración a todos. El que en verdad conoce a Dios: lo conoce en amor, en justicia, en misericordia, en juicio, en bondad, en mansedumbre, en fé, en toda buena obra; y no solamente en nombre como hoy día lo confiesan. Dios es conocido en Espíritu y no por nombre y ceremonias como ahora lo presentan.

Ay de la confianza de este pueblo: porque será puesta en

llamas, y no podrá resistir el Juicio de Dios. El que teme a Dios y obra su justicia, obedeciendo a su palabra: este no teme al fin, ni tiembla al ver el mundo puesto en llamas: porque su esperanza es espíritu y vida; el hombre que hace el bien que agrada a los ojos de Dios: este tiene su casa y su vida fundada en roca; y nada lo escandaliza. Toda la confianza de los rebeldes, no pasará en el juicio de Dios ni estará firme el amor de los profesos ante la ira que viene. Como se derrite la cera ante el calor del sol: así el amor y la fe falsa, serán derretidos ante el juicio de Dios; y los falsos predicadores no hallarán palabras para hablarle al pueblo en aquél día. Los que ahora pasa por cristianismo no podrá estar firme de aquí en pocos días: en aquél día sabrán todos los cabezas y jefes de las gentes, qué cosa es "palabra de Dios" y qué cosa es "Mandamiento de Dios."

La justicia que ahora hay: ésta arderá, esta se quemará; como también el amor que ahora hay, será abrazado en llamas porque no es el amor de Dios. Los templos y ceremonias es lo único que ahora toma el lugar de la justicia. Pero ¿quién recibe beneficio de esta gloria de los hombres? La viuda y el huérfano, no reciben beneficio de tantos templos. Todos reconcentran sus intereses de dar solamente en templos: y entre más templos se multiplican, mas descuidan a las viudas. Y todo esto porque de los grandes reciben las ordenes. ¿Guardará Dios silencio al ver todo este mal? ¿Halla Dios favor en estos hijos rebeldes y arrogantes? Como los ojos aborrecen al humo: así Dios aborrece las obras de este pueblo arrogante e hipócrita. Porque solo hacen bien donde tienen interes propio. Pero esto también el mundo y los hijos de las tinieblas hacen: y de una manera mejor y más sagaz. Cristo nos enseñó a amar aun a nuestros enemigos: pero ahora el hermano no ama ni aun a su propio hermano, menos al enemigo. El hermano en Cristo, como el hermano en la fe, de igual manera pleitean; nadie hace un bien a su prójimo. ¿Quién es el hijo que da la ayuda a su propio padre? todos emprestan dinero cuando mucho: pero dado, ni un solo centavo. Y si no fuera que los predicadores amenazaran a las gentes con el juicio de Dios: ni ellos mismos ganaran el pan, ni recibieran el diezmo que ellos han impuesto como tributo. Digo "Como tributo" porque las gentes no lo dan como fruto de amor, ni tampoco voluntariamente; antes lo ven como un tributo por pertenecer a la Iglesia. Esto hiede a la presencia de Dios; y es cosa vergonzosa; porque todos defienden sus propios bienes, pero nadie aboga por el mudo y por el igorante. Los hijos arrogantes y disolutos, desobedientese a los padres: así son puestos como embajadores de Cristo; y estoy cierto que si los cabezas de estos grupos fueran reyes de la tierra: no querían embajadores hipócritas y disolutos. Partos prematuros, son los predicadores que ahora toman la palabra de Dios en sus bocas mentirosas; hombres codiciosos, son los que ahora enseñan al pueblo: ¿y qué podrán enseñar estos hombres? Que si pasaran un examen por las manos de Dios; aun la tierra abriría su boca para tragarlos como hizo con Coré y su séquito. Por esta razón, la justicia de Dios perdió su fuerza en la tierra de los vivientes; porque hombres ciegos tomaron el lugar de los jueces: y hombres asalariados interpretan la Ley de Dios.

Hombres que nunca han conocido el amor de Dios: ni la misericordia; hombres que no saben lo que es juicio y justicia; estos han sido puestos para enseñar la vida de Dios que fue revelada en Cristo Jesús. Por eso aun hasta los pequeños de la tierra hacen el mal como hacer el bien; y beben el mal como beber agua. Todos han torcido el derecho, a causa de los falsos enseñadores que ahora por todas partes se amontonan. Si esto es así: ¿quién podrá desmentir estas palabras y salir con bien delante de Dios? Acérquese, y venga a juicio con Dios; Por Dios hablo, y no por los hombres; Mi salario está en los cielos; y aunque no haya salario para mí: esto me conviene hablar, porque desde el principio deberíamos de servir a Dios sin interés cual alguno: porque mi interés es Cristo, y mi salario es la vida eterna. Ay de los que venden la palabra de Dios, y cambia el juicio y la justicia por pan que perece.

¿FALTAN MAESTROS?

Los maestros se han multiplicado, los profetas abundan en la tierra; la tierra está llena de enseñadores; todos garantizan vida eterna, todos prometen la paz duradera. La tierra ha sido sorprendida por la plaga más grande; la plaga que no solo ha podrido a la tierra sino hasta los habitantes, es la plaga de los profetas asalariados; los maestros que contienden en pura historia, que se dividen en vana opinión. Esta plaga ha hecho daño en la tierra. Dios esperaba uvas dulces de su pueblo, y fruto bueno: pero en cambio, vino fruto malo y uvas amargas y silvestres. Estos maestros ocupan el tiempo, contendiendo en lo pasado, y la palabra del Espíritu, la cual es el mandamiento de Dios es ignorado. Los médicos se ocupan en los vivos, pero no en los muertos; pero los profetas de hoy, se ocupan en lo muerto, en lo que ya pasó; se ocupan en narrar la historia, y pintar cuadro de varios colores, a fin de tener a sus oyentes atentos. El mandamiento del Espíritu, la santa voluntad de Dios ha sido del todo ignorado y escarnecida; y procuran curar el alma de los pecadores con palabras vanas, y promesas que no se cumplen. Todos dicen: "Ya no pequeis," "ya no pequeis," pero nunca descubren al pecado, ni lo llaman por nombre a fin de que los pecadores sepan lo que es pecado; ¿quién conoce pecado y lo puede distinguir en estos días obscuros? Todos a una vez, están llenos de malicia, de soberbia; todos buscan la misma cosa; todos buscan riquezas, y las entrañas las han cerrado al pobre y al huérfano. La ley no es historia; la voluntad de Dios no ha pasado; de esto hablemos, y ocupemos a nuestras almas en hacer la voluntad de nuestro Dios, la cual es que amemos no solo a nuestros hermanos, sino aun a nuestros enemigos; Pero si no hacemos bien a nuestros hermanos ¿podremos hacer bien a nuestros enemigos? Las gentes han dejado el santo mandamientos, a causa de los asalariados; todos resisten al Espíritu de Dios porque han sido conducidos por caminos engañosos. A la santa Ley de Dios le han llamado "Sermón del Monte" pero ¿de dónde vino este nombre? Los apóstoles no le dieron este nombre; ¿por qué es que la gente ha ignorado la palabra de Dios? Todos escarnecen los mandamientos de Dios, y quieren vivir y progresar en el bien sin ejecutar la voluntad de Dios.

Las gentes confiesan por todas partes, y de todos los movimientos, que no están haciendo la voluntad de Dios y que no están obedeciendo a Dios según sus mandamientos; ahora ¿porqué es que los profetas y los maestros de las gentes dicen al contrario, que sí están obedeciendo?

¡Oh! hermanos míos, ¿qué no miran las gentes en pleito? ¿Que no ven a todos disputando y divididos en palabras y opiniones? ¿Y en qué se distinguen los unos de los otros? ¿no visten todos con gala y con soberbia? No comen todos en mesas de ricos? ¿No van todos, tanto unos como otros, tras la figura y el color? ¿No enseñan todos su soberbia aun en el tacón de sus zapatos? ¿No procuran todos de enseñar sus propias figuras, sus propias caras? ¿Quién no adorna su cara para ganar el ojo de la mujer de su prójimo? Pueblo ignorante, escucha la voz de tu Dios, que te dice: "Salid pueblo mío" no toqueis lo inmundo. Todo el mundo será puesto en llamas y en completa confusión y desolación, por nuestra causa; porque nosotros dejamos que pereciera la Ley de Dios; nuestros cuerpos soponían ser templos del Espíritu Santo, y habitación del altísimo; nuestros cuerpos suponían ser casas y habitaciones del amor, y de la misericordia, de la justicia, de los santos juicios de Dios; pero ahora ¿Qué es lo que habita en el corazón de los hombres? Malicia, envidia, egoismo, soberbia, palabras torpes, murmuración, y toda obra repugnante.

¿Por qué condenar al bautista? ¿Por qué condenar al pentecostal? ¿Por que condenar al adventista? ¿Y por qué condenar a las diferentes organizacioes? ¿Quién puede levantar la mano contra algún credo o movimiento? ¿No tratan todos de agradar a Dios? ¿No leen todos la "Biblia"? Miremos el espíritu que ha arruinado a todo el mundo: Amor propio, soberbia, la cual todos la tienen, envidia, desobediencia a Dios nuestro criador; El haber dejado la justicia y la misericordia, esto nos arruinó. ¿No estamos todos los moradores del mundo sentenciados a muerte si es que no obedecemos a Dios? ¿Quién es aquel que no ha quebrado la voluntad de Dios? ¿Dónde está aqul que está obedeciendo a Dios en todos sus santos mandamientos?

¿Amparas tu a la viuda, al huérfano? ¿Das de tu pan al hambriento, y repartes de la mucha ropa que tienes a los necesitados? ¿está tu mente limpia? ¿No piensas mal de la mujer de tu prójimo? Responde, y levanta la mano. ¡Oh pueblo cubierto de rebeldía! Humilla tu alma, cierra tu boca; levanta tu cabeza y mira el arrepentimiento de los ninivitas; ¿quieres perdón? pues perdona a tu enemigo primero; y ya no hables contra tu hermano, el cual con dificultad anda buscando la misma puerta que tu buscas. ¿No hay un solo Juez de toda la tierra? ¿Pues quién eres tú que juzgas a otro? ¿Tienes mayor amor que él? ¿Haces mejores obras que él? Pues ¿de qué te jactas, si es que no conoces todavía lo que es el amor de Dios? ¿Guardas tu los mandamientos de Dios? De otra manera eres un mentiroso y no hay nada de verdad en ti.

Hermanitos míos, consideremos los tiempos; ya se está acortando la vida del hombre, ya los años terminarán; seámos sabios de corazón y miremos nuestra triste condición. Necesitamos a Dios. ¿No necesitamos todos la misma agua para vivir? ¿No comemos todos la misma comida de la tierra a fin de vivir? pues ¿por qué? no alimentar a nuestras almas de la misma fuente de Sabiduría, del amor de Dios, de la misericordia. Vistámonos de entrañas de misericordia.

¿PARA QUIEN ES LA MISERICORDIA?

Es muy cierto que Dios prometió guardar el "Pacto de la Misericordia" con su pueblo; pero él lo especificó, y dijo: "Con los que me aman y guardan mis mandamientos." Dios nunca ha prometido guardar su pacto con los que no le aman ni guardan sus mandamientos.

Los discípulos guardaron la palabra de Dios que Cristo les habló; y por esto les dijo: "Ya vosotros sois limpios por la palabra que os he hablado." Estos hombres y mujeres en verdad que habían obedecido a la palabra de Dios que Cristo había hablado. Porque la palabra que Cristo siempre hablaba era del Padre, como él mismo lo dijo: "La palabra que habéis oído, no es mía, sino del Padre que me envió." Pero en estos días la palabra de Dios, es menospreciada por los cabezas y los pastores de las mismas gentes. Por eso es que la palabra no nos limpia ni nos trae conocimiento; aquellos tenían fé en la palabra de Dios; Basta con la palabra. Pues así como nos basta el oír la palabra sola sobre algún falso o palabra que se diga de nosotros para creerla: así nos debiera de bastar la palabra de Dios sola para que nosotros la creamos.

Dios no nos puede santificar por su palabra, como nos dice Cristo en Juan 17:17. Porque no creemos a la palabra. No obstante, la gente está creída que sí cree a Dios; pero los hechos desmienten. Aquí está la razón por qué Dios no puede guardar el pacto ni la misericordia con nosotros; No le tememos, pero ni guardamos sus Mandamientos. Y esto no lo habló solo Dios en el Antiguo Testamento, sino que también Cristo lo dijo: (Jn. 14:21-24): "El que tiene mis mandamientos y los guarda, aquél es el que me ama; y el que me ama, será amado de mi Padre y yo le amaré y me manifestaré a él." y este mismo Apóstol Juan dijo: "si alguno dice que le ha conocido, y no guarda sus mandamientos: el tales es mentiroso y no hay verdad en él." ¿Cómo podremos estar en su amor sin guardar sus mandamientos? Cuando mismo Cristo dijo: "Si guardaréis mis mandamientos estaréis en mi amor; como yo he guardado los mandamientos de mi Padre y estoy en su amor!

Por eso es que la palabra de estos días solo nos limpia de vicios y costumbres. Pero los pensamientos malos, las palabras arrogantes y vanas como los hechos malos y desagradables no solo a Dios: sino que también son hechos que no amparan a la viuda ni al huérfano, tampoco al pobre y al extranjero pueden hacer bien: todo esto no quita. Y ¿por qué) Porque los mandamientos que las gentes guardan y obedecen, son mandamientos y acuerdos de hombres que aman sus vientres, y agradan al ojo, y mucho se sacrifican por puestos y títulos firmados por la mano de hombres peores que ellos. Si el pueblo de Dios guardara la Palabra de Dios: la viuda no fuera despreciada por la iglesia y alimentada por el gobierno y el "Wellfare." Si guardaramos los mandamientos de Dios que Cristo nos habló: los hijos cristianos no deshonraran a sus padres; Si obedeciéramos a Dios en su consejo: nuestros ojos no estuvieran puestos en templos grandes, en carros nuevos, en casas espaciosas, en vestiduras de príncipes, y en toda cosa vana. Otra cosa testificaría el pobre, el extranjero y el huérfano a nuestro favor: Si estuviéramos guardando el mandamiento de Dios; pues que no sabemos ni qué cosa es misericordia; y ¿cómo pues alcanzaremos misericordia? ¿Con quién hemos hecho misericordia? Pues que ni a nuestros mismos padres hemos hecho bien: cuando menos a los que nos aborrezcan. Cristo dijo que los misericordiosos alcanzarían misericordia; pero no dijo que los hipócritas alcanzarían Misericoria. La misericordia no se ve en el templo, la misericordia no se ve en los cantos ni en las oraciones; tampoco se ve la misericordia en ceremonias vanas de hombres, tampoco en ayunos y predicaciones: antes la misericordia se ve al hacer el bien a los pobres imposibilitados, a la viuda y al huérfano; La misericordia se ve en el perdón, en el dar, en el servir a nuestros semejantes; la misericordia se ve en el dar al enfermo como al necesitado con sacrificio, y no de lo que nos sobra.

Pero todo esto se há perdido de la tierra de los vivientes: acausa de los que han tomado la rienda de la ley; porque estos que están como ejemplos del pueblo, obran sin misericordia; y la misma gente están tan impuesta y acostumbrada que ya no lo echan de ver. Pero por esto está escrito." Juicio sin misericordia será hecho con el que no hiciere misericordia. Quien hace y conoce la misericordia, no teme a nada: porque la misericordia se gloría contra el juicio y contra la Ley; porque no hay palabra ni Ley de Dios que condene la Misericordia: esto es, la Misericordia que es según Dios. Porque no puede haber Misericordia en el hombre sin antes conocer a Dios y a su hijo el cual nos reveló la verdad del Padre. Pero sí hay tal cosa, como conocer el evangelio de estos días y la conversión de estos días; y no tener misericordia. Porque la tierra está llena de este pueblo. Y los pobres de la tierra, como las viudas y los huérfanos dan testimonio contra la que ahora se llama "iglesia de Cristo." La misericordia y la verdad no guardan, aun a los reyes de la tierra. Y con clemencia sustentan sus propios tronos; cuanto mas el cristiano vivirá si permaneciere en ella. (Prov. 20:28). Por eso también Cristo lo dijo, que en peña firme, edifica el que oye la palabra y la ejecuta. Aun David, dice que Dios es bueno para con el bueno, y limpio para con el limpio. Como también íntegro para con el íntegro; pero Dios se muestra rígido para con el perverso (2 Sam. 22:26). Y ¿quién podrá justificarse ahora que venga la ira de Dios? ¿Quién es el que piensa que no es digno de la ira que viene? Levántese.

LA JUSTICIA DE ESTA GENERACION

Ay de los que van junto con la nación fuerte; y ay de los que confían en la energía atómica. Esta nación ha dejado a su Dios, y ay de los profetas que no la corrigieron; porque Dios mismo puso hombres, y levantó profetas para que la humillaran con palabras de sabiduría; pero en vez de anunciarle la justicia de Dios; ellos mismos hicieron negocio con ella. Por eso, está nación se apartó para hacer iniquidad y violencia. Fueron más fuertes los hombres de las tinieblas que los hombres de la luz; pudieron más los ciegos que los que decían tener ojos.

Los hijos de los malos pudieron más que los hijos de los buenos; esta fama salió por toda la tierra; se divulgó la ruina y la derrota de los cristianos por toda la tierra; Pereció el celo por la justiica; murió el vigor de los corazones; y todos se fueron tras la hermosura de esta grande Nación. Si de este pueblo hipócrita, ingrato, injusto, sin fruto bueno, y sin testimonio compone Dios a su Iglesia: aborrezco el día en que yo conocí a este pueblo; lejos sea de que Dios justifique a un pueblo que recibió una verdad tan grande y tan preciosa, y que ahora se porta con un despotismo tan grande, y con un corazón tan soberbio. ¡Oh grandes de la tierra, que detienen la verdad, e impiden a la justicia para que no se haga manifiesta. ¿Qué mal es el que hago? Vuestra jutsicia no tiene color ni figura. De vuestra misericordia ni los más miserables alcanzan; ¿quién alcanza beneficio de vuestro amor? Por cierto que ni vuestros propios familiares dan testimonio a favor vuestro; cuanto menos vuestros enemigos. ¿Ha recibido la viuda algún bien de vosotros? ¿Ha recibido el mundo algún beneficio de vuestros ejemplos? ¿Habéis enseñado al mundo como vestir con honra y descencia? ¿Se ha modificado algún creyente con vuestras palabras de sabiduría y de humildad? ¿No hablan todos con soberbia por causa vuestra? Las gentes han aprendido a poner todo su corazón y todas las fuerzas y todo el entendimiento para conseguir los antojos de la carne, porque esto aprendieron de los Profetas alquilads. ¡Oh profetas alquilados! Si sois de Dios, pues sufrid esta injuria, nada perderéis. Maestros asalariados, tened paciencia, y soportad este reproche que yo en mi locura hablo; ya que este nombre se les da a todos los que reprenden. ¿Por qué pues condenan a los enemigos de Jeremías, simplemente porque recibían salario? ¿Qué no es mayor vuestro salario que el de aquellos? Por cierto que aquellos falsos profetas no andaban con la pompa que vosotros andáis; ni los vientres de ellos estaban tan amplios como los vuestros; tenían mejor cortesía aquellos (ya que la cortesía es una capa de la hipocresía) que vosotros.

Sufrid esta palabra maestros y profetas, porque a mi sangre entró el celo de Dios, y de mi corazón se apoderó lo que yo no quería: Vosotros enseñáis que vuestro Cristo no abrió su boca cuando se le acusaba: pues ¿por qué la abrís vosotros contra esta palabra falsa? ¿No es el salario, veustro interés? ¿enseñaríais aun sin salario por amor a Cristo el cual no recibió salario, sino una corona de espinas? ¡Oh profetas mayores, ¿qué no veis a todos los profetas pequeños, corriendo tras de vuestro fijo salario? Por esto se abandonó la misericordia, y el amor perdió su fuerza en el corazón de las gentes.

¿De dónde fuimos nosotros cortados, de un Cordero, o de un lobo? ¿quién es nuestro ejemplo, un humilde, o un soberbio? Escudriñar vuestros corazones, según la palabra de Dios, y hallaréis grande pecado envuelto en vuestras entrañas. Ciertamente que en vano se multiplicaron las Biblias, y por demás fueron la muchedumber de profetas; pues que todos han sido cortados con la misma palabra; y todos buscan la misma cosa: fama, gloria, posesión.

Ay de los que han atesorado aquí en la tierra; grande será su pérdida; muchas serán sus lágrimas. Buscad oro fino, dando a los pobres; abrid vuestros ojos negando las cosas del mundo; ¿por qué mutilais vuestras vidas en lo que no es? ¿Por qué arrojais vuestros días por las cosas que pronto pasarán? ¿No véis el ejemplo que dejáis para vuestros seguidores?

Ya pronto se le dará el poder a la bestia, y ¿dónde quedará vuestra soberbia con la cual escarnecéis a los mandamientos de Cristo? ¿Qué será de vuestros tronos y grandes nombres, cuando aparezca la voluntad de Dios en aquél humilde galileo? Mirad como vuestros puestos y títulos han podrido y saquiado vuestros corazones; desapareció la humildad y la misericordia cuando los hombres inventaron sillas grandes en las cuales se sentaron a fin de que los hombres les temieran. Y así las gentes temen a los hombres, no por sus vidas santas que vivan, sino por el lugar y trono que ocupan.

Bienaventurados los que también en estos días tengan hambre y sed de justicia. Pocos misericordiosos quedan en la tierra, pero bienaventurados ellos porque alcanzarán misericordia; no hay promesa que los hipócritas e injustos alcanzarán misericordia; antes como dice Santiago: "Juicio sin misericordia será hecho con aquel que no usa de misericordia." Por mucho tiempo se ha hablado del amor de Dios, y los pueblos no han querido vivir en este amor de Dios; ahora las gentes probarán de la ira de Dios. Y esto, porque no quisieron el amor: recibirán la ira de Dios.

LOS PECADORES VAN ADELANTE

El Estado tuvo que urdir una idea para dar de comer a los ancianos, que estaban quedando en la tierra sin alimento; el estado vió que los padres ancianos estaban quedando sin alimento y sin quien los alimentasen, y así fué el estado movido a misericordia, para dar el alimento a padres que quedaban en el abandono, sin tener quien les diera el alimento; todos estos padres, eran padres ancianos de hijos fuertes, de cristianos saludables, pero que estaban muy ocupados en sus propio bienes; y por eso no podían ayudar a sus propios viejos.

El Estado nunca hubiera proporcionado tal plan, si es que no hubiera visto tantos ancianos abandonados por la Iglesia de Jesucristo. El Estado fué exegido a mirar por los ancianos porque la Iglesia estaba muy ocupada levantando templos para agardarle a Dios. El pueblo de Dios debiera de cubrir su rostro de vergüenza; si el estado no alimentara a los ancianos, y no hubieran los hijos de las tinieblas urdido este plan, para dar de comer a los ancianos y viudas: ¿Qué haría la Iglesia? sería movida a misericordia? No. En los hogares se ve la maldición, porque los hijos llamados cristianos, en vez de ayudar a sus padres y darles lo necesario, solamente emprestan dinero a sus padres, como si sus padres fueran extranjeros; pero no dan a sus padres ni un centavo nada. ¿No es esto espantoso? ¿Tenemos razón luego de ir a Dios y pedir misericordia? Antes Dios ha sido longánime, que no nos ha quitado de la tierra; somos un pueblo indigno de habitar este buen planeta. No somos pueblo propio para vivir en esta tierra; hemos corrompido a toda la creación. Busco en mi ignorancia un testimonio, que testifique a favor de la Igelsia, pero en vano: porque no lo he podido hallar. No hay quien se ponga en frente y se atreva defender a la Iglesia de sus grandes abominaciones; ¿quién justificará a esta generación? Los mismos ciegos del mundo, no se atreven a dar testimonio de ella para bien. Los justos de la tierra no teman, no escandilicen a sus propias almas al oír o leer esta palabra. Pero sí aconsejo a los pequeños y debilitados a que se esfuercen para que sean dignos de escapar de la ira que abrazará a toda la tierra, y de estar en pie sin temblar, ante la presencia de Cristo el rey de toda la tierra. Si el justo con mucha dificultad se salva en estos días, ¿a dónde aparecerá los que no aman, los que no tienen misericordia, los que se alimentan con pensamientos malos? Digámosle al justo que por su justicia vivirá; pero que el hipócrita no se engañe a sí mismo: porque todas las cosas hechas en oculto, Dios las pondrá, a luz de todos, y él dará a cada uno según su propia obra.

En vano fué derramada la sangre de Cristo por esta mala generación; muchos pasados lograron el perdón, y agradecieron andando en el temor de Dios y en novedad de vida; pero este pueblo, no se ha limpiado: antes quitaron el valor de la sangre para que otros también pasaran sobre la sangre.

El justo está firme, y nada lo puede mover; el justo no se

escandaliza con estas palabras; él está confiado en el temor de Dios. Sus obras son limpias y dignas de ser alabadas: como las obras de Dorcas, como las obras de Cornelio. Pero ¿quién codicia las obras de los cristianos presentes? ¿Qué intercesión podrá oír Dios a favor de esta generación? ¿La intercesión de Moisés? ¿La de Daniel? ¿La de Abraham? No, Dios ha sido levantado de su santo lugar por nuestra causa; nosotros lo hemos provocado. El fin viene y nadie lo puede tener, las Oraciones no valen, porque los labios de los que oran, hablan mentira contra su propio hermano. Las Oraciones ya no valen, porque son oraciones vanas; oraciones sin temor de Dios.

El ingrato que no usa de misericordia con los huérfanos y las viudas, ¿alcanzará misericordia de Dios? Nunca se oyó tal cosa sobre la tierra, porque Dios es justo, y él defiende a la viuda y al huérfano. Volvámonos al que nos informó, dejemos nuestra rebeldía; despojémonos de toda soberbia, y hallaremos gracia delante de Dios. Abramos nuestro corazón a la palabra de Dios; y dejemos el lucro del mundo; todo pasará de aquí en muy pocos días; ¿porque negarle a nuestra alma la salvación? En el tiempo de nuestro Señor, también había lucho según aquellos días; también había ropa de gala, y comidas mejores que otras. Pero nuestro maestro dejó lo mejor por lo peor; dejó el lucro y escogió el pesebre. ¿O sería casualidad que Cristo naciera en pesebre? ¿Sería descuido de Dios que Cristo naciera en pesebre? No, Lo que para el hombre es riqueza, para Dios es inmundicia y torpeza. ¿Si las riquezas son buenas, porque pues las negó Cristo? ¿Por qué las llamó Pablo "estiércol"? Oh ciego, ¿no veis el fin de todas estas cosas? Tomad lo que permanece; y no engañéis a vuestras almas con cosas ilusorias. Amad justicia, haced el bien, de mañana; recread vuestras almas haciendo misericordias. ¿Por qué llenad a vuestros corazones de nombres dulces, pero vacíos? Dejad que el Espíritu de Dios habite en vosotros, y que fructifique a vida eterna; humillad a vuestra voluntad antes que llegue el día en el cual por la fuerza tendréis que rendirla.

Mirad, ¿que ha pedido Dios de nosotros? ¿alguna obra difícil? ¿ha demandado de nosotros alguna obra como las que él hizo en los seis días de su creación? No, solo pide de nosotros lo que podemos hacer. ¿No podemos perdonar? ¿No podemos amar a nuestro semejante? Seguro que sí podemos; pero el orgullo que se ha apoderado de nuestra alma nos impide. Dejad pues esto que arruina nuestra alma. Despidamos al egoísmo, la ira, la malicia.

¿DONDE ESTA EL SABIO?

¿A quién imitaremos para aprender justicia? ¿Quién nos enseñará como amar? ¿Quién sobre la tierra es digno de ser imitado? ¿Quién entre los cabezas? ¿Hay hombre de seso, que nos enseña juicios limpios? Descurran por las calles, busquen entre los pueblos, entren a los templos, y pregunten por hombres sabios; pregunten por un hombre que le interese el juicio de Dios.

Busquen un hombre que no venda la palabra de Dios; un hombre que mire por el oprimido, uno que no sea asalariado. Levantad bandera ahí en el lugar donde le hallaréis; gritad y dad las nuevas, para que de él aprendamos todos los que necesitamos a Dios. El día se ha hecho obscuro; el sol de justicia ha caído, y ¿quién tomará nuestra mano para que nos conduzca entre las tinieblas? Buscad ojos que no vayan tras la recompensa, buscad labios que no hable engaño ni exageren; buscad oídos que no se inclinen a la vanidad, y de estos ojos limpios aprenderemos el bien, de estos labios verdaderos oiremos los juicios de Dios los cuales son limpios y sanos para el alma; ¿Dónde está la escuela de justicia? ¿Dónde está el colegio de la misericordia? Llevadnos allá. ¿Dónde está un hombre que no sea movido por lo terrenal? ¿Dónde está el hombre que no sea movido por la opinión de un pueblo, como el que está ya para ser consumido por la ira de su hacedor? Busquen el hombre que no tenga sus ojos en las cosas que el insensato está inventando. Buscad un hombre que no se escandalice por los mandamientos de Dios y su hijo. Un hombre queremos, que no busque su propio bien. Este hombre no se levantará, hasta que aparezca el Rey de Reyes, el cual regirá la tierra con vara de hierro. ¿Y en aquél día ¿dónde estarán los que reciben cólicos por esta palabra escrita? No os asusteis con estas simples palabras; dejad vuestro susto y miedo para el día cuando vereis cara a cara vuestros propios pecados e injusticias. Dios se ha levantado de su santo lugar, porque los grandes de la tierra han detenido la justicia; han hecho que el justo tropiece, no han dado lugar a la misericordia, sino que como nubes negras se levantan amenazando a todo aquél que quiera hacer justicia y juicio. Han hecho que el pequeño tropiese, aun en la oración, porque han enseñado a orar en público. Los injustos han contristado y muerto al que quería vivir en temor, y luego dicen. ¿Pero en qué hemos hecho mal al justo? Con vuestras propias leyes ligáis el alma del inocente, con vuestra mala conducta; en vuestro rostro no hay más que pura burla y sarcasmo; la verdad la habláis con burla y broma; mas la mentira la habláis con seriedad.

¿Cómo no iba a caer el ciego que principiaba en el camino? ¿Quién de los que principian la vida escapará? Con tanta fuerza en vuestras hechicerías? Bienaventurado el que escape y obre justicia, porque Dios le pondrá en lugar alto; dichoso el hombre que se libre de las muchas tretas de la antigua babilonia. Decid al justo, que ya pronto dominará; el que en verdad hará justicia; decidle, que ya no más, regirá el asalariado. Yo pronto, y muy pronto: los reinos de los príncipes, vendrán a ser los reinos de nuestro Señor y Salvador Cristo el Rey.

Ay de las mujeres que han sido puestas para red, para ruina del hombre; Ay de las que se adornan con toda suerte de adorno. ¿Qué perfume, que pomito, que adorno no usa la mujer? Nuestras mujeres fueron también adornadas como las hijas de babilonia; los ojos del hombre son humillados ante la hermosura y la compostura de las mujeres. ¿Cuál es el hombre que escapa de la poderosa figura, con la cual la mujer ha sido adornada? ¿Qué no hay sabios entre las cabezas? ¿No hay quien se disguste con la inmundicia y con la soberbia de la mujer? Decidle a la mujer que así no agrada a Dios, decidle que Dios la pondrá en vergüenuza y en grande humillación. El adorno de la mujer ha proporcionado y abierto más, la puerta del adulterio. ¿Acaso son los hombres limpios de corazón, para que no sean lastimados con la figura y la apariencia de la mujer? ¿Acaso son tan limpios que no les molesta la desnudez de la mujer? No, por cierto; antes alimentan sus apetitos corruptos, y sus ojos de ellos como no se hartan de ver lo ajeno, no estorban a este gran mal; esto hablo, no de los pecadores que saben y admiten que entre las hijas de Babilonia se desarroya. Y todos esto para detener el mal, y establecer justicia y honra n la tierra. Pero estos atalayas ciegos, no saben detener el mal; antes: en vez de atacar el mal, atacan el bien, y dan paso libre al mal que entre las hijas de Babilonia se desarrolla. Y todos estos hacen, apoyánodse en la palabra de Dios; y dicen: Dios no es contra la soberbía de la mujer, ni tampoco aborrece Dios las aromas y los pomitos con los cuales la mujer se adorna; tampoco aborrece Dios las vestiduras transparentes que nuestras hijas visten. ¡Cómo se ha multiplicado el pecado en la tierra! Pereció la decencia y la honra de la mujer; se fué la vergüenza y el respeto de la mujer ajena.

La mente del hombre fue embotada, y ¿quién le dirá a la mujer el mal que está causando en la tierra?

¿DONDE ESTA NUESTRO FRUTO?

Los pasados escogieron el mandamiento del Espíritu Santo, pero está generación ha escogido las promesas con un corazón lleno de avaricia; los pasados escogieron el servir a la humanidad, pero esta gente ha escogido el ser servida; por esto el derecho pereció de la tierra y la justicia no se puede ver. Esto levantó a Dios de su lugar; al ver que los grandes se enseñoreaban y maltrataban a los pequeños. Dios miró desde su morada que los sabios perdieron el sentido, y se fueron también tras la vanidad; por esto Dios quemará la obra del hombre, porque el hombre con su propia obra se ha engañado, y ha descuidado la vida y el camino a causa de las cosas que conciernen al vientre y al cuerpo. ¿No es esto lo que pertenece a los insensatos? A esto se debe las muchas divisiones; porque nadie se ha dividido para poder ser más manso o humilde; nadie se ha dividido para hacer mayor misericordia, o para obrar más y mejor justicia. Antes cada uno de los que se han dividido, por la gloria y por los tronos se han dividido. Nada se ha mejorado con tanta división. El mundo no ha recibido ningún beneficio; ni aun los creyentes se han mejorado en alguna de las muchas divisiones. Antes todo esto es el fruto de nuestra rebeldía. Esto no aprendimos de Cristo. Nuestra división debe de ser en espíritu, y no en palabras y nombres, como opiniones humanas. Y separarnos, no de algunos creyentes, porque lleven algún nombre hechiso: sino que nuestra separación debe d ser, separación del mundo. Si el mundo aborrece, nosotros debemos de amar. Si el mundo roba y quita, nosotros debemos de dar y servir. Si el mundo se goza en ver, oír, y hablar lo malo; pues nosotros debemos de gozarnos en ver, oír, y hablar lo bueno; aquello que agrada a Dios; aquellos que aprendimos de Cristo.

¿Habló Cristo fuera de la voluntad de Dios? ¿quebró e ignoró Cristo las palabras de su padre? Pues ¿que de nosotros? Por eso dijo Cristo al padre "Padre santifícalos con tu verdad, tu palabra es la verdad" (Juan 17:17). En otra parte dijo el Señor "En esto es glorificado mi padre, en que lleveis mucho fruto." ¿Y dónde está nuestro fruto? y ¿qué clase de fruto nos pide el Señor? ¿Ceremonias? ¿Cantos dulces de labios? ¿Oraciones vanas y largas? Templos grandes y finos? No, este no fué el fruto que el hijo de Dios tuvo antes, el fruto de la vida de Cristo fué dar de comer al hambriento, espiritual y materialmente. La vida de Cristo produjo amor, misericordia, justicia, fe, mansedumbre y templanza. Estos frutos agradaron al padre; ¿y el nuestro? Ni nuestros propios hermanos apetecen el fruto que nosotros estamos dando. Dios libranos; haznos ver nuestra miseria que es pobre, ciega, desnuda y muy miserable. Dios santo, abre nuestros ojos antes de que llegues con el fuego consumidor; porque ¿quién podrá estar firme: con rebeldía, contra ti?

Dinero y riquezas no tengo; fama y nombre menos, porque mi nombre anda en los pies de muchos; esta palabra es la única que hay en mi corazón; si esta palabra no lo reciben, pues no tengo más que ofrecerles. Pero esta palabra será fuerte testimonio contra todos los rebeldes, que en los últimos días traten de excusarse delante de Mi Dios. No habrá sangre ajena en mis manos, por cuanto yo ví el fin, y lo notifique a todas las gentes. ¿Quién podrá decir que fué inocente, después de que lea las palabras de este libro. Porque hablo verdad en Dios, y no miento, que todos hablan mentira, cada uno con su prójimo. El mismo esposo escucha muchas cosas de su esposa; y lo mismo hace la esposa con su esposo. Y cosas que debieran de encubrir no encubren. No miento, con decir que el hombre se ha pervertido con pensamientos malos, y su corazón no cesa de pensar el mal; los ojos de todos están hinchados de adulterio; no dejan mujer hermosa y compuesta que no codicien. ¿Es de soportarse todo esto? ¿Lo pasarán el que pesa los pensamientos? ¿Las oraciones de estos hombres serán aceptas delante del ojo limpio que ve y considera toda su creación? !¿Cómo podemos llamarnos buenos siendo malos? ¿Cómo podemos llamarnos nuevas creaturas, sin tener obras nuevas que agraden a Dios. Esto es lo que ha encendido el furor de Dios. Llorad, lamentad, por vuestras miserias que os alcanzarán, borrad vuestro nombre de entre las gentes, antes que seamos confundidos y sorprendidos por la justicia de Dios. Los que oran en público, y gritan buscando al Señor, sin obrar justicia ni hacer misericordia: ¿Por qué engañáis así a vuestras almas?

Haced bien, buscad justicia, amad como Cristo nos mandó y nos enseñó. Sobrellevad al ignorante, a fin de que también Dios nos mire con ojos de compasión. Amad a todos; ya no es tiempo de que el hombre ande con sus ojos levantados, y con su boca abierta.

Miremos al mundo, está temblando ante su creador, y las montañas ya sienten la grande visita de su Hacedor; sintamos esta grande visita del norte.

LOS ENEMIGOS DE LA CRUZ

No haplo de las leyes que hacen perfecto al sol, porque el sol nunca ha dejado las leyes que Dios le marcó para que anduviera en ellas. El sol no tiene necesidad que nadie le enseñe, porque Dios le enseñó su camino y el lo ha guardado hasta este día. No hablo tampoco de las leyes que sujetan a la tierra, al viento, a las nubes y a todas las cosas que Dios formó con su mano poderosa y terrible: todas estas cosas guardan la voluntad de Dios, y hacen como les fué ordeando desde el principio; y sin las leyes que Dios les preparó para que anduviesen en ellas, todas estas cosas perecerían en un momento, y causarían un basto y terrible desorden en toda la creación de Dios. Pero siendo que todas estas cosas permanecen en la voluntad de Dios, no hay pues necesidad de hablar de ellas, ni tampoco de las leyes que las gobiernan y las sujetan. Antes por el contrario. Yo hablo a hombres y no a bestias; hablo con gente animada, y no con cosas inanimadas. Hablo con un pueblo que fue hecho a la imagen a la semejanza de Dios. Y como todas las cosas recibieron las leyes que marcan el camino para cada una: así también el hombre recibió una santa Ley; el hombre recibió una vida nueva para que anduviese según la estatura de esta nueva vida. Cristo fué la nueva vida por la cual el hombre debe de controlar al hombr que tiene fe en Dios y que ama a Dios; porque sin fé es imposible agradar a Dios; y el que no ama no conoce a Dios. Y el que no guarda sus mandamientos no le ama. (Juan 14:21-24). Y por el contrario: el que guarda sus mandamientos está en su amor: ("Si guardareis mis mandamientos, estaréis en mi amor; como yo también he guardado los mandamientos de mi padre, y estoy en su amor." (Juan 15:16).

Aquí está la caída y la ruina de todo el mundo. Cuando el hombre quiso salvarse sin obedecer a Dios fracasó, y el egoismo mismo lo traicionó. Los hombres buscan los templos, para hacer el bien; todos creen que el amor crece con ir al templo y ser devoto con los ritos del templo. Pero todos estos esfuerzos en verdad que son humanos, los cuales Dios nunca los mandó; Los hombres han recibido su salvación hechisa dentro de los templos; por eso es que no dan fruto de amor, de misericordia, de mansedumbre, de justicia. La Salvación que Dios dá, y la obra del Espíritu Santo es una vida nueva; no compuesta solamente de cantos y oraciones, sino que de frutos santos, obras santas, juicios santos, amor santo. De esto hemos caído, porque hemos dejado el santo camino que Dios le marcó al hombre. Todas las cosas que Dios crió y formó, guardan el orden y el mandamiento de Dios, menos el hombre. El hombre cada día inventa nuevas leyes, tratando de parar el mal que él mismo se ha acarriado por haber dejado el mandamiento de Dios.

Por todas partes los hombres se afanan por inventar leyes, por las cuales el pueblo se pueda mejorar; pero por lo que se ve, estas leyes solo acarrean beneficios a los que las inventan pero ninguna de estas leyes protejen a la viuda, o al huérfano; estas leyes no amparan ni ayudan a los pequeños de la tierra: antes por el contrario, los justos son oprimidos y mal tratados por las leyes que cada día salen. Estas cosas, de las cuales DIOS habló, en un tiempo fueron muy populares; los apostoles no ignoran los santos mandamientos que Cristo les habló y les mandó; las cuales por lo que se ve, fueron dados a todos, para siempre, hasta que Cristo regrese. Estos mandamientos, que os recuerdo; no fueron desdeñados por nuestros padres. En este mismo camino del cual habla, los antepasados hallaron la paz; en estas leyes ellos se deleitaron. No solamente se gozaban en llamar a Cristo: "Señor, Señor," y en confesarlo como ahora se hace: sino que ellos le obedecían y guardaban todos los mandamientos que de Cristo recibieron.

Yo quiero estar limpio delante de Dios, y por eso hablo en **el temor de Dios de la violencia que la Iglesia hace en estos** últimos días: seré culpable si no digo y hablo lo que mis ojos ven, y lo que mis oídos oyen. Que sepan, y un día confiesen que hubo quien les hablara y les dijera que estaban mal, y muy lejos de Dios. Los hipócritas se han multiplicado en la tierra; y estos son los que atacan el derecho de Dios; estos malos asalariados son los que le hacen guerra a la verdadera Cruz de Cristo; por esto los hombres aborrecen la vida de Cristo. Sino aborreceis la vida de Cristo: ¿por qué no viven la vida que Cristo pide de nosotros? Dejad el salario, cada uno de vosotrso: y defended al pobre, haced bien a los oprimidos de la tierra, defendamos los derechos de Dios. Si alguno ama la vida, y quiere ver días buenos, en lo que está para venir: tema a Dios de todo el corazón y haga el bien de Dios. Cada uno de los que quieren hacer el bien y salvar la vida, si es que ya cree en Cristo y ama a Dios, busque los mandamientos que Dios nos dió, a fin de que tuvieramos vida. Porfiad de todo corazón, por entrar por la puerta estrecha; y en estos días está más estrecha que nunca, porque la maldad es más. Apuremos a nuestras almas, antes de que aparezca la ira de Dios, y no haya quien nos defienda, ni quien escape. Porque días de venganza se aproximan; día de ira es el que ya se ve: todos los rebeldes serán quitados; y los que substituyeron las leyes de Dios por mandamientos humanos también recibirán terrible castigo; escape cada uno, y redimamos los días haciendo misericordia y justicia con los oprimidos de la tierra. Y ay de los que escarnecen y desdeñan estas palabras: porque hablo en días malos, y estas palabras los sabios la comerán y pondrán sus almas en libertad. Dios sea con los de corazón humilde y espíritu quebrantado.

No hablo de cosas que abundan; ni de palabras suaves las cuales engañan el alma. Antes digo que grande es el juicio que nos va a sorprender; porque Dios hará venganza de todas sus santas palabras. Las cuales el mismo dijo que traerían salvación o condenación.

Hablo a los que esperan el día del Señor; me dirijo a los que se llaman del nombre de Dios y que se llaman hijos de Dios; ¿Si no habéis guardado el temor de Dios, y si no habéis obedecido en nada al Señor: Para que esperar el día del Señor? Ay de los que esperan el bien sin haber hecho misericordia con nadie. Ay de los que esperan el rapto sin habr guardado los mandamiento de Dios. Ay de los que esperan ver a Cristo cara a cara, sin haber amado a sus prójimos de la manera que Cristo nos mandó que los amasemos. Ay de los que dicen: Yo no puedo guardar los mandamientos de Dios". Porque en aquel día temblarán como tembló el rey Belsazar, Cada uno se esfuerza y alcanza las cosas que quiere; pero nadie se aflige por las cosas del alma. Todos van en pos de los terrenal. Ay de los que dicen: "No por obras para que nadie se glorie" porque en aquel día, les pesará no haber obrado con justicia y con misericordia para con sus semejantes. En aquel día descubrirán que ellos mismos escogieron la muerte; y ellos mismos hicieron pacto con la muerte como lo hizo Irael. Porque habiendo tenido la palabra de Dios en vuestros hogares, no la pusisteis por obra. Cuando el pueblo teme a su Dios, guarda las leyes de su Dios; y cuando el pueblo guarda las leyes de su Dios, la vida de Aquel pueblo agrada a su Dios; y cuando la vida del pueblo agrada a los ojos de Dios, aun sus cantos y oraciones son oídos. Pero, cuando el pueblo retira su oído para no oír el santo mandamiento: aun sus oraciones y solemnidades son abominación a la presencia de Dios. (Prov. 28:9).

Todos hablan mentira; cada uno exagera cuando le conviene; pero nadie cree a la verdad. Si hay habitantes aun en la tierra, que todavía tienen oídos para oír; estos, vuélvanse a Dios y obren el bien. Los hijos rebeldes, a los padres; y las hijas violentas, a sus madres; la mujer que ahora habla tanto como el mismo hombre: guarde su boca, y vuélvase a la honra de la mujer. Porque cada uno ha perdido su honra, y nadie ordena sus caminos a los ojos de Dios.

Las notas ordenadas, gobiernan los sonidos y así vienen a formar la música dulce al oído; así el hombre que ordena sus caminos según los mandamientos de Dios, sus hechos son gobernados por el Espíritu de la Ley de Cristo: y así vienen a formar una nota dulce y agradable a los ojos de Dios. Pero ay de los que quieren vivir la vida de Cristo sin temer al mandamiento de Dios; porque es como quien busca fruto en un árbol seco. Digo a los sabios de la tierra; toleradme un poco, y sufrid mis palabras; porque para esto quedé en la tierra. Yo sé que el hombre que reprende en la tierra nos es apreciado. Y estas palabras por pocos son recibidas. De esto no estoy ignorante, porque el que puso las palabras en mi boca, él mismo permitió a mis ojos el ver la condición de su pueblo; y me hizo ver que los más aborrecerían estas palabras, y un muy pequeño número recibiría la corrección. ¿Por qué ser tan rebeldes? ¿Pereceremos también en el mismo error de Israel? También Israel pensaba que estaba bien: también los fariseos pensaban que estaban bien. Pero ¿no se arrepintió Nínive al oír el consejo de Dios? ¿Por qué dejar que los ninivitas se levanten contra nosotros en el día grande de Dios? Ningún bien hemos hecho en la tierra. ¿De qué pues nos gloriaremos? Prestemos oído al consejo que el profeta Jeremías daba al pueblo de Israel, el cual también pensaba que estaba bien: Decía el Profeta: "No se alabe el sabio de su sabiduría, ni el fuerte en su fuerza, ni el rico en su riqueza; mas si alguno se alaba, alábese en esto: En conocerme que yo soy Jehová, que hago misericordia, juicio y justicia en la tierra: Porque estas cosas quiero, dice Jehová."

Días vienen, en los cuales toda nuestra valentía perecerá, toda nuestra sabiduría perecerá también; en aquél día también nuestras riquezas perecerán. ¿Y cuál será nuestro refugio y nuestro amparo? cuáles obras estarán a nuestra parte. No hemos cumplido aquello, para lo cual fuimos puestos; antes, el bien que nos pertenecía lo abandonamos; y por demás fueron los mandamientos que Cristo nos dió; en vano fueron las palabras por las cuales Cristo murió.

En vano fué para esta generación el nuevo pacto; Los consejos de Dios, ningún provecho ha traído a este pueblo tardo y rebelde. Antes ellos, como Israel en su rebeldía: formaron sus propios mandamientos, en los cuales no hay vida, sino división y contención. todos difieren en credo y opinión: pero en cuanto a obra y espíritu, todos se parecen y todos aman las vanidades de este mundo. Todos son iracundos, violentos para responder; cada uno se alimenta con pensamientos malos, y abre sus ojos a la mujer ajena; y ¿quién se avergüenza de esto? por cierto no hay quien se escandalice, antes todos se sienten en lo propio al hacer el mal y codiciar lo ajeno.

¿Con qué medicina sanará este pueblo? ¿Qué no hay remedio? Las campañas que los hombres dan para traer avivamiento entre este pueblo, no han hecho bien; antes hacen que este pueblo claudique y vacile con su paso de muerte. ¿Por qué no buscar la mejor medicina para vuestras almas? Abramos el oído a la palabra del altísimo, el cual guarda con su palabra todas las cosas hasta este día. ¿No podrá limpiarnos con su palabra como limpio a los apóstoles que mezclaron fe a la palabra? (Juan 15:3). Israel no mezcló fe a la palabra que Dios les dió a ellos (Heb. 4:2). Por eso no les aprovechó la palabra. Tengamos fe en la palabra de Dios y obremos justicia en los pocos días que nos restan, no sea que Dios visite a la tierra y nadie escape.

EL PUEBLO VENCIDO

Las tinieblas de la maldad y violencia, se han hecho más intensas; el mal se ha hecho más fuerte que nunca, y las armas del diablo y reino de Satanás están más poderosas que nunca. ¿Quién podrá resistir a la maldad de estos de estos días: con el evangelio tan débil que se está hablando? Los pecadores se están haciendo más fuertes, y los cristianos se están haciendo más débiles que nunca; las armas de Satanás están más fuertes en estos días que las armas de los cristianos. Por eso es que no hay Amor, por eso es que no hay Mansedumbre y Humildad; los cristianos no pueden dar estos frutos del Espíritu, porque están muy débiles, y han dejado la Sabiduría.

Los cristianos se ocupan más en las cosas del mundo y del vientre, que en las cosas del alma; les puede más la carne que el espíritu; les puede más el cuerpo que el alma. ¿Qué fuerza hay entre los cristianos en estos días? Por todas partes, el mundo ha vencido al cristiano, y lo ha derrotado. Los hombres más grandes y más avanzados en la ciencia humana: son los que el diablo usa para corromper las mentes de los cristianos. El espíritu de confusión ha penetrado en el corazón de los cristianos, y todos los cristianos se han tornado en clientes y comerciantes de la grande Babilonia. Los cristianos se han embriagado de los deleites de la grande babilonia; y todos artífice de artes vanas de la vida, ha hallado ganancia entre los cristianos; Los inventores de los pomitos, de los perfumes, de las ropas y telas finas; los inventores de comidas deleitosas y vanas, bebidas dulces; los inventores de aparatos para transmitir el engaño, el pasatiempos, el ruido y la música y todo sonido agradable a la carne; todos estos inventores se han enriquecido con la grande babilonia, en la cual también los cristianos sin Fe y sin Amor de Dios están incluídos; porque ¿cuál es el cristiano que no se deleita en las vanidades de la vida? ¿cuál es el cristiano que no está endeudado por cosas vanas? La fuerza del cristiano está invertida en puras vanidades. Si en estas cosas que acabo de mencionar no hay mal: ¿pués por qué es que Dios las condena en la grande madre de las fornicaciones? (Rev. 18:12). (Isa. 3:16-24). Si estas cosas engañaron a los antíguos, ¿no engañarán nuestras almas también? Si Dios condenó estas cosas en las vidas de aquellos que todavía no tenían el alto conocimiento que nosotros tenemos. ¿No las condenará mucho más en nuestras vidas? Por cierto que sí.

El diablo tiene a los cristianos bien ocupados en toda arte vana; los tiene ocupados en las cosas que destruyen el alma, y embotan las mentes. Por ejemplo: Tenemos los reporteros del periódico y ¿qué clase de reportes nos dan todos los días? Uno o dos buenos reportes, pero los demás son puros anuncios de las vanidades de la vida; anuncios de deleites y cosas que los cristianos no debieran ni saber. Estos reporteros vienen a ser, más bien como mujeres que llevan y traen para irritar el alma pacifica; estos reporteros, ocupan las páginas en incidentes y ocurrencias de las mas innecesarias. Y lo peor es que los cristianos están ocupados durante el día en hablar de las cosas que salen en el papel, cosas vanas y sin ninguna edificación. Cuando estos reporteros podían más bien, hablar de hechos importantes, de verdad; pero ellos reportan estas vanas cosas porque han hallado que los cristianos tienen hambre de cosas vanas y sin sabiduría. El radio y el periódico son los medios más grandes, para que los maestros más insensatos inculquen y trasmitan sus venenos a la sangre del cristianismo; por supuesto que los cristianos nada de malo ven en el radio y el periódico, pero cuando aparezca el Señor: entonces sabrán el gran mal que estos instrumentos de Satanás hicieron en el corazón de los cristianos. Los artífices más sabios en el mal, han sido escogidos para pintar mujeres desnudas, para dibujar figuras y apariencias de las más poderosas. ¿Y quién no es trastornado con estas figuras? Si los cristianos estuvieran con el antiguo Evangelio, y enseñadores santos y celosos: si los predicadores de la palabra fueran sabios, y entendidos: entonces si hubiera cristianos que pudieran reistir el arte de Satanás, y las fuerzas de las tinieblas. Pero con este cristianismo tan débil y opaco: ¿quién podrá hacerle frente a la fuerza de las tinieblas? Los artistas dibujan mujeres con caras más bellas que ni las que existen, para de esta manera trastornar las mentes, y envenenar las intenciones; ¿Y qué resistencia están haciendo los sabios de la tierra? antes ellos mismos son víctimas de estas artes, y se alimentan con figuras malas. Los hombres llamados de Dios y enseñadores, van a las barberías para cortarse el pelo, y así ven mujeres desnudas por completo, en los calendarios y comparando estas mujeres desnudas con sus propias esposas; pues dicen ellos: ciertamente que mi esposa anda bien vestida, y con vergüenza. Pero no saben que sus propias mujeres a la vista de Dios y los verdaderos cristianos, son y andan como mujeres malas y sin ninguna vergüenza. Las mujeres públicas y rameras del tiempo de los apóstoles, se vestían mejor, que las llamadas cristianas de nuestros días. ¿Y es casualidad esto? ¿Es pasajero? ¿Ignora Dios nuestras maneras de vestir? ¿Soy yo el primero que hablo de la desnudez de la mujer? ¿Soy yo el único fanático de los que han denunciado el pecado? Ciertamente que el mal que la Iglesia está causando en la tierra, no le será pasado; por eso es que viene grande ira por toda la tierra habitada. Los ojos de los enseñadores, son malos e impuestos a ver la deshonra en el pueblo: por eso es que a ellos no les importa nada de como ande la mujer. ¡Oh qué ruina tan grande! que desastre tan terrible el que se ha acarriado la Iglesia; por esto vendrá miseria y hambre sobre toda la tierra; muerte y lloro, angustia y apriete; terror y clamor, sobre todos los que se mofan de la vida santa.

LA FALSA CONFIANZA

El nombre de Cristo, por todas partes ha sido infamado; y ha llegado a un nivel el nombre de Cristo; que aun los mismos hijos del diablo se llaman de este nombre; los hijos de perdición se llaman Cristianos. Nadie más es culpable por esta grande deshonra mundial contra Dios: que los hombres que están al frente con la palabra de Dios; ¿Cuál es la marca que distingue al Cristiano verdadero de un cristiano hipócrita? No hay marca que distinga al uno del otro; solo que los unos han dejado algunos vicios que los otros no. Pero tanto los unos como los otros están vacíos de la misericordia de Dios; tanto los unos como los otros aborrecen la Humildad y el Amor de Dios, que es la Cruz de Cristo. Hombres malos, son los que se llaman Cristianos en estos últimos días; pero estos mismos que se llaman cristianos: son peores que los fariseos que crucificaron a Cristo; con la diferencia que aquellos crucificaron el cuerpo de Cristo solamente; mas estos han crucificado la palabra de Dios y la vida Espiritual de Cristo, y la han substituído por una vida arrogante, y llena de soberbia; en el cristianismo presente hay lugar para toda clase de gente y hombres: arrogantes, malos y perjuros. Hijos rebeldes con sus padres pasan como cristianos. Mujeres y hombres ingratos, sin afecto natural; sin temor de Dios; hombres y jóvenes implacables y sin misericordia; aborrecedores de lo bueno y santo. Maliciosos; sucios de pensamiento y de palabra; crueles para con los pobres y huérfanos; generación mala de palabra, de hecho, de pensamiento; no conocen lo que es temor de Dios; porque ni sus líderes lo conocen. Gente murmuradora, es la que ahora ocupa el lugar de Cristianos. Gente de malos pensamientos y adutlerina son los que ahora ocupan los púlpitos que pertenecían a hombres santos y celosos. Estos son los que han traído infamia a la palabra de Dios, y al santo nombre de Cristo; porque ahora todos profesan creer en el nombre de Cristo; estos son los que han hecho nulo el sacrificio de Cristo; estos han quitado el valor de la sangre de Cristo, y solo la han usado para tomar libertad en el pecado. Los hijos se han hecho más grandes que los padres; ¿no es esto vergonzoso? y ¿no es esta nuestra culpa? Hombres blasfemos, son los que ahora llevan la palabra de Dios por salario; estos mismos son los que han adelantado la ira de Dios, provocándole e irritándole. Todo tiene valor en estos días, menos el nombre de Cristo; todos pagan mucho dinero por lo terrenal, menos por el nombre de Cristo; todos sacrifican por sus propios caprichos, menos por el nombre de Cristo; todos sacrifican por sus propios caprichos, menos por el nombre de Cristo; el nomber de Cristo es de poca significancia en estos días. Y cualquier hipócrita, cargado de pecado, se llama del hombre de Cristo; y así el nombre de Cristo viene a ser infamado y ultrajado. ¿Y quién se escandaliza porque los malvados se llamen cirstianos? por cierto nadie; porque todos por igual, están cargados de pecados y de malicia. Todos se alimentan con la misma clase de pensamiento; cada uno murmura contra su hermano. Por haber dejado al Dios vivo, y por haber hecho nulo el Grande Sacrificio de Cristo: es que el mundo será puesto en llamas; y los cristianos serán entregados en manos del mismo diablo. Dios traerá Juicio Justo sobre esta nación, como también sobre las otras que ocupan la tierra. La confianza y el orgullo de la Iglesia falsa (cristianismos sin temor de Dios) será puesto en llamas; ciertamente que la iglesia confía en que esta nación está fuerte, y que nadie le puede hacer nada; pero esta confianza se tornará en cenizas. Dios mismo, le dará permiso especial (como se lo dió a Nabucodonosor), a la bestia; el anticristo tendrá el derecho sobre los que ahora se llaman Cristianos, sin tener Amor de Dios, ni conocer lo que es misericordia. Y ¿dónde aparecerán los cristianos de nombre ¿Estarán firmes los que ahora dirigen al pueblo a un precipicio con todo engaño? ¿Podrán estos estar de pie, ante el Justo Juicio de Dios, el cual vendrá con grande ira? ¿Quién estará limpio ante la presencia de Dios? Ciertamente que los de limpio corazón nada temerán; y los que fueron santificados por la sangre de Cristo y por su Santa Palabra, tampoco serán confundidos; antes sin temor, podrán estar de pie en la venida de Cristo; pero no así los que escarnecieron los mandamientos de Cristo. Estos últimos, hipócritas, sabrán y entonces echará de ver que ellos mismos dejaron la verdadera vida, por una vida vacía y muerta.

LOS SIERVOS DE BABILONIA

¿Quién es la gran Babilonia? ¿Quiénes son los ciudadanos de la gran Babilonia? ¿Cómo hablan estos ciudadanos? ¿Cómo ven, cómo oyen y que oyen? ¿Cómo cantan, cómo oran? Estos ciudadanos: de labios, honran a Dios; este pueblo de Babilonia, codicia, y tiene un corazón de piedra para con los pobres. Todas las gentes de esta gran babilonia busca su propio bien; cada uno va tras la vanidad; así fueron enseñanodos por esta gran ramera, a vestir con soberbia, a andar con soberbia, a hablar con soberbia, y todos viven en soberbia.

Este pueblo instruído en el error, no sabe hablar verdad, no ama verdad, no piensa en la verdad; nada se le da a este pueblo al ver la verdad en tierra. Por esta gran ramera y madre de las fornicaciones, todos los pueblos aprendieron a orar en vano, a cantar de labios, y a leer la Biblia sin aprovechar nada ni obedecer los mandamientos de Dios; de esta gran babilonia todos aprendieron a hacer las cosas en público, porque ella misma es una mujer pública.

¿Qué cosa hacen los cristianos en secreto? Las malas obras las hacen en secreto; pero toda ceremonia hacen en público para ser vistos. Ay de esta generación, porque sobrepujaron las obras de los fariseos; esta generación, de labios alaban a los profetas antiguos, de labios alaban a Abraham, a Moisés, a Daniel, a Cristo, a Juan el Bautista, a Pablo y sus sufrimientos. Pero con sus hechos aborrecen a los profetas, y con sus obras malas de envidia y de soberbia hacen manifiesto que son enemigos de todos los que sufrieron; son enemigos de la Cruz de Cristo, y no dejan a nadie vivir como los antiguos. Pero la ira de Dios la cual pronto será puesta en manifiesto, les desmentirá, y los pondrá en vergüenza. Todos apoyan el comercio de la gran Babilonia, y ellos mismos han hecho que la maldad prospere; nadie es culpable, solo la Iglesia apóstata, ella ha llenado a toda la tierra de Hipocrecía, de apariencia y de toda obra engañosa. ¿Para qué culpar un solo movimiento y hacerlo responsable de toda la maldad que hay en la tierra? ¿No está el mismo Espíritu en todos? ¿No buscan todos las mismas cosas? Dinero, gloria, nombre, honra y toda cosa que perece; y no satisfechos con esto, cada uno mira y codicia la mujer de su hermano, la mujer de su prójimo, ¿no es esto vergonzoso?

Nadie se niega a sí mismo, (solo de labios). Antes nada le niegan al ojo, nada le niegan al oído, nada le niegan a la lengua; todos hablan y oyen y ven lo que más les conviene. Nada le niegan a sus ojos altivos y codiciosos. ¿En qué pues se ha negado esta mala generación? ¿Quién ampara al pobre? ¿Quién se deleita en hacer el bien a sus hermanos o a sus enemigos? ¿Se podrá olvidar la madre del fruto de su vientre? Pues este pueblo que fué educado en la gran Babilonia, se ha olvidado del mandamiento de Dios; Nadie llora por la palabra de Dios, nadie gime por ver los mandamientos en tierra. Todos están ocupados en comprar lo mejor, en comer lo mejor, en vestirlo mejor, en vivir en la mejor casa. ¡Oh pueblo torcido e insensato, abre tus ojos, y mira lo que has hecho. ¿No ves que estás despojado del amor? ¿No echas de ver que estás mucho muy pobre ante la presencia de Dios? ¿No echas de ver que la misericordia no te acompaña, la justicia no está contigo? ¿Quién pues está a tu lado?

¿Quien será tu abogado? pues que has dejado el santo mandamiento de Cristo. Si alguno dice que ha conocido a Cristo, y no guarda sus mandamientos: el tal es mentiroso y no hay verdad en él (1 Juan 2:4).

Miremos, que hemos hecho muy mal, hemos violado el bien de Dios. Y ¿qué se beneficia el pobre con todos nuestros cantos y oraciones? Todos nuestros cantos y oraciones ¿podrán reconciliarnos con Dios? ¿Qué beneficio saca Dios, de nuestras vanas alabanzas?

Hombre ciego, abre tus ojos para que veas que estás vestido de soberbia, detén tu pie, y medita en el camino santo, y descubrirás que vives en envidia, y que no hay amor en tus entrañas.

Ya no se identifique nadie por nombre y palabras vanas. Si alguien quiere identificar o revelar su cristianismo, revélese e identifíquese como Dios es revelado e identificado; ¿cómo se revela Dios? Cristo nos dijo cómo: "Sed misericordiosos como vuestro padre Celestial es misericordioso." Dios se identifica en obra y no solo en palabra. Dios se identifica en el sol, en la lluvia, ¿y cómo? Dándola a todos, sin hacer acepción de personas.

¿Y nosotros obramos como hijos de él? No, antes cada uno

va tras su propio bien; y nadie imita a Cristo en perdonar, en servir, en dar, en sobrellevar, en amar, en aquello que hace la paz.

Antes todos se han envanecido en cantos y ceremonias en público a fin de ser vistos; ¿no es este el espíritu de la gran ramera, y Madre de todas estas abominaciones? Los fariseos también aprendieron a hacer sus obras en público de la misma madre (Babilonia la grande).

Las enfermedades se han multiplicado en los cuerpos físicos, pero la ciencia Médica también ha multiplicado las medicinas para combatir a la enfermedad. Pero ahora que se ha multiplicado el pecado en la Iglesia como Cristo lo dijo, ¿en qué sentido es ha multiplicado la sabiduría en los profetas para combatir al pecado multiplicado? en ningún sentido, antes todos se han hecho vanos, y se han conformado con el pecado multiplicado. Los profetas se han hecho torpes, y se han envanecido en sus discursos vacíos; ¿y qué bien han hecho en al tierra Nada, antes la mujer ha perdido su vergüenza, su honra, su respeto, su decencia); y los hijos ¿qué han sacado de estos discursos vacíos? nada, antes, los hijo han perdido su respeto al padre, se han hecho desobedientes, violentos, rspondones, se han corrompido en pensamientos y palabras sucias e inmundas; desde pequeños hacen lo malo en secreto; y así han perdido su gloria como niños.

Lo secreto se hace en público, y lo público se hace en secreto. Hablo a maestros, hablo con sabios; ¿Pero qué es sabiduría? ¿qué se un sabio? ¿Cómo vive un sabio? ¿cómo habla y piensa un sabio? ¿Cuál es el fruto de la sabiduría? ¿cuáles sus síntomas? ¿Carece el sabio de amor, de justicia, de misericordia, de humildad? Estas cosas son los frutos de un sabio, o hijo de Dios. El hombre que no tiene misericordia, amor justicia y temor de Dios: este hombre es un árbol seco y sin fruto. ¿Seremos sabios? "El sabio de corazón recibe los mandamientos, mas el loco de labios caerá" (Prov. 10:8). Aquí está nuestra caída, aquí comenzó nuestra ruina; cuando dejamos los mandamientos de Dios. El sabio recibe la corrección, el sabio ama la misericordia. El sabio no es asalariado; ni se pueden alquilar los sabios. Busquemos en la historia, ¿qué sabio fué asalariado? ¿recibió Moisés salario por sacar el pueblo de Egipto? Aun ni Sócrates el anciano griego, recibió salario, ni tampoco quiso. Los sabios no se hallan por dinero; ellos tienen a Dios en su corazón, pues que Dios mismo es la sabiduría, y por eso estos hombres sabios ponen sus vidas por las gentes que aman a Dios; Busquemos sabios que hablen a este pueblo, y que les digan que han dejado a su Dios.

Todas las cosas van a arder en la ira de Dios, en el día que Dios visite la tierra.

¿DONDE ESTA LA FE?

Han llegado los días de los cuales Cristo habló. Ha desaparecido la fe de sobre la tierra. La virtud de la fe se acabo. El amor ha venido a ser algo aborrecible, el amor es muy oculto para la gente de estos días; los cristianos se han enajenado, se han hecho extraños al amor.

En le fé no hay virtud, en la virtud que hay no hay ciencia, y en la ciencia que hay no hay templanza, y en la templanza que hay, no hay temor de Dios, y en el poco temor que hay, no hay amor fraternal, y en el poco amor fraternal, que hay, no hay caridad. Sin fe es imposible agradar a Dios; ¿y por qué es imposible agradar a Dios? ¿Qué cosa pues agrada a Dios? sabemos que su hijo le agradó. ¿Y porqué agradó Cristo Jesús a su Padre? Agradó porque vivió en la voluntad del padre, y siempre hizo aquello que agrada al padre. ¿Cuáles cosas agradan al padre? La vida en amor verdadero y puro; la vida llena de misericordia como Cristo la vivió; Quién ama como Cristo amó, este agrada a Dios. ¿Quien perdona como Cristo perdonó, este agrada a Dios. ¿Y que diremos de estos días? ¿Perdonamos? ¿Amamos? Cristo amó a sus enemigos, pero nosotros no amamos ni a nuestros propios hermanos. Aquí está la evidencia que no hay fe; el que tieen fe en Dios, obedece a Dios. Quien obedece a Dios en su santa voluntad y mandamientos, este tiene fe; por eso es que sin fe es imposible agradar a Dios. Por fe debemos de obedecer a todo lo que Dios nos manda, por fe tenemos que guardarnos limpios, por fe tenemos que amar a nuestros enemigos. Es la fe la que mueve todo nuestro ser o debe de moverlo; porque Dios no está en persona entre nosotros; es decir no le vemos con nuestros ojos carnales; es fe la que necesitamos para creer en él, es fe la que necesitamos para perdonar, para amar, para sufrir. Sin fe no podemos agradar a Dios, porque sin fe no hacemos lo que él manda, y no haciendo lo que él manda, pues ¿Cómo le vamos agradar? por eso es que hemos ignorado y dejado la voluntad de Dios (sus mandamientos que nos dió por su hijo porque no tenemos fe. Somos un pueblo incrédulo y no obdecemos; pretendemos tener fe, pero solo en aquellas cosas que queremos; tales como cuando estamos enfermos, entonces si queremos creer. Pero Dios no puede ser burlado, Dios sabe bien que esta generación no le ama a él.

Esta presente generación no le importa de los pobres, de las viudas, de los oprimidos; No tiene fe para amparar al oprimido, no tiene fe para amar a su hermano, menos para amar a sus enemigos; no tiene fe para visitar a los necesitados no tiene fe para guardar su ojo malo de ver a la mujer ajena; no tiene fe este pueblo para guardar su corazón de los pensamientos malos; no tiene fe para obedecer ninguno de los mandamientos de Dios en Cristo; pero cuando cae en cama, o cuando se está muriendo, pronto hace lo que el pueblo de Israel en los tiempos antiguos: Pronto llora a Dios, y pronto pide que oren por él. Y los hombres de los cuales Cristo profetizó que andarían haciendo muchos milagros en su nombre, engañan a este pueblo rebelde y malvado: diciéndole, que solo crea que puede ser sano, y será sano.

Las promesas que pertenecen al pueblo de Dios humilde y obe-

94

diente, se las apropian ellos mismos, como si no fueran bien rebeldes, y como si estuvieran en el centro de su voluntad.

Por todo el mundo ha salido la hipocresía de este pueblo, ajeno a la verdad; no hay nación, que no haya corrompido con sus mentiras; a la mujer le han quitado su gloria y su vergüenza; a los niños e hijos los han enseñado como rebelarse contra sus padres; y ¿qué bien han hecho en el mundo? Todos los milagros que en los últimos días se iban a hacer, iban a ser en el nombre de Cristo; es sencillo saber que los obradores de estos últimos días son hijos de error; porque andan haciendo grande comercio con la palabra de Dios, y a muchos los engañan.

¿Viven estos hombres la vida de Cristo? ¿Llevan en sus vidas humildad? ¿Aman a los menesterosoos? cuidan y enseñan al pueblo a que haga bien? No, el bien lo reciben ellos mismos; comenzaron bien, como muchos, pero pronto los puso el diablo bajo sus pies; pronto los hizo el diablo doblar la rodilla a mammon. Pronto les entenebreció los ojos. Oremos, a todos los justos y pequeños os ruego por amor a esta pobre generación que roguemos a Dios, que envie unos cuantos hombres que no sean asalariados, unos cuantos que enseñen el camino de Dios sin reserva ni poner escondrijos como los hombres que ahora lo hacen sin temor de Dios.

Dios busca hombres que aborrezcan las tinieblas, hombres que no amen las dádivas ni los presentes. Hombres que entiendan los tiempos, y que denuncien el pecado que hay en la iglesia.

Ya no son tiempos de conformarnos con ceremonias, con gritos y lágrimas fingidas; con todas las tradiciones paganas hemos resistido al Espíritu de Dios. Cuando el Espíritu de Dios no está en un pueblo, aquél pueblo no tiene amor para con su prójimo, no hace derecho ni justicia; y aquí está la razón por qué esta generación no tiene ni justicia pero ni amor de Dios. Hijos sin fé son los que adoran a Dios en estos días; todos hablan mucho, todos dicen mucho; en los templos hablan mucho, en los templos cantan mucho, en los templos profesan amar a Dios; pero en la calle, en la casa, en el mundo son hijos sin fe, hijos rebeldes.

Ay de esta mala gente, porque ¿quién la librará de la ira que viene? ¿Quién intercederá por ellos? Todos serán sorprendidos, cuando los santos juicios de Dios aparezcan. No es de admirarse que el mundo se corrompa y crezca en maldad; pero sí es de admirarse de que un pueblo como el que ahora se llama cristiano, y que habiendo conocido el camino de la justicia que es Cristo: se torne a la violencia, a la maldad, a toda obra sucia en secreto. Ay de este pueblo porque grande serán los juicios contra él; y ¿quién lo librará en aquella hora?

¿En que nos alabará Dios? ¿En qué nos agradece? ¿Hemos obedecido sus santas palabras para que esté contento con nosotros? Antes, hemos trocado su santa gloria, le hemos dado menos honra que al hombre; todos temen al hombre más que a Dios, y le creen más al hombre que a Dios.

El hombre falso, el profeta mentiroso dice que hay paz y

seguridad para los cristianos, pero esto es mentira, en estas palabras no hay verdad. Dios está descontento y enojado con los que pasan por su nombre, porque no le obedecen en nada; han descuidado todo lo que él les mandó.

Esta violencia nuestra ha levantado a las naciones unas contra otras, porque faltó el amor puro, faltó la justicia de sobre la tierra; dejamos al príncipe de paz, y todos nos hemos dividido, unos contra otros, aun entre los mismos familiares. Pero lo peor es que estamos divididos: no por causa de amor, ni por causa de justicia y derecho, sino que por caprichos y opiniones.

Esto ha deshonrado la palabra de Dios, por esta razón cayó el derecho y la justicia a tierra. Salgamos de la gran babilonia, los que teman a Dios, hagan bien, humillen sus almas, no murmuren, no juzguen a nadie porque estamos en días malos, en los cuales todos hemos faltado y ofendido a Dios; No condenen, ni hagan prejuicio; perdonen y aman de todo corazón. Volvamos a los derechos antiguos, al temor antiguo de Dios, al perdón antiguo, al amor antiguo, a la justicia antigua, a la misericordia antigua, a la mansedumbre antigua; hagamos bien a aquellas personas que Cristo nos mandó y nos encargó diciendo: "Cuando hagas cena o banquete, no invites a tus hermanos, ni a tus vecinos ricos, ni a tus amigos, porque ellos te regresarán el bien y no tendrás nada en aquel día: mas cuando tu haces banquete o cena, invita a los pobres, a los ciegos, a los mancos, a los menesterosos; porque estos no tienen con que recompensarte, mas se te recompensará en la resurrección de los justos." Levantemos la sendas caídas, andemos con derecho; es tiempo de volvernos a Dios el cual entregó a su Hijo amado.

¿Por qué poner los ojos en aquello que será destruído con la ira de Dios?? ¿Por qué desperdiciar nuestras fuerzas en riquezas que no duran? No perdamos nuestro tiempo, no engañemos nuestras pobres almas; tiempo es de restituir al agraviado, es tiempo de poner en libertad al oprimido, dándole lo que nosotros amamos, sirviéndole como queremos que otros nos sirvan a nosotros.

Es tiempo de hacer la voluntad de Dios con solicitud. Es tiempo de ignorar al mundo con todas sus hermosas y vanidosas ofertas, es tiempo de despreciar las cosas que nos han engañado, ¿Por qué tirar nuestro dinero y gastar nuestra fuerza y nuestro tiempo solo por ir tras el mundo y aquellos que les gusta la pompa? ¿No fuimos puestos nosotros para andar con humildad en todas nuestras cosas y en nuestras obras? ¿Por qué ir en vestido, en comida, y en casa como los ciudadanos de la gran Babilonia? Cada uno cierre sus ojos a las cosas que su vecino poseé, no condiciemos, ya más. Si su hermano va tras pompa y lujo, déjelo; ¿Por qué imitar al soberbio? ¿Por qué imitar al vanidoso? Imitemos más bien al humilde y al manso; ¿porqué buscar compañía soberbia y ligera? ¿Por qué no buscan más bien compañía sufrida y despreciada, compañía humilde y de temor? El justo por su fe y su justicia vivirá, ¿y quién levantara la mano contra él? Mas estas palabras son a un pueblo falso, a un pueblo mentiroso, a un pueblo que ha dejado la vida por la muerte; Bienaventurado aquél que recibe estas palabras con temor y humildad. Benditos de Dios sean todos los que no sean escandalizados en estas palabras.

Hijos e hijas de Babilonia, ¿Porque no obedecéis a vuestro padre legítimo? Dejad a la que ahora llamáis madre, porque ella no es vuestra madre; viviendo con ella habéis aprendido toda obra de mentira y de engaño; viviendo con ella habéis aprendido a no tener misericordia, por que ella es una mujer dura y de mal corazón. Ella no se compadece de nadie, porque pasa el tiempo adornando su casa, y buscando bienes para tener valor delante de sus Amantes.

Ella no tiene piedad del huérfano ni del oprimido, antes despoja a todos los que ella puede a fin de celebrar sus festividades con pompa y lujo; en estos días todos se han embriagado de sus entrañas duras, y por eso ya no se hallan los justos en la tierra. Esta mala mujer ha puesto en destierro a todo justo que clama por justicia. El egoismo, la soberbia, la envidia, la ira y toda mentira son virtudes de esta mala mujer que ha engañado a todo el mundo. Por eso nuestros mismos hijos se levantan contar nosotros, las hijas son violadas por llamados cristianos nuestras mujeres son deseadas por todos, porque las hemos vestido con ornamento de codicia, las hemos proporcionado al ojo lascivioso; ¿no es esto así? Esto aprendimos de la gran ramera. Los padres perdieron el interés de instruir a sus hijos en los santos caminos. Yo pongo por testigo a la misma palabra de Dios, que no miento; antes hablo palabras de verdad, y estas palabras no son para hacer comercio, ni para venderlas; son para que el justo salga de esta gran iglesia apóstata, no en opinión, sino que en hechos; son palabras que ayudan al hombre a salir de la avaricia, de la soberbia, de la envidia y de todo egoísmo. Las palabras vendidas no llevan misericordia, las palabras vendidas por dinero no llevan buen propósito; el hombre que compra las palabras: también las vende más delante; mas el hombre a quien le son dadas las palabras: él también las da. Estas palabras no las he comprado, por eso tampoco las vendo. Dirá alguien, lo dado no tiene valor, mas lo comprado si tiene. Pero siempre entended que esas son palabras de mercaderes falsos, hombres embotados; discípulos de la gran ramera. Todo justo guárdese de los comerciantes, ciudadanos de la gran ramera; y haga bien comenzando en su hogar.

LAS OBRAS DESPRECIADAS

Cristo vino para hacer bien a la humanidad, vino para enseñar el amor: no en palabra solamente, sino que en obra y en Espíritu; vino a enseñarnos qué es "Misericordia," y hacer manifiesto el juicio y la justicia del reino de Dios. Por esto, y solo por esto nos dió el Señor mandamientos; y nos marcó toda palabra y obra de amor y misericordia. (Efe. 2:10).

A esto se refirió el Apóstol PABLO cuando dijo: "Porque somos hechura suya, criados en Cristo Jesús; para buenas obras las cuales Dios preparó para que anduviésemos en ellas."

Es muy cierto que nadie se salva por obras: y nuestras buenas obras nunca borrarían nuestros malos hechos pasados. Pero para esto fuimos salvos, y para esto nos reconcilió la Sangre de Cristo: para andar en los caminos y en las obras que el Padre nos preparó para que anduviésemos en ellas. Mismo Cristo el Hijo de Dios anduvo en estas santas obras; vivió según los caminos que el padre le marcó, y en nada ofendió a Dios. ¿Por qué no andar nosotros en los mismos caminos? El que dice que fué salvo por gracia, y no anda en los caminos que Dios marcó, es porque no le ha amanecido, y todavía esta en las tinieblas; tal vez tendrá salvación, pero no la que Dios dá, sino que esta persona ha recibido salvación de los hombres, pero no de Dios.

En estos últimos días, todos se excusan; y para no andar en los caminos de Dios, dicen que las buenas obras no salvan. Pero ¿quién dice que las buenas obras salvan? Nadie ha dicho tal cosa; antes, las buenas obras, son frutos de los que en verdad son salvos. El que cree que ama en estos días: mire el amor de Cristo y a la manera que Cristo amó al mundo, y avergüence, confundase, porque el amor es la cosa más barata en estos días. El que dice que ama, y no tiene misericordia de los huérfanos, de las viudas, de los extranjeros y de todos los necesitados y afligidos: es mentiroso y no hay verdad en él; antes engaña a su pobre alma. El que dice que ama y no vive en paz con sus familiares: este tal es mentiroso. Pero ¿quién es aquel que vive en paz con sus padres o con sus familiares? Por esta razón el fin del mundo y de todos los rebeldes es inevitable; porque hemos corrompido toda la tierra, hemos dejado los santos mandamientos de Dios, y hemos obedecido a mandamientos de hombres que no tienen entendimiento del Dios Vivo; antes todos estos hombres que no han dado los mandamientos que ahora tenemos, son hombres que aman lo terrenal y que no hablan verdad, antes mienten los unos a los otros como hijos sin fe. Todos dicen. "Por gracia somos salvos" y no por obras para que nadie se gloríe." Tardos para entender el bien: El mismo que dijo estas palabras ¿no dijo también (vestíos de entrañas de misericordia, de benignidad, de humildad, de mansedumbre, de tolerancia? (Col. 3:12).

¿No fué la sangre de Cristo derramada para formar un Pueblo celoso de buenas obras? ¿Dónde pues está este pueblo celoso de buenas obras? ¿No le dijo Pablo el mismo apostol a Tito: "Muéstrate en todo por ejemplo de buenas obras"? ¿Por qué pues todos le huyen a las buenas obras? Cada uno busca su propio bien, y todos han descuidado el amor de Cristo el cual hace bien al prójimo, el cual amor, para las divisiones. ¿Qué pueblo estaba tan dividido como esta generación, profesando y reclamando el mismo Cristo? Si todos tuvieran el mismo amor de Cristo, no fueran tantos grupos y pueblos divididos: antes todos fueran uno, como somos llamados a formar un solo cuerpo, por cuanto por un mismo Espíritu debemos de ser movidos y enseñados. Pero ¿qué sucede en estos días? Todos son maestros, todos son enseñadores amontonados; que han torcido el derecho de Dios: primero mira por el débil y flaco, y luego ve por los fuertes y grandes; el derecho de Dios primero mira por las viudas, por los pobres de la tierra, y luego mira por los hijos de Dios. Todos hemos irritado a Dios, por volvernos enemigos de la "Cruz." ¿Quién pelea a favor de los mandamientos de Cristo? Cada uno forma sus caprichos y funda sus convicciones en palabras históricas, pero que no contienen el santo mandamiento de Dios dado por labios de Cristo mismo. ¿No dice el mismo apóstol de Cristo: "La ira de Dios viene sobre los hijos de rebelión, los cuales son movidos por Avaria, por mala concupiscencia, por inmundicia.... (Col. 3:5, 6). Miremos pues, por cuales cosas hemos caído de la verdadera gracia; todo mundo se preocupa por las cosas de la vida. Esto nos llevó a la glotonería, y a toda obra de inmundicia y de concupiscencia. Por eso somos llamados un pueblo muerto y sin fe: porque no tenemos obras; nosotros decimos que estamos ricos y que no tenemos necesidad de que nadie nos dé consejo: pero no sabemos que estamos ciegos y desnudos en cuanto a justicia y misericordia de Dios. Dios les habla en revelación a las siete Iglesias de Asia, las cuales representan a una misma Iglsia en un proceso continuo. Habla a estas Iglesias, y a las siete les dice: "Yo conozco tus obras." Y también a las siete les dice: "Al que venciere" y a las siete les dice: "El que tiene oídos para oír, oiga. Todo esto quiere decir: en primer lugar: que él nos juzga y nos pesa, nos condena o nos justifica, por nuestras propias Obras. En segundo lugar, la condición que él pone a luz de todos es que: "Al que venciere" es decir, el que vence al mundo, el que vence al verdadero Egoísmo, el que vence al verdadero hombre viejo, el que vence a la envidia, a la soberbia, al pecado. ¿Y podrá vencer uno al mundo sin guardar los mandamientos de Dios? ¿Podrá vencer uno al mundo con toda la concupiscencia de la vida sin andar en el amor de Dios que es Cristo mismo? Y finalmente, "al que tiene oídos para Oír, oiga." en otras palabras, el mandamiento de Dios y sus caminos son para todos los que tienen oídos. Solamente el que no tiene oídos puede ser excusado al no guardar la voluntad de Dios la cual es formada de todos sus santos mandamientos que su hijo nos dió.

Ay de los hijos de la luz, porque serán sorprendidos; ay de los que esperan bendición, porque les vendrá grande y pesada maldición; ay de los que tienen la ley en sus manos, porque con la misma ley serán arrancados. La ley y la doctrina del espíritu perdieron su valor en el corazón de los hombres, a causa de aquellos que no querían sufrir. Los soberbios arrebataron la ley, y molieron las carnes de los justos. Los malos son muchos, pero si algún asalariado teme a Dios y ama justicia, no se levante contra esta palabra, no sea que también a él lo arrebate el fuego de la ira de Dios. Todo el que teme a Dios, sufra estas palabras y vuélvase a Dios. Yo aconsejo a los que esperan el regreso del hijo de Dios, que humillen a sus almas, y levanten el derecho. Nadie confíe en palabras de hombres que no temen a Dios ni guardan los mandamientos de Dios; antes cada uno, confíe en Dios, y con temor y temblor obedezca a Dios en todos sus santos mandamientos que él nos habló por su santo hijo Jesús. Cada uno haga misericordia, hable verdad con pocas palabras, aparte sus ojos de la vanidad, humille su corazón a la justicia de Dios; deléitese cada uno en los derechos de Dios; imitemos a Cristo en medio de está mala generación; reconciliemos nuestras almas a Dios nuestro creador antes que desnude su brazo de venganza, y nadie pueda librar. Y vosotros, oh cabezas y líderes, hablad el derecho de Dios sin reservad nada; ya no engañéis a los humildes de la tierra. Trabajad por derecho y justicia y no por salario. Esperen en Dios, que él dá mejor salario. Dad ejemplo a los que quieren la vida, y no busquéis ropa de gala; los que visten con ropas finas en las casas de los reyes están. No toca a vosotros el vestir con ropas costosas, ni el andar como hachas encendidas por los caminos. Porque por estas colicias, perece la humildad y la mansedumbre de la tierra. Aprended de Nínive, la cual con gran temor se arrpintio, y se volvió su Dios. No seáis duros de cerviz, no resistáis la corrección de Dios. ¿Por qué recibid el mismo salario de los fariseos? ¿Por qué perecemos como Sodoma y Gomorra? ¿Qué no hay manera de ecapar? Dios ha hecho camino, andemos por él. Los cielos y la tierra, los cuales siempre han atestiguado contra los rebeldes: serán testigos, una vez más, que os he hablado y os he denunciado vuestra grande maldad y rebeldía Cristo habló de estos tiempos, pero ¿porque no escapar de ellos? Que nos se cumpla en nosotros la profecía, escapemos de la ira de Dios. ¿Qué pide Dios de nosotros? Solo que no busquemos nuestro propio bien, y que hagamos juicio y justicia? ¿Es la misericordia cosa pesada? Estas cosas pide Dios de nosotros; ¿Por qué resistirle? El mundo nos ha engañado, y todo nuestro dinero lo hemos empleado en la vanidad; casas grandes fué lo que condiciamos, carros nuevos y costosos, comidas de reyes y ropas de príncipes nos quitaron nuestra vista de la cruz de Cristo; por estas cosas nosotros erramos; volvamos a los caminos antiguos. Abramos los ojos a la luz de Dios, prestemos oídos a los mandamientos de Dios; cada uno ordene sus caminos en el temor de Dios, y ya no murmure contra nadie. Todos estamos en la misma, y todos hemos irritado a Dios porque no hemos hecho según su santa voluntad; nadie quiere ser el menos, antes cada uno ama el primado y el ser estimado por todos. Grande es el mal que hemos hecho en la tierra; y por nuestra culpa que perdimos nuestro sabor como sal de la tierra, los malos se multiplicaron en la tierra y la maldad se hizo mucha.

¿Con qué responderemos a Dios? ¿Y qué argumento usaremos? Somos malos, y solo la cortesía nos queda; pero con la

100

cortesía no se alimenta la viuda, ni tampoco el huérfano recibe bien de la cortesía; despojemos esta capa de hipocresía, y vistámonos con ropas de justicia. Oh burladores ,¿hasta cuando distinguiréis la verdad de la mentira? ¿Hasta cuándo recibiréis la sana corrección? Yo soy ignorante en muchas cosas; pero la grande rebeldía de la Iglesia me ha hecho hablar; Temo a vosotros, y en mi corazón hay miedo a causa de vuestra soberbia; pero ¿quién al ver lo que mis ojos ven podría detener sus palabras? Vaciad la sangre de mis venas, pero vuestra rebeldía permanecerá; y el fuego por vosotros viene.

LO CAIDO

Lo que se conquista con la espada, con la espada se tiene que cuidar y proteger; lo que se conquista con amor, con amor se tiene que cuidar y proteger. Lo que se conquista con la espada, no se puede proteger con la espada.

Si el amor de Cristo nos trajo a Dios, es menester que nos guardemos en el amor de Cristo. Si con medios humanos y ceremonias humanas nos trajeron a Cristo, con estas mismas nos podrán guardar, pero no en Dios, sino en el amor de los hombres. Todo corazón que fué movido por el Espíritu de Dios, todo Corazón que fué movido por el Evangelio de Cristo: este corazón no se rebela contra las leyes del Espíritu Santo. Pero todo hombre que fué persuadido por fuerzas humanas e intereses humanos, esta persona no le interesa mucho o nada por la voluntad de Dios, es decir, mientras esté haciendo la voluntad de los hombres. La persona nacida de nuevo, que ha nacido según Dios. esta persona se deleita en las cosas que pertenecen al reino de Dios; para este hijo de Dios, el servir y el amar, no le es cosa fastidiosa, porque el amor de Dios está perfectamente en él; Hermanos, es menester no escarnecer las virtudes del Espíritu Santo el cual nos guiará a toda Justicia y a toda verdad si nosotros le damos lugar humillándonos; Los males del diablo y las fuerzas de las tinieblas se hacen fuertes cada día; nosotros debemos de dar lugar a Dios, que le gobierne nuestras almas; esto aunque nos cueste pasar por lugares parecidos al "Getsemaní" en esto es glorificado Dios; porque si Dios fué gloficado cuando su hijo pasó por estas horas amargas. ¿Qué no será glorificado al pasar nosotros también por estas? Humillemos pues a nuestras almas, para que Dios sea servido y y glorificado en el tabernáculo de su Espíritu, que es nuestro cuerpo mortal. Con todo el corazón pues, levantemos lo que está caído, el amor de Dios, al humildad de espíritu, la mansedumbre del alma; Dios es con aquellos que de Corazón quieren hacer lo recto delante de sus ojos; y no se avergüence de hacer bien al alma de aquellos que no se avergüenzan del ejemplo que Cristo nos dejó, y que no se averguenzan de obedecer a sus santos mandamientos. ¿Por qué avergonzarnos de los santos mandamientos que Cristo nos dió por el mismo Espíritu? ¿A caso los apóstoles ignoraron los mandamientos de Cristo y del Espíritu Santo? ¿No amó Pablo a sus Enemigos como Cristo lo mandó a sus seguidores? ¿No sufrió Pablo juntamente con los profetas que fueron antes que él? Es menester que nosotros ignoremos las fuerzas del mundo, y los métodos humanos que el diablo nos ofrece: el que confía en mano de hombre alcanza la maldición, y tarde que temprano caerá, y descubrirá que no puede contra los malos pensamientos, contra la envidia, contra la soberbia, contra la mentira de los labios, contra las pasiones locas y vanas. En estos días sabemos que todo el mundo se va tras las obras y maravillas que el hombre ha hecho con sus propias manos, y las maravillas de Dios son ignoradas. ¿No es esto algo penoso a los ojos de Dios? Dura cosa es esta, y grande el mal que nosotros el pueblo de Dios hemos hecho. Dios quiere que volvamos a las primeras obras y que le demos honra con nuestras vidas; humillando a nuestras almas al Dios y padre de nuestros espíritus. Hermanos y queridos compañeros de peregrinación, ¿Por qué no sacrificar lo que nos queda, por las cosas y riquezas del alma? El hombre que Dios formó, es una maravilla y es un milagro; porque Dios nos dió un corazón para poder entender, y fuerzas para poder decidir, ¿por qué usar estas fuerzas y este corazón para ganar las cosas terrenales que nuestra carne busca? ¿Acaso no se acaban estas cosas? ¿Dónde está lo que poseían nuestros padres? y ¿lo que nosotros poseíamos tiempo pasado, ¿Dónde está? Todo se pasó. Sí, todo se pasa. ¿No pudiéramos llenar estos corazones que Dios nos ha dado de riquezas Celestiales? Vistamos pues a nuestras almas y nuestras vidas con el amor de Dios y con la humildad de Cristo para poder servir a nuestro Dios. El amor no se mira en palabras ni en cantos, el amor se ve en Obras de justicia; el amor se ve y se siente; el amor no se oye. ¿Para qué hablar el amor? Si lo poseemos nosotros, pues el hermano y la viuda y el huérfano dará testimonio, y también Dios será hallado en nuestras peticiones; porque él ha dicho: "Bienaventurados los Misericordiosos. Porque ellos alcanzarán Misericordia" y también nos dice por el mismo Espíritu : "Juicio sin misericrdia, será hecho con aquél que no usare de misericordia." Hermanos, amados y deseados de Dios, miremos que ya no es tiempo de entretener nuestros últimos días en obras de los hombres y en tradiciones de los hombres. Dios es contra las tradiciones de los hombres, porque por estas tradiciones los hombres se apartan del verdadero camino de Dios, y los hombres dejan de temerle a causa que se olvidan de sus Santos Mandamientos en los cuales el hombre no halla sino bien. ¿Acaso hemos hallado falta en los mandamientos que Cristo nos dejó? Los mandamientos de Cristo, ¿qué no son para los hijos de Dios como lo fué Cristo y también él los cumplió con todo temor y reverencia? Dejando pues toda malicia y amargura de contienda, sirvamos a Dios, obedeciendo su santa palabra la cual como han dicho todos sus santos como también su santo hijo, que ésta su Santa Palabra nos podía hacer sabios y salvados; no escarnezcamos con nuestra conducta a la palabra de Dios, porque Cristo nos dejó dicho que por esta misma palabra ibamos a ser Juzgados. Cristo nos vino a salvar, no solo de los vícios que los hombres han inventado ahora pronto, sino que nos vino a salvar de cosas que son tan viejas como el mismo diablo, como es la envidia y la soberbia. De estas cosas tenemos que huir. En estos días muchos son enseñados a huir de los vícios, pero no más allá. Cristo quiere hacernos libres con su verdad: de la mentira, de la ira, estas cosas son las que destruyen naciones enteras; estas cosas son las que combaten en nuestra carne; levantemos nuestros corazones en busca de esta libertad. Una libertad completa. En la Salvación que los hombras ofrecen en estos días, no se halla el bien que Dios quiere de sus hijos; solamente ellos hallan, porque alcanzan sacar el diezmo de las gentes, pues esto no es malo, pero han dejado de ofrecer la Salvación, en la cual no solo ellos alcanzarían bien, sino que la viuda y el huérfano y Dios también alcanzarían bien en verdad. Dios oye a todo aquél que gime por una Salvación real y como la que sus santos apóstoles predicaban y ofrecían a las almas hambrientas por la justicia de Dios; pero ahora no se puede ofrecer por un hombre que él mismo no la conoce. ¿Quién ofrece lo que no tiene? Nomás el diablo porque el es mentiroso desde el principio. Hermanos yo les ruego en estos últimos días, y con temor en mi corazón les digo, que echen mano a la salvación que el hijo de Dios nos trajo. Yo sé que muchos ya están contentos con lo que poseen, pero esto no quire decir que todos están contentos; hay muchos corazones que no están contentos con lo que tienen. Estos pocos que no están contentos serán saciados del amor de Dios si le obedecen.

Cristo mismo nos dijo: "El que tiene mis mandamientos y los guarda, aquél es el que me ama, y el que me ama será amado de mi Padre, y yo le amaré y me manifiestaré a él." En estos días que desgracia tan grande y que mal tan grande: el que las gentes no tienen ni entienden los mandamientos de Cristo, ni si quiera de memoria, mucho menos en sus vidas; este mal es grande. ¿Qué podemos esperar después que nosotros hemos dejado el santo mandamiento del Dios Santo? Por eso está el mundo lleno de ira y de confusión, y de división; y esto comenzando con los llamados cristianos. Los judíos estaban lejos de Dios cuando Cristo apareció por primera vez, pero no estaban tan divididos como lo estamos nosotros; y ¿por qué? ¿Será esto casualidad? ¿No dice la palabra misma de Dios que por la rebeldía en la tierra los príncipes se multiplican? Por el mismo pecado se hacen muchos líderes. Y es que los judíos no se llamaban hijos de Dios, solo se llamaban hijos de Abraham; pero en estos días todos los que pasamos por cristianos nos llamamos hijos de Dios; esto es más que llamarnos hijos de Abraham como lo hacían los judíos, ¿Pero les valió esto delante de Cristo? ¿No les llamó Cristo hijos del diablo, el cual los había convertido con tradiciones humanas? Miremos pues, de dónde están dependiendo nuestras almas en estos días. Ya no hay mucho tiempo para estar claudicando con nuestras almas. Ay de aquel que sabe que los mandamientos de Dios son para los hijos de Dios y no los hace, ni vive con temor. Os recuerdo, hermanos, que se recuerden del consejo que Cristo nos dió, al decir "Aprended de mí, que soy manso y humilde de corazón." El mal más grande que nos estorba para entender nuestra pobre estatura, y ver nuestro propio mal es el que Cristo nos declara donde dice: "Tú dices, yo estoy rico, y no tengo necesidad de nada; pero no sabes, que estas ciego, y desnudo, y pobre."

Dice el Espíritu Santo que nosotros no sabemos que estamos ciegos; este mismo mal había en los fariseos; es decir también los fariseos no sabían que estaban ciegos. Y dice el Espíritu que nosotros creemos que estamos ricos en las cosas de Dios; pero esto es lo que nosotros creemos; todo mundo cree que está bien; y esto es porque todos tienen el nombre de Dios en sus bocas; nadie admite corrección. Dios corrige al que admita corrección, y a los otros rebeldes no los corrige hasta el postrer tiempo, cuando alcanzará a todos los soberbios en el fuego de su ira. Admitamos hermanos míos, toda la corrección de Dios. ¿Qué no es verdad que estamos llenos de avaricia, de soberbia, de ira, de venganza, de malicia, de pensamientos sucios, de mentiras en nuestros labios? ¿NO es esto así? ¿Todavía nos vamos a negar? Todavía vemos que ya se acerca el mal que nosotros nos hemos acarriado, y no queremos admitir. ¿Por qué hermanos míos? No confiemos en mano de hombre ni en nuestro propio corazón. Porque nuestros corazones nos va a negar si confiamos en él; y si Dios nos dice que estamos lejos de él y que estamos ciegos y desnudos y pobres: ¿No vamos a creer esto? Todavía vamos a seguir confiando en nuestro propio corazón mentiroso? No; dejemos esta falsa confianza; busquemos a Dios con lloro y ayuno; ¿para que negar a nuestras pobres almas? Todos se sacrifican por sus propios intereses, todos se atreven a grandes peligros, por las cosas terrenales, Pero ¿por qué no sacrificar de la misma manera por nuestras almas, por el bienestar de la vida eterna? Nuestros hijos van detras de nosotros, y ellos van embriagándose del mismo consejo que nosotros hemos cogido del mundo; ¿Para qué arrojar a nuestros hijos a un precipicio tan lóbrigo, a un crepúsculo tan incierto como lo es el falso cristianismo presente? el cual Dios arrojará a su izquierda.

EL ENTENDIDO ENTENDERA

Aconsejo a los pequeños de la tierra, a los que creen que necesitan consejo, pues que yo sé que a los grandes de la tierra no puedo aconsejar: pues que ni Cristo mismo los pudo aconsejar. A los que están sobre el mando y sobre las almas, yo no puedo aconsejar, y no tengo nada de bueno para ellos. Pero a los pequeños de la tierra; a los que temen a Dios si quiero aconsejar, porque ellos conocen la voz del buen pastor: decir ellos conocen cuando es palabra de Dios; y al oirla la obedecen, porque ellos temen a Dios; y ellos están listos a hacer todo lo que el alto Dios mande. Que creamos como dicen las escrituras; y oigamos a lo que el Espíritu Santo nos aconseja: "Que no sepamos más de lo que está escrito." Vamos a mirar por el pobre antes que Cristo venga y nos halle en el mal del cual él nos advirtió; luchemos por ser hallados en las cosas que él nos mandó que nos ocupasemos; demos de comer al menesteroso; no buscando ventajas e intereses propios. Ya no es tiempo de ver a quien le estamos hacindo el bien; echemos la ira fuera de nuestro hogar; echemos fuera la venganza; ya no dejemos que reine en nuestros hogares los malos pensamientos y las bocas mentirosas; echemos todo lo que Dios abomina; y en cambio vendrá a morar en nuestra casa la paz de Dios y hallaremos el amor perfecto de Cristo Jesús.

La malicia que por tanto tiempo la hemos descuidado y ha hecho morada en nuestros corazones, abramos la puerta de nuestro corazón y echémosla fuera para siempre; esto no hace bien en el templo del Espíritu Santo el cual es nuestro cuerpo y por medio del cual Dios se glorifica.

Esto aconsejo a los que temen a Dios, y a los que se hallan escasos de consejos. Dios es con todos los humildes de Corazón, y da garcia a aquellos que se compadecen del pobre; Dios mira que nosotros ya no nos deleitamos en ayudar al necesitado; esto es un gran mal a los ojos del justo Juez de toda la tierra; el cual hace bien a todos; y quiere que todos los hombres sean salvos y que tengan pastos verdes, alimentos para sus chiquitos, que el mismo les dá. Miremos esto y temamos a Dios, yo les ruego hermanos míos. Miremos cuan grande amor trajo Cristo al mundo. Echemos mano a este amor; vistámonos con el amor de Cristo, y quitémonos las vestiduras de maldad, de envidia, de ira, de amargura, de amor propio; estoy cierto que Dios no desecha a los que se esfuerzan por hallar la justicia de Dios: porque Cristo mismo dijo: "Buscad primeramente el reino de Dios y su justicia." Ya tenemos la justicia de los hombres, pero ¿qué bien nos ha hecho? Hemos aprendido a buscar nuestro propio bien, y dejar la necesidad de nuestro prójimo, el cual Cristo nos enseñó que lo amaramos como a nosotros mismos. Las muchas fuerzas que estamos empleando para buscar con el mundo entero las cosas de la vida y las comodidades, son fuerzas tiradas al viento, y todo es vanidad de vanidades; hagamos bien a todos y empleemos todas nuestras fuerzas y nuestro entendimiento por las cosas de arriba; los mansos de corazón heredarán las moradas de Dios, pero los rebeldes que ignoraron el consejo de Dios no tendrán derecho a estas moradas preparadas para los de corazón manso, para los que amaron más a sus hermanos que sus propias almas; estos son los que serán los primeros en aquel día. No dejemos que la palabra de Dios permanezca donde los hombres la han puesto; juntos todos los humildes de la tierra levantemos la palabra de Dios en nuestras propias vidas. Esto agradara a Dios, como le agradó la vida de su hijo en el cual halló Dios contentamiento. Despojémonos de los ojos altivos, de los labios mentirosos; de la soberbia del corazón; y ya no confiemos en palabra de mentira, llamándonos lo que no somos; pero humillando a nuestras almas con lágrimas y con ayuno, Dios mandará ayuda para nuestras almas; y confortamiento para nuestro espíritu, por medio de us Santo Espíritu. Cobremos ánimo; y no temamos a las injurias de los soberbios; también nuestro Señor y todos los profetas que amaron el reino venidero, sufrieron a causa de la justicia; porque en todo tiempo el humilde es puesto para ser escarnecido; no temamos. Que más sufrió el que nos Amó y se dió por nosotros. Adelante pues; no mirando a lo que se ve, ni intimidiéndonos con las amenazas del diablo, el cual no tiene entrada al reino de Nuestro Dios. Amemos el don de Dios y la vida venidera. No desechemos el consejo de Dios el cual está en la palabra de Dios; el consejo que los soberbios han olvidado, y han solo aprendido las promesas de Dios; las cuales no les pertenecen a ellos, sino a los mansos de la tierra; el diablo ha embotado los sentidos de aquellos que aman lo terrenal, y les ha dado las escrituras que a el mismo le parecen propias para negar a todos los que sienten lo terrenal.

No miremos al que nos hable, sino que temamos a la palabra de Dios; porque Dios mora con aquel que teme a su Santa Palabra ;así que no temamos obedecer los santos mandamientos, y no resistamos al Espíritu el cual nos quiere siempre guiar a toda verdad de Dios y a toda justicia.

PALABRAS A LA ULTIMA GENERACION

¿Para qué tratar de tapar y ocultar el mal que hay? No hay con qué cubrirlo. La hija es contra su madre, la madre contra su hija; el hijo contra su padre y el padre contra su hijo; la nuera y la suegra no viven tres días en paz; los pastores y sus ovejas no se aman con amor de Dios; y ¿para qué tratar de encubrir todo este mal, cuando el mismo mundo no se distingue de los que hoy día se llaman cristianos? La Iglesia es toda una llaga; ¿De qué hablaremos que no la ofendamos? y corrección no aprecia, no ama el castigo de su Creador; ¿Con qué la curaremos, que no le duela? Las llagas de Jesucristo las cuales curan si nos envestimos de ellas, no las quiere; Prefiere sufrir por sus propios caprichos; y por sus antojos de deleite terrenal. Paga hasta con la vida. Como un niño se corrompe con muchos juguetes, y el tiempo que debe de usar en hacer la voluntad de sus padres lo pasa jugando; así la Iglesia, pasa el tiempo que debe de usar en la voluntad de Dios, en las cosas que solo engañan y quitan el tiempo que uno necesita para ganar la vida eterna. ¿Qué aparato, qué invención, qué juguete, que vanidad no entretiene y roba el tiempo a los llamados cristianos? Todo aman, menos la justicia; todo codician, menos la humildad; por todo se sacrifican y hasta que enferman, menos por la Cruz de Cristo. Levanten testigos contra estas palabras, y ¿quién podrá condenar estas palabras? ¿Acaso miro yo mejor que mi Dios? ¿Soy más escrupuloso yo que mi Dios? Si con la pequeña porción de su Espíritu que él ha depositado en mí, miro y alcanzo ver tantas cosas, amarguras de violencias que ni yo viviría con ellas: Cuanto más mi Dios, el ʰcual es santo, y no puede tolerar al hipócrita, ni da por inocente al culpable. Por esto mismo los ojos de esta generación no se hartan de ver; el ojo de cada uno está puesto en la mujer de su prójimo. La boca de esta generación de todo habla, menos de amor y de misericordia; no habla de estas cosas, porque ellos las abominan y pueden vivir sus propias vidas sin la necesidad de estas cosas; pero cuando llegue el día grande de la ira, todos buscarán misericordia de Dios, pero no la hallarán; por cuanto ellos mismos la escarnecieron en un tiempo, el cual era oportuno y único. Hermanitos, a todos los que teméis el nombre de Dios, os hablo, en el amor de Dios, y para bien vuestro; salid de los engaños de las tinieblas; ¿por qué malgastar el tiempo bueno que Dios nos ha brindado? ¿Por qué pondremos el corazón en las cosas que van a pasar en la ira de Dios? Si las cosas en las cuales el pueblo de Dios está gastando su alma y su dinero valieran, pues Dios no las quemaría; ¿por qué engrandecer nuestro nombre, y vestir nuestra vida, con cosas que aun Salomón abominó? ¿Por qué no conseguir oro puro de Dios, y sabiduría sólida de arriba? Es tiempo de echar el pan a las aguas, que luego pronto lo hallaremos en un buen tiempo y lugar; es tiempo de que nos llamen locos, por justa causa; pero ¿quién es aquel que en estos días no le huye al escarnio y a la burla de los ciegos y torpes?

Es tiempo de error, de burla, de vanidad, de codicia, de locura; todos reclaman lo mejor, y poseen lo peor que en la historia se ha registrado. Aquellos que reclaman el Espíritu de Dios, aborrecen todo lo que es del Espíritu de Dios; y ¿por qué es esto? Todo se halla, menos: la Caridad, el gozo del Espíritu, la paz de Cristo la cual es por el mismo Espíritu, tolerancia, benignidad, bondad, fe, mansedumbre y templanza. ¿Es acaso una casualidad que estas cosas no se hallen en el pueblo de Dios? ¿No debiera de ser esto nuestra vestidura? ¿Hallaremos pues estas cosas en el mundo? Si en el mundo no las hay, ¿Dónde pues las buscaremos? o ¿no es tiempo de producir tal fruto? Si es que tenemos el Espíritu de Dios? ¿Es culpable Dios de que no tengamos estas cosas? o ¿no seremos más bienn nosotros los culpables? y es que el mundo nos ha robado el alma, y el corazón nuestro ha sido llenado de todo antojo carnal, y de toda envidia y codicia por las cosas que valen mucho dinero; y las cosas que son del Espíritu, las cuales son gratis, no codiciamos. La tierra se ha corrompido exactamente como dijo Cristo; bienaventurado el que cree a lo que Cristo dijo. Todos buscan dinero, y los más están usando la palabra de Dios para ganar su pan, y comprar las vanidades solo para vivir más comodamente; nunca en la historia había dejado tanta ganancia la palabra de Dios, a los hombres que la emplean para ganar su pan; por esto ha perdido la palabra de Dios su valor en las manos de los impíos; y el pequeño queda desamparado, siendo que la palabra de Dios es la única que alivia y alimenta a los

107

pequeños. ¿A quién vemos que vaya tras la humildad y la mansedumbre de Cristo; como habló él que aprendieramos, y fueramos tras las cosas que él amó? ¿Cuándo habló Cristo diciendo que el pueblo de los últimos días estaría bien en amor y en la FE? ¿Por qué pues enseñan los hombres y dicen al pueblo que les viene la paz eterna? Cuando en verdad lo que les sorprenderá será tinieblas y confusión, de aquí en muy pocos días. Yo sé que estas palabras lastiman; hieren el corazón de muchos que están al frente de las gentes; pero ¿Dónde está pues la humildad? ¿Dónde la paciencia y la mansedumbre? Pus ¿qué no debe de sufrir estas palabras el pueblo de Dios a fin de sanar? Si alguno se enoja, más bien se debiera de avergonzar. No hablo de la propiedad de nadie en particular, si hablo mal, contra Dios estoy hablando, porque el es dueño, y no los que dirigen al pueblo. No estoy escarneciendo el vestido de nadie, ni la casa, ni el automóvil; ¿por qué pues se enojan? El vestido, la casa, el automóvil, es vuestra importancia, pero de ello no hablo antes hablo de las cosas de Dios; lo que ha sido olvidado.

¿Contra quién pues van estas palabras? El espíritu de Dios no es contra el que ama justicia, no es contra el que perdona a su hermano; ni contra el que hace el bien a su prójimo, al pobre, al necesitado, al huérfano; esta palabra no es contra los mansos de la tierra, ni contra los humildes de corazón. ¿Contra quién pues van estas palabras? ¿Acaso van contra algún movimiento? ¿contra alguna organización o secta? Lejos sea; Dios está irritado contra los que lo irritan, contra los que quiebran sus leyes, contra los que apoyan el mal en las manos de los que hacen el mal. ¿A caso no está la soberbia en toda la tierra? ¿No hinche el egoismo el corazón de los creyentes en estos días? ¿No está el corazón del hombre lleno en estos días de malicia? ¿y esto, es solo en algún movimiento, o alguna organización religiosa? No, la codicia tiene al mundo en llamas de enemistad y odio. Por este mismo espíritu de error, las gentes están divididas; ¿quién tiene amor, quién tiene misericordia de los que perecen? acerquese a Dios, y él le enseñará justicia y verdad. La malicia en el corazón, el egoismo y la soberbia nos ha distanciado de Dios. Estas palabras son y hablan contra los que aborrecen, contra los que hacen acepción de personas, contra los que no perdonan, contra los murmuradores, contra los que no obedecen a sus padres. ¿Es acaso casualidad que Dios este irritado contra los moradores? ¿Será Dios injusto porque va a destruir a la tierra con los rebeldes? ¿Son los borrachos los que han irritado a Dios? ¿Son los inconversos los que han hecho a Dios que se enoje? ¿Quién pues es aquel que ha irritado a Dios? Los rebeldes de la tierra, aquellos que han dejado sus mandamientos por tierra; miremos que hemos dejado el derecho del criador, hemos dejado el camino del que hizo el sol la tierra, y todo lo que respira. ¿Quién ha propagado el amor, el temor de Dios? ¿quién es aquel que le puede, al ver la justicia por tierra; acerquese a la luz de Dios.

A nosotros que hemos conocido el nombre de Cristo y el

amor de Dios, nos convenía detener el derecho de Dios. Pero por nuestra causa el derecho cayó a tierra, y luego la maldad se multiplicó el mal entró aun en el corazón de los pequeños; de esto nos hará Dios culpables.

Somos réos, culpables de grandes delitos; porque habiendo sido enseñados por el hijo de Dios, nos tornamos de los caminos de vida; y nada se nos dió cuando el mal entró a la Iglesia.

En estos días el sabio de corazón, pone su mano en la boca; el que teme a Dios, tapa sus oídos, acausa de tanta maldad oída; los humildes de corazón, cierran sus ojos, acausa de la fuerza que hay en las obras malas de los hombres. Pero, ¿qué de esta generación? ¿Cierra sus ojos al mal, sus oídos; tapa su boca? NO, antes los ojos de esta presente generación, se abren más a lo malo; su boca habla los pensamientos abominables que su corazón piensa. A lo malo llaman bueno; y a lo bueno aborrecen. ¿Quién se regocija en hacer el bien? ¿Quién halla deleite en usar de misericordia? Por esto mismo la palabra de Dios perdió su valor para el corazón del hombre; El hacer la voluntad de Dios era el alimento de Cristo; pero ahora todos escarnecen la voluntad de Dios, la cual es para nuestro propio bien. Todos le huyen a la Cruz de Cristo; Por eso el corazón de esta generación ha sido entenebrecido, y vuelto en piedra; y nadie se compadece del afligido. Cada uno se alimenta con el mundo; cada uno vé y codicia aquello que Dios aborrece; aborrece y abomina el ojo codicioso, Dios no puede ver el corazón que maquina pensamientos malos. ¿Por qué están todas las gentes en deuda terrenal? ¿Nos hemos endeudado a causa de la viuda? ¿A causa del pobre, a causa del afligido, o a causa de la misericordia? No, antes por nuestros antojos estamos endeudados; es la codicia, el mundo y la soberbia la que nos ha hecho que caigamos en tan grandes deudas. ¿No habla la misma historia? ¿Hubo acaso, antes de nosotros, una generación tan endeudada como lo es esta presente generación? ¿Y son nuestras deudas a causa de que haya mucha necesidad y pobreza sobre la tierra? No, antes, por ir tras el mundo y el rico; por no ser menos que nuestro enemigo, al cual llamamos hermano, por esto estamos en deuda; por esto nos matamos, por esto hemos olvidado el amor, la misericordia.

Esta generación, en nada imita a Cristo. Todos quieren conseguir las cosas como "Simón el Mago". Ya no engañemos a nuestras almas; ya no confiemos en nuestro corazón; volvamos a Dios; ¿Por qué dejar el consejo de Dios? ¿Por qué pisotear la sabiduría? ¿Por qué resistir al Espíritu? Aborrezcamos el prejuicio; retiremos la murmuración, pues que todos estamos iguales delante de Dios; porque todos hemos dejado la justicia y la misericordia, le fe no fingida y el temor de Dios. Ya no extendamos el dedo; ¿qué no viene ya el fin? ¡Oh pueblo ciego y torpe!, ¿Qué no ves que ya se te han acortado tus días? Recoje tu dedo; cierra tu boca; tus oídos y tus ojos retiralos del mal, ¿qué no ves el fin que ya se te acerca? ¿No dijo Cristo el Rey: "Porque por tus palabras serás justificado, y por tus pala-

bras serás condenado (Mat. 12:37).
Por el poco amor de Dios que queda en vuestros corazones, os ruego que cerréis vuestras bocas; ¿para qué aumentar más la condenación? Humillemos a nuestras almas, y prestemos oídos a los consejos antiguos por los cuales nuestros padres fueron salvos. Ya no ayudemos a propagar las vanidades del mundo, comprando y vendiendo todo lo que forma orgullo en nuestros corazones; ¿o no sabéis que todas estas cosas vanas han hecho que nuestras almas tropiezen? Nuestros corazones no encierran bien de Dios, porque hemos dejado entrar lo que Dios abomina.
¿Para qué pues llamarle SEÑOR a Cristo, si no le obedecemos? Estas palabras se levantarán contra nosotros, en el día del juicio.

DESCENDIENTES DE LOS FARISEOS

Nosotros hemos madurado el pecado en la tierra; con nuestra ignorancia, con nuestra soberbia, con nuestra envidia por poseer y comprar, hemos apurado a la maldad. El diablo viendo el tiempo maduro y oportuno, nos dió la democracia, en la cual hacemos como queremos, en la cual nació y se desarrollo más el hambre por poseer; con la democracia, se abrieron más trabajos, hubo más dinero, más gastos, más ambición, más comida, y todos ansieron por mejorar la vida terrenal; el vientre creció y se hizo más amplio. Los inventores viendo en las gentes hambre de cosas vanas, hambre de curiosidades, se pusieron a inventar; por eso todos alaban a la democracia; no porque haya más justicia entre la gente, pero porque hay más glotonería. No se hace la gente más misericordiosa al estar bajo un presidente demócrata, antes entre más haya, más se cierran las entrañas de los que se llaman hijos de Dios. Y ahora por ser un pueblo protegido por una nación tan grande y tan fuerte como lo es "Los estados Unidos, por esto la Iglesia está confianda, de que nadie la puede asustar; pero esto es cosa mala, y por esta causa la gente no busca a su Dios; pues se ve equipada de todo lo necesario; aunque no tenga el amor de Dios y ni sepa el juicio de Dios, no le apura nada. Dios va a castigar a esta nación, para derribar la soberbia de la Iglesia. ¿Cuándo había la desconfianza que ahora hay? ¿Cuándo hablaba la mujer de su marido como ahora habla? ¿Cuándo en la historia el hombre había amado el oro terrenal como en estos días? Los llamados cristianos, caminan por los caminos, como hachas encendidas, caminan por los caminos, con una velocidad tan grande, que parece que alguien se está muriendo en sus casas, pero sucede que cuando llegan a casa se hechan en las camas. Los hijos de las tinieblas, no tienen que aprender de los hijos de la luz; porque al contrario; los hijos de la luz van tras los hijos de las tinieblas. Los cristianos que no creen en el matar y en la guerra, están trabajando por el gobierno, ocupados en haciendo bombas atómicas, aviones con los cuales arrojar las bombas; los cristianos están trabajando por el gobierno por interés de ganar el dinero que necesitan para comprar sus carros nuevos y amejorar sus habitaciones terrestres, aunque están apresurando la guerra, y la ira de Dios; de esto nada se les da a los cristianos. Es cosa dura la que un hijo de Dios mira en estos últimos días; cierto es que solo los muy valientes y los verdaderos sabios de corazón pueden escapar de los últimos engaños grandes y mortales.

No hablo a los hijos de las tinieblas, que pasan por pecadores o inconversos; hablo a los que pasan por cristianos. Son días de humillar el alma; días son de renunciar las cosas que nos han engañado por tanto tiempo, antes de que venga la ira de Dios; ¿para qué esperar como esperó Lot? Hermanos, volvámonos a nuestro padre que nos formó; pidamos perdón; seamos sabios de Corazón y andemos en las sendas antiguas. ¿Por qué avergonzarnos de esas sendas? Todos los profetas anduvieron por esos santos caminos. ¿Para qué confiar en obras de hombres, que Dios nunca nos pidió? La confianza de esta generación está en cantos y ceremonias que Dios nunca demandó. Justicia ordenó de nosotros; y dijo: "Si vuestra justicia no fuere mayor que la justicia de los escribas y de los fariseos, no entraréis al reino de los Cielos." Ellos también cantaban, ellos también oraban, ellos también ayunaban, ellos también pagaban sus diezmos; pero nada de esto les valió cuando Cristo vino. ¿Cómo saldremos nosotros? Una cosa tengo por maravilla a mis ojos; y es que en aquellos días había más vergüenza en las mujeres y en los niños; en aquellos días había más devoción hacia las cosas de Dios. En aquellos días se hacían más limosnas; fuera con trompeta o sin trompeta; pero el caso es que estos días ni con trompeta, menos sin trompeta. En vano es la escritura en estos días; no la creen las gentes por cuanto los que la hablan no la obedecen. ¿Pues de qué nos limpió la sangre de Cristo? ¿cuáles pecados nos quitó el perdón de Dios? ¿No continúa la envidia, la soberbia, la injusticia y todo pensamiento malo en nosotros. ¿Se agradará Dios de un pueblo sin fruto de justicia? ..

Aun ni los pueblos paganos, han creído en desamprar a la viuda y al huérfano; y aun las bestias del campo son movidas a misericordia más fácil que la presente generación. Hablo al pueblo que ha conocido el derecho de su Dios; hablo con aquellos que dicen que han sido lavados con la sangre de Jesucristo. Para escarnecer me puso Dios, y ¿quién me podrá sacar de este asiento? Mi carne tiembla un tanto al pensar del pueblo con quien hablo, porque sé que no entiende la razón de Dios; no soy inocente, sé lo que me vendrá a causa de esto, porque los enemigos de la cruz, están más fuertes que nunca. No ignoro lo que me acarrean estas palabras, no de los borrachos, no de los ladrones de este mundo; pero de los llamados cristianos. Pero pronto vendrá mi testigo, el cual sacará más a luz lo que ahora hablo por letra. Jefes y mayores, ¿por qué no inclinan el oído? ¿No son los humildes de corazón los más grandes a la presencia de Dios? ¿No se humilló David? ¿No se humilló Salomón? o ¿son vuestras cabezas más sabias que las del Rey Josías, y otros santos hombres de Dios los cuales se humillaron de todo corazón? ¿No levantó Dios las cabezas de estos hombres por haberse humillado? Volvamos a la voz de la Justicia, ¿cuál en nuestra justicia presente? ¿Dónde están nuestras obras buenas para que los hombres glorifiquen a Dios? Ni los ciegos dan testimonio a favor de nosotros. Suframos esta palabra y busquemos refugio antes que sea tarde. ¿No es Dios el que viene con grande destrucción? Pues ¿por qué se ha irritado Dios? Acaso son los borrachos los que han irritado a Dios? ¿No es antes su pueblo el cual se llama de su nombre santo? No estamos obrando las obras de nuestro Dios.

¿Habló Cristo contra Juan el bautista, simplemente porque Juan no andaba con él? o ¿habló Juan contra Cristo? ¿No habló Pablo contra las divisiones? ¿No hablaron los profetas de la justicia que Cristo iba a traer? ¿Se ha contradicho Dios en algunos de los tiempos? Siempre Dios ha tratado de unir a sus hijos, y ha tratado de establecer entre ellos buena voluntad: por eso mismo entregó a su amado hijo, a fin de que aprendieran de su hijo como vivir en comunión los unos para con los otros; Dios nunca ha querido que los hombres los cuales todos vienen de una misma sangre vivan en disputas y en debates, y en contiendas, las cuales crecen y vienen a ser divisiones en palabra, y más tarde divisiones en espíritu, y más tarde vienen a formarse grandes guerras entre los mismos. ¿Por qué pues los hijos de Dios que han conocido su Santa Palabra no se pueden ver, no se aman, no se ayudan los unos y los otros? ¿No es esto el resultado de la soberbia? Y la sobrebia ¿qué no es el resultado del abandonar la humildad y la mansedumbre de Cristo? Volvámonos pues a Cristo y aprendamos de él. Ya no nos engañemos; hablemos verdad; están los hogares llamados cristianos llenos de odio, de riña, de envidia, el hijo le empresta al padre, la hija le empresta a la madre, pero nadie le da a su padre, a su madre; nadie hace bien; y si entre el pueblo hay quien haga bien, los otros le escarnecen, y le ultrajan; por esto la tierra esta contra los moradores, y ya no soporta la ediondes de los vientos.

Por todas partes la tierra le rehusa al Sembrador, y le niega la bendición, pero ni por eso abre los ojos el morador; ni por esto vuelve en sí el hombre. ¿De qué manera podrá Dios hablar con el morador de la tierra? Si les manda castigo, se lo atribuyen al diablo; si el diablo les da riquezas como las que le ofreció a Cristo en el monte de la tentación, pues entonces se lo atribuyen que Dios se los ha dado. Y de esta manera no admite este pueblo la corrección del alma.

Notemos, como ha crecido el mal entre nosotros, y como nosotros cooperamos para que crezca más. Como crecen las cosas terrenales las cuales se ven; así mismo crecen las cosas espirituales las cuales no se ven, pero que hacen más mal que las que se ven. El hombre que formó una de las cosas terrenales (el automovil) murió ya, pero el automovil quedo, y los hombres que quedaron le aumentaron, en la figura y en el color. La mujer que fabricó el vestido que trajo deshonra, ya murió, pero el vestido quedó, y las mujeres que quedaron, ellas le aumentaron, en la figura y en el color.

Así son las leyes malas que han entrado por hombres malos; el hombre que inventó muchos de los acuerdos que desmienten a Cristo y al Espíritu Santo ya murió, pero aquellos acuerdos quedaron detrás de él, y los que quedaron aumentaron y le añadieron a las leyes humanas. Así la soberbia, de igualmente ha ido creciendo y aumentando; cada generación le ha ido aumentando a la herencia de sus antepasados; y de esta manera el pecado se ha multiplicado de tal manera que ahora pocos podrán escapar de él. Salid valientes, salid de la ciudad de pecado; huid de la gran babilonia; ¿por qué participar en sus pecados, y en sus plagas que le vendrán?

Nuestros malos hechos han hecho que aun nuestros cantos y oraciones sean abominables a la presencia de Dios. Nuestro egoismo nos ha separado de la humildad de Cristo. Ya no somos sufridos. De todo nos defendemos; y nada sufrimos; ¿qué es esto? ¿nos mandó acaso Dios, que nos defendieramos de toda palabra? ¿Es tiempo de callar, es tiempo de guarda silencio. No conviene hablar en estos días. El que es limpio, guardese limpio, y si puede, límpiese más. Pero al que esté sucio, dejadlo, que se ensucie más; se pasó el tiempo de tratar de limpiar a otro. Nadie se engañe, poniendo sus ojos en otros, o en los pecadores; creyendo que él está ya limpio, y que puede limpiar a otro. Quita tu pecado primero, barre la maldad que en ti hay, y luego mirarás en limpiar a otro. Pero no te engañes, tienes soberbia, y grande iniquidad; atiende a la justicia, y mira por tu hogar, mete a tus hijos primero; porque si no tienes pasión con los que son hueso de tus huesos, y carne de tu carne: ¿cómo podrás tener piedad de otros que no son nada tuyos. Haz justicia y verdad, y tus hijos entrarán a la vida; ellos podrán ver y conocer la verdadera justicia.

Los libros se han multiplicado, y la venta de ellos ha crecido sobre manera grande; pero la ira que se aproxima, ¿quién la ha acarriado? ¿No han limpiado los libros? ¿No hemos recibido bien de tanto libro? ¿Será esta la ciencia a la cual el Angel se refirió? Se está pasando el día. El juicio grande se acerca; los elementos de la tierra están ya listos, las naciones ya no soportan el comercio de la Iglesia; y la ira de Dios ha llegado a su colmo. El Cordero de Dios ya no puede soportar los gritos de los oprimidos los gemidos de los pequeñitos; el Cordero que manifestó todo su amor al derramar su santa e inocente sangre, este mismo va a manifestar su terrible ira; y ¿quién podrá estar firme o justificarse delante de él? Todos los Templos y las ceremonias, ¿podrán apaciguar su ira? ¿Escaparán los que se tapan en cantos y oraciones vanas?

LA JUSTICIA PERDIDA

"Los reinos del mundo han venido a ser los reinos de Jesucristo."

Estas fueron las palabras que el angel habló. Esto es lo que los humildes de la tierra están esperando con todo el corazón; los pobres en espíritu están gimiendo por este evento; y todos los que aman la Justicia anhelan este gran evento y prodigioso cambio, en el cual los grandes de la tierra serán humillados y los pequeños de la tierra serán puestos en lugares altos; este será el día cuando ya no más reinará el brazo del hombre; ni admirarán la obra del hombre en lugar de admirar la Obra de Dios. Ya se ve la aurora de este gran día, día de regocijo para los que amaron al Señor de todo el Corazón, para aquellos que le obedecieron y que lo hicieron con paciencia; aquellos que no se cansaron de hacer el bien, aunque les costó amargura y muchas pruebas a causa de los infieles que no amaban al Señor, ni le temían de corazón.

Este día va a confundir a muchos y saldrán avergonzados; en este día muchos van a descubrir que las palabras que Cristo nos habló, las estuvieron ignorando, y dieron más aprecio a las enseñanzas de hombres y temieron más a lo que los hombres mandaban que a lo que Dios ordenó. Este reino, el cual no tendrá fin, no admitirá ciudadanos rebeldes; ni entrarán en el los que se avergonzaron de la humildad, de la pobreza, de la vida, del huérfano, y de la mansedumbre que Cristo nos enseñó; a este reino no entrarán los inventores de maldad.

Cristo, el cual fué el príncipe de los pobres; el amigo de los pequeñitos, el que no tuvo donde reclinar su cabeza: este mismo Cristo será rey en este reino, en el cual reinará la justicia; no la justicia que los hombres ahora llaman justicia, sino la verdadera Justicia, en la cual no hay grande ni pequeño, sino todos son iguales. Cuando Cristo vino a la tierra la primera vez, todos los grandes de la tierra no lo recibieron, antes fueron confundidos; la soberbia que en ellos había les hizo rechazar la vida de Cristo, y no quisieron recibir a Cristo como un ejemplo para la libertad, como la vida que agrada a Dios; ni le quisieron tener por Señor. Antes sin tener nada de amor, creyeron que ellos tenían lo que agrada a Dios; se desvanecieron en la nada que ellos poseían; cuando Cristo vino por primera vez, él sabía que venía a un mundo ciego, a un pueblo cargado de maldad; él sabía que había pecado, y al ver que en el mundo había mucha maldad, él no se escandalizó, antes ya esperaba él que ellos estuvieran en tal condición; y vino para perdonarles; es decir, a aquellos que le recibieran, a aquellos que admitieran que estaban en necesidad, y que no estaban contentos con lo que habían recibido de los hombres. Perdonó a todos los pecadores, y les dió un nuevo camino, para que anduviesen en él. Pero ahora que el venga, no tolerará a los rebeldes; no perdonará a los que no le obedecieron y que hicieron nulos todos sus mandamientos, y que trataron de justificarse con una profesión falsa y sin frutos de justicia. En esta venida de nuestro Señor, muchos irán a ser sorprendidos, a causa de la terrible justicia de Dios.

Juan, un hombre enviado por Dios, hablaba a los que salían para ser bautizados por él; y les decía: "Haced frutos dignos de arrepentimiento," Juan no se había criado en los templos de los judíos; él no había recibido el espíritu de los fariseos, mas bien no fué desarrollado en el mismo espiríritu por el cual los fariseos eran movidos. Dios no quería que él fuera empapado de las enseñanzas de aquellos hombres; los cuales habían hecho nulo el consejo de Dios y habían establecido tradiciones y mandamientos de hombres en los cuales, no se miraba amor ni justicia de Dios. Si Juan se hubiera criado en las enseñanzas de elloso; pues no hubiera visto mal entre ellos; antes se hubiera conformado como todos estaban conformes. Un hombre movido por enseñanzas de hombres no hubiera hablado lo que Juan habló. Juan no se dejó engañar como los hombres en estos días; ni miraba sus alabanzas, sus oraciones, sus ayunos, sus templos; antes miraba, que los grandes reinaban sobre las espaldas de los pequeños; y miraba que no había misericordia entre la gente, y esto era porque los que enseñaban, no enseñaban el amor de Dios ni lo tenían. Hoy en estos últimos días los templos, y las ceremonias hechas en un espíritu muerto y sin celo, sin amor, nos contentan, y estamos satisfechos con que los templos estén llenos de gente; pero esto no engañó a Juan; porque Juan era un hombre de Dios; Juan sabía que aquellos no eran frutos de arrepentimiento; sabía que los templos y las ceremonias son las más grandes apariencias; y que es el engaño más grande, si es que esto no es hecho en el Espíritu, y con temor de Dios. Y Juan hablaba con los fariseos y los escribas que salían para ser bautizados por él; no piensen, les decía Juan: que son hijos de Abraham; Este espíritu que engañaba a los fariseos, haciendoles creer que ellos eran hijos de Abraham es el mismo que en estos días esta en los corazones de los hombres, haciéndoles creer que son hijos de Dios. No, dijo Juan, Ya el hacha está puesta a la raíz del árbol, y todo árbol que no lleve buen fruto, será cortado, y echado al fuego. SI, cuando se trata de fruto, y de dar buen fruto todos los corazones tiemblan y tienen miedo; todos le huyen a esta palabra; ¿Por qué es que los cristianos no quieren oír de fruto bueno y fruto malo? ¿Será casualidad? Cristo dijo: "En esto es glorificado mi Padre, en que llevéis mucho fruto, y seáis así mis discípulos." Por todas partes hallo que la gente no quiere oír de fruto. Fue esto, lo que sorprendió a las gentes que oyeron a Juan el Bautista; cuando él les habló de fruto, se hallaron en angustia, y pronto dijeron: ¿Qué haremos? Juan les habló de algo que ni pensaban ellos; "El que tenga dos tunicas, dele una al que no tiene." Esto parece curioso, y sin valor; y en verdad es porque se ha olvidado el amor y se ha desaparecido de los corazones de los Cristianos; porque hemos dejado lo mejor; y por esta razón se ha olvidado, porque escarnecen las enseñanzas de los hombres de Dios; Cristo no desmintió lo que Juan habló en aquella ocasión; antes habló, y dijo: "Haced bien a los que os aborrecen." "Sed misericordiosos como vuestro Padre Celestial es misericordioso."

Se necesita amor para cumplir y ejecutar lo que Juan habló y lo que Cristo confirmó; los soberbios de la tierra escarnecieron el consejo que Dios les dió por labios de Juan, Juan no les decía que creyeron en Dios, porque ellos pensaban que ya creían, sino que les hablaba de las cosas que los hijos de Dios deben de hacer. Este amor se había desaparecido de la tierra; y a esto vino Cristo a poner en libertad a los que estaban oprimidos por el diablo; y denunciar a los llamados hijos de Dios; estos que se llamaban hijos de Dios, no tenían las obras de Dios; por eso Cristo los denunció, como hijos del diablo; esto por supuesto no les pareció a los fariseos, porque ellos pensaban que eran los mejores de toda la tierra; pues en verdad que parecían que ellos eran los mejores; porque ellos eran los que levantaban los templos, y eran ellos los que hablaban de la Ley de Moisés; eran ellos los que cantaban, los que hacían las más largas Oraciones, los que ayunaban, los que pagaban el diezmo: y luego recibir este reproche de un Hombre tan humilde como lo era Cristo, pues esto en verdad que parecía muy ridículo; pero como esto ya pasó a la historia, todos lo creemos; pero ¿qué de nuestra propia condición? Estamos en una condición muy pobre y sin frutos de arrepentimiento. Los unicos frutos que ahora se pueden manifestar, son los vicios que dejamos; pero Juan les hablaba, de frutos, es decir de obras; no les hablaba de vicios, porque ya ellos los habían dejado, y esto lo sabemos que en verdad era así. Juan no era ni podía ser engañado fácilmente, porque él no buscaba su propio bien, como ahora. Juan tenía el Espíritu de Dios, y este mismo Espíritu de Dios le iluminaba, para que él descubriera la maldad de ellos. Les decía: "Levantad lo caído, enderezad lo torcido." ¿Qué cosa estaba caída? ¿Qué cosa estaba torcida? La Ley de Dios estaba caída, la Justicia de Dios estaba torcida. Y ¿quién había torcido esta Justicia de Dios? Los fariseos la habían torcido. Sí, No es el borracho ni el ladrón que tuerce la Justicia de Dios, porque ellos no enseñan, ni se llaman del nombre de Dios; ni infaman tampoco el Nombre de Dios. Antes los que tienen la Ley de Dios, son precisamente los que la pueden levantar, o la pueden humillar.

Cristo habló y dijo, que en estos ultimos días la maldad iba a ser mucha; y que todos iban a venir en su nombre; y en efecto, en estos ultimos días, ¿quién es aquel que no viene en el nombre de Cristo? ¿Quién es aquel que admita de por sí, que es falso o hipócrita?

EL BIEN PASA POR MAL

El mundo se ha rebelado contra el Hijo de Dios; los hombres han dejado el consejo del Cristo que murió y se entregó por ellos. Cada uno se ha olvidado del mandamiento de vida, y no hay quien aprecie ni quien tema al consejo de Dios; nosotros, nuestros enseñadores y nuestros príncipes y presidentes: hemos hecho inicuamente, hemos pecado, nos hemos rebelado dejando el **santo mandamiento y el camino de Justicia**; y no hay quien clame, ni quien se queje a causa de tanta maldad. La vida que Cristo nos reveló, el dechado en santo lo hemos mutilado; y todos aborrecen lo santo, lo decente, lo humilde, lo justo; y en cambio cada uno procura el mal de su prójimo; cada uno se ale**gre en la ruina de su hermano**, hijo de su misma madre. El Cristo verdadero, él que murió en la cruz del calvario en la ciudad de Jerusalem: este es el que ha sido dejado, y contra este: todos se han levantado; cada uno haciendo lo que Cristo abomina. Y ahora, solo un Cristo histórico ha quedado, y de labios usan de su nombre para engañar a los pobres de la tierra. Todos juntos, todos son de un mismo espíritu de error, y todos aman el mal y el mal camino. No hay quien use de Misericordia para con su prójimo. A los ojos de este Cristo y de Dios: no hay Concilios ni movimiento. Todos son hijos de perdición, todos aman lo malo, arrebatan el mal y lo tragan como algo que fuera de beneficio. Todos codician, todos arrebatan, todos piensan el mal en sus corazones; no hay quien piense a favor de la justicia, del **Juicio, de la Misericordia**. Ya sobre la tierra no hay quien mire y le pueda por el caído ni por el afligido. Cada uno se ha hecho un capitalista, un príncipe, un dictador; pero nadie mira por el inválido. No hay más que obras de Satanás, y cada uno se disculpa con la "Cruz roja" con el "Salvación Army" con "El Well Fare" pero todos estos grupos son tretas y engaños, para despojar a las gente; al pobre lo envían con las manos vacías. El dinero que recogen, lo emplean en aparatos de los más modernos y más vanos; emplean el dinero que recogen con engaño, en oficinas vanidosas y muebles de los más lujosos. Por esta razón la Iglesia se ha dormido, y los obreros no enseñan el bien y la Misericordia a las gentes. Antes todos se disculpan en esos grupos engañadores. Dios es testigo de todo esto, porque él también tiene ojos como nosotros; y mira por toda la tierra.

Toda las naciones lo han dejado; cada uno ignora al hijo de Dios, y no hay quien consulte a Dios para andar derecho. Cada uno procura la ayuda de Dios: pero solo para andar más ligero y para robar a su hermano. Por eso es que la ira del Cordero, y el furor de Dios ha llegado a su fin, y no hay quien detenga el brazo de Dios para destruir la tierra con sus falsos habitantes. La ira del cordero consumirá a todos los mentirosos, y abrazará a todos los violentos que vivieron en vanidad, confiando en templos y en palabras vanas. Sabed que el Hijo de

Dios está ariado en extremo, nadie sea inocente que el furor de Dios acabará con todos los injustos; que para enseñar usaron la palabra de Dios y para robar a los afligidos usaron los dichos de Cristo. El fin está sobre nosotros; cada uno descubrirá que Dios no puede ser burlado. Porque Dios comenzara su Santo y Justo Juicio por la casa santa, por los que se llaman de su nombre. Dios dará su pago a todos los que enseñaban a las congregaciones como rebelarse contra los santos Mandamientos de Dios: los cuales fueron dados por su hijo Jesús. ¿Y qué será del oro y la plata que los injustos recogen de los pobres con engaño? ¿Dónde aparecerá el que anda en carro de príncipes? ¿Los que visten con gala y levantan casas altas con dinero del pobre? Ningun Mandamiento de Cristo está ejecutando el pueblo que se llama del nombre de Dios; ni mandamiento grande, pero ni mandamiento pequeño; todos los que dirigen, respondan a esto. ¿Cuál es el mandamiento que los adoradores están ejecutando? ¿Dónde está el sabio, para qué responda? Si uno solo mandamiento estuvieran ejecutando: la Misericordia no estuviera por tierra: La justicia no estuviera ignorada.

Todos se han hecho vanos, predicándole a un pueblo rebelde e injusto: puras promesas. Ciertamente que esta generación no es digna ni da la promesa más pequeña; de otra manera Dios no dejaría que el Juicio santo llegará a su pueblo. Pero es su pueblo que de día y de noche le alaba de puros labios; pero su corazón está lleno de pensamientos malos y de toda avaricia. El corazón de este pueblo que canta y ora en público para ser visto, se alimenta con pensamientos ajenos y abominables, no teme codiciar la mujer de su más cercano. ¿Dónde pues están los sabios para que le diga a esta mala y torcida generación que su fin ha llegado. Porque Dios así lo ha dicho por sus santos profetas que fueron antes de nosotros. ¿Y quién podrán justificar a esta mala generación que come carne de su prójimo? Cada uno de los cabezas dice: "la obra vá creciendo, y Dios está bendiciendo nuestro movimiento." Y de esta manera se creen estar ricos y sin necesidad. Pero no saben los ciegos: que están pobres y muy miserables en todo lo que pertenece al reino de Dios. Cada uno mira el número de sus seguidores, y cada uno confía y depende del número de creyentes: pero ciegos como los fariseos. No saben que todavía no saben ni lo que es Misericordia: mucho menos conocer lo que es Justicia.

¿Qué cosa de Cristo tiene esta generación; Misericordia no la conoce, Justicia, Amor, Humildad, Mansedumbre, Sabiduría, Temor de Dios, Juicio? Ciertamente que nada de esto tiene este pueblo malo y desobediente. Por esta razón la tierra se infisionó de iniquidad y toda obra mala. Se acabaron los que conocían la Justicia y la Misericordia; se acabaron los hombres de Fe, por eso fué que la verdad fué torcida, y el Juicio no salió recto; La Justicia no apareció, y el hombre que temía a Dios fué puesto en prisión de los concilios de hombres injustos. Este gran mal ha hecho que el Cordero se irrite, y de aquí en pocos días, aun los grandes y ricos gritarán, y arrojarán el dinero y todo aquello en que confiaban. Llorarán como niños, gritarán por los montes como toros enojados; y no habrá quién los defienda: porque ellos no defendieron el oprimido de manos de los opresores; antes consentían en todo lo malo; y luego se vestía de apariencia con cantos religiosos y oraciones largas.

El día de Dios viene, y los hipócritas saldrán de sus escondrijos; entonces reconocerán que la obra de sus manos fué más pesada y mala que la obra de los fariseos. Y sin duda que los de Sodoma y Gomorra condenarán a esta generación, porque ellos no tuvieron el conocimiento que esta gente tuvo. Ay de los que ahora gritan y saltan de gusto: porque el día se les tornará en tinieblas, y la risa se les volverá llanto como de primogénito. Ay de los que ahora tienen todo lo necesario, sin mirar por su prójimo: porque en el día de Dios, todo les faltará; y con la misma medida que midieron: también ellos serán medidos. Porque Juicio sin Misericordia es hecho: con todos los que no hacen Misericordia. La tierra está llena de murmuración, y cada uno se ha hecho enemigo de su hermano. Murmuración en labios de la madre, en la boca de los hijos, en la nuera, en el padre, en los nietos, en los abuelos, en los tíos, en los sobrinos, en los amigos, en los vecinos, en la esposa, en el yerno; y no hay quien haya escapado de esta plaga: que por causa de los falsos y asalariados la tierra se inficionó. Todos escarnecen como niños necios y sin educación: cuando hablan de su enemigo, es tanto el odio ciego: que no dejan parte de su cuerpo que no lo describan; hablan de sus ojos, hablan de su boca, hablan de su nariz; y con desdén describen a su enemigo como describir a una misma bestia. En esto se ve la necedad y la torpeza a donde nos han arrojado los falsos y torpes enseñadores.

Aun los que reportan en los periódicos diarios: cuando hablan de su enemigo rojo, describen con desprecio hasta su última cosa. Y no dejan cosa en la cara de sus enemigo que no describan con odio y deprecio. ¿A causa los sabios se portan de esta manera? ¿Habla la historia de algun sabio que haya describido con odio y desprecio la facción de su enemigo? ¡Nunca!

Esta nación de predicadores, escarnecer la pobreza de las otras naciones; e insultan las costumbres de sus naciones vecinas; siendo que las costumbres de las otras naciones son más limpias y decentes. ¿O hay alguna nación mas inmoral que esta? Oh pueblo arrogante, tu que has edificado tu morada sobre las nubes, tu que te jactas porqué piensas un día llegar a conocer otros planetas: de arriba serás arrojado, y tu caída será más fuerte que la de alemania; más humillada serás que Japón; porque el que te va a arrojar por tierra: es el que todo lo puede —es tu Creador; el mismo que te metió a esta tierra él mismo te pondrá por tierra.

Reies L. Tijerina

NOTES

Introduction

1. Tijerina, *Mi lucha por la tierra*, 32.
2. Cargo, *Lonesome Dave*, 191.
3. "Reies Lopez Tijerina Dies at 88," http://www.latimes.com/local/obituaries/la-me-reies-lopez-tijerina-20150123-story.html; Sam Roberts, "Reies Tijerina, 88, Dies; Led Chicano Property Rights Movement," https://www.nytimes.com/2015/01/28/us/reies-tijerina-88-dies-led-chicano-property-rights-movement.html; Phaedra Haywood, "Land Grant Activist Reies Lopez Tijerina dies at 88," http://www.santafenewmexican.com/land-grant-activist-reies-lopez-tijerina-dies-at/image_9b336f3d-5ced-5af7-bb04-565a5c552321.html.
4. Gutiérrez, "Introduction," in Tijerina, *They Called Me "King Tiger,"* xvi.
5. See Meier and Rivera, *The Chicanos*, 184, 257–80; Acuña, *Occupied America*, 222–45.
6. Montoya, *Translating Property*; Gómez, *Manifest Destinies*; Scarborough, *Trespassers on Our Own Land*, 246–54; Carlson, *The Spanish-American Homeland*, 13–20.
7. Rosenbaum, *Mexicano Resistance in the Southwest*.
8. Phil Smith interview with Jake Kosek, December 11, 1999, as quoted in Kosek, *Underhistories*, 43.
9. Tijerina, *Mi lucha por la tierra*, 135. Henceforth, all quotations from this book are my own translations.
10. National Broadcasting Corporation, *Reies Tijerina: The Most Hated Man in New Mexico*. 1969.
11. Tijerina, *They Called Me "King Tiger."*
12. Albuquerque FBI SAC to Director, June 9, 1967, RTP, Box 2, File 16, 1,111.
13. Oropeza, "Becoming Indo-Hispano," 180–206, especially 202; Mariscal, *Brown-Eyed Children of the Sun*, especially 97–139.
14. "Former Alliance Grant May Try to Take Over Vast Southwest," *Albuquerque Journal* (May 28, 1967), E-8.

Chapter 1

1. Castro, *The Spaniards*.
2. Much of the Tijerina family's genealogy was collected by Reies in his

unpublished manuscript, *My Life, Judaism, and the Nuclear Age* (1986), 4–6. See also Archivo General de Indias, *Catálogo de pasajeros a Indias durante los siglos XVI, XVII y XVIII*; Tijerina Family Geneology, accessed August 25, 2006, http://genforum.genealogy.com/tijerina/messages/34.html.

3. Alberro, *Inquisición y sociedad en México 1571–1700*, 172; M. Cohen, *The Martyr Luis de Carvajal*; Gitlitz, *Secrecy and Deceit*; Hordes, *To the End of the Earth*; Gilman and Shain, *Jewries at the Frontier*; Tobias, *A History of Jews in New Mexico*.

4. Cohen, op. cit.; Tobias, op. cit.
5. Gardner, *¡Grito!*, 33.
6. Ibid.
7. On the Texas Revolution see Davis, *Lone Star Rising*; Jenkins, ed., *The Papers of the Texas Revolution, 1835–36*.
8. "Polk Requests a Declaration of War Against Mexico, May 11, 1846," accessed September 17, 2019, https://faculty.chass.ncsu.edu/slatta/hi453/polk.htm.
9. Griswold del Castillo, *The Treaty of Guadalupe Hidalgo*.
10. Stephens as quoted in Hietala, *Manifest Design*, ix.
11. Rodríguez, *Memoirs of Early Texas*, 75.
12. Hammett, *The Empresario*, 25, 28, 58–59, 189–90; Seguín, *Personal Memoirs of John N. Seguín*, 18.
13. Montejano, *Anglos and Mexicans in the Making of Texas, 1836–1986*, 26–27.
14. Horsman, *Race and Manifest Destiny*, 217.
15. Hietela, *Manifest Design*, 162.
16. McNeill, "Tijerina: Flashback to A Forgotten Frontier," 37.
17. Ibid., 39–40.
18. Richardson and Pisani, *Batos, Bolillos, Pochos, and Pelados*, 8–9.
19. Cortina as quote in Montejano, op.cit., 32.
20. Sonnichsen, *The El Paso Salt War*; García, *Desert Immigrants*, 13, 156–57.
21. Johnson, *Revolution in Texas*, 80–81.
22. Gibson and Jung, *Historical Census Statistics on Population*, table E-7.
23. De León and Stewart, *Tejanos and the Numbers Game*, 33.
24. Foley, *The White Scourge*, 28–29.
25. As quoted in Foley, *The White Scourge*, 36.
26. Fox, *The Three Worlds of Relief*, 73–94; Taylor, *Mexican Labor in the United States*, 521.
27. Stimpson Jr., *My Remembers*, 70–71.
28. Gardner, *¡Grito!*, 31.
29. Jarman Hagood, *Mothers of the South*; Conrad, *The Forgotten Farmers*, 1–5.
30. "Another Biographical Sketch," RTP, Box 53, File 43, 4.
31. "Memorias que siguen conmigo, que han influenciado mi vida," RTP, Box 53, File 43, 1.
32. "Additional Biographical Sketch," RTP, Box 53, File 43, 7–8.
33. Gardner, *¡Grito!*, 31, 36; "La Vida de Reies," RTP, Box 53, File 43, 2.

34. "Additional Biographical Sketch," RTP, Box 53, File 43, 5–8; Nabokov, *Tijerina and the Courthouse Raid*, 196.
35. Gardner, *¡Grito!*, 36.
36. Richardson and Pisani, 17.
37. Nabokov, 195.
38. "Memorias que siguen conmigo, que han influenciado mi vida," RTP, Box 53, File 43, 5. See also Tijerina interview with Rudy V. Busto, April 1990, as quoted in Busto, *King Tiger*, 37.
39. Busto, 37.
40. Gardner, *¡Grito!*, 32.
41. Conrad, 10.
42. Stimpson Jr., passim.
Gardner, *¡Grito!*, 32.
43. Richardson and Pisani, 9.
44. "Biography," RTP, Box 53, File 43, 2.
45. Nabokov, 194.
46. Gardner, *¡Grito!*, 32.
47. Ibid.
48. Ibid.
49. Jenkinson, *Tijerina*, 19.
50. Gardner, *¡Grito!*, 32, 36.
51. Nabokov, 194.
52. Gardner, *¡Grito!*, 36.
53. Busto, 36.
54. PNP, Box II, File 22, Item 16; Collado, "Reies Tijerina: Heroe o Malhechor?" 1, 3. On work conditions see Menefee, *Mexican Migratory Workers of South Texas*.
55. Gardner, *¡Grito!*, 36.
56. McLean and Thompson, *Spanish and Mexican in Colorado*, 17, 50.
57. Ibid.
58. Coalson, *The Development of the Migratory Farm Labor System in Texas*, 56–67; Jarman Hagood, 52–111; Stimpson Jr., passim.
59. Gardner, *¡Grito!*, 32.
60. Busto, 36.
61. Gardner says that Herlinda López died in 1934, while Nabokov notes Reies was six years old when his mother died, which would place her death in 1933. Her death certificate lists April 21, 1931, as the date, making Reies four-and-a-half years old at the time. See "Death Certificate: Herlinda López," in RTP, Box 54, File 25, as well as "Memorias que siguen conmigo, que han influenciado mi vida," RTP, Box 53, File 43, 5–6. On Herlinda's death see Gardner, *¡Grito!*, 36; Nabokov, 196.
62. De León and Stewart, 56–57.
63. Clark, *The Latin Immigrant in the South*, 33.
64. McLean and Tomson, 10.

65. McCombs, *From Over the Border*, 55.
66. Letter from Antonio Tijerina to Reies, March 2, 1972, RTP, Box 54, File 28.
67. "Memorias que siguen conmigo, que han influenciado mi vida," RTP, Box 53, File 43, 8.
68. McLean and Thomson, 29–30; Deutsch, *No Separate Refuge*, 107–61.
69. Dennis Nodín Valdés, *Al Norte*; Valdés, *Barrios Norteños*; Vargas, *Proletarians of the North*; J. García, *Mexicans in the Midwest, 1900–1932*.
70. "La Vida de Reies," RTP, Box 53, File 43, 7.
71. Richardson and Pisani, 22.
72. Ibid., 25.
73. Ibid., 22.
74. Ibid.
75. Ibid.
76. Ibid., 23.
77. Ibid., 25.
78. Ibid., 27.
79. Ibid.
80. McLean and Thompson, 29–32; Deutsch, 107–61.
81. Richardson and Pisani, op. cit., 25.
82. Ibid., 19.
83. Gardner, *¡Grito!*, 36; Busto, 38.
84. Jenkinson, *Tijerina*, 17.
85. Richardson and Pisani, op. cit., 20.
86. "Another Biographical Sketch," RTP, Box 53, File 43, biographical, 3–4.
87. Ibid., 5.
88. Ibid., 6–7.
89. Ibid.
90. Ibid.
91. "School Record: Frank Johnson Elementary School," RTP Box 53, File 43; "Another Biographical Sketch," RTP, Box 53, File 43, 7.
92. PNP, Box 2, File 22, Item 18, 5.
93. Autobiographical, "La Vida de Reies," RTP, Box 53, File 43, 3–4.
94. Ibid., RTP, Box 53, File 43, 5–6.
95. Gardner, *¡Grito!*, 37–38.
96. PNP, Box 2, File 22, Item 18, 5.
97. Gardner, *¡Grito!*, 38.
98. Autobiographical, "La Vida de Reies," RTP, Box 53, File 43, 7–9.
99. "La Vida de Reies," RTP, Box 53, File 43, 9; María Escobar, interview with Ramón Gutiérrez, September 23, 2006, Albuquerque, NM.
100. "Biography," RTP, Box 53, File 43, 2, 6.
101. PNP, Box 2, File 22, Item 18, 5.
102. Nabokov, 196–97.

Chapter 2

1. Parham, *The Life of Charles F. Parham*, 2–53.
2. Ibid., 36.
3. Ibid., 51. See also Blumhofer, *Restoring the Faith*, 70–87; Robeck Jr., *The Azusa Street Mission and Revival*, 39–52.
4. Ibid., 17–47.
5. Ibid, 44.
6. Ibid., 66–67.
7. Bartleman, *How Pentecost Came to Los Angeles*, as quoted in Azusa Street Testimonies: Frank Bartleman, 2, accessed August 23, 2010, http://www.azusastreet.org/AzusaStreetBartleman.htm.
8. "Weird Babel of Tongues," *Los Angeles Daily News*, April 18, 1906, as quoted in Robeck, 76.
9. *Los Angeles Daily News*, April 19, 1906, part 2, 1, as quoted in MacRoberts, 54.
10. Charles F. Parham published a similarly titled newspaper. The two should not be confused.
11. Seymore, *Apostolic Faith* 1, no. 1 (September 1906), 2.
12. Ibid., 1.
13. Bartleman, *How Pentecost Came to Los Angeles*, as quoted in Azusa Street Testimonies: Frank Bartleman, 2, accessed August 23, 2010, http://www.azusastreet.org/AzusaStreetBartleman.htm.
14. Ibid., 1.
15. Azusa Street Testimonies: A. G. Garr, 2, accessed August 23, 2010, http://www.azusastreet.org/AzusaStreetGarr.htm.
16. Bartleman, *How Pentecost Came to Los Angeles*, as quoted in Azusa Street Testimonies: Frank Bartleman, 2, accessed August 23, 2010, http://www.azusastreet.org/AzusaStreetBartleman.htm.
17. *Apostolic Faith* 2, no. 1 (January 1907), 1.
18. Ibid., 1.
19. Florence Crawford quoted in Azusa Street Testimonies, 1–3, accessed August 23, 2010, http://www.azusastreet.org/AzusaStreetCrawford.htm.
20. Bartleman, *How Pentecost Came to Los Angeles*, as quoted in Azusa Street Testimonies, 3, accessed August 23, 2010, http://www.azusastreet.org/AzusaStreetBartleman.htm.
21. *Apostolic Faith* 1, no. 1 (December 1906), 1.
22. Bartleman, *How Pentecost Came to Los Angeles*, as quoted in Azusa Street Testimonies, 1, accessed August 23, 2010, http://www.azusastreet.org/AzusaStreetBartleman.htm.
23. A. A. Boddy as quoted in Hollenwegger, *The Pentecostals*, 24.
24. *Apostolic Faith*, September 1906, 1, as quoted in McGee, "This Gospel . . . Shall Be Preached," 45.

25. Harris, *Spoken by the Spirit*. On glossolalia, see Anderson, *Vision of the Disinherited*, 10–27; Samarin, "The Linguisticality of Glossolalia," 49–75.

26. Remarks of George N. Eldridge in *The Tenth Annual Report of the Christian and Missionary Alliance* (March 31, 1907), 166, quoted in McGee, op. cit., 60.

27. C. Parham, *A Voice Crying in the Wilderness*, 83, 91–100; S Parham, op. cit., 148, 154–55, 160, 168.

28. Charles F. Parham, "Free Love," *Apostolic Faith* (December 1912), 4, as quoted in Blumhofer, *Restoring the Faith*, 56.

29. Blumhofer, *Restoring the Faith*, 56; Sanders, *Saints in Exile*, 29–30.

30. Bartleman, *How Pentecost Came to Los Angeles*, 58–9; Espinosa, "'El Azteca,'" 597–616.

31. The baptism of Abundio and Rosa López was reported in the *Apostolic Faith*, in November 1906.

32. While the church originally called itself an "Asamblea" or assembly, it changed its name to "Iglesia" in 1944.

33. Ramírez, "Borderlands Praxis," 573–96; and Ramírez, *Migrating Faith*.

34. Espinosa, "Brown Moses," 263–95; and Espinosa, *Latino Pentecostals in America*.

35. McGee, *"This Gospel . . . Shall Be Preached,"* 74–82.

36. Allen, *Missionary Methods*. See also Forman, "A History of Foreign Mission Theory in America," 63–80.

37. Beaver, "A History of Mission Strategy," 7–28; Luce, "Paul's Missionary Methods," *Pentecostal Evangel*, January 8, 1921, pp. 6–7; January 22, 1921, 6, 11; February 5, 1921, 6–7.

38. Luce, *Latter Day Evangel*, December 1930, 22, as quoted in Sánchez Walsh, *Latino Pentecostal Identity*, 49.

39. Luce, "Latin American Bible Institute," *Pentecostal Evangel*, December 13, 1937, 7, as quoted in Sánchez Walsh, 54.

40. Kelty, "Needs of Bible Institute," *Pentecostal Evangel*, August 27, 1927, 11, as quoted in Sánchez Walsh, 51.

41. Busto, *King Tiger*, 88.

42. María Escobar interview with Ramón A. Gutiérrez, September 23, 2006; Luce, *Hermeneutica*; Luce, *Estudios de las Evidencias Cristianas*; Luce, *El Mensajero y Su Mensaje*; and Luce and Ball, *Himnos de Gloria y Triunfo*.

Chapter 3

1. Savage, *The Spirit Bade MeGo*, 25, 51–54.
2. "La Vida de Reies," RTP, Box 53, File 43, 9; "Biography," RTP, Box 53, File 43, 2.
3. "La Vida de Reies," RTP Papers, Box 53, File 43, 1–2.
4. "Biography," RTP, Box 53, File 43, 3.
5. Luce, *Probad los Espiritus, Si Son de Dios*, prologue, n.p.
6. Luce, *The Messenger and His Message*.

7. Ibid., vi.
8. Ibid., 11.
9. Ibid., 42.
10. Ibid., 35.
11. Ibid., 54.
12. Ibid., 74–83.
13. Ibid., 18, 11.
14. "Biography," RTP, Box 53, File 43, 2; "La Vida de Reies," RTP, Box 53, File 43.
15. Ibid.
16. Reies López Tijerina, interview with Ramón Gutiérrez, July 21, 2005.
17. "Biography," RTP, Box 53, File 43, 3.
18. "Reies López Tijerna Latin American Bible Institute transcript," ASP, Box 1, File 18.
19. "Biography," RTP, Box 53, File 43, 10–12.
20. Maria Escobar, interview with Ramón Gutiérrez, September 23, 2006.
21. "Biography," RTP, Box 53, File 43, 3.
22. "Biography," RTP, Box 53, File 43, 4; Reies López Tijerina, interview with Ramón Gutiérrez, August 20, 2009.
23. "Biography," RTP, Box 53, File 43, 3.
24. Ibid., 5.
25. President Harry S Truman's Announcement of the Dropping of an Atomic Bomb on Hiroshima, Press Release, August 6, 1945, accessed August 22, 2015, https://millercenter.org/the-presidency/presidential-speeches/august-6-1945-statement-president-announcing-use-bomb.
26. Ibid.
27. William L. Laurence, a *New York Times* journalist, witnessed the testing of the atomic bomb at Alamogordo, New Mexico, on July 15, 1945, and describes the light in his book *Dawn Over Zero*, 9–10; Edward Rabinowitch, a chemist at the University of Chicago who worked on the Manhattan Project offers the "fireball" metaphor in "Five Years After," 3.
28. Robert Lewis as quoted in David McNeill, "Hiroshima," *The Independent*, August 6, 2010, 1.
29. *Santa Fe New Mexican*, August 6, 1945, 1; President Harry S Truman as quoted in Geddes and Wendt, eds., *The Atomic Age Opens*, 38.
30. Ibid.
31. Ibid.
32. Dower, *War without Mercy*.
33. "Biography," RTP, Box 53, File 43, 5; Gardner, *¡Grito!*, 39.
34. President Harry Truman Diary, as quoted in Boyer, *Fallout*, 32, 240.
35. "Biography," RTP, Box 53, File 43, 7.
36. María Escobar Chávez, interview with Ramón A. Gutiérrez, September 23, 2006.
37. "Biography," RTP, Box 53, File 43, 3, 6–8.

38. Gardner, ¡Grito!, 38–39; "Reies López Tijerina Latin American Bible Institute Transcript," in ASP, Box 1, File 18.
39. "Biography," RTP, Box 53, File 43, 11–12; Reies López Tijerina, interview with Ramón Gutiérrez, August 20, 2009.
40. María Chávez, interview by José Angel Gutiérrez, videotape 2000; "Biographical Sketch," RTP, Box 53, File 43, 4.

Chapter 4

1. Gardner, ¡Grito!, 39.
2. María Escobar, interview with José Angel Gutiérrez; María Escobar, interview with Ramón A. Gutiérrez, September 23, 2006; "The Land, Reies and the Indo-Hispano People," RTP, Box 53, File 43; "Biography," RTP, Box 53, File 43, 12.
3. Ibid.
4. María Escobar, interview with Ramón Gutiérrez, September 23, 2006. Very similar facts are recorded in an interview José Angel Gutiérrez conducted with David Tijerina on June 28, 2000, 3.
5. María Escobar, interview with R. Gutiérrez.
6. Ibid.
7. Ibid.
8. María Escobar Chavez, interview with José Angel Gutiérrez.
9. "A Cause to Die For," NTP, unpublished mss., November 2, 2007, 52.
10. Sánchez Walsh, *Latino Pentecostal Identity*, 79.
11. Ibid.
12. "Biography," RTP, Box 53, File 43, 13–14.
13. On dispensationalism see "Christian Fundamentalism," Encyclopaedia Britannica Online, accessed July 17, 2016; "Biography," RTP, Box 53, File 43, 13–14.
14. Gardner, ¡Grito!, 39.
15. "Biography," RTP, Box 53, File 43, 13–14.
16. Ibid., 15–16; Gardner, ¡Grito!, 39.
17. "Biography," RTP, Box 53, File 43, 15–16.
18. Ibid., 15.
19. Ibid.
20. "Biography," RTP, Box 53, File 43, 16–17; José Angel Gutiérrez interview with Reies "David" Hugh Tijerina, 2000, 1; Gardner, ¡Grito!, 39.
21. María Escobar, interview with Ramón A. Gutiérrez; María Escobar, interview with José Angel Gutiérrez.
22. "The Land, Reies and the Indo-Hispano People," RTP Box 53, File 43, 3–4.
23. "Biographical Sketch," RTP, Box 53, File 43, 1–2.
24. Gardner, ¡Grito!, 44; María Escobar, interview with Ramón A. Gutiérrez.
25. "Biographical Sketch," RTP, Box 53, File 43, 2–4.

26. Busto, *King Tiger*, 43; María Escobar, interview with Ramón Gutiérrez.
27. María Escobar, interview with José Angel Gutiérrez, 6.
28. Boyer, *By the Bomb's Early Light*.
29. María Escobar, interview with Ramón Gutiérrez.
30. Hymn #3, "Jesus Vendra Otra Vez," in Ball, *Himnos de Gloria*, n.p., my translation.
31. Tijerina, "Lost Justice," in *¿Hallará fe en la tierra . . . ?*
32. María Escobar, interview with Ramón Gutiérrez.
33. Harding, *The Book of Jerry Falwell*, 57–8.
34. "Faith Without Mercy."
35. Ball, *Himnos de Gloria*, n.p. hymn no. 78.
36. New Testament taken from *The New American Bible* (New York: World Publishing, 1970).
37. "The Ignored Sacrifice."
38. Azusa Street Testimonies: E. S. Williams and Florence Crawford, accessed August 23, 2006, http://www.azusastreet.org; María Escobar, interview with Ramón Gutiérrez.
39. RTP, Box 54, File 28.
40. Ibid.
41. Azusa Street Testimonies: A. G. Garr, accessed August 23, 2006, http://www.azusastreet.org/AzusaStreetGarr.htm.
42. María Escobar, interview with Ramón A. Gutiérrez.
43. David Tijerina, interview with José Angel Gutiérrez, 2.
44. Service, *The Hunters*.

Chapter 5

1. Pagels, *Revelations*, 133–70.
2. Friesen, *Imperial Cults and the Apocalypse of John*, 150.
3. This sociohistorical analysis of Revelation is largely influenced by Pagels and Fiorenza, *Revelation: Vision of a Just World*; Kovacs and Rowland, *Revelation: Blackwell Bible Commentaries*.
4. In the Old and New Testaments, this woman represents God's people (Gen. 37: 9–11). Later, the Virgin Mary, as immaculately conceived, would be described with very similar language.
5. The most extensive feminist reading of Revelation is by Rossing, *The Choice Between Two Cities*. See also Malina, *The New Jerusalem in the Revelation of John*.
6. Mayo, *"Those Who Call Themselves Jews"*; Friesen, "Sarcasm in Revelation 2–3: Churches, Christians, True Jews, and Satanic Synagogues," 127–46; Buell, *Why This New Race? Ethnic Reasoning in Early Christianity*.
7. N. Cohen, *The Pursuit of the Millennium*.

8. King Jr., *The Radical King*; Boesak, *Comfort and Protest*; Berrigan, *The Nightmare of God*.

9. Lamadrid, "Reconsidering Reies López Tijerina," 430.

Chapter 6

1. Gardner, *¡Grito!*, 39; "Biography," RTP, Box 53, File 43, 15.

2. The only extant copy of *Hallará Fe en La Tierra . . . ?* can be found in RTP, Box 54, File 2. Historian Rudy V. Busto asserts that the book was published in April 1954, which is wrong. The oldest sermon in the book is dated November 22, 1954. Given the length of time it would have taken to publish the book, it had to have been printed no earlier than 1955. Busto counts forty-three sermons. *Will He Find Any Faith on Earth . . . ?* contains forty-five sermons with distinct titles. See Busto, *King Tiger*, 224, notes 69, 99.

3. I analyzed these sermons employing Voyant Tools, a content analysis software program that produces word frequencies, among other things. *Will He Find Any Faith on Earth . . . ?* contains 64,000 words, give or take, added as footnote clarifications of my own. God is mentioned 1,034 times, followed by 434 invocations of Jesus Christ. Reies imagines God primarily as a stern law-giving king, who was due obedience because of his commandments (190) and laws (116), which together totals 306 uses. God's judgment (95) will be exercised on those who do not accept his commandments. The virtues that lead humanity to salvation are love (322), mercy (290), justice (284), faith (201), humility (106), wisdom (42), and honor (71). Satan and the devil (216) estrange women and men from God through arrogance (163), vanity (114), egoism, selfishness, and haughtiness (42), avarice and greed (25), adultery and fornication (23), drinking and drunkenness caused by the consumption of liquor (22), and gluttony (3). Using language directly from Revelation, Reies decries the sins of Babylon's inhabitants (72), the seductions of its lecherous whore (32), and Jerusalem's Pharisees (50) who colluded with the beast (18) to have Jesus killed. He invoked the words of Old Testament prophets—Moses (10), Isaiah (6), Jeremiah (4), and Daniel (4)—recounting how each had tried to restore God's covenant with Israel and the Israelites (25) and failed. But like the residents of Sodom and Gomorrah (6) and those of Nineveh (6), who ignored God's laws, they eventually were judged and harshly punished.

4. Appendix 1 reprints the original sermons in Spanish and in English translation.

5. Luce, *The Messenger and His Message*. The Spanish translation of this book is still available as *El Mensajero y Su Mensaje*.

6. Luce, *El Mensajero y Su Mensaje*, 10, 27, 11.

7. "The Clamor of the Earth."

8. "The Clamor of the Earth"; "The Just One's Clamor."

9. Gardner, *¡Grito!*, 39; "Biography," RTP, Box 53, File 43, 15.

10. "The Clamor of the Earth."

11. "The Clamor of the Earth"; "Confusion and Shame."

12. "Faith Without Mercy."
13. "The Clamor of the Earth; Confusion and Shame."
14. "The Lost Justice."
15. "Let Us Return to Our Maker."
16. "The People Without Honor."
17. "The Evil in the Seat of the Good."
18. "Faith Without Mercy."
19. "Who Will Be Saved?"; "The Enemies of the Cross."
20. "The Provocateurs of Judgment"; Gardner, ¡Grito!, 39, emphasis in the original.
21. "The Enemies of the Cross."
22. "The Lost Love."
23. "The Faith of Our Times."
24. "The Lost Image."
25. "The Lost Wise Man."
26. "The Captive People—Leave, Leave."
27. "Descendants of the Pharisees."
28. "The Clamor of the Earth."
29. "The Lost Wise Man."
30. "The Prudent Will Understand."
31. "The Arrogant of This Generation."
32. "The Servants of Babylon."
33. "Faith Without Mercy."
34. "The Clamor of the Earth"; "The Faith of Our Times"; "The Lost Wise"; "The Captive People—Leave, Leave"; "Shame and Confusion"; "Listen Wise Ones"; "The Provocateurs of Judgment"; "The People Without Honor"; "The Enemies of the Cross."
35. "The Captive People—Leave, Leave."
36. "The Provocateurs of Judgment."
37. "The Clamor of the Earth."
38. "The Faith of Our Times."
39. "Shame and Confusion."
40. "The Enemies of the Cross."
41. "The People Without Honor."
42. "The Servants of Babylon."
43. "The Lost Wise Man."
44. "The Captive People—Leave, Leave."
45. "The Weapons of Babylon."
46. "Descendants of the Pharisees."
47. "The Clamor of the Earth."
48. "The Lost Wise Man."
49. "The Prudent Will Understand."
50. "The Lost Image."

51. "The Day of God."
52. "Who Will Be Saved?"
53. "The Lost Image."
54. "Who Will Be Saved?"
55. "The Yearning of Those Who Adore."
56. Rossing, *The Choice Between Two Cities*.
57. "The Unfaithful Spouse."
58. Ibid.
59. Ibid.
60. Ibid.
61. "Do We Lack Teachers?"
62. "Words to the Last Generation."
63. "The Faith of Our Times."
64. "False Confidence."
65. "The Merciful One Was Missing."
66. "To Whom Does Justice Belong?"
67. "The Unfaithful Spouse."
68. "The Just One's Clamor."
69. "This Generation's Justice."
70. "The Real Salary."
71. Ibid.
72. "The Enemies of the Cross."
73. "What Is Mercy?"
74. "The Lost Justice."
75. "Justice that Does not Perish."
76. "The Clamor of the Earth."
77. "The Ignored Sacrifice."
78. "Listen Wise Ones," 4; "The Faith of Our Times."
79. "The Merciful One Was Missing."
80. "Where Is Our Benefit?"
81. "The Arrogant of this Generation."
82. Larson, *Summer of the Gods*.
83. Harding, 62.
84. Ibid., 65, 77.
85. "The Arrogant Generation."
86. "Where is Faith?"
87. Spittler describes the Bible as a "sacred meteor" in "Scripture and the Theological Enterprise," 63.
88. William Seymour, *Apostolic Faith*, October 1906, 4, as quoted in Wacker, "Playing for Keeps," 196–219, quotation on 200.
89. Brumback, *Suddenly . . . from Heaven*.
90. "The Servants of Babylon."

91. "Confusion and Shame."
92. The anthropological dimensions of honor and shame have been most extensively studied in Peristiany, ed., *Honour and Shame*; Pitt-Rivers, *The People of the Sierra*; R. Gutiérrez, *When Jesus Came, the Corn Mothers Went Away*.
93. "The Faith of Our Times."
94. "The Captive People—Leave, Leave."
95. Ibid.
96. "The Clamor of the Earth."
97. "The Lost Image."
98. "The Faith of Our Times."
99. The divorce date is listed in a report from Joe Padilla to Santos Quintana regarding Reies's parole request, dated August 18, 1970, in ASP, Box 1, File 4.
100. "The Merciful One Was Missing."
101. "Faith Without Mercy."
102. "Where Is the Wise Man?"
103. "The Lost Image."
104. Ibid.
105. "The Vanquished People."
106. Ibid.
107. "The Servants of Babylon."
108. "The Provocateurs of Judgment."
109. "The Vanquished People."
110. "Descendants of the Pharisees."
111. "The Provocateurs of Judgment."
112. "Descendants of the Pharisees."
113. Ibid.
114. "The Provokers of Judgment."
115. "Good Passes for Evil."
116. "The Provokers of Judgment."
117. Ibid.

Chapter 7

1. Tijerina, *Mi lucha por la tierra*, 27.
2. Ibid.; Gardner, *¡Grito!*, 45.
3. Tijerina, *Mi lucha por la tierra*, 27; María Escobar interview with Ramón Gutiérrez; Reies Tijerina, *My Life, Judaism, and the Nuclear Age* (unpublished manuscript, 1986), 25.
4. Reies Tijerina, as quoted in Tony Hillerman in *The Great Taos Bank Robbery and Other True Stories of the Southwest*, 138.
5. Rose Tijerina as quoted in Oropeza, *The King of Adobe*, 51.
6. Adam Saytanides interview with Rose Tijerina, 2004.

7. Tijerina, *Mi lucha por la tierra*, 27.
8. María Escobar, interview with Ramón Gutiérrez; Reies Tijerina, interview with Ramón Gutiérrez; Gardner, *¡Grito!*, 45.
9. María Escobar, interview with José Angel Gutiérrez, 62; Tijerina, *Mi lucha por la tierra*, 28.
10. Gardner, *¡Grito!*, 45–46.
11. "Tijerina Family History" appears to be a police report in ASP, Box 1, File 18; the reference to "desert rats" comes from David Tijerina, interview with José Angel Gutiérrez, 9.
12. María Escobar, interview with José Angel Gutiérrez, 7; David Tijerina, interview with José Angel Gutiérrez, op. cit. 7–8.
13. María Escobar, interview with José Angel Gutiérrez.
14. Tijerina, *Mi lucha por la tierra*, 38.
15. Ibid., 30.
16. There are several versions of Reies's revelation, his Grand Vision, his transformative life-changing dream. See Jenkins, *Tijerina*, 22; Gardner, *¡Grito!*, 47; Busto, *King Tiger*, 19–20, 121–30; Reies Tijerina, interview with Adam Saytanides, passim.
17. Ibid., 32.
18. Tijerina, *Mi lucha por la tierra*, 33.
19. Laurie Coyle interview with Lillian De La Torre (María Moreno's daughter), telephone conversation.
20. Simón Serna letter to Tijerina, 1963 (incorrectly dated during processing as 1967), RTP, Box 42, File 2.
21. Tijerina, *Mi lucha por la tierra*, 34–35; Gardner, *¡Grito!*, 44; Nabokov, *Tijerina and the Courthouse Raid*, 201, 210.
22. Tijerina, *Mi lucha por la tierra*, 34–36.
23. Rose Tijerina, interview with Adam Saytanides; Oropeza, *The King of Adobe*, 61, 64.
24. Rose Tijerina, interview with Adam Saytanides.
25. Ibid.
26. Oropeza, *King of Adobe*, 52.
27. Rose Tijerina, interview with Adam Saytanides.
28. Reies Tijerina interview with Rose Diaz, June 12–13, 2001, *Guide to the Photo Collection in the Reies López Tijerina Papers*, Center for Southwest Research, University of New Mexico, 8.
29. Soleri, *The Bridge Between Matter and Spirit Is Matter Becoming Spirit*.
30. David Tijerina, interview with José Angel Gutiérrez, 10.
31. Tijerina, *Mi lucha por la tierra*, 40.
32. Offense Report, Pinal Co. Sheriff's Office, Grand Theft, March 19, 1957, in ASP, Box 1, File 18.
33. "Tijerina Family History" in ASP, Box 1, File 18, 3.

Chapter 8

1. Markiewicz, *Ejido Organization in Mexico 1934–1976*; Whetten, *Rural Mexico*, 124–215, ejido distribution statistics, 125.
2. Kosek, *Underhistories*, 1, 224–25.
3. Ibid., 13.
4. Ibid., 14.
5. González, *The Spanish-Americans of New Mexico*, 99.
6. ASP, Box 1, File 18, 69.
7. RTP, Box 59, File 6.
8. The Alianza's stationary carried this motto on its letterhead. See RLT Papers, Box 4, File 15, for examples.
9. Transcript of Treaty of Guadalupe Hidalgo (1848), www.ourdocuments.gov.
10. Alianza minutes, RLT Papers Box 1, File 13; RLT Papers Box 1, File 1. The Alianza's building was purchased as a swap by Los Caballeros de las Indias, under the names of Cristóbal López Tijerina, Santiago Anaya, and Rudy Marez, surrendering ownership of "160 acres of land located NW quarter section 20 township seven south range seven east of the Gila and Salt River Base and Meridian Pinal County Arizona," on June 24, 1964.
11. RTP, Box 1, File 3.
12. "Fight for Lost Lands Goes to Washington," *News Chieftain* 92, no. 17 (May 8, 1964), 1.
13. See the Alianza's minutes, its initial press releases, and "Mensaje a todos los heraderos de las Mercedes Reales," which is the transcript of a KLOS radio broadcast. All are in RLT Papers Box 1, File 1. See, too, "Fight for Lost Lands Goes to Washington," *News Chieftain* 92, no. 17 (May 8, 1964), 1.
14. The Alianza's membership rolls can be found in Boxes 4–31 of the RTP.
15. See "Alliance Planned," *Sacramento Bee*, October 21, 1967, in JMP Box 238, File 18.
16. "Alliance Planned," *Sacramento Bee*, October 21, 1967, JMP, Box 238, File 18. NBC, *Reies Tijerina: The Most Hated Man in New Mexico*, 1969.
17. US Department of Agriculture food surplus distributions were often composed of bricks of cheese, butter, and powdered milk. For farmers who had once owned cows and had fresh milk, this was quite a humiliation.
18. Personal recollection. Also reproduced in Richard Gardner, *¡Grito!*, 93.
19. Tijerina, *They Call Me "King Tiger,"* 71.
20. María Escobar, interview with Ramón Gutiérrez.
21. "Voz de la Justicia," KABQ Radio Station, Albuquerque, NM, April 23, 1965.
22. Tijerina, *Mi lucha por la tierra*, 116–17.
23. Mantler, *Power to the Poor*, 181.
24. "Marchers Decide to Remain Until Campbell Returns Home," *New Mexican* (Santa Fe), July 5, 1966; "12 Marchers Await Return of Governor," *New Mexican* (Santa

Fe), July 7, 1966; "Governor to Send Petition from Marchers to Johnson," *New Mexican* (Santa Fe), July 11, 1966.

25. "Governor to Send Petition from Marchers to Johnson."
26. Tijerina, *Mi lucha por la tierra*, 125.
27. *Albuquerque Journal* (September 4, 1966), A-4, in RTP, Box 2, File 15.
28. Alianza, "NEWS BULLETIN-RELEASE," in RTP, Box 2, File 15 (no date).
29. Albuquerque FBI SAC to Director, October 17, 1967, in RTP, Box 2, File 15.
30. Gardner, *¡Grito!*, 127; Kosek, *Understories*, 44.
31. Tijerina as quoted in Gardner, *¡Grito!*, 48.
32. Both quoted in ibid., 44, 48.
33. Albuquerque FBI SAC to Director, February 21, 1967, in RTP, Box 2, File 15; Don Victoriano Chavez to President Johnson, January 5, 1967, and Ernesto Chavez to City of Albuquerque, April 7, 1967, both in RTP, Box 47, File 19.
34. Hoover to Secret Service, February 21, 1967, RTP, Box 2, File 15, 1,024.
35. Tijerina to Gonzales, March 25, 1967, in Vigil, *The Crusade for Justice*, 30–31.
36. Albuquerque FBI SAC to Director, April 17, 1967, in RTP, Box 2, File 16.
37. Nabokov, *Tijerina and the Courthouse Raid*, 17–18.
38. For oral histories with the participants of these events, see Scarborough, *Trespassers on Our Own Land*; Ruben Sálaz Márquez, *New Mexico: A Brief Multi-History*, 451.
39. Nabokov, *Tijerina and the Courthouse Raid*, op. cit., 106.
40. Albuquerque FBI SAC to Director, June 2, 1967, in RTP, Box 2, File 16, 1076.
41. DeLoach to Wick, June 6, 1967, in RTP, Box 2, File 16, 1,085.
42. Hoover to Albuquerque FBI, June 7, 1967, in RTP, Box 2, File 16, 1,098–1,111.
43. Vina Windes, "Research Reveals Little Information about 'King Tiger,'" *New Mexican*, June 8, 1967, 1.
44. Scarborough, *Trespassers on Our Own Land*, op. cit., 128–63.
45. Grayson Jr., "Tijerina: The Evolution of a Primitive Rebel," 464–66.
46. "Day of Triumph in Tierra Amarilla," *El Grito del Norte* (Española, NM), January 11, 1969, 7.
47. Blawis, *Tijerina and the Land Grants*, op. cit.
48. Ibid.
49. Stang, "Reies Tijerina: The Communist Plot to Grab the Southwest," *American Opinion* (October 1967), 1–22; "Terror Grows: 'War on Poverty' Supports Castroite Terrorists," *American Opinion* (March 1968), 1–17; "New Mexico: The Coming Guerilla War," *American Opinion* (March 1969), 3–16.
50. Della Rose, "Spanish-American Rebel Leader, Tijerina, Faces Prison Sentence in Land Grant Battle," *Los Angeles Free Press*, November 17, 1967, 1; John Gregory Dunne and Joan Didion, "King Tiger," *Saturday Evening Post*, April 20, 1968, 22; Reies López Tijerina, "Remarks," 97–105, quotation on p. 100.
51. Gitlin, *The Sixties*, 245; Hall, "On the Tail of the Panther, I, 59–78; For Senator

James Eastland's incendiary response to the National Conference for New Politics, read his entry into the *Congressional Record* of a number of documents in the hands of the Senate's Internal Security Subcommittee, September 22, 1967, 26, 537–40.

52. Mantler, *Power to the Poor*, 65–66.
53. Gitlin, *The Sixties*, op.cit., 245; Hall, "On the Tail of the Panther," op. cit. 59–78.
54. King Jr., *Where Do We Go from Here*, 31.
55. Convention Program, RTP, Box 1, File 22.
56. Documents relating to the 5th Annual Alianza Convention, October 19–22, 1967, in RTP, Box 1, File 22.
57. Gardner, *¡Grito!*, 223–25.
58. For the peace treaty's articles see Maulana Ron Karenga, "Gente de Color: Vamos a Sobrevivir; People of Color We Shall Survive," in RTP, Box 34, File 24.
59. For this mythology of white ancestry see Montgomery, *The Spanish Redemption*; and Montgomery, "The Trap of Race and Memory," 478–513.
60. Blawis, *Tijerina and the Land Grants*, 100; Gardner, *¡Grito!*, 100–101.
61. Churchill and Vander, eds., *The COINTELPRO Papers*; O'Reilly, *"Racial Matters"*; Haas, *The Assassination of Fred Hampton*.
62. Gutiérrez, "Tracking King Tiger: The Political Surveillance of Reies López Tijerina by the Federal Bureau of Investigation"; Correia, "'Rousers of the Rabble' in the New Mexico Land Grant War," 561–83.
63. The best overall analysis of the Poor Peoples' Campaign can be found in Mantler, *Power to the Poor*, op. cit. Most of the archival material on Tijerina's participation in the march is in RTP, Box 31, Files 20–28, Box 32, Files 1–7.
64. Blawis, *Tijerina and the Land Grants*, 107–25.
65. Transcripts of federal trial stemming from the takeover of the Echo Amphitheatre can be found in RTP, Box 39, Files 2–15.
66. Nabokov, *Tyerina and the Courthouse Raid*, 264.
67. "Instruction on the Right of Citizens' Arrest Given by the Court in the Case of the State of New Mexico v. Reies Tijerina," in Blawis, *Tijerina and the Land Grants*, 181.
68. Tijerina, *My Life, Juda-ism, and the Nuclear Age*, 178.
69. The details of court actions against Reies López Tijerina are spelled out meticulously in a letter from Will Wilson, an assistant attorney general in the US Department of Justice, to Harvard Law Professor Vern Countryman, on April 13, 1971, in RTP, Box 40, File 14. The incarceration dates for his State of New Mexico charges see J. Gutiérrez, *Tracking King Tiger*, 257.
70. Muñoz, *Youth, Identity and Power*.
71. R. Gutiérrez, "Community, Patriarchy and Individualism," 44–72.
72. "Torture of Tijerina," *El Grito del Norte*, October 8, 1970. Tijerina's complaints about the psychotropic drugs he was given to sedate him come from Tijerina, *Mi lucha por la tierra*, 351–90.

73. "Chicano Leader Speaks: Tijerina Pleads for Global Justice, Unity," *Chase*, September 17, 1971, 1 in RTP, Box 32, File 15.

74. RTP, Box 32, File 13; Rose Diaz Interview with Reies López Tijerina (June 14, 2002), 55, 58–59.

75. Press release in RTP, Box 32, File 22.

76. Resolutions in RTP, Box 32, File 36.

77. Tijerina, *My Life, Juda-ism, and the Nuclear Age*, 98.

78. Rose Diaz, interview with Reies López Tijerina, 55, 58–59, 61–63.

79. Tijerina, "Remarks," 97–105, quotation on 101.

80. "Proposal Submitted to the Campaign for Human Development on Behalf of the Pueblo de San Joaquin de Chama by the Institute for the Research and Study of Justice," January 15, 1981, in RTP, Box 32, File 10.

81. RTP, Box 59, Files 24–30.

Chapter 9

1. Tijerina, "From Prison: Reies López Tijerina," 215–22.
2. Tijerina, *They Called Me "King Tiger,"* 160.
3. Gutiérrez, *Tracking King Tiger*, 283.
4. Ibid., 290.
5. The prescription drugs listed on Tijerina's prison medical record were Thorazine, Atropine, Tetracycline, Stelazine, Zactrin, Melloril, Methylpyriline, Maslex, Strazine, Artane, Sod Salicylate, Haldol, Naslicilate Dulcolax, Compazine, Hale, Darvin, Vdrlin, Xylocaine, ampicillin, Demerol, and Nembutal. Ibid., 290.
6. Dr. Leonardo García-Buñuel to Reies Tijerina Jr., August 4, 1970, RTP, Box 54, File 7.
7. Dr. Leonardo García-Buñuel to Judge Howard Bratton, December 6, 1970, both letters in RTP, Box 54, File 7.
8. Ibid.
9. Ibid.
10. For the letters between Reies and Patsy while he was in prison, see RTP, Box 55, Files 1–2.
11. Rachel Tijerina letter to Reies, June 1970 in RTP, Box 55, File 8.
12. Tijerina, *Mi lucha por la tierra*, 355–59.
13. Ibid., 380–82.
14. "Reies López Tijerina Speech at the 20th Anniversary of the Revolution in Tierra Amarilla, June 6, 1987." Special thanks to Enrique Lamadrid for giving me a transcript copy of this speech.
15. Ibid.; Tijerina "Remarks," 97–105
16. Tijerina, *My Life, Juda-ism, and the Nuclear Age*, 175, 185, 230, 259.
17. Tobias, *A History of Jews in New Mexico*; Hordes, *To the End of the Earth*.
18. *Encyclopaedia Judaica* (Jerusalem: Encyclopaedia Judaica/Keter Publishing

House; New York: Macmillan, 1971–1982), 17 vols. On this *Encyclopaedia*, see Levy, "The Making of the *Encyclopaedia Judaica* and the Jewish Encyclopedia."

19. Tijerina's used "Juda-ism" throughout his book manuscript, from the Spanish *Judá*, with "ism." For purposes of clarity herein I substituted Judaism as the faith, Judah or Judea as the place, and only kept "Juda-ism" in direct quotations from his manuscript.

20. Tijerina, *My Life, Juda-ism, and the Nuclear Age*, 48, 57.
21. Fenton, *Old Canaan in A New World*.
22. Tijerina, *My Life, Juda-ism, and the Nuclear Age*, 57.
23. Ibid., 53. Shem was the oldest son of Noah; Ham, although placed between Shem and Japeth by Tijerina, was probably Noah's youngest son.
24. Ibid., 48, 54, 55–56, 60, 63.
25. Ibid., 60. See Genesis 9:20–27 for Noah's curse.
26. Ibid, 63, 58. Nimrod was the son of Cush, grandson of Ham, son of Noah (Gen. 10:8–12; 1 Chron. 1:10).
27. Ibid., 266–67.
28. Ibid., 48–49.
29. Ibid., 49, 66, 179.
30. Ibid., 49–50.
31. Ibid., 52–53.
32. "Act of Surinam (August 17, 1665)," in Mendes-Flohr and Reinharz, eds., *The Jew in the Modern World*, 16–17.
33. Tijerina, *My Life, Juda-ism, and the Nuclear Age*, 187, 272.
34. Feiner, *The Jewish Enlightenment*.
35. Tijerina, *My Life, Juda-ism, and the Nuclear Age*, 208.
36. Pagels, *The Origin of Satan*.
37. Tijerina, *My Life, Juda-ism, and the Nuclear Age*, 274.
38. Ibid., 208.
39. Ibid., 67, 303, 312.
40. Ibid., 62, 67, 297, 301–3, 312.
41. Meltzer, "The Children of Jacob," 58–71.
42. ASP, Box 1, Files 18, 22, and Box 1, File 8, 44–53
43. ASP, Box 1, Files 18, 22, and Box 1, File 8, 44–53.
44. Tijerina, *Mi lucha por la tierra*, 116–17.
45. Simon Romero, "60's Latino Militant Now Pursues a Personal Quest," *New York Times*, May 5, 2006.
46. Reies to Esperanza Tijerina, RTP, Box 55, File 3.
47. María Escobar, interview with José Angel Gutiérrez, 19.
48. David Tijerina, interview by José Angel Gutiérrez, 15–16; Noah Tijerina, *A Cause to Die For*, unpublished book manuscript, 2007, in NTP, 52.
49. N. Tijerina, *A Cause to Die For*, 23.
50. Noah Tijerina, interview with José Angel Gutiérrez, 5.
51. N. Tijerina, *A Cause to Die For*, 23.

52. Ibid.
53. Noah Tijerina, interview with José Angel Gutiérrez, 23.
54. Rose Tijerina Duran, interview with José Angel Gutiérrez, 7.
55. Gutiérrez, Meléndez, and Noyola, *Chicanas in Charge*, 69–70.
56. Mexico City trip explained by Reies Tijerina, *Mi lucha por la tierra*, 101; Rose Tijerina interview with Lorena Oropeza, as quoted in *The King of Adobe*, 90–92.
57. Rose Tijerina Duran, interview with José Angel Gutiérrez, 36–39.
58. Ibid., 56–70.
59. Ibid., 30. The quotation in Spanish reads: "Que yo iba ser el vaso de donde la Alianza, de la causa, iba tomar de mi. Que yo era el vaso de la causa."
60. Larry Calloway, "Skeletons of the Past Live With Her," *Albuquerque Journal*, June 5, 1992, in RTP, Box 55, File 6.
61. "Washington Jr. High School Student Grievances," April 1968, RTP, Box 55, File 8.
62. "Address of Daniel E. Tijerina," in Rinzler ed., *Manifesto: Addressed to the President of the United States from the Youth of America*, 189–93.
63. Letter from Daniel to Reies, September 3, 1971, RTP Papers, B55, F7.
64. Ibid., RTP Papers, B55, F7.
65. Rose Tijerina Duran, interview with José Angel Gutiérrez, 6.
66. Ibid., 10.
67. N. Tijerina, *A Cause to Die For*, 92, 127.
68. Ira de Alá letter to Reies, March 4, 1970, RTP Papers B55, F10.
69. Letter from María Escobar to Reies, [circa 1971] RTP, Box 54, File 32.
70. Order to Show Cause, March 29, 1974, RTP, Box 55, File 9.
71. Rose Tijerina Duran, interview with José Angel Gutiérrez.
72. María Escobar, interview with José Angel Gutiérrez, 22–23.
73. Ibid., 45; N. Tijerina, *A Cause to Die For*, 47.
74. N. Tijerina, *A Cause to Die For*, 8–9.
75. Ibid., 16.
76. Report issued by New Mexico's Attorney General David L. Norvell, RTP, B54, File 11, 6.
77. Rose Tijerina, interview with José Angel Gutiérrez, 32–34.
78. Ibid., 136.
79. N. Tijerina, *A Cause to Die For*, 15–16.
80. Ibid., 15–16.
81. Ibid., 17.
82. Ibid., 14–16, 22–24, 37–38.
83. María Escobar, interview with José Angel Gutiérrez, 49.
84. N. Tijerina, *A Cause to Die For*, 11, 28.
85. Ibid., 199.

Epilogue

1. For María Varela's and my presentations, see Brick and Parker, eds., *A New Insurgency*, 80–84.

2. Nabokov, *Tijerina and the Courthouse Raid*, op. cit., 106.
3. Ibid., 15–16; Gardner, *¡Grito!*, 39.
4. Nabokov, *Tijerina and the Courthouse Raid*, op. cit., 15.
5. "Biography," RTP, Box 53, File 43, 15–16.
6. Ibid.
7. Tijerina, *Mi lucha por la tierra*, 75, 85, 95, 126, 178, 222, 320, 357, 402, 551.
8. Tijerina, *My Life, Juda-ism, and the Nuclear Age*, 221, 202–3.
9. "Governor to Send Petition from Marchers to Johnson," *New Mexican* (Santa Fe), July 11, 1966.
10. ASP, Box 1, File 18, 22, and Box 1, File 8, 44–53.
11. Rose Tijerina Duran, interview with José Angel Gutiérrez, 6.
12. Reies Tijerina to María Varela, September 14, 1967, RTP, Box 41, File 1.
13. María Varela interview with Gordon Mantler, cited in *Power to the Poor*, 179–80.
14. King Jr., *Where Do We Go From Here*, 31.
15. Matthew García, *From the Jaws of Victory: The Triumph and Tragedy of Cesar Chavez and the Farm Worker Movement* (Berkeley: University of California Press, 2014); Luis León, *The Political Spirituality of Cesar Chavez: Crossing Religious Borders* (Oakland: University of California Press, 2015).
16. Tijerina, *My Life, Juda-ism, and the Nuclear Age*, 221.

Appendix 1

1. Ancient Assyrian city in Upper Mesopotamia that because of its wickedness, God planned to destroy. Then they heard God's word, repented, and were spared.
2. *Glossolelia*, or speaking in tongues
3. The biblical citation in the original was incorrect and is now corrected above.
4. John 14:15.
5. The quotation is incorrectly cited. It comes from 2 John 1:6.
6. Tijerina's original sermon here cites Proverbs 21:12. The quotation comes from verse 13, which has been corrected above.
7. This quotation comes from Philippians 4:9, not verse 8, which I have corrected above.
8. Tijerina's statement is incorrect. The first atom smasher was constructed by the Westinghouse Electric Corporation in Forest Hills, Pennsylvania, in 1937.
9. Korah led a contingent of 249 men in a rebellion against Moses and were severely punished by God, who killed all 250 by fire. See Numbers 16:1–41.
10. In the original Spanish-language text of these sermons, this exact sentence is repeated. I have deleted it here suspecting it was an editorial error.

BIBLIOGRAPHY

Manuscript Collections

Center for Southwest Research, Zimmerman Library, University of New Mexico, Albuquerque (CSR).
    Joseph M. Montoya Papers (MSS 386), cited as JMP.
    Peter Nabokov Papers (MSS 93 BC), cited as PNP.
    Alfonso Sanchez Papers (MSS 803), cited as ASP.
    Noé Tijerina Papers (MSS 859 SC), cited as NTP.
    Reies Tijerina Papers (MSS 654 BC) cited as RTP.
    Reies López Tijerina, *La Historia de la Casa de Israel* (1984).
    Reies López Tijerina, *My Life, Juda-ism, and the Nuclear Age* (1986).
Nettie Lee Benson Latin American Collection, University of Texas Libraries, University of Texas at Austin.
    José Angel Gutiérrez Papers, Reies Tijerina Bureau of Prisons, Box 3 of accession #2018–12.

Interviews

David Tijerina, interview with José Angel Gutiérrez, June 28, 2000, Albuquerque. Center for Southwest Research, Zimmerman Library, University of New Mexico, Albuquerque (CSR).
María Escobar, interview with José Angel Gutiérrez, videotape 2000. Center for Southwest Research, Zimmerman Library, University of New Mexico, Albuquerque (CSR).
María Escobar, interview with Ramón Gutiérrez, September 23, 2006, Albuquerque. In author's possession.
Noah Tijerina, interview with José Angel Gutiérrez, July 12, 2012, Albuquerque. Center for Southwest Research, Zimmerman Library, University of New Mexico, Albuquerque (CSR).
Reies López Tijerina, interview with Adam Saytanides, (circa 1992), Taos, New Mexico. In author's possession.
Reies López Tijerina, interview with Ramón Gutiérrez, August 20, 2009, Juárez, Chihuahua, México. In author's possession.
Reies López Tijerina, interview with Ramón Gutiérrez, July 21, 2005, Uruapán, Michoacán, México. In author's possession.

Reies López Tijerina, interview with Rose Diaz, June 12–13, 2001. *Guide to the Photo Collection in the Reies López Tijerina Papers*, Center for Southwest Research, University of New Mexico, 8.

Rose Tijerina Duran, interview with José Angel Gutiérrez, July 3, 2000, Albuquerque Center for Southwest Research, Zimmerman Library, University of New Mexico, Albuquerque (CSR).

Published Sources

Acuña, Rodolfo. *Occupied America: The Chicano's Struggle Toward Liberation.* New York: Harper & Row, 1972.

Alberro, Solange. *Inquisición y sociedad en México 1571–1700.* México: Fondo de Cultura Económica, 1988.

Allen, Roland. *Missionary Methods: St. Paul's or Ours?* 2nd ed. Grand Rapids, MI: Wm. B. Eerdmans, 1962.

Anderson, Robert Mapes. *Vision of the Disinherited: The Making of American Pentecostalism.* New York: Oxford University Press, 1979.

Archivo General de Indias. *Catálogo de pasajeros a Indias durante los siglos XVI, XVII y XVIII.* Madrid: Imprenta Espasa-Calpe, s.a., 1930.

Ball, Henry C. *Himnos de Gloria: Cantos de Triunfo.* Miami: Editorial Vida, 1985, originally published 1923.

Bartleman, Frank. *How Pentecost Came to Los Angeles: As It Was in the Beginning.* Los Angeles: Frank Bartleman, 1925.

Beaver, R. Pierce. "A History of Mission Strategy." *Southwestern Journal of Theology* 12 (Spring 1970), 7–28.

Bell Blawis, Patricia. *Tijerina and the Land Grants: Mexican Americans in Struggle for Their Heritage.* New York: International, 1971.

Berrigan, Daniel. *The Nightmare of God: The Book of Revelation.* Yonkers, NY: Rose Hill Books, 1983.

Blumhofer, Edith L. *Restoring the Faith: The Assemblies of God, Pentecostalism, and American Culture.* Urbana: University of Illinois Press, 1993.

Boesak, Allan A. *Comfort and Protest: Reflections on the Apocalypse of John of Patmos.* Philadelphia: Westminster, 1987.

Boyer, Paul. *By the Bomb's Early Light: American Thought and Culture at the Dawn of the Atomic Age.* New York: Pantheon Books, 1985.

———. *Fallout: A Historian Reflects on America's Half-Century Encounter with Nuclear Weapons.* Columbus: Ohio State University Press, 1998.

———. *When Time Shall Be No More: Prophecy Belief in Modern American Culture.* Cambridge, MA: Belknap, 1992.

Brick, Howard, and Gregory Parker, eds. *A New Insurgency: The Port Huron Statement and Its Times.* Ann Arbor: Maize, 2015.

Brumback, Carl. *Suddenly . . . from Heaven: A History of the Assemblies of God.* Springfield, MO: Gospel, 1961.

Buell, Denise Kimber. *Why This New Race? Ethnic Reasoning in Early Christianity*. New York: Columbia University Press, 2005.
Busto, Rudy V. *King Tiger: The Religious Vision of Reies López Tijerina*. Albuquerque: University of New Mexico Press, 2005.
Carlson, Alvar W. *The Spanish-American Homeland: Four Centuries in New Mexico's Río Arriba*. Baltimore: Johns Hopkins University Press, 1990.
Cargo, David Francis. *Lonesome Dave: The Story of New Mexico Governor David Francis Cargo*. Santa Fe: Sunstone, 2010.
Castro, Américo. *The Spaniards: An Introduction to their History*. Berkeley: University of California Press, 1971.
Churchill, Ward, and Jim Vander, eds. *The COINTELPRO Papers: Documents from the FBI's Secret Wars Against Domestic Dissent*. Boston: South End, 1990.
Clark, Elmer T. *The Latin Immigrant in the South*. Nashville, TN: Cokesbury, 1924.
Coalson, George O. *The Development of the Migratory Farm Labor System in Texas: 1900–1954*. San Francisco: R & E Research Associates, 1977.
Cohen, Martin A. *The Martyr Luis de Carvajal: A Secret Jew in Sixteenth-Century Mexico*. Albuquerque: University of New Mexico Press, 2001.
Cohen, Norman. *The Pursuit of the Millennium: Revolutionary Millenarians and Mystical Anarchists of the Middle Ages*. New York: Oxford University Press, 1957.
Collado, A. B. "Reies Tijerina: Hero or Malhechor?" *El Hispano* 2, no. 8 (August 8, 1967): 1, 3.
Conrad, David Eugene. *The Forgotten Farmers: The Story of Sharecroppers in the New Deal*. Urbana: University of Illinois Press, 1965.
Correia, David. *Properties of Violence: Law and Land Grant Struggle in Northern New Mexico*. Athens: University of Georgia Press, 2013.
———. "'Rousers of the Rabble' in the New Mexico Land Grant War: *La Alianza Federal de Mercedes* and the Violence of the State." *Antipode* 40, no. 2 (2008), 561–83.
Davis, William C. *Lone Star Rising: The Revolutionary Birth of the Texas Republic*. New York: Free Press, 2004.
De León, Arnoldo, and Kenneth L. Stewart. *Tejanos and the Numbers Game: A Socio-Historical Interpretation from the Federal Censuses, 1850–1900*. Albuquerque: University of New Mexico Press, 1989.
Deutsch, Sarah. *No Separate Refuge: Culture, Class, and Gender on an Anglo-Hispanic Frontier in the American Southwest, 1880–1940*. New York: Oxford University Press, 1987.
Dower, John. *War Without Mercy: Race and Power in the Pacific War*. New York: Pantheon, 1986.
Espinosa, Gastón. "Brown Moses: Francisco Olazábal and Mexican American Pentecostal Healing in the Borderlands." In *Mexican American Religions: Spirituality, Activism, and Culture*, edited by Gastón Espinosa and Mario García, 263–95. Durham, NC: Duke University Press, 2008.
———. "'El Azteca': Francisco Alazábal and Latino Pentecostal Charisma, Power and Faith Healing in the Borderlands." *Journal of the American Academy of Religion* 67, no. 3 (1999), 597–616.

———. *Latino Pentecostals in America: Faith and Politics in Action*. Cambridge, MA: Harvard University Press, 2014.
Feiner, Shmuel. *The Jewish Enlightenment*, Chaya Naor, trans. Philadelphia: University of Pennsylvania Press, 2002.
Fenton, Elizabeth. *Old Canaan in A New World: Native Americans and the Lost Tribes of Israel*. New York: New York University Press, 2020.
Foley, Neil. *The White Scourge: Mexicans, Blacks and Poor Whites in Texas Cotton Culture*. Berkeley: University of California Press, 1997.
Forman, Charles W. "A History of Foreign Mission Theory in America." In *American Missions in Bicentennial Perspective*, edited by R. Pierce Beaver, 63–80. South Pasadena, CA: William Carey Library, 1977.
Fox, Cybelle. *The Three Worlds of Relief: Race, Immigration, and the American Welfare State from the Progressive Era to the New Deal*. Princeton, NJ: Princeton University Press, 2012.
Friesen, Steven J. *Imperial Cults and the Apocalypse of John: Reading Revelation in Ruins*. New York: Oxford University Press, 2001.
———. "Sarcasm in Revelation 2–3: Churches, Christians, True Jews, and Satanic Synagogues." In *The Reality of Apocalypse: Rhetoric and Politics in the Book of Revelation*, edited by David L. Barr, 127–46. Atlanta: Society of Biblical Literature, 2006.
García, Juan R. *Mexicans in the Midwest, 1900–1932*. Tucson: University of Arizona Press, 1996.
García, Mario T. *Desert Immigrants: The Mexicans of El Paso, 1880–1920*. New Haven, CT: Yale University Press, 1981.
García, Matthew. *From the Jaws of Victory: The Triumph and Tragedy of Cesar Chavez and the Farm Worker Movement*. Berkeley: University of California Press, 2014.
Gardner, Richard. *¡Grito!: Reies Tijerina and the New Mexico Land Grant War of 1967*. New York: Harper & Row, 1970.
Geddes, Donald Porter, and Gerald Wendt, eds. *The Atomic Age Opens*. New York: Pocket Books, 1945.
Gibson, Campbell, and Kay Jung. *Historical Census Statistics on Population Totals by Race, 1790 to 1990, and by Hispanic Origin, 1970 to 1990, for the United States, Regions, Divisions, and States*. Washington, DC: US Census Bureau, 2002. Table E-7.
Gilman, Sander L., and Milton Shain. *Jewries at the Frontier: Accommodation, Identity, Conflict*. Urbana: University of Illinois Press, 1999.
Gitlin, Todd. *The Sixties: Years of Hope, Days of Rage*. New York: Bantam, 1987.
Gitlitz, David M. *Secrecy and Deceit: The Religion of Crypto-Jews*. Albuquerque: University of New Mexico Press, 1996.
Gómez, Laura E. *Manifest Destinies: The Making of the Mexican American Race*. New York: New York University Press, 2007.
González, Nancie L. *The Spanish-Americans of New Mexico: A Heritage of Pride*. Albuquerque: University of New Mexico Press, 1967.

Grayson, George W. Jr. "Tijerina: The Evolution of a Primitive Rebel." *Commonweal* (July 28, 1967), 464–66.
Griswold del Castillo, Richard. *The Treaty of Guadalupe Hidalgo: A Legacy of Conflict.* Norman: University of Oklahoma Press, 1990.
Gutiérrez, José Angel. Introduction to *They Called Me "King Tiger": My Struggle for the Land and Our Rights,* by Reies López Tijerina. Houston, TX: Arte Público, 2000.
———. "Tracking King Tiger: The Political Surveillance of Reies López Tijerina by the Federal Bureau of Investigation." Paper presented at the 23rd National Association for Chicana and Chicano Studies, March 20–23, 1996.
———. *Tracking King Tiger: Reies López Tijerina and the FBI.* East Lansing: Michigan State University Press, 2019.
Gutiérrez, José Angel, Michelle Meléndez, and Sonia Adriana Noyola. *Chicanas in Charge: Texas Women in the Public Arena.* Lanham, MD: Altamira, 2007.
Gutiérrez, Ramón A. "Community, Patriarchy and Individualism: The Politics of Chicano History." *American Quarterly* 45, no. 1 (March 1993), 44–72.
———. *When Jesus Came, the Corn Mothers Went Away: Marriage, Sexuality, and Power in New Mexico, 1500–1846.* Stanford, CT: Stanford University Press, 1991.
Haas, Jeffrey. *The Assassination of Fred Hampton: How the FBI and the Chicago Police Murdered a Black Panther.* Chicago: Chicago Review, 2010.
Hall, Simon. "On the Tail of the Panther: Black Power and the 1967 Convention of the National Conference for New Politics." *Journal of American Studies* 37, no 1 (2003), 59–78.
Hammett, A. B. J. *The Empresario: Don Martín de León.* Waco: Texian Press, 1973.
Harding, Susan Friend. *The Book of Jerry Falwell: Fundamentalist Language and Politics.* Princeton, NJ: Princeton University Press, 2000.
Harris, Ralph W. *Spoken by the Spirit: Documented Accounts of "Other Tongues" from Arabic to Zulu.* Springfield, MO: Gospel, 1973.
Hietala, Thomas R. *Manifest Design: Anxious Aggrandizements in Late Jacksonian America.* Ithaca, NY: Cornell University Press, 1985.
Hillerman, Tony. *The Great Taos Bank Robbery and Other True Stories of the Southwest.* New York: Perennial, 2001.
Hollenwegger, Walter J. *The Pentecostals.* London: SCM, 1972.
Hordes, Stanley M. *To the End of the Earth: A History of the Crypto-Jews of New Mexico.* New York: Columbia University Press, 2005.
Horsman, Reginald. *Race and Manifest Destiny: The Origins of American Racial Anglo-Saxonism.* Cambridge, MA: Harvard University Press, 1981.
Jarman Hagood, Margaret. *Mothers of the South: Portraiture of the White Tenant Farm Women.* New York: W. W. Norton, 1939.
Jenkins, John H., ed. *The Papers of the Texas Revolution, 1835–36.* Austin: Presidial, 1973.
Jenkinson, Michael. *Tijerina: Land Grant Conflict in New Mexico.* Agora Hills, CA: Paisano, 1968.

Johnson, Benjamin Heber. *Revolution in Texas: How a Forgotten Rebellion and Its Bloody Suppression Turned Mexicans into Americans*. New Haven, CT: Yale University Press, 2003.
King Jr., Martin Luther. *The Radical King*. Edited by Cornel West. Boston: Beacon, 2015.
———. *Where Do We Go from Here: Chaos or Community?* Boston: Beacon, 1968.
Kosek, Jake. *Underhistories: The Political Life of Forests in Northern New Mexico*. Durham, NC: Duke University Press, 2006.
Kovacs, Judith, and Christopher Rowland. *Revelations: Blackwell Bible Commentaries*. Oxford, UK: Blackwell, 2004.
Lamadrid, Enrique. "Reconsidering Reies López Tijerina: The Ethnopoetics of the Rise of a Prophet and His Fall from Grace." *New Mexico Historical Review* 92, no. 4 (Fall 2017), 401–52.
Larson, Edward J. *Summer of the Gods: The Scopes Trial and America's Continuing Debate over Science and Religion*. New York: Basic Books, 1997.
Laurence, William. *Dawn Over Zero: The Story of the Atomic Bomb*. London: Museum Press, 1947.
———. *Luis León, The Political Spirituality of Cesar Chavez: Crossing Religious Borders*. Oakland: University of California Press, 2015.
Levy, David B. "The Making of the Encyclopaedia Judaica and the Jewish Encyclopedia." Proceedings of the 37th Annual Convention of the Association of Jewish Libraries, 2002.
Luce, Alice E. *Estudios de las Evidencias Cristianas*. Miami: Editorial Vida, 1965.
———. *Hermeneutica: Introducción Biblica*. Miami: Editorial Vida, 1964.
———. *El Mensajero y Su Mensaje*. Miami: Editorial Vida, 1953.
———. *The Messenger and His Message: A Handbook for Young Workers on the Preparation of Gospel Addresses*. Springfield, MO: Gospel Publishing, 1925.
———. *Probad los Espiritu. Si Son de Dios*. San Antonio, TX: Casa Evangélica de Publicaciones, 1900.
Luce, Alice E., and Henry C. Ball. *Himnos de Gloria y Triunfo*. Miami: Editorial Vida, 1985.
Malina, Bruce J. *The New Jerusalem in the Revelation of John: The City as Symbol of Life with God*. Collegeville, MN: Liturgical, 1995.
Mantler, Gordon K. *Power to the Poor: Black-Brown Coalition and the Fight for Economic Justice, 1960–1974*. Chapel Hill: University of North Carolina Press, 2013.
Mariscal, George. *Brown-Eyed Children of the Sun: Lessons from the Chicano Movement, 1965–1975*. Albuquerque: University of New Mexico Press, 2005.
Markiewicz, Dana. *Ejido Organization in Mexico 1934–1976*. Los Angeles: UCLA Latin American Center Publications, 1980.
Mayo, Philip L. *"Those Who Call Themselves Jews": The Church and Judaism in the Apocalypse of John*. Eugene, OR: Pickwick, 2006.
MacRobert, Iain. The Black Roots of White Racism in Early Pentecostalism. New York: St. Martin's Press, 1988.
McCombs, Vernon Monroe. *From Over the Border: A Study of the Mexicans in the United*

States. New York: Council of Women for Home Missions and Missionary Education Movement, 1925.
McGee, Gary B. *"This Gospel . . . Shall Be Preached": A History and Theology of Assemblies of God Foreign Missions to 1959*. Springfield, MO: Gospel, 1986.
McLean, Robert N., and Charles A. Thompson. *Spanish and Mexican in Colorado: A Survey of the Spanish Americans in the State of Colorado*. New York: Board of the National Missions of the Presbyterian Church in the U.S.A., 1924.
McNeill, Don. "Tijerina: Flashback to A Forgotten Frontier." *Village Voice* (August 1, 1969), 37–40.
Meier, Matt S., and Feliciano Rivera. *The Chicanos: A History of Mexican Americans*. New York: Hill & Wang, 1972.
Meltzer, David J. "The Children of Jacob: Using Evolutionary Biology to Explore Genesis." *CCAR Journal: A Reform Jewish Quarterly* (Fall 2002), 58–71.
Mencken, H. L. *A Religious Orgy in Tennessee: A Reporter's Account of the Scopes Monkey Trial*. Hoboken, NJ: Melville, 2006.
Mendes-Flohr, Paul, and Jehuda Reinharz, eds. *The Jew in the Modern World: A Documentary History*. New York: Oxford University Press, 2010.
Menefee, Selden C. *Mexican Migratory Workers of South Texas*. Washington, DC: Federal Works Agency, WPA, 1941.
Montejano, David. *Anglos and Mexicans in the Making of Texas, 1836–1986*. Austin: University of Texas Press, 1987.
Montgomery, Charles. *The Spanish Redemption: Heritage, Power and the Loss of New Mexico's Upper Rio Grande*. Berkeley: University of California Press, 2002.
———. "The Trap of Race and Memory: The Language of Spanish Civility in the Upper Rio Grande." *American Quarterly* 52 (Fall 2000), 478–513.
Montoya, María E. *Translating Property: The Maxwell Land Grant and the Conflict in the American West, 1840–1900*. Berkeley: University of California Press, 2002.
Muñoz, Carlos. *Youth, Identity and Power: The Chicano Movement*. New York: Verso, 1989.
Nabokov, Peter. *Tijerina and the Courthouse Raid*. Albuquerque: University of New Mexico Press, 1969.
National Broadcasting Company. *Reies Tijerina: The Most Hated Man in New Mexico*. TV documentary (videotape), 1969.
O'Reilly, Kenneth. *"Racial Matters": The FBI's Secret Folder on Black America, 1960–1972*. New York: Free Press, 1989.
Oropeza, Lorena. "Becoming Indo-Hispano: Reies López Tijerina and the New Mexican Land Grant Movement." In *Formations of United States Colonialism*, edited by Alyosha Goldstein, 180–206. Durham, NC: Duke University Press, 2014.
———. *The King of Adobe: Reies López Tijerina, Lost Prophet of the Chicano Movement*. Chapel Hill: University of North Carolina Press, 2019.
Pagels, Elaine. *The Origin of Satan*. New York: Random House, 1995.
———. *Revelations: Visions, Prophecy, and Politics in the Book of Revelation*. New York: Viking, 2012.

Pagels, Elaine, and Elisabeth Schüssler Fiorenza. *Revelation: Vision of a Just World*. Minneapolis, MN: Fortress, 1991.
Parham, Charles F. *A Voice Crying in the Wilderness*. Baxter Springs, KS: Joplin, 1944.
Parham, Sarah E. *The Life of Charles F. Parham*. Joplin, MO: Tri-State, 1930.
Peristiany, J. G., ed. *Honour and Shame: The Values of Mediterranean Society*. Chicago: University of Chicago Press, 1965.
Pitt-Rivers, Julian. *The People of the Sierra*. Chicago: University of Chicago Press, 1966.
Rabinowitch, Edward. "Five Years After." *Bulletin of the Atomic Scientists* 7, no. 1 (January 1951), 3–5, 12.
Ramírez, Daniel. "Borderlands Praxis: The Immigrant Experience in Latino Pentecostal Churches." *Journal of the American Academy of Religion* 67, no. 3 (1999), 573–96.
———. *Migrating Faith: Pentecostalism in the United States and Mexico in the Twentieth Century*. Chapel Hill: University of North Carolina Press, 2015.
Reich, David. *Who We Are and How We Got Here: Ancient DNA and the New Science of the Human Past*. New York: Pantheon, 2018.
Richardson, Chad, and Michael J. Pisani. *Batos, Bolillos, Pochos, and Pelados: Class and Culture on the South Texas Border*. Austin: University of Texas Press, 1999.
Rinzler, Alan ed. *Manifesto: Addressed to the President of the United States from the Youth of America*. New York: Macmillan, 1970.
Robeck, Cecil M. *The Azusa Street Mission and Revival: The Birth of the Global Pentecostal Movement*. Nashville: Nelson Reference & Electronic, 2006.
Rodríguez, José María. *Memoirs of Early Texas*. San Antonio: Passing Show, 1913.
Rosenbaum, Robert J. *Mexicano Resistance in the Southwest: "The Sacred Right of Self Preservation."* Austin: University of Texas Press, 1981.
Rosenzweig, Roy, and David Thelen. *The Presence of the Past: Popular Uses of History in American Life*. New York: Columbia University Press, 1998.
Rossing, Barbara R. *The Choice Between Two Cities: Whore, Bride, and Empire in the Apocalypse*. Harrisburg, PA: Trinity, 1999.
Samarin, William J. "The Linguisticality of Glossolalia." *Hartford Quarterly* 3, no. 4 (Summer 1968), 49–75.
Sánchez Walsh, Arlene. *Latino Pentecostal Identity: Evangelical Faith, Self, and Society*. New York: Columbia University Press, 2003.
Sanders, Cheryl J. *Saints in Exile: The Holiness-Pentecostal Experience in African American Religion and Culture*. New York: Oxford University Press, 1996.
Savage, Kenzy. *The Spirit Bade Me Go (Simon Peter, Acts 11:12): Rambling with Kenzy—Hebrews 11:8*. Kearney, NE: Morris, 2000.
Scarborough, Mike. *Trespassers on Our Own Land: Structured as an Oral History of the Juan P. Valdez Family and of the Land Grants of Northern New Mexico*. Indianapolis, IN: Dog Ear, 2011.
Seguín, Juan Nepomuceno. *Personal Memoirs of John N. Seguín: From the Year 1834 to the Retreat of General Woll from the City of San Antonio in 1842*. San Antonio: Ledger Book & Job Office, 1858.

Service, Elman R. *The Hunters*. Englewood Cliffs, NJ: Prentice-Hall, 1979.
Soleri, Paolo. *The Bridge Between Matter and Spirit Is Matter Becoming Spirit: The Arcology of Paulo Soleri*. Garden City, NY: Anchor, 1973.
Sonnichsen, C. L. *The El Paso Salt War*. El Paso: Texas Western, 1961.
Spittler, Russell P. "Scripture and the Theological Enterprise: View from a Big Canoe." In *The Use of the Bible in Theology: Evangelical Options*, edited by Robert K. Johnston, 56–77. Atlanta: John Know, 1985.
Stimpson Jr., Eddie. *My Remembers: A Black Sharecropper's Recollections of the Depression*. Denton: University of North Texas Press, 1996.
Taylor, Paul S. *Mexican Labor in the United States: Dimmit County, Winter Garden District of South Texas*. Berkeley: University of California Press, 1930.
Tijerina, Reies López. "From Prison: Reies López Tijerina." In *The Chicanos: Mexican American Voices*, edited by Ed Ludwig and James Santibañez, 215–22. Baltimore: Penguin, 1971.
———. *Mi lucha por la tierra*. México, DF; Fondo de la Cultura Económica, 1978.
———. "Remarks." In *Memoria de Encuentro Chicano México: 1988*, edited by Axel Ramírez, 97–105. México: Universidad Autónoma de Mexico, Centro de Enseñanza para Estranjeros, 1992.
———. *They Called Me "King Tiger": My Struggle for the Land and Our Rights*. Translated and edited by José Angel Gutiérrez. Houston: Arte Público, 2000.
Tobias, Henry Jack. *A History of Jews in New Mexico*. Albuquerque: University of New Mexico Press, 1990.
Valdés, Dennis Nodín. *Al Norte: Agricultural Workers in the Great Lakes Region, 1917–1970*. Austin: University of Texas Press, 1991.
———. *Barrios Norteños: St. Paul and Midwestern Mexican Communities in the Twentieth Century*. Austin: University of Texas Press, 2000.
Vargas, Zaragosa. *Proletarians of the North: A History of Mexican Industrial Workers in Detroit and the Midwest, 1917–1933*. Berkeley: University of California Press, 1993.
Vigil, Ernesto B. *The Crusade for Justice: Chicano Militancy and the Government's War on Dissent*. Madison: University of Wisconsin Press, 1999.
Wacker, Grant. "Playing for Keeps: The Primitivist Impulse in Early Pentecostalism." In *The American Quest for the Primitive Church* edited by Richard T. Hughes, 196–219. Urbana: University of Illinois Press, 1988.
Whetten, Nathan L. *Rural Mexico*. Chicago: University of Chicago Press, 1948.

INDEX

Page numbers in italic text indicate illustrations.

Abernathy, Ralph, 179, *180*
Abraham (biblical), 200–201, 203
Acts of the Apostles, 47, 50, 92
African Americans, 2–3, 29, 162, 169, 177–78, 231; in Pentecostal movement, 49–50
Alberro, Solange, 21
Albuquerque Journal, 164, 167, 175, 180–81, 186, 214, 221
Alianza Federal de Mercedes, 1, 3, 9–10, 13; Escobar in, 153, 208–9, 217–18; formation and incorporation of, 17, 152–53, 224; on Indo-Hispanos, 153–55, *155*, *156*, 206, 208, 228; "Information from the Alianza Federal de Mercedes" in *News Chieftain*, 159–61; Kit Carson National Forest occupation, 17, 166, 177, 183, 224, 227–28; marches and rallies, 162–63, *165*, 168; media strategy, 231; membership growth, 1960s, 157; motto of, 153, *158*; National Constitution of, 154; national conventions, 164, 168–69, 176–78, 231–32; *Noticias de la Alianza Federal de Mercedes* of, 11; Romero, P., rape allegations and, 218–19; scripted meetings of, 1963-166, 158–59; Tierra Amarilla Courthouse Raid, 5, 169, 183, 186, 188, 209, 214, 216, 224–25, 228; Tijerina children and, 209–10, 212, 214, 216–18; on Treaty of Guadalupe Hidalgo, 153–54, 159, 162
Alianza Federal de Pueblos Libres, 166–71, 173, 176, 179, 183–84, 186
Allen, Roland, 58
American imperialism, 75, 105, 114, 122, 224, 233
American Southwest: Chicano movement and, 174; colonizers of, 232; ethnic Mexicans in, 1–2, 4, 141; Jews in, 199; Mexican American in, 6–7, 171, 176; property rights in, 5
Anaya, Santiago, 219
Anderson, Mad Bear, *180*
Anglo-Jewish alliance, Tijerina, R. L., on, 204–7
Anglo-Jewish League, 204
anticolonial struggles, 12–13, 104
antiracism, 175
anti-Semitism, 6, 20, 197, 228–30
Apocalypse, 54; atomic bomb and, 3, 71–72, 133, 206–7; Revelation on, 71, 97, 102, 133, 206–7, 227; Tijerina, R. L., on, 7, 71–72, 109, 111, 131–33
Apostolic Faith, 46, 48–49, 54, 57–58, 113; Assemblies of God on, 122–23; Tijerina, R. L., on return to, 123. *See also* Pentecostalism
Apostolic Faith (newspaper), 51–53
The Apostolic Light (*La Luz Apostólica*), 58
Aragón, Duke, *155*

533

arcology, 144
Arizona, 131–32
Arizona State Board of Education, 136
Armageddon, 101, 116
Armonía Fraternal monument, 188, *189*
La Asamblea Apostólica de la Fe en Cristo Jesús, 55
Assemblies of God, 3, 7, 10, 94, 107, 192; on Apostolic Faith, 122–23; First General Council, 58; LABI and, 16, 45–46, 59–60, 63–64, 72–73, 75; Luce and Ball in, 58–61; Mexicans and, 58–60, 63–64, 72, 77–78; missionaries, 58–59, 75–77; NAE, 122; origins of, 57–61; Pentecostalism and, 16, 57, 76–77; Tijerina, R. L., church leaders and, 111–12, 129; Tijerina, R. L., expelled from, 84–85, 95, 110, 113, 141, 226–27; Tijerina, R. L., ministry in, 75–76, 78–84; Tijerina, R. L., on materialism of, 113; women in, 61, 72–73, 77–78
Assemblies of God Bible Institute, 68
atomic bombs, 127, 183, 198; Apocalypse and, 3, 71–72, 133, 206–7; Cold War and, 85–86, 133; Hiroshima, 69–71, 86, 95, 105, 109, 133; Nagasaki, 70–71, 86, 95, 105, 109, 133; Tijerina, R. L., on Jews and, 204, 206
Axelrod, Beverley, 173, 181
Aztlán, 174, 184, 231–32
Azusa Street Mission, 50–55

Babylon, 6, 12, 101–5, 113–16, 200–201
Ball, Henry A., 58–60
Ballard, William, 146
Banyacya, Tomas, 177
Barrajas, María Luisa, 142–44, 210
Bartleman, Frank, 50–53, 55
Basón, Ester, 68
Berean Bible Institute, 59

Bethel Bible School, 47–49
Bible: Bethel Bible School, on literal truth of, 48–49; evangelical Christians on, 122; LABI on, 64–66, 198; Pentecostals on, 56; in sermons, of Tijerina, R. L., 91; Tijerina, R. L., introduced to, 44–45, 64; Tijerina, R. L., on, 110, 221–22; on women, 78. *See also specific books*
Billy Graham Crusades, 121
Black Panthers, 174, 225
Black Power movement, 10, 176, 178, 231–32
Blawis, Patricia Bell, 173
Boddy, A. A., 53
Boesak, Allan, 104
braceros, 86
Bradbury, Norris, 183
Bratton, Howard C., 193–94
Brotherhood Awareness movement, 187–88, *189*, 197, 229, 233
Brumback, Carl, 123
Buckner Fanning Christian School, 42
Burger, Warren, 183
Burke, Tarana, 232
Busto, Rudy V., 510n2
Byers, Bill, 138

Calhoun, John C., 24
Campbell, Jack M., 163
Canjilón lakes, 168
capitalism, 113–14, 125–26, 128–29, 131, 173
"The Captive People—Leave, Leave" (Tijerina, R. L.), 114
Carabajal de Valenzuela, Romana, 55
Cargo, David, 5, 170, 194, 213–14
Carmichael, Stokely, 231
Catholic Church and Roman Catholicism, 36–37, 59–60, 94, 203–4
Catholics, 37, 81, 161

A Cause to Die For (Tijerina, N.), 218
Chávez, Alfonso, 181
Chávez, César, 6–7, 184–85, 232
Chávez, Don Victoriano, 167
Chávez, Eduardo, 154, 167
Chávez, María Escobar. *See* Escobar, María
Chicana feminists, 184–85
Chicano movement, 6–7, 174, 184–85, 231–32
children, of Tijerina, R. L., 81–84, 132–37, 143–44, 186, 193, 208–22; Alianza Federal de Mercedes and, 209–10, 212, 214, 216–18; as migrant workers, 94; sexual abuse of, 140–41, 212–14, 218–21, 232; on Valley of Peace, 209, 212
Christian evangelicals, 47–48
Church of Jesus Christ Latter-Day Saints, 139–40, 200
civil rights: conference, in Washington, DC, 1971, 218; leader, Tijerina, R. L., as, 173–74, 232; movement, 6–7; for racialized minorities, 11
Civil Rights Act of 1964, 179–80, 231
Civil War, US, 2–3
"The Clamor of the Earth" (Tijerina, R. L.), 108–10
Clark, Elmer T., 37
Cleaver, Eldridge, 181
COINTELPRO, 179
Cold War, 85–86, 133
colonialism, 113, 122; imperialism and, 12; Revelation, in revolutionary movements against, 104; of Roman Empire, 6, 12, 97, 99, 126–27
colonization: of Mexico, 138–39, 232; of New Spain, 4–5, 7–8, 232; of Texas, 223
Columbus, Christopher, 204
Comfort and Protest (Boesak), 104
communal land grants (*mercedes*), 3, 7–9, 16, 26, 139, 154. *See also* Alianza Federal de Mercedes; land grants
communism, 128–29, 171, 174
Communist Party USA (CPUSA), 173
Confraternity of Our Lord Jesus Nazaren, 139
Constantine, 122
Constitution, Mexico, 1917, 149
Constitution, US, 149, 159
conversion process, 91–94
Cortina, Juan Nepomuceno, 26
Cortina Wars, 25–26
Cota, Epifano, 56
cotton farming, in Texas, 28–31, 33, 80, 82, 223
CPUSA. *See* Communist Party USA
Crawford, Florence, 52–53
Crusade for Justice, 6–7, 175
Cruz, José, 107
Cruz, Manuel de la, 81
Cuban Revolution, 1959, 173

The Daily World, 173
death, of Tijerina, R. L., 5
democracy, capitalism and, 128
Deuteronomy, 203
Diego, Juan, 141
dispensationalism, 79
Domenici, Pete, 188
Domínguez, Ezekial, 181
Domínguez de Mendoza, Tomé, 161–62
Domitian, 98

Echeverría Álvarez, Luís, 213
Echo Creek Amphitheatre invasion, 166–67, 175, 181–82, 186
Einstein, Albert, 206
Eldridge, George N., 54
El Monte, California, 80–82
emancipated slaves, 2–3
Encyclopaedia Judaica, 197, 199
"The Enemies of the Cross" (Tijerina, R. L.), 111–12

Escobar, María, 9, 75–86, 93–94, 108, 125, 227; in Alianza Federal de Mercedes, 153, 208–9, 217–18; Barrajas and, 142–43; divorce from Tijerina, R. L., 161, 208, 210–11, 216–17, 230; at LABI, 72–73, 77–78; Tijerina, R. L., abusing and mistreating, 143, 209–11, 215–17, 232; Tijerina, Rose, and, 213; at Valley of Peace, 132–35, 143

essays and columns, by Tijerina, R. L., 159–62

evangelical Protestants, 121–22, 129

evangelism, of Tijerina, R. L., 78–95, 97, 136–38, 141, 152, 158, 212

Exodus, Book of, 147

"Faith Without Mercy" (Tijerina, R. L.), 89

"False Confidence" (Tijerina, R. L.), 90

familial governance, 123–24

FBI. *See* Federal Bureau of Investigation

Featherstone, Ralph, 177–78

Federal Alliance of Free Towns. *See* Alianza Federal de Pueblos Libres

Federal Alliance of Land Grant Heirs. *See* Alianza Federal de Mercedes

federal and state trials, of Tijerina, R. L., 181–84

Federal Bureau of Investigation (FBI), 4, 136; file on Tijerina, R. L., 205–7, 221, 228–99; Hoover at, 9–10, 13, 167, 170–71, 175–76, 179, 205, 225, 228; on Kit Carson National Forest invasion and occupation, 17, 166, 177; surveillance of New Left Anti-War National Conference for New Politics, 175–76; Valley of Peace surveillance by, 171, 205; Watergate and, 205

federal prison: Medical Center for Federal Prisoners, Springfield, 183, 192–96, 216–18, 226; "My Letter from Prison" on, 191; schizophrenia diagnosis and psychiatric treatment in, 183–84, 192–96, 206, 221, 226, 228; Tijerina, R. L., after release from, 185–88, 190, 196, 216–17

feminists, 184–85

Ferdinand (king), 20

First Nations of New Mexico, 5

Forest Rangers, 150, 166, 181

Forest Service, US, 8–9, 146, 150–51, 164, 166, 181, 183

Frank Johnson School, 43–44

fundamentalists, 121–22

Galindo, Samuel, 44–45

García, Guadalupe, 56

García, Vicente, 56

García-Buñuel, Leonardo, 193–94

Garr, A. G., 51–52

gender, 123–26, 184–85

genealogical research, of Tijerina, R. L., 198–99, 206–7, 222

Genesis, Book of, 188, 207

GI Bill of Rights, 7

glossolalia, 48–54, 56, 59, 93

Gómez, Fred, 46, 78–79

Gonzales, Rodolfo "Corky," 6–7, 167–68, 175, 180, 184

"Good Passes for Evil" (Tijerina, R. L.), 128

Graham, Billy, 121, 127

Grayson, George W., Jr., 172–73

Great Depression, 6, 8, 29–30, 33–35, 56, 223

Green, Robert B., 37

El Grito de Dolores, 173

El Grito del Norte, 173, 181, 185

Guerilla Warfare (Guevara), 13

Guevara, Ernesto "Che," 13, 173, 178

Gutiérrez, José Angel, 6–7, 12, 212

¿Hallará Fe en la Tierra . . . ? (Will He

Find Any Faith on Earth . . . ?) (Tijerina, R. L.), 12, 16, 81, 105, 510nn2–3. *See also* sermons, by Tijerina, R. L.,
Haskalah, 204–6, 229
Henry VIII (king), 205
Hernández, María, 20, 199
Higgs, William, 181, 186, 220
Hiroshima, 69–71, 86, 95, 105, 109, 133
Hispanos, of New Mexico: Alianza Federal de Mercedes and, 153, 163; foreigners on, 152; Jews and, 170, 198; revivals among, 75; US Forest Service and, 150–51. *See also* Indo-Hispanos
La Historia de la Casa de Israel (Tijerina, R. L.), 197
Hitler, Adolf, 66, 191
Holy Spirit baptism, 60, 75, 78–79; John the Baptist and, 110–11; Pentecostalism and, 47–54, 56; Tijerina, R. L., and, 86, 88, 92–93, 105, 110–11, 224
Hoover, J. Edgar: at FBI, 9–10, 13, 167, 170–71, 175–76, 179, 205, 225, 228; Nixon and, 205
The Hour of Decision, 121
House of Israel and House of Judah, 199–201, *202*, 203–4, 207
Howard, Charles, 26
How Pentecost Came to Los Angeles. How It Was in the Beginning (Bartleman), 55
Hurst, William D., 164, 166

Iberian Peninsula, 19–20, 199, 204
imperialism, 12–13, 26, 103, 113–14, 122
indios, 22
individualism and personal freedom, 142
Indo-Hispanos, 178–79, 184, 188, 190; Alianza Federal de Mercedes on, 153–55, *155*, *156*, 206, 208, 228; Jews and, 196, 199–201, 203, 206, 228–30; "My Letter from Prison" on, 191; Tijerina, David, on living conditions of, 215; Tijerina, R. L., on land of, 195–97, 206, 231
"Information from the Alianza Federal de Mercedes" column, by Tijerina, R. L., 159–61
Institute for the Research and Study of Justice, 186–87, 190
Instituto Bíblico Latino Americano. See Latin American Bible Institute
Isabella (queen), 20
Isaiah, Book of, 208
Islam and Muslims, 201, 203–4
Israel, 99; Babylon, Roman Empire and, 114–15; Judah and, 199–201, *202*, 203–4, 207; Six Day War and, 228–29

Jáuregui, Guadalupe, 132
Jenkins, Myra Ellen, 163–64, 230
Jeremiah, 115
Jerusalem, destruction of temple of, 99–100, 115, 157
Jesus Christ: crucifixion of, 98–99, 207; Jewish followers of, 98–99, 104; Last Supper, 213; in New Testament, 97; Revelation on, 100–103; Roman Empire and, 98–99; Tijerina, R. L., on childhood dream about, 225–26
Jesus movement, in first century CE, 97–100, 105
Jewish diaspora, 198–99
Jewish War of 66–70 CE, 99
Jews: anti-Semitism and, 6, 20, 197, 228–30; Haskalah and, 204–6, 229; Hispanos and, 170, 198; Indo-Hispanos and, 196, 199–201, 203, 206, 228–30; Jesus followers, 98–99, 104; Roman Empire and,

Jews (*continued*)
228; Spain and, 20, 203–4; Tijerina, R. L., as "psychiatrist" of, 197, 230; Tijerina, R. L., on Anglo-Jewish alliance, 204–7; Tijerina, R. L., on atomic bomb and, 204, 206; Tijerina, R. L., on history of, 190–91, 197–99, 228
Jim Crow, 24, 46, 54, 85, 223
John, Gospel of, 92
John of Patmos, 7, 12, 16, 75, 97–103, 105, 113–14, 126–27
Johnson, Lyndon B., 163, 167, 175–77, 179–80
John the Baptist, 110–11
Joseph (biblical), 199–201, *202*, 203–4
Juárez, Santiago, 166
Judah, Israel and, 199–201, *202*, 203–4, 207
Judaism: Babylon and, 200–201; Christianity and, 199–200; Spanish Inquisition and, 21; Tijerina, R. L., on history of, 198–201, *202*, 203–4, 207
"The Just One's Clamor" (Tijerina, R. L.), 89

Karenga, Maulana Ron, 177–78
Kelty, H. Mary, 60
King, Coretta Scott, 1–2, 137
King, Martin Luther, Jr., 19, 137, 163, 207, 231; "Letter from a Birmingham Jail," 104, 191; on Poor People's March on Washington, 1, 176, 179, *180*
Kingdom of New Mexico, 8, 15, 139, 161
Kit Carson National Forest, 17, 150, 166, 177, 183, 224, 227–28
Ku Klux Klan, 34–36, 55

LABI. *See* Latin American Bible Institute
Laduke, Jack, 220
land grants, 5, 206; as free city-states, 167; in New Mexico, 8–9, 141–42, 144, 149–51, 159–64, 166–68, 174–75, 182, 184, 222, 227; restorationism and, 224; in Texas, Anglos stealing land and, 24–25; Texas Rangers and, 24; Tomé de Dominguez, 14; US government on, 8–9, 155
land rights, 149, 210
land tenure, in New Mexico, 138–39, 151, 157, 163, 184, 230
Laredo, Texas, 21–24, 76
Larrazolo, Paul, 182–83, 225
Latin American Bible Institute (LABI): Anglo teachers, on Mexican students at, 65; Assemblies of God and, 16, 45–46, 59–60, 63–64, 72–73, 75; on Bible, 64–66, 198; Escobar at, 72–73, 77–78; Luce and, 64–66; Luce and Ball establishing, 59–60; Mexicans at, 63–65, 68, 78; Pentecostal revivals and, 63; racism and segregation at, 68; on Revelation, 113; Savage at, 63, 68, 73–75; Tijerina, R. L., at, 10–13, 16, 45–46, 63–64, 66–69, 72–75, 80–81, 88, 143, 226; women at, 68, 72–73, 78
Latter Day Evangel, 59
laws of Moses, 21, 120, 198, 207–8
Laws of the Indies, 142, 145, 149, 159
Lee, Edward, 49–50
Lee, Mattie, 49–50
León, Martín de, 23
"Letter from a Birmingham Jail" (King, M. L.), 104, 191
"Let Us Return to Our Maker" (Tijerina, R. L.), 88
Lewis, Robert, 70
Leyba, Tobias, 168–69
liberation theology, 104
"Listen Wise Ones" (Tijerina, R. L.), 90
Llorente, Francisco, 55

López, Abundio, 55
López, Herlinda, 19, 29–30, 32–34, 36–39, 503n61
López, Luis, 55
López, María, 39
López, Rosa, 55
Los Angeles Daily Times, 50–51
Los Angeles Times, 170–71
"The Lost Justice" (Tijerina, R. L.), 110–11
Lovato, Cristino, 139, 145
Luce, Alice E., 58–61, 64–66, 108
Lujan, Manuel, 188
Luke, Gospel of, 109
La Luz Apostólica (*The Apostolic Light*), 58

Malcolm X, 176, 225
Manifesto (Marx), 128
"Manifesto to the Oppressed Peoples of America," 26–27
Mares, Rodolfo, 132, 136–37, 147
Martín, José María, 23
Martinez, Elizabeth, 173
Martínez, Vicente, 132
Martínez, Zebedeo, 138
Marx, Karl, 128
Mata, Manuel, 132, 136–37
materialism, 82–83, 87, 112–13
Mathas, John, 32
Matthew, Gospel of, 99, 191
McCombs, Vernon Monroe, 38
McLean, Robert N., 38
Meagher, Ed, 170
MECHA. See *Movimiento Estudiantil Chicano de Aztlán*
Mecham, G. V., 146
Medical Center for Federal Prisoners, Springfield, MO, 183, 192–96, 216–18, 226
Mendoza, Alvino, 83
mercedes (communal land grants), 3, 7–9, 16, 26, 139, 154. *See also* Alianza Federal de Mercedes; land grants

Meredith, James, 181
The Messenger and His Message (Luce), 65, 108
mestizos, 22
#MeToo, 232
Mexican Americans: in American Southwest, 6–7, 171, 176; civil rights, 6; history of political activism, 184–85; Mexican immigrants and, 36; rights of, US government and, 152; teachers, 214–15; Tijerina, R. L., and, 86, 141, 174–75; against Vietnam War, 13–14
Mexican Catholics, 36–37
Mexican immigrants, 29, 36, 38
mexicanos: Gospel message for, 79; religious options of, 94; in Texas, 26, 31, 33, 35–36
Mexican Revolution, 27, 56, 76, 149
Mexicans: in American Southwest, 1–2, 4, 141; Assemblies of God and, 58–60, 63–64, 72, 77–78; at Azusa Street Mission, 55; in California, 39; Catholic Church and, 36, 59–60; conversions at Pentecostal revivals, of Tijerina, R. L., 94; families of, Tijerina, R. L., on, 124, 210; at LABI, 63–65, 68, 78; in Pentecostal movement, 55–56; poverty of, structural origins of, 7, 157; public educational system and, 135; in Texas, 27–29, 36–37, 76, 82; Tijerina, R. L., preaching to, 111–12, 136–37
Mexican Texans (*Tejanos*), 16, 22–29, 31, 33–34, 39–40
Mexican War, 1, 3, 7, 150; Treaty of Guadalupe Hidalgo ending, 5, 9, 23, 141–42, 149, 152–53
Mexico: colonization of, 138–39, 232; Constitution, 1917, 149; land reform in, 149; New Mexico and,

Mexico (*continued*)
141–42, 149; Pentecostalism in, 55; Spain and, 4–5, 7–8, 22, 138–39, 149–50; surveillance of Tijerina family by, 176; *Tejanos* in, 24; Texas and, 22–23; Tijerina, R. L., in, 141–43
Mexico City, 141–43, 210, 212, 218
Michigan: sugar beet production in, 38–41, 43, 45, 75, 79–80; Tijerina family in, 38–41, 43–45, 75
Militant, 174
Mi lucha por la tierra (Tijerina, R. L.), 11–12, 147, 194–95, 227–29
ministry, of Tijerina, R. L., 75–76, 78–82
Missionary Methods: St. Paul's or Ours? (Allen), 58
Montoya, Joseph, 178–79, 186, 188, 225, 233
Moreno, Luis, 132, 140
Moreno, María, 132, 140
Moses (biblical), 5–6, 12, 45, 131–32, 142, 188; in Exodus, 147; law of, 21, 120, 198, 207–8; in Pentateuch, 222
Movimiento Estudiantil Chicano de Aztlán (MECHA), 174
Muhammad, Elijah, 176, 231
"My Letter from Prison" (Tijerina, R. L.), 191
My Life, Juda-ism, and the Nuclear Age (Tijerina, R. L.), 107, 197–201, 202, 203–5, 229–30
Myrick, Eunice, 153

NAE. *See* National Association of Evangelicals
Nagasaki, 70–71, 86, 95, 105, 109, 133
Naranjo, Benny, 169–70, 225
National Association of Evangelicals (NAE), 121–22
National Council of Churches, 122
National Prayer Breakfasts, 122

National Youth Conference, 184
Native Americans, 5, 12–13, 177–78, 231–32
NBC, 10
New Jerusalem, 85, 87, 92; in Revelation, 102–5, 113–14, 138; Tijerina, R. L., on, 113–14, 116, 123
New Left Anti-War National Conference for New Politics, 1966, 175–76, 178, 231
New Mexican, Sante Fe, 163, 171
New Mexico: Brotherhood Awareness Week in, 187–88; Cargo on "economic Darwinism" in, 5; First Nations of, 5; Hispanos of, 75, 150–52; Kingdom of New Mexico, 8, 15, 139, 161; land grants in, 8–9, 141–42, 144, 149–51, 159–64, 166–68, 174–75, 182, 184, 222, 227; land tenure in, 138–39, 151, 157, 163, 184, 230; Mexican War and, 3; Mexico and, 141–42, 149; national forests in, 150–51, 166; state police, 218–19, 228; Texans in, 161; Tijerina, R. L., arriving in, 17; Tijerina, R. L., in, speeches by, 151–52; US Forest Service and, 150; Visalia Dream on, 138–39, 141. *See also* Hispanos, of New Mexico
New Mexico State Penitentiary, 172–73, 183
News Chieftain, Albuquerque, 11, 159–62
New Spain, 4–5, 7–8, 20–21, 154, 232
Newsweek Magazine, 174
New York Times, 170–71, 228–29
Nixon, Richard, 195–96, 205, 215
Noll, Jerry, 181
Norvell, David, 186, 219
Numbers, Book of, 138

Ocampo, Ramón, 55
Olazábal, Francisco, 56
Old Testament prophets, 199

Oppenheimer, Robert, 206
Otero, Ray, 219
Ozman, Agnes, 48

Pagels, Elaine, 206
Palestine, 12–13, 99, 229
parents, of Tijerina, R. L., 29–30, 32–38, 41, 43–45, 64, 66, 68
Parham, Charles Fox, 47–49, 51, 55
patriarchy, 123–24, 185, 207, 209
Pelton, Dan, 136
Pentecost, 47, 50–51, 54, 61, 72
Pentecostal Evangel, 60
Pentecostalism, 11, 46; African Americans, in movement, 49–50; Assemblies of God and, 16, 57, 76–77; Azusa Street Mission, in early movement, 50–55; on Bible, 56; birth of movement, 48; on end-time, 131; on first-century Christianity, 122; glossolalia and, 48–54, 56; Holy Spirit baptism and, 47–54, 56; Mexicans, in movement, 55–56; Parham, in early movement, 47–49, 51, 55; on Protestant denominationalism, 56–57; racism and segregation, in early movement, 49, 55; on rapture, 133; reformism, 110; on Revelation, 97, 105; schisms within movement, 57; Seymour, in early movement, 49–51, 55; theology and evangelization methodology, 58, 60; theology of, Tijerina's "new interpretation" of, 111; Tijerina, R. L., as preacher, 107–9, 131, 151–52, 224
Pentecostal revivals, 78, 226; LABI and, 63; Tijerina, R. L., staging, 86–94, 158, 171
"The People Without Honor" (Tijerina, R. L.), 111
Pepper, Max, 194
Peter, Allen, 150

Pilate, Pontius, 98–99, 157
Pile, William A., 164
Pinal County School Board, 135, 144
"El Plan Espiritual de Aztlán," 184
Polk, James, 23
Poor People's March on Washington, 1, 176, 179–81, *180*
primitivism, 112, 122–24, 151, 224
Probe the Spirits, to Assure They Are God's (Luce), 64–65
property-owning citizens (*vecinos*), 7–8, 22, 154
property rights, 5, 7–8
Protestant churches, 75, 113, 120–21, 131, 136, 164
Protestantism, 56–57, 118, 121–22
Protestants, 45; Catholics and, 37, 81, 161; evangelical, 121–22, 129; Spain and, 203–4; white, 37
"The Provokers of Judgment" (Tijerina, R. L.), 128
psychiatrists, Tijerina, R. L., on, 195–97, 230
psychopathy, Tijerina, R. L., on, 195, 197
public school, 135–36
Pueblo de San Joaquín del Rio de Chama, 164, 166–68, 183, 190, 205, 209, 224, 227–28
Pueblo Revolt, 1680, 162

Quinn, John, 171
Qur'an, 134

racism, 11, 24, 39–40, 46; in early Pentecostal movement, 49, 55; at LABI, 68
the rapture, 133–34
Raza Unida Party, 6–7
Reagan, Ronald, 105, 229
Rebelde, Dolores, 213
Reies Tijerina Papers, at University of New Mexico's Zimmerman Library, 14

Reies Tijerina: The Most Hated Man in New Mexico, 10, 218
restorationism, 112, 122–24, 151, 224
Revelation, Book of, 2–3, 11, 95; on Apocalypse, 71, 97, 102, 133, 206–7, 227; on Armageddon, 101, 116; on Babylon, 6, 101–5, 113–14; inclusion in New Testament, 97–98, 104; on Jesus Christ, 100–103; by John of Patmos, 7, 12, 16, 75, 97–98, 100–103, 105, 113–14, 126–27; on Last Judgment, 92; in liberation theology, 104; Luce on, 65; on New Jerusalem, 102–5, 113–14, 138; Pentecostal movement on, 97, 105; on Pilate, 157; Roman Empire and, 98, 103, 126–27; in sermons, of Tijerina, R. L., 87, 111, 113, 129; Tijerina, R. L., and, 104–5, 111, 195–96, 232–33
Rivera, Dan, 170, 182, 224–25
Rivera, Vicky, 67–69, 73–74, 143
Roman Empire, 13, 75, 114, 173; colonialism of, 6, 12, 97, 99, 126–27; Jerusalem temple destroyed by, 99–100, 115; Jews and, 228; Revelation and, 98, 103, 126–27
Romero, Jessie, 166
Romero, Patricia, 161–62, 169, 182–83, 186, 194, 209, 217–21
Rosales, Rosa, 31
Rusk, Dean, 167

Saiz, Nick, 170, 182
Salazar, Eulogio, 170, 186, 188
Salazar, Francisco, 166
Salt War of 1877, 26
Sánchez, Alfonso, 152, 168–71, 182–83, 224–25, 227–28
Santa Fe National Forests, 150
Santa Fe New Mexican, 70
Santa Fe Ring, 164

Saspamco, Texas, 63
Savage, Kenzy, 63, 68, 73–75
schizophrenia diagnosis and treatment, of Tijerina, R. L., 10, 17, 183–84, 192–95, 206, 221–22, 226, 228
school experience, of Tijerina, R. L., and siblings, 41–44
Scopes trial, 1925, 121
Seguín, Juan, 23–24
sermons, by Tijerina, R. L., 87–91, 104–5, 107; against American materialism, capitalism, and consumerism, 112–14, 120, 125–26, 128–29; on atomic bombs, 127; on Babylon, 114–16; "The Captive People— Leave, Leave," 114; on charity, 119–20; on church and state, 121–22; against church leaders, 111–12, 118–19, 129; "The Clamor of the Earth," 108–10; on communism, 128–29; on current events, 127–29; "Faith Without Mercy," 89; "False Confidence," 90; on familial governance, 123–24; on gender roles and hierarchies, 123–26; "The Just One's Clamor," 89; "Let Us Return to Our Maker," 88; "Listen Wise Ones," 90; "The Lost Justice," 110–11; *The Messenger and His Message* and, 108; against pastoral salaries, 119–20, 125; "The People Without Honor," 111; against popular media, 126–27; Revelation and, 87, 111, 113, 129; "The Enemies of the Cross," 111–12; "Where Is Our Benefit?," 89; "Who Will Be Saved?," 111, 116–18; "The Yearning of Those Who Adore," 90
Serna, Simón, 132, 140
Service, Elman R., 94
sexual abuse and sexual assault, 140–41, 157, 212–14, 218–21, 232

sexual liberation, 184–85
Seymour, William J., 49–51, 55, 122–23
sharecropping and sharecroppers, 28–29, 33–35, 43, 46, 223
Shears, Bob, 25–26
Shedd, Frank, 145–46
siblings, of Tijerina, R. L., 29–31, 41–45, 66–68, 76–77, 131, 186, 223
Six Day War, 228–29
Smith, Joseph, 200, 208
Smith, Philip, 9, 181
SNCC. *See* Student Nonviolence Coordinating Committee
social justice, 1–2
Soleri, Paolo, 144
Soul on Ice (Cleaver), 181
Southern Christian Leadership Council, 176, 179
Soviet Union, 85–86, 128, 133
Spain: Catholic Church and, 203–4; Iberian Peninsula, 19–20, 199, 204; Jews and, 20, 203–4; Kingdom of New Mexico, 8, 15; Laws of the Indies, 142, 145, 149; Mexico and, 4–5, 7–8, 22, 138–39, 149–50; Protestants and, 203–4; Tijerina family from, 19–20
Spanish Inquisition, 21
Spanish language, 11–12, 42–44, 46, 151
speaking in tongues, 48–54, 56, 59, 93
speeches, by Tijerina, R. L., 151–52, 157–59, 160, 165, 185, 187
Stang, Alan, 174
Stephens, Alexander, 23
Stevens, Albert, 34–35
Stimpson, Eddie, 30
Student Nonviolence Coordinating Committee (SNCC), 173–74, 181, 231
Suddenly . . . from Heaven (Brumback), 123
sugar beet production, 38–41, 43, 45, 75, 79–80

Surinam Act of 1665, 204

Taylor, Walter, 181
Tejanos (Mexican Texans), 16, 22–29, 31, 33–34, 39–40
televangelists, 121
television, Tijerina, R. L., on, 162, 171, 231
Templo Cristiano, 63, 76–77
Teotihuacán, 142
Texans, New Mexicans on, 161
Texas: Anglos and *Tejanos* in, 22–29, 31, 33–34, 37; Anglos stealing land in, 24–26; central, grasslands of, 28; colonization of, 223; cotton farms and farmers in, 28–31, 33, 80, 82, 223; ethnic Mexicans in, 27–29, 36–37, 76, 82; independence, 1836, 23; Jim Crow, 223; mexicanos in, 26, 31, 33, 35–36; Mexico and, 22–23; population demographics, 1821-1930, 27–28; sharecroppers in, 33–34; *Tejano* revolution in, 26–27
Texas Rangers, 24, 26, 35, 37, 150
Texas Revolution, 16
Texerina, Diego, 20, 199
Texerina, José, 20–21
Thessalonians, Book of, 92, 200
They Called Me "King Tiger" (Tijerina, R. L.), 12
Third World liberation movements, 12
Thomson, Charles A., 38
Tierra Amarilla, 138–39, 145, 168–70, 172–73; Courthouse, 5, 169, 181–83, 186, 188, 209, 214, 216, 224–25, 228
Tijerina, Anselmo, 43, 46, 66–67, 141
Tijerina, Antonio, 29–30, 32, 34–38, 41, 43; death of, 68; illness and laying on of hands, 93, 226; LABI and, 64, 66, 69
Tijerina, Cristóbal, 38, 171, 181
Tijerina, Daniel, 214–15
Tijerina, David, 81, 193, 210, 215

Tijerina, Della, 216
Tijerina, Margarito, 43, 66–67, 141, 145–46
Tijerina, Noah, 78, 210–11, 216–18, 220–22
Tijerina, Rachel, 194, 214–15, 218
Tijerina, Reies López, *158, 160, 165, 180*. See also specific topics
Tijerina, Rose, 133, 140, 210–20, 230–31
Tijerina, Santiago, 21–22, 24–25, 45
Tomé de Dominguez land grant, 14
Topeka, Kansas, 47–49, 57
Treaty of Guadalupe Hidalgo, 145, 213, 224; Alianza Federal de Mercedes on, 153–54, 159, 162; Mexican War and, 5, 9, 23, 141–42, 149, 152–53
Treaty of Peace, Harmony, and Mutual Assistance, 178, 231–32
Trinity test, of atom bomb, 71–72
Trujillo, Manuel, 145
Truman, Harry S., 70–72
La Tuna Federal Prison, 192

United States (US), 152; Civil War, 2–3; Constitution, 149, 159; Forest Service, 8–9, 146, 150–51, 164, 166, 181, 183; on land grants, 8–9, 155; Tijerina, R. L., on Anglo-Jewish alliance in, 204–5
University of New Mexico, Zimmerman Library at, 12–15
US Immigration Quota Acts of 1921 and 1924, 27

Valdez, Juan, 170
Valdez, Juanita, 39–40, 145
Valdez, Zebedeo, 132
valientes, 67, 77
Valladares, Esperanza García, 209
Valley of Peace (*Valle de Paz*), 3, 16, 129; Anglo neighbors and, 135–36, 144, 146–47; arrests at, 145–47; Escobar at, 132–35, 143; FBI surveillance of, 171, 205; first residents of, 132–33; flooding, 137; Heralds of Peace at, 16, 133–36, 139–40, 143–44, 152–53, 208, 212; land value of, 144; nuclear war preparations at, 133–34; school and, 135–36, 144; Serna on, 140; sexual abuse of children at, 140–41, 212; Tijerina children on, 209, 212; Visalia Dream and, 138, 227
Varela, María, 224, 231
Vásquez, Nasario, 38
Vásquez de Coronado, Francisco, 188, *189*
vecinos (property-owning citizens), 7–8, 22, 154
Vega, Albert, 220–21
Vergara, Santana, 142
Vespasian, 99
Vietnam War, 12–15, 175, 179, 184, 215
Virgin of Guadalupe, 141
Visalia Dream, of Tijerina, R. L., 11, 16–17, 137, 149, 153, 209; New Mexico and, 138–39, 141; Valley of Peace and, 138, 227
The Voice of Justice (*La Voz de la Justicia*), 161
Voting Rights Act of 1965, 179–80, 231
La Voz de la Justicia (The Voice of Justice), 161

Washington Post, 205
Watergate, 205
Weber, Max, 58
"Where Is Our Benefit?" (Tijerina, R. L.), 89
White, Lawrence, 136
White House Conference on Children and Youth, 1971, 215
white supremacy and white supremacists, 11, 35, 37, 111–12, 216, 223
"Who Will Be Saved?" (Tijerina, R. L.), 111, 116–18
Will He Find Any Faith on Earth . . . ?

(¿Hallará Fe en la Tierra . . . ?) (Tijerina, R. L.), 12, 16, 81, 105, 510nn2–3. See also sermons, by Tijerina, R. L.,
Works Progress Administration, 43
World War II, 61, 66–71, 85, 105, 112, 114, 223; evangelical Protestants after, 121; labor reorganization during, 123; Tijerina brothers in, 226

Yaegley, William, 171
"The Yearning of Those Who Adore" (Tijerina, R. L.), 90
"You and I," 91–92

Zapata, Emiliano, 13, 173
Zimmerman Library, at University of New Mexico, 12–15

www.ingramcontent.com/pod-product-compliance
Lightning Source LLC
Chambersburg PA
CBHW051155300426
44116CB00006B/322